AMERICAN WARPLANES
of WORLD WAR II

AMERICAN WARPLANES
of WORLD WAR II

Editor: David Donald

Aerospace Publishing Ltd
AIRtime Publishing Inc.

Published by
Aerospace Publishing Ltd
179 Dalling Road
London W6 0ES
England

Published under licence in USA and
Canada by
AIRtime Publishing Inc.
10 Bay Street
Westport, CT 06880
USA

Aerospace **ISBN: 1 874023 72 7**
AIRtime **ISBN: 1-880588-21-8**

Distributed in the UK,
Commonwealth and Europe by
Airlife Publishing Ltd
101 Longden Road
Shrewsbury
SY3 9EB
England
Telephone: 01743 235651
Fax: 01743 232944

Distributed to retail bookstores in the
USA and Canada by
AIRtime Publishing Inc.
10 Bay Street
Westport, CT 06880
USA
Telephone: (203) 838-7979
Fax: (203) 838-7344

US readers wishing to order by mail,
please contact
AIRtime Publishing Inc. toll-free at
1 800 359-3003

Publisher: Stan Morse

Editor: David Donald

Associate Editors:
  Chris Bishop
  Tim Senior

Sub Editors:
  Trisha Palmer
  Karen Leverington

Authors: David Donald
  René J. Francillon
  Gordon Swanborough
  Peter R. March
  Bill Gunston

Artists: John Weal
  Keith Fretwell

Colour reproduction:
Universal Graphics Pte Ltd

Printed in Italy

WORLD AIR POWER JOURNAL is
published quarterly and provides
an in-depth analysis of
contemporary military aircraft
and their worldwide operators.
Superbly produced and filled
with extensive colour
photography, World Air Power
Journal is available by
subscription from:

(UK, Europe and
Commonwealth)
Aerospace Publishing Ltd
FREEPOST
PO Box 2822
London W6 0BR
Telephone: 0181-740 9554
Fax: 0181-746 2556
(no stamp needed within the UK)

(USA and Canada)
AIRtime Publishing Inc.
Subscription Dept
10 Bay Street
Westport, CT 06880
USA
Telephone: (203) 838-7979
Fax: (203) 838-7344
Toll-free number in USA:
1 800 359-3003

CONTENTS

Aeronca L-3 Grasshopper

The US Army Air Corps had been slow to appreciate the value of light aircraft for employment in an observation/liaison role, but information received from Europe in late 1940, where World War II was already more than a year old, highlighted their usefulness. Consequently, in 1941 the US Army began its own evaluation of this category of aircraft, obtaining four commercial light-planes from each of three established manufacturers, namely Aeronca, Piper and Taylorcraft. For full field evaluation larger numbers of these aircraft were ordered shortly afterwards, to be deployed in the US Army's annual manoeuvres which were to be held later in the year. It took very little time for the service to appreciate that these lightweight airplanes had a great deal to offer, both for rapid communications and in support of armed forces in the field.

The name Aeronca Aircraft Corporation had been adopted in 1941 by the company established in late 1928 as the Aeronautical Corporation of America. One of its most successful products was the Model 65 high-wing monoplane, developed to meet commercial requirements for a reliable dual-control tandem two-seat trainer. The four of these aircraft supplied initially to the USAAC became designated **YO-58**, and these were followed by 50 **O-58**, 20 **O-58A** and 335 **O-58B** aircraft, serving with the USAAF (established on 20 June 1941). In the following year the 'O' (Observation) designation was changed to 'L' (Liaison), and the O-58, O-58A and O-58B desig-

Above: This Aeronca Grasshopper wears the standard olive drab finish used as the basic colour for USAAC aircraft until camouflage schemes were introduced after America entered World War II. This is an L-3B.

nations became respectively **L-3**, **L-3A** and **L-3B**. An additional 540 aircraft were delivered as L-3Bs, and 490 **L-3C**s were manufactured before production ended in 1944. The designations **L-3D/-3E/-3F/-3G/-3H/-3J** were applied to civil Model 65s with varying powerplant installations, which were pressed into military service when the United States became involved in World War II.

Most L-3s were generally similar, with small changes in equipment representing the variation from one to another. All shared the welded steel-tube fuselage/tail unit with fabric covering, and wings with spruce spars, light alloy ribs and metal frame ailerons, all fabric-covered. Landing gear was of the non-retractable tailwheel type, with the main units divided

and incorporating oleo-spring shock absorbers in the side vees.

With the requirement for a trainer suitable for glider pilots, Aeronca developed an unpowered version of the Model 65. This retained the wings, tail unit and aft fuselage of the L-3, but introduced a new front fuselage providing a third seat forward for an instructor, the original tandem seats being used by two pupils; all three occupants had similar flying controls and instruments. A total of 250 of these training gliders was supplied to the USAAF under the designation **TG-5**, and three supplied to the US Navy for evaluation were identified as **LNR**. Production of Aeronca liaison aircraft continued after the war, with planes supplied to the USAF under the designation **L-16**.

Above: Sporting the name 'Junior' and a shark's tooth embellishment complete with a staring eye on the engine cylinder-head fairing, this is an example of the L-3C, final production version of the Aeronca Grasshopper.

Specification
Type: two-seat light liaison and observation monoplane
Powerplant: one 65-hp (48-kW) Continental O-170 flat-four piston engine
Performance: maximum speed 87 mph (140 km/h); cruising speed 46 mph (74 km/h); service ceiling 10,000 ft (3050 m); range 200 miles (322 km)
Weights: empty 835 lb (379 kg); maximum take-off 1,300 lb (590 kg)
Dimensions: span 35 ft 0 in (10.67 m); length 21 ft 0 in (6.40 m); height 7 ft 8 in (2.34 m); wing area 158 sq ft (14.68 m²)

Beechcraft XA-38

The Model 28 represented something of a departure for Beech, which had hitherto produced transports and trainers. Two examples of this twin-engined attack aircraft were ordered in 1943 under the designation **XA-38**, with the names Grizzly and Destroyer tentatively mooted. The aircraft showed some similarity to other Beech designs, but was basically new. It was a large twin-engined low-wing monoplane, the fuselage accommodating a three-man crew. Defensive armament consisted of upper and lower remotely-controlled gun turrets, while the main offensive weapon was a 75-mm cannon mounted in the nose with the

barrel projecting forwards. Underwing racks could mount bombs or rockets, while additional forward-firing machine-guns were fitted. The two aircraft were delivered for evaluation in 1945, but the end of the war killed any chance of procurement.

Specification
Type: prototype three-seat attack aircraft
Powerplant: two 2,300-hp (1715-kW) Wright R-3350-43 Cyclone radial piston engines
Performance: maximum speed 376 mph (605 km/h)
Weight: maximum take-off 35,264 lb (15995 kg)
Dimensions: wing span 67 ft 4 in (20.52 m); length 51 ft 9 in (15.77 m)

The second prototype of the Beech XA-38, which made its first flight on 22 September 1945, was the only one to carry a full cannon armament and two gun turrets. An unarmed first prototype had made its first flight on 7 May 1944.

Beechcraft C-45/AT-7/AT-10/F-2 family

First flying on 15 January 1937, the civilian Model 18 met only modest success pre-war, but the adoption of the type by the US armed forces paved the way for massive production and continued success in both civil and military fields long after the war.

The first US Army Air Corps order, placed during 1940, was for the supply of 11 aircraft under the designation **C-45** for use as staff transports, these being generally similar to the civil Model B18S. Subsequent procurement covered 20 **C-45A**s for use in a utility transport role, with interior and equipment changes being made in the 223 **C-45B**s that followed. The USAAF designations **C-45C**, **C-45D** and **C-45E** were applied respectively to two impressed B18S civil aircraft, two AT-7s completed for transport duties, and six AT-7Bs similarly modified. Major and final production version for the USAAF was the seven-seat **C-45F**, with a slightly longer nose and of which no fewer than 1,137 were built. All of the foregoing C-45 designations were changed to a new UC-45 category in January 1943. A small number of drone directors converted from UC-45Fs and given the designation **CQ-3** became, instead, **DC-45F**s.

In 1941, the USAAF adopted the Beech Model 18 for navigation training tasks under the designation **AT-7 Navigator**. It was equipped with three positions for trainee navigators plus a dorsal astrodome. A total of 577 was built, being followed by six **AT-7A**s with float landing gear and a large ventral fin. Nine **AT-7B**s, basically winterised AT-7s, were built to USAAF order. Final version of the Navigator was the **AT-7C** with a different powerplant, the R-985-AN-3, production totalling 549. Those surviving after the war were redesignated **T-7**.

Following the AT-7, another version of the Model 18 appeared in the AT (advanced trainer) category during 1941. This was the **AT-11 Kansan** (originally named Kansas), procured by the USAAF as a bombing and gunnery trainer. It incorporated a small bomb bay, had small circular portholes in place of the standard rectangular cabin win-

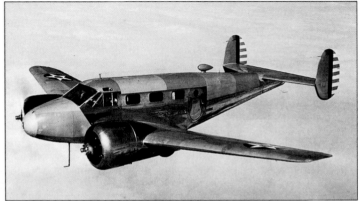

Above: The US Navy JRB-1, used to control pilotless drones, featured a raised cabin top to allow a good all-round view for the radio operator. This aircraft also has a port side door hatch to permit the use of cameras from the cabin.

This is one of 1,137 UC-45F Expeditors delivered to the USAAF from 1943 onwards, making this the most-produced of all the many military derivatives of the Beech Model 18. The cabin provided seats for six passengers in addition to the crew of two.

A formation of AT-11 Kansans flies on a training mission over the USA. This C-45 derivative featured a bomb-aiming position in the nose and internal stowage for practice bombs, as well as nose and dorsal guns for the bombing and gunnery training role.

Left: An AT-11 Kansan lands at Laredo, Texas, on 15 August 1943. In the bombardier training role many AT-11s had the dorsal turret replaced by a Perspex fairing, but this example carries the turret with a pair of 0.3-in (7.62-mm) machine-guns to fulfil the gunnery training role also.

dows, a redesigned nose to provide a bomb-aiming position, and two 0.3-in (7.62-mm) machine-guns, one in the nose, the other in a dorsal turret. Production to USAAF orders totalled 1,582 of which 36 were converted for navigation training as **AT-11A**s. Twenty-four AT-11s ordered by the Netherlands for service in the Netherlands East Indies were instead taken on charge by the USAAF. Surviving AT-11s were redesignated **T-11** after the war, and a few were modernised under the **T-11B** designation.

Last of the US Army Air Force's wartime versions of the Beech Model 18 were photographic reconnaissance **F-2**s, 14 civil Model B18s being purchased and converted with cabin-mounted mapping cameras and oxygen equipment. They were supplemented later by 13 **F-2A**s with four cameras, converted from C-45As, and by 42 **F-2B**s, which were conversions from UC-45Fs; these had additional camera ports in both sides of the fuselage.

US Navy and Marine Corps procurement of the Model 18 also totalled over 1,500 examples. The initial **JRB-1** was equivalent to the F-2, the **JRB-2** was a transport and the **JRB-3** and **JRB-4** were similar to the C-45C and UC-45F. The **SNB-1**, **SNB-2** and **SNB-3** were retrospective designations applied to aircraft similar to the AT-11, AT-7 and AT-7C respectively. The three last variants were the **SNB-2H** air ambulance, **SNB-2P** photo-reconnaissance aircraft, and **SNB-3Q** ECM trainer.

Specification
Beechcraft C-45
Type: six-seat utility transport
Powerplant: two Pratt & Whitney R-985-AN-1 Wasp Junior radial piston engines, each rated at 450 hp (336 kW)
Performance: maximum speed 215 mph (346 km/h); service ceiling 20,000 ft (6095 m); range 700 miles (1125 km)
Weights: empty 5,890 lb (2671 kg); maximum take-off 7,850 lb (3560 kg)
Dimensions: wing span 47 ft 8 in (14,53 m); length 34 ft 3 in (10.44 m); height 9 ft 8 in (2.95 m); wing area 349 sq ft (32.42 m²)

The US Navy bought 15 JRB-2 six-seat transports before the war began, and then added 328 JRB-4s that were transferred from USAAF contracts for the C-45F. An additional 23 JRB-3s were the equivalent of C-45Bs.

Beechcraft AT-10 Wichita

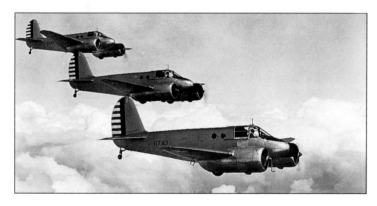

The AT-10 was designed for ease of production, and was largely of wooden construction – a first for USAAF trainers. Globe Aircraft added 600 to Beech Aircraft's own total of 1,771 aircraft of this type.

The rapid expansion of US training facilities in 1941 created a sudden need for trainer aircraft at a time when it seemed likely that raw materials, notably aluminium and magnesium alloys, would have to be conserved for first-line types. An engineering team led by Beech's T.A. Wells evolved the Beech Model 26, which was the first all-wood trainer to be accepted by the US Army Air Force. This was given the designation **AT-10 Wichita**. The design

avoided, where possible, the use of compound curves and of hot moulding processes for the structure's sub-assemblies, allowing them to be subcontracted to non-specialist woodworking firms; 85 per cent of the airframe was manufactured on this basis, with final

Left: About half of all USAAF multi-engined pilots received their transitional training on the Beech AT-10 (seen here pre-war). The aircraft was rapidly developed as the USAAF expanded during 1941.

assembly by Beech at Wichita.

Metal airframe parts were limited to engine nacelles and cowlings, and panelling around the cockpit section. Perhaps the most interesting innovation was the use of wooden fuel tanks lined with synthetic rubber. For operation as a multi-engined conversion trainer, the Wichita was equipped with dual controls and an autopilot, and entry to the cockpit was via rearward-sliding side windows.

The AT-10 was powered by two 295-hp (220-kW) Lycoming R-680-9 engines, and by 1943

Beech had completed four contracts, for 150, 191, 1,080 and 350 aircraft respectively, bringing the total built at Wichita to 1,771. The last of these was delivered on 15 September 1943. Beech then supplied engineering and production data to the Globe Aircraft Corporation of Dallas, Texas, so that another 600 could be manufactured.

Specification
Type: two-seat advanced trainer
Powerplant: two 295-hp (220-kW) Lycoming R-680 radial piston engines
Performance: maximum speed 198 mph (319 km/h); service ceiling 16,900 ft (5150 m); range 770 miles (1239 km)
Weights: empty 4,750 lb (2155 kg); maximum take-off 6,130 lb (2781 kg)
Dimensions: span 44 ft 0 in (13.41 m); length 34 ft 4 in (10.46 m); wing area 298 sq ft (27.68 m²)

Bell P-39 Airacobra

The P-39 Airacobra was one of the outstanding examples of an aircraft which on paper seemed likely to be a world-beater, but which in practice turned out to be an also-ran. Radical in arrangement, it did have some excellent qualities, and eventually matured as an excellent ground-attack fighter which saw much action in different parts of the world.

Bell Aircraft was formed in 1935 by three key men who remained behind in Buffalo after the Consolidated Company moved to San Diego. In June 1936 they began to design a revolutionary new fighter, which they named the Airacobra. The two most unusual (but not unique) features were that the engine was mounted on the centre of gravity, above the wing and behind the pilot, and the new 'tricycle' type of landing gear was fitted. The unusual location of the engine was expected to confer several advantages. One obvious benefit was improved manoeuvrability, the heavy engine being located in the centre of the aircraft instead of being swung round on an extremity. All-round pilot vision was considerably improved, especially when taxiing; conventional fighters had a giant nose that completely blocked forward view. The new form of landing gear was expected to offer many advantages, including much easier handling on take-off and landing and eliminating the possibility of nosing over, which was increasingly becoming a major problem with high-power fighters with large propellers. It also facilitated the installation of concentrated firepower in the nose, including a large cannon firing through the hub of the propeller.

Cannon-carrier

Bell put together a detailed proposal to the US Army Air Corps. The list of advantages looked impressive, and the Army was especially eager to find a fighter that could carry the powerful T-9 cannon of 37-mm calibre developed by AAC (American Armament Corporation). Such a gun could go in the nose of the Lockheed P-38, but this was a big aircraft with two engines. The Bell proposal fitted the heavy gun into a small, agile machine. On 7 October 1937 the Army ordered a prototype of the Airacobra as the **XP-39**. There has been much confusion over the date of the first flight, but the XP-39 actually flew on 6 April 1938.

It was a beautiful-looking aircraft, with a shiny metal skin and almost perfect streamlining. The 1,150-hp (858-kW) Allison V-1710-17 liquid-cooled V-12 engine was installed just behind the cockpit, where it provided protection against attack from astern. On the left was a big air inlet and fairing over a General Electric B-5 turbo-supercharger. On the right side was a smaller air duct housing the coolant radiator and oil cooler. The roomy cockpit offered almost perfect all-round visibility, and its most unusual feature (apart from being in a level attitude on the ground) was that it had a car-type door on each side, with a wind-down window. The landing gear and split flaps were electrically operated, all control surfaces were fabric-covered, and all exterior riveting was of the flush type.

The XP-39 carried no armament or armour, and weighed only 5,550 lb (2517 kg) in flying trim. Together with the turbo-equipped engine this resulted in scintillating performance, the maximum speed being 390 mph (628 km/h) at a height of 20,000 ft (6100 m); this was reached in only five minutes. It is not surprising that, on 27 April 1939, the Army ordered 12 **YP-39A** service-test aircraft, plus one YP-39A without turbo-supercharger. However, the XP-39 was lent

Above: In its P-39D version, the Airacobra entered USAAF service early in 1941 and first saw combat with the 8th Pursuit Group in New Guinea a year later. Early promise of the radical Bell fighter was never fully realised in operational deployments.

Above: The prototype of the Airacobra series, the XP-39, is seen here in its original form, with air intakes for the carburettor and turbo-superchargers on the fuselage sides. With these intakes and the turbos later removed, it became the XP-39B.

Above: This is an early production example of the Airacobra, without wing armament. The elegant lines of the original Bell Model 11 are evident in this illustration, but the performance of production Airacobras, especially when tested by the RAF, was disappointing.

to the National Advisory Committee for Aeronautics at Langley Field, and NACA (predecessor of NASA) recommended over 60 modifications. The most significant was the elimination of the turbo-supercharger. The United States considered that the country's geographical position made it invulnerable to attack by high-altitude bombers, so the only possible missions for an American fighter would be close support and ground (or anti-ship) attack. Accordingly, the engine was changed to a V-1710-39 rated at 13,300 ft (4054 m).

The other major changes were to move the coolant radiators to the

9

Four 0.3-in (7.62-mm) wing guns plus two 0.5-in (12.7-mm) guns in the nose, together with a 20-mm hub cannon, gave these P-39D-1-BEs a substantial punch. They could also carry a 250-lb (113.5-kg) or 500-lb (227-kg) bomb under the fuselage in lieu of a drop tank.

roots of the wings, with leading-edge inlets, and the carburettor air inlet to the top of the fuselage; to reduce the span and increase the length; to redesign the canopy to have greater length and reduced height; and to add fairing doors over the mainwheel wells. Altogether the NACA changes resulted in a significant reduction in drag, but the deletion of the turbo greatly reduced the maximum speed and all high-altitude performance, the time to 20,000 ft (6100 m) being increased to 7½ minutes. At low levels there was little difference, and manoeuvrability was improved, so all 13 service-test aircraft were built as **YP-39B**s with the recommended changes.

Armour and armament

When the first YP-39B (40-27) flew on 13 September 1940 it also featured a significantly broader fin. The engine was a V-1710-37, rated at 1,090 hp (813 kW) at 13,300 ft (4054 m), and armament was installed, together with cockpit armour. The armament comprised a 37-mm T-9 cannon with 15 rounds, two 12.7-mm guns with 200 rounds each and two 7.62-mm guns each with 500 rounds. The four machine-guns were mounted in the top of the nose. All the modifications increased the gross weight to 7,235 lb (3282 kg), further reducing maximum speed to 368 mph (592 km/h). This did not greatly bother the Army, which on 10 August 1939 ordered 80 production aircraft. These were to be designated **P-45**, but the political climate did not allow what seemed to be a 'new' fighter, so the designation was changed to **P-39C**.

The first P-39C (40-2971) flew in January 1941. By this time, however, the Army had studied combat reports from Europe and decided that the Airacobra was inadequately protected; thus, only 20 of the first 80 were completed as P-39Cs. On 13 September 1940, the day on which the YP-39B first flew, the Army ordered 344 **P-39D**s. On the following day it ordered the last 60 C models to be completed as Ds. Among the changes were the provision of improved armour, self-sealing fuel tanks (reducing capacity from 170 to 120 US gal/645 to 454 litres), a bulletproof windscreen, and revised armament. The 7.62-mm guns were removed, but four similar guns, each with 1,000 rounds, were fitted in the outer wings. The ammunition box for the 37-mm gun was doubled in capacity, to 30 rounds. Empty weight was increased by 245 lb (111 kg), and performance fell further.

Back on 13 April 1940, the British had ordered no fewer than 675 of what seemed to be a wonderful aircraft (having believed Bell's XP-39 figures were typical of production aircraft). Originally to be called Bell Caribou I, the RAF Airacobra I was similar to the P-39D apart from the cannon being a long-barrelled Hispano 20-mm with 60

Specification
Bell P-39Q Airacobra
Type: single-seat fighter
Powerplant: one 1,200-hp (895-kW) Allison V-1710-83 liquid-cooled V-12 piston engine, driving a three-bladed Curtiss propeller
Performance: maximum speed 386 mph (621 km/h) at 9,500 ft (2895 m); cruising speed 200 mph (322 km/h); service ceiling 36,000 ft (10973 m); range 650 miles (1045 km)
Weights: empty 5,610 lb (2545 kg); maximum take-off 8,400 lb (3810 kg)
Dimensions: wing span 34 ft 0 in (10.36 m); length 30 ft 2 in (9.19 m); height 11 ft 10 in (3.61 m); wing area 213 sq ft (19.79 m²)
Armament: one 37-mm cannon firing through hub; two 0.5-in (12.7-mm) machine-guns in fuselage upper decking; provision for two more machine-guns in wing pods (usually deleted on Soviet aircraft) and ventral rack for one 500-lb (227-kg) bomb

Above: Final production version of the Airacobra was the P-39Q, which introduced 0.50-in (12.7-mm) guns in underwing fairings.

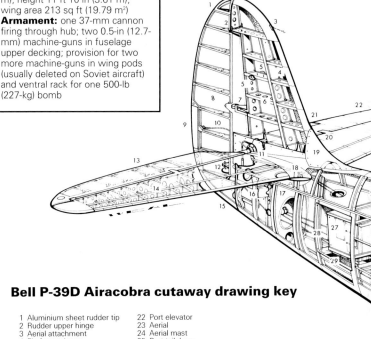

Bell P-39D Airacobra cutaway drawing key

1 Aluminium sheet rudder tip
2 Rudder upper hinge
3 Aerial attachment
4 Fin forward spar
5 Tall navigation lights
6 Fin structure
7 Rudder middle hinge
8 Rudder
9 Rudder tab
10 Rudder tab flexible shaft
11 Elevator control quadrant
12 Rudder control quadrant
13 Starboard elevator
14 Starboard tailplane
15 Rudder lower hinge
16 Control cables
17 Fuselage aft frame
18 Diagonal brace
19 Fin root fillet
20 Elevator hinge fairing
21 Elevator tab (port only)

22 Port elevator
23 Aerial
24 Aerial mast
25 Port tailplane
26 Aft fuselage semi-monocoque structure
27 Radio installation
28 Access panel
29 Radio equipment tray
30 Control quadrant
31 Oil tank armour plate
32 Aft fuselage/central chassis bulkhead
33 Engine oil tank
34 Prestone (cooler) expansion tank

35 Carburettor intake fairing
36 Carburettor intake shutter housing
37 Engine accessories
38 Central chassis web
39 Frame
40 Starboard longitudinal fuselage beam
41 Exhaust stubs
42 Allison V-1710-35 Vee 12-cylinder engine
43 Engine compartment decking

44 Aft-vision glazing
45 Crash turnover bulkhead
46 Turnover bulkhead armour plate
47 Auxiliary air intake
48 Ventral Prestone (coolant) radiator
49 Rear main spar/centre section attachment
50 Cylindrical oil radiator
51 Ventral controllable shutters
52 Auxiliary spar/centre section attachment

Left: This pre-Pearl Harbor photograph shows P-39Cs of the 31st Pursuit Group, then based at Selfridge Field, Michigan. Improved P-39D versions reached this and other Groups before combat use began. First in action were P-39s of the 8th Pursuit Group in New Guinea, early 1942.

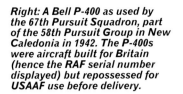

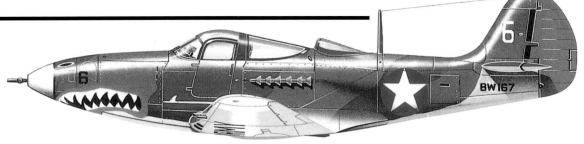

Right: A Bell P-400 as used by the 67th Pursuit Squadron, part of the 58th Pursuit Group in New Caledonia in 1942. The P-400s were aircraft built for Britain (hence the RAF serial number displayed) but repossessed for USAAF use before delivery.

53 Hoses
54 Shutter control rod access doors
55 Starboard mainwheel well
56 Mainwheel leg/rear main spar attachment point
57 Wing structure
58 Port flap structure
59 Aileron tab control link fairing
60 Aileron trim tab
61 Aileron servo tab
62 Wing rib
63 Starboard navigation light
64 Ammunition tanks
65 Two 0.3-in (7.62-mm) machine-guns

66 Inboard gun ammunition feed chute
67 Machine-gun barrels
68 Mainwheel door fairing
69 Starboard mainwheel
70 Axle
71 Mainwheel fork
72 Torque links
73 Mainwheel oleo leg
74 Wing fuel cells (6)
75 Fuel filler cap
76 Mainwheel retraction spindle
77 Fuel tank gauge capacity plate
78 Fuel tank access plate
79 Forward main spar
80 Oil cooler intakes
81 Intake duct rib cut-out
82 Wing centre-section
83 Aileron control cables

84 Undercarriage gear motor
85 Aileron control quadrant
86 Undercarriage emergency handcrank
87 Coolant radiator/oil temperature shutter controls
88 Sutton harness
89 Pilot's seat
90 Armoured glass turnover bulkhead frame
91 Cockpit entry doors
92 Internal rear-view mirror
93 Gunsight
94 Armoured glass windscreen
95 Steel plate armour overlap
96 Instrument panel frame
97 Control column
98 Control column yoke/drive shaft
99 Nosewheel retraction chain coupling

Right: Early production P-39Q-1-BEs await action at the south-east end of the runway on Makin Island in the Gilberts, late 1943.

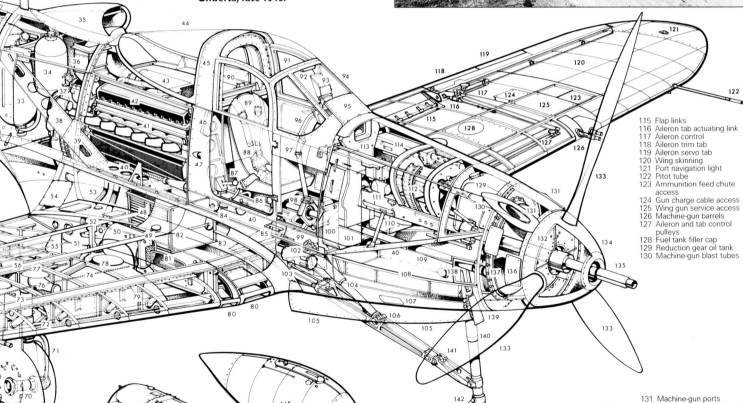

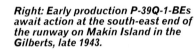

115 Flap links
116 Aileron tab actuating link
117 Aileron control
118 Aileron trim tab
119 Aileron servo tab
120 Wing skinning
121 Port navigation light
122 Pitot tube
123 Ammunition feed chute access
124 Gun charge cable access
125 Wing gun service access
126 Machine-gun barrels
127 Aileron and tab control pulleys
128 Fuel tank filler cap
129 Reduction gear oil tank
130 Machine-gun blast tubes

100 Rudder pedal assembly
101 Fuselage machine-gun ammunition tank
102 Nosewheel drive motor
103 Nosewheel retraction strut forged 'A'-frame attachments
104 Retraction screw
105 Nosewheel doors
106 Link assembly
107 Access plate
108 Nosewheel well
109 Drive shaft
110 Cannon aft support frame
111 37-mm M4 cannon breech
112 Circular endless belt-type cannon magazine (30 rounds)
113 Cockpit forward armoured plate
114 Two 0.5-in (12.7-mm) fuselage machine-guns

131 Machine-gun ports
132 Reduction gear box frontal armour
133 Three-bladed Curtiss Electric constant speed propeller
134 Spinner
135 Cannon muzzle
136 Blast tube access
137 Reduction gear casing
138 Nosewheel link
139 Nosewheel door forward fairing
140 Nosewheel oleo
141 Link assembly
142 Torque links
143 Axle fork
144 Rearward-retracting nosewheel
145 Ventral stores, options including auxiliary fuel tank, or;
146 Two-man life raft

Bell P-39 Airacobra

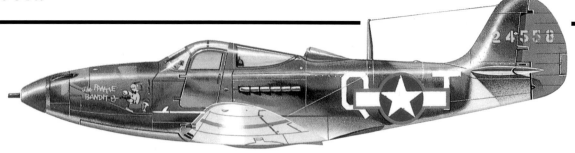

'Little Rebel' was the 29th production P-39Q-1-BE, and was the first Airacobra to reach the Gilbert Islands. It is seen here landing on Makin Island on 13 December 1943. Nearly 5,000 P-39Qs were built, making this the most-produced of all Airacobra versions.

small differences, all having the 1,325-hp (988-kW) Dash-63 engine. The next 240 Gs were built as **P-39M**s with an engine giving better performance at height, but worse performance lower down.

The first really massive production comprised 2,095 **P-39N**s. Almost all went to the Soviet Union, where they were popular as ground-attack aircraft, being found tough and able to return after suffering very severe battle damage. Most had the four wing fuel cells supplied as an optional kit, so that if range was unimportant the low-level performance could be marginally increased. Armour replaced a rear sheet of curved armour-glass, and altogether gross weight was reduced from 9,100 to 8,750 lb (4128 to 3969 kg).

The most important production variant of all was the **P-39Q**, output of which totalled 4,905, bringing total Airacobra production to 9,558. The initial **Q-1** sub-type replaced the four wing machine-guns with two underwing gondolas housing single 12.7-mm weapons. Fuel capacity and weight of armour shuttled between previous values, while some sub-types had four-bladed propellers. From the **Q-20** block the underwing guns were often omitted, the Soviet authorities considering one 37-mm and two 12.7-mm sufficient and the small gain in performance and agility to be valuable.

Allied air force use

By 1943 the P-39 was rapidly being replaced in US Army Air Force units, but it was being delivered to numerous units in other Allied air forces. By far the most important remained the IAP fighter regiments of the Soviet air forces, including many elite Guards units. The P-39Q served on all sectors of the Eastern Front right up to the final Battle of Berlin. A total of 165, almost all of them Q models, were supplied to the Free French air force, serving in Italy and southern France in 1944-45. The last USAAF unit was the 332nd Fighter Group which, equipped with 75 P-39Qs, joined the 15th Air Force in Italy in February 1944. Over 220 Ns and Qs were supplied to units of the Italian Co-Belligerent Air Force in 1944, operating mainly in northern Italy and over the Balkans. Bell did considerable work on the **P-76**, intended to be powered by the Continental IV-1430 inverted engine. The laminar-wing XP-39E was planned to test this engine, but the programme was dropped. Much earlier, in 1938, Bell had designed the **XFL-1 Airabonita** for the US Navy, with a shorter fuselage, tail-wheel landing gear, carrier equipment and many other changes. Carrier trials (which were failed) took place in February 1941. Later in the war, however, the US Navy did receive seven **F2L** Airacobras and a P-39Q-10 modified as the **XTDL-1**. All these were target drones, although much of the flight testing took place with human pilots. The production radio-controlled target was to have been the **A-7**, but this was never completed.

The last versions were two-seaters, almost all converted at service units. Most were **TP-39F**s and **RP-39Q**s, the former being a dual-control version. In each case the extra cockpit was added in front of the first, the armament being removed and the canopy hinging to the side. To maintain directional stability the dorsal fin fillet was enlarged and a long shallow ventral fin was added.

rounds, and all six machine-guns being Brownings of 7.7 mm. The first aircraft was test-flown in England on 6 July 1941, and by September No. 601 Squadron had re-equipped with the unusual US fighter. But by this time it was realised that it was useless as a fighter for the RAF, being 33 mph (53 km/h) slower than advertised and having totally inadequate high-altitude performance. On 10 October 1941 four of No. 601's aircraft flew a strafing mission over northern France, shooting up invasion barges. There were 19 other deficiencies, including lethal carbon monoxide concentration in the cockpit after firing the guns, random errors in the compass after firing the cannon, and an unacceptably long take-off run of 2,250 ft (686 m). The Airacobra was withdrawn, and of the British order 212 were diverted to the Soviet Union, 54 were lost at sea and 179 were taken over by the US Army as **P-400**s, most of which were rushed to bolster the defences of northern Australia and New Guinea. Nearly all the remainder, about 200 aircraft, were handed to the US 8th Air Force in England in 1942.

Production in 1941-42 centred on **P-39D-1**s, **D-2**s, **D-3**s and **D-4**s. All had provision for a 75-US gal (284-litre) drop tank or 500-lb (227-kg) bomb, and they respectively introduced a dorsal fin fillet and 20-mm M1 gun, V-1710-63 engine of 1,325 hp (988 kW), armoured oil and glycol radiators (these were earlier Ds rebuilt), and two cameras in the rear fuselage. There were still such deficiencies as lack of high-altitude gun heaters and gun hydraulic chargers and a tendency for oil to seep over the canopy from the propeller gearbox. The **P-39E** tested the laminar-flow wings later used on the P-63 KingCobra. The **P-39F**, 229 of which were built, had an Aeroproducts (instead of Curtiss) propeller and had the 12-stub exhaust first seen on the P-400. No G/H/I versions were built, but there were 25 **P-39J**s with automatic engine boost control and most features similar to the F. Bell delivered 210 **P-39K**s and 250 **P-39L**s, all ordered as Gs but with

This P-39Q-5 was converted to an unarmed TP-39 training variant, with a second cockpit ahead of the first and added fin area.

The P-39Q-5 sub-variant had increased wing fuel tankage and also carried a high-capacity tank under the fuselage.

This single example of the XFL-1 Airabonita, essentially a P-39 with a tailwheel undercarriage, was tested by the US Navy in 1940.

Bell P-59 Airacomet

The XP-59 designation was initially assigned to the Bell company Model 16, a twin-boom, propeller-driven pusher fighter developed from the firm's unbuilt XP-52. The fighter would have been powered by a 2,000-hp (1491-kW) Pratt & Whitney R-2800 engine driving six-bladed Hamilton Standard dual-rotation contra-rotating propellers. The aircraft was futuristic in appearance, with a bullet-shaped nose, but was nonetheless a holdover from the past.

When the project was cancelled at an early stage, re-issuing the XP-59 designation seemed a sensible way to guard the secrecy of one of the most hush-hush projects of the war, the **Bell P-59 Airacomet**, the first American jet fighter. Roughly contemporary with the Heinkel He 178 and Gloster E.28/39 but flown only after the later Messerschmitt Me 262 and Gloster Meteor, the P-59 Airacomet was to be an American vehicle for the British Whittle jet engine.

Because the UK was so far ahead of the USA in gas turbine development, the UK supplied the General Electric Company with specifications of what became the 2,000-lb (8.89-kN) thrust I-16 powerplant, later redesignated J31-GE-5. On 5 September 1941 Bell was tasked to build the XP-59A airframe,

the company Model 27. The first of three XP-59As (42-108784/108786) was trucked in secrecy to Muroc Dry Lake, California, draped in tarpaulin and with a fake propeller to conceal its revolutionary power source. First flight of the **XP-59A** was achieved on 1 October 1942 with Bell's chief test pilot, Robert M. Stanley, at the controls. The first military flight was by Brigadier General Laurence C. Craigie on 2 October 1942.

The twin-jet, mid-wing, tricycle-gear XP-59A offered only modest improvement in performance over the best propeller-driven fighters of the early 1940s, but USAAF planners recognised that jet power was the wave of

Top: The first of two YP-59As. Above: The XP-59A was fitted with a dummy propeller and canvas covers for security reasons when flooding at Muroc Dry Lake in April meant that it had to be removed promptly by road to nearby Hawes Field and then to Harpers Lake.

Right: The third XP-59A arrived at Muroc at the end of April 1943. The first two aircraft had meanwhile been building test hours slowly for the previous six months or so.

Left: First of the production Airacomets, this P-39A-BE came from the 50-strong batch delivered by August 1945. Plans to build 350 had been cut back progressively in the course of 1944. All the P-59As and P-59Bs emerged in overall natural metal finish.

Above: The XP-59A was first flown at Muroc on 1 October 1942. The serial number, 42-108784, was not applied to the aircraft until after testing began; the finish is the standard USAAF olive drab on upper surfaces and neutral grey beneath.

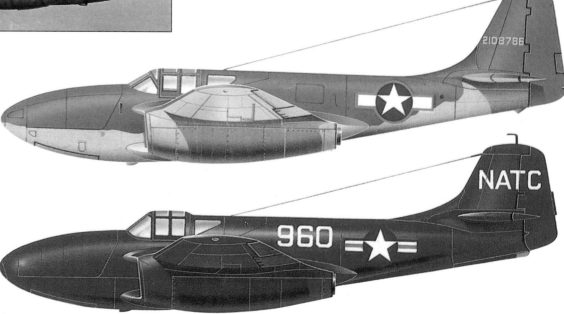

Right: Two YP-59As (and three P-59B-1s) were transferred to the US Navy, which retained the USAAF designation for these aircraft. Illustrated here is BuNo. 63960, originally 42-108778, repainted post-war and fitted with the P-59B-style fin and rudder.

Bell P-59 Airacomet

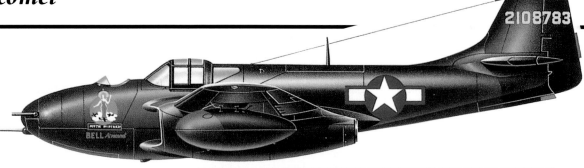

the future. Following the three test aircraft which had been powered by British-built engines designated I-A, 13 service-test **YP-59A**s (42-108771/108783) flew with the I-16. Production orders followed for 20 **P-59A** aircraft (44-22609/22628). The **XP-59B** was originally to have been a single-engined variant, but the 30 **P-59B**s completed (44-22629/22658) of 80 originally ordered retained the twin-jet layout with only minor changes. A sole YP-59A (42-108773), in 'trade' for a Gloster Meteor flown by the USAAF, was shipped to the British test centre at Farnborough with RAF serial RJ362/G, and evaluated only briefly. The US Navy designation **XF2L-1** is sometimes quoted for machines tested at NATC Patuxent River, Maryland, and the three P-59Bs in Navy markings (4422651, 44-22657/22658) did acquire bureau numbers (64100, 64108/ 64109), but the P-59B nomenclature was retained.

All production had been completed by the end of the war and many Airacomets were assigned to the USAAF's 412th Fighter Group for use as drones or controllers, some aircraft having a second open cockpit in the nose for an observer. In fact, it was in this unique open cockpit that Lawrence Bell made his first ride in a jet aircraft. No P-59, however, ever reached fully operational status or saw combat.

Specification
Bell P-59B
Type: single-seat jet fighter
Powerplant: two 2,000-lb (8.89-kN) thrust General Electric I-16 (J31-GE-5) centrifugal-flow turbojet engines
Performance: maximum speed 409 mph (658 km/h); cruising speed 375 mph (603 km/h); service ceiling 46,200 ft (14082 m); range 400 miles (644 km)
Weights: empty 8,165 lb (3704 kg); maximum take-off 13,700 lb (6214 kg)
Dimensions: span 45 ft 6 in (13.87 m); length 38 ft 2 in (11.62 m); height 12 ft 0 in (3.66 m); wing area 385.8 sq ft (35.84 m²)
Armament: one 37-mm M4 cannon and three 0.5 in (12.7 mm) machine guns in nose

Above: Photographed in December 1944, 'Smokey Stover' was the second P-59A-BE. Underwing drop tanks shown in this illustration have a capacity of 150 US gal (568 litres) each, stretching the aircraft's range to 520 miles (837 km).

Furthest from the camera in this photo, 'Reluctant Robot' was the 10th YP-59B, 42-108780, modified for use as a drone to help to develop radio-control equipment. In the foreground is 'Mystic Mistress', the two-seat drone controller.

Bell P-63 KingCobra

The Bell P-63 KingCobra was a wholly new fighter design using the essential layout of the P-39 Airacobra and introducing the laminar-flow wing and taller tail tested on the XP-39E. The USAAF ordered two **XP-63** prototypes (41-19511/19512) in June 1941, powered by the 1,325-hp (988-kW) Allison V-1710-47 engine located behind the pilot and driven by an extension shaft. The first machine flew on 7 December 1942, but was lost in an accident a few weeks later. The **XP-63A** (42-78015)

was originally conceived as a Merlin engine testbed under the designation **XP-63B,** but became instead a third prototype powered by a 1,325-hp (988-kW) Allison V-1710-93. The XP-63A was actually the fastest KingCobra built, attaining 426 mph (685 km/h) on military power at 20,000 ft (6096 m), but air combat was not to be the type's forte: the KingCobra was envisaged for the ground-attack role and for export, primarily to the Soviet Union.

The production **P-63A**, 1,825

of which were built in numerous sub-variants with minor changes in armament, armour and ordnance, was followed in 1943 by the **P-63C** with an 1,800-hp (1342-kW) Allison V-1716-117 engine with water injection. One P-63A (42-68937) was tested by the UK's Royal Air Force as the KingCobra Mk I (FR 408). The first P-63C (42-70886) introduced a distinctive small ventral fin intended to improve lateral stability characteristics. The sole **P-63D** (43-11718) was configured with a bubble canopy and

increased wingspan. The first **P-63E** (43-11720,) with minor changes, was followed by 12 further examples before contracts for 2,930 were cancelled at war's end. One **P-63F** (43-11719) introduced the V-1710-135 powerplant and, while a second was cancelled, survived to be H. L. Pemberton's mount in the 1947 Cleveland Air Races with civil registration NX1719.

Ferried to the USSR via Alaska and Iran, the P-63 KingCobra proved a potent attack aircraft and tank-buster. P-

The single example of the P-63D was distinguished by the rearwards-sliding bubble canopy and the slightly increased wing span.

This is one of the two P-63F-1s, which were readily identified by the taller fin and rudder, and which had increased engine power.

Several configurations of 'butterfly' or 'V' tails were tested by Bell on P-63s such as this, using the XP-63N designation.

63s also served with Free French forces. The relatively few aircraft retained by the USAAF were used primarily for training, and none is thought to have seen combat.

In 1945 and afterwards, P-63 KingCobras were used as flying targets, painted bright red, piloted, and shot at by other fighters using frangible bullets. These 'robot' **RP-63A** and **RP-63G** aircraft were insulated with a protective covering of duralumin alloy, bulletproof windscreen and canopy glass, a steel grille over the engine air intake, steel guards for the exhaust stacks, and thick-walled, hollow propellers. When a hit was scored by an attacking aircraft, a red light blinked to confirm impact, causing one RP-63A (42-69654) to be nicknamed 'Pinball'. For more than 25 years

A P-63A-9-BE flies on test close to its home, the Bell Aircraft Corporation plant at Buffalo, NY. The A-9 block of aircraft featured an increase in the number of rounds carried for the nose-mounted 37-mm cannon.

an RP-63G (45-57295) has been on outdoor display at Lackland AFB, Texas. This unique piloted target was redesignated **QF-63G** in 1948, although the 'Q' prefix usually denotes an unmanned drone.

The sole **XP-63H** was converted from a P-63E to test new internal systems. Two P-63s without specific designations were modified to test the V-shaped tail configuration more familiarly associated with the Beechcraft Bonanza. A sole P-63 was rebuilt with swept-back wings and test-flown by the US Navy, known as the **L-39**. A handful of standard aircraft were also tested by the Navy, although the **F2L** designation was not taken up.

Although total KingCobra production was a respectable 3,362 airframes, 2,456 being delivered to the Soviets, the type must be included among the second rank of wartime fighters and remembered as Bell's last great success in the fighter field.

Specification
Bell P-63A

Type: single-seat fighter
Powerplant: one 1,325-hp (988-kW) Allison V-1710-93 liquid-cooled 12-cylinder Vee piston engine driving a four-bladed propeller
Performance: maximum speed 410 mph (660 km/h) at 25,000 ft (7620 m); cruising speed 378 mph (608 km/h); service ceiling 43,000 ft (13106 m); range 450 miles (724 km)
Weights: empty 6,375 lb (2892 kg); maximum take-off 10,500 lb (4763 kg)
Dimensions: span 38 ft 4 in (11.68 m); length 32 ft 8 in (9.96 m); height 12 ft 7 in (3.84 m); wing area 248 sq ft (23.04 m²)
Armament: one 37-mm cannon and four (two wing-mounted and two nose-mounted) fixed forward-firing 0.5-in (12.7-mm) machine guns, plus up to three 522-lb (237-kg) bombs

Bell XP-77

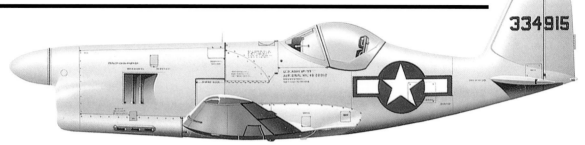

The first Bell XP-77 escaped being scrapped, and emerged in 1947 with fresh markings. This illustration shows it in its original form. The Ranger engine looked disproportionately large.

The **Bell XP-77**, an all-wood lightweight fighter made from Sitka spruce, patterned after racers of the 1930s and intended to operate from grass runways, was an astonishingly attractive machine. Yet when the first of two XP-77s (43-34915/34916) flew on 1 April 1944 at Niagara Falls, New York, with Jack Woolams at the controls, it was not unfitting that the date was April Fools' Day.

Initially, the idea of a small, cheap, all-wood fighter built with few strategic materials had

held high appeal. In early 1941 Larry Bell's upstate New York fighter team had begun work on a plane at first called the 'Tri-4', shorthand for an informal USAAF requirement for '400 hp, 4,000 lb, 400 mph'. On 16 May 1942, the USAAF ordered 25 'Tri-4' aircraft. Delays, technical problems with subcontracting plywood construction, and disappointing wind-tunnel tests caused the manufacturer to suggest by early 1943 that the number of machines on order be reduced to six. In May 1943, the USAAF

pared this figure to two, seeing the XP-77 as having no operational utility but as being useful in lightweight fighter research.

Beginning in July 1944, the second XP-77 was tested at Eglin Field, Florida. Spin problems led to a crash of this aircraft on 2 October 1944, which the pilot survived but the programme did not. Plagued by noise and vibration, an unexpectedly long take-off run, and general performance "inferior to the present fighter aircraft employed by the USAAF" (according to a report of the time), the XP-77 was killed by administrative fiat on 2 December 1944. The prototype went to Wright Field, then back to Eglin, then to Wright again. It was seen at post-war displays wearing spurious markings and its

This is one of the few photos that were taken of the second XP-77. An unusual feature was manually operated flaps.

final disposition is unknown. Described in a wartime promotional release as "an engine with a saddle on it", this effort ended up being another of the many 1941-45 programmes which failed to produce an operational aircraft.

Specification
XP-77
Type: single-seat fighter
Powerplant: one 520-hp (388-kW) Ranger XV-770-7 air-cooled 12-cylinder inverted-Vee piston engine driving a two-bladed propeller
Performance: maximum speed 330 mph (531 km/h); initial climb rate 3,600 ft (1097 m) per minute; service ceiling 30,100 ft (9174 m); range 550 miles (885 km)
Weights: empty 2,855 lb (1295 kg); maximum take-off 4,029 lb (1828 kg)
Dimensions: span 27 ft 6 in (8.38 m); length 22 ft 10 in (6.97 m); height 8 ft 2 in (2.5 m); wing area 100 sq ft (9.29 m²)
Armament: two 0.5-in (12.7-mm) fixed forward-firing machine-guns plus provision for one bomb or other ordnance up to 300 lb (136 kg) in weight

Boeing P-26

Devoid of unit markings, this was one of the last P-26As in service. It was retained as a hack with the 18th PG at Wheeler Field until early 1942.

It was in 1931 that Boeing presented proposals to the US Army for a diminutive monoplane fighter (the **Boeing Model 248**) around the well-tried Pratt & Whitney R-1340 nine-cylinder air-cooled radial engine. Construction of the first prototype started in January 1932, its first flight being made on 20 March before being delivered for service trials at Wright Field. All three prototypes were successful in their various trials and were accorded the successive designations **XP-26**, **Y1P-26** and finally **P-26**.

All P-26As were modified with curiously high headrest fairings, as shown here. Later versions followed suit.

On 11 January 1933 the US Army Air Corps and Boeing signed a contract for 111 examples of this improved design (the **Model 266**), to be designated the **P-26A**. As P-35s and P-36As entered service with home-based front-line squadrons, the P-26 was moved further afield, initially to the Panama Canal Zone and soon after to Wheeler Field, Hawaii. The 37th Pursuit Group received P-26s in 1940, its 31st Squadron still flying them

in 1942 (after the outbreak of World War II). One other group, the 18th, flew P-26s from Wheeler Field between 1938 and 1941, but they had been discarded in favour of P-40s by the time of the Japanese attack on Pearl Harbor.

Returning to the development of the P-26 itself, the addition of 25 aircraft to the original order brought changes to the powerplant. The first two aircraft, designated **P-26B**s and first flown on 10 January 1935, were powered by R-1340-33 engines with fuel injection, and were followed by 23 **P-26C**s, also with R-1340-33 engines but initially without fuel injection.

Specification
Boeing P-26A
Type: single-seat fighter
Powerplant: one 500-hp (373-kW) Pratt & Whitney R-1340-27 nine-cylinder air-cooled radial piston engine
Performance: maximum speed 234 mph (377 km/h) at 6,000 ft (1830 m); initial climb rate 2,360 ft (719 m) per minute; service ceiling 27,400 ft (8350 m); normal range 360 miles (579 km)
Weights: empty 2,271 lb (1031 kg); maximum take-off 3,012 lb (1366 kg)
Dimensions: span 27 ft 11 in (8.52 m); length 23 ft 10 in (7.26 m); height 10 ft 5 in (3.17 m); wing area 149.5 sq ft (13.89 m²)
Armament: two synchronised forward-firing 0.3-in (7.62-mm) machine-guns on sides of nose, plus provision to carry up to two 100-lb (45-kg) or five 30-lb (13.6-kg) bombs under fuselage and wings

Boeing XB-15/XC-105

However determined the majority of Americans might have been to maintain the nation's long-established policy of isolation, there were still numbers of radicals, in both the United States government and services, who realised that almost certainly the day would dawn when the USA would have to become involved in warlike activities. Given such circumstances, one of the essential weapons would be an advanced strategic bomber, and in the US Army men like Colonels Hugh Knerr and C.W. Howard were working steadily away in the 1930s to ensure, to the best of their capability, that when that moment came such a bomber would be available. This thinking had led to the introduction into service of bombers like the Boeing B-9, and the Martin B-10 and B-12. While it was appreciated that these did not represent the ideal, they prepared the way for the procurement of a true strategic bomber.

In 1933 came the US Army's requirement for a design study of such an aircraft: a range of 5,000 miles (8050 km) was included in the specification to provide long-range strategic capability. Both Boeing and Martin produced design studies, but it was the former company which received the US Army's contract for construction and development of their **Model 294**, under the designation **XB-15**. When this monoplane flew for the first time, on 15 October 1937, it was then the largest aircraft to be built in the USA.

As might be expected, it introduced a number of original features, including internal passages within the wing to permit minor engine repairs or adjustments in flight; two auxiliary power units within the fuselage to provide a 110-volt DC electrical system; sleeping bunks to allow for 'two-watch' operation; and the introduction of a flight engineer into the crew to reduce the pilot's workload. Intended to be powered by engines of around 2,000 hp (1491 kW), which did not materialise for some years, the actual powerplant comprised four 1,000-hp (746-kW) Pratt & Whitney Twin Wasp Senior radial engines, which meant that

The XB-15's engines were R-1830-11s, among the first versions of what later was just called the Twin Wasp.

performance was far below that estimated. Purely an experimental aircraft, it was, however, provided with cargo doors and flown as a cargo transport during World War II, under the designation **XC-105**.

Specification
Type: long-range bomber/transport
Powerplant: four 1,000-hp (746-kW) Pratt & Whitney Twin Wasp Senior radial piston engines
Performance: maximum speed 195 mph (314 km/h); service ceiling 18,900 ft (5760 m); range 5,130 miles (8256 km)
Weight: maximum take-off 92,000 lb (41731 kg)
Dimensions: span 149 ft 0 in (45.42 m); length 87 ft 11 in (26.80 m); height 18 ft 0 in (5.49 m)

Boeing B-17 Flying Fortress

The original Model 299 prototype is shown here, with R-1690 Hornet engines. The switch to the R-1820 Cyclone lost Pratt & Whitney orders for over 70,000 engines.

When viewing this earlier generation of Boeing classics, even the most sceptical observer cannot divorce the B-17 from the wartime fields of East Anglia, the strains of Glenn Miller and the monumental air battles fought over German cities from late 1942. However, there was a lot more to the B-17 than just its 8th Air Force service.

The vast armadas of the US 8th Air Force, equipped mainly with the Boeing B-17, ranged far and wide over Germany and occupied Europe in 1942-45, bombing individual factories and other precision targets and also whittling away at the fighter strength of the Luftwaffe

A B-17C of the 7th Bomb Group with, beyond, a B-17B of the 19th with the older 'C' (pre-May 1940) style of unit designator on the fin. The photograph was taken in January 1941.

In December 1941 this B-17D served with the 14th BS, 19th BG, at Clark Field, Luzon, Philippines. Only a few aircraft from this theatre escaped to Australia.

Boeing B-17 Flying Fortress

The B-17F, with a moulded Plexiglas nose, was the first version built in enormous numbers. This 1942 picture shows the then-standard olive drab camouflage with yellow serial and European theatre code letters.

in some of the largest and bloodiest air battles in all history. In 1934, such battles could not have been foreseen. The only targets within range of US bombers were in such unlikely places as Canada, Mexico and small British islands. In the Depression money was tight, and the new monoplane Martin Bomber appeared to be all that was needed.

When the US Army Air Corps put out a request for a new multi-engined bomber, a few far-sighted engineers at the Boeing Airplane Company decided to interpret 'multi-engined' as meaning not two engines (as had generally been done before) but four. Admittedly, they did this mainly in order to get more height over the target, but it had the effect of making the Boeing **Model 299** significantly larger than its rivals. Design began on 18 June 1934, and the prototype made a very successful first flight in the hands of Les Tower at Boeing Field on 28 July 1935. The main purpose of the new bomber was to defend the United States by bombing an invasion fleet (the only plausible kind of target), and it was the nature of this mission, rather than heavy defensive armament, that resulted in Boeing eventually registering the name 'Flying Fortress'.

Triumph and disaster

On 20 August 1935 the impressive aircraft, unpainted except for US Army Air Corps rudder stripes and civil registration NX13372, flew nonstop to Wright Field at an average speed faster than the maximum possible speed of its twin-engined rivals. On the first officially observed flight before the USMC evaluation officers, on 30 October 1935, the great bomber took off, climbed far too steeply, stalled and dived into the ground, bursting into a ball of fire. The accident was

caused entirely by someone having omitted to remove the external locks on the elevators, and although the immediate winner of the official trials had to be the Douglas B-18, the much greater potential of the great Boeing bomber resulted in a service-test order for 13, designated **Y1B-17**, placed on 17 January 1936.

These had many changes, especially to the landing gear, armament and in having 930-hp (694-kW) Wright Cyclone engines instead of 750-hp (560-kW) Pratt & Whitney Hornets. In 1937 the machines were delivered to the 2nd Bombardment Group at Langley Field, which subsequently flew almost 10,000 hours with no serious trouble and did more than any other unit in history to solve the problems of long-distance bombing, especially at high altitude. A 14th aircraft was built as the **Y1B-17A** with engines fitted with General Electric turbo-superchargers, which increased the speed from 256 mph (412 km/h) to 311 mph (500 km/h) and raised the operating height to well over 30,000 ft (9145 m).

Results with the **B-17** (as the Y1B was called after its test period was complete) were so good that the USMC not only fought for massive production numbers, in the teeth of opposition from the US Navy, but also with Boeing collaboration even planned a next-generation bomber which became the B-29. US Navy anger was so intense that production numbers had to be scaled down, and the production batch of the first series model, the **B-17B**, numbered only 39. These had numerous minor changes as well as a redesigned nose and large rudder, and were the first aircraft in the world to enter service with turbocharged engines. The B-17B entered service in 1939 and was the fastest, as well as the highest-flying, bomber in the world. The US Army Air Corps had by this time embarked on a major programme of perfecting long-range strategic bombing by day, using the massed firepower of a large formation to render interception hazardous. It was expected that, because of the B-17's speed and height, opposing fighters would be hard-pressed to keep up and would present an almost stationary (relative to the bombers) target that could be blasted by the fire from hundreds of machine-guns.

Greater power and speed

Boeing and Wright Field continued to improve the B-17, and in 1939 an additional 39 were ordered under the designation **B-17C**. These were much heavier, weighing 49,650 lb (22520 kg) compared with about 43,000 lb (19505 kg) for a B-17, because of increased armour, self-sealing tanks, heavier defensive armament (with twin 0.5-in/12.7-mm guns above and, in a new ventral 'bathtub', twin 0.3-in/7.62-mm guns in the nose and new flush side gun positions) and

Probably taken in 1941 during the activation of a new bomb squadron, this photograph shows B-17Es of the second production block, all of which had the newly developed Sperry manned ball turret.

This aircraft, 42-3259, was a **B-17F** of the 40th block built by Douglas at Long Beach. As 'Snafu', it served with the 332nd Bomb Squadron of the 94th Bomb Group.

B-17E 41-9023 was 'Yankee Doodle', which made headlines around the world by, on 17 August 1942, carrying General Ira C. Eaker, 8th Air Force Commander, on the first US raid on Europe.

This **B-17F-40-BO** had medium-green sprayed at random over the basic olive drab. It served with the 359th Bomb Squadron, 303rd Bomb Group from Molesworth, Cambridgeshire.

extra equipment. Despite the greater weight, the fitting of 1,200-hp (895-kW) engines made this the fastest of all versions, with a maximum speed of 320 mph (515 km/h). In spring 1941 a batch of 20 was assigned to the RAF, following 15 months of negotiations which finally resulted in the aircraft being supplied in exchange for complete information on their combat performance (this was prior to the 1940 Lend-Lease Act). As RAF **Fortress Mk I**s they had a disastrous and mismanaged career which dramatically reduced their numbers to a handful (about nine), which were transferred to Coastal Command and the Middle East.

Further extensive internal improvements, a new electrical system and engine-cowl cooling gills led to the **B-17D**, of which 42 were ordered in 1940. This was the latest model in service at the time of Pearl Harbor (7 December 1941), when 30 were destroyed on the ground at Hickam Field and at Clark Field, Philippines, the following day.

By this time Boeing had developed a visually different model which incorporated all the lessons learned in World War II in Europe. Called **Boeing 2990**, it entered US Army Air Force service in December 1941 as the **B-17E**. Its most striking change was the much larger tail, with a giant dorsal fin and long-span tailplane giving better control and stability at high altitude. Armament was completely revised, with paired 0.5-in (12.7-mm) guns in a powered turret behind the cockpit, in a ventral turret at the trailing edge, and in a new manual turret in the tail. Another pair of guns could be fired by hand from the roof of the radio compartment, and with a single hand-aimed gun at each waist position this made a total of 10 heavy machine-guns, plus two 0.3-in (7.62-mm) guns aimed from the nose.

Further improvements in armour and equipment all helped to increase gross weight to 54,000 lb (24494 kg), so cruising speed inevitably fell from 231 to only 210 mph (372 to 338 km/h). This was the first B-17 in large-scale production, and deliveries totalled 512, including 45 sent to the RAF as Fortress Mk IIAs.

Massive production

On 30 May 1942 Boeing flew the first **B-17F,** incorporating many changes which allowed gross weight to soar to 65,000 lb (29484 kg) with a potential bombload for short ranges of 20,800 lb (9435 kg), although on normal combat missions the load seldom exceeded 5,000 lb (2268 kg). The only obvious external change on the F model was the more pointed nose moulded in one piece of Plexiglas. This type went into production not only at Boeing but also in a great nationwide pool with assembly lines at Douglas (Long Beach) and Vega (a Lockheed subsidiary at Burbank). Boeing built 2,300 of this model, and Douglas and Vega added 605 and 500 respectively.

With the B-17E and B-17F the US 8th Air Force built up its early strength in England. The first combat mission was flown on 17 August 1942 by 12 B-17Es of the 97th Bomb Group against a marshalling yard near Rouen. This was the small beginning to the greatest strategic striking force ever created, which was to lead to a three-year campaign in the course of which 640,036 tons of bombs were dropped on German targets. At the cost of grievous losses, supremacy was eventually obtained even over the heart of Germany in daylight.

By far the most numerous model of B-17 was the last one. The **B-17G** was the final result of bitterly won combat experience, and

The XB-40 escort version can most readily be identified by the fact that the single gun in the top of the radio compartment was replaced by a second dorsal turret.

B-17E 41-2593 was converted into the first XC-108 transport. Named 'Bataan', it had 38 seats, and served as General Douglas MacArthur's personal transport.

among other changes it introduced a chin turret firing ahead with twin accurately-aimed 0.5-in (12.7-mm) guns. Previously, German fighters had brought down many B-17s with head-on attacks, but the B-17G, with the chin turret plus two more 0.5-in (12.7-mm) cheek guns (and possibly the dorsal turret) firing ahead, was a tougher proposition. The B-17G had enclosed waist positions, much greater ammunition capacity and, like most B-17Fs, paddle-blade propellers to handle the greater weight and prevent too much deterioration in performance. Most B-17Gs had improved turbochargers which actually increased service ceiling to 35,000 ft (10670 m), but these bombers were so heavy that the cruising speed fell to 182 mph (293 km/h). This increased the time the gigantic formations were exposed to rocket and cannon attack by the German fighters; conversely, of course, it lengthened the time the B-17 guns could destroy those fighters.

Electronic versions

Boeing built 4,035 B-17Gs, Douglas 2,395 and Vega 2,250, a total of 8,680. The total of all versions was 12,731, of which 12,677 were formally accepted by the USAAF. The B-17F was used by the RAF as the **Fortress Mk II** and the B-17G as the **Fortress Mk III**, the main user being Coastal Command. Some were modified with a radar in place of the chin or ball turret, and for use against surfaced U-boats a 40-mm Vickers S gun was fitted in a nose mount. The only electronic device often carried by USAAF B-17s was the early H2X or Mickey Mouse radar used for bombing through cloud. This set's scanner was normally housed in a retractable radome under the nose or in place of the ball turret.

The ball turret, a retractable installation on the B-24 Liberator, was fixed on the B-17. Originally the B-17E had been fitted with a drumtype ventral turret aimed by a gunner in the fuselage, sighting via a periscope. This was soon replaced by the aptly-named spherical ballturret made by the Sperry company. The gunner had to climb into

B-17E No. 41-2401 was rebuilt by Vega as the XB-38 with Allison V-1710-89 liquid-cooled powerplants. The radiators were in the leading edge between each pair of engines. Performance on test in May 1943 was impressive, but an engine fire soon destroyed the aircraft.

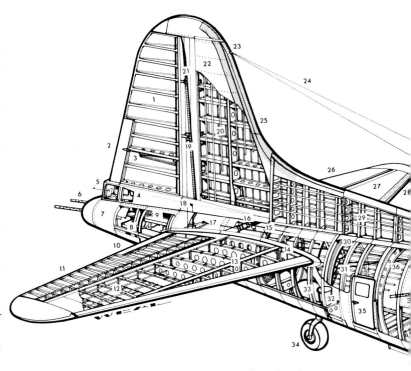

Boeing B-17F Flying Fortress cutaway drawing key

1 Rudder construction
2 Rudder tab
3 Rudder tab actuation
4 Tail gunner's station
5 Gunsight
6 Twin 0.5-in (12.7-mm) machine-guns
7 Tail cone
8 Tail gunner's seat
9 Ammunition troughs
10 Elevator trim tab
11 Starboard elevator
12 Tailplane structure
13 Tailplane front spar
14 Tailplane/fuselage attachment
15 Control cables
16 Elevator control mechanism
17 Rudder control linkage
18 Rudder post
19 Rudder centre hinge
20 Fin structure

21 Rudder upper hinge
22 Fin skinning
23 Aerial attachment
24 Aerials
25 Fin leading-edge de-icing boot
26 Port elevator
27 Port tailplane

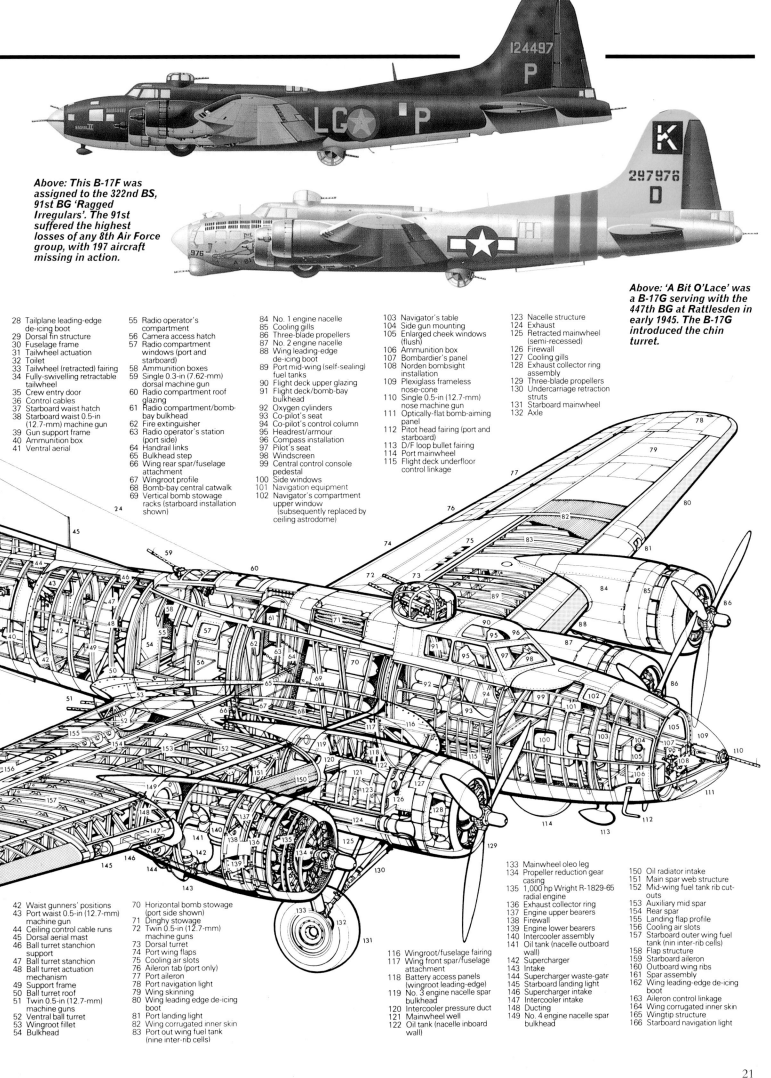

Above: This B-17F was assigned to the 322nd BS, 91st BG 'Ragged Irregulars'. The 91st suffered the highest losses of any 8th Air Force group, with 197 aircraft missing in action.

Above: 'A Bit O'Lace' was a B-17G serving with the 447th BG at Rattlesden in early 1945. The B-17G introduced the chin turret.

28 Tailplane leading-edge de-icing boot
29 Dorsal fin structure
30 Fuselage frame
31 Tailwheel actuation
32 Toilet
33 Tailwheel (retracted) fairing
34 Fully-swivelling retractable tailwheel
35 Crew entry door
36 Control cables
37 Starboard waist hatch
38 Starboard waist 0.5-in (12.7-mm) machine gun
39 Gun support frame
40 Ammunition box
41 Ventral aerial

55 Radio operator's compartment
56 Camera access hatch
57 Radio compartment windows (port and starboard)
58 Ammunition boxes
59 Single 0.3-in (7.62-mm) dorsal machine gun
60 Radio compartment roof glazing
61 Radio compartment/bomb-bay bulkhead
62 Fire extinguisher
63 Radio operator's station (port side)
64 Handrail links
65 Bulkhead step
66 Wing rear spar/fuselage attachment
67 Wingroot profile
68 Bomb-bay central catwalk
69 Vertical bomb stowage racks (starboard installation shown)

84 No. 1 engine nacelle
85 Cooling gills
86 Three-blade propellers
87 No. 2 engine nacelle
88 Wing leading-edge de-icing boot
89 Port mid-wing (self-sealing) fuel tanks
90 Flight deck upper glazing
91 Flight deck/bomb-bay bulkhead
92 Oxygen cylinders
93 Co-pilot's seat
94 Co-pilot's control column
95 Headrest/armour
96 Compass installation
97 Pilot's seat
98 Windscreen
99 Central control console pedestal
100 Side windows
101 Navigation equipment
102 Navigator's compartment upper window (subsequently replaced by ceiling astrodome)

103 Navigator's table
104 Side gun mounting
105 Enlarged cheek windows (flush)
106 Ammunition box
107 Bombardier's panel
108 Norden bombsight installation
109 Plexiglass frameless nose-cone
110 Single 0.5-in (12.7-mm) nose machine gun
111 Optically-flat bomb-aiming panel
112 Pitot head fairing (port and starboard)
113 D/F loop bullet fairing
114 Port mainwheel
115 Flight deck underfloor control linkage

123 Nacelle structure
124 Exhaust
125 Retracted mainwheel (semi-recessed)
126 Firewall
127 Cooling gills
128 Exhaust collector ring assembly
129 Three-blade propellers
130 Undercarriage retraction struts
131 Starboard mainwheel
132 Axle

42 Waist gunners' positions
43 Port waist 0.5-in (12.7-mm) machine gun
44 Ceiling control cable runs
45 Dorsal aerial mast
46 Ball turret stanchion support
47 Ball turret stanchion
48 Ball turret actuation mechanism
49 Support frame
50 Ball turret roof
51 Twin 0.5-in (12.7-mm) machine guns
52 Ventral ball turret
53 Wingroot fillet
54 Bulkhead

70 Horizontal bomb stowage (port side shown)
71 Dinghy stowage
72 Twin 0.5-in (12.7-mm) machine guns
73 Dorsal turret
74 Port wing flaps
75 Cooling air slots
76 Aileron tab (port only)
77 Port aileron
78 Port navigation light
79 Wing skinning
80 Wing leading edge de-icing boot
81 Port landing light
82 Wing corrugated inner skin
83 Port out wing fuel tank (nine inter-rib cells)

116 Wingroot/fuselage fairing
117 Wing front spar/fuselage attachment
118 Battery access panels (wingroot leading-edge)
119 No. 3 engine nacelle spar bulkhead
120 Intercooler pressure duct
121 Mainwheel well
122 Oil tank (nacelle inboard wall)

133 Mainwheel oleo leg
134 Propeller reduction gear casing
135 1,000 hp Wright R-1829-65 radial engine
136 Exhaust collector ring
137 Engine upper bearers
138 Firewall
139 Engine lower bearers
140 Intercooler assembly
141 Oil tank (nacelle outboard wall)
142 Supercharger
143 Intake
144 Supercharger waste-gate
145 Starboard landing light
146 Supercharger intake
147 Intercooler intake
148 Ducting
149 No. 4 engine nacelle spar bulkhead

150 Oil radiator intake
151 Main spar web structure
152 Mid-wing fuel tank rib cut-outs
153 Auxiliary mid spar
154 Rear spar
155 Landing flap profile
156 Cooling air slots
157 Starboard outer wing fuel tank (nin inter-rib cells)
158 Flap structure
159 Starboard aileron
160 Outboard wing ribs
161 Spar assembly
162 Wing leading-edge de-icing boot
163 Aileron control linkage
164 Wing corrugated inner skin
165 Wingtip structure
166 Starboard navigation light

Boeing B-17 Flying Fortress

Boeing B-17 variants

Model 299/XB-17: company-funded prototype armed with five 0.3-in machine-guns

Y1B-17: 13 pre-production aircraft for evaluation; GR-1820-39 engines and 8,000-lb bombload

Y1B-17A: single aircraft completed with GR-1820-51 supercharged engines

B-17: redesignation of Y1B-17s in service with 2nd BG

B-17A: redesignation of Y1B-17A

B-17B: similar to Y1B-17 but with enlarged flaps and rudder, redesigned nose transparency and hydraulic brakes; 1,000-hp R-1820-65 engines

B-17C: self-sealing fuel tanks introduced, crew armour fitted and side gun blisters deleted; ventral gun blister replaced by bathtub fairing; 38 built (20 to RAF as Fortress Mk I)

B-17D: similar to B-17C but with revised electrics and more armour protection; 42 built (plus 18 conversions from B-17C)

B-17E: first model with redesigned and enlarged tail surfaces; revised armament of one 0.3-in gun in nose, two waist 0.5-in guns, and nose, chin and tail turrets each with two 0.5-in guns; 512 built

B-17F: similar to B-17E but with moulded Plexiglas nosecone and modified engine cowlings; late-production aircraft powered by 1,380-hp GR-1820-97 engines and featuring increased fuel capacity and underwing bomb racks; total 2,300

XB-17F: one B-17F used by NACA for tests

ZB-17F: designation of remaining B-17Fs after 1948

B-17G: as B-17F but featuring a chin turret with two 0.5-in guns; provision for additional armament and staggered waist gun positions; later aircraft with revised tail turret and better supercharging; 8,680 built

CB-17G: transport conversion of B-17G

DB-17G: drone director version, originally designated CQ-4

EB-17G/JB-17G: one aircraft (originally EB-17G) converted with flight deck moved aft and 5,500-shp XT35W turboprop in nose; later tested other engines with Curtiss-Wright; one more JB-17G produced for Pratt & Whitney

SB-17G: redesignation of B-17H

TB-17G: crew trainer conversion of B-17G

VB-17G: staff transport conversion of B-17G

XB-17G: single B-17G employed on test duties

B-17H: conversion of about 12 B-17Gs with air-droppable lifeboat under belly for air-sea rescue role; redesignated SB-17G in 1948

TB-17H: projected trainer version for air-sea rescue role

QB-17L: target drone conversion of B-17G

QB-17N: similar to QB-17L but lacking TV transmitters

DB-17P: at least four B-17Gs converted as drone directors; later redesignated QB-17P

XB-38: single B-17E re-engined with four V-1710-89 inline engines for trials

XB-40: one B-17F converted as armed escort with 10 0.5-in machine-guns

TB-40: four B-17Fs converted to train crews for YB-40s

YB-40: 20 B-17Fs converted as escort bombers, with two dorsal and two ventral turrets in addition to the chin and tail armament

BQ-7: about 25 B-17Es and B-17Fs converted as flying-bombs; later redesignated QB-17G, and a further variant was the MB-17G

XC-108: one B-17E converted for General MacArthur's personal use; all armament removed, extra windows and 38 seats fitted

YC-108: one B-17F converted as staff transport

XC-108A: one B-17E converted without armament and with side cargo door fitted

XC-108B: one B-17F converted to serve as unarmed tanker

F-9: 16 B-17Fs converted for reconnaissance with cameras in bomb bay; subsequently redesignated FB-17F and then RB-17F

F-9A: 25 B-17Fs with alternative camera installations

F-9B: redesignation of F-9As after modification of camera installation; later FB-17F/RB-17F

F-9C: 10 B-17Gs converted with camera installations in both chin and bomb bay positions; subsequently redesignated FB-17G and then RB-17G

PB-1: single B-17F transferred to the US Navy; later modified to B-17G standards and later to unarmed trials configuration

PB-1G: 17 B-17Gs transferred to US Coast Guard for air-sea rescue role; brought up to SB-17G standards

PB-1W: 30 B-17Gs transferred to US Navy and fitted with APS-20 search radar in ventral radome

This B-17G is painted as 'A Bit O'Lace', of the 447th BG, which flew 83 missions from Rattlesden, Norfolk. Wing chevron was blue and the two fuselage bands (from January 1945) were green. The photograph below shows a B-17G-25-VE of the 364th BS, 305th 'Can Do' BG.

this and squat with his knees fully bent for perhaps five or six hours. A belly landing could flatten the ball-turret and its occupant, and there were many occasions when – because of combat damage – the turret doors jammed and a belly landing would have killed the ball-turret gunner. Normal procedure for a belly landing was to get the gunner out and then, using special tools, disconnect the whole turret from the aircraft and let it fall free. On one occasion a B-17 returned with severe combat damage and jammed landing gears, and near its home airfield it was found that the special tools were not on board. The executive officer of the station was notified by radio; within minutes he had grabbed a set of tools and taken off. For more than two hours he circled in close formation with the stricken B-17 trying to pass the tools on the end of a cable. He succeeded.

In 1942 various special versions of B-17 were produced by Vega to serve as escort fighters. The first was the second Boeing-built B-17F, which was rebuilt as an **XB-40** with many armament changes including a second dorsal turret and a bomb bay full of ammunition. It was followed by 20 **YB-40**s with even heavier armament, including quadruple gun mounts at nose and tail and a total of as many as 30 guns of up to 37- or 40-mm calibre. So heavy were these 'fighters' that they could not even keep formation with the B-17 bombers, and although they flew nine combat missions in 1943 they were judged unsuccessful.

In 1943 Boeing converted the ninth production B-17E to have liquid-cooled Allison engines of 1,425 hp (1063 kW) each; these naturally resulted in improved performance, but it remained a one-off prototype (designated **XB-38**). Another unique machine was the plush **XC-108** VIP transport which began life as a B-17E (41-2593) but was converted for General Douglas MacArthur, Supreme Commander in the Pacific, with a comfortable interior for 38 passengers. The **XC-108A** was a similar conversion but for cargo, with a large door on the left side. The **YC-108** was a VIP conversion of a B-17F, and the **XC-**

Above: Escorting fighters, probably P-38s, weave high contrails as B-17Fs of the 390th Bomb Group head for a target in 1943.

Left: B-17G-55-DL 44-6537 lets go a complete load of what are probably fragmentation bombs. It served with the 340th Bomb Squadron, 97th Bomb Group, 15th Air Force, in the Italian theatre.

108B was a B-17F tanker which ferried fuel over the 'Hump' from India to China.

The **F-9**s were a batch of 16 B-17Fs rebuilt by United Airlines at Cheyenne as strategic reconnaissance machines with from six to 10 cameras in fuselage installations. Another 45 B-17Fs were converted as **F-9A**s or **F-9B**s, while 10 B-17Gs were turned into **F-9C**s, the post-war designation for survivors being **FB-17** up to 1947 and **RB-17** thereafter. One B-17F served with the US Navy, and late in the war 40 B-17Gs were transferred to the US Navy to pioneer the technique of AEW (airborne early warning) with the newly developed APS-120 radar in a vast chin blister; this variant was designated **PB-1W**.

A strange wartime rebuild was the Aphrodite cruise missile conversion in which war-weary B-17Fs and B-17Gs were stripped of everything that could be removed and packed with 10 tons of Torpex, a British explosive with 50 per cent greater blasting power than Amatol. Under the project names 'Perilous' and 'Castor', many tests were made, the take-off being made by two pilots in an open cockpit who

then baled out to leave the Fortress (official designation **BQ-7**) under radio control from an accompanying aircraft such as a B-17 or PV-1. Though 11 combat launches were made on German targets the idea was judged too perilous after one BQ-7 had made a crater more than 100 ft (30 m) in diameter in England and another had broken radio link and orbited a British city before heading out to sea.

In 1944 British experience was used in converting B-17Gs into B-17H air/sea rescue aircraft with an airborne lifeboat and search radar; post-war, these were designated **SB-17G**. Other post-war variants included the **CB-17** and **VB-17** transports, **TB-17** trainers, radio-guided **QB-17** versions and **DB-17** radio director aircraft. These soldiered on with the USAF after its formation in 1947, and also with various minor air forces.

No history of the B-17 would be complete, however, without reference to its exciting cloak-and-dagger operations with I/KG 200, the clandestine *Gruppe* of the Luftwaffe. The B-17, mainly the G model, was its most important captured type, used for numerous long-range missions under the cover designation **Dornier Do 200**. These machines carried out daring operations throughout Europe, from Norway to Jordan and the Western Desert. They were not specifically intended to deceive the Allies, and wore German markings; they were used just because they were better for the job than any German aircraft.

Above: From 1944 a total (originally planned to be 130) of 12 B-17Gs were converted into ASR (air/sea rescue) aircraft, most carrying an airborne lifeboat and much special equipment, including radar in place of the chin turret. Designated B-17H, they were restyled SB-17G in 1948.

Left: Escorted by a solitary P-51B, B-17Gs of the 381st Bomb Group head back to Ridgewell. Most are from the 532nd Bomb Squadron, but the aircraft nosing in at extreme left is from the 533rd.

Boeing B-17F-40 Flying Fortress 359th BS, 303rd BG, 8th AF, Molesworth, 1942-45

The most famous American bomber of World War II was actually conceived as a defensive aircraft: when in 1934 the Army issued a specification for a multi-engined anti-ship bomber it was because the hostile nations appeared to be within bombing range of the USA. In Britain, more than anywhere else in the world, the B-17 evokes vivid memories of courageous aircrew who day after day – despite horrific losses – continued to attack strategic targets in Europe for three gruelling years, until the war was won.

Armament

The defensive armament of the B-17F was normally 12 0.5-in (12.7-mm) machine-guns. The 'E' was the first Fortress to incorporate power-driven turrets and a tailgun position. The 'F' model was similar to the 'E' model, but fitted with additional fuel tanks and with external racks under inner wings for a maximum of two 4,000-lb (1815-kg) bombs over short ranges. This version incorporated modifications based on RAF experience. Two guns were 'cheek' mountings, one on each side of the plastic nose; two in an electrically-operated turret on top of the fuselage, just aft of the pilot's cockpit; one manually-operated, firing through the top of the fuselage above the radio operator's compartment; two in a Sperry electrically-operated 'ball' turret below the fuselage, just aft of the trailing edge of the wing; two on hand-operated mountings and firing through side ports; one on each side of the fuselage midway between wings and tail; and two in the extreme tail.

Powerplants

The original Model 299 was powered by Pratt & Whitney Hornet R-1690E engines of 559 kW (750 hp), but all subsequent production models had versions of the Wright Cyclone R-1820. The B-17B had 746-kW (1,000-hp) Wright R-1820-51 engines with exhaust-driven superchargers, and the B-17C Fortress Mk I featured Wright R-1820-65 engines that developed 895 kW (1,200 hp). These were nine-cylinder air-cooled radials of 1,823-cu in (29.88-litre) capacity and had forged aluminium-alloy heads, with the fins machined out and with the application of Wright 'W' fin to the cylinder barrels. A Stromberg Model PD12K10 injection downdraught fully-automatic non-icing carburettor was located on top of the supercharger rear section. Later B-17F Fortress Mk IIs and the B-17G Fortress Mk III had the 895-kW (1,200-hp) R-1820-97 engines. General Electric Type B-22 exhaust-driven turbochargers were installed in the undersides of the engine nacelles. Propellers were Hamilton Standard three-bladed constant-speed of 11 ft 7 in (3.54 m) diameter. Self-sealing fuel tanks were carried in the wings; normal fuel capacity, carried in six tanks in the inner wing sections, totalled 1,700 US gal (6435 litres). Nine self-sealing auxiliary feeder tanks were fitted in the outer wings, and two self-sealing droppable ferry tanks could be carried in the bomb bay. Maximum capacity of all wing tanks was 2,780 US gal (10523 litres). There was a self-sealing hopper oil tank in each engine nacelle, the total oil capacity being 148 US gal (560 litres).

Specification
Boeing B-17F-25-BO
Type: heavy bomber with crew of eight to 10
Powerplant: four 1,200-hp (895-kW) Wright R-1820-97 Cyclone radial piston engines
Performance: maximum speed 295 mph (475 km/h); initial climb rate 900 ft (274 m) per minute; service ceiling 36,000 ft (10975 m); combat radius with 5,000-lb (2270-kg) bombload 800 miles (1287 km)
Weights: empty (typical) 34,000 lb (15422 kg); loaded (normal) 56,000 lb (25400 kg); (war overload from 1943) 72,000 lb (32660 kg)
Dimensions: span 103 ft 9 in (31.6 m); length 74 ft 9 in (22.8 m); height 19 ft 2 in (5.85 m); wing area 1,420 sq ft (131.92 m²)
Armament: maximum bombload 9,600 lb (4355 kg), later increased to 17,600 lb (7983 kg); defensive firepower normally 12 guns of 0.5-in (12.7-mm) calibre

Crew

Normal crew complement was nine, but could be more. The bomb-aimer's compartment was in the extreme nose. The pilot's compartment, seating two side by side with dual controls, was in front of the leading edge of the wings; aft of the pilot's position was an upper electrically-operated turret. The radio operator's position was amidships. The gun positions were aft of the wings, one electrically-operated turret beneath the fuselage and one position in the extreme tail.

Markings

In the summer of 1943 42-5177 had medium green blotching on olive drab upper surfaces. The effects of the English weathering appears to have given it a purplish hue. Lettering at this time was in yellow, black being used after the switch on 1 January 1944 to natural metal finish. With the inscription *Fast Woman* on the nose, this depicts the period prior to July 1943 when the national insignia changed. 'BN' relates to the 303rd Bomb Group (others in the group were GN, PU and VK). 'U' on the fuselage, which in this instance stood for 'Uncle', is repeated on the tailfin.

Boeing B-29 Superfortress

No other aircraft ever combined as many technological advances as the B-29. Designed for a specific strategic task, it later spawned the double-deck Stratocruiser airliner and the KC-97 tanker/transport, and laid the foundations for the super-successful Boeing airliner series. It also provided the Soviet Union with the starting block for the entire Tupolev heavy aircraft lineage, when US aircraft force-landed on Soviet territory at the end of the war. By reverse-engineering, Tupolev managed to produce the Tu-4 copy, and from it developed a huge range of bombers and airliners. It is probable that a detailed analysis of the Soviet 'Blackjack' swing-wing bomber of the 1980s would unearth design features that can be traced right back to the B-29.

Even more amazing was that the Boeing B-29 Superfortress was started more than three years before the USA entered World War II, in October 1938. In one of his last acts before he was killed in a crash at Burbank, the US Army Air Corps Chief of Staff, General Oscar Westover, had officially established a requirement for a new super-bomber to succeed the Boeing B-17, at a time when the B-17 itself was being denied funds by the Congress. Despite a totally negative reaction from the War Department, procurement chief General Oliver Echols never gave up in his fight to keep the superbomber alive, and it had the backing of 'Hap' Arnold, Westover's successor. The bomber was to be pressurised to fly very quickly at high altitude: the figures for speed (390 mph; 628 km/h), range (5,333 miles; 8582 km) and military load were staggering.

Design solutions

At the Boeing Airplane Company in Seattle there was, at least, experience of large pressurised aircraft, unlike all other companies, but there seemed no way to reconcile the conflicting factors. For most of 1939 the answer seemed to be to fit Pratt & Whitney's slim sleeve-valve liquid-cooled engines inside the wing, but newly hired George Schairer soon pointed out that as the biggest drag item was the wing, the best course was to make the wing as small as possible and not try to put engines inside it. (Thus began a basic philosophy which saw sharp contrast between the Boeing B-47 and the British V-bombers, and has continued to today's Boeing Models 757 and 767.) How does one pressurise a fuselage containing enormous bomb doors? The answer was to make the colossal bomb bays unpressurised and link the front and rear pressure cabins by a sealed tunnel. Chief engineer

The capture of the Marianas islands was fundamental to the success of the strategic bombing campaign against Japan, which had previously been undertaken on a small scale from less-than-ideal bases in China. From October 1944 the islands of Guam (illustrated), Saipan and Tinian groaned under the weight of a huge armada of B-29s.

Above: Destined to remain with Boeing as a test vehicle throughout the war, the first of the three XB-29 prototypes was readied for its maiden flight at Boeing Field, Seattle, on 21 September 1942. It was finished in the then-standard olive drab and neutral grey.

Above: The Wright R-3350 twin-row radial engines served the Superfortress well for the whole of its career, but the potential value of other powerplants was not ignored. This YB-39 was the first of the YB-29s re-engined with inline Allison V-3420-11 engines.

Wellwood Beall was first to crawl through the mock-up tunnel in January 1940.

By March 1940 the demands had increased, including 16,000 lb (7258 kg) of bombs for short-range missions, powered turrets, and far more protection including armour and self-sealing tanks. Weight had already leapt in stages from 48,000 to 85,000 lb (21773 to 38556 kg), and with the fresh demands the design finally rounded out at a daunting 120,000 lb (54432 kg). With just 1,739 sq ft (161.55 m²) of wing, the wing loading was going to be 69 lb/sq ft (336.9 kg/m²), about double the figure universally taken in 1940 as the desirable limit. Test pilot Eddie Allen was happy that the Boeing Model 345 would be flyable (just) if it had the biggest and most powerful high-lift flaps ever thought of, to reduce take-off and landing speeds to about 160 mph (257 km/h), which was about double the equivalent speed of such familiar machines as the B-17 and Supermarine Spitfire.

As the BEF was rescued from the beaches at Dunkirk the new

Above: With its Seattle factories committed to production of the B-17, Boeing put its new superbomber into production at a massive new factory at Wichita, Kansas. The first Superfortresses built there were the 14 service-test YB-29s, which – like the XB-29 prototype – had regular USAAF finish. Fully armed, they had R-3350-21 engines and three-bladed propellers.

Above: The 29th production model Superfortress built at Wichita, this B-29-1-BW was in service with the 486th Bomb Group as part of the 58th Bomb Wing (Heavy) in India in November 1944. Stripped of armament, it was used to fly fuel over 'the Hump' to the B-29 bases in China. The name 'Esso Express' is suitably descriptive – and 30 camel-shaped mission symbols on the nose were indicative of the intensity of these dangerous operations.

Left: Superfortresses entered combat service in the Pacific area in mid-1944, hitting Japan's mainland at Yarrata on 15 June. More than 17,000 tons of bombs would be dropped by B-29s in the next 14 months. Here, B-29s – apparently of the 314th Bomb Wing – approach the distinctive twin runways of North Field, Guam, in the Marianas Group, at the conclusion of a 3,000-mile mission.

Whatever opinions are now held on the decision to drop a second atom bomb on Japan in August 1945, public sentiment at the time was universally in favour. It was Nagasaki's misfortune, though, that the intended target for 'Bock's Car' carrying 'Fat Man' was cloud-obscured.

Boeing B-29 Superfortress cutaway drawing key

1 Temperature probe
2 Nose glazing
3 Optically flat bomb aiming panel
4 Bombsight
5 Windscreen panels
6 Forward gunsight
7 Bombardier's seat
8 Pilot's instrument console
9 Control column
10 Co-pilot's seat
11 Pilot's seat
12 Side console panel
13 Cockpit heating duct
14 Nose undercarriage leg strut
15 Steering control
16 Twin nosewheels
17 Retraction struts
18 Nosewheel doors
19 Underfloor control cable runs
20 Pilot's back armour
21 Flight engineer's station
22 Forward upper gun turret, four 0.5-in (12.7-mm) machine-guns, 500 rpg
23 Radio operator's station
24 Chart table
25 Navigator's instrument rack
26 Fire extinguisher bottle
27 Forward lower gun turret, two 0.5-in (12.7-mm) machine-guns, 500 rpg
28 Ventral aerial
29 Navigator's seat
30 Hydraulic system servicing point
31 Access ladder
32 Forward cabin rear pressure bulkhead
33 Armoured bulkhead
34 Pressurised tunnel connecting front and rear cabins
35 Astrodome observation hatch
36 Forward bomb racks
37 Bomb hoisting winches
38 Catwalk

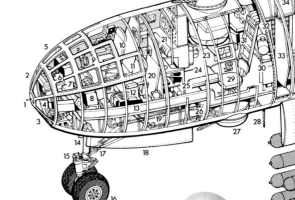

bomber was designated the **B-29**, and in August the US Army Air Corps provided funds for two (later three) prototypes. Work was rushed ahead, but nobody knew how to stop guns and propeller mechanisms from freezing at far more than 30,000 ft (9145 m), which Boeing was confident the aircraft could reach. The intense wing loading was all against the designers, but using four monster Wright R-3350 Duplex Cyclones, each with not one but two of General Electric's best turbochargers and driving 16-ft 7-in (5.05-m) Hamilton Standard four-bladed propellers, the propulsion was equal to the task.

Fuselage structure

Behind the nose section were two giant bomb bays, from which an electric sequencing system released bombs alternately from front and rear to preserve the centre of gravity position. Between the two bays was a ring forming the structural heart of the aircraft and integral with the main wing box, the strongest aircraft part built up to that time. On the wing were four monster nacelles, which Schairer showed to have less drag than engines buried in a bigger wing. After four main gears had been studied, a way was found to fold simple two-wheel gears into the inboard nacelles. Fowler flaps were screwed out electrically to add 21 per cent to area of the wing, fighting a wing loading which by September 1940 reached 71.9 lb/sq ft (351.1 kg/m²) and climbed to a frightening 81.1 lb/sq ft (396 kg/m²) by the time of the first combat mission.

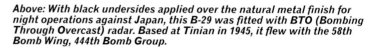

Behind the wing the rear pressure cabin had three sighting stations linked to two upper and two lower turrets, each with twin 0.5-in (12.7-mm) machine-guns. The electric fire control was normally set so that the top station controlled either or both of the upper turrets, the side stations the lower rear turret, and the bombardier the forward lower turret, but control could be overridden or switched (because gunners could be knocked out in action). In the extreme tail was another gunner driving a turret with two 0.5-in (12.7-mm) guns and a 20-mm cannon.

In any case, over 2,000 B-29s were to be built before this turret could come into production, because immediately after Pearl Harbor a colossal manufacturing programme was organised, involving vast new

Above: With black undersides applied over the natural metal finish for night operations against Japan, this B-29 was fitted with BTO (Bombing Through Overcast) radar. Based at Tinian in 1945, it flew with the 58th Bomb Wing, 444th Bomb Group.

plants across the nation. Major parts were made in over 60 new factories, the enormous nacelles - each as big as a P-47 - coming from a new Cleveland facility operated by the Fisher Body Division of General Motors. Final assembly was organised at three of the world's largest buildings, Boeing at Wichita, Martin at Omaha and Bell at Marietta (today the same building houses the Lockheed Georgia Company). Later, yet another line was set up at Boeing Renton. All this had been organised before the olive-drab **XB-29** (41002) had

Boeing B-29 Superfortress

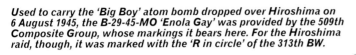

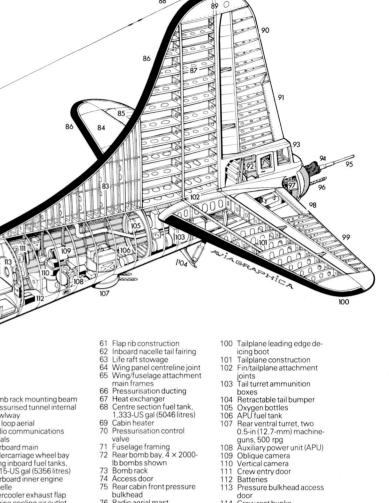

Used to carry the 'Big Boy' atom bomb dropped over Hiroshima on 6 August 1945, the B-29-45-MO 'Enola Gay' was provided by the 509th Composite Group, whose markings it bears here. For the Hiroshima raid, though, it was marked with the 'R in circle' of the 313th BW.

39 Bomb rack mounting beam
40 Pressurised tunnel internal crawlway
41 D/F loop aerial
42 Radio communications aerials
43 Starboard main undercarriage wheel bay
44 Wing inboard fuel tanks, 1,415-US gal (5356 litres)
45 Starboard inner engine nacelle
46 Intercooler exhaust flap
47 Engine cooling air outlet flaps
48 Engine cowling panels

49 Hamilton Standard 4-bladed constant-speed propellors, 16 ft 7 in diameter
50 Propeller hub pitch change mechanism
51 Starboard outer engine nacelle
52 Exhaust stub
53 Wing outboard fuel tanks, 1,320 US gal (4991 litres) maximum internal fuel load 9363-US gal including bomb bay ferry tanks
54 Wing bottom skin stringers
55 Leading edge de-icing boots
56 Starboard navigation light
57 Fabric-covered aileron
58 Aileron tab
59 Flap guide rails
60 Starboard Fowler-type flap

61 Flap rib construction
62 Inboard nacelle tail fairing
63 Life raft stowage
64 Wing panel centreline joint
65 Wing/fuselage attachment main frames
66 Pressurisation ducting
67 Heat exchanger
68 Centre section fuel tank, 1,333-US gal (5046 litres)
69 Cabin heater
70 Pressurisation control valve
71 Fuselage framing
72 Rear bomb bay, 4 × 2000-lb bombs shown
73 Bomb rack
74 Access door
75 Rear cabin front pressure bulkhead
76 Radio aerial mast
77 Upper gun turret sighting hatch
78 Upper gunner's seat
79 Remote gun controller
80 Radio and electronics racks
81 Upper gun turret, two 0.5-in (12.7-mm) machine-guns, 500 rpg
82 Rear pressure bulkhead
83 Fin root fillet
84 Starboard tailplane
85 Starboard elevator
86 Leading edge de-icing boots

87 Tailfin construction
88 HF aerial cable
89 Fin tip fairing
90 Fabric covered rudder construction
91 Rudder tab
92 Pressurised tail gunners compartment
93 Armoured glass window panels
94 Tail gun camera
95 20-mm cannon, 100 rounds
96 Twin 0.5-in (12.7-mm) machine guns, 500 rpg
97 Remotely controlled ball turret
98 Elevator tab
99 Port fabric covered elevator construction

100 Tailplane leading edge de-icing boot
101 Tailplane construction
102 Fin/tailplane attachment joints
103 Tail turret ammunition boxes
104 Retractable tail bumper
105 Oxygen bottles
106 APU fuel tank
107 Rear ventral turret, two 0.5-in (12.7-mm) machine-guns, 500 rpg
108 Auxiliary power unit (APU)
109 Oblique camera
110 Vertical camera
111 Crew entry door
112 Batteries
113 Pressure bulkhead access door
114 Crew rest bunks
115 Toilet
116 Radio communications tuning units
117 Remote gunsight
118 Gun aiming blister
119 Gunner's seat, port and starboard
120 Voltage regulator
121 Bomb door hydraulic jacks
122 Rear bomb bay doors
123 Port Fowler flap
124 Flap shroud ribs
125 Rear spar
126 Outer wing panel joint
127 Aileron tab
128 Fabric covered aileron construction
129 Wing tip fairing
130 Port navigation light
131 Wing stringers
132 Outer wing panel ribs
133 Front spar
134 Leading edge nose ribs
135 Leading edge de-icing boots
136 Port wing fuel tank bays
137 Engine nacelle firewall
138 Nacelle construction
139 Engine mounting frame
140 Twin mainwheels
141 Main undercarriage leg strut
142 Mainwheel leg pivot mounting
143 Port mainwheel bay
144 Hydraulic retraction jack
145 Nacelle tail fairing
146 Self-sealing oil tank, 85 US gal (322 litres)
147 Hydraulic reservoir
148 Mainwheel doors
149 Exhaust stub
150 Exhaust driven turbo-supercharger
151 Intercooler
152 Engine cooling air exit flaps
153 Exhaust collector ring
154 Wright Cyclone R-3350-57A, 18-cylinder, two-row radial engine
155 Engine intake ducting
156 Forward bomb bay doors
157 20 × 500-lb (227 kg) bombs, maximum bomb load 20,000-lb (9072 kg)

Photo-reconnaissance was a vital adjunct to the success of bombing missions. For this purpose, the USAAF acquired 113 camera-equipped F-13As (and four TF-13A trainers) by converting B-29 and B-29A bombers. Post-war, they became FB-29As in 1945 and RB-29As in 1948.

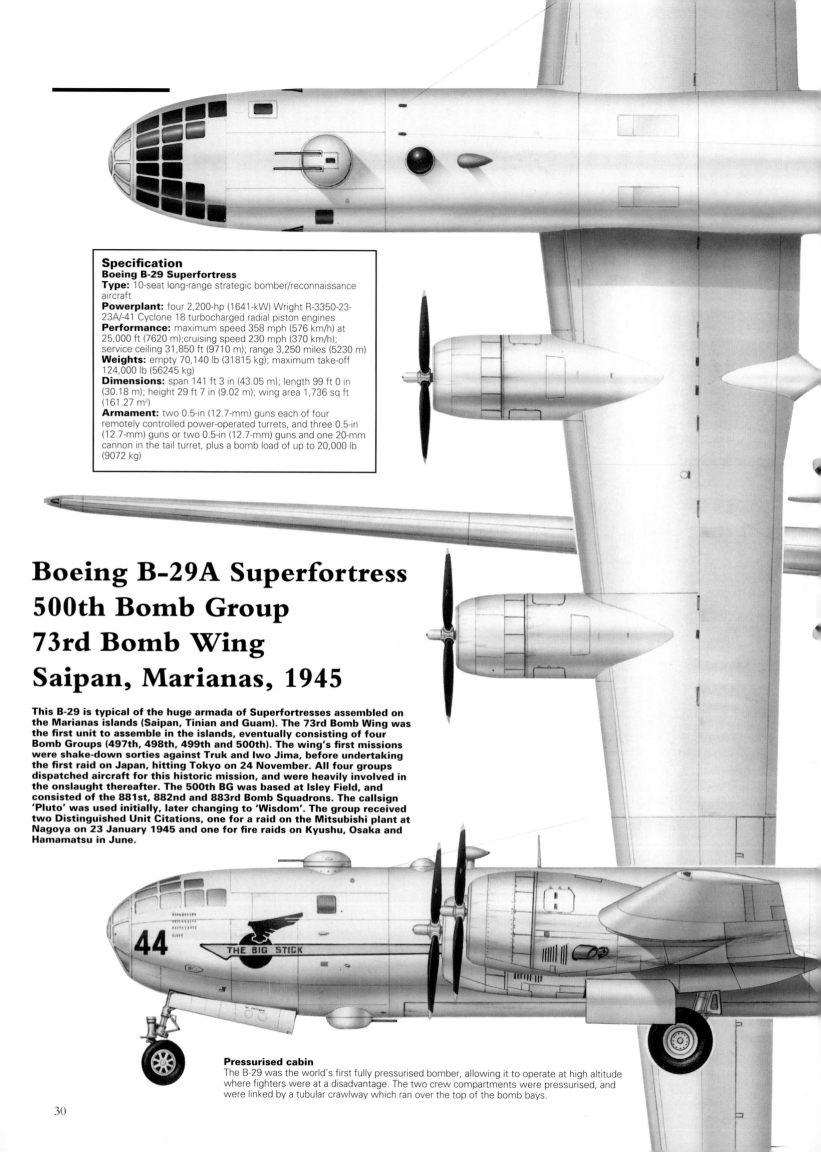

Specification
Boeing B-29 Superfortress
Type: 10-seat long-range strategic bomber/reconnaissance aircraft
Powerplant: four 2,200-hp (1641-kW) Wright R-3350-23-23A/-41 Cyclone 18 turbocharged radial piston engines
Performance: maximum speed 358 mph (576 km/h) at 25,000 ft (7620 m);cruising speed 230 mph (370 km/h); service ceiling 31,850 ft (9710 m); range 3,250 miles (5230 m)
Weights: empty 70,140 lb (31815 kg); maximum take-off 124,000 lb (56245 kg)
Dimensions: span 141 ft 3 in (43.05 m); length 99 ft 0 in (30.18 m); height 29 ft 7 in (9.02 m); wing area 1,736 sq ft (161.27 m²)
Armament: two 0.5-in (12.7-mm) guns each of four remotely controlled power-operated turrets, and three 0.5-in (12.7-mm) guns or two 0.5-in (12.7-mm) guns and one 20-mm cannon in the tail turret, plus a bomb load of up to 20,000 lb (9072 kg)

Boeing B-29A Superfortress
500th Bomb Group
73rd Bomb Wing
Saipan, Marianas, 1945

This B-29 is typical of the huge armada of Superfortresses assembled on the Marianas islands (Saipan, Tinian and Guam). The 73rd Bomb Wing was the first unit to assemble in the islands, eventually consisting of four Bomb Groups (497th, 498th, 499th and 500th). The wing's first missions were shake-down sorties against Truk and Iwo Jima, before undertaking the first raid on Japan, hitting Tokyo on 24 November. All four groups dispatched aircraft for this historic mission, and were heavily involved in the onslaught thereafter. The 500th BG was based at Isley Field, and consisted of the 881st, 882nd and 883rd Bomb Squadrons. The callsign 'Pluto' was used initially, later changing to 'Wisdom'. The group received two Distinguished Unit Citations, one for a raid on the Mitsubishi plant at Nagoya on 23 January 1945 and one for fire raids on Kyushu, Osaka and Hamamatsu in June.

Pressurised cabin
The B-29 was the world's first fully pressurised bomber, allowing it to operate at high altitude where fighters were at a disadvantage. The two crew compartments were pressurised, and were linked by a tubular crawlway which ran over the top of the bomb bays.

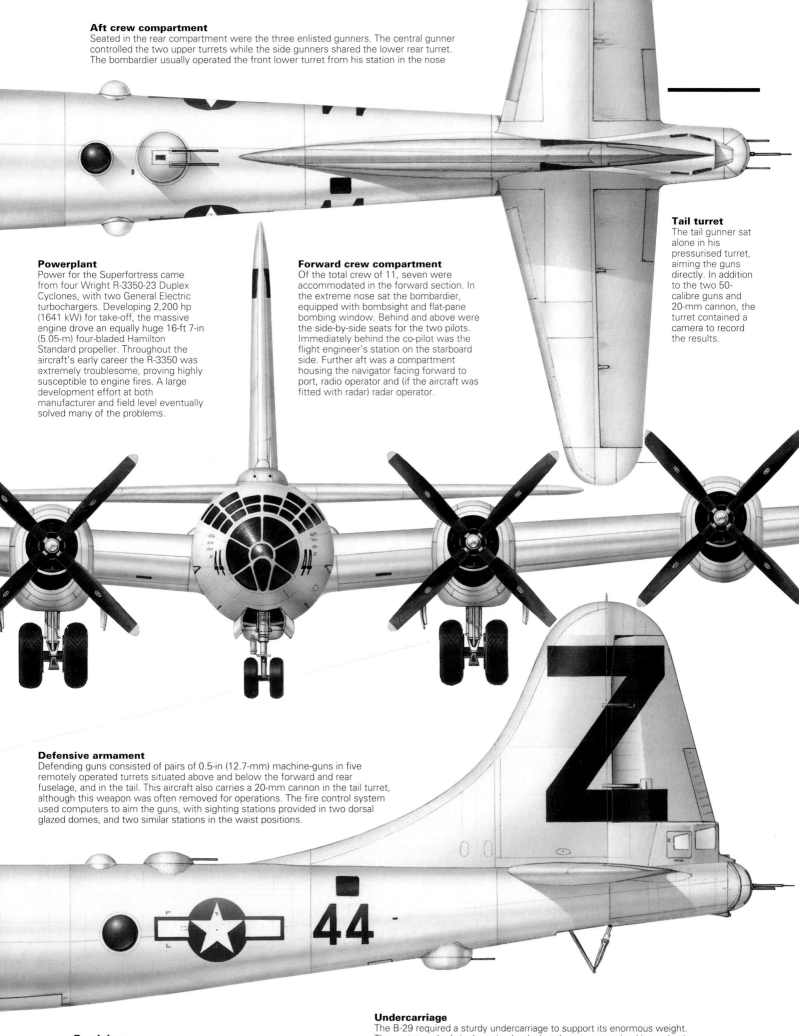

Aft crew compartment
Seated in the rear compartment were the three enlisted gunners. The central gunner controlled the two upper turrets while the side gunners shared the lower rear turret. The bombardier usually operated the front lower turret from his station in the nose

Tail turret
The tail gunner sat alone in his pressurised turret, aiming the guns directly. In addition to the two 50-calibre guns and 20-mm cannon, the turret contained a camera to record the results.

Powerplant
Power for the Superfortress came from four Wright R-3350-23 Duplex Cyclones, with two General Electric turbochargers. Developing 2,200 hp (1641 kW) for take-off, the massive engine drove an equally huge 16-ft 7-in (5.05-m) four-bladed Hamilton Standard propeller. Throughout the aircraft's early career the R-3350 was extremely troublesome, proving highly susceptible to engine fires. A large development effort at both manufacturer and field level eventually solved many of the problems.

Forward crew compartment
Of the total crew of 11, seven were accommodated in the forward section. In the extreme nose sat the bombardier, equipped with bombsight and flat-pane bombing window. Behind and above were the side-by-side seats for the two pilots. Immediately behind the co-pilot was the flight engineer's station on the starboard side. Further aft was a compartment housing the navigator facing forward to port, radio operator and (if the aircraft was fitted with radar) radar operator.

Defensive armament
Defending guns consisted of pairs of 0.5-in (12.7-mm) machine-guns in five remotely operated turrets situated above and below the forward and rear fuselage, and in the tail. This aircraft also carries a 20-mm cannon in the tail turret, although this weapon was often removed for operations. The fire control system used computers to aim the guns, with sighting stations provided in two dorsal glazed domes, and two similar stations in the waist positions.

Undercarriage
The B-29 required a sturdy undercarriage to support its enormous weight. The prototype had single mainwheels, but these were revised in production aircraft to a twin-wheel arrangement, retracting forwards into the engine nacelle. The nosewheel retracted backwards to lie in a well below the forward crew compartment. To protect the rear fuselage in the case of over-rotation, the B-29 had a retractable tail bumper.

Bomb bay
Up to 20,000 lb (9072 kg) of bombs could be carried in two bomb bays situated each side of the centre section. Bombs were usually carried in vertical stacks. The space between the bomb bays was used to mount the APQ-13 or Eagle bombing radar in aircraft so equipped.

Above: The four guns in the upper front barbette provided a small visible clue to the B-29A-BN variant built at Renton in a run totalling 1,119. Other differences from the B-29 concerned the structural design of the wing/fuselage attachment.

Left: Aircraft of the 500th Bomb Group ('Z' on tail), part of the Saipan-based 73rd Bomb Wing, participate in a firebomb raid on Yokohama on 29 May 1945. Attacks of this kind, particularly on Tokyo itself, caused more casualties than the atom-bomb raids.

even flown, but from the first flight, on 21 September 1942 (initially using three-bladed propellers), it was clear that the B-29 was going to be a winner. It could so easily have been what test pilots then called 'a dog', and one of the firms delegated to build B-29s was convinced that Boeing's figures were far too optimistic and that the whole programme was a giant mistake. What made the B-29, by 1942 named Superfortress, now vitally important was that it was obviously going to be the only aircraft with the range to attack Japan.

To say that the good results of ship 41-002 were a relief would be an understatement. Far more money ($3 billion) had been invested in the B-29 programme long before its wheels left the ground than in

Boeing B-29 Superfortress variants

XB-29: three prototypes (41-002, 41-003 and 41-18335), powered by R-3350-13 engines with three-bladed propellers; one static test airframe also
YB-29: 14 service-test aircraft with R-3350-21 engines driving four-bladed propellers; armament fitted
B-29: main production model built by Boeing Wichita, Bell and Martin Omaha; powered by R-3350-23 engines of 2,200 hp (R-3350-41 and -57 in later aircraft); tail turret with three guns, either three 0.50-in or two 0.50-in and one 20-mm cannon
B-29A: 1,119 production aircraft similar to B-29 but with wing span increased to 142 ft 3 in (43.36 m), four-gun forward dorsal turret and R-3350-57 or -59 engines; built at Boeing Renton
FB-29A: redesignation of F-13A in 1945
RB-29A: redesignation of FB-29A in 1948
TB-29A: crew trainer version of B-29A
ETB-29A: single aircraft (44-62093) converted post-war to carry EF-84E fighters from the wingtips
B-29B: 310 production aircraft built by Bell with all but tail armament removed; R-3350-51 engines
EB-29B: single B-29B converted to carry XF-85 Goblin parasite fighter
B-29C: proposed variant with later R-3350 engines; 5,000 on order were cancelled
B-29D: major redesign with enlarged vertical fin and R-4360-35 engines; redesignated B-50
XB-29E: single B-29 modified to test new fire control system
B-29F: six post-war lightened and winterised aircraft for service in Alaska; believed to have been used on reconnaissance missions over the Soviet Union
XB-29G: one B-29B converted for use as engine testbed
XB-29H: one B-29A used for armament trials
YB-29J: six B-29 used for engine

trials with modified nacelles
RB-29J: two YB-29Js subsequently used for reconnaissance; also known as **FB-29J**
YKB-29J: two YB-29J converted with Boeing flying boom
CB-29J: single B-29 converted for cargo transport
KB-29M: B-29 and B-29A converted as single-point drogue refuellers
B-29MR: B-29s converted as receiver aircraft
KB-29P: B-29s converted as flying-boom tankers
YKB-29T: one KB-29M converted with triple-point refuelling capability
DB-29: drone director conversion
GB-29: aircraft modified to act as launch platforms for X-1 and other research aircraft
QB-29: radio-controlled target conversion
SB-29: 16 B-29s converted for long-range rescue duties with air-droppable lifeboat
WB-29: weather reconnaissance conversions
XB-39: one YB-29 re-engined with V-3420-11 engines
XB-44: single B-29A re-engined with R-4360-33 engines; armament restricted to two tail guns; became XB-29D and prototype for B-50 series
F-13A: B-29s and B-29As converted for long-range photo-reconnaissance role; redesignated FB-29A in 1945 and RB-29A; later adopted signals intelligence role
TF-13A: four trainer versions of F-13A
RB-13A: F-13A redesignated in 1945
FB-13A: RB-13A redesignated in 1948
P2B-1S: two B-29As transferred to US Navy as radar picket aircraft; extra fuel and large radar in bomb bay
P2B-2S: two similar US Navy aircraft with equipment changes; P2Bs later used as launch platforms for research aircraft

any other project in the history of any nation. At the same time the technical snags were severe, and they multiplied. Many, such as powerplant fires and runaway propellers, were highly dangerous, and three months into the flight programme the prototypes had logged just 31 of the 180 hours scheduled.

Even when the Superfortresses trickled and then poured off the lines, they were so complex that nobody in uniform fully understood them. All went to a modification centre at Salina, Kansas, where over 9,900 faults in the first 175, urgently needed for the new 20th Bomb Wing, were bulldozed right by a task force of 600 men in 'The Battle of Kansas'. Sheer manpower and the USA's mighty industrial power forced the obstacles out of the way, and the B-29s not only began racking up the hours but their baffled crews gradually learned how to manage them, how to fly straight and level in a goldfish bowl without continuously using instruments, and above all how to get something faintly resembling the published range with heavy bombloads. Air miles per pound of fuel were improved by exactly 100 per cent between January and March 1944. And the complex systems grew reliable in the ultra-cold of 33,000 ft (10060 m).

On 5 June 1944 the first combat mission was flown from Kharagpur, India, to Bangkok; the worst problem was an unexpected tropical storm. On 15 June the first of the raids on Japan was mounted, from Chengdu (one of many newly bulldozed B-29 strips in China) to the Yawata steel works. The specially created 20th Air Force grew in muscle, and in October 1944 the first B-29s arrived on newly laid runways on the Marianas islands of Tinian, Saipan and Guam, just taken from the enemy. The numbers grew swiftly as the mighty plants back home poured out B-29s and **B-29As** with 12 in (30 cm) more span and the four-gun front turret, while Bell added 311 **B-29Bs** with all armament stripped except that in the tail, making a considerable difference in reduced weight and complexity. The B-29B was made possible by the patchy fighter opposition, and many Superfortresses were similarly stripped in the field.

Moreover, the commander of the XXI Bomber Command, Major General Curtis LeMay, boldly decided to bomb Tokyo by night from low level, with a full load of incendiaries. There were many reasons for this, but the chief ones were that it promised much greater bombloads and the elimination of bombing errors attributable to jet-stream winds. This policy, totally at variance with the idea of high-altitude day formations, resulted in the greatest firestorms the world has ever seen, and the biggest casualties ever caused by air attack. They were far greater than the 75,000 of Hiroshima, hit by the 20-kT 'Little Boy' atom bomb dropped on 6 August 1945 from Colonel Paul Tibbets' B-29 'Enola Gay', or the 35,000 of Nagasaki hit by the 20-kT 'Fat Man' dropped on 9 August from 'Bock's Car'. The war ended five days later.

Many modifications

Only by the incredibly bold decision to go into the biggest multi-company production programme ever organised long before the first flight did the B-29 manage to make so large a contribution to World War II. By VJ-Day more than 2,000 were actually with combat crews, and although 5,000-plus were cancelled days later the manufacturing programme was slowed progressively, and did not close until May 1946, by which time 3,960 B-29s had been built. Hundreds were modified for different tasks, and many were launched on new careers as air/sea rescue aircraft, turbojet testbeds or tankers, which kept them busy for another decade or more.

Boeing Model 314

As early as January 1935, Pan American Airways had signified to the US Bureau of Air Commerce its wish to establish a transatlantic service and, despite its ownership of the large Martin M-130 and Sikorsky S-42 long-range four-engined flying-boats, the airline wanted a new aircraft for the route. Boeing submitted a successful tender to the Pan American specification, and a contract for six **Boeing 314**s was signed on 21 July 1936. The manufacturer used features of the earlier XB-15 heavy bomber, adapting the wing and horizontal tail surfaces for its 82,500-lb (37421-kg) gross weight flying-boat, which could accommodate up to 74 passengers in four separate cabins. The engines were not the 1,000-hp (746-kW) Pratt & Whitney R-1830 Twin Wasps of the XB-15, but 1,500-hp (1119-kW) Wright GR-2600 Cyclone 14s, which gave the machine a maximum speed of 193 mph (311 km/h). The fuel capacity of 4,200 US gal (15898 litres) conferred a maximum range of 3,500 miles (5633 km); some of the fuel was stored in the stabilising sponsons, which also served as loading platforms.

The first Boeing 314 took off on its maiden flight on 7 June

1939, this original version having a single fin and rudder, later replaced by twin tail surfaces to improve directional stability. These proved to be inadequate, and the original centreline fin was restored, without a moveable rudder.

Pan American ordered another six aircraft which were designated **Model 314A**, improved by the installation of 1,600-hp (1193-kW) Wright Cyclone 14s with larger-diameter propellers, an additional 1,200 US gal (4542 litres) of fuel capacity, and a revised interior. The first 314A flew on 20 March 1941 and delivery was complete by 20 January 1942. Five of the original order were retrospectively converted to 314A standard in 1942.

Not only was the Boeing Model 314A one of the biggest production aircraft of its day, but its Cyclone 14AC1 engines were the first in the world regularly to use 115/145-grade fuel; Pan American calculated that the costly fuel was worthwhile in increased payload over long ranges. The last 314A is seen here in wartime Navy camouflage after briefly serving as an Army C-98.

Of Pan American's nine 314/314As, four were requisitioned by Army Transport Command and given the military designation **C-98**. They were little used, however, and in November 1942 one was returned to the airline. The other three were transferred to the US Navy to join two acquired direct from Pan American; the airline provided crews for the US Navy's **B-314** operations, and the aircraft were partially camouflaged but operated with civil registrations.

Specification
Type: long-range flying boat transport
Powerplant: (B-314A) four 1,600-hp (1193-kW) Wright R-2600 Cyclone 14 radial piston engines
Performance: maximum speed 193 mph (311 km/h) at 10,000 ft (3050 m); cruising speed 183 mph (295 km h); service ceiling 13,400 ft (4085 m); range 3,500 miles (5633 km)
Weights: empty 50,268 lb (22801 kg); maximum take-off 82,500 lb (37421 kg)
Dimensions: span 152 ft 0 in (46.33 m); length 106 ft 0 in (32.31 m); height 27 ft 7 in (8.41 m); wing area 2,867 sq ft (266.34 m²)

Boeing XF8B

US Navy carriers operating in the Pacific during World War II were very vulnerable to air attack. When it became clear that the US Navy might have to deploy its carriers close to the Japanese mainland to support an invasion, and so bring the valuable ships within easy range of land-based aircraft, the service looked to find a long-range fighter-bomber that could engage the enemy from safer waters further offshore.

The requirement was communicated to Boeing, which immediately began its design of the **Model 400**. Submitted to the US Navy, Boeing's design study was sufficiently interesting to warrant a contract for three **XF8B-1** prototypes, awarded on 4 May 1943. The first of these aircraft made its initial flight during November 1944, and was immediately seen to be the largest single-seat piston-engined fighter to be built in the USA. It

subsequently proved to be one of the most powerful single-seat fighters ever developed, for its powerplant consisted of the mighty Pratt & Whitney XR-4360-10 four-row 'corn-cob' engine. This drove two contra-rotating three-bladed propellers. The XF8B-1 performed well, but it was not until after VJ-Day that the remaining two prototypes were flown and delivered. By that time interest in tactical aircraft powered by reciprocating

engines had all but vanished, so the F8B programme was terminated.

Specification
Type: long-range carrier-based fighter-bomber
Powerplant: one 3,000-hp (2237-kW) Pratt & Whitney XR-4360-10 radial piston engine
Performance: maximum speed 432 mph (695 km/h); service ceiling 37,500 ft (11430 m); range 2,800 miles (4506 km)
Weights: empty 13,519 lb (6132 kg); maximum take-off 20,508 lb (9302 kg)
Dimensions: wing span 54 ft 0 in (16.46 m); length 43 ft 3 in (13.18 m); height 16 ft 3 in (4.95 m); wing area 489 sq ft (45.43 m²)
Armament: six 0.50-in (12.7-mm) or six 20-mm cannon in wings; up to 3,200 lb (1451 kg) of bombs

Today it is hard to recall that Boeing was originally famous for fighters. The XF8B-1, the first of which is seen here, was one of the biggest and most powerful single-piston-engined fighters ever built. The Douglas Skyraider – likewise at first dismissed as obsolete because of its piston engine – showed that the Model 400 might have been a most valuable aircraft.

Boeing XPBB-1 Sea Ranger

Even before the USA's entry into the war, the frequent appearance of German U-boats and surface raiders close to US coastal waters made the US Navy conscious of the fact that a long-range maritime patrol aircraft was a necessity. As a result Boeing was approached to evolve the design of a suitable aircraft, the company's resulting **Model 344** proving to be the largest twin-engined flying-boat to be built and flown by any of the combatant nations.

Boeing had already gained considerable experience of flying-boat construction from its earlier days, culminating in the superb Model 314 'Clippers' with which Pan American Airways had inaugurated dependable services across the North Atlantic and Pacific.

Boeing's design proved acceptable to the US Navy, and a contract for the construction of a prototype, under the designation **XPBB-1**, was awarded on 29 June 1940. This aircraft flew for the first time on 5 July 1942 and proved to be of fairly conventional design and construction. It had a wing very similar to that of its Boeing stablemate, the B-29, the prototype of which was being built simultaneously.

Changed ideas regarding maritime patrol aircraft brought cancellation of the order for the US Navy's **PBB-1 Sea Rangers**, the role being adequately undertaken by land-based aircraft.

The XPBB-1 is always included in any listing of the world's biggest twin-piston-engined aircraft. This picture was taken in 1944, by which time the XPBB was dubbed 'the Lone Ranger'.

Specification
Type: long-range maritime patrol/bomber flying boat
Powerplant: two 2,300-hp (1715-kW) Wright R-3350-8 Cyclone radial piston engines
Performance: maximum speed 228 mph (367 km/h) at 14,200 ft (4330 m); cruising speed 158 mph (254 km/h); patrol speed 127 mph (204 km/h); service ceiling 22,400 m (6830 m); maximum range 6,300 miles (10140 km); maximum endurance 72 hours
Weights: empty 41,531 lb (18838 kg); maximum take-off 101,130 lb (45872 kg)
Dimensions: span 139 ft 8½ in (42.58 m); length 94 ft 9 in (28.88 m); height 34 ft 2 in (10.41 m); wing area 1,826 sq ft (169.64 m²)
Armament: eight 0.50-in (12.7-mm) machine-guns (in bow, waist and tail positions), plus up to 20,000 lb (9072 kg) of bombs

Boeing/Stearman PT-13/-17/N2S Kaydet

The Stearman Aircraft Company, formed by Lloyd Stearman in 1927, became identified as the Wichita Division of the Boeing Airplane Company in 1939. As early as 1933 the company began design and construction of a new training biplane, derived from the earlier Stearman Model C; built as a private venture, this was first flown in December 1933 and, designated as the Stearman X70, was submitted as a contender in 1934 to meet a US Army Air Corps requirement for a new primary trainer.

The first service to show interest in this aircraft was the US Navy, which in early 1935 contracted for the supply of 61 Stearman Model 70s under the designation **NS-1** (Trainer, Stearman, 1). These, however, received a different powerplant, for the US Navy had in storage a quantity of 225-hp (168-kW) Wright J-5 (R-790-8) radial engines which were specified for installation in this initial order, the company changing the model number of aircraft so equipped to Model 73. The X70 supplied for US Army evaluation was subjected to protracted testing and eventually, in early 1936, the USAAC contracted for the supply of 26 aircraft under the designation **PT-13** (Primary Trainer, 13). These, powered by 215-hp (160-kW) Lycoming R-680-5 engines, were the first of the Stearman Model 75s.

This cautious approach by the US Army should not be considered as a reflection upon the capability of the new trainer. The truth of the matter was that at that period the USAAC had little money to spend on new aircraft: not only had this service to be as certain as possible that it was procuring the best available, but even then was only able to procure small quantities. Soon, however, the fortunes of war were to bring Boeing contracts for thousands of the Stearman-designed trainers and although, officially, the aircraft were Boeing Model 75s from 1939, they were persistently regarded as Stearman 75s throughout the war. The name **Kaydet**, bestowed later by Canada and adopted generally in reference to these aircraft, was also unofficial except in Canada.

This attractive two-seat biplane was of mixed construction, the single-bay wings being basically of wood with fabric covering, the remainder of welded steel-tube structure with mostly fabric covering.

Landing gear was non-retractable tailwheel type, the divided cantilever main units having cleanly faired oleo-spring shock absorbers. The powerplant was to vary considerably throughout a production run which lasted until early 1945, and during which well over 10,000 examples were built.

USAAC procurement continued with 92 **PT-13A**s delivered from 1937, these having improved instrumentation and 220-hp (164-kW) R-680-7 engines, and by the end of 1941 the USAAF had received an additional 255 **PT-13B**s with R-680-11 engines and only minor equipment changes. The designation **PT-13C** was allocated in 1941 to six PT-13As which were converted by the addition of equipment necessary to make them suitable for night or instrument flight. A change of powerplant, the 220-hp (164-kW) Continental R-670-5 engine installed in a PT-13A type airframe, brought the designation **PT-17**, and 3,519 of these were built during 1940 to meet the

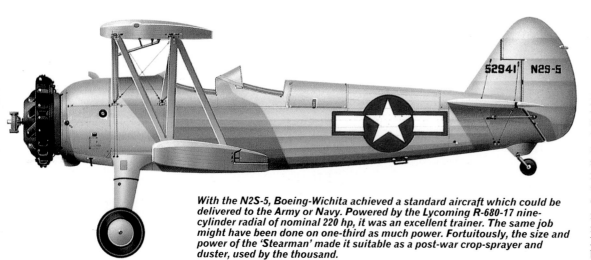

With the N2S-5, Boeing-Wichita achieved a standard aircraft which could be delivered to the Army or Navy. Powered by the Lycoming R-680-17 nine-cylinder radial of nominal 220 hp, it was an excellent trainer. The same job might have been done on one-third as much power. Fortuitously, the size and power of the 'Stearman' made it suitable as a post-war crop-sprayer and duster, used by the thousand.

This aircraft was probably the first PT-13B, delivered to the Army in October 1939. It bears the fin designator MD, indicating a test unit in the Materiel Division at Wright Field.

enormous demand for training aircraft. Eighteen PT-17s were equipped with blind-flying instrumentation under the designation **PT-17A**, and three with agricultural spraying equipment for pest control became **PT-17B**s. Aircraft remaining in service after 1948 were assigned the designation **T-17**.

US Navy procurement during this same period included a first batch of 250 Model 75s with Continental R-670-14 engines, designated **N2S-1**, followed by 125 with Lycoming R-680-8 engines as **N2S-2**. **N2S-3**s, totalling 1,875, had Continental R-670-4 engines, and 99 aircraft diverted from US Army PT-17 production plus 577 similar aircraft on US Navy contracts were designated **N2S-4**. For the first time both the US Army and US Navy had a common model in

1942, basically the PT-13A airframe with a Lycoming R-680-17 engine, and these had the respective designations **PT-13D** and **N2S-5**. These were to be the last major production variants for the US forces, the US Army receiving 318 and the US Navy 1,450. A shortage of engines in 1940-41 had, however, produced two other designations: **PT-18** and **PT-18A**. The first related to 150 aircraft with the PT-13A type airframe and a 225-hp (168-kW) Jacobs R-755-7 engine, and the six PT-18As were six of the PT-18s converted subsequently with blind-flying instrumentation. The designation **PT-27** applied to 300 aircraft procured by the US Army for supply under Lend-Lease to the Royal Canadian Air Force. A small number of these, and of the N2S-5s supplied to the

Standard Army training colours in 1928-42, seen on this PT-17, were yellow wings and blue fuselage. From April 1942 trainers were doped all silver. The PT-17 was powered by the seven-cylinder Continental R-670-5.

Above: The R-680 engine of an N2S-2 is hand-cranked at a US Navy primary pilot-training school. This version, delivered in April-October 1941, was almost identical, apart from the paint scheme, to the Army PT-13 with the same engine.

US Navy, had cockpit canopies, cockpit heating, full blind-flying instrumentation and a hood for instrument training. In North America the Stearman Kaydet retains an aura of nostalgia which Britons equate with such aircraft as the de Havilland Tiger Moth, or Germans with the Bücker trainers. When declared surplus at

the war's end many served with the air forces of other nations, and large numbers were converted for use as agricultural aircraft.

Specification

Type: two-seat primary trainer
Powerplant: one 220-hp (164-kW) Lycoming R-680-17 radial piston engine
Performance: maximum speed 124 mph (200 km/h); cruising speed 106 mph (171 km/h); service ceiling 11,200 ft (3415 m); range 505 miles (813 km)
Weights: empty 1,936 lb (878 kg); maximum take-off 2,717 lb (1232 kg)
Dimensions: span 32 ft 2 in (9.80 m); length 25 ft 0 in (7.63 m); height 9 ft 2 in (2.79 m); wing area 297 sq ft (27.59 m²)

Brewster F2A Buffalo

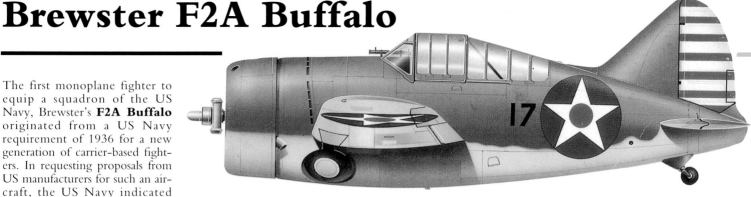

The first monoplane fighter to equip a squadron of the US Navy, Brewster's **F2A Buffalo** originated from a US Navy requirement of 1936 for a new generation of carrier-based fighters. In requesting proposals from US manufacturers for such an aircraft, the US Navy indicated requirements which included monoplane configuration, wing flaps, arrester gear, retractable landing gear and an enclosed cockpit. Clearly, this specification recognised the fact that the carrier-based biplane was nearing the end of its useful life.

Proposals were received from Brewster, allocated the designation **XF2A-1**, Grumman (XF4F-1) and Seversky (XFN-1),

but of these the only significant aircraft in the long term was the Grumman design, which was initially of biplane configuration and given serious consideration by the US Navy as an insurance policy against the possible failure of new-fangled monoplanes.

A prototype of the Brewster XF2A-1 was ordered on 22 June 1936, and this flew for the first time in December 1937. While bearing a distinct family resemblance to the XSBA-1 of 1934, the new fighter appeared to be tubbier and stubbier, but a com-

Among the Buffaloes that saw action, and proved to be outclassed by such Japanese types as the Army Ki-43 and Navy A6M, were the F2A-3s of US Marine Corps squadron VMF-221. This aircraft from the unit shows the standard light grey and non-specular blue-grey of the period, though the red inside the star and the striped rudder lasted only to 15 May 1942.

parison of dimensions showed this to be something of an illusion. Of mid-wing monoplane configuration, it was of all-metal construction, except for fabric-covered control surfaces. Hydraulically operated split flaps were provided, and the main units of the tailwheel type landing gear retracted inwards to be housed in fuselage wells. The powerplant consisted of a 950-hp (708-kW) Wright XR-1820-22 Cyclone radial engine, driving a Hamilton three-blade metal propeller.

Service testing of the prototype

Left: Dated 8 March 1942, this US Navy photograph shows F2A-2s of the US Navy peeling off from echelon. The unit was probably VF-3, the only one left flying the F2A at that time.

Above: A small number of B-339D and B-439C fighters served in Australia in 1942 with the US Army Air Force. This one had a Netherlands East Indies number, and another was RAAF A51-16.

began in January 1938, and on 11 June the US Navy contracted with Brewster for the supply of 54 **F2A-1**s. Deliveries of these started 12 months later, nine aircraft going almost immediately to equip US Navy Squadron VF-3 aboard USS *Saratoga*. The available balance of 44 aircraft was, sympathetically, declared surplus to requirements and, instead, supplied to Finland which was then fighting off the might of the Soviet Union.

An improved version was ordered by the US Navy in early 1939, this having a more powerful engine, an improved propeller and built-in flotation gear. Designated **F2A-2**s, these began to enter service in September 1940. They were followed by **F2A-3**s with more armour and a bulletproof windscreen, and these two production versions were to equip US Navy Squadrons VF-2 and VF-3, and US Marine Corps Squadron VMF-221. A number were used operationally in the Pacific, notably by the Marines during the Battle of Midway, but as the type was overweight, unstable and of poor manoeuvrability, it was no match for opposing Japanese fighters.

Specification
Type: single-seat land- or shipbased fighter
Powerplant: (F2A-3) one 1,200-hp (895-kW) Wright R-1820-40 Cyclone radial piston engine
Performance: maximum speed 321 mph (517 km/h) at 16,500 ft (5030 m); cruising speed 258 mph (415 km/h); service ceiling 33,200 ft (10120 m); range 965 miles (1553 km)
Weights: empty 4,732 lb (2146 kg); maximum take-off 7,159 lb (3247 kg)
Dimensions: span 35 ft 0 in (10.67 m); length 26 ft 4 in (8.03 m); height 12 ft 1 in (3.68 m); wing area 208.9 sq ft (19.41 m²)
Armament: four 0.50-in (12.7-mm) machine-guns, plus two 100-lb (45-kg) bombs

Left: This aircraft appears to be the same as the leader in the peel-off picture. But it is clearly an F2A-3, not an F2A-2, and the photograph is dated August 1942, at which time all Navy F2As had been transferred to the Marine Corps.

Brewster SBA/SBN

It was not until 1934 that Brewster became involved in the design and prototype construction of its first aircraft, a two-seat scout bomber required by the US Navy for service aboard the carriers USS *Enterprise* and *Yorktown*, which were scheduled for launch in 1936. Designated **XSBA-1**, this emerged as a clean looking mid-wing monoplane of all-metal construction except for its control surfaces, which were fabric-covered. Trailing-edge flaps were provided to simplify shipboard operations. The powerplant of the prototype consisted of a single 750-hp (559-kW) Wright R-1820-4 Cyclone radial engine, and other features included hydraulically retractable tailwheel type landing gear and internal stowage for bombs.

The XSBA-1 flew for the first time on 15 April 1936, but flight testing was to indicate that more power was necessary to provide satisfactory performance. In 1937, therefore, a 950-hp (708-kW) XR-1820-22 Cyclone engine was installed, and after tests the US Navy had no hesitation in ordering the type into production. But Brewster had inadequate production facilities, and it was decided that the 30 aircraft which the US Navy required would be built by the Naval Aircraft Factory (NAF) in Philadelphia.

The Brewster-designed scout/bomber built by the NAF was given the designation **SBN-1**, and deliveries to the US Navy extended from November 1940 to March 1942. By that time more advanced designs were

An unusual feature of the XSBA-1 prototype was its long-chord cowl, around the single-row Cyclone engine. The production SBN had a short cowl, as well as a deeper cockpit canopy, taller vertical tail and other changes. By the time they were delivered it would have been suicidal to use these aircraft in action.

becoming available, and production of SBNs came to an end. These aircraft were used by US Navy Squadron VB-3 when they first entered service, and most were later employed for training. Squadron VT-8 used its SBN-1s for training on board USS *Hornet*.

Specification
Type: two-seat carrier-based scout-bomber/trainer
Powerplant (SBN-1): one 950-hp (708-kW) Wright XR-1820-22 Cyclone radial piston engine
Performance: maximum speed 254 mph (409 km/h); service ceiling 28,300 ft (8625 m); range 1,015 miles (1633 km)
Weight: maximum take-off 6,759 lb (3066 kg)
Dimensions: span 39 ft 0in (11.89 m); length 27 ft 8 in (8.43 m); height 8 ft 7 in (2.64 m); wing area 259 sq ft (24.06 m²)
Armament: one 0.30-in (7.62-mm) gun on flexible mount in rear of cockpit, plus up to 500 lb (227 kg) of bombs in internal bay

Brewster SB2A Buccaneer

With the SBA, virtually off its hands, Brewster was able to turn to the design of an improved version. The aim was to produce a more effective scout-bomber with heavier armament, increased bombload and higher performance; this dictated a slightly larger airframe and the installation of a more powerful engine.

A single prototype **XSB2A-1** was ordered by the US Navy on 4 April 1939, and this flew for the first time on 17 June 1941. By then the company had already received several production orders, comprising 140 for the US Navy, 162 for the Netherlands and a total of 750 for the RAF, after a British purchasing mission of 1940 was convinced of the excellence of the design. Procurement for the USAAF was also intended and the designation **A-34** allocated, but the contract was cancelled before any production resulted.

The intention of providing heavier armament was realised without difficulty, the US Navy's **SB2A-1 Buccaneer**s having eight 0.30-in (7.62-mm) machine-guns, six forward-firing and two on a flexible mounting

Not many photographs were taken of SB2As in the insignia introduced in June 1943. This US Navy photograph of March 1944 appears to show an SB2A-4 in fully operational trim, though by this time only a handful were still airworthy, used as hacks on utility missions. A few were converted as target tugs, while 90 ex-British Bermudas transferred to the Army as A-34s were grounded in 1944.

in the aft cockpit. Unfortunately, performance was far below that anticipated and the larger, much heavier aircraft lacked manoeuvrability. Despite this the US Navy continued to procure small numbers, acquiring 80 **SB2A-2**s with armament changes and 60 **SB2A-3**s. These latter aircraft, intended for carrier operations, featured folding wings and an arrester hook. The 162 aircraft built for the Netherlands were also taken over by the US Navy, and these were given the designation **SB2A-4** and transferred to the US Marine Corps for use in a training role. They were to serve a useful purpose in establishing the US Marines' first night-fighter squadron, VFM(N)-531.

Deliveries of aircraft for the RAF began in July 1942; supplied under Lend-Lease, these were identified as **Bermudas** in RAF service, but their performance was such that they were completely unsuitable for combat operations. As a result, most were converted for target towing duties, and second-line deployment, so far as is known, was the fate of all the 771 aircraft produced by Brewster.

Specification
Type: two-seat land- or carrier-based scout-bomber
Powerplant: one 1,700-hp (1268-kW) Wright R-2600-8 Cyclone radial piston engine
Performance: maximum speed 274 mph (441 km/h) at 12,000 ft (3660 m); cruising speed 161 mph (259 km/h); service ceiling 24,900 ft (7590 m); range without bombload 1,675 miles (2696 km)
Weights: empty 9,924 lb (4501 kg); maximum take-off 14,289 lb (6481 kg)
Dimensions: span 47 ft 0 in (14.33 m); length 39 ft 2 in (11.94 m); height 15 ft 5 in (4.70 m); wing area 379 sq ft (35.21 m²)
Armament: (SB2A-2) two 0.50-in (12.7-mm) fuselage-mounted machine-guns and four 0.30-in (7.62-mm) guns (two in wing and two in aft cockpit on flexible mount), plus up to 1,000 lb (454 kg) of bombs

Above: The SB2A was one of the worst aircraft of World War II. These SB2A-4s were photographed in early 1943 in active service as Scout Trainers at Vero Beach, Florida. Later that year the Navy terminated all such use, and all existing contracts.

Bristol Beaufighter

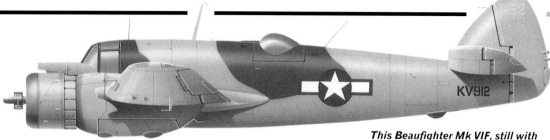

In the wake of the Munich Agreement of 1938, when UK Prime Minister Neville Chamberlain returned to the UK waving a 'piece of paper' (peace pact) that he believed had resolved the Czech-German crisis, promising "peace in our time", the British aircraft industry gained a short breathing space in which to do its utmost to strengthen the Royal Air Force. The need for a heavily-armed fighter, suitable for the long-range escort or night-fighter roles, was a significant gap in its inventory. This requirement was placed high on the list of priorities and Roy Fedden and Leslie Firse of the Bristol Aircraft Company proposed a compromise design to fill this need.

The wings, tail unit and landing gear of the in-production Bristol Beaufort were to be united by a new fuselage and to be powered by two of the company's Hercules sleeve-valve radial engines in wing-mounted nacelles. The draft proposal, submitted to the Air Ministry in October 1938, was adopted with such alacrity that the first prototype was in the air just under nine months later on 17 July 1939. Known to Bristol as the **Type 156**, but far better known as the **Beaufighter**, it proved sufficiently important to the RAF that

the British production totalled 5,562 aircraft.

In view of the large number built there were several variants, and of these the **Beaufighter Mk VIF** was the only version to find short-term service with the US Army Air Force. This occurred in the Mediterranean theatre during 1942-43, at a period when the USAAF was desperately in need of night-fighter aircraft. In an inter-service arrangement between the RAF and USAAF, the 12th Air Force gained for its 1st Tactical Air Command sufficient Beaufighter Mk VIFs to equip four squadrons (414th, 415th, 416th and 417th NFS). These saw extensive ser-

This Beaufighter Mk VIF, still with its RAF serial of KV912, served in Corsica with the USAAF 416th NFS. It was fitted with AI (airborne interception) radar Mk IV.

vice during the German withdrawal from North Africa, especially in providing night air cover during the army landings at Anzio and Salerno, and were retained by the USAAF until the war's end.

Specification
Beaufighter Mk VIF
Type: two-seat night/long-range fighter
Powerplant: two 1,670-hp (1245-kW) Bristol Hercules radial piston engines
Performance: maximum speed 333 mph (536 km/h) at 15,600 ft (4755 m); maximum cruising speed 276 mph (444 km/h) at 15,000 ft (4570 m); service ceiling 26,500 ft (8075 m); range, internal fuel 1,480 miles (2382 km)
Weights: empty 14,600 lb (6622 kg); maximum take-off 21,600 lb (9798 kg)
Dimensions: span 57 ft 10 in (17.63 m); length 41 ft 8 in (12.70 m); height 15 ft 10 in (4.83 m); wing area 503 sq ft (46.73 m²)
Armament: four 20-mm cannon in nose and six 0.303-in machine-guns in wings

This Beaufighter Mk VIF, fitted with AI Mk IV radar, was one of a substantial number initially taken on 12th Air Force charge as stopgaps, pending arrival of the P-61. In fact, most continued to be operational until VE-Day.

Budd RB/C-93 Conestoga

The **Budd Conestoga** reflected the early anxiety during World War II to find alternative construction materials for aircraft manufacture in case there was a shortage of the extensively used aluminium alloys. Consequently the Budd Conestoga was primarily built of stainless steel, and was the first large aircraft to be constructed from this material.

Intended for use as a cargo carrier, the Conestoga was developed by Budd Manufacturing Company in collaboration with

the US Navy. The high-set wing was mostly of stainless steel stressed-skin construction, but the trailing edges of the outer panels and the control surfaces were fabric-covered. The tail unit was similar, but the fuselage was all steel. It incorporated an electrically-operated loading ramp under the upswept tail, allowing vehicles to be driven straight into the 8 ft x 8 ft (2.44 m x 2.44 m) cargo hold. By mounting the flight deck high in the nose, the hold maintained these dimensions

for an impressive 25 ft (7.62 m). As an alternative to bulky cargo, 24 fully-equipped paratroops could be carried, or in the ambulance role there was room for 24 litters and 16 seated casualties.

In August 1942 the US Navy awarded Budd a contract for 200 of these transports under the designation **RB-1**, and USAAF interest brought an additional contract for 600 aircraft designated **C-93**. The first prototype flew on 31 October 1943, but production delays, cost overruns and a

realisation that there would be no aluminium shortage brought cancellation of the USAAF contract. Shortly after, the US Navy cut its requirement to just 25. By the war's end only 17 had been delivered, and were not used operationally. The remainder were cancelled. Of the 17 built, at least 14 were used by civilian operators post-war.

Specification
Type: cargo or troop transport
Powerplant: two 1,200-hp (895-kW) Pratt & Whitney R-1830-92 Twin Wasp radial piston engines
Performance: maximum speed 197 mph (317 km/h); range 700 miles (1127 km) with full payload
Weights: empty 20,156 lb (9143 kg); maximum take-off 33,860 lb (15359 kg)
Dimensions: wing span 100 ft 0 in (30.48 m); length 68 ft 0 in (20.73 m); height 31 ft 9 in (9.68 m); wing area 1,400 sq ft (130.06 m²)

The 17 production RB-1 s were assigned BuAer numbers 39292-39308. This photograph, dated 2 May 1944, shows the civil-registered prototype, NX41810. About half of each of the three wheels projected when retracted.

Cessna T-50 Bobcat

Cessna Aircraft's first twin-engined lightplane, built and flown in 1939, was a five-seat commercial transport typical of many very similar aircraft which became fairly common in the USA during the late 1930s. Designated Cessna **Model T-50** by the company, it was of low-wing cantilever monoplane configuration and of mixed construction. Wings and tail unit were of wood, the latter with fabric covering; the fuselage, however, was a welded steel-tube structure with fabric over lightweight wooden skinning. Retractable tailwheel-type landing gear and wing trailing-edge flaps were both electrically actuated.

In 1940 the military potential of this aircraft, as a trainer suitable for the conversion of pilots from single-engined to twin-engined types, became apparent almost simultaneously to two North American nations. First was Canada, which acquired a machine of this type for the Commonwealth Joint Air Training Plan, and 550 aircraft were supplied under Lend-Lease, these being designated **Crane 1A**.

The second requirement was for the US Army Air Corps which, in late 1940, contracted for the supply of 33 T-50s for service evaluation, allocating to them the designation **AT-8**. These were powered by two 295-hp (220-kW) Jacobs R-680-9 radial engines, but service trials showed that these were unnecessarily powerful for use in a two-seat trainer, and when in 1941 the first real production contracts were placed, less powerful engines by the same manufacturer were specified.

The initial production version, designated **AT-17**, was equipped with Jacobs R-755-9 engines driving wooden propellers. A total of 450 was built, and these aircraft were followed into production by 223 of the generally similar **AT-17A**, which differed by having Hamilton-Standard constant-speed metal propellers. The later **AT-17B** (466 built) had some equipment changes, and the **AT-17C** (60 built) was provided with different radio for communications. The final production variant was the **AT-17D**, of which 131 were built with minor equipment changes. The **AT-17E**, **AT-17F** and **AT-17G** designations related to AT-17, AT-17A and AT-17B respectively after gross weight was restricted to 5,300 lb.

The original use of Cessna T-50s had been in a light transport role, and in 1942 the USAAF decided that these aircraft would be valuable for liaison/communication purposes and as light personnel transports. Production of this variant totalled 1,354, the aircraft being named **Bobcat** and given the designation **C-78**, later changed to **UC-78**. Sixty-seven were transferred to the US Navy as **JRC-1**s. In addition, 17 commercial T-50s were impressed for service with the USAAF under the designation **UC-78A**.

The USAAF's requirement for the two-seat conversion trainers had been difficult to predict, and when it was discovered in late 1942 that procurement contracts very considerably exceeded the training requirement, Cessna was

A US Army Air Force AT-17B cruises over the vast flat land of the Midwest where it was built. Training aircraft were doped silver, with anti-reflective black above the nose and inner side of the cowlings and nacelles. Instructor and pupil had remarkably small aileron/elevator control wheels.

requested to fulfil the outstanding balance of the AT-17B and AT-17D models as **UC-78B** and **UC-78C** Bobcats respectively. Both were virtually identical, but differed from the original UC-78s by having two-bladed fixed-pitch wooden propellers and some minor changes of installed equipment. Production of these two versions amounted to 1,806 UC-78Bs and 327 UC-78Cs.

Specification
Cessna UC-78

Type: five-seat light transport
Powerplant: two 245-hp (183-kW) Jacobs R-755-9 radial piston engines
Performance: maximum speed 195 mph (314 km/h); cruising speed 175 mph (282 km/h); service ceiling 22,000 ft (6705 m); range 750 miles (1207 km)
Weights: empty 3,500 lb (1588 kg); maximum take-off 5,700 lb (2585 kg)
Dimensions: span 41 ft 11 in (12.78 m); length 32 ft 9 in (9.98 m); height 9 ft 11 in (3.02 m); wing area 295.0 sq ft (27.41 m²)

Above: This aircraft, 42-58125, was the 16th of the 1,354 C-78s built, redesignated UC-78 (utility cargo) in January 1943.

Right: USAAF 42-58507 came later in the same batch. Standard finish for the UC-78 was olive drab. Many were used as personal transports by senior officers, and these were often unofficially called UC-78 Brasshat. All UC-78s, unlike later versions, had Hamilton Standard variable-pitch propellers.

Consolidated B-24 Liberator

More effort, more aluminium and more aircrew went into the Consolidated **B-24 Liberator** than into any other aircraft ever built. The prototype Liberator did not even fly until after the beginning of World War II, and the last (except for the PB4Y-2 model) came off the assembly line before the end of the war; yet, in between, deliveries of some 15 major variants totalled 18,188, or 19,203 including spares. This compares with 12,731 B-17s and 7,366 Lancasters.

Particularly in the matter of range, which to some degree stemmed from its having an unusually efficient wing, the Liberator gave the Allies capabilities they would not otherwise have possessed. Early in the war the first Liberators, in RAF markings, were the first aircraft to make North Atlantic crossings a matter of everyday routine. In 1942 a more developed version closed the gap in the Western North Atlantic, where U-boats had been able to operate beyond the range of other RAF aircraft. On countless occasions Liberator formations made attacks on targets that could be reached by no other Allied bomber until the advent of the B-29. Though primarily a heavy bomber, the Liberator was also a most effective fighter (it shot down about 2,600 enemy aircraft), the leading Allied oceanic patrol and anti-submarine aircraft, and the leading Allied long-range cargo transport.

Hard to handle

At the same time it was a most complicated and advanced machine, leading to prolonged pilot training programmes and, on occasion, to severe attrition. It was demanding to fly, even to a pilot fully qualified on the type, and eventually operated at such high weights that take-offs became marginal even with full power on all engines. Flight stability was also marginal, and escape from a stricken machine was extremely difficult once the pilot or pilots had let go of the controls. Moreover, though more modern and in most ways more efficient than the B-17, the overloaded late-model B-24s were hardly any improvement over their more primitive partners, and several commanders, including 'Jimmy' Doolittle, famed commanding general of the 8th Air Force, preferred the old B-17.

In fact the B-24s might have been B-17s, because in October 1938 Consolidated Aircraft Corporation was asked if it would set up a second-source production line of the Boeing bomber. Consolidated had moved three years earlier from icy Buffalo in New York State to

Just one month after making its first flight from Lindbergh Field at San Diego, California, the XB-24 displays its purposeful lines. At this time it lacked turbo-superchargers, self-sealing fuel tanks and armour. Six 0.3-in (7.62-mm) guns were singly mounted.

sunny San Diego in California, and was well placed to expand its large new plant. But chief engineer Isaac M. 'Mac' Laddon had already made studies for long-range bombers and was confident of producing a superior design. Part of this confidence rested on the wing patented by David R. Davis; this had a particularly deep section, with sharp camber and a reflex curve on the underside, and was almost as slender as the wing of a sailplane. Tunnel tests confirmed Davis' claim that this wing offered from 10 to 25 per cent less drag than ordinary wings, but no full-scale wing had flown. Laddon had designed a giant flying-boat, the Model 31, and this was to fly in spring 1939 with a Davis wing. Pending its measured drag figures, he quickly drew a heavy bomber with the same wing and tail but a new fuselage with a futuristic smooth nose and tricycle landing gear. Under the mid/high-mounted wing were two bomb-bays, each as large as that of a B-17.

The commanding general of the US Army Air Corps, H.H. 'Hap' Arnold, studied the plans of the **Model 32** in January 1939 and told Laddon to go ahead, and "build a bomber that will fly the skin off any rivals." Consolidated received a contract for the Model 32, designated **XB-24**, on 30 March 1939. It was to be able to reach 300 mph (483

Among the most memorable of missions flown by Liberators in the course of the war was the attack on the Concordi Vega oil refinery at Ploesti, Romania, in June 1944. 15th Air Force B-24Js are seen here under heavy anti-aircraft fire on a later Ploesti mission.

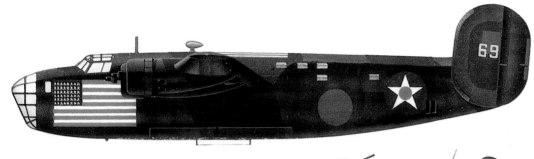

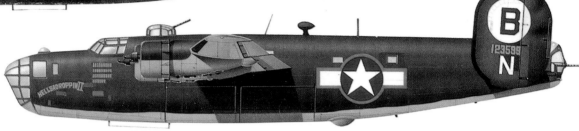

Left: The stars and stripes of the USA are prominently displayed on the fuselage of this LB-30B VIP transport, diverted from a British contract and still in RAF night-bomber finish, with roundels and fin flashes overpainted.

Right: A B-24D in the markings of the 93rd Bomb Group, Eighth Air Force, operating from Hardwick, Norfolk. The long-serving 93rd flew more missions than any other B-24 Group in the Eighth.

Above: One – probably the first – of the seven YB-24s ordered by USAAC in March 1939. Only one of them reached the Air Corps; the other six went to Britain as Liberator Mk Is in exchange for an equal number of British-contract LB-30s relinquished to the USAAC.

Above: The XB-24B, serial 39-680, was in fact the original XB-24, modified to have turbo-supercharged R-183C-41 engines, self-sealing tanks and full protective armour. By 1945, when this photo was taken, it had also acquired outsize windows in the transport role.

Right: The B-24D – this example was delivered from the Convair line in 1942 – was the first Liberator variant to achieve mass production. San Diego built 2,409 of the 'D' variant; another 303 came from Fort Worth, also run by Consolidated, and 10 were built by Douglas at Tulsa before later models followed. In all, 18,188 Liberator variants were produced, exceeding the production quantity of every other heavy bomber.

km/h), 35,000 ft (10670 m) and 3,000 miles (4828 km). The Model 31 flying-boat flew on 5 May 1939, and met the promised drag figures. Design of the Model 32 went ahead quickly, though it was drastically altered to have a conventional nose with the navigator and bombardier in the front and a side-by-side cockpit further back with a stepped windscreen. The first XB-24 (US Army serial 39-680) made a successful flight from Lindbergh Field on 29 December 1939.

This prototype was modern and impressive rather than beautiful, with a deep and stumpy fuselage and very large oval fins and rudders contrasting with the graceful wing. The engines were 1,100-hp (821-kW) Pratt & Whitney R-1830-33 Twin Wasps with geared superchargers, though it was planned to fit turbo-superchargers later to increase the speed from the achieved 273 mph (439 km/h) to beyond the contractual figure.

Crew access

Each of the bomb-bays could carry 4,000 lb (1814 kg) of bombs, with a catwalk down the centre to provide structural strength and crew access to the rear fuselage. To enter the aircraft the usual drill was to flick a small hydraulic lever on the right side of the bay. This opened the bomb doors, which rolled up the outside of the fuselage like a roll-top desk, the moving sections driven by large sprockets working directly on the corrugated inner stiffening skins. Then the crew of seven climbed onto the catwalk, the pilots, navigator, bombardier and radio operator going forward and three gunners aft. Armament comprised five hand-held machine-guns. Apart from the general complexity of the systems, and the extremely advanced

Minneapolis-Honeywell autopilot, features included 12 flexible fuel cells in the wing, Fowler flaps and unusual main gears comprising single legs curved round the outside of single very large wheels which retracted hydraulically outwards to lie flat in the wing, where the wheel projected below the undersurface and needed a fairing.

In March 1939 the US Army Air Corps ordered seven **YB-24s**, and these were delivered in 1940 with additional fuel and equipment and pneumatic de-icer boots, but without fixed outer-wing slots. Only a month later, in April 1939, the French ordered 175 Model 32s in a version designated **32B7**, but the country collapsed before delivery and the UK took on this contract while ordering 165 on its own account. Of the 165, 25 were retained by the US Army and eventually 139 were delivered to the RAF as the **LB-30** (Liberator British type 30), with the British designation **Liberator Mk II**. These were developed to British requirements and had self-sealing tanks, ample armour, R-1830-S3C4G engines driving Curtiss instead of Hamilton propellers, a lengthened nose, and completely re-thought equipment including 11 0.303-in (7.7-mm) Browning guns, eight of them in mid-upper and tail Boulton Paul electric turrets. Serial numbers began at AL503. The second LB-30 was completed as the personal transport of Prime Minister Churchill, with the name Commando, unpainted bright finish and (in 1943) the tall single fin also used on the US Navy RY-3 transport and PB4Y-2 (its designation was Liberator C.Mk IX).

In parallel, Consolidated began to deliver the former French order from March 1941, converted from metric to RAF instruments and gear and known as the **LB-30MF**. RAF serial numbers of these began at AM258, and the basic designation was **Liberator Mk I**. These air-

craft served in many roles, including crew training, military transport, Atfero (Atlantic Return Ferry Service) transport between Prestwick and Montreal, civil BOAC services (joint RAF serials and civil registration) mainly on the route round Europe to Egypt, and with Coastal Command on long-range patrol, some aircraft having a belly installation of four 20-mm cannon firing ahead in addition to normal ASW weapons and ASV Mk I radar. The much better Mk II Liberators also served with Coastal Command, but were employed mainly as bombers in the Middle East and India.

Engine change

Thus all early deliveries went to the UK, but the US Army Air Corps (US Army Air Force from June 1941) received nine (of an order for 36) **B-24A**s which introduced hand-held 0.5-in (12.7-mm) guns but retained Dash-33 engines. The turbocharged Dash-41 engine first flew on the original prototype in late 1940 in characteristic new cowlings of flattened oval shape, with the air ducts and oil coolers along the sides and the exhaust piped to the turbocharger on the underside of the nacelle under the wing. To absorb the power at high altitude, paddle-bladed propellers were fitted (invariably a Hamilton of 11 ft 7 in/3.53 m diameter, with no spinner). As modified, the prototype became the **XB-24B**, other changes including self-sealing tanks and armour. These changes were all incorporated in nine **B-24C**s (ordered as B-24As) delivered in 1941, which also had two American power turrets, a Consolidated in the tail and a Martin just aft of the cockpit, each with two 0.5-in (12.7-mm) guns, as well as three hand-held 0.5-in (12.7-mm) guns in the nose and waist positions.

The B-24C was the basis of the first mass-produced variant, the **B-24D**, which had Dash-43 engines, two further nose guns plus a tunnel ventral gun (10 0.5-in/12.7-mm guns in all), increased outerwing tanks and a bombload of 8,800 lb (3992 kg) or, as an overload with reduced fuel, eight 1,600-lb (726-kg) bombs (total 12,600 lb/5806 kg). From the start the B-24D was cleared to 56,000 lb (25402 kg) and by mid-1942 it was operating at 60,000 lb (27216 kg), making it the heaviest aircraft in production in the USA (the Halifax and Lancaster had just been cleared to the same weight).

Plans were rushed ahead for production on a scale never before seen. The San Diego plant had already been approximately tripled in size. A vast new factory was built in 1941 outside Fort Worth, Texas; a few miles away at Dallas a large facility was built for North American Aviation, which among other types built the B-24G. By July 1942 Douglas was in volume production at Tulsa, and by August 1942 the largest factory in the United States was on stream for Ford Motor Co. at Willow Run, near Detroit, Michigan. It produced 200 complete B-24s each month, plus a further 150 sets of parts for other assembly lines.

Naval use

The B-24D saw service in every theatre, and in 1942-43 was by far the most important long-range bomber in the Pacific area. By late 1942 it equipped 15 anti-submarine squadrons (using radar-equipped aircraft) all round the North Atlantic. In July 1942 the US Navy was permitted to share B-24 deliveries, and in August 1943 the Army ASW squadrons were transferred to the US Navy, which eventually operated 977 **PB4Y-1** Liberators as well as large numbers of **RY-1** and **RY-2** transports. These were the equivalent of the US Army **C-87A** and **C-87**, which were designed almost overnight as the result of the need for long-haul transports in the evacuation of the Dutch East Indies and went into production at the new Fort Worth plant in April 1942. Named **Liberator Express**, the C-87 and RY family had 20 easily removed seats and tie-downs for up to 10,000 lb (4536 kg) of

Garish markings were adopted for 'assembly ships' that were used to help squadrons of the 8th Air Force to formate before the start of a mission. This (right) is the 458th Bomb Group's 'Spotted Ape', perhaps the most eye-catching of all such aircraft.

Consolidated B-24J Liberator cutaway key

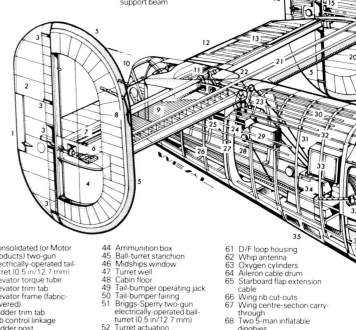

1 Rudder trim tab
2 Fabric-covered rudder
3 Rudder hinges (metal leading-edge)
4 Starboard tailfin
5 Leading-edge de-icing boot
6 Starboard rudder horn
7 Rudder push-pull tube
8 Rear navigation light
9 Tailplane stringers
10 Consolidated (or Motor Products) two-gun electrically-operated tail-turret (0.5 in/12.7 mm)
11 Elevator torque tube
12 Elevator trim tab
13 Elevator frame (fabric-covered)
14 Tab trim tab
15 Tab control linkage
16 Rudder post
17 Light-alloy rudder frame
18 HF aerial
19 Tailfin construction
20 Metal-covered fixed surfaces
21 Tailplane front spar
22 Port elevator push-pull tube
23 Elevator drive quadrant
24 Elevator servo unit
25 Rudder servo unit
26 Ammunition feed track (tail turret)
27 Fuselage aft main fuse
28 Walkway
29 Signal cartridges
30 Longitudinal 'Z'-section stringers
31 Control cables
32 Fuselage intermediate secondary frames
33 Ammunition box
34 Aft fuselage camera installation
35 Lower windows
36 'Waist'-gun support mounting
37 Starboard manually-operated 'waist'-gun (0.5 in/12.7 mm)
38 'Waist' position (open)
39 Wind deflector plate
40 'Waist' position hinged cover
41 Port manually-operated 'waist'-gun (0.5 in/12.7 mm)
42 Dorsal aerial
43 Ball-turret stanchion support beam
44 Ammunition box
45 Ball-turret stanchion
46 Midships window
47 Turret well
48 Cabin floor
49 Tail-bumper operating jack
50 Tail-bumper fairing
51 Briggs-Sperry two-gun electrically-operated ball-turret (0.5 in/12.7 mm)
52 Turret actuation mechanism
53 Bomb-door actuation sprocket (hydraulically-operated)
54 Bomb-door corrugated inner-skin
55 Bomb-bay catwalk (box keel)
56 Bomb-bay catwalk vertical channel support members (bomb release solenoids)
57 Bomb-door actuation track and rollers
58 Wing rear spar
59 Bomb-bay access tunnel
60 Fuselage main frame/bulkhead
61 D/F loop housing
62 Whip antenna
63 Oxygen cylinders
64 Aileron cable drum
65 Starboard flap extension cable
66 Wing rib cut-outs
67 Wing centre-section carry-through
68 Two 5-man inflatable dinghies
69 Flap hydraulic jack
70 Flap/cable attachments
71 Hydraulically-operated Fowler flap
72 Wing rear spar
73 Port mainwheel well and main fairing
74 Engine supercharger waste-gate
75 Three auxiliary self-sealing fuel cells (port and starboard)
76 Wing outer section
77 Aileron gear boxes

Consolidated B-24 Liberator

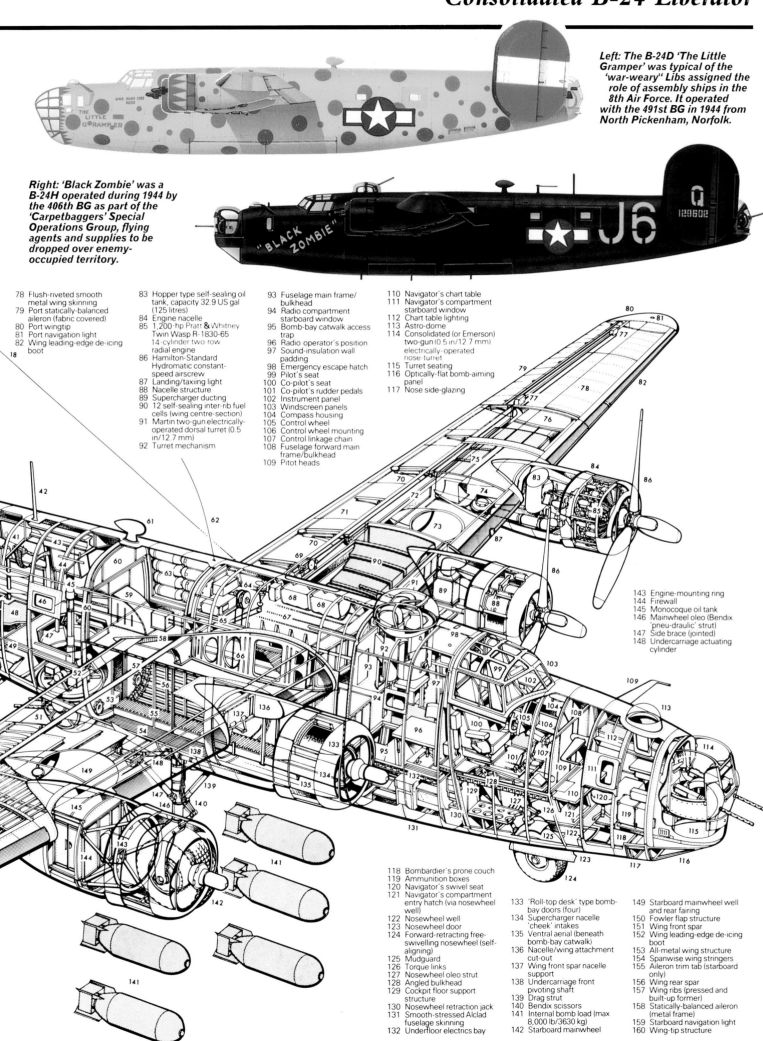

Left: The B-24D 'The Little Gramper' was typical of the 'war-weary'' Libs assigned the role of assembly ships in the 8th Air Force. It operated with the 491st BG in 1944 from North Pickenham, Norfolk.

Right: 'Black Zombie' was a B-24H operated during 1944 by the 406th BG as part of the 'Carpetbaggers' Special Operations Group, flying agents and supplies to be dropped over enemy-occupied territory.

78 Flush-riveted smooth metal wing skinning
79 Port statically-balanced aileron (fabric covered)
80 Port wingtip
81 Port navigation light
82 Wing leading-edge de-icing boot
83 Hopper type self-sealing oil tank, capacity 32.9 US gal (125 litres)
84 Engine nacelle
85 1,200-hp Pratt & Whitney Twin Wasp R-1830-65 14-cylinder two-row radial engine
86 Hamilton-Standard Hydromatic constant-speed airscrew
87 Landing/taxiing light
88 Nacelle structure
89 Supercharger ducting
90 12 self-sealing inter-rib fuel cells (wing centre-section)
91 Martin two-gun electrically-operated dorsal turret (0.5 in/12.7 mm)
92 Turret mechanism
93 Fuselage main frame/bulkhead
94 Radio compartment starboard window
95 Bomb-bay catwalk access trap
96 Radio operator's position
97 Sound-insulation wall padding
98 Emergency escape hatch
99 Pilot's seat
100 Co-pilot's seat
101 Co-pilot's rudder pedals
102 Instrument panel
103 Windscreen panels
104 Compass housing
105 Control wheel
106 Control wheel mounting
107 Control linkage chain
108 Fuselage forward main frame/bulkhead
109 Pitot heads
110 Navigator's chart table
111 Navigator's compartment starboard window
112 Chart table lighting
113 Astro-dome
114 Consolidated (or Emerson) two-gun (0.5 in/12.7 mm) electrically-operated nose-turret
115 Turret seating
116 Optically-flat bomb-aiming panel
117 Nose side-glazing

143 Engine-mounting ring
144 Firewall
145 Monocoque oil tank
146 Mainwheel oleo (Bendix 'pneu-draulic' strut)
147 Side brace (jointed)
148 Undercarriage actuating cylinder

118 Bombardier's prone couch
119 Ammunition boxes
120 Navigator's swivel seat
121 Navigator's compartment entry hatch (via nosewheel well)
122 Nosewheel well
123 Nosewheel door
124 Forward-retracting free-swivelling nosewheel (self-aligning)
125 Mudguard
126 Torque links
127 Nosewheel oleo strut
128 Angled bulkhead
129 Cockpit floor support structure
130 Nosewheel retraction jack
131 Smooth-stressed Alclad fuselage skinning
132 Underfloor electrics bay
133 'Roll-top desk' type bomb-bay doors (four)
134 Supercharger nacelle 'cheek' intakes
135 Ventral aerial (beneath bomb-bay catwalk)
136 Nacelle/wing attachment cut-out
137 Wing front spar nacelle support
138 Undercarriage front pivoting shaft
139 Drag strut
140 Bendix scissors
141 Internal bomb load (max 8,000 lb/3630 kg)
142 Starboard mainwheel
149 Starboard mainwheel well and rear fairing
150 Fowler flap structure
151 Wing front spar
152 Wing leading-edge de-icing boot
153 All-metal wing structure
154 Spanwise wing stringers
155 Aileron trim tab (starboard only)
156 Wing rear spar
157 Wing ribs (pressed and built-up former)
158 Statically-balanced aileron (metal frame)
159 Starboard navigation light
160 Wing-tip structure

Consolidated B-24 Liberator

The last C-87 produced at San Diego is shown here. Some 286 of these transport versions of the Liberator came from Fort Worth and San Diego, including six VIP C-87As. They served in all the war theatres, and notably over 'The Hump' from Burma to China.

Two hundred and nine B-24s were converted to C-109 tankers, primarily to carry fuel over 'The Hump' for use by B-29 Superfortresses. The C-109s were able to carry an extra 2,036 US gal (7707 litres) of gasoline in fuselage tanks. A few – as illustrated – served in Europe.

cargo loaded through a 6-ft (1.83-m) square door on the left side at the rear; a single gun was kept at the tail for a while, but from late 1942 the transports were unarmed. The RAF designation was Liberator C.Mk VII. The C-87A/RY-1 was a VIP model with a luxurious interior normally seating 16. The **C-87B** was an armed transport, while the **C-87C/RY-3/Liberator C.Mk IX** was a 1943 model with a tall single fin, lengthened fuselage and oval cowlings with the major axis upright, the air trunks being at top and bottom.

Attacking in Europe

Total production of the B-24D, excluding transports, was 2,738, 2,409 of these coming from San Diego. The most famous exploit of this model was the first of several long-range attacks on the oil refineries at Ploesti, Romania, on 11-12 June 1942 by a dozen aircraft from a special detachment under Colonel H. A. Halverson, which formed the nucleus of the 9th Air Force. Many others went to 8th Air Force bomb groups in England, flying their first mission against Lille on 9 October 1942. No fewer than 37 RAF squadrons operated the equivalent **Liberator Mks III** (British purchase) and **IIIA** (Lend-Lease), mostly with the Martin top turret but retaining the Boulton Paul tail turret with four 0.303-in (7.7-mm) guns, in Coastal, Bomber and Far East Commands. Coastal Command also used the **Mk V** with chin and retractable ventral radars, ASV arrays, Leigh light, extra fuel and special equipment, which sometimes included eight forward-firing rockets carried on stub wings on each side of the forward fuselage.

The B-24D was developed through block numbers up to 170, bringing in the Dash-65 engine and the Briggs-Sperry retractable ball turret (in place of the tunnel gun), which were to remain standard on subsequent bomber versions. Gross weight climbed to 71,200 lb (32296 kg), much heavier than any other Allied bomber except the B-29, and quite unanticipated when the B-24 was designed. Even the most gentle turns were best made on the autopilot, as the controls were heavy and sluggish, and at weights much in excess of 60,000 lb (27216 kg) any rapid manoeuvre was impossible.

The **B-24E** (RAF **Liberator Mk IV**) had Curtiss propellers and was the first model built at Willow Run; later some B-24Es were made at Fort Worth and Tulsa. The **C-109** was a gasoline tanker conversion of the B-24E (later of the B-24D also) able to carry 2,900 US gal (10978 litres) of fuel in metal tanks in the fuselage, linked to a single socket in the side of the fuselage and with an inert-gas safety

system. Later models had Mareng bag tanks, and their main use was to ferry fuel 'over the Hump' from Burma into China, especially to support B-29 missions. The **XF-7** was a rebuilt B-24D with extra tankage and a large installation of reconnaissance cameras, from which the later **F-7** reconnaissance versions were derived, and two one-off experimental prototypes were the **XB-24F** and **XB-41**. The XB-24F was fitted with thermal de-icing, and it is surprising it was not adopted because rubber-boot de-icers were useless if punctured by shell splinters and needed thousands of man-hours of inspection The XB-41 was a 'destroyer' (escort fighter) carrying 14 guns in twin dorsal, chin and tail turrets and duplicated waist positions, and extra ammunition.

One of the definite shortcomings of the B-24 in combat proved to be its vulnerability to head-on attack. At best there were only three hand-held guns in the nose, and despite progressive modification to the armour the internal protection was so poor that, both in Europe and over the Pacific Ocean, numerous waist gunners were killed by shells entering at the nose and often killing the pilots en route. Some pilots took to carrying slabs of sheet armour held in front of their bodies by hand during crucial periods. One B-24E (42-7127) was fitted with a nose turret and powered lateral barbettes low on the fuselage sides, flying in this form on 30 June 1943. By the time it flew the decision had been taken to make nose turrets standard, and the vast floods of orders for B-24D and **B-24G** models were switched to have turrets. North American's B-24G line had the turret from the start, the selected type being the Emerson A-15; 430 of the B-24G model were built. A new optical bombing station was built in under the turret, and to give the navigator sufficient room and house the 1,200

Above: A single tail unit gave the B-24 improved handling and a better field of fire for the tail guns. This XB-24N was followed by seven YB-24Ns in May/June 1945, but contracts for 5,169 B-24Ns then on order were cancelled at war's end.

Left: A pair of B-24Ms in service with the 494th Bomb Group approaches the target near Cebu City, on Cebu Island in the Philippines, on 25 March 1945. The last Liberator model built in large quantities, the 'M' variant was distinguished by a lightweight tail turret.

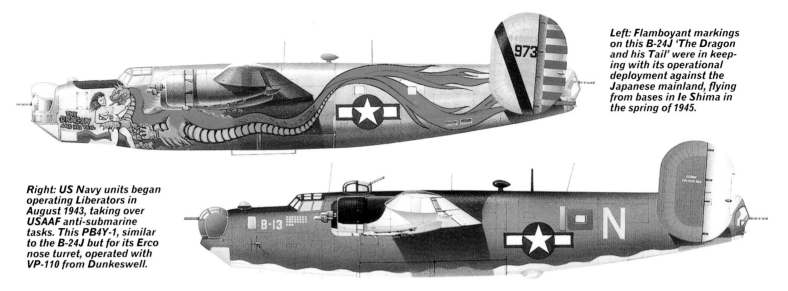

rounds of nose-turret ammunition the nose was extended by 10 in (0.254 m). Fitting the nose turret to an extended nose was the last major modification.

Those bought under 1941 and early 1942 contracts were designated **B-24H**, and the 738 built at Forth Worth retained the flat-fronted Emerson electric nose turret as used on the B-24G. The 1,780 built at Willow Run and 582 from Tulsa had the sloping-front Consolidated hydraulic turret, the first Tulsa block being the last B-24s not to have the Dash-65 engine. Called **Liberator Mk VI**, the RAF and Commonwealth versions usually had the Boulton Paul tail turret, so that all four turrets were of different makes. Made in much larger numbers than any other variant, the **B-24J** was initially merely a rationalised B-24G or B-24H, with the new C-1 autopilot and M-9 bomb sight and, usually, the A-6A (Consolidated) or A-6B (Motor Products) nose turret.

From spring 1944 all five plants delivered aircraft to USAAF service depots where any of a wide range of tail armament and equipment schemes could be installed according to the destination theatre. Those for the US Navy, the PB4Y-1, which originally had a B-24D-type nose, switched to the A-6A turret and then, for the main run in 1944, to the near-spherical Erco nose turret. From April 1944 B-24s were unpainted, and the only significant modifications after that were the introduction of the improved General Electric (B-22 type) turbocharger, giving higher performance at altitude, and a lightweight Consolidated M-6A twin-gun tail 'stinger' (basically manual, with hydraulic assistance, and with a wider field of fire than a turret) which resulted in the designation **B-24L**. San Diego built 417 of these, and Willow Run 1,250. Some were again rebuilt as B-29 gunner trainers with that aircraft's complex remote sighting and barbette armament, under the designation **RB-24L**; later they received additional radar as the post-war **TB-24L**. The many British variants were designated Liberator Mk VI, Coastal Command models being the **GR.Mk VI** and **GR.Mk VIII** (the **C.Mk VII** was a Liberator Express transport series and the C.Mk IX was similar to the US Navy RY-3 with the tall single fin).

Tail redesign

In March 1943 Consolidated had merged with Vultee to form Convair, and the last major wartime variant was the **B-24M** with a lightweight Motor Products tail turret, Convair building 916 and Willow Run 1,677. Among the experimental versions were the **XB-24P** and the Ford-built **XB-24Q** with a radar-controlled remotely sighted tail stinger, which led to that fitted to the B-47. These were the last of the familiar models with the original tail.

As far back as 1942 it had been clear that a single fin would be better, and on 6 March 1943 a converted B-24D flew with the fin and rudder of a Douglas B-23. After refinement the whole tail end of this machine was grafted onto another aircraft (42-40234, originally a B-24D but with a nose turret) to become the **XB-24K**. Ford also fitted 1,350-hp (1007-kW) Dash-75 engines, and the result was a bomber that was considerably faster, had more than double the full load rate of climb and much better power of manoeuvre.

Convair were busy with further major improvements including longer nacelles housing larger oil tanks, an Emerson ball nose turret and lightweight ball turret in the tail, a completely new cockpit window arrangement giving better pilot view, and a further refined tail. This became the next standard model after the B-24J, the **B-24N**. Thousands were ordered, the **XB-24N** flying in November 1944, but only seven **YB-24N**s had flown when production stopped on 31 May

Above: The US Navy received 977 **PB4Y-1** patrol bombers, early examples being B-24Ds transferred from the USAAF. Later aircraft were the equivalent of the B-24J, as illustrated here, and had the Erco nose turret mounting twin guns. Service use continued until 1951.

Above: The name 'Privateer' was adopted by the Navy for this **PB4Y-2** development of the B-24, which featured a lengthened fin and rudder as planned for the B-24N. Intended for low/medium-altitude use, the PB4Y-2s lacked engine turbo-superchargers.

1945, 5,168 being cancelled.

Independently, the US Navy had been developing an optimised patrol version with the even taller single fin of the RY-3, low-rated engines without turbochargers and a further lengthened and completely rearranged fuselage. Work began on 3 May 1943, and the first prototype of the **PB4Y-2 Privateer** flew on 20 September that year. Absence of turbochargers resulted in the engine cowls being made oval vertically instead of horizontally, but the main differences lay in the capacious fuselage which resulted in an overall length of 74 ft 7 in (22.73 m) with accommodation for a crew of 11. Armament comprised 12 guns in a Consolidated tail turret, fore and aft Martin dorsal turrets, an Erco nose turret and Erco twin-gun waist blisters. The internal bomb-bay was basically that of the B-24, but ASM-N-2 Bat radar-homing anti-ship missiles could be carried on underwing attachments, and there were extensive maritime sensors. A total of 736 production Privateers was delivered by October 1945, some being converted into other versions including the **PB4Y-1G** for the Coast Guard, with no guns but more extensive glazing and a mass of special avionics. In 1951 the PB4Y-2s were redesignated **P4Y**, and several were used by the Coast Guard as **P4Y-2G**s. One variant, the **P4Y-2K** target, even survived to become the **QP-4B** under the 1962 unified designation system.

Consolidated B-24D Liberator
376th Bomb Group
47th Bomb Wing, 1943

Aircraft 42-40664 was a B-24D-85-CO, built at San Diego in 1942 and operated by the 15th Air Force in Cyrenaica. The 376th, the 'Liberandos', took a wrong turning on the run-in to the Ploesti oilfields on 1 August 1943 and went straight on for Bucharest, which had intense flak but few targets. The bombers were painted in desert pink, and like all North African-based aircraft had yellow-ringed insignia and RAF-style tail flashes. 'Teggie Ann' was the name of an equally famous B-24D (41-23754) which in the hands of the 93rd BG of the 8th Air Force was the first B-24 of any type to fly in action from England for the first time on 9 October 1942 in an attack on Lille.

Consolidated B-24 Liberator variants

USAAF variants
XB-24: Model 32 prototype
YB-24: seven pre-production aircraft with many small changes
B-24A: first US Army version, with six 0.5-in (12.7-mm) guns but otherwise similar to Liberator Mk I; used mainly as transports
XB-24B: Model 32/XB-24 rebuilt with turbocharged engines in flattened elliptical cowlings used on most subsequent versions
B-24C: production B-24B with new 0.5-in (12.7-mm) twin-gun turrets behind cockpit and in tail
B-24D: first mass-produced version, progressively greater bombload and armament; final blocks with three nose guns, two (rarely four) waist guns and twin guns in retractable ventral ball turret in addition to dorsal and tail turrets
TB-24D: redesignation of AT-22 trainer
B-24E: Ford-built variant with minor changes
XB-24F: test B-24D with thermal instead of pneumatic de-icers
B-24G: North American-built version of B-24D; lengthened fuselage with nose turret
B-24H: mass-produced variant of B-24G with minor changes
B-24J: mass-produced bomber standard production 1943-44
XB-24K: rebuild of B-24D with experimental single-fin tail
B-24L: production B-24J with twin manually-controlled tail guns
RB-24L: a number of B-24L converted for B-29 gunnery training
TB-24L: RB-24Ls converted to act as radar trainers
B-24M: production B-24J with lightweight tail turret
ZB-24M: remaining B-24Ms on USAF charge, redesignated in 1948 to recognise their 'obsolescence'
XB-24N: one prototype bomber with single fin, new nose and cockpit, and many other improvements
YB-24N: seven pre-production single-fin bombers
B-24N: production variant of YB-24N; cancelled
XB-24P: single B-24D converted for airborne fire control research
XB-24Q: single B-24L converted to test B-47 remotely-sighted tail guns
XB-41: single B-24D converted as heavily-armed escort bomber; 14 0.5-in (12.7-mm) machine-guns
AT-22: five C-87s converted for flight engineer training
BQ-8: a small number of high-time B-24Ds and Js were converted as radio-controlled bombs for use against Japanese targets; no operational use
C-87 Liberator Express: rebuild of B-24D as 25-passenger transport
C-87A: VIP transport version of C-87 with 16 seats or 10 berths
C-87B: projected armed transport with five 0.5-in (12.7-mm) machine-guns
C-87C: designation reserved for

USAAF version of RY-3; not used
XC-109: single B-24E converted to unarmed fuel tanker
C-109: over 200 B-24D/J/Ls converted to fuel tanker
XF-7: single B-24D converted with 11 cameras in nose, bomb bay and tail positions
F-7: four B-24Ds converted for reconnaissance; essentially similar to XF-7
F-7A: 86 B-24Js converted with three cameras in nose and three in bomb bay
F-7B: 47 B-24J, five B-24L and 71 B-24M converted with six cameras in bomb bay

Royal Air Force variants
LB-30: transport derivative of Liberator Mk II
LB-30A: British transport versions similar to YB-24 but unarmed
Liberator Mk I: various models mainly converted in UK for Coastal Command with ASV radar and ventral cannon installation
Liberator Mk II: improved bomber, longer nose, two Boulton Paul four-gun turrets, first operationally ready variant
Liberator Mk III: equivalent of B-24D
Liberator Mk IV: equivalent of B-24E
Liberator GR.Mk V: modification of Liberator Mk IV with extra fuel and ASW equipment
Liberator Mk VI/VIII: versions of B-24J; operated in bomber, transport and maritime variants
Liberator C.Mk VII: RAF version of C-87
Liberator C.Mk IX: RAF equivalent of RY-3

US Navy variants
PB4Y-1: equivalent to B-24D
PB4Y-1P: 65 PB4Y-1s converted for photo-reconnaissance; redesignated P4Y-2P in 1951
PB4Y-2 Privateer: development of PB4Y-1 with lengthened fuselage, single fin, additional fuel and R-1830-94 unsupercharged engines; redesignated P4Y-2 in 1951
PB4Y-2B: several PB4Y-2s converted to carry Bat anti-ship missiles; also known as PB4Y-2M and redesignated P4Y-2B in 1951
PB4Y-2S: designation of PB4Y-2 with surface search radar; redesignated P4Y-2S in 1951
P4Y-2G: nine P4Y-2 transferred to US Coast Guard; armament removed and extra glazing added
P4Y-2K: radio-controlled drone conversion of P4Y-2; redesignated QP-4B in 1962
P4Y-2P: photo-reconnaissance conversion of P4Y-2
RY-1: equivalent of C-87A VIP transport
RY-2: equivalent of C-87 passenger transport
RY-3: transport forerunner of PB4Y-2 with lengthened fuselage and tall single fin

POWERPLANTS
The initial B-24As were fitted with four P&W R-1830-33 Twin Wasp 14-cylinder two-row radial air-cooled engines which produced 1,200 hp (895 kW) at 2,700 rpm. The Liberator Mk II (LB-30) had four P&W R-1830-S3C4Gs with two-speed superchargers and driving Curtiss Electric full-feathering propellers.

100 TEGGIE ANN

CONFIGURATION

Fundamental features included the long and aerodynamically efficient Davis wing (high-aspect ratio), with Fowler flaps and fuel cells between the spars. The tall main landing gears featured single wheels and legs retracting outwards to lie inside the wing. A nosewheel undercarriage was an important feature. The stumpy fuselage had a large central bomb bay with roller-shutter doors – the front and rear fuselage being joined across the bay by a catwalk.

Specification
Consolidated-Vultee B-24D-85-CO
Type: heavy bomber with crew of 10
Powerplant: four 1,200-hp (895-kW) Pratt & Whitney R-1830-43 Twin Wasp radial piston engines
Performance: maximum speed 303 mph (488 km/h); initial climb 1,100 ft (335 m) per minute; operating radius with 5,000-lb (2268-kg) bombload 1,080 miles (1730 km); service ceiling 28,000 ft (8540 m)

Weights: empty 33,980 lb (15413 kg); maximum take-off 60,000 lb (27216 kg)
Dimensions: span 110 ft 0 in (33.52 m); length 66 ft 4 in (20.22 m); height 17 ft 11 in (5.46 m); wing area 1,048 sq ft (97.36 m²)
Armament: one (usually three) 0.5-in (12.7-mm) nose gun, two 0.5-in guns in dorsal turret, two in tail turret, two in retractable ball turret, and two in waist positions; plus a maximum internal bombload of 8,000 lb (3629 kg)

Consolidated B-32 Dominator

For precisely the same requirement to which Boeing designed the B-29, Consolidated evolved a competing proposal, and each company was awarded a contract to build three prototypes: those ordered from Consolidated were allocated the designation **XB-32**.

The first prototype made its maiden flight on 7 September 1942, two weeks before the first XB-29. The second and third followed on 2 July 1943 and 9 November respectively. Like the XB-29 these featured pressurisation and remotely-controlled gun turrets, but each differed in some fairly major aspect of its configuration. The first had a rounded

The three XB-32s are even less remembered than the totally redesigned B-32. Here Army Air Corps 41-141, the first, is running up on the San Diego ramp in 1942. Planned armament was 14 0.5-in guns in seven barbettes.

fuselage nose and twin fins and rudders based on those of the B-24 Liberator. The second retained this tail unit but had a modified fuselage nose with a stepped windscreen for the flight deck. The third prototype retained this fuselage design but introduced a large single fin and rudder, and this was the basic configuration as finalised for production aircraft.

Somewhat smaller than the B-29, the **B-32** was of cantilever high-wing monoplane configuration, and powered by four Wright Cyclone 18 radial engines of the same series used for the B-29. Landing gear was of the retractable tricycle type, and two cavernous bomb bays could carry 20,000 lb (9072 kg) of bombs. Accommodation was provided for a standard crew of eight.

Consolidated was to experience extensive problems in the

development of the B-32, to the extent that it was not possible to begin the delivery of production examples until November 1944, almost eight months after XX Bomber Command B-29s had been deployed on forward bases in China. Even then, production aircraft (of which 74 were built) had the intended pressurisation system and remotely-controlled gun turrets deleted.

In the final analysis, only 15 of these aircraft were to become operational before VJ-Day, these equipping the USAAF's 386th Bombardment Squadron based on Okinawa. A total of 40 **TB-32**s was also produced for training purposes, but with the end of the war all versions were very soon withdrawn from service.

AAF No. 42-108476 was the sixth of the 74 B-32 Dominators to be completed. The turrets comprised nose, tail, forward, and aft dorsal and ventral.

Specification
Type: long-range strategic bomber
Powerplant: four 2,200-hp (1641-kW) Wright R-3350-23 Cyclone radial piston engines
Performance: maximum speed 357 mph (575 km/h) at 25,000 ft (7620 m); service ceiling 35,000 ft (10670 m); range with maximum bombload 800 miles (1287 km); maximum range 3,800 miles (6115 km)
Weights: empty 60,272 lb (27339 kg); maximum take-off 111,500 lb (50576 kg)
Dimensions: span 135 ft 0 in (41.15 m); length 83 ft 1 in (25.32 m); height 33 ft 0 in (10.06 m); wing area 1,422 sq ft (132.10 m²)
Armament: 10 0.50-in (12.7-mm) machine-guns in five turrets, plus up to 20,000 lb (9072 kg) of bombs

Consolidated PBY Catalina

Left: Looking remarkably clean, with no visible floats, blisters or radar, BuNo. 0121 was the 20th of the 60 PBY-1s, with 900-hp Twin Wasp engines. It became No. 9 aircraft in squadron VP-11.

Below: In November 1939 Consolidated first flew the XPBY-5A. This was converted from a PBY-4 and was the first of the amphibian variants (denoted by the 'A' suffix).

The **Consolidated Catalina** was one of the slowest combat aircraft of World War II; wags said its crews needed a calendar rather than a stopwatch in order to rendezvous with a convoy. Flown in 1935, it was no longer young even at the outbreak of war, and the US Navy had already ordered a next-generation boat (the Martin PBM) to succeed it. But the well-loved 'Cat' happened to be rather hard to beat. In 1938 it had been recognised by the Soviet Union as superior to anything created by their own designers, and it was built there under licence throughout the war. More than that, the original US machine blossomed forth in many new versions which to the end of the war outsold all the newer replacements. More Catalinas were built than any other flying-boat or floatplane in history.

A CATALINA, NAVY 'DUMBO', PATROLS ALONG ALEUTIAN COAST.

The genesis of the **PBY**, as the aircraft was known to US forces, lay in a 1933 requirement by the US Navy for a new long-range patrol flying-boat. At that time the principal aircraft in this category was the Consolidated P2Y, designed at Buffalo by Isaac M. 'Mac' Laddon, a gifted seaplane engineer and a director of Consolidated Aircraft. To meet the new demand he cleaned up the P2Y by giving it an almost cantilever wing mounted above the shallow but broad hull on a central pylon housing the flight engineer. The wing differed from that of the P2Y by having a regular centre-section and tapered outer panels, all of stressed-skin all-metal construction (ailerons were fabric-skinned). A unique feature was that the wingtip floats were mounted on pivoted frames which could be retracted electrically so that in flight the floats formed the wingtips. The hull, likewise all-

This PBY-5A amphibian, equipped with British ASV (air-to-surface vessel) radar, was photographed while on patrol along the Aleutian Islands coast in early 1943. Surprisingly, as this was a front-line theatre, no armament is visible.

metal, was quite different from that of most large boats in being all on one deck, with a broad semi-circular top. In the bow was a mooring compartment and transparent sighting window with a venetian blind giving sea water protection. The bow cockpit was a turret with large all-round windows in production aircraft, with a machine-gun above. Two pilots sat side-by-side in the wide cockpit with large windows all round. Aft of the wing were left and right gunner's stations, each with a sliding hatch. Unlike the P2Y the tail was clean and simple, with the horizontal tail mounted well up the single fin. The powerplant

This PBY-5A, not fitted with radar, was photographed in January 1945 landing (the PBY had no flaps) with its anti-submarine bombs still on board. Clouds of mud are being thrown up from the airstrip at Amchitka, in the Aleutians. The date was January 1943.

This PBY-1 is seen taxiing out, possibly at NAS Pensacola. A crewman is on the wing, waist hatches are open, and the pilot has full up-elevator and full left aileron. The biplane is an N3N Canary.

switched from Cyclones to the new two-row Pratt & Whitney Twin Wasp, neatly cowled on the centre-section with cooling gills and driving Hamilton variable-pitch propellers.

With the massive order for 60, Consolidated had plenty of work to support its 2,000-mile (3220-km) move to San Diego, in southern California, where weather was fine all through the year. In October 1935 the XP3Y made a non-stop flight of almost 3,500 miles (5633 km) from Coco Solo to San Francisco. It then went on to participate in the dedication of the giant new San Diego plant on 20 October before returning to Buffalo to be modified to PBY standard with a broad rounded rudder, de-icer boots on all leading edges (with pull-out steps up the leading edge of the fin), full armament and combat equipment. It flew again in March 1936 and reached US Navy squadron VP-11F at the same time as the first production machines in October 1936. Unquestionably this was the best patrol flying-boat in the world at that time.

In July 1936 Consolidated received a contract for 50 **PBY-2**s with all four wing racks stressed to 1,000-lb (454-kg) loads and with 0.5-in (12.7mm) guns in the waist positions. In November 1936 an order followed for 66 **PBY-3**s with R-1830-66 Twin Wasps uprated from 900 to 1,000 hp (671 to 746 kW), and in December 1937 a contract followed for 33 **PBY-4**s, all but one with large bulged transparent

Probably in the Aleutians, this 'Cat', a PBY-4 or PBY-5 without radar, appears to be heading for the very close deserted shore. One hopes that the ship from which the photograph was taken was not doing the same!

Though these four (including the photographer's aircraft) were all radar-equipped Black Cats, they were not amphibians but straight PBY-5s. Like all the mass-produced versions, the Twin Wasps were uprated to 1,200 hp, enabling take-off weight to be higher than in early variants.

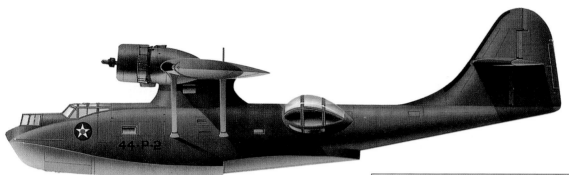

Left: One of the first PBY-5s, with 1,200-hp engines, a redesigned vertical tail and many other improvements. No fewer than 16 Navy squadrons were flying the PBY-5 by the end of 1941.

blisters instead of lateral sliding hatches for the beam gunners and with 1,050-hp (783-kW) engines. Two more PBYs were sold in 1937 to explorer Dr Richard Archbold, who named them *Guba I* and *Guba II* (Motu word for a sudden storm). *Guba II* spent an arduous year in New Guinea, finally making the first flight across the Indian Ocean to survey the route known in World War II as the 'horseshoe route' on which hundreds of military and BOAC Catalinas were to fly. It then crossed Africa and the Atlantic, the first aircraft to circle the globe near the Equator. *Guba I* was sold to a Soviet expedition led by Sir Hubert Wilkins which flew 19,000 miles (30600 km) through the worst weather in the world fruitlessly searching for S. A. Levanevskii, who vanished near the North Pole on 13 August 1937. So outstanding was the Model 28 in this work that the **Model 28-2** was put into production at Taganrog on the Azov Sea as the **GST** (civil transport version, **MP-7**), over 1,000 being used in World War II with 950-hp (709-kW) engines in Polikarpov I-16 type shuttered cowlings and with Soviet equipment and armament.

Another **Model 28-5** (PBY-4) was bought by the British Air Ministry and tested at Felixstowe as P9630, proving so outstanding that it was adopted as a standard boat for Coastal Command. Named **Catalina Mk I** – a name later adopted by the US Navy – the first RAF variant was similar to the latest US Navy type, the **PBY-5** with 1,200-hp (895-kW) R-1830-92 engines, an order for 200 of which had been placed on 20 December 1939. No flying-boat – in fact no large US Navy aircraft – had ever been ordered in such quantities, and the vast open-ended British orders called for massive extra capacity. British officials helped arrange for licence production by Canadian Vickers at Cartierville (Montreal) and Boeing of Canada at Vancouver. The San Diego plant also much more than doubled in size and was joined by a larger plant a mile down the road building B-24s.

On 22 November 1939 Consolidated flew a PBY-4 rebuilt as the **XPBY-5A** with retractable tricycle landing gear. This excellent amphibian conversion was a great success and had only a minor effect

One of the latest versions was the Boeing PB2B-2, based on the PBN with a redesigned airframe of which the most visible changes were the bow and vertical tail. Most, including BuNo. 44241 depicted, were equipped with centimetric-wavelength radar in a neat pod above the cockpit.

This is one of the small number of conversions of PBY-4 and PBY-5 Catalinas to the mine warfare role. A special electric-generating plant supplied a large current to cables inside the ring to explode magnetic mines. As the aircraft had to fly over the minefield at low level, this was a dangerous job.

on performance. The final 33 PBY-5s were completed as **PBY-5A**s, and another 134 were ordered in November 1940. At the time of Pearl Harbor (7 December 1941) the US Navy had three squadrons of PBY-3s, two of PBY-4s and no fewer than 16 flying the new PBY-5. Before sunrise on that day a PBY crew spotted the periscope of a Japanese submarine at Pearl Harbor, marked it with smoke and guided the destroyer USS *Ward,* which sank it – the first US shots of World War II over an hour before the air attack began. By this time a further 586 PBY-5s had been ordered, and the export list had risen to 18 for Australia, 50 for Canada, 30 for France and 36 for the Netherlands East Indies. In 1942 another 627 PBY-5As were added, of which 56 were to be **OA-10**s for the USAAF, used for search and rescue. The first Lend-Lease batch for the RAF comprised 225 non-amphibious **PBY5B**s (**Catalina Mk IA**s) followed by 97 **Catalina Mk IVA**s, fitted in Britain with ASV Mk II radar. RAF Catalinas usually had a Vickers K (VGO) machine-gun in the bow and twin 0.303-in (7.7-mm) Brownings in the waist blisters.

RAF Catalina operations began in spring 1941 with Nos 209 and 210 Squadrons, and one of the first to become operational was a machine of No. 209 from Castle Archdale which on 26 May 1941

Consolidated PBY Catalina

A photograph taken in early 1943 from a seaplane tender in the Aleutians, showing a **PBY5** being winched alongside for refuelling. The flying-boat is on an operational patrol, with anti-submarine bombs under the wings. The colour scheme at this time was sea blue and white.

Consolidated PBY-5A Catalina cutaway drawing key

1 Starboard tailplane
2 Tailplane leading edge de-icing
3 Tail navigation light
4 Starboard fabric-covered elevator
5 Elevator tab
6 Rudder trim tab
7 Fabric-covered rudder construction
8 Tailcone
9 Elevator push-pull control rod
10 Rudder control horn
11 Tail mooring point
12 Lower fin structure integral with tail fuselage
13 Tailplane centre section attachment
14 Upper fin construction
15 Aerial cables
16 Fin leading edge de-icing
17 Port tailplane
18 Cooling air intake
19 Rear fuselage frame and stringer construction
20 Ventral tunnel gun hatch
21 0.3-in (7.62-mm) machine gun
22 Fuselage skin plating

was far out over the Atlantic, with the crew under Pilot Officer Briggs being checked out by a 'neutral' lieutenant in the US Navy. Suddenly they spotted a giant warship; it was the *Bismarck,* which had eluded all pursuers for 31½ hours. Despite heavy flak the Catalina radioed the battleship's position and kept her in view until another Catalina from No. 240 Squadron took over and guided the British fleet to the spot. Apart from this epic, almost all Coastal Command missions by more than 650 Catalinas were against U-boats, many of the 15- to 20-hour trips ending at Grasnaya (Murmansk) and Arkhangelsk protecting convoys supplying the Soviet Union. The only shortcoming of the Catalina was that its slow speed often gave a U-boat time to dive after being spotted. By 1943 they stayed on the surface, bristling with flak, and two Catalina skippers won the VC, one posthumously, for pressing home their attacks on heavily armed U-boats under almost unbelievable conditions.

Life was equally tough in the Pacific where the Catalina was from 7 December 1941 by far the most important US patrol aircraft. In the northern campaign along the Aleutians many Catalinas had to make overloaded downwind take-offs in blizzards at night, with ice over the windscreen. The PBY was the first US aircraft (other than the obsolete Douglas B-18) to carry radar. They fulfilled diverse missions including those of torpedo-bomber, transport and glider tug. Perhaps the most famous of all Catalinas were the Black Cat PBY-5A amphibians which, painted matt black, roamed the western Pacific from December 1942, finding Japanese ships of all kinds by radar at night and picking up Allied survivors from ships and aircraft in boats and dinghies. In addition to radar, bombs, depth charges and fragmentation grenades, the Black Cats often carried crates of empty beer bottles whose eerie whistling descent deterred Japanese gunners and caused wasted time looking for unexploded bombs.

By late 1941 the Cartierville plant was in full production. Canadian Vickers delivered 230 amphibians ordered as **PBV-1A**s but actually passed to the USAAF as **OA-10A**s, as well as 149 **Canso I** amphibians for the RCAF. Boeing, which came on stream later, built 240 **PB2B-1**s, mainly as **Catalina Mk IVB**s for the RAF, RAAF and RNZAF, and 17 Catalinas and 55 Cansos for the RCAF. Yet another plant was brought into the programme in 1941 to produce its own improved models. The NAF (Naval Aircraft Factory) at Philadelphia had been the source of all US Navy flying-boat designs, and its experience enabled it to improve on 'Mac' Laddon's design in a way that

23 Target-towing reel
24 Flare launch tube
25 Rear fuselage bulkhead
26 Bulkhead door
27 0.5-in (12.7-mm) beam machine gun
28 Starboard beam gun cupola
29 Cupola opening side window
30 Flexible gun mounting
31 Port beam gun cupola
32 Gunner's folding seat
33 Semi-circular gun platform
34 Walkway
35 Hull bottom V-frames
36 Wardroom bulkhead
37 Crew rest bunks
38 Wardroom
39 Starboard mainwheel
40 Hull planing bottom step
41 Planing bottom construction
42 Fuselage skin plating
43 Mainwheel housing

44 Hydraulic retraction jack
45 Telescopic leg strut
46 Fore and aft wing support struts
47 Wing mounting centre pylon construction
48 Pylon tail fairing
49 Starboard wing integral fuel tank, capacity 875 US gal (3312 litres)
50 Fuel jettison pipe
51 1000-lb (454-kg) bomb
52 Smoke generator tank
53 Trailing edge ribs
54 Fabric covered trailing edge
55 Rear spar
56 Aileron trim tab
57 Starboard retractable wing-tip float
58 Float support struts
59 Retraction linkage
60 Fabric-covered starboard aileron
61 Static discharge wicks
62 Wing-tip aerial mast
63 Float up-lock
64 Float leg housing
65 Starboard navigation light

66 Leading edge de-icing boot
67 Float retracting gear
68 Front spar
69 Wing rib/stringer construction
70 ASV radar aerial
71 Outer wing panel attachment joint
72 Wing lattice ribs
73 Bomb carrier and release unit
74 Two 500-lb (227-kg) bombs
75 Leading-edge nose ribs
76 Position of pitot tube on port wing
77 Landing lamp
78 Landing lamp glare shield
79 Starboard engine nacelle fairing
80 Hydraulic accumulator
81 Engine oil tank
82 Fireproof bulkhead
83 Exhaust stub
84 Engine bearer struts
85 Detachable engine cowlings
86 Curtiss Electric three-bladed constant-speed

propeller, 12-ft (3.66-m) diameter
87 Propeller hub pitch-change mechanism
88 Pratt & Whitney R-1830-92 Twin Wasp two-row radial engine
89 Aerial cable lead-in
90 D/F loop aerial
91 Oil cooler
92 Control runs through pylon front fairing
93 Pylon step
94 Engineer's control panel
95 Flight engineer's seat
96 Wing mounting fuselage main frame
97 Radio and radar control units
98 Cabin heater
99 Front cabin walkway
100 Port main undercarriage leg strut
101 Torque scissor links
102 Port mainwheel
103 Mk 13-2 torpedo
104 450-lb (204-kg) depth charge

105 Forward fuselage frame construction
106 Navigator's seat
107 Radio/radar operator's seat
108 Radio rack
109 Cabin side window
110 Autopilot servo controller
111 Navigator's chart table
112 Fuselage chine member
113 Cockpit bulkhead
114 Co-pilot's seat
115 Pilot's seat
116 Pilot's electrical control panel
117 Sliding side window
118 Engine cowling cooling air gills
119 Port engine nacelle
120 Cockpit roof escape hatch
121 Overhead throttle and propeller controls
122 Windscreen wipers
123 Curved windscreens
124 Instrument panel
125 Control column yoke and handwheels
126 Rudder pedals
127 Cockpit flooring

128 Nose undercarriage hatch doors
129 Nosewheel bay
130 Port aileron
131 Nosewheel
132 Port retractable wing-tip float
133 Float support struts
134 Nosewheel forks
135 Leading edge de-icing boot
136 Nosewheel forks
137 Nose undercarriage retraction jack
138 Front gunner/bomb aimer's station
139 Curtained bulkhead
140 Gunner's footboards
141 Spare ammunition containers
142 Front rotating gun turret
143 0.3-in (7.62-mm) machine gun
144 Bomb aimer's instrument panel
145 Drift sight
146 Bomb aiming window with protective blind
147 Anchor cable

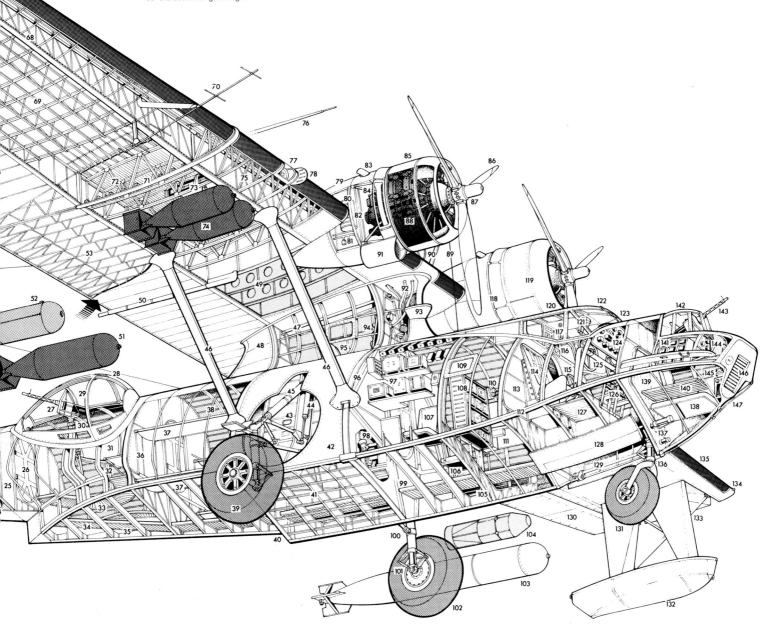

Consolidated PBY Catalina

could have been done by the parent company had it not been for the frantic demand for production. The NAF Catalina, the **PBN-1**, had a wing restressed for 38,000-lb (17237-kg) gross weight, with increased tankage, redesigned wingtip floats and struts, and a new hull with a longer and sharper bow, 20° step amidships, and rear step extended about 1.52 m (5 ft) aft; most obvious of the changes was the tall vertical tail, with a horn-balanced rudder, and armament was generally increased to three or more 12.7-mm (0. 5-in) machine-guns (only the ventral tunnel retained the rifle-calibre gun) with a rounded bow turret and improved continuous-feed magazines. Another change was a redesigned electrical system of increased capacity, with the batteries moved from the leading edge down to the hull.

The NAF itself delivered 138 **PBN-1 Nomad**s, and Consolidated (by this time Convair) opened yet another plant at New Orleans to build the best Catalinas of all, the amphibious version of the PBN.

Called **PBY-6A**, this usually carried a centimetric radar in a neat pod above the cockpit, and the bow turret usually had twin 12.7-mm (0.5in) guns. An order was placed for 900, but the end of the war cut this to 48 for the Soviet Union (which also received all but one of the PBNs), 75 as **OA-10B**s for the USAAF and 112 for the US Navy. Fifty more were delivered by Boeing from Vancouver as **PB2B-2**s, designated **Catalina Mk VI** by the RAF.

Total production of all versions of the Consolidated Model 28 considerably exceeded 3,000. Of these 2,398 were delivered by Consolidated Aircraft and Convair (the March 1943 name for the merged Consolidated and Vultee-Stinson companies). Some 892 were built by the NAF and by the two Canadian plants, and 27 were built in the Soviet Union.

This is a PBY-6A, BuNo. 46642. More than 300 engineering changes distinguished this final version from the PBY-5A, about half being concerned with armament, electronics and equipment. Like the PBN it was cleared to a maximum weight of 38,000 lb, five tons heavier than early versions.

This PBY-5A, and another in the background plus numerous Lockheed PV-1s, were all operating in the Aleutian Islands in the summer of 1943. The colour scheme at that time was non-specular sea blue, and the national marking had a red border. The man between the engines is standing on the step on the leading edge of the wing pylon to warn the tractor driver of any wingtip obstructions.

Consolidated PB2Y Coronado

This PB2Y-5 shows the mixture of darker non-specular sea blue merging into pale grey-blue lower down, with undersurfaces white. This was the ultimate patrol-bomber version, with Catalina-type R-1830-92 engines giving high power at low altitudes.

Plans for the development of a maritime patrol bomber larger than the PBY Catalina were drawn up by the US Navy very soon after the first flight of the Catalina's XP3Y-1 prototype. The aim was to procure a patrol flying boat with increased performance and good weapon load capability, Consolidated and Sikorsky each receiving a contract for the construction of a prototype for evaluation. Sikorsky's XPBS-1, ordered on 29 June 1935, flew for the first time on 13 August 1937. Despite a number of new features (it was, for example, the first US military aircraft with both nose and tail turrets), it was the Consolidated **XPB2Y-1** which, when evaluated following a first flight on 17 December 1937, was regarded as the more suitable for production. As at that time the US Navy had no funds for immediate procurement of any of these aircraft, Consolidated were to have almost 15 months in which to rectify the shortcomings revealed by initial flight tests.

Most serious of the problems was lateral instability, which the company attempted to rectify by the addition of two oval-shaped fins, mounted one each side of the tailplane. This was a move in the right direction, but stability

was still far from satisfactory and was finally resolved by the design of a new tail unit, first with circular endplate fins and rudders and, finally, by endplate fins and rudders similar to those of the B-24 Liberator.

The other problem concerned the hydrodynamic performance of the flying-boat's hull; fortunately, the procurement time-scale allowed Consolidated to redesign the hull, this being deeper than that of the prototype, with a much-changed nose profile.

Eventually, on 31 March 1939, the US Navy were able to order six of these aircraft, given the designation **PB2Y-2** and the name **Coronado**, and delivery of these to US Navy Squadron VP-13 began on 31 December 1940. They were impressive aircraft, powered by four 1,200-hp (895-kW) Pratt & Whitney R-1830-78 Twin Wasp radial engines mounted on the high-set cantilever wing. Construction was all-metal, and interesting features included stabilising floats which retracted to form wingtips in flight, and bomb bays formed in the deep-section wing. Accommodation was provided for a crew of nine.

These PB2Y-2s were used for service trials, leading to the procurement of the **PB2Y-3**

Coronado, following the conversion of one of the PB2Y-2s as a prototype **XPB2Y-3**. They differed by having R-1830-88 engines, increased armament, and the provision of self-sealing tanks and armour. A total of 210 of this version was built, late production aircraft being equipped with ASV (Air-to-Service Vessel) radar.

Ten of the aircraft, designated **PB2Y-3B**, were supplied to the RAF and based initially at Beaumaris, Anglesey, intended for service with Coastal Command. Their stay there was only brief, for they were transferred to No. 231 Squadron of Transport Command, and used from June 1944 to operate freight services.

Variants in US service, converted from PB2Y-3s, included 31 **PB2Y-3R** transports, fitted with single-stage supercharged R-1830-92 engines; one **XPB2Y-4** converted by the experimental installation of Wright R-2600 Cyclone engines; **PB2Y-5**s with increased

fuel capacity and R-1830-92 engines; and a number of **PB2Y-5H** casualty-evacuation aircraft which saw service in the Pacific theatre, with military equipment removed to provide accommodation for 25 stretchers.

Specification

Type: long-range flying-boat bomber
Powerplant: (PB2Y-3) four 1,200-hp (895-kW) Pratt & Whitney R-1830-88 Twin Wasp radial piston engines
Performance: maximum speed 223 mph (359 km/h) at 20,000 ft (6095 m); cruising speed 141 mph (227 km/h) at 1,500 ft (460 m); service ceiling 20,500 ft (6250 m); range with 8,000-lb (3629-kg) bombload 1,370 miles (2205 km); maximum range 2,370 miles (3814 km)
Weights: empty 40,935 lb (18568 kg); maximum take-off 68,000 lb (30844 kg)
Dimensions: span 115 ft 0 in (35.05 m); length 79 ft 3 in (24.16 m); height 27 ft 6 in (8.38 m); wing area 1,780 sq ft (165.36 m²)
Armament: two 0.50-in (12.7-mm) machine-guns in each of bow, dorsal and tail turrets, and one 0.50-in (12.7-mm) gun in each of two beam positions, plus up to 12,000 lb (5443 kg) of weapons including bombs, depth bombs and torpedoes in bomb bays

Above: Though retaining its radar, this PB2Y-5H is an unarmed ambulance conversion. All Dash-5 versions had four-bladed inboard propellers.

Left: The principal patrol-bomber version was the PB2Y-3, of which this is an early example without radar. Four of the maximum load of 12 1,000-lb bombs were carried externally.

Consolidated P4Y Corregidor

In 1938 Consolidated designed its **Model 31** flying-boat. This featured a deep hull with a high-set wing and tailplane, the latter mounting a pair of endplate fins similar to those fitted to the B-24. The 'Davis' wing was fitted, this being a high aspect ratio surface with constant taper, offering extremely efficient range performance, highly necessary for either civilian or military uses.

The prototype was completed in May 1939, and flown soon after. With war breaking out in Europe, Consolidated elected to develop the type purely for military use. The designation was **XP4Y-1**, and the unofficial name **Corregidor** was bestowed on the type. Nearly three years of redesign elapsed it was ready for service testing. Trials showed that the XP4Y-1 was a suitable basis for quantity production, and a batch of 220 was ordered. Shortages of the Cyclone engine led to the cancellation of the programme in the summer of 1943.

Specification
Type: long-range maritime patrol flying-boat
Powerplant: two 2,300-hp (1715-kW) Wright R-3350-8 Cyclone 18 radial piston engines
Performance: maximum speed 247 mph (398 km/h); service ceiling 21,400 ft (6520 m); range 3,280 miles (5279 km)
Weights: empty 29,334 lb (13306 kg); maximum take-off 48,000 lb (21772 kg)
Dimensions: wing span 110 ft 0 in (33.53 m); length 74 ft 1 in (22.58 m); height 25 ft 2 in (7.67 m); wing area 1,048 sq ft (97.36 m²)

Armament: (intended) one 37-mm cannon in bow turret, two 0.50-in (12.7-mm) machine-guns in dorsal and tail turrets plus up to 4,000 lb (1814 kg) of weapons carried externally

Free of official involvement, designers of the Consolidated Model 31 were able to combine their own long experience of hull design with the newly-patented Davis high-aspect ratio wing.

Consolidated TBY (Vought TBU) Sea Wolf

Competing against Grumman in late 1939 to provide the US Navy with a new torpedo-bomber, Vought was awarded a contract on 22 April 1940 to design and develop a prototype to the same requirement. Allocated the designation **XTBU-1**, this flew for the first time on 22 December 1941, and was delivered to the US Navy for evaluation in March 1942.

Of mid-wing configuration, it was of all-metal construction and provided with retractable tail-wheel undercarriage. Accommodation was provided for a crew of three, pilot, radio operator and rear gunner being housed under a long glazed canopy which terminated in the rear turret. The powerplant was a 2,000-hp (1491-kW) Double Wasp driving a three-bladed constant-speed propeller. Enclosed accommodation for a torpedo was provided in the lower fuselage, and there was a forward-firing fixed gun in addition to defensive armament.

US Navy testing confirmed that the performance of the XTBU-1 was considerably better than that of the rival Grumman TBF Avenger, and it was decided to procure the type without delay. However, Vought was unable to meet the production demand due its limited production capacity, so the programme was handed over to Consolidated, who were to build 1,100 aircraft in a new factory at Allentown, Pennsylvania, under the designation **TBY-2 Sea Wolf**. The contract was dated 6 September 1943.

Consolidated production aircraft were generally similar to the prototype, although two more fixed guns were added and a radome for search radar was mounted under the starboard wing. The first of these entered service in November 1944, and only saw service in the training role before VJ-Day brought cancellation of the remaining contracts, including a follow-on batch of 600 improved **TBY-3s**. Only 180 TBY-2s were built.

Designed by Chance Vought Aircraft, the Sea Wolf was intended to complement the Grumman TBF Avenger, but the type never became operational.

Specification
Consolidated TBY-2
Type: three-seat carrierborne torpedo-bomber
Powerplant: one 2,000-hp (1491-kW) Pratt & Whitney R-2800-22 Double Wasp radial piston engine
Performance: maximum speed 306 mph (492 km/h); service ceiling 27,200 ft (8290 m); range 1,500 miles (2414 km)
Weight: maximum take-off 16,247 lb (7370 kg)
Dimensions: wing span 57 ft 2 in (17.42 m); length 39 ft 0 in (11.89 m); height 15 ft 6 in (4.72 m)
Armament: three 0.50-in (12.7-mm) machine-guns firing forward, one 0.50-in (12.7-mm) machine-gun in dorsal turret, one 0.3-in (7.62-mm) machine-gun in ventral position plus one torpedo in internal weapons bay

Consolidated Vultee P-81

The Consolidated Vultee **XP-81** (its newly-merged builder soon to be better known as Convair) was the first American aircraft powered by a turboprop engine. Ordered by the USAAF on 11 February 1944, the XP-81 was intended as a long-range escort fighter using compound power with one 1,650-shp (1230-kW) General Electric TG-100 turboprop and one 3,750-lb (16.68-kN) thrust Allison I-40 jet engine eventually designated J33-A-5. When delays with the turboprop powerplant were encountered, the prototype XP-81 (44-91000) was flown on 11 February 1945 with a Packard V-1650-7 Merlin installed temporarily in the nose.

The first flight with the intended turboprop engine followed on 21 December 1945 and, to the astonishment of pilots and observers, the turboprop provided no advantage in performance over the Merlin. A second XP-81 (44-91001) flew in early 1946 to join the first machine in exploring the potential for this unusual powerplant, but several factors (war's end, the disappointing results with the TG-100, and the evident superiority of pure jet designs) resulted in cancellation of an order for 13 **YP-81** service-test aircraft.

Specification
Type: single-seat fighter

Powerplant: one 1,650-shp (1230-kW) General Electric TG-100 (XT-31) turboprop engine driving a four-bladed propeller, plus one 3,750-lb (16.68-kN) thrust Allison I-40 (J33-A-5) turbojet engine
Performance: maximum speed 507 mph (816 km/h) at 20,000 ft (6096 m); cruising speed 275 mph (442 km/h); initial climb rate 4,600 ft (1402 m) per minute; service ceiling 35,500 ft (10820 m); range 2,500 miles (4023 km)
Weights: empty 12,755 lb (5785 kg); maximum take-off about 28,000 lb (12700 kg)
Dimensions: span 50 ft 6 in (15.39 m); length 44 ft 10 in (13.67 m); height 14 ft 0 in (4.27 m); wing area 425 sq ft (39.48 m²)
Armament: six 0.5-in (12.7-mm) machine-guns or six 20-mm cannon planned but not installed, plus provision for up to 3,200 lb (1451 kg) of underwing bombs or rockets

Noteworthy as the first turboprop-engined aircraft to fly in the US, the Convair Model 102 was designed to escort B-29s on operations in the Pacific, but the war ended before production could begin. The first of two XP-81 prototypes is illustrated.

Convair XA-41

During 1943 Convair designed an all-metal single-seat close support aircraft under the designation Convair **Model 90**. Intended to meet a USAAF requirement, a single prototype was ordered under the designation **XA-41**, and this was flown for the first time on 11 February 1944.

A cantilever mid-wing monoplane, it had an oval-section fuselage, conventional tail unit and retractable tailwheel landing gear. The wing featured dihedral on the outer panels, and was intended to mount heavy cannon. A wide range of other stores was intended for carriage on wing pylons or in a weapons bay in the lower fuselage. Although it was tested by both the USAAF and the US Navy, no production was ordered, and the sole flying example ended its days serving as an engine test-bed with Pratt & Whitney.

Specification
Type: single-seat close support aircraft

Powerplant: one 3,000-hp (2237-kW) Pratt & Whitney R-4360-9 Wasp Major radial piston engine
Performance: maximum speed 363 mph (584 km/h); service ceiling 29,300 ft (8930 m); range 800 miles (1287 km)

Weights: empty 13,336 lb (6049 kg); maximum take-off 24,188 lb (10971 kg)
Dimensions: wing span 54 ft 0 in (16.46 m); length 48 ft 8 in (14.83 m); height 13 ft 11 in (4.24 m); wing area 544 sq ft (50.54 m²)

The Model 90 was intended as a dedicated low-level attack bomber, but fighter-bombers fulfilled the role and only one of the two XA-41 prototypes was completed, as an engine testbed.

Culver PQ-8/A-8

In the USA, the Culver **LCA Cadet** lightplane was selected by the US Army Air Corps in 1940 as being suitable for development as a radio-controlled target to satisfy a requirement for anti-aircraft artillery training. The first of these acquired for test purposes (41-18889) was allocated the designation **A-8** (later **XPQ-8**). This was a low-wing monoplane with retractable tricycle-type landing gear, and powered by a 100-hp (75-kW) Continental O-200 flat-four engine. Successful testing resulted in a production order for 200 similar **PQ-8**s, and at a later date an additional 200 were ordered as **PQ-8A** (later Q-8A), this version being equipped with a more powerful engine.

The US Navy had a similar training problem for the anti-aircraft gunners of its warships, and in late 1941 acquired a single example of the US Army PQ-8A for evaluation. An order for 200 similar aircraft, designated **TDC-2**, was placed with Culver in 1942.

Specification
Type: radio-controlled target aircraft
Powerplant: (PQ-8A) one 125-hp (93-kW) Continental O-200-1 flat-four piston engine
Performance: maximum speed 116 mph (187 km/h)

Weight: empty 720 lb (327 kg); maximum take-off 1,305 lb (592 kg)
Dimensions: span 26 ft 11 in (8.20 m); length 17 ft 8 in (5.38 m); height 5 ft 6 in (1.68 m); wing area 120 sq ft (11.15 m²)

The Culver Cadet lightplane was an early candidate for the USAAF programme to acquire cheap, easily-operated aircraft for use as radio-controlled target drones. The original A-8 designation changed to PQ-8 in 1942.

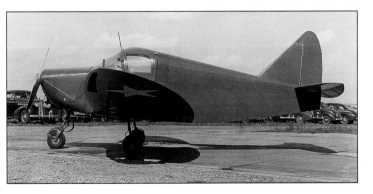

Culver PQ-14

Use of the Culver PQ-8/-8A and TDC-2, by the USAAF and US Navy respectively, left little doubt that targets of this nature improved very considerably the accuracy of those anti-aircraft units which had ample opportunity to train with such devices. The real problem associated with use of the PQ-8 was that its maximum speed of 116 mph (187 km/h) was completely unrealistic in 1941-42, when attacking fighters and bombers could demonstrate speeds that were, respectively, three and two times that of the PQ-8.

To meet this requirement, Culver developed during 1942 an aircraft designed specifically to serve as a target aircraft. With a general resemblance to the PQ-8, it was of low-wing monoplane configuration and had a similar tail unit; the control surfaces of the aerofoils were, however, larger in area to ensure much improved response and manoeuvrability when under radio control. The landing gear was of the retractable

tricycle type. The powerplant comprised a Franklin O-300 flat-six engine, of greater power to provide increased performance.

In early 1943 the USAAF acquired a single prototype for evaluation under the designation **XPQ-14**. This proved satisfactory from the maintenance, launch and flight aspect, and a batch of 75 **YPQ-14A**s was ordered for service trials in its target aircraft role. Proving successful, the **PQ-14** was ordered into large-scale production and the USAAF was to acquire 1,348 **PQ-14A**s, of which 1,201 were transferred to the US Navy, being designated **TD2C-1** in that service. A heavier version was built subsequently, the USAAF acquiring an initial batch of 25 for service trials as **YPQ-14B**s, and following these up with the procurement of 1,112 **PQ-14B**s for training units. A single example with a Franklin O-300-9 engine was designated **PQ-14C**. In 1948 surviving drones were redesignated **Q-14A** and **Q-14B**.

Specification
Type: radio-controlled target aircraft
Powerplant (PQ-14A): one 150-hp (112-kW) Franklin O-300-11 flat-six piston engine
Performance: maximum speed 180 mph (290 km/h)
Weight: maximum take-off 1,820 lb (826 kg)
Dimensions: span 30 ft 0 in (9.14 m); length 19 ft 6 in (5.94 m); height 7 ft 11 in (2.41 m)

Good experience with the PQ-8 led the USAAF to seek a larger development from Culver. This emerged in early 1943 in prototype form and led to production of more than 2,000 PQ-14 variants. Over half of these were eventually transferred to the Navy (as illustrated), where they took the designation TD2C-1. Overall red finish made the drones easily visible as unmanned targets.

Curtiss A-12 Shrike

To meet a US Army attack bomber requirement which was formulated in 1929, the Curtiss **XA-8 Shrike** made its maiden flight in June 1931. It was an impressive aircraft for its time: the first Curtiss all-metal low-wing monoplane, with such advanced features as automatic leading-edge slots and trailing-edge flaps. The wing was strut- and wire-braced, and the main landing gear comprised two fully-enclosed trousered units, these fairings also housing two 0.3-in machine-guns. Pilot and observer-gunner were accommodated in widely separated cockpits, the former under a fully enclosed canopy and the latter protected by an extended windscreen. Power was provided by a 600-hp (447-kW) Curtiss V-1570C inline engine with a radiator beneath the nose, slightly forward of the wing leading edge.

The **A-8**, powered by a Prestone-cooled V-1570-31 each of 600 hp, created something of a sensation in US aviation circles when they went into service with the 3rd Attack Group at Fort Crockett, Texas in April 1932.

The US Army had ordered an additional 46 Shrikes under the designation **A-8B**, but maintenance problems with the liquid-cooled engines of the A-8s led to

the new aircraft being powered by Wright R-1820-21 radial air-cooled engines of 670 hp (500 kW), resulting in the new designation **A-12**. These aircraft retained the open pilot's cockpit with faired headrest which had been introduced on the A-8 production batch, and carried the same machine-gun armament and bombload. In an attempt to improve co-operation between pilot and observer, the rear cockpit was moved forward with its glazed covering forming a continuation of the fuselage decking immediately behind the pilot's cockpit.

After long service with the US Army's attack groups the Shrikes were relegated to second-line units in 1939, but nine A-12s still remained in service in Hawaii when Pearl Harbor was attacked in December 1941.

Specification
Type: two-seat attack (light bomber) aircraft
Powerplant: one 690-hp (515-kW) Wright R-1820-21 Cyclone radial piston engine
Performance: maximum speed 177 mph (285 km/h) at sea level; service ceiling 15,150 ft (4620 m); range 510 miles (821 km)
Weights: empty equipped 3,898 lb (1768 kg); maximum take-off 5,756 lb

Final development in a series of two-seat ground attack aircraft for the USAAC with the name Shrike, the A-12 differed in having an air-cooled radial engine. A few were at Pearl Harbor in December 1941, but were not engaged in action.

(2611 kg)
Dimensions: span 44 ft 0 in (13.41 m); length 32 ft 3 in (9.83 m); height 9 ft 4 in (2.84 m); wing area 284.00 sq ft (26.38 m²)
Armament: five 0.3-in (7.62-mm) machine-guns, four with limited adjustment in landing gear fairings and one on a ring mounting operated by observer/gunner, plus provision for four 122-lb (55-kg) or 10 30-lb (13.6-kg) bombs on underwing racks

Curtiss A-14/A-18 Shrike II

The Curtiss Model 76 twin-engined attack monoplane was a company venture contemporary with the Curtiss Hawk 75 prototype. Bearing civil registration X15314, the Model 76 made its maiden flight in September 1935 powered by two experimental Wright XR-1510 twin-row radial engines. It was a cantilever mid-wing monoplane of all-metal construction, except for fabric covering on the moving control surfaces and rear wing section. All three units of the tailwheel landing gear were retractable, each wheel remaining partially exposed when retracted. Great care had been taken to achieve the best possible aerodynamic shape, and the two crew members were seated under a smooth glazed canopy. The fuselage bomb bay had provision for a total bombload of 600 lb (272 kg). Four 0 3-in (7.62-mm) machine-guns were mounted in the nose, with a fifth on a flexible mounting for operation by the observer.

After appraisal by the US Army Air Corps at Wright Field, the Model 76 was returned to Curtiss and fitted with 775-hp

(578-kW) Wright R-1670-5 Cyclone radials with constant-speed propellers, in this form receiving the USAAC designation **XA-14**. The US Army was sufficiently impressed to order 13 of a developed version of the XA-14 under the new designation **Y1A-18**, given the name Shrike II by Curtiss in July 1936. All 13 had been delivered by October 1937. Essentially refined versions of the earlier aircraft, they were powered by two 850-hp (634-kW) Wright R-1820-47 Cyclones and carried part of their bombload in bays located in the wings.

The **A-18** went into service with the 8th Attack Squadron, 3rd Attack Group; with that unit the type pioneered low-flying formation attacks on ground targets, but for economy reasons no further A-18s were ordered. Surviving aircraft (a number having been written off as a result of landing gear weaknesses) were retired from first-line service in 1940 and diverted to operational training; the final A-18 in flying condition was grounded in 1943.

Specification
Curtiss A-18
Type: twin-engined attack monoplane

After the 8th Attack Squadron won the M.F. Harmon Efficiency Trophy in the annual contest at Barksdale in 1939, its Y1A-18s were marked with the 'E' for efficiency.

Powerplant: two 850-hp (634-kW) Wright R-1820-47 Cyclone radial piston engines
Performance: maximum speed 247 mph (398 km/h); service ceiling 28,650 ft (8370 m); range 651 miles (1048 km)
Weights: empty equipped 9,410 lb (4268 kg); maximum take-off 13,170 lb (5974 kg)
Dimensions: span 59 ft 6 in (18.14 m); length 41 ft 0 in (12.50 m); height 11 ft 6 in (3.51 m); wing area 526.00 sq ft (48.87 m²)
Armament: five 0.3-in (7.62-mm) machine-guns, plus 600 lb (272 kg) of bombs

Curtiss AT-9 Jeep I

In 1940, and with Europe already at war, the US Army Air Corps knew that it was essential to begin preparations for the very real possibility of war. The only positive action which could be taken at that time was to intensify the training programme so that a maximum number of active and reserve flying crews would be available if the need arose.

The US Army had already begun evaluation of the Cessna T-50 as an 'off-the-shelf' twin-engined trainer which would prove suitable for the transition of a pilot qualified on single-engined aircraft to a twin-engined aircraft and its very different handling technique.

For the more specific transition to a 'high-performance' twin-engined bomber it was considered that something less stable than the T-50 was needed. However, Curtiss-Wright had anticipated this requirement in the design of their **Model 25**, a twin-engined pilot transition trainer which had the take-off and landing characteristics of a light bomber aircraft. The Model 25 was of low-wing cantilever monoplane configuration, pro-

Rapid USAAC expansion and the introduction of a new generation of twin-engined medium bombers such as the B-25 and B-26 led to a need for a dedicated fast training twin. Curtiss responded by modifying the CW-19 wing to be used with a new fuselage. Its name, Jeep, from a strip cartoon character, preceded its use for the Army utility vehicle.

vided with retractable tailwheel-type landing gear, and powered by two Lycoming R-680-9 radial engines, with Hamilton-Standard two-bladed constant-speed metal propellers. The single prototype acquired for evaluation had a welded steel-tube fuselage structure, and the wings, fuselage and tail units were fabric-covered.

Evaluation proving satisfactory, the type was ordered into production under the designation **AT-9**. These production examples differed from the prototype by being of all-metal construction. A total of 491 AT-9s was produced, and these aircraft were followed into service by 300 **AT-9A**s which had R-680-11 engines and revised hydraulics. These remained in use for a comparatively short time, for the USA's involvement in World

War II in late 1941 resulted in the early development of far more effective training aircraft.

Specification
Type: twin-engined advanced trainer
Powerplant: two 295-hp (220-kW) Lycoming R-680-9 radial piston engines

Performance: maximum speed 197 mph (317 km/h); cruising speed 175 mph (282 km/h); range 750 miles (1207 km)
Weights: empty 4,600 lb (2087 kg); maximum take off 6,000 lb (2722 kg)
Dimensions: span 40 ft 4 in (12.29 m); length 31 ft 8 in (9.65 m); height 9 ft 10 in (2.99 m); wing area 233 sq ft (21.65 m²)

Curtiss C-46/55/113 Commando

Above: The sole CW-20T prototype of the C-46 family is shown in its original twin-finned configuration, as flown in 1940. After a single fin and rudder had been fitted, it became the C-55 and was sold to BOAC.

C urtiss' capable C-46 has always had to live in the shadow of the C-47. Sharing the latter's airliner origins, it was larger, heavier and more expensive, factors which counted against it in wartime. It made a name for itself in the Far East and Pacific theatres and, after the war, went on to see action again over Korea and even Vietnam.

Development of the Curtiss-Wright **CW-20**, later to become the **C-46** and at the time the costliest project ever undertaken by its well-known builder, began in 1936 under chief designer George A. Page. A new generation of airliners was due to replace the Curtiss Condor and other biplane types. Although the Douglas DC-3 was entering service with American Airlines and other carriers, the CW-20 seemed to offer promise as a larger, longer-range commercial ship, powered by two 1,650-hp (1230-kW) Pratt & Whitney R-2800-17 Double Wasp 18-cylinder radial engines. For maximum internal stowage, the CW-20 was designed with a cross-section of two circular segments, or lobes, intersecting at a common chord line, giving the mistaken impression of a 'double decker'.

Construction of the CW-20 was begun, in advance of actual airline contracts, at Curtiss's St Louis, Missouri, plant. The **CW-20T** prototype, NX19436, or c/n 101, powered by two 1,600-hp (1193-kW) Wright R-2600 Cyclone engines and distinguished by a cumbersome twin-fin empennage, was first flown on 26 March 1940 by Edmund T. (Eddie) Allen. Curtiss revealed the existence of the new aircraft on 11 April 1940 and made one of history's forgotten gestures by giving the CW-20 the name 'Substratosphere Transport'. For Americans, the aircraft's real potential was not obvious until 7 December 1941, when Pearl Harbor sidetracked the CW-20's airline career and took it into uniform.

The aircraft was a conventional, cantilever low/mid-wing monoplane transport with semi-monocoque fuselage, fully retractable landing gear, and cabin windscreen flush with its fuselage contour. The crew numbered four. Fairing plates on the prototype CW-20 which had smoothed over the indentation at the double-lobe fuselage intersection were discarded on subsequent machines, it having been found that the fairing provided no reduction in aerodynamic drag. The CW-20 prototype soon acquired, as the **CW-20A**, the cantilever single fin

rudder and tail unit which characterised every machine to follow, the twin-tail configuration having proven inadequate in tests.

Although shown to airline executives and noted flying as a 'civilian' in natural metal over New York City, the prototype was impressed into USAAF service on 20 June 1941 as the sole **C-55** (41-21041) and, three months later, was sold to British Overseas Airways Corporation (BOAC) with the registration G-AGDI, and named *St Louis*. Alarmed by its deficiencies in air transport (the word airlift was not used then), the US Army Air Forces (USAAF) was attracted by the cavernous double-bubble fuselage of the Curtiss design. The main compartment could accommodate (in addition to general cargo) 40 fully-equipped troops, up to 33 stretchers, five Wright R-3350 engines or their equivalent tonnage in other freight. In September 1940, the USAAF ordered 200 C-46s, company designation **CW-20B**. The basic design was fixed and plans to pressurise the aircraft were dropped. A wing fuel-leak problem was resolved through field modification only much later.

Production was shifted to Curtiss's Buffalo, New York, plant where the first C-46 (41-5159) was delivered to the USAAF on 12 July 1942.

Further orders followed. The **C-46A** (CW-20B) model, from the 26th production airframe onwards, introduced a large cargo-loading door, a cargo floor, and fold-down seats along the cabin wall; 1,491 were built by Curtiss at Buffalo, St Louis and Louisville, Kentucky. The USAAF planned to use a second manufacturer, Higgins Industries, Inc., of New Orleans, Louisiana, to build 500 C-46As plus 500 Curtiss C-76 Caravans, the latter a mostly wood design intended to benefit from its lack of reliance on strategic materials. When it became clear that sufficient steel would be available, the latter machine failed to reach production and in the end Higgins built only two C-46A airframes, the first (43-43339) being delivered 1 October 1944.

The **XC-46B** (43-46953) was a conversion (**CW-20B-1**) of a Louisville-built C-46A with 2,100-hp (1566-kW) Pratt & Whitney R-2800-34W engines and a 'stepped' windshield which broke the clean flush lines of the fuselage. No clear historical detail has survived regarding the C-46C, which may have been another experimental C-46A conversion fitted with rocket-assisted take-off gear. The flush windshield was retained in the **C-46D** (CW-20B-2), which had double loading doors; 1,410 of the machines were built at Buffalo.

The stepped windshield, the only true distinguishing feature among all C-46 models, was reintroduced with the **C-46E** (**CW-20B-3**), which was powered by R-2800-75 engines and employed the three-bladed Hamilton Standard propeller rather than the four-bladed Curtiss Electric propeller used in most C-46 models. In later years the two propeller types would be virtually interchangeable, with operators preferring the slightly less efficient three-bladed type because of its greater reliability. Only 17 examples of the distinctive, stepped-windshield C-46E were built.

The Buffalo-manufactured **C-46F** (**CW-20B-4**) reverted to the original windshield profile and cargo doors. The sole **C-46G** (4478945), company designation **CW-20B-5**, was powered by R-2800-34Y engines and was later modified as the sole **XC-113** to test the Curtiss-Wright TG-100 gas turbine, although it is unclear whether this testbed ever actually flew. Variants of the Curtiss Commando which were never built at all include the **C-46H**, intended to have twin tailwheels, the **C-46J**, with stepped windscreen, and the **XC-**

Curtiss C-46/55/113 Commando

Although the C-46 saw service in almost every theatre of the war, the greater majority of those built served in Asia. This scene at Saipan in the Marianas in June 1944 shows a Commando operating in the role of air ambulance, when it could carry up to 33 stretchers.

In a photo dated 24 June 1944, the first two C-46s to land at Aslito, Saipan, are seen sharing parking space with a P-61 Black Widow (left) and a squadron of P-47 Thunderbolts (distant right). Olive drab and neutral grey finish was standard at this period.

46K, to have been powered by Wright R-3350 engines. Three **XC-46L** conversions with R-3350s were built and flown.

In 1942, the USAAF began to employ C-46s on South Atlantic ferry operations. Lawrence Rogers, a wartime ATC sergeant, recalls the aircraft arriving and departing Accra being "an impressive sight", although Rogers is less cheerful about the machine he saw explode in mid-air moments after lift-off: "That was impressive in a different way." USAAF Troop Carrier Command (separate from ATC) took delivery of C-46s in 1943 at Baer Field, Fort Wayne, Indiana. Because of its range and durability the C-46, although used in airborne operations in Europe, went primarily to the Asian and Pacific theatres.

The Curtiss C-46 Commando is best known as the mainstay of the massive air transport supply effort undertaken from the Assam region of India to supply friendly forces in south-west China. Flying the 'Hump', as this treacherous crossing of the Himalayan massif became known, was a task fraught with peril for the men and C-46s of Colonel Edward H. Alexander's India-China Wing of ATC. The aircraft were loaded and flown under the most primitive conditions, their fuel pumped by hand from drums, the Assam airfields largely unpaved and transformed into quagmire by monsoons which poured down half the year. On the 500-mile (805-km) Assam-Chunking route, C-46s had to haul cargo over ridgelines looming at 12,000 to 14,000 ft (3660 to 4265 m), even though ice began to form on the wings at 10,000 ft (3050 m). In August 1942, using a few C-47s, the USAAF had been able to transport only 170,000 lb (77110 kg) of cargo over the India-China route; by December 1943, with many C-46s, the figure rose to 25.18 million

lb (11.42 million kg). Short on spare parts, flying in unbearable wet and cold with minimal navigation aids, taking off at maximum overload weight, the C-46 crews were a lifeline to Chiang Kai-shek's Chinese forces and General Claire Chennault's 14th Air Force at a time when the Japanese were active all around. During one of these flights Captain Wally A. Gayda shot down at close range a Japanese fighter, apparently a Nakajima Ki-43, by firing a Browning automatic rifle through his C-46 front cabin window and killing the pilot.

About 40 C-46As were assigned USAAF serials but were completed with BuAer numbers, as **R5C-1**s for the US Marine Corps, serving at first with MAG-35 in the south-west Pacific. A few remained in service with the USMC during the 1950-53 Korean conflict. Contrary to most accounts, a few R5C-1s were ultimately transferred from the US Marines to the US Navy, at least one becoming an **R5C-1T** trainer at NAS Memphis, Tennessee, in about 1954.

C-46s continued in widespread USAAF service after VJ-Day, especially with Troop Carrier Command. Some were employed in tests of glider-towing techniques, including 'hard' tows with the gliders coupled close behind the tug. The C-46 is not thought to have been a factor in the Berlin Airlift, but was widely used by the newly independent US Air Force (USAF) well past the late 1940s. The C-46E was declared obsolete in 1953, apparently as a result of its paucity and lack of com-

From mid-1944, the USAAF dispensed with painted finishes on many of its aircraft, unless particular operational needs dictated otherwise. In this photo, C-46As display both the painted and the natural metal finish, the latter reducing maintenance cost and enhancing speed.

monality with flush-windscreen models, but C-46A, C-46D and C-46F airframes continued with USAF Reserve squadrons. **TC-46D** trainers served with USAF Air Training Command as late as 1955.

Long-lasting airframes continued in USAF markings well past the 1950s. In addition, the USAF employed private operator Civil Air Transport (CAT) to fly civil-registered C-46s on military charter flights, an example being Taiwan-registered B-858, originally a C-46D (44-78405). A counter-insurgency (COIN) version of the C-46 was developed in the early 1960s for USAF's 1st Air Commando Wing for combat operations in South Vietnam, although little actual modification of the airframe appears to have taken place and, unlike the 'gunship' C-47, it was unarmed. These were diverted to the Panama Canal Zone where they served as late as June 1968, the apparent cut-off date for American military C-46s.

Specification
Curtiss C-46 Commando
Type: medium-range passenger/cargo transport
Powerplant: two 2,100-hp (1566-kW) Pratt & Whitney R-2800-34 Double Wasp 18-cylinder radial piston engines driving three-bladed Hamilton Standard propellers
Performance: maximum speed 270 mph (435 km/h) at 10,000 ft (3048 m); cruising speed 235 mph (378 km/h) at 9,000 ft (2743 m); service ceiling 22,000 ft (6706 m); range 1,800 miles (2897 km)
Weights: empty 29,300 lb (13290 kg); maximum take-off 50,000 lb (22680 kg)
Dimensions: span 108 ft 0 in (32.92 m); length 76 ft 4 in (23.27 m); height 21 ft 9 in (6.63 m); wing area 1,358 sq ft (126.16 m²)

Three of the USAAF's major transport aircraft types of World War II keep company on a near-flooded hardstanding. From the right are a painted and a natural-metal-finished C-46, a Douglas C-47 Skytrain and, at the end of the line, a C-87 Liberator Express.

In 1944, Curtiss converted the first C-46A-1-CS from the St Louis plant to this XC-46B configuration, the principal new features of which were a stepped windscreen (productionised in the C-46D) and R-2800-34W engines with water injection to boost take-off power.

Curtiss-Wright C-76 Caravan

During 1941 Curtiss received a contract from the US Army covering the design and construction of an all-wooden military transport. Like a number of aircraft built in the USA during the period, it was one of a series constructed in prototype form to develop manufacturing techniques for new-generation all-wood aircraft as an insurance policy against future shortages of light alloys, a circumstance which did not arise.

The initial contract called for 11 **YC-76** pre-production aircraft to be built to the Curtiss-Wright **CW-27** initial design, and this medium-size twin-engined transport had some resemblance to the earlier, larger C-46 Commando. Most noticeable change concerned the monoplane wing, which in the Commando was of low-wing and in the **Caravan** of high-wing configuration. Landing gear

was of retractable tricycle type, and powerplant comprised two Pratt & Whitney R-1830 Twin Wasp engines in wing-mounted nacelles. Accommodation was provided for a total of 23 persons, including the flight crew.

The first YC-76 made its initial flight on 1 January 1943, and, in addition to the original contract, follow-up orders were received for five **C-76** production and nine **YC-76A** revised service test aircraft, all of which were delivered during 1943. Production was terminated when it was clear that a serious shortage of light alloy was unlikely, 175 **C-76A**s then on order being cancelled.

Specification
Type: medium military transport
Powerplant: two 1,200-hp (896-kW) Pratt & Whitney R-1830-92 Twin Wasp radial piston engines
Performance: maximum speed 192

mph (309 km/h); service ceiling 22,600 ft (6890 m); range 750 miles (1207 km)
Weights: empty 18,300 lb (8301 kg); maximum take-off 28,000 lb (12701 kg)
Dimensions: span 108 ft 2 in (32.97 m); length 68 ft 4 in (20.83 m); height 27 ft 3 in (8.31 m); wing area 1,560.0 sq ft (144.92 m²)

Aptly named Caravan, the Curtiss CW-27 responded to a USAAF request for aircraft using non-critical materials for as much as the airframe as possible. Primarily of wooden construction, the C-76 (this is the fifth production example) was not needed.

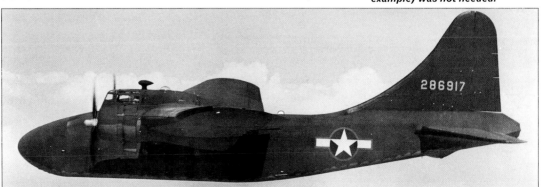

Curtiss O-52 Owl

In the late 1930s the US Army notified Curtiss-Wright of its requirements for a two-seat observation aircraft. The resulting configuration suggests that more than an observation role was envisaged by the specification, for it was very different to any other Curtiss design, and efforts had clearly been made to confer good low-speed manoeuvrability and landing characteristics.

Identified as the **Model 85** by Curtiss, the design was for a high-wing monoplane with one streamlined bracing strut on each side. Construction was all-metal, except that ailerons and tail control surfaces were fabric-covered. Good low-speed handling came from the provision of full-span automatic leading-edge slots interconnected with wide-span trailing-edge flaps; when the slots were extended the flaps were lowered automatically. The land-ing gear was of the retractable tailwheel type, with the main units retracting into wells in the lower sides of the fuselage. Dual controls were standard, and inward-folding doors in the floor of the observer's cockpit were provided to facilitate the use of a camera. The retractable turtle back, which the company had developed for the SOC Seagull, was also incorporated, to ensure that the observer had a maximum field of fire for his flexibly-mounted machine-gun. Powerplant consisted of a Pratt & Whitney Wasp radial engine.

Ordered into production in 1939, some 203 Owls were built for the US Army under the des-ignation **O-52**, with deliveries beginning in 1940. None, how-ever, was used in first-line ser-vice, all being directed for use in a training role. Nineteen were delivered to the Soviet Union.

Specification
Type: two-seat observation aircraft
Powerplant: one 600-hp (447-kW) Pratt & Whitney R-1340-51 Wasp radial piston engine
Performance: maximum speed 220 mph (354 km/h); cruising speed 192 mph (309 km/h); service ceiling 21,000 ft (6 400 m); range 700 miles (1127 km)
Weights: empty 4,231 lb (1919 kg); maximum take-off 5,364 lb (2433 kg)
Dimensions: span 40 ft 9 in (12.43 m); length 26 ft 4 in (8.03 m); height

Up to the outbreak of the war, the USAAC believed in the operational value of two-seat heavy observation aircraft. The Curtiss Model 85, bought by the Air Corps as the O-52, was the last such type; a few survived into 1941.

9 ft 3 in (2.83 m); wing area 210.4 sq ft (19.55 m²)
Armament: one 0.30-in (7.62-mm) synchronised forward-firing machine-gun and one 0.30-in (7.62-mm) machine-gun on flexible mount

Curtiss P-36 Hawk

Through the hot summer of 1934, Curtiss-Wright's chief engi-neer Don Berlin toiled at his drawing board to create a fighter he hoped would be well ahead of its rivals. The **Model 75** was a stressed-skin cantilever low-wing monoplane, fitted with hydraulically-operated split flaps and main landing gears which retract-ed directly to the rear, the wheels turning 90° to lie flat in the wing. The cockpit was enclosed by a sliding canopy, while on the nose was the new 900-hp (671-kW) Wright XR-1670 twin-row engine in a compact small-diameter cowling. The only traditional feature was the armament, of one machine-gun of 0.50-in calibre and one of 0.30-in.

Sadly for Berlin, designers all over the world had similar ideas, and the US Army initially picked the rival Seversky IXP. Curtiss got the decision postponed, and at a further competition in April 1936 offered the **Model 75B**, with the large-diameter Wright Cyclone R-1820-G5 and an improved cockpit with the rear fuselage scalloped to give a

Above: Although the Curtiss Model 75 failed to win the USAAC contest for which it was designed in 1935, it was successful in a further competition two years later and became progenitor of a long series of fighters, widely used throughout the war. This is the original H-75 in its second form, when fitted with a P & W R-1535 engine.

Left: When first evaluated by the USAAC, the Curtiss Model 75 lost out to the competing Seversky P-35. As a consolation, however, Curtiss did receive an order for three Y1P-36s, based on the Model 75 but powered by the same P&W R-1830 engine as the P-35. As a result, a year later the Curtiss fighter was selected for production in larger quantities than its Seversky rival.

Above: It is October 1939; Europe is now at war, and the US is looking to its defences around the world. With a minimum of identification markings, three P-36As take off for a morning patrol in the Canal Zone.

Right: Operating in early 1940 with the 20th Pursuit Group, this P-36 has the Group designator (PT) on the fin and the yellow cowling of the 79th Pursuit Squadron, whose insignia is on the fuselage side. Aircraft serial numbers were not prominently displayed; the '21' is the aircraft-in-group number.

rear view. The Army still preferred Seversky, ordering its fighter as the P-35, but the Curtiss had some good points, so an order was placed for three further Model 75s designated **Y1P-36**, powered by the two-row Pratt & Whitney R-1830 Twin Wasp driving the new Hamilton hydraulic constant-speed propeller. These were delivered in spring 1937, and the Army test pilots were enthusiastic.

Meanwhile, Curtiss had also fought for export customers. Recognising that many air forces were not ready for all the new features, Curtiss quickly rebuilt the original 75B as a simplified export model called the Hawk 75, the most obvious change being fixed landing gear.

The Hawk 75 proved a success from the start. Even the prototype was purchased by China, which bought 112 more, and other major customers included Thailand (with 23-mm Madsen cannon in underwing gondolas) and Argentina. Meanwhile, following its good reception by Wright Field, the US Army Air Corps placed an order on 7 July 1937 for 210 **P-36A**s - the biggest American fighter contract since 1918.

Basically, the P-36A was a perfectly sound aircraft, with good handling and manoeuvrability, although in terms of flight performance

A diversity of camouflage schemes is displayed on 15 P-36As of the 27th Pursuit Squadron, part of the 1st PG based at Selfridge Field, Michigan. Every aircraft is different, painted for their appearance at the 1939 National Air Races; none of the schemes was used operationally.

Curtiss P-36 Hawk

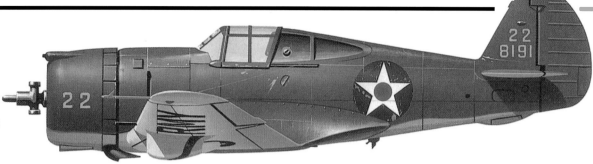

Despite the many different patterns and colours of camouflage displayed on P-36s participating in regular war games up to 1940, the only operational finish used after 1941 was the regulation olive drab/neutral grey, as on this P-36C.

and firepower it was already outclassed by such European fighters as the Spitfire and Bf 109D. Worse, from the start of its combat duty in the late spring of 1938, the P-36A was troubled by a host of problems which caused it to be repeatedly grounded.

While working their way through the contract for 210 aircraft, Curtiss made 81 major and minor changes to try to eradicate faults and improve the P-36's fighting ability. The **XP-36B** was temporarily fitted with a more powerful Twin Wasp. The **P-36C** designation was applied to the last 30 aircraft, which had the even more powerful 1,200-hp (895-kW) Twin Wasp R-1830-17, and an added 0.30-calibre gun in each wing, whose spent cases were collected in prominent boxes under the wings. The **XP-36D** was the No. 174 aircraft modified with two 0.50-calibre fuselage guns and four 0.30-calibre in the wings. The **XP-36E** was the 147th aircraft fitted with new outer wings housing eight 0.30-calibre guns. The **XP-36F** was the No. 172 P-36A fitted with underwing gondolas housing the Danish 23-mm Madsen cannon, each with 100 rounds, as used by Thai **Hawk 75N**s. This reduced maximum speed from 311 to only 265 mph (500 to 426 km/h).

In March 1941 Curtiss-Wright rolled out the 1,095th and last of the radial-engined Hawk monoplane series. Among the late customers were China (**Hawk 75A-5**), Norway (**75A-6**), the Netherlands (**75A-7**), Norway again (**75A-8**), Peru (**75A-8**s redesignated **P-36G**) and Iran (**75A-9**). Most of the Hawk 75's combat experience was provided by French, Dutch, British and Finnish pilots, although by chance a few saw combat in the Pacific during the early days of the war with Japan. They were soon relegated to a fighter training role.

Specification
Curtiss P-36A Hawk
Type: single-seat pursuit fighter and advanced trainer
Powerplant: one 1,050-hp (783-kW) Wright R 1830-13 piston engine
Performance: max speed 298 mph (480 km/h) at 915 ft (3000 m); cruising speed 267 mph (430 km/h); service ceiling 32,808 ft (10000 m); range 807 miles (1300 km)
Weights: empty weight 4,565 lb (2070 kg); gross weight 5,952 lb (2700 kg)
Dimensions: wing span 37 ft 5 in (11.4 m); length 28 ft 6 in (8.7 m); height 12 ft 2 in (3.7 m)
Armament: two 0.030-in machine-guns

In December 1938, Curtiss added a single 0.3-in (7.62-mm) machine-gun in each wing of a P-36A, which then became the XP-36C; the final 30 production aircraft were built to the same standard. Ammunition was held in the underwing boxes outboard of the undercarriage leg fairings.

Above: Production of the P-36, which was never named by the USAAC but was known as Mohawk in the RAF, totalled 210 against Army contracts. Of these, two became XP-40 and XP-42 prototypes. After 178 P-36As, Curtiss delivered 30 P-36Cs; one such is illustrated.

Curtiss P-40 Warhawk

Encouraged by the performance being demonstrated by European interceptors powered by liquid-cooled inline engines, the Curtiss-Wright Corporation decided, in 1938, to substitute an 1,160-hp (865-kW) supercharged Allison V-1710-19 in the current Wright radial-powered P-36A, retaining the 10th production example (30-18) for the trial installation. Redesignated the **XP-40**, this aircraft was first flown in October 1938 and evaluated at Wright Field the following May, in competition with the Bell XP-39 and Seversky XP-41. As originally flown the XP-40 featured a radiator located under the rear fuselage, but this was moved forward to the nose, together with the oil cooler. In all respects other than the powerplant the new aircraft remained unchanged from the P-36A, being an all-metal, low-wing monoplane whose main landing gear units retracted rearwards into the wings, the mainwheels turning through 90 degrees to lie flush with the undersurfaces. Armament remained the paltry pair of 0.3-in (7.62-mm) machine-guns in the wings.

Although the other prototypes evaluated with the XP-40 later led to successful service fighters, the Curtiss-Wright aircraft was selected for immediate production and a contract was signed for 524 **P-40s**, worth almost $13 million and at that time the largest order ever placed for an American fighter. Production got under way late in 1939 with 200 aircraft known as the **Hawk 81A** for the USAAC, powered by the 1,040-hp (776-kW) Allison V-1710-33 engine and distinguishable by the absence of wheel disc plates and by the carburettor air intake above the nose. The first three aircraft served as prototypes (occasionally known as **YP-40s**) and subsequent machines were delivered to the 33rd Pursuit Squadron, moved to Iceland on 25 July 1941.

Production continued at Buffalo, NY, with the **P-40B**. Some 131 were produced, introducing cockpit armour and an armament of four 0.3-in (7.62-mm) wing guns and two 0.5-in (12.7-mm) nose guns. When Japan struck in December 1941 there were 107 P-40s and P-40Bs present in the Philippines, but such was the measure of surprise achieved that only four managed to take off. Within four days the number of these fighters (flown by the 20th and 34th Pursuit Squadrons) had fallen to 22. The RAF **Tomahawk Mk IIA** corresponded to the P-40B (**Hawk 81A-2**), and the majority of the 110 aircraft dispatched went directly to the Middle East. One hundred other Tomahawk Mk IIAs were diverted from RAF contracts to China, for service with the American Volunteer Group.

A prime example of evolution rather than revolution in fighter design, the Curtiss P-40 family was destined to serve widely throughout World War II. Its origin lay in the radial-engined P-36 Mohawk, the prototype XP-40 being the 10th P-36A re-engined with an Allison V-1710.

The next variant was the **P-40C** (**Hawk 81A-3**), which introduced self-sealing fuel tanks; only 193 were produced for the USAAC, but this was the RAF's principal Tomahawk version, the **Mk IIB**. Out of a total of 945 produced under this designation, 21 were lost in transit at sea and 73 were delivered directly to the USSR. With a maximum weight of 8,058 lb (3658 kg), compared with 6,870 lb (3119 kg) for the XP-40, the **P-40C** was the slowest of all the production variants, possessing a top speed of only 328 mph (528 km/h) at 15,000 ft (4590 m). When it arrived in North Africa late in 1941 it was found to be much inferior to the Messerschmitt Bf 109E and only marginally better than the Hawker Hurricane Mk I, and was therefore primarily used in the ground-attack role.

The **P-40D** (**Hawk 87A-2**) brought a major redesign of the nose (hence the new company designation) with the introduction of the

Displaying the short-lived red-bordered 'star-and-bar' insignia of July-September 1943, this Warhawk was flying from Randolph Field. The serial number identifies it as a P-40E-1, a repossessed Kittyhawk Mk IA built for Lend-Lease to Britain; a P-40K-type fin has been fitted.

Allison V-1710-39 engine with external-spur reduction gear, permitting the nose to be shortened by 6 in (15.24 cm). The nose cross-section area was reduced, and the radiator moved forward and deepened; the main landing gear was shortened, the four wing guns were changed to 0.5-in (12.7-mm) calibre and the nose guns were deleted. Provision was also made for a rack capable of carrying a 500-lb (227-kg) bomb or 52-US gal (197-litre) drop tank under the fuselage. The P-40D had a top speed of 360 mph (580 km/h), but only 23 were produced for the USAAC.

The **P-40E** (**Hawk 87A-3**) was the first Warhawk (as the whole P-40 series was named in American service) to be produced in large quantities after Pearl Harbor. It introduced an armament of six 0.5-in (12.7-mm) wing machine-guns, and accompanied the first American fighter squadrons to the UK in 1942, as well as those in the Middle East. With an all-up weight of 8,840 lb (4013 kg), it had a top speed of 354 mph (570 km/h), which was roughly the same as that of the Spitfire Mk VC with tropical filter. Production totalled 2,320 on American contracts plus 1,500 for the RAF as the **Kittyhawk Mk IA**; many of the latter were diverted directly to the RAAF, RNZAF and RCAF.

Merlin tested

With dimensions approximately the same as the Allison V-1710, the Rolls-Royce Merlin, whose production had assumed enormous proportions by 1941, was selected for the P-40. During that year a production P-40D (40-360) was experimentally fitted with a Merlin 28, resulting in the designation **XP-40F** (**Hawk 87D**); although the weight increased to 9,460 lb (4295 kg), the more powerful British engine raised maximum speed to 373 mph (600 km/h) at 18,000 ft (5500 m). This version was distinguishable by the absence of the carburettor air intake above the nose, the downdraught intake of the Allison being replaced by the updraught trunk of the Merlin. The revised ducting was developed on the third production aircraft (4113602) as the **YP-40F**.

The first 260 aircraft employed the same fuselage as the P-40E, but the progressive increase in the forward keel area had introduced a progressive reduction in directional stability, so later **P-40F**s featured a rear fuselage lengthened by 20 in (51 cm). Maximum weight of the production aircraft had crept up to 9,870 lb (4480 kg) and its top speed dropped to 364 mph (586 km/h).

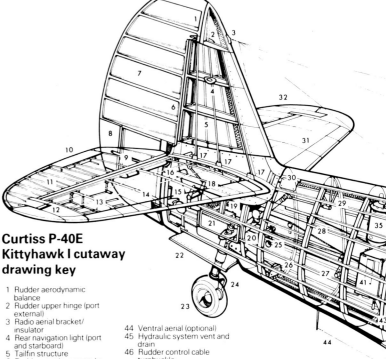

Curtiss P-40E
Kittyhawk I cutaway
drawing key

1 Rudder aerodynamic balance
2 Rudder upper hinge (port external)
3 Radio aerial bracket/insulator
4 Rear navigation light (port and starboard)
5 Tailfin structure
6 Rudder post/support tube
7 Rudder structure
8 Rudder trim tab
9 Rudder trim tab push-rod (starboard external)
10 Elevator tab
11 Elevator structure
12 Elevator aerodynamic balance
13 Tailplane structure
14 Rudder lower hinge
15 Elevator control horn
16 Tab actuator flexible drive shafts
17 Tailplane attachment lugs
18 Elevator control horn
19 Tab control rear sprocket housing/chain drive
20 Tailwheel retraction mechanism
21 Access panel
22 Tailwheel door
23 Retractable tailwheel
24 Tailwheel leg
25 Lifting point
26 Tailwheel lower attachment
27 Trim control cable turnbuckles
28 Elevator control cables
29 Tailwheel upper attachment
30 Access panel
31 Port tailplane
32 Port elevator
33 Radio aerials
34 Monocoque fuselage structure
35 Hydraulic reserve tank
36 Automatic recognition device
37 Aerial lead-in
38 Radio aerial mast
39 Hand starter crank stowage
40 Radio bay access door (port)
41 Radio receiver/transmitter
42 Support frame
43 Battery stowage

44 Ventral aerial (optional)
45 Hydraulic system vent and drain
46 Rudder control cable turnbuckle
47 Oxygen bottles
48 Radio equipment installation (optional)
49 Hydraulic tank
50 Hydraulic pump
51 Wingroot fillet
52 Streamline ventral cowl
53 Wing centreline splice
54 Fuselage fuel tank, capacity 51.5 Imp gal (234 litres)
55 Canopy track
56 Fuel lines
57 Rear-vision panels
58 Pilot's headrest
59 Rearward-sliding cockpit canopy
60 Rear-view mirror (external)
61 Bullet-proof windshield
62 Instrument panel coaming
63 Electric gunsight
64 Throttle control quadrant
65 Trim tab control wheels
66 Flap control lever
67 Pilot's seat
68 Elevator control cable horn
69 Seat support (wing upper surface)
70 Hydraulic pump handle
71 Control column
72 Rudder pedal/brake cylinder assembly
73 Bulkhead
74 Oil tank, capacity 10.8 Imp gal (49 litres)
75 Ring sight
76 Flap control push-rod rollers
77 Aileron control cables
78 Aileron cable drum
79 Aileron trim tab drive motor
80 Aileron trim tab
81 Port aileron
82 Port navigation light
83 Pitot head
84 Wing skinning
85 Ammunition loading panels
86 Bead sight
87 Coolant expansion tank,

capacity 2.9 Imp gal (13 litres)
88 Carburettor intake
89 Engine bearer support attachment
90 Air vapour eliminator
91 Hydraulic emergency reserve tank
92 Junction box
93 Engine support tubes
94 Engine mounting vibration absorbers
95 Exhaust stacks
96 Cowling panel lines
97 Allison V-1710-39 engine
98 Carburettor intake fairing
99 Propeller reduction gear casing

Curtiss P-40 Warhawk

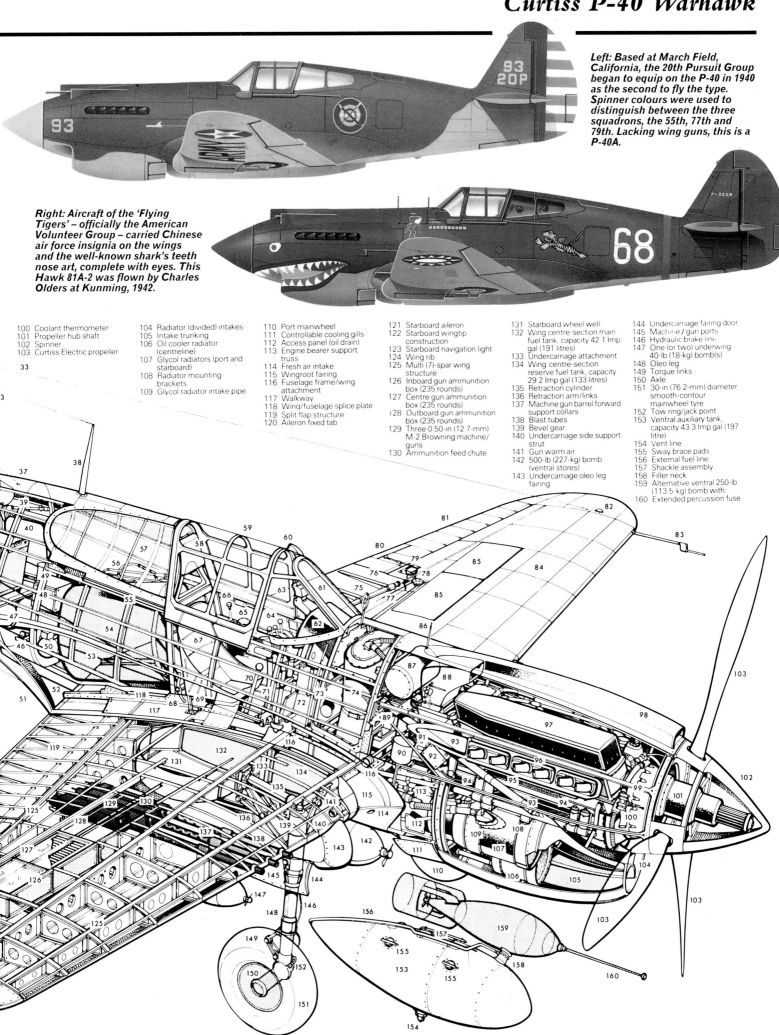

Left: Based at March Field, California, the 20th Pursuit Group began to equip on the P-40 in 1940 as the second to fly the type. Spinner colours were used to distinguish between the three squadrons, the 55th, 77th and 79th. Lacking wing guns, this is a P-40A.

Right: Aircraft of the 'Flying Tigers' – officially the American Volunteer Group – carried Chinese air force insignia on the wings and the well-known shark's teeth nose art, complete with eyes. This Hawk 81A-2 was flown by Charles Olders at Kunming, 1942.

100 Coolant thermometer
101 Propeller hub shaft
102 Spinner
103 Curtiss Electric propeller
104 Radiator (divided) intakes
105 Intake trunking
106 Oil cooler radiator (centreline)
107 Glycol radiators (port and starboard)
108 Radiator mounting brackets
109 Glycol radiator intake pipe
110 Port mainwheel
111 Controllable cooling gills
112 Access panel (oil drain)
113 Engine bearer support truss
114 Fresh air intake
115 Wingroot fairing
116 Fuselage frame/wing attachment
117 Walkway
118 Wing/fuselage splice plate
119 Split flap structure
120 Aileron fixed tab
121 Starboard aileron
122 Starboard wingtip construction
123 Starboard navigation light
124 Wing rib
125 Multi (7)-spar wing structure
126 Inboard gun ammunition box (235 rounds)
127 Centre gun ammunition box (235 rounds)
128 Outboard gun ammunition box (235 rounds)
129 Three 0.50-in (12.7-mm) M-2 Browning machine/guns
130 Ammunition feed chute
131 Starboard aileron
132 Wing centre-section main fuel tank, capacity 42.1 Imp gal (191 litres)
133 Undercarriage attachment
134 Wing centre-section reserve fuel tank, capacity 29.2 Imp gal (133 litres)
135 Retraction cylinder
136 Retraction arm/links
137 Machine gun barrel forward support collars
138 Blast tubes
139 Bevel gear
140 Undercarriage side support strut
141 Gun warm air
142 500-lb (227-kg) bomb (ventral stores)
143 Undercarriage oleo leg fairing
144 Undercarriage fairing door
145 Machine / gun ports
146 Hydraulic brake line
147 One (or two) underwing 40-lb (18-kg) bomb(s)
148 Oleo leg
149 Torque links
150 Axle
151 30-in (76.2-mm) diameter smooth-contour mainwheel tyre
152 Tow ring/jack point
153 Ventral auxiliary tank, capacity 43.3 Imp gal (197 litre)
154 Vent line
155 Sway brace pads
156 External fuel line
157 Shackle assembly
158 Filler neck
159 Alternative ventral 250-lb (113.5-kg) bomb with:
160 Extended percussion fuse

Left: When Allied forces landed in North Africa in November 1942 during Operation Torch, USAAF P-40 units already in area were augmented by squadrons flown from US aircraft-carriers. The 'stars and stripes' insignia, as on these P-40F-20s, was for the benefit of French ground forces.

Below: These P-40Fs were probably serving in a US-based training unit. The 'F' model was the first of the Warhawks to receive the Packard-built Rolls-Royce Merlin 28, the V-1650-1.

Produced in parallel with the last P-40Fs was the **P-40K** with the marginally more powerful Allison V-1710-73 (1,325 hp/988 kW), which increased the top speed to 366 mph (589 km/h), thereby giving it an edge over the Bf 109E in Europe and North Africa, and over the Mitsubishi A6M in the Far East. More power was added in the **P-40M** with the introduction of the V-1710-81 engine producing 1,360 hp (1015 kW). Some 1,300 P-40Ks (originally intended for Lend-Lease to China) and 600 P-40Ms were produced for the USAAF. RAF versions of the P-40F were the **Kittyhawk Mks II** and **IIA**, of which 330 were produced as an interim measure by converting USAAF aircraft. It was intended to transfer these back in due course to American squadrons, but in the end only 80 were returned to the USAAF. A total of 616 **Kittyhawk Mk III**s, equivalent to the P-40M, was delivered to the RAF.

Further variants

A number of other interim versions had meanwhile been produced or planned. Some 45 **P-40G**s had been built, combining the Kittyhawk fuselage with RAF Tomahawk wings and six 0.5-in (12.7-mm) wing guns; all were retained by the USAAF. The **P-40J** was intended to use a turbocharged Allison but was not built owing to the introduction of the Rolls-Royce Merlin. The Packard (Merlin) V-1650-1 was fitted in the **P-40L**, of which 700 were produced for the USAAF in 1943 (but none for the RAF), some of these aircraft having two guns, armour and some fuel removed to improve performance.

The definitive Warhawk was the **P-40N**, which entered production towards the end of 1943 and started delivery to the USAAF in March the following year. Reverting to the Allison engine, this was a lightweight version with the front fuselage fuel tank omitted. The early production blocks from -1 to -15, of which 1,977 were built, were armed with only four wing guns and weighed 8,850 lb (4081 kg) all-up. These were followed by 3,023 aircraft in the blocks -20 to -35 with V-1710-99 engines, with armament restored to six guns and provision to carry a 500-lb (227-kg) bomb on belly shackles. The final production version, in the -40 block, was powered by the V-1710-115 and had wing racks to carry two additional 500-lb (227-kg) bombs; 1,000 of this variant were ordered, but production of the Warhawk was terminated in September 1944 when only 220 had

been completed. Some 588 were produced for the RAF, equivalent to the P-40N-20, as the **Kittyhawk Mk IV**.

In 1944, following the introduction of the Merlin in the P-51, there existed a heavy demand on spares for this engine and so 300 P-40Fs and P-40Ls were converted to take the V-1710-81, their designations being altered to P-40R-1 and R-2 respectively.

Three experimental **XP-40Q**s were produced with V-1710-121 engines and the radiators moved to the wings. The first, a converted P-40K (42-9987) with four-bladed propeller, was followed by another converted P-40K (42-45722) and a P-40N (43-24571) with clear-view 'bubble' canopies; 42-45722 later had its wings clipped to 35-ft 3-in (10.79-m) span and its radiator moved back to the nose position, and in this configuration it was the fastest of all Warhawks, with a top speed of 422 mph (679 km/h) at 20,500 ft (6273 m). Finally, a small number of P-40Es and P-40Ns were converted to two-seat trainers under the designation **TP-40N**.

The P-40M-1 (this one, semi-derelict, was photographed shortly after the war had ended) introduced an Allison V-1710-81 engine and some other small changes.

A standard P-40K-10 retained by Curtiss for development of new cooling systems and revised cowling lines, as shown here, took the designation XP-40K.

Last of the production P-40 variants, the P-40Ns had Allison V-1710-81 engines and lightened airframes. The D/F loop behind the radio mast on this example was non-standard.

Left: 'Lighthouse Louie' was the P-40L-5-CU Warhawk flown in Tunisia by Lt Col Gordon H. Austin in the HQ Flight of the 325th Fighter Group. The 'sand-and-spinach' finish, with sky blue undersides, was standard in the desert.

Right: The 11th Fighter Squadron, 343rd FG, was flying P-40Es in the Aleutians, Northern Pacific, in 1942. Known as the 'Aleutian Tiger', the nose art was adopted as a tribute to Claire Chennault, leader of the 'Flying Tigers'.

Fitted with a second cockpit well to the rear of the pilot, and dual controls, several P-40N-30s were modified for training and 'hack' use, with the designation R-40N.

One of the most elegant of all the Warhawks, this XP-40Q (the second of three) was also the fastest, achieving 422 mph (679 km/h) at a height of 20,500 ft (6248 m).

The first XP-40Q (a modified P-40K) had the standard canopy with a high rear fuselage, but a revised cooling system, similar to the XP-40K, and a four-bladed propeller.

Warhawks of the USAAF served on almost all fronts during World War II with many pursuit and fighter groups, among them the 8th and 49th Groups of the US Fifth Air Force in the Far East between 1942 and 1944; the 15th and 18th Fighter Groups of the US Seventh Air Force between 1941 and 1944; the 57th and 79th Fighter Groups of the US 9th Air Force in the Mediterranean theatre between 1942 and 1944; the 51st Pursuit Group with the US Tenth Air Force in India and Burma between 1941 and 1944; and the 27th and 33rd Fighter Groups of the US 12th Air Force in the Mediterranean between 1942 and 1944. They also provided the backbone of the USAAF's fighter defences protecting the Panama Canal between 1941 and 1943, serving with the 16th, 32nd, 36th, 37th and 53rd Pursuit Groups.

While it might be suggested that the P-40 remained in service with the USAAF in secondary war theatres in order to allow delivery priorities to be bestowed upon more advanced aircraft (such as the P-38, P-47 and P-51), in combat theatres the prolonging of Warhawk production as late as 1944 - by which time its performance was thoroughly pedestrian among current fighters - has never been satisfactorily explained, especially having regard to the very large numbers built.

Be that as it may, many Tomahawks and Kittyhawks were also delivered against contracts for the RAF, RAAF, RCAF, RNZAF and SAAF; the relatively small number of squadrons so equipped is largely explained by the fact that a large proportion of the aircraft purchased by Britain were diverted to the USSR during 1942 and 1943 (2,091 of the 2,430 aircraft said to have been dispatched arriving safely). During the last two years of the war the United States supplied 377 P-40s (mostly P-40Ns) to China, while in 1942 some P-40Es were delivered to Chile, and 89 P-40Es went to Brazil the following year.

Production of all P-40s totalled 16,802, including 4,787 on British contracts.

Specification
Curtiss P-40N-20 Warhawk
Type: single-seat interceptor and fighter-bomber
Powerplant: one 1,360-hp (1015-kW) Allison V-1710-81 inline piston engine
Performance: maximum speed 378 mph (609 km/h) at 10,500 ft (3210 m); climb to 15,000 ft (4590 m) in 6 minutes 42 seconds; service ceiling 38,000 ft (11630 m); normal range 240 miles (386 km)
Weights: empty 6,000 lb (2724 kg); maximum take-off 8,850 lb (4018 kg)
Dimensions: span 37 ft 4 in (11.42 m); length 33 ft 4 in (10.2 m); height 12 ft 4 in (3.77 m); wing area 236 sq ft (21.95 m²)
Armament: six 0.5-in (12.7-mm) machine-guns in wings and provision for one 500-lb (227-kg) bomb under fuselage

Curtiss P-40 Warhawk variants

XP-40: prototype converted from P-36A with V-1710-19 engine
P-40: 200 production aircraft built with V-1710-33 engine and all-up weight of 7,215 lb (3277 kg)
P-40A: one example converted from P-40 as a photo-reconnaissance aircraft
P-40B: retaining the V-1710-33, the P-40B introduced armour and increased armament; all-up weight 7,600 lb (3450 kg); 131 built
P-40C: 193 built for USAAC; similar to P-40B but introduced self-sealing tanks; weight increased to 8,058 lb

(3658 kg)
P-40D: 23 built for USAAC; V-1710-39 engine with deepened radiator; 0.5-in wing guns and underwing store racks added
P-40E: major variant similar to P-40D but with six wing guns; 2,320 built
TP-40E: two P-40Es converted as two-seat trainers
XP-40F: P-40D converted with Rolls-Royce Merlin 28
P-40F: production version with Packard-built Merlin; 1,311 built for USAAF with all-up weight 9,870 lb (4480 kg); later production aircraft

with rear fuselage stretch
P-40G: small number of P-40 fuselages joined with Model 81A-2 wings
P-40K: 1,300 built; Allison V-1710-73 engine; small dorsal fairing; all-up weight 10,000 lb (4540 kg)
TP-40K: one P-40K converted to two-seat trainer
P-40L: Merlin-powered version with reduced fuel, armour and armament; 700 built
P-40M: 600 built; similar to P-40K but with V-1710-81 engine
P-40N: 5,210 built; initially similar to P-40M but with only four guns, and reduced weight; mid-production

aircraft with V-1710-99 engine and late production with V-1710-115, flame-dampers and metal-covered ailerons
TP-40N: 30 P-40Ns converted as two-seat trainers
XP-40Q: three prototypes with V-1710-121 engine, four-bladed propeller, four wing guns and leading-edge radiators; second and third aircraft with cut-down rear fuselage, bubble canopy and clipped wings
P-40R: 300 P-40Fs and P-40Ls re-engined with V-1710-81 and used for training

Curtiss XP-55 Ascender

The **Curtiss XP-55 Ascender** is perhaps best known of the three pusher fighters built for a 1941 competition in response to US Army 'Request for Data R40-C' dated 20 February 1940 (the others being the Vultee XP-54 and Northrop XP-56). A flying wing in most respects, albeit with a small fuselage and a canard foreplane (with only the horizontal portion of this surface forward of the wing), the XP-55 went through numerous design changes at Curtiss's plant at St Louis, Missouri. Like its competitors it was long-delayed getting into the air, although it eventually carried out a test programme which involved four airframes.

Curtiss built a full-scale flying testbed, the company **Model CW-24B**, powered by an 850-hp (633-kW) Menasco C65-5 engine. The fabric-covered CW-24B went to a new US Army test site, the ultra-secret airfield at Muroc Dry Lake, California, for 1942 tests. These revealed serious stability problems which were only partly resolved by moving its vertical fins further out from their initial midway position on the swept-back wing.

The full-sized XP-55 fighter was ordered in fiscal year 1942, based on the proven 1,475-hp (1100-kW) Allison V-1710-F23R engine being used for the first time as a pusher. The XP-55 used a single-rotation three-bladed propeller instead of the coaxial, contra-rotating type which had been planned and which was, in fact, employed with the parallel Northrop XP-56.

The first of three XP-55 aircraft (42-78845/78847) was delivered on 13 July 1943 and underwent early flights at Scott Field, Illinois. It was found that excessive speed was required in the take-off run before the nose-mounted elevator could become effective. Before this problem could be addressed, the first machine was lost during spin tests at St Louis on 15 November 1943, the pilot parachuting to safety.

The second XP-55 was flown in St Louis on 9 January 1944. The third followed on 25 April 1944, and soon after went to Eglin Field, Florida, for tests of its nose-mounted 0.5-in (12.7-mm) machine-guns. The XP-55 had the advantage of being constructed largely from non-strategic materials and for a time a jet version, the company **Model CW-24C**, was contemplated. Lingering problems, including generally poor stability, remained unsolved when the third XP-55 was returned to Wright Field, Ohio, for further tests continuing into 1945.

On 27 May 1945, at a Wright Field air show and bond rally attracting a crowd of more than 100,000, the third XP-55 took off to give a public flying display. Captain William C. Glascow flew across the field leading five other fighters in formation. Glascow made one roll before the crowd,

Failing at first to obtain AAF backing for its CW-24 fighter proposal, Curtiss built a low-powered proof-of-concept vehicle at its own expense – this CW-24B. Tests at Muroc started on 2 December 1941 and proved promising, and led to an order for three XP-55 fighter prototypes.

began another, and suddenly dived into the ground inverted. The pilot was thrown from the wreckage but suffered mortal injuries, and a nearby motorist was also killed.

Few aircraft contributed more to advancing technology while remaining trouble-plagued and failing to reach production.

Specification
XP-55
Type: single-seat fighter
Powerplant: one 1,475-hp (1100-kW) Allison V-1710-F23R liquid-cooled 12-cylinder Vee piston engine driving a three-bladed pusher propeller
Performance: maximum speed 390 mph (627 km/h) at 19,300 ft (5883 m); climb to 20,000 ft (6096 m) in 7.1 minutes; service ceiling 34,600 ft (10546 m); range 490 miles (789 km)
Weights: empty 6,354 lb (2882 kg), maximum take-off 7,330 lb (3324 kg)
Dimensions: span 44 ft 6 in (13.56 m); length 29 ft 7 in (9.02 m); height 10 ft 0 in (3.05 m); wing area 235 sq ft (21.83 m²)
Armament: four 0.5-in (12.7-mm) nose-mounted fixed forward-firing machine-guns

Second of the three XP-55s, flown on 9 January 1944, was in the same 'B' configuration as the first, which was lost eight weeks earlier. The name 'Ascender' was a polite version of the obvious soubriquet for a tail-first design.

Curtiss P-60

The **P-60** designation applies to a family of widely different Curtiss fighters, each reflecting the urgency of the builder's unsuccessful effort to develop a P-40 replacement. Although only four airframes carried out the P-60 programme, no fewer than nine designations were involved: XP-60, XP-60A, YP-60A, P-60A, XP-60B, XP-60C, XP-60D, XP-60E and YP-60E. The programme ran from early 1941 to December 1944 and was Curtiss's last gasp in the propeller-driven fighter field, an ambitious but unfocused effort which involved several engines, propellers and canopy configurations.

The **XP-60** (42-79245) was a low-wing, conventional-gear fighter developed from the uncompleted XP-53 but powered by a 1,300-hp (969-kW) Packard V-1560-1 licence-built Merlin, belatedly determined by the USAAF to be the best engine available in 1941. This airframe flew on 18 September 1941. With all Merlin-related resources soon committed to the P-51 Mustang programme, the USAAF then decided to employ the ubiquitous 1,425-hp (1063-kW) Allison V-1710-75 in planned production-model P-60s. On 31 October 1941, 1,950 such fighters were ordered. Soon, however, it became evident that Curtiss' Buffalo, New York, plant could be more usefully employed building P-47G Thunderbolts and the contract was cancelled. Three **XP-60A** airframes were tested with the Allison powerplant before being re-engined. The proposed **YP-60A**, which would have had a 2,000-hp (1491-kW)

Seeking to replace the P-40 with an improved single-engined fighter, Curtiss came up with the Model 90 proposal in 1941 and gained an order for 1,950. Essentially a P-40D with laminar-flow wing, the XP-60 remained only a prototype.

Pratt & Whitney R-2800-10 radial, was another variation which did not result in a finished airframe. The **XP-60B** was to have been the original machine with a shift from Merlin to Allison power, but apparently this change was never made.

The **XP-60C** - converted in 1943 from one of the three Allison test ships - employed the R-2800 radial. This was the sole example tested with Curtiss Electric contra-rotating propellers. The **XP-60D** was the original machine retaining its Merlin but with enlarged tail surfaces and other minor changes. The **XP-60E** was another R-2800 radial-powered variant. Last in the series was the **YP-60E**, another conversion, again R-2800 radial-powered but now uncamouflaged and with bubble canopy, the result being formidable competition to the Curtiss P-40Q for the claim of most beautiful fighter ever built.

In November 1942, the US Army ordered 500 Pratt & Whitney-powered P-60 fighters, but the production contract was soon set aside in favour of other priorities. The P-60 programme

ended by mid-1944, the last airframe being scrapped on 22 December 1944.

Specification
XP-60C
Type: single-seat fighter
Powerplant: one 2,000-hp (1491-kW) Pratt & Whitney R-2800-53 air-cooled 18-cylinder radial piston engine driving a six-bladed Curtiss Electric contra-rotating propeller unit
Performance: maximum speed 386 mph (621 km/h) at sea level; climb to 10,000 ft (3048 m) in 3.7 minutes; service ceiling 36,000 ft (10972 m); range 615 miles (990 km)
Weights: empty 8,698 lb (3945 kg); maximum take-off 10,525 lb (4774 kg)
Dimensions: span 41 ft 4 in (12.60 m); length 34 ft 1 in (10.39 m); height 15 ft 0 in (4.57 m); wing area 275 sq ft (25.55 m²)

Between 1942 and 1944, Curtiss built a series of fighter prototypes under the XP-60 designation. All were Model 95s, and differed from the earlier Model 90 XP-60 in having different engines and revised armament. None achieved production status. The airframe illustrated began as the XP-60B, intended to have an Allison V-1710 engine, but flown as the XP-60E with a P&W R-2800 radial.

Curtiss XP-62

The **Curtiss XP-62** was the final propeller-driven fighter built by its manufacturer and the second largest single-seat fighter of orthodox layout developed during World War ll, its dimensions being exceeded only by the Boeing XF8B naval fighter. The XP-62 was ordered by the USAAF on 27 June 1941 as a

vehicle for the 2,300-hp (1715-kW) Wright R-3350 radial engine. Initial plans called for delivery of one XP-62 and one **XP-62A** and later for 100 production **P-62** fighters, but it was clear almost from the beginning that the design was overweight, underpowered, and an uneconomical alternative to continued

Curtiss production of the P-47G Thunderbolt. Because it would be an effective testbed for dual-rotation propellers and a pressurised cabin, it was decided on 18 July 1942 to proceed with a sole airframe, the remaining machines on order being cancelled.

Development of the XP-62's cabin pressurisation system was

delayed and the aircraft did not fly until early 1944. By then even the XP-62's value as a test ship was marginal, and the programme was terminated after a few hours' flying time. Although the unbuilt XP-71 and the jet XF-87 still lay ahead, the great days of Curtiss as a leading fighter manufacturer were to become history.

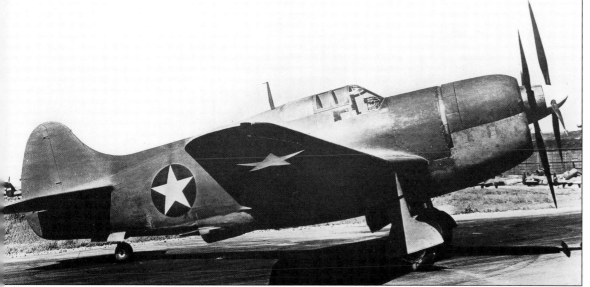

Specification
Type: single-seat fighter
Powerplant: one 2,300-hp (1715-kW) Wright R-3350-17 Cyclone air-cooled 18-cylinder twin-row radial engine driving a six-bladed dual-rotation propeller unit
Performance: (estimated) maximum speed 448 mph (721 km/h) at 27,000 ft (8230 m); initial climb rate 2,000 ft (610 m) per minute; service ceiling 35,700 ft (10880 m); range 710 miles (1143 km)
Weights: empty 11,773 lb (5340 kg); maximum take-off 14,660 lb (6649 kg)
Dimensions: span 53 ft 8 in (16.36 m); length 39 ft 6 in (12.04 m); height 16 ft 3 in (4.95 m); wing area 420 sq ft (39.02 m²)

With a 2,300-hp Wright R-3350-17 swinging a contra-prop, the XP-62 featured a turbo-supercharger and a pressurised cockpit. The heaviest of the Curtiss single-seat fighters, it flew in July 1943 but offered no advantages over other fighters.

Curtiss XF14C

Looking for more effective carrier-based fighters, the US Navy ordered from Curtiss in June 1942 two experimental fighter prototypes. Given the company designation **Model 94**, one (US Navy designation **XF14C-1**) was to be powered by a new Lycoming H-2470-4 engine, and the other (**XF14C-2**) by a Wright XR-3350. As the Lycoming engine was not available in time, only the XF14C-2 was completed, this being of similar configuration to the XP-62 but without a pressurised cockpit. First flown in late 1943, it was delivered to the US Navy for testing in mid-1944, but by that time the requirement had been satisfied and no further examples were built.

Specification
Type: single-seat carrier-based fighter
Powerplant: one 2,300-hp (1715-kW) Wright XR-3350-16 radial piston engine
Performance: maximum speed 418 mph (673 km/h); service ceiling 39,800 ft (12130 m); range 1,530 miles (2462 km)

Weights: empty 10,531 lb (4777 kg); maximum take-off 14,950 lb (6781 kg)
Dimensions: wing span 46 ft 0 in (14.02 m); length 37 ft 9 in (11.51 m); height 17 ft 0 in (5.18 m); wing area 375 sq ft (34.84 m²)
Armament: four 20-mm cannon

A non-standard all-white finish enhanced the appearance of the sole prototype of the cannon-armed Curtiss XF14C-2. Slow development meant that the Grumman F6F and Vought F4U fulfilled the Navy's requirement.

Curtiss SBC Helldiver

In 1932, the US Navy ordered a new two-seat fighter prototype from Curtiss. Designated **XF12C-1**, this flew for the first time in 1933 as a two-seat parasol-wing monoplane with retractable landing gear, powered by a 625-hp (466-kW) Wright R-1510-92 Whirlwind 14. At the end of the year it was decided to use the aircraft in a scout capacity, and its designation was changed to **XS4C-1**. In January 1934 it became a scout-bomber and a Wright R-1820 Cyclone was installed. Trials followed, but during a dive test in September 1934 there was structural failure of the wing and the **XSBC-1**, as it was now designated, was damaged extensively.

The parasol wing was clearly unsuitable for the dive-bombing requirement, and a new prototype was ordered as the **XSBC-2**, with biplane wings and a 700-hp (522-kW) Wright R-1510-12 Whirlwind 14. When, in March 1936, this engine was replaced by an 825-hp (615-kW) Pratt & Whitney R-1535-82 Twin Wasp Junior, the designation changed to **XSBC-3**. Production **SBC-3**s, of which the US Navy ordered 83 on 29 August 1936, were generally similar, were armed with two

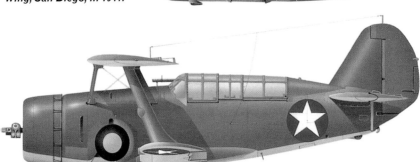

Right: By order dated 30 December 1940, all US Navy shipboard aircraft were to be given an overall light grey finish. This SBC-4 (BuAer No. 1287) was serving as a command liaison and transport aircraft with the 1st Marine Aviation Wing, San Diego, in 1941.

Left: By mid-1942, all US Navy aircraft were finished in a non-specular blue-grey on upper surfaces with light grey undersides. This SBC-3 in the US Navy Reserve service sports the post-May 1942 insignia, with red removed from the star and no rudder stripes.

0.30-in (7.62-mm) machine-guns and could carry a single 500-lb (227-kg) bomb beneath the fuselage. First deliveries, to Navy Squadron VS-5, were made on 17 July 1937, and the type was also to equip Squadrons VS-3 and VS-6.

The last SBC-3 on the production line was used as the prototype of an improved version. With a more powerful Wright R-1820-22 engine, and the ability to carry a 1,000-lb (454-kg) bomb, this was

designated **XSBC-4**. Following an initial contract of 5 January 1938, the first of 174 production **SBC-4**s for the US Navy was delivered in March 1939. Because of the desperate situation in Europe in early 1940, the US Navy diverted 50 of its SBC-4s to France but these were received too late to be used in combat. Five of them were recovered for use by the RAF, being assembled in Britain in August 1940, and were issued to RAF Little Rissington for allocation as ground trainers under the designation **Cleveland**. The US Navy's deficiency of 50 aircraft was made good by delivery of 50 out of the 90 aircraft which had been in production for France. Retaining the SBC-4 designation, these differed from standard in having self-sealing fuel tanks.

On the eve of US entry into World War II, SBC-4s of VS-8 (lead aircraft) and VB-8 from USS Hornet engage in manoeuvres over South Carolina.

By the time the USA became involved in World War II, the SBC-3s had become obsolescent, but SBC-4s were then in service with US Navy Squadrons VB-8 and VS-8 on board the USS *Hornet* and with US Marine Squadron VMO-151. The type performed useful work with second-line and training units.

Specification
Type: two-seat carrier-based scout-bomber
Powerplant: (SBC-4) one 950-hp (708-kW) Wright R-1820-34 Cyclone 9 radial piston engine
Performance: maximum speed 237 mph (381 km/h) at 15,200 ft (4635 m); cruising speed 127 mph (204 km/h); service ceiling 27,300 ft (8320 m); range with 500-lb (227-kg) bomb 590 miles (950 km)
Weights: empty 4,841 lb (2196 kg); maximum take-off 7,632 lb (3462 kg)
Dimensions: span 34 ft 0 in (10.36 m); length 28 ft 4 in (8.64 m); height 12 ft 7 in (3.84 m); wing area 317 sq ft (29.45 m²)
Armament: one 0.30-in (7.62-mm) forward-firing and one 0.30-in (7.62-mm) machine-gun on flexible mounting, plus one 500-lb (227-kg) or one 1,000-lb (454-kg) bomb

Curtiss SB2C Helldiver

The **Curtiss SB2C**, one of the few members of the long and proud series of Curtiss dive-bombers to bear the name **Helldiver** (officially or unofficially), was intended to be a great war-winner to replace the ancient SBD. Unlike the Douglas product, created by Ed Heinemann working under John K. Northrop, the marvellous new Curtiss had a mighty new two-row engine, an internal weapon bay and a mass of fuel and new equipment all packaged into a tight space. After Pearl Harbor it became the focus of a gigantic nationwide production programme intended to blast the Japanese from the Pacific. The only thing wrong was the aircraft itself. To a man, the US Navy preferred the old SBD, which simply kept on in the forefront of the battle.

The other mass-produced Navy Curtiss of World War II was the SO3C Seamew, and it is doubtful if two less-successful aircraft have ever been built in numbers. This experience played a major part in the decline of the once pre-eminent names of Curtiss and Wright in the immediate post-war era, and this was allowed to happen by the US Army and US Navy customers.

In fact the Seamew was designed by a team under the famed chief engineer, Don R. Berlin, while the SB2C was the creation of a newly formed group under Raymond C. Blaylock. As its designation reveals, the SB2C was planned as a scout bomber, for operation from US Navy carriers. The 1938 specification was extremely comprehensive and allowed little room for manoeuvre. The type had to be a stressed-skin cantilever monoplane, and the wing had to be raised from the low position in order to allow the accommodation of an internal weapon bay beneath it. This bay did not have to accommodate a torpedo, but it did have to take a 1,000-lb (454-kg) bomb and a wide range of other stores, and be closed by hydraulically-operated bomb doors. There had to be tandem accommodation for a crew of two, a large amount of fuel (various ranges and mission radii were specified)

Early testing of the XSB2C-1 led to the introduction of a longer fuselage and enlarged tail surfaces; in this guise, illustrated, tests resumed in October 1941. The use of chrome yellow on the upper wing surfaces was standard Navy practice until camouflage was introduced at the end of 1941, and helped improve visibility in the event of a ditching.

and comprehensive radio and other gear including a hefty camera in the rear cockpit. The structure had to be stressed for dive-bombing, and the aircraft had to be carrier-compatible, with folding wings, catapult hooks and an arrester hook. The specified engine was the Wright R-2600 14-cylinder Cyclone.

Poor performance

Not unnaturally, the prototype **XSB2C-1** came out looking rather like its rival, the Brewster XSB2A-1 Buccaneer; and, if such a thing were possible, the latter was an even poorer aircraft than the Curtiss. In fact, the US Navy had such faith in the Buffalo-based company that it placed a firm order for 200 **SB2C-1**s before the prototype made its first flight on 18 December 1940. The single prototype, BuNo 1758,

A group of SB2C Helldivers head out on another mission in the Pacific, with F6F Hellcats flying top cover. As the designed successor for the SBD Dauntless, the Helldiver proved initially disappointing, with little improvement in speed, and better range and load-carrying abilities spoiled by poor handling and low serviceability.

Left: Assigned to a training unit in the US Navy, this Helldiver engages in a dive-bomb attack, The weapon is a 1,000-lb (454-kg) bomb; two of these, or a single 1,600-lb (726-kg) bomb, could be carried in the capacious bomb bay, which was a feature of the original Navy request issued during 1938. A torpedo or two depth-charges could be carried alternatively, and smaller bombs or depth charges were later added as underwing options. Defensive armament was two 20-mm cannon in the wings and a pair of 0.3-in (7.62-mm) guns in the rear cockpit.

had been ordered on 15 May 1939, and the big production order came on 29 November 1940. Thus, as 1941 dawned Curtiss had a single shiny prototype which occasionally flew, on the strength of which 14,000 workers were being hired for a vast new plant rapidly taking shape at Columbus, Ohio (later NAA and today Rockwell). Plans were already afoot for two further giant production programmes, at Canadian Car & Foundry at Fort William and Fairchild Aircraft at Longueil, Montreal. Curtiss announced that "The Helldiver is the world's most efficient dive-bomber; it carries twice the bombload, has double the firepower, is at least 100 mph faster, remains in flight 4½ hours longer and can operate 600 miles further away from its base than any type now in use. We will build 1,000 or more, at the rate of 80 a month."

Such confidence overlooked the fact that the SB2C was riddled with problems. Some were the normal ones of immaturity, affecting almost all the functioning items and particularly the R-2600-8 engine and 3.66-m (12-ft) Curtiss Electric three-bladed propeller. More serious were the deeper faults of the aircraft itself, which resulted in structural weaknesses, generally poor handling, shockingly inadequate stability (especially in yaw and pitch) and unacceptable stall characteristics. Yet the strange thing is that the first prototype looked almost the same as all the production machines. Even the fact that the tail had to be enlarged was not immediately obvious.

Features of the XSB2C-1 included a large wing with all its taper on the trailing edge. On the trailing edge were large flaps split into lower and upper portions, again divided into inboard and outboard sections on the manually folded outer wings. In normal flight the upper flap sections were hydraulically locked to form the upper surface of the wing, the lower part functioning as a normal split flap. For dive-bombing the upper flaps were unlocked by moving the selector lever

to a different position, the hydraulic jacks then opening both flaps fully above and below. This held the dive to 354 km/h (220 mph) but buffeted the tail so violently that the pilot feared structural failure (which often did occur, though not necessarily from the buffet). The ailerons, which in most versions had greater chord than the flaps, were unusual in having aluminium skin above and fabric below. In line with the ailerons on the leading edge were large slats which were pulled open by a cable connection to the landing gears, so that at low speeds in the traffic pattern the handling, especially lateral control, was almost acceptable. The US Navy did pass the sluggish ailerons, but in 1944 the British rejected it out of hand, and that was after four years of improvement.

Engine failure

Unfortunately, BuNo. 1758 crashed quite early, on 8 February 1941, the cause being engine failure on the approach. Like many aircraft of its day the SB2C suffered violent changes in trim with application of flap, dive brakes, gear down or changes in engine power. In the case of this aircraft the forces needed on the stick were at the limit of what most pilots could apply, and very high friction in the control circuits did not help, so it was small wonder that control was lost when the engine cut. But with a gigantic production programme fast taking shape Curtiss simply had to carry on with flight test, so 1758 had to be urgently rebuilt. Almost every part was changed, the fuselage being about 1 ft (0.305 m) longer, the tail areas almost 30 per cent larger and numerous shapes subtly altered. The poor stability led to the expensive addition of an autopilot. Thanks to combat reports from Europe the fuel tanks in the fuselage and inner wings were made of the self-sealing type, local armour was added and the forward-firing armament changed from two 0.5-in (12.7-mm) guns above the cowl-

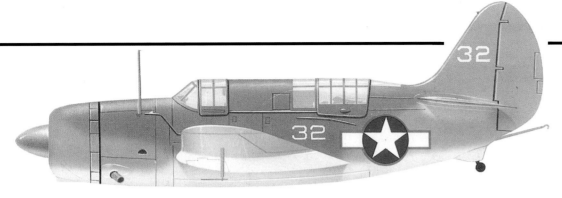

ing to four of these guns in the wings. The rear cockpit was redesigned with improved collapsible decking to improve the field of fire of the observer's single 0.5-in (12.7-mm) gun. Later this gun was replaced by observer armament of twin 0.3-in (7.62-mm) guns, each with no less than 2,000 rounds, with traverse round the mounting ring effected by an hydraulic motor. Wing racks were added for bombs of up to 325-lb (147-kg) depth-bomb size. These and other changes did not all come in at once, but most had at least been agreed on paper by the time the prototype resumed flight testing on 20 October 1941.

So enormous was the production scheme that, coming on top of dozens of others throughout North America, it fell seriously behind. Curtiss had agreed to begin deliveries in December 1941, but by this time no production machine was even being assembled. Worse, on 21 December 1941 the sole prototype broke up in the air while on dive-bombing tests, pilot B.T. Hulse managing to escape by parachute. By this time further changes had been demanded, and another 900 Helldivers had been ordered for the US Army Air Force as **A-25 Shrikes**, with carrier gear deleted, pneumatic tailwheels and many other changes. Everyone worked round the clock to try to speed the programme, and eventually the first SB2C-1 was completed at Port Columbus in June 1942. The US Navy did not fail to notice that 10 days earlier the far better Grumman TBF Avenger had gone into

*An SB2C-1 from **USS Yorktown (CV-10)** cruises over the Born Islands. Bombed-up, the Helldiver is heading for action some time in 1944, some of the type's early unpleasant characteristics having been overcome, or at least accommodated by the growing experience of flight and ground crews who had struggled to reduce accident attrition rates.*

action, though its design had been started almost two years later than the bug-ridden SB2C.

Urgent testing of the first six production machines revealed that in many respects they were worse than the prototype, the great increase in weight (empty weight rose from 7,122 lb/3230 kg to some 10,220 lb/4636 kg) without change in the engine resulting in an aircraft described at NAS Anacostia as "extremely sluggish". But by this time the trickle of production machines was fast building up, and to avoid political scandals some had to be delivered, so US Navy attack squadron VS-9 began to equip with SB2C-1s in December 1942. In fact political scandals had to be accepted; this was wartime, and there seemed to be so many poor or late programmes that the Truman Committee on the National Defense Program was set up to examine what was going on. This committee finally compiled a damning report on the SB2C, and among other things managed to divert the A-25s to other customers, though many did briefly wear US Army colours.

Subsequently production of the SB2C progressed through the many variants listed separately. Only the original order for 200 applied to the SB2C-1 model, and all of these were retained in the USA for training purposes. The **SB2C-1A**, which appeared in 1943, was the

Above: More than 7,100 Helldivers were built, with Fairchild Aircraft's Canadian branch and Canadian Car & Foundry supplementing Curtiss' own production. By a large margin, therefore, production of the type exceeded the quantity of any other dive-bomber built in the US or by any other nation – despite the inadequacies of its performance in its intended role.

Right: This pair of SB2C-3s come from USS Yorktown (CV-10), as indicated by the diagonal white stripe on the fin. A diversity of white markings was used in 1944-45 to identify the aircraft flying from the many aircraft-carriers engaged in the Pacific war. These aircraft are in the three-tone non-specular finish, with star-and-bar markings in white and blue.

Curtiss SB2C Helldiver

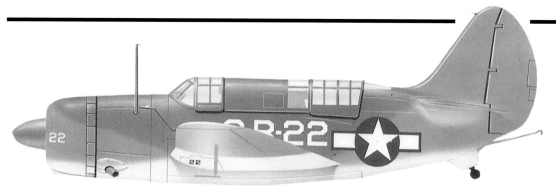

In June 1944, Navy squadron VB-8 replaced the original VB-17 aboard USS Bunker Hill (CV-17) to begin operations against Saipan. At this stage, squadron indicators – based on pre-war practice – were still in use, as here, with '8-B' on the fuselage of aircraft number '22'.

non-navalised A-25A after transfer to the US Marine Corps, with whom many saw action still painted in olive drab. The **SB2C-1C** introduced several armament improvements, including the option of removing the bomb doors and carrying a torpedo on an external truss, but little use appears to have been made of this. The major SB2C-1C change was to replace the four wing guns by two 20-mm cannon, each with 400 rounds loaded from above the wing. Immediately ahead of the magazines were extra 37.4-Imp gal (170-litre) auxiliary tanks, and at full load the SB2C-1C, the first model to go into action, was inferior in many performance respects to the old SBD, which was far nicer to fly, and safer.

Rabaul strike

The first action was flown by a bomber squadron, VB-17, operating from USS *Bunker Hill*. The SB2Cs flew the second strike mounted on 11 November 1943 against the big Japanese base at Rabaul, New Guinea. They were painted in the sea blue and white scheme then common, though by this time aircraft on the line were being finished in gloss midnight blue, usually with a bold white three-figure Modex number on the nose.

A welcome small improvement in performance in the **SB2C-3** resulted from fitting the more powerful R-2600-20 engine, its extra power being absorbed by an improved Curtiss Electric propeller with four blades and fitted with root cuffs. Towards the end of the war it became common to omit the spinner, though this was often done at unit level. Certainly by 1944, when the SB2C-3 appeared, the Helldiver was well established in service, and at least was becoming operationally effective, though crashes, inflight break-ups and carrier landing accidents continued at the very top of the 'league table'. Everyone in the US Navy called this aircraft 'The Beast' and said its designation stood for 'Son of a Bitch, 2nd Class', though pilots who became experienced on it came to think this appellation unfair.

Like most wartime programmes, production became a flood after most of the tougher fighting had been done, and the **SB2C-4**, which did not appear until summer 1944, was the most numerous version of all. From the pilot's viewpoint the chief new feature of this model was that both upper and lower wing flaps were perforated, looking like a sieve. This had virtually no effect on their drag in dive-bombing but did slightly reduce the tremendous tail buffet, which many pilots claimed affected

Starting in 1942, the Curtiss-operated factory at St Louis built 900 Helldivers for the USAAF under the designation A-25A, with arrester gear removed and other small changes. Most served as RA-25A trainers and target-tugs, with 410 later transferred to the Marine Corps.

Curtiss SB2C-4 Helldiver cutaway drawing key

1 Curtiss Electric four-bladed constant-speed propeller
2 Spinner
3 Propeller hub mechanism
4 Spinner backplate
5 Propeller reduction gearbox
6 Carburettor intake
7 Intake ducting
8 Warm air filters
9 Engine cowling ring
10 Oil cooler intake
11 Engine cowlings
12 Wright R-2600-20 Cyclone 14 radial engine
13 Cooling air exit louvres
14 Exhaust collector
15 Exhaust pipe fairing
16 Oil cooler
17 Engine accessories
18 Hydraulic pressure accumulator
19 Boarding step
20 Cabin combustion heater
21 Engine oil tank (25 US gal/ 94.6 litre capacity)
22 Engine bearer struts
23 Hydraulic fluid tank
24 Fireproof engine compartment bulkhead
25 Aerial mast
26 Starboard wing fold hinges
27 Wing fold hydraulic jack
28 Gun camera
29 Rocket projectiles (4.5-in/ 11.43-cm)
30 Starboard leading edge slat (open)
31 Slat roller tracks
32 Slat operating cables
33 Starboard navigation light
34 Formation light
35 Starboard aileron
36 Aileron aluminium top skins
37 Aileron control mechanism
38 Starboard dive brake (open position)
39 Windshield
40 Bullet proof internal windscreen
41 Reflector gunsight
42 Instrument panel shroud
43 Cockpit coaming
44 De-icing fluid tank
45 Instrument panel
46 Pilot's pull-out chart board
47 Rudder pedals
48 Control column
49 Cockpit floor level
50 Engine throttle controls
51 Pilot's seat
52 Oxygen bottle
53 Safety harness
54 Armoured seat back
55 Headrest
56 Pilot's sliding cockpit canopy cover
57 Jury strut
58 Wing folded position
59 Fixed bridge section between cockpits
60 Fuel tank filler cap
61 Fuselage fuel tank (110 US gal/416 litre capacity)
62 Fuselage main longeron
63 Handhold
64 Fuselage frame and stringer construction
65 Autopilot controls

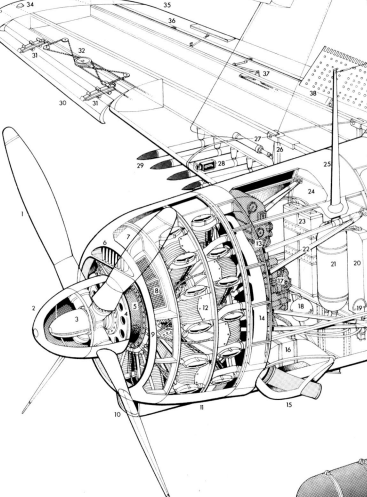

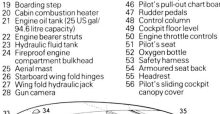

66 Sliding canopy rail
67 Aerial lead-in
68 Radio equipment bay
69 Life raft stowage
70 APG-4 low-level bombing radar
71 Gunner's forward sliding canopy cover
72 Gun mounting ring
73 Gunner's seat
74 Footrests
75 Ammunition boxes
76 Armour plate
77 Wind deflector
78 Twin 0.3-in (7.62-mm) machine-guns
79 Retractable turtle decking
80 Gun rest mounting
81 Folding side panels
82 Upper formation light
83 Fin root fillet
84 Starboard tailplane
85 Deck handling handhold
86 Fabric-covered elevator
87 Remote compass transmitter
88 Tailfin construction
89 Aerial cable
90 Sternpost
91 Rudder construction

92 Fabric skin covering
93 Trim tab
94 Balance tab
95 Elevator trim tab
96 Elevator construction
97 Tailplane construction
98 Tailplane spar root fixing
99 Deck arrester hook
100 Arrester hook damper
101 Tail navigation light
102 Tailwheel leg strut
103 Solid tyre tailwheel
104 Leg fairing
105 Rear fuselage frames
106 Tailplane control cables
107 Lifting bar
108 Gunner's floor level
109 Wing root trailing edge fillet
110 Aft end of bomb bay
111 Rear spar centre section fixing
112 Wing walkway
113 Port upper surface flap dive brake
114 Rear spar hinge joint
115 Split trailing edge flaps
116 Balance tab
117 Aileron hinge control
118 Aileron trim tab
119 Lower surface fabric skinning
120 Wing rib construction
121 Wing tip construction

122 Port navigation light
123 Pitot tube
124 Automatic leading edge slat (opens with undercarriage operation)
125 Slat riblets
126 Slat operating cables
127 Main spar
128 Leading edge nose ribs
129 500-lb (226.8-kg) bomb
130 Rocket projectiles (4.5-in/ 11.43-cm)
131 Drop tank (58 US gal/219.5 litre capacity)
132 Wing fold joint line
133 Main undercarriage leg fairing doors
134 Drag strut
135 Port mainwheel
136 Shock absorber leg strut
137 20-mm wing cannon
138 Cannon barrel fairing
139 Undercarriage leg pivot mounting
140 Wing fold spar hinge joint
141 Cannon ammunition box
142 Auxiliary fuel tank (45 US gal/170 litre capacity)
143 Fuel filler cap
144 Centre section fuel tank (105 US gal/397.5 litre capacity)
145 Front spar/fuselage attachment joint
146 Main undercarriage wheel well
147 Retractable catapult strop
148 Approach light
149 Bomb doors (open)
150 Bomb door hydraulic jack
151 Displacement gear jack
152 H-type bomb displacement arm
153 1,000-lb (453.6-kg) bomb

A big improvement in combat effectiveness of the Helldiver came with the introduction of the SB2C-4, of which model Curtiss built 1,985 examples at its Columbus plant. Underwing provision was made for eight HVARs, and perforated dive brakes were introduced.

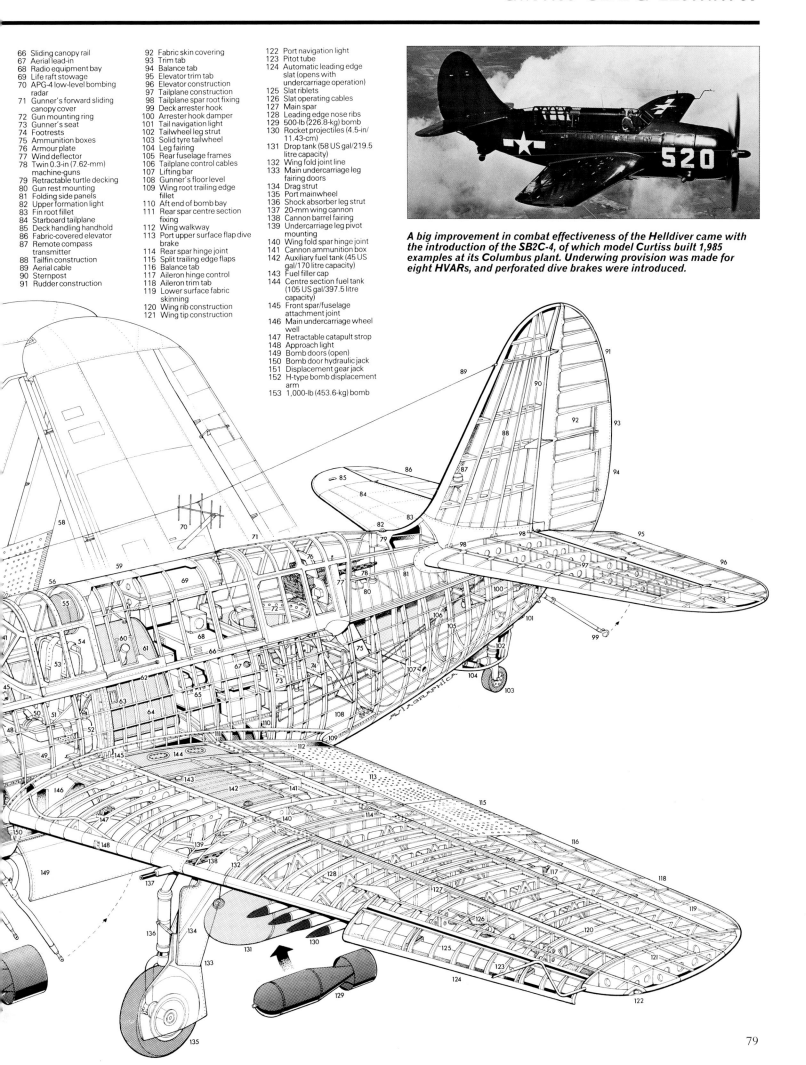

Powerplant

The prototype XSB2C-1 had a 1268-kW (1,700-hp) Wright Double Cyclone R-2600-8 engine. This was a newly-developed but conventional two-row, 14-cylinder, air-cooled radial. It had the regular 6.125-in (155.6-mm) bore but a new stroke of 6.312-in (160.2-mm), giving 2,603-cu in (42.7-litre) capacity. The R-2600 became a major wartime engine, of which over 50,000 were made by Wright at a plant in Cincinnati. The SB2C-3, which began to appear in 1944, had the uprated R-2600-20 that developed 1417 kW (1,900 hp) and was geared and supercharged. A four-bladed Curtiss constant-speed, fully-feathering propeller was fitted. The SB2C-5, which did not go into production, had the 1566-kW (2,100-hp) R-2600-22 engine.

Curtiss SB2C-3 Helldiver CV-19, CVG-7 USS *Hancock*, 1943/44

The Helldiver was by far the most successful Allied dive-bomber of World War II. But despite its great accomplishments in the Pacific theatre, the Helldiver was never popular with aircrew – the designation was said to mean 'Son of a Bitch, 2nd Class'. Its basic handling and stability was poor, and most crews preferred the old SBD Dauntless, which was now replaced by the SB2C but remained in production alongside the Curtiss type. The SB2C-3 illustrated wears the old sea blue, intermediate sea blue and insignia white camouflage. It shows the plain (unperforated) flaps originally fitted, which caused a severe buffet when used as dive brakes; from the SB2C-4, the flaps were perforated. There are bomb racks fitted at the extremity of the fixed portion of its wing, but there is no provision for rockets under the folding outer wings. Also missing is the APG-4 automatic low-level bombing system, fitted to many US Navy carrier-based bombers from 1944.

Armament

The prototype XSB2C had two cowling guns, but production aircraft featured four 0.50-in (12.7-mm) machine-guns in the wings. After the first 200 SB2C-1s, fixed armament was again changed to two 20-mm cannon in the SB2C-1C version. In addition, the Helldiver had two 0.30-in (7.6-mm) guns in the rear cockpit and an internal bombload of 1,000 lb (454 kg). The SB2C-4 had wing fittings for eight 5-in (127-mm) rockets or up to 1,000 lb (454 kg) of bombs (in addition to the internal load). The SB2C-4E version was fitted with radar. Some versions featured a single 0.50-in (12.7-mm) gun in the rear cockpit instead of the twin 0.30-in (7.6-mm) guns.

Undercarriage

For carrier landings a substantial undercarriage was a necessity. The retractable mainwheels comprised two Curtiss oleo-pneumatic shock-absorber struts that were raised inwardly into the undersides of the wings, the apertures being closed by fairings attached to the struts and wheels. Retraction was hydraulic. The steerable tailwheel was partly retractable, with a pronounced fairing at its base. A single SB2C-1 was converted as an XSB2C-2 with twin floats.

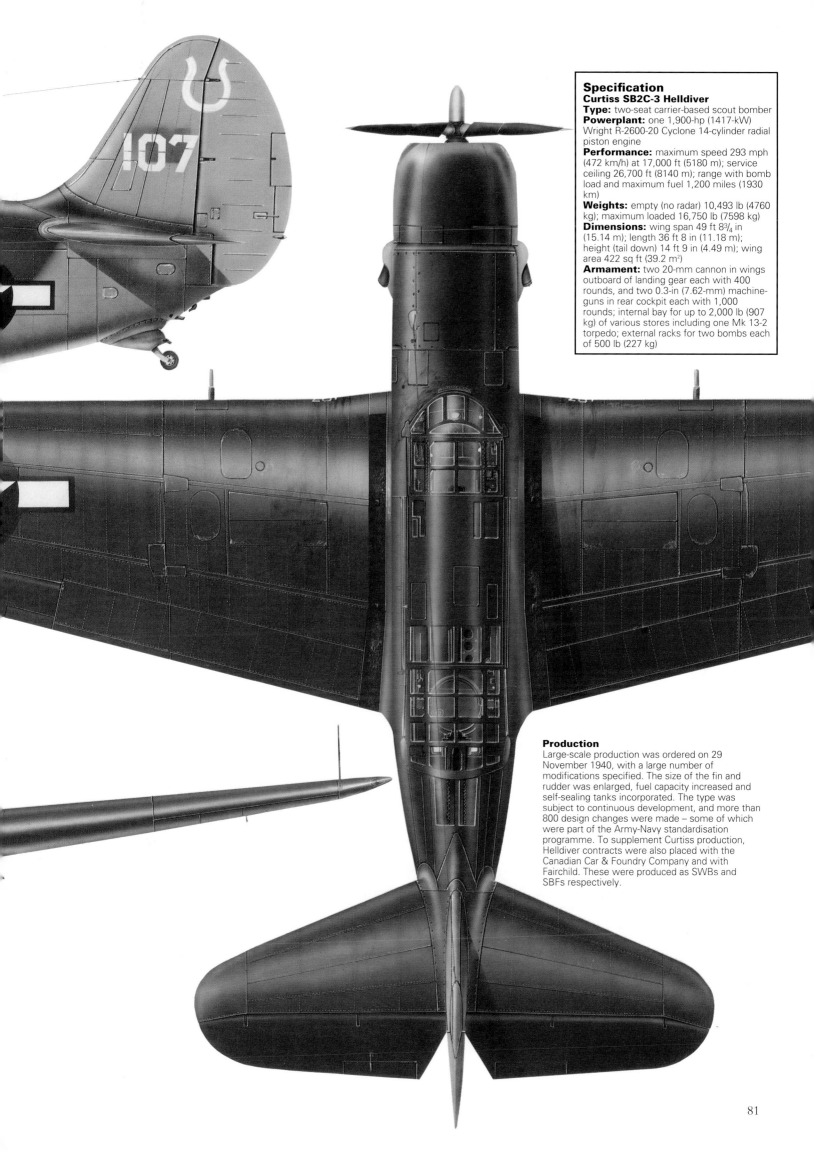

Specification
Curtiss SB2C-3 Helldiver
Type: two-seat carrier-based scout bomber
Powerplant: one 1,900-hp (1417-kW)
Wright R-2600-20 Cyclone 14-cylinder radial
piston engine
Performance: maximum speed 293 mph
(472 km/h) at 17,000 ft (5180 m); service
ceiling 26,700 ft (8140 m); range with bomb
load and maximum fuel 1,200 miles (1930
km)
Weights: empty (no radar) 10,493 lb (4760
kg); maximum loaded 16,750 lb (7598 kg)
Dimensions: wing span 49 ft 8¾ in
(15.14 m); length 36 ft 8 in (11.18 m);
height (tail down) 14 ft 9 in (4.49 m); wing
area 422 sq ft (39.2 m²)
Armament: two 20-mm cannon in wings
outboard of landing gear each with 400
rounds, and two 0.3-in (7.62-mm) machine-
guns in rear cockpit each with 1,000
rounds; internal bay for up to 2,000 lb (907
kg) of various stores including one Mk 13-2
torpedo; external racks for two bombs each
of 500 lb (227 kg)

Production

Large-scale production was ordered on 29
November 1940, with a large number of
modifications specified. The size of the fin and
rudder was enlarged, fuel capacity increased and
self-sealing tanks incorporated. The type was
subject to continuous development, and more than
800 design changes were made – some of which
were part of the Army-Navy standardisation
programme. To supplement Curtiss production,
Helldiver contracts were also placed with the
Canadian Car & Foundry Company and with
Fairchild. These were produced as SWBs and
SBFs respectively.

Curtiss SB2C Helldiver

Curtiss SB2C Helldiver variants

XSB2C-1: single prototype (BuNo 1758) with R-2800-8 engine; rebuilt or modified several times; armament of two nose machine-guns and one machine-gun in rear cockpit
SB2C-1: first production version with four wing machine-guns; total 200
SB2C-1A: designation applied to A-25A; subsequently used again for 410 ex-USAAF A-25As for US Marine Corps
SB2C-1C: first version with 20-mm wing guns and hydraulic flaps; total 778
XSB2C-2: single aircraft (00005) tested with twin Edo floats; intended as reconnaissance bomber
XSB2C-3: one aircraft (00008) re-engined with R-2600-20
SB2C-3: production version with R-2600-20, four-bladed propeller and APG-4 low-level bomb system; total 1,112
SB2C-3E: SB2C-3 aircraft fitted with APS-4 3-cm radar in pod
SB2C-4: similar to SB2C-3 but with underwing hardpoints for rockets and up to 1,000 lb (454 kg) of bombs; 2,045
SB2C-4E: SB2C-4 with APS-4 radar pod
XSB2C-5: two SB2C-4s converted with increased

internal fuel capacity and other minor modifications
SB2C-5: production version of XSB2C-5; total 970 with 2,500 cancelled
XSB2C-6: two SB2C-3s completely rebuilt with longer fuselage housing more fuel and powered by a 2,100-hp (1566-kW) Pratt & Whitney R-2800-28 Double Wasp
SBF-1: Fairchild-built SB2C-1; total 50; one used for trials as XSBF-1
SBF-3: Fairchild-built SB2C-3; total 150
SBF-4E: Fairchild-built SB2C-4E; total 100
SBW-1: CCF-built SB2C-1; total 38
SBW-1B: CCF-built Lend-Lease aircraft of SB2C-1C standard for the UK; total 28, of which 26 delivered
SBW-3: CCF-built SB2C-3; total 413
SBW-4E: CCF-built SB2C-4E; total 270
SBW-5: CCF-built SB2C-5; total 85 with 165 cancelled
A-25A Shrike: US Army version of SB2C-1 with various changes; total 900, of which 410 to USMC, 270 to US Navy and 10 to RAAF
Helldiver Mk I: Fleet Air Arm SBW-1B, 26 delivered as JW100/125, most to No. 1820 Sqn but rejected for operational use

A group of Helldivers return to their home carrier in tranquil skies after completing a bombing mission over Chichi-Jima, July 1944. Anticipating their imminent approach to the carrier deck, several aircraft have their arrester hooks already extended.

their ability to see the target and aim the dive! Operational effectiveness was considerably increased in this version by strengthening the wing and providing for the carriage of either two drop tanks, two 500-lb (227-kg) bombs or eight 5-in (127-mm) rockets.

The final production Helldiver was the **SB2C-5**, with slightly increased internal fuel capacity (an extra 29 Imp gal/132 litres). Most of the Columbus versions had more or less exact counterparts built by the two Canadian companies.

Curtiss was only too keenly aware of the indifferent qualities of the SB2C, and many years after the war the company president, Guy Vaughan, said it was "one of the biggest of the wartime crosses we had to bear."

After the war, Helldivers did not vanish overnight. A few continued flying with the US Navy Reserves and with various test units until at least 1947, often being used to tow targets. Others were operated in the attack role by the French Aéronavale, the navies of Italy and Portugal and the air forces of Greece and Thailand. French Helldivers played a significant role in the war in Indo-China, which did not collapse until 1954. One cannot blame the SB2C for that.

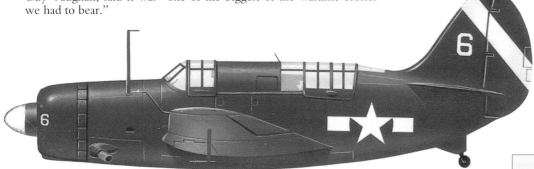

Left: In June 1944, the US Navy made its final large-scale change to its standard aircraft finishes, introducing glossy sea blue overall for carrier-based aircraft. This SB2C-3 was serving with VB-80 aboard USS Hancock (CV-19) off Iwo Jima in February 1945.

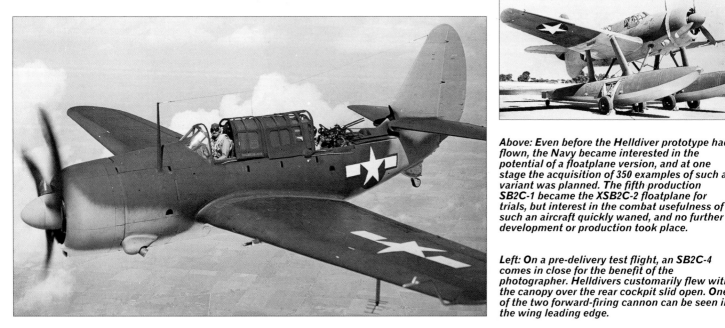

Above: Even before the Helldiver prototype had flown, the Navy became interested in the potential of a floatplane version, and at one stage the acquisition of 350 examples of such a variant was planned. The fifth production SB2C-1 became the XSB2C-2 floatplane for trials, but interest in the combat usefulness of such an aircraft quickly waned, and no further development or production took place.

Left: On a pre-delivery test flight, an SB2C-4 comes in close for the benefit of the photographer. Helldivers customarily flew with the canopy over the rear cockpit slid open. One of the two forward-firing cannon can be seen in the wing leading edge.

Curtiss SOC Seagull

An SOC-3 leaves the catapult of a US Navy cruiser during an attack on Wake Island, 5/6 October 1943. Designed in 1933, the Seagull seemed as much of an anachronism by 1941 as Britain's Fairey Swordfish – and, like its British contemporary, it gave valiant service throughout the war.

Last of the Curtiss biplanes to be used operationally by the US Navy, the **SOC Seagull** had a service history which very nearly duplicates that of the Royal Navy's Fairey Swordfish torpedo-bomber. Both originated in 1933, both should have become obsolescent during the early stages of World War II; and both remained operational until the end of the war, superbly surviving later designs intended to replace them.

The US Navy's requirement for a new scouting/observation aircraft was circulated to US manufacturers in early 1933, resulting in proposals from Curtiss, Douglas and Vought. A competing prototype was ordered from each under the respective designations of XO3C-1, XO2D-1 and XO5U-1, but it was the **XO3C-1**, ordered on 19 June 1933 and first flown in April 1934, which was ordered into production as the **SOC-1**. This changed

Right: A distinctive yellow ring around the US star insignia on this SOC-3 indicates that it was operating in the North African theatre at the time of Operation Torch, November 1942. The radioman/gunner stands to drop a message from the rear cockpit.

designation reflected the combination of scout and observation roles.

When first flown, the prototype was equipped with amphibious landing gear, the twin mainwheels being incorporated in the central float. However, standard production aircraft were built as floatplanes, with non-retractable tailwheel-type landing gear optional; but in any event they were easily convertible from one configuration to the other. Construction was mixed, with wings and tail unit of light alloy, a welded steel tube fuselage structure, and a mixture of light alloy and fabric covering. Other features of the design included braced biplane wings

which could be folded for shipboard stowage; the upper was the 'business' wing, carrying full-span Handley Page leading-edge slots, trailing-edge flaps and ailerons. The pilot and gunner/observer were accommodated in tandem cockpits, enclosed by a continuous transparent canopy with sliding sections for access. To provide a

maximum field of fire for the flexibly-mounted gun in the rear cockpit, the turtleback could be retracted.

Deliveries of the first SOC-1 production aircraft began on 12 November 1935. These were powered by 600-hp (447-kW) Pratt & Whitney R-1340-18 Wasp engines, and the first

A feature of the Curtiss SOC Seagull, in common with other US Navy scouting biplanes, was its interchangeable float-wheel undercarriage, aircraft usually changing to wheels when their parent ships were in port. From 1941, some wheeled versions also operated from escort carriers.

Curtiss SOC Seagull

squadrons to become fully equipped with the type comprised Scouting Squadrons VS-5B/-6B/-9S/-10S/-11S/-12S. Production of 135 SOC-1s was followed by 40 **SOC-2**s, supplied to contract with wheeled landing gear, and minor improvements in detail, and with R-1340-22 Wasp engines. A total of 83 **SOC-3**s was built, the aircraft being generally similar to the SOC-1. SOC-2s and -3s, after modification to install arrester gear during 1942, were redesignated **SOC-2A** and **SOC-3A** respectively. Curtiss also built three aircraft virtually the same as the SOC-3 for service with the US Coast Guard; these were acquired by the US Navy in 1942 and equipped with arrester gear to bring them up to SOC-3A standard. In addition to the SOC Seagulls built by Curtiss, 44 were produced by the Naval Aircraft Factory at Philadelphia. Basically

To replace the Seagull, the Navy sought development of a more advanced scout monoplane, as represented by the Curtiss SO3C. However, the planned successor failed to come up to expectations, and Seagull biplanes, in the process of retirement, were recalled to serve until the end of the war.

the same as the Curtiss-built SOC-3, these were designated **SON-1** or, if fitted with arrester gear, **SON-1A**.

Following termination of SOC production in early 1938, Curtiss became involved in the development and manufacture of a successor, designated SO3C Seamew. However, when the operational performance of the Seamew proved unsatisfactory it was withdrawn from first-line service, and all available SOCs were brought back into operational service, con-

tinuing to fulfil their appointed role until the end of the war.

Specification
Type: two-seat scout/observation aircraft
Powerplant: (SOC-1) one 600-hp (447-kW) Pratt & Whitney R-1340-18 Wasp radial piston engine
Performance: (floatplane) maximum speed 165 mph (266 km/h) at 5,000 ft (1525 m); cruising speed 133 mph (214 km/h); service ceiling 14,900 ft (4540 m);

range 675 miles (1086 km)
Weights: (floatplane) empty 3,788 lb (1718 kg); maximum take-off 5,437 lb (2466 kg)
Dimensions: span 36 ft 0 in (10.97 m); length 26 ft 6 in (8.08 m); height (floatplane) 14 ft 9 in (4.50 m); wing area 342 sq ft (31.77 m²)
Armament: one 0.30-in (7.62-mm) forward-firing machine-gun and one 0.30-in (7.62-mm) gun on flexible mount, plus external racks for up to 650 lb (295 kg) of bombs

Curtiss SO3C Seamew

In 1937 the US Navy invited proposals for the design of a scout monoplane which would offer improved performance over the Curtiss SOC Seagull then in operational service. In accordance with what at that time had become fairly conventional practice, it was required for operation from either ships at sea or land bases, which meant that easily interchangeable float/wheel landing gear was essential. From the proposals received, both Curtiss and Vought were awarded prototype contracts in May 1938 under the respective designations XSO3C-1 and XSO2U-1. The latter prototype, powered by a

550-hp (410-kW) Ranger XV-770-4 engine, was duly flown in competition, but it was the Curtiss design which was ordered into production.

One must assume that the performance of the Vought prototype left much to be desired, for the Curtiss **XSO3C-1**, first flown on 6 October 1939, was found to have serious instability problems. These were resolved finally by the introduction of upturned wingtips and increased tail surfaces, but the resulting aircraft in its landplane form was almost certainly the ugliest aircraft to be produced by the Curtiss company. Of all-metal construction, except for

In its production form, the SO3C-1 featured redesigned, upturned wingtips and increased fin area – changes that were indicative of early handling problems. However, few of the 141 SO3C-1 models saw active service, many being converted to radio-controlled target drones.

Third distinct Curtiss design to bear the name Seagull, the Model 82 was designed in 1938 to provide a successor for the SOC scout biplane. The prototype, illustrated, flew on 6 October 1939 and was tested in both landplane and single-float seaplane configuration.

fabric-covered control surfaces, the aircraft had wide-span split trailing-edge flaps, and the crew of two was accommodated in tandem enclosed cockpits. The float-

plane landing gear comprised a large single-step central float and strut-mounted wingtip stabiliser floats. The wheeled landing gear was conspicuous by having large streamlined fairings, and picking up on to the central float attachment points the main units were located so far aft that an undignified nose-up position on the ground and difficult ground handling resulted. An unusual feature was attachment of the front section of the dorsal fin to the top of the aft cockpit sliding hatch: when the hatch was slid forward the fin lost its foremost section. The prototype and production **SO3C-1**s, initially named **Seagull**, were powered by a 520-hp (388-kW) Ranger V-770-6 engine.

SO3C-1 production aircraft

began to enter service on board USS *Cleveland* in July 1942, and 300 were built before production was switched to the **SO3C-2**. This differed in having equipment for carrier operations, including an arrester hook, plus an under-fuselage rack on the landplane version to mount a 500-lb (227-kg) bomb. Production of this model totalled 456, of which 250 were allocated to Britain under Lend-Lease, although British records would seem to suggest that only 100 were received. The designation of the version originally intended for the Royal Navy was **SO3C-1B**, but those actually delivered were **SO3C-2C**s, with a more powerful engine, 24-volt electrical system and improved radio. Wheeled aircraft were equipped with hydraulic brakes. In British service these aircraft were designated **Seamew**, a name subsequently adopted by the US Navy, but none were used operationally in

An unusual feature of the SO3C was that a portion of the dorsal fin remained attached to the forward-sliding segment of the rear cockpit canopy. From a total of 795 SO3Cs built, 280 went to Britain, where the service name was Seamew or, for a radio-controlled target drone version, Queen Seamew.

Great Britain. Instead, they equipped Nos 744 and 745 Training Squadrons, based at Yarmouth, Canada, and Worthy Down, Hampshire, respectively, for the instruction of air gunners/wireless operators.

The unsatisfactory performance of the SO3C-1 in the US Navy led to its withdrawal from first-line service. Many were converted for use as radio-controlled targets, 30 being assigned to Britain, where they were designated **Queen Seamew** and used to supplement the fleet of de Havilland Queen Bee target aircraft.

In an attempt to retrieve the

situation, Curtiss introduced in late 1943 a lighter-weight variant equipped with the more powerful SGV-770-8 engine; designated **SO3C-3**, only 39 were built before production ended in January 1944. Plans to introduce an SO3C-3 variant with arrester gear, and production by the Ryan Aeronautical Corporation of SO3C-1s under the designation **SOR-1**, were cancelled.

Specification
Type: two-seat scout/observation aircraft
Powerplant: (SO3C-2C) one 600-hp (447-kW) Ranger SGV-770-8 inline

piston engine
Performance: (floatplane) maximum speed 172 mph (277 km/h) at 8,100 ft (2470 m); cruising speed 125 mph (201 km/h); service ceiling 15,800 ft (4815 m); range 1,150 miles (1851 km)
Weights: (floatplane) empty 4,284 lb (1943 kg); maximum take-off 5,729 lb (2599 kg)
Dimensions: (floatplane) span 38 ft 0 in (11.58 m); length 36 ft 10 in (11.23 m); height 15 ft 0 in (4.57 m); wing area 290 sq ft (26.94 m²)
Armament: (floatplane) one 0.30-in (7.62-mm) forward-firing machine-gun and one 0.50-in (12.7-mm) machine-gun on flexible mount, plus two 100-lb (45-kg) bombs or 325-lb (147-kg) depth charges beneath wings

Curtiss SC Seahawk

Development of the Curtiss SC Seahawk began in June 1942, when the US Navy requested the company to submit proposals for an advanced wheel/float scout aircraft. The easily convertible landing gear was required so that the aircraft could be operated from aircraft-carriers and land bases or be catapulted from battleships, and they were needed to replace the rather similar Curtiss Seamew and Vought Kingfisher which stemmed from 1937 procurements to satisfy a similar role. The Curtiss design proposal was submitted on 1 August 1942 but it was not until 31 March 1943 that a contract for two **XSC-1** prototypes was issued.

The XSC-1 was low-wing monoplane configuration and of all-metal construction. The wings had considerable dihedral on their outer panels, were provided with strut-mounted wingtip stabiliser floats, and were foldable for shipboard stowage. The main units of the tailwheel-type landing gear

Undaunted by the failure of the SO3C Seagull, the USN sought a further scout seaplane in 1943, contracting for prototypes of Curtiss' Model 97 in March 1943. Unlike its predecessors the SC Seahawk was a single-seater; development of ASH radar and other sensors made the role of an observer dispensable. This SC-1 was alongside USS Alaska (CB-1).

shared common attachment points with the larger single-step central float. If desired, auxiliary fuel could be accommodated in the central float. The powerplant comprised a 1,350-hp (1007-kW) Wright R-1820-62 Cyclone 9 radial engine.

The first prototype made its maiden flight on 16 February 1944, and was followed by 500 production **SC-1 Seahawks** which had been contracted in June 1943. All production aircraft were delivered as landplanes, the stabiliser floats and Edo central float being purchased separately and installed as and when required by the US Navy.

Delivery of production aircraft began in October 1944, the first of these equipping units aboard USS *Guam*. A second batch of 450 SC-1s was contracted, but of these only 66 had been delivered before contract cancellation at VJ-Day.

Meanwhile, an improved version had been developed using one of the original prototypes for modification. Changes included the installation of a 1,425-hp (1063-kW) R-1820-76 engine, provision of a clear-view cockpit canopy and jump seat behind the pilot, and changes in rudder and fin profile. The modified prototype, designated **XSC-1A**, led to receipt of a contract for similar

SC-2s, but only 10 had been delivered by the war's end.

Specification
Type: single-seat scout or ASW aircraft
Powerplant: one 1,350-hp (1007-kW) Wright R-1820-62 Cyclone 9 radial piston engine
Performance: maximum speed 313 mph (504 km/h) at 28,600 ft (8715 m); cruising speed 125 mph (210 km/h); service ceiling 37,300 ft (11370 m); range 625 miles (1006 km)
Weights: empty 6,320 lb (2867 kg); maximum take-off 9,000 lb (4082 kg)
Dimensions: span 41 ft 0 in (12.50 m); length 36 ft 4½ in (11.09 m); height 12 ft 9 in (3.89 m); wing area 280 sq ft (26.01 m²)
Armament: two 0.50-in (12.7-mm) machine-guns, plus two underwing bomb racks with a combined capacity of 650 lb (295 kg)

First operational examples of the SC-1 Seahawk were assigned to USS Guam in October 1944. The finish was the then-standard three-tone non-specular blue/blue/white, as on this example. Overall gloss sea blue soon followed.

Curtiss SNC Falcon

Under the designation **SNC**, the US Navy ordered in 1940 a variant of the Curtiss-Wright CW-21, the SNC indicating that it was required for deployment in the Scout Trainer category. By comparison with the CW-21 it had a very different fuselage to provide accommodation for a crew of two, and since the training role did not require such high performance as the CW-21 fighter, a very much lower-powered engine was installed.

Of all-metal construction, except for fabric-covered ailerons, the SNC had retractable landing gear of the tailwheel type; this was identical to that of the early manufacture CW-21s, with the main units retracting aft to be housed in split fairings beneath the wings. The major emphasis, however, had been to ensure that both accommodation and equipment should be suitable for an advanced training role. The tandem cockpits were enclosed by one extended canopy, the forward cockpit being intended for the pupil; dual flight controls were standard; and full instrumentation was duplicated so that the **Falcon**, as the SNC was unofficially named, could be used for instrument flight training. In addition, machine-guns and light bombs on underwing racks, could be installed when needed for gunnery or bombing training, and there were provisions for a radio transmitter and receiver and for an oxygen supply.

An initial contract for 150 of these trainers was placed in November 1940, and subsequent contracts for 150 and five aircraft brought numbers built to 305 before production was terminated.

Development of the Model CW-22 was initiated by Curtiss as a company venture in 1940, intended to provide a military basic trainer by using features of the CW-19B and the CW-21. Named Falcon, the CW-22 attracted US Navy backing with an order for 305 as scout trainers.

Specification
Type: two-seat advanced multi-role trainer
Powerplant: one 420-hp (313-kW) Wright R-975-E3 Whirlwind 9 radial piston engine
Performance: maximum speed 201 mph (323 km/h); cruising speed 195 mph (314 km/h) at 2,500ft (760m); service ceiling 21,900 ft (6675 m); range 515 miles (829 km)
Weights: empty 2,610 lb (1184 kg); maximum take-off 3,626 lb (1645 kg)
Dimensions: span 35 ft 0 in (10.67 m); length 26 ft 6 in (8.08 m); height 7 ft 6 in (2.29 m); wing area 174.3 sq ft (16.19 m²)
Armament: one forward-firing 0.30-in (7.62-mm) machine-gun and light bombs on underwing racks as required for training purposes

de Havilland Mosquito/F-8

Britain's most versatile warplane of World War II was supplied to the USAAF in some numbers under Reverse Lend-Lease arrangements, primarily to fulfil reconnaissance requirements. In October 1943 the British government agreed to supply 120 Mosquitoes to the USAAF as bombers, these being **B.Mk XX**s from Canadian production with 1,460-hp (1089-kW) Packard-built Merlin 31/33s. However, the RAF's needs for these bomber aircraft was so great that the numbers were revised to 90 B.Mk XXs from Canada and 30 fighter-bomber from British production. The B.Mk XXs were intended in USAAF use for the reconnaissance role, and were given the **F-8** designation to reflect this. In the event only 40 of these aircraft were delivered as F-8s, and they suffered from numerous problems. Only 11 of this number were dispatched to England for 8th AF service, being assigned initially to the 375th Servicing Squadron at Watton. They were not to see active service in US hands, and were passed on to the RAF in return for PR.Mk XVIs.

Over 100 of the much better **Mosquito PR.Mk XVI** were supplied by Britain to the 8th Air Force from early 1944, and this became the main US operational variant. The PR.Mk XVI was a pressurised high-altitude version which introduced a small astrodome for celestial navigation. It was powered by the two-stage Merlin 72/73 or 76/77. A handful of **T.Mk III** dual-control trainers were also supplied for conversion and continuation training.

The principal operational unit was the the 25th Bomb Group of the 8th Air Force, operating from Watton in Norfolk. The group had three squadrons, one of which (652nd BS) flew the Boeing B-17G. The 653rd Bomb Squadron (Light) and 654th Bomb Squadron (Special Purpose) operated the PR.Mk XVI from April 1944. The 653rd was principally concerned with weather reconnaissance, and its aircraft for this task featured red tail surfaces. The Mosquito was chosen for its high speed for operations in areas where heavy fighter opposition could be expected. The 654th operated PR.Mk XVIs with H2X radar for reconnaissance, and 12 aircraft fitted for chaff dispensing. The latter role became more important as the war progressed, the Mosquitoes laying a chaff screen ahead of the bomber formations to disguise their approach.

A shadowy unit which operated the Mosquito PR.Mk XVI was the 856th Bomb Squadron (36th

More than 70 Mosquito PR.Mk XVIs served with the USAAF in Europe, for photo-reconnaissance duties. This example flew with the 653rd Bombardment Squadron (Light), a part of the 25th Bombardment Group (R) in the 8th Air Force at Watton, Norfolk, in 1944/45.

BS prior to August 1944), part of the Special Operations Group – better known as the 'Carpetbaggers' – which operated from Harrington on missions into Europe to support clandestine resistance and surveillance work. The unit flew seven PR.Mk XVIs, equipped to communicate with agents and Resistance groups in occupied territory. Forty such missions were conducted under Operation Red Stocking, while Operation Skywave accounted for a further six sorties.

Specification
de Havilland
Mosquito PR.Mk XVI
Type: two-seat unarmed reconnaissance aircraft
Powerplant: two Rolls-Royce Merlin 72/73 12-cylinder piston engines, each rated at 1,710 hp (1276 kW)
Performance: maximum speed 408 mph (657 km/h)
Weights: maximum take-off 25,917 lb (11756 kg)
Dimensions: wing span 54 ft 2 in (16.50 m); length 41 ft 6 in (12.65 m); height 15 ft 3 in (4.65 m); wing area 454.0 sq ft (42.18 m²)

During 1943, the USAAF acquired 40 Canadian-built Mosquitoes (five B.Mk VII and 35 B.Mk XX) and converted them for photo-reconnaissance, with the designation F-8. Two Fairchild K-17 or K-22 cameras were fitted in the forward bomb bay, and additional fuel tanks in the rear bay.

Douglas A-20 Havoc

When they fashioned their **Model 7B** in 1938, designers Jack Northrop and Edward Heinemann of Douglas Aircraft at El Segundo, California, had not even been told that the US Army wanted twin engines, let alone tricycle gear, on an attack aircraft. The contract they won for a prototype was a reluctant one, and the snub-nosed, scoop-bellied machine driven by twin Pratt & Whitney R-1830C engines of 1,100 hp (820 kW) which made its first flight on 26 October 1938 gave little hint of the type's promise, its life being all too brief before a fatal crash on 23 January 1939.

By January 1940, when the Armée de l'Air began operating the type with its 19th and 32nd Air Groups, initially in Morocco and later in metropolitan France, the UK was interested in the machine and the US Army had placed an order. For the remainder of its career there was confusion and overlap between the company term DB-7 and the USAAF designation **A-20**, and between the popular names **Boston** and **Havoc**. Many RAF machines officially had both names, the UK's involvement beginning with a 20 February 1940 contract for 150 aircraft, soon raised to 300 and eventually totalling 781, which became the **DB-7B Boston Mk III** to distinguish them from the 200 French and 18 Belgian **DB-7 Boston Mk I**s and 249 French DB-7A **Boston Mk II**s diverted to the UK after the fall of France.

Crew positions

Though armament, intended mission and modifications varied widely, the Boston/Havoc twin-engine, shoulder-wing monoplane was fixed in its essential configuration virtually from the beginning. Pilots transitioning from 'tail-draggers', and so new to tricycle gear, sat high and comfortable and proceeded straight down the taxiway with a commanding view, the cockpit being located forward of the propeller arc for this reason.

With Heinemann's improvements following the Model 7B prototype came, too, a handicap which would remain with the Boston/Havoc series: because of the narrowness of the fuselage, each crewman was fixed in his own position, unable to exchange places with the other. Injury or death to the pilot would require the nose bombardier and dorsal gunner to bail out. On some machines, for emergencies, token dual controls in the rear gunner's compartment consisted of stick, rudder pedals and throttle, although the gunner had landing problems if an immobilised pilot could not communicate his vision through the intercom.

The essential design was conventional, with a slender, aluminium alloy, semi-monocoque fuselage and a single-spar, aluminium-alloy wing with fabric-covered control surfaces. Armament varied, but the

Progenitor of the A-20 series, the Douglas Model 7B featured a glazed nose for bomb-aiming, with four forward-firing 'package' guns on the fuselage sides or a 'solid' nose mounting six guns for ground attack, in addition to dorsal and ventral guns and internal bombs.

basic design called for fixed forward-firing machine-guns in various combinations while the rear gunner operated a pivoted 0.303-in (7.7-mm) machine-gun in both dorsal and ventral locations, each stocked with 500 rounds of ammunition. Two tandem bomb-bays could accommodate a load of 1,200 lb (544 kg) of bombs, a typical machine having two vertical racks for six 100-lb (45-kg) bombs. Up to 2,000 lb (907 kg) could be carried over shorter distances.

In 1940, as the RAF received deliveries of aircraft originally intended for France, night-fighters were badly needed. It was decided that some Boston Mk IIs would be converted locally as night-fighters or intruders. These received flame-trap engine exhausts and four British

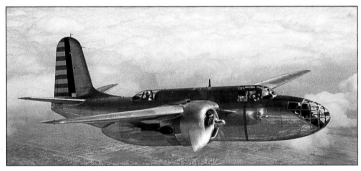

Above: Examples of the Douglas DB-7B were already in service with the Armée de l'Air in France by the time the first A-20 for the USAAC left the Douglas plant at El Segundo in 1940. Photo shows the first A-20A.

Left: Douglas A-20G Havocs of the 671st Bombardment Squadron, 416th BG, part of the 9th Air Force, cross the English Channel on a combat mission during the build-up to D-Day in 1944. Tight formations were maintained in order to provide concentrated defensive fire against attacking enemy fighters.

Flying over Los Angeles in 1941, these Havocs – apparently A-20As – are finished in the then-standard olive drab over upper surfaces and sides, with neutral grey undersides. Tail insignia had been deleted in February 1941; the red centre in the star marking went in May 1942.

0.303-in (7.7-mm) machine-guns mounted in the lower forward fuselage, plus a single Vickers 'K' gun in the rear cockpit. The glazed nose was retained. With the RAF's No. 23 Squadron, these low-level night intruders commenced sorties over Europe in the winter of 1940-41. Nicknamed variously 'Rangers' and 'Moonfighters', these aircraft were officially designated the **Havoc Mk I (Intruder)**. Later machines with no fewer than 12 0.303-in (7.7-mm) nose guns and with airborne intercept radar became the **Havoc Mk II (Night Fighter)**.

These craft functioned well as RAF night-fighters in the period just following the Battle of Britain. In December 1940 the **Havoc Mk III**, later renamed **Havoc Mk I (Pandora)**, operated against Nazi attackers while rigged with a 2,000-ft (610-m) cable with an explosive mine at its end. An air-to-air kill was actually scored by Sergeant Wrat of No. 93 Squadron in aircraft AX913 before this bizarre method outlived its usefulness.

Turbinlite development

Almost as bizarre was the Turbinlite, the nose-mounted night lamp devised by Wing Commander W. Helmore as a 2,700 million candle-power searchlight for the nose of the **Havoc Mk II (Turbinlite)** aircraft. Batteries were carried in the Havoc's bay, but because of their weight this night-fighter variant was unarmed. The Havoc was to home in on a German attacker and, at a 3,000-ft (914-m) distance, illuminate it for accompanying Hawker Hurricanes, which eventually served side-by-side with the Douglas machine in RAF squadrons. Ten such squadrons roamed the night using this useless 'search and kill' technique until December 1942. Far too much effort was expended in trying to aim beams of light, when bullets would have been more effective. It scored one victory: an RAF Stirling.

To add to the confusion of names, British-ordered DB-7B Boston Mk IIIs which began to arrive in May 1941 were locally modified as night-fighters to become the **Boston Mk III (Intruder)**. These

In its A-20G-1-DO version, the Havoc mounted four 20-mm M2 cannon plus two 0.5-in (12.7-mm) machine-guns in the nose. Most examples of this type went to the Soviet Union, which received a total of 3,066 A-20s direct from the US and others by local transfers.

could carry a gun pack containing four 20-mm Hispano cannon beneath their fuselages. The Royal Canadian Air Force's No. 418 Squadron at Debden, formed in November 1941, operated this type, as did No. 605 Squadron RAF. Thereafter the role of the Boston/Havoc as a night-fighter waned, and RAF Bomber Command used the Boston Mk III on the offensive, including No. 88 Squadron's search for the battle-cruiser *Scharnhorst* in February 1942. Boston crews flew a few missions against Germany itself but usually struck targets in France, the Netherlands and Belgium. RAF Boston crews were particularly courageous in the raid on the Philips radio works at Eindhoven on 6 December 1942. Eventually, heavier bombers with greater load-carrying capability eclipsed the Boston as a bomber in the European theatre, though the type soldiered on performing other duties, such as smoke-laying off the Normandy beaches in 1944. Improved **Boston Mk IV** and **Boston Mk V** aircraft with power-operated dorsal turrets fought in the Middle East and Italy.

Douglas Boston Mk III cutaway key

1. Starboard fabric covered elevator
2. Starboard tailplane
3. Elevator tab
4. Tail navigation and signal lights
5. Tailcone
6. Rudder tab
7. Fabric covered rudder construction
8. Rudder hinges
9. Pitot tube
10. Fin tip fairing
11. Aerial cable
12. Port elevator
13. Port tailplane
14. Fin leading edge
15. Tailfin construction
16. Elevator hinge control
17. Rudder hinge control
18. Fin attachment joints
19. Tailplane stub attachment
20. Tailplane root fillet
21. Tail bumper
22. Tailcone construction
23. Rear fuselage/tailcone joint frame
24. Fin root fillet
25. Flare launcher tube
26. Reconnaissance flares
27. Ventral hatch cover, open
28. Rear gunner's side window
29. Reconnaissance camera
30. Vickers 0.303-in (7.7-mm) ventral machine-gun
31. Spare ammunition containers
32. Map case
33. Upper identification light
34. Dorsal gun stowage doors
35. Dorsal gun mounting ring
36. Twin Browning 0.303-in (7.7-mm) machine-guns
37. Armour plated screen
38. Rear gunner's cockpit enclosure
39. Rear gunner's seat
40. Rear emergency control column
41. Trailing aerial reel
42. Wing root trailing edge fillet
43. Starboard inboard flap
44. Rear spar attachment joint
45. Radio racks
46. Rear gunner's canopy cover, open position
47. Radio receiver
48. Cabin heater pack
49. Propeller de-icing fluid tank
50. D/F loop aerial
51. Aerial mast
52. Radio transmitters
53. Main spar attachment joint
54. Inboard wing panel construction
55. Main undercarriage wheel well housing
56. Hydraulic flap jack
57. Nacelle tail fairing
58. Outer flap construction
59. Main spar
60. Outer wing panel attachment joint
61. Wing ribs
62. Aileron tab
63. Fabric covered aileron construction
64. Formation light
65. Starboard navigation light
66. Leading edge nose ribs
67. Wing stringer construction
68. Mainwheel doors
69. Starboard mainwheel
70. Undercarriage leg strut
71. Mainwheel pivot mounting struts
72. Hydraulic retraction jack
73. Engine exhaust
74. Sloping fireproof bulkhead
75. Engine bearer struts
76. Cooling air exit flaps
77. Exhaust collector ring
78. Detachable engine cowlings
79. Hamilton Standard three-bladed, constant speed propeller, 11 ft 3 in (3.43-m) diameter
80. Propeller hub pitch change mechanism
81. Propeller reduction gearbox
82. Wright GR-2600-A5B Cyclone, two-row radial engine
83. Upper cooling air duct
84. Carburettor air intake
85. Starboard oil tank, 19-Imp gal (86-litre) capacity
86. Fuel filler cap
87. Inboard main fuel tank, 110-Imp gal (500-litre) capacity
88. Bomb door central hydraulic jack
89. Wing root fillet
90. Cockpit heater duct
91. Bomb doors
92. Forward pair of 500-lb (227-kg) bombs, maximum bomb load 2,000 lb (907 kg)
93. Lower fuselage box beam construction
94. Bomb carrier
95. Bomb hoist winches
96. Bomb bay top decking
97. Cockpit entry hatch aft extension
98. Port inboard main fuel tank, 110-Imp gal (500-litre) capacity
99. Engine nacelle fairing

Douglas A-20 Havoc

With the first aircraft snapped up by France and the UK (including 16 ordered by Belgium), other purchasers came later, including the USAAF with its order for the **A-20 Havoc**. A few A-20s were sent to the Dutch on Java in 1942, some of these being captured by the Japanese. The USSR received no fewer than 3,125 Boston/Havoc aircraft (as compared with 1,800 for the UK and 1,962 operated by US forces) and these were delivered via transit points as distant as Fairbanks, Alaska, and Tehran, Iran. Though it seems doubtful, some American pilots believe they encountered Soviet Lend-Lease Havocs flown by their adversaries in the early days of the Korean War. After 1945 Boston/Havoc aeroplanes appeared in a number of countries, and one of the best-preserved such machines in the world today is located at the Air and Space Museum in Brasilia, restored to post-war Brazilian air force markings.

The USAAF A-20, **A-20A** and **A-20B** Havocs saw little action, although numerous A-20Bs ended up in Soviet colours. Some of the

Left: Modified from an A-20G-5-DO, this is a P-70B-2, carrying centimetric radar in the nose fairing to permit use in the night-fighter training role. For this purpose, the P-70B-2 remained unarmed.

Above: This model was the first of 59 P-70 night fighters, carrying AI Mk IV radar, with wing- and nose-mounted aerials. A ventral tray mounts four 20-mm cannon, and the aircraft is finished in matt black overall.

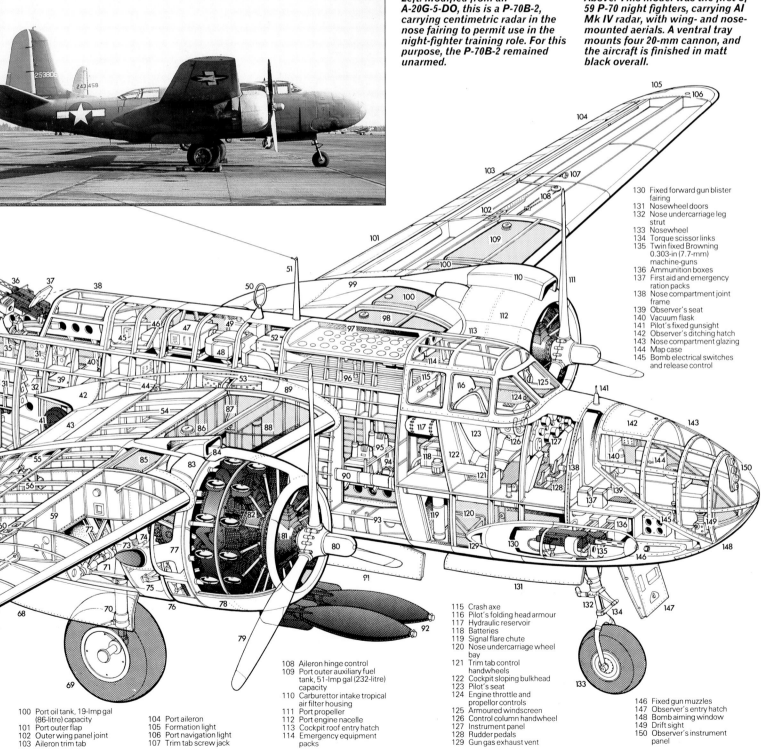

100 Port oil tank, 19-Imp gal (86-litre) capacity
101 Port outer flap
102 Outer wing panel joint
103 Aileron trim tab
104 Port aileron
105 Formation light
106 Port navigation light
107 Trim tab screw jack
108 Aileron hinge control
109 Port outer auxiliary fuel tank, 51-Imp gal (232-litre) capacity
110 Carburettor intake tropical air filter housing
111 Port propeller
112 Port engine nacelle
113 Cockpit roof entry hatch
114 Emergency equipment packs
115 Crash axe
116 Pilot's folding head armour
117 Hydraulic reservoir
118 Batteries
119 Signal flare chute
120 Nose undercarriage wheel bay
121 Trim tab control handwheels
122 Cockpit sloping bulkhead
123 Pilot's seat
124 Engine throttle and propellor controls
125 Armoured windscreen
126 Control column handwheel
127 Instrument panel
128 Rudder pedals
129 Gun gas exhaust vent
130 Fixed forward gun blister fairing
131 Nosewheel doors
132 Nose undercarriage leg strut
133 Nosewheel
134 Torque scissor links
135 Twin fixed Browning 0.303-in (7.7-mm) machine-guns
136 Ammunition boxes
137 First aid and emergency ration packs
138 Nose compartment joint frame
139 Observer's seat
140 Vacuum flask
141 Pilot's fixed gunsight
142 Observer's ditching hatch
143 Nose compartment glazing
144 Map case
145 Bomb electrical switches and release control
146 Fixed gun muzzles
147 Observer's entry hatch
148 Bomb aiming window
149 Drift sight
150 Observer's instrument panel

Douglas A-20 Havoc

Above: Eight A-20B-DLs – this is one of them – were transferred from the USAAF to the USN and were then given the designation BD-2, and were used for target-towing and general utility duties. One other Havoc, originally the YF-3 reconnaissance variant, became the sole BD-I.

Above: This A-20G-20 was in service with a unit of the Ninth Air Force, which took its place alongside the Eighth Air Force in operations in the European Theater of Operations and flew more than 100,000 combat missions in the run-up to D-Day.

earliest Havocs built were converted as **P-70** night-fighters. All Segundo and Long Beach production transferred to Douglas' Santa Monica, California, facility in 1941, where the **A-20C** model emerged, powered by two 1,600-hp (1193-kW) R-2600-23 engines.

It was the A-20C which arrived in England in June 1942 with the USAAF's 15th Bomb Squadron, seeing action over the Continent and later in North Africa. This and other combat squadrons soon began to acquire the **A-20G** solid-nose model, which dispensed with a bombardier in favour of nose armament eventually comprising six 0.5-in (12.7-mm) guns. The similar **A-20H** model had 1,700-hp (1268-kW) R-2600-29 engines.

Pacific action

In the Pacific, Havocs first saw action when they came under fire in the December 1941 Pearl Harbor attack. A-20As modified by Major 'Pappy' Gunn of the 3rd Bomb Group to carry heavy nose armament were used for low-level strafing in New Guinea. Against the Germans, Havocs ranged across North Africa, then began striking targets in Sicily and on the Italian boot. USAAF Havocs fought on in Normandy and across Europe to Berlin, although the more advanced Douglas A-26 Invader replaced the Havoc in some squadrons by VE-Day.

The final major operational variants of the USMF Havoc were the **A-20J** and **A-20K**, which returned to a glazed nose of a new and more streamlined frameless type. Some A-20Ks were painted all black for night interdiction missions. Representative operators in the European theatre of operations included the 47th, 409th, 410th and 416th Bomb Groups, and in the Pacific the 3rd, 312th and 417th Bomb Groups. The last Havoc built (7,385 by Douglas, 140 by Boeing) rolled off the Santa Monica production line on 20 September 1944.

What was it like to fly the Boston/Havoc at the height of its operational career? "Sensational!" is the word used by one pilot who remembers. Instruments, hydraulics and electrical systems on the Boston/Havoc were regarded as being of a very good quality. Visibility from the pilot's perch in his cockpit was excellent.

The pilot entered the cockpit by opening a unique, 7-ft (2.13-m) hinged, fold-out hatch and lowering himself into his seat. His cabin floor was foam-carpeted, all pipes and wires were protected behind insulation, and the roomy, armoured cockpit provided a 'sports car'

Below: An A-20G-1-DO bears the 'white star' marking that prevailed from May 1942 to July 1943. Thereafter a white rectangle was added to each side of the blue disc, with a red (and later blue) border added. Some A-20G versions mounted six guns in the nose.

In the closing stages of the war and in the early post-war period, Havocs were adapted for the training role. This, for example, is a TA-20K-15-DO, with armament removed and a yellow rudder and fuselage band indicating its training application.

In the A-20K version of the Havoc, the transparent bomb-aimer's nose first introduced on the A-20J was combined with the airframe and powerplant of the A-20H. The final A-20K, delivered on 20 September 1944, was also the last DB-7/A-20 built. Of the 413 A-20Ks produced, 90 went to the RAF under Lend-Lease and were known as Boston Mk Vs.

feel. On glazed-nose variants, the bombardier sat well forward with a door in the bottom for entry and exit.

Apart from the remarkable taxiing qualities mentioned earlier, the Havoc had in many respects the feel of a single-seat aircraft, and could indeed be taken 'upstairs' by the pilot alone. The aeroplane needed a full take-off roll, but having attained 110 mph (177 km/h) it fairly leaped from the runway. The landing gear retracted very quickly because of the hydraulic accumulator. and the initial rate of climb was impressive. Once aloft, the machine manoeuvred with great agility and, apart from its high top speed of around 335 mph (539 km/h), was in every respect a first-rate performer.

The high, single-rudder tail unit was astonishingly responsive to the pilot's pressure on the pedals, a brief experiment with a twin rudder tail on the 131st DB-7 Boston having been found to offer no improvement. Some pilots found the Boston/Havoc a bit too powerful for easy control, at least on letdown and final approach, and felt that the brakes were not effective enough and needed changing too often. It was not a forgiving machine when it came to ending a fast landing in a full stop on a short runway.

British success with this aircraft type as a night-fighter may have inspired the USAAF's decision to convert early A-20 Havocs to the P-70 night-fighter standard. Seizing the opportunity offered by the availability of British air intercept radar, the first A-20 (39-735) was modified to **XP-70** standard in 1942. A further 59 A-20 aircraft were

converted to P-70s, while 13 A-20Cs received the **P-70A-1** nomenclature and 26 A-20Gs were designated **P-70A-2**. Further conversions were the sole **P-70B-1** and a small number of **P-70B-2**s.

Throughout the P-70 programme various attempts were made to refine and develop the night-fighting capability of the aircraft, but while these were going on Northrop (the firm which designer John Northrop had restarted in 1938) was designing its own twin-engine night-fighter from the ground up, and in the end the P-61 Black Widow offered considerable performance advantages over the P-70. The P-70 was used primarily for training, although a few saw combat in the Pacific.

The 'foto' reconnaissance designation **F-3** was applied to camera-carrying Havocs after a proposal for an 'observation' derivative, the **O-53**, was cancelled. A single A-20 (39-741) was revamped to become the **XF-3**, carrying cameras in the fuselage bay, while two further machines became **YF-3**s with various optical and camera installations. The potential of the Havoc as an intelligence-gathering platform, especially because of its good performance at low altitude, was obvious. Once 'bugs' were worked out of the photo-reconnaissance configuration, 46 A-20J and A-20K aircraft were modified to become **F-3A**s. The relatively small number of F-3A reconnaissance craft actually saw a disproportionate employment in battle, and one F-3A Havoc was the first Allied aircraft to touch down at Itazuke air base in Japan following the 15 August 1945 surrender.

Left: This dramatic picture captures the A-20 doing what it did best: low-level bombing. Such raids were mounted against a variety of targets in the Pacific theatre, including shipping and, as here, Japanese airfields. The enemy bomber which has so far escaped the Havoc's attentions is a Mitsubishi G4M 'Betty'.

Right: This A-20B operated with the 84th Bomb Squadron, 47th BG, at Mediouna in Morocco in December 1942. Large patches of brown have been applied over the original olive drab to provide a makeshift desert camouflage. The A-20B was the first version built at Long Beach.

Specification
Douglas A-20G Havoc
Type: two/three seat light attack bomber
Powerplant: two 1,600-hp (1193-kW) Wright R-2600-23 Double Cyclone radial piston engines
Performance: maximum speed 339 mph (546 km/h) at 12,400 ft (3780 m); cruising speed 272 mph (439 km/h); initial climb rate 2,910 ft (887 m) per minute; service ceiling 25,800 ft (7865 m); range 1,090 miles (1754 km) with normal bombload
Weights: empty 15,984 lb (7265 kg); maximum take-off 27,200 lb (12338 kg)
Dimensions: span 61 ft 4 in (18.69 m); length 48 ft 0 in (14.63 m); height 17 ft 7 in (5.36 m); wing area 464.0 sq ft (43.11 m²)
Armament: six fixed forward-firing 0.5-in (12.7-mm) machine-guns in the nose, two 0.5-in (12.7-mm) machine-guns in the power-operated dorsal turret and one manually-operated 0.5-in (12.7-mm) machine-gun in the ventral position, plus up to 3,000 lb (1364 kg) of bombs

Powerplant
The initial version featured the Pratt & Whitney Twin Wasp R-1830-S3C4G which gave 1,200 hp (895 kW) at 2,700 rpm on take-off. The first of the DB-7 series to be built to a US Army specification had two 1,500-hp (1119-kW) Wright Cyclone R-2600-7 engines, with exhaust-driven turbo-superchargers. The A-26G was fitted with two 1,600-hp (1193-kW) Wright R-2600-23 14-cylinder radial air-cooled engines with two-speed superchargers.

Douglas DB-7/A-20 variants
A-20C: 808 built as part of Lend-Lease programme, primarily for delivery to RAF as Boston Mk IIIAs and to the Soviet air force, but a substantial number were taken over by USAAF after 7 December 1941 to establish A-20 training groups in the US
A-20D: projected lightweight model with R-2600-7 engines
A-20E: 17 A-20As modified with R-2600-11 engines and other refinements
XA-20F: single A-20A modified with 37-mm cannon in nose and two remotely operated turrets
A-20G: major production version based on A-20D airframe but with R-2600-23 engines; solid nose for four 20-mm cannon or six 0.5-in (12.7-mm) machine-guns; 2,850 built, later blocks introducing twin-gun Martin dorsal turret
CA-20G: post-war transport conversion
A-20H: similar to A-20G but with R-2600-29 engines; 412 built
TA-20H: handful of A-20Hs used for training
A-20J: based on A-20G but with frameless glazed nose; slightly longer; 450 built
TA-20J: trainer conversion of A-20J
A-20K: similar to A-20H but with A-20J glazed nose; 413 built
TA-20K: trainer conversion of A-20K
XF-3: single A-20 fitted with cameras in rear portion of bomb bay
YF-3: two A-20s with cameras and rear manned turret
F-3A: 46 A-20J and A-20K converted for photo-reconnaissance tasks
O-53: reconnaissance version of A-20B; 1,489 ordered but subsequently cancelled
XP-70: conversion of A-20 to night-fighter role with solid nose housing AI radar, four 20-mm cannon in ventral pack, R-2600-11 engines and accommodation for pilot and radar operator
P-70: 59 A-20s converted for use as night-fighter trainers
P-70A-1: 13 A-20Cs converted to night-fighters with R-2600-23 engines and six or eight 0.5-in (12.7-mm) machine-guns in ventral tray
P-70A-2: 65 night-fighter trainer conversions of A-20G; all moveable guns removed
P-70B-1: one A-20G with SCR-720 centimetric radar in modified solid nose and six guns in blisters each side of the forward fuselage
P-70B-2: 105 night-fighter conversions from A-20G and A-20J with SCR-720 or SCR-729 radar and guns in ventral tray
BD-1: designation of single A-20A transferred to USMC for target tug/utility duties
BD-2: eight A-20Bs transferred to USMC

Development
Development of the A-20 was swift and service delivery to France, via Casablanca, began early in 1940. Despite its advanced design and contrast with contemporary French equipment it got quickly into action, some 80 seeing action before the collapse of France. A huge depot was set up at Burtonmead for modifying American aircraft, and through here passed hundreds of DB-7s in 1940-41. Small numbers served with the US Navy as the DB-1 and -2. By 1943 production was centred on a new series of which the basic model was the A-20G. Most A-20s operated at low or medium level, in almost all theatres of war, making level bombing runs and, in some areas, using their heavy front armament to good effect in low-level attacks on surface targets.

Camouflage

The early A-20s had their upper surfaces camouflaged in a factory pattern of olive drab 41 and medium green 42. The US-built night fighters were finished in flat black overall. Olive and 'desert' pink were often used in camouflage schemes applied locally in North Africa from November 1942. The addition of 'invasion stripes' to the rudder was common to the 9th Air Force's 647th BS, 410th BG while operating from the UK after D-Day.

Douglas A-20 Havoc
646th Bomb Squadron
410th Bomb Group, Gosfield, 1944

The A-20 was first flown on 26 October 1938 and attracted the attention of the French Purchasing Commission in the USA, eventually ordering 170 of the DB-7 version. Before the fall of France in June 1940 about half of the order had been delivered. The balance was taken over by the UK and these were known as the Boston Mks I and II; some were modified for night intruder and night fighter duties and known as the Havoc. The Boston Mk III was the designation applied to 300 British-ordered DB-7Bs. The A-20 was the definitive version for the USAAF, and when the last Havoc came off the production line on 28 September 1944 a total of 7,385 had been built. This total included export versions and some 3,125 Havocs went to Russia – only some 800 less than the US Army. USAAF 43-10195 (illustrated) has one of a sub-block of 93 A-20G-35s built in 1943 at the main Douglas plant at Santa Monica.

Configuration

The A-20 was a twin-engined bomber, with wings mounted high on the fuselage sides and with a tricycle undercarriage. Big Pratt & Whitney Twin Wasp radial engines were faired with long nacelles underslung on the wing. The fuselage was comparatively deep with a narrow cross-section and 'stepped' cockpit and dorsal gun position.

Operational service

Although A-20s were serving overseas with Army squadrons before the end of 1941, the A-20C was the first model to see combat in the hands of the 15th Bombardment Squadron. This unit arrived in the UK in May 1942 and went into action on 4 July. The 15th BS, and others which followed it to Europe and North Africa, eventually served with the 9th and 15th Air Forces, achieving considerable success in the tactical and intruder role. In addition to service in Europe and North Africa, the A-20Gs and A-20Hs saw operation in the Pacific theatre, principally in the low-altitude attack role.

Douglas A-26 Invader

<D>esigned as a replacement for the A-20 Havoc by the superb engineering team under Edward H. Heinemann at Douglas' El Segundo, California, facility, the prototype **XA-26** (42-19504) took to the air on 10 July 1942 with Ben Howard at the controls. The outward appearance of the **Invader** would change little, but the first machine was unusual in having camouflage and large propeller spinners.

Heinemann began from the outset with three variants: the XA-26 (later **A-26C**) bomber with a glazed nose for the bomb-aimer, the **A-26A** night-fighter with radar and four ventral 20-mm cannon, and the **XA-26B** with a solid gun-nose for the ground-attack role. The night-fighter version was short-lived, but bombers churned from the Douglas production lines at Long Beach, California, and Tulsa, Oklahoma.

The **A-26B** had six 0.5-in (12.7-mm) machine-guns in the nose (later increased to eight), remotely controlled dorsal and ventral turrets each with two 0.5-in (12.7-mm) guns and up to 10 more 12.7-mm (0.5-in) guns in underwing and underfuselage packs. Heavily armoured and able to carry up to 4,000 lb (1814 kg) of bombs, the A-26B with its maximum speed of 355 mph (571 km/h) at 15,000 ft (4570 m) was the fastest Allied bomber of World War II. Some 1,355 A-26B models were followed by 1,091 **A-26C** machines with a bomb-aimer's glazed nose.

Early difficulties

Rushed into combat with the 553rd Bomb Squadron at Great Dunmow in England by September 1944 and soon also operating in France and Italy, the Invader was flying air-to-ground missions against the Germans before its bugs were ironed out. Pilots were delighted with its manoeuvrability and ease of handling, but the A-26 began life with a needlessly complex and fatiguing instrument array, a weak nose gear that collapsed easily, and an early cockpit canopy that was difficult to hold in the 'open' position for bail-out. Time and attention resolved these problems, and A-26 pilots took pride in mastering a demanding but effective bombing machine.

In the European theatre of operations, Invaders flew 11,567 sorties and dropped 18,054 tons of bombs. The A-26 was also nimble enough to hold its own when intercepted by fighters. Major Myron L. Durkee of the 386th Bomb Group at Beaumont in France was credited with the probable kill of a Messerschmitt Me 262 jet fighter on 19 February

A feature of the Douglas A-26 was the variety of interchangeable noses designed for its use. This formation from the 386th BG includes glazed-nose A-26Cs (nearest camera) of the 554th BS and A-26Bs of the 553rd BS. Both versions carry eight additional guns in underwing packs.

The XA-26-DE prototype, first flown on 10 July 1942, featured the transparent bombardier-type nose. At this stage, the designed armament for such a variant comprised forward-firing 0.5-in (12.7-mm) guns and two similar guns each in dorsal and ventral turrets.

The prototype Invaders – this is the XA-26-DE – were distinguished by unusually large propeller spinners. The engines were 2,000-hp P&W R-2800 radials which, in successively improved versions, would power all the main production variants of the Douglas twin.

Right: The 'RG' codes identify this A-26B-15-DT 'Stinky' as an aircraft of the 552nd BS, 386th BG, at Beaumont-sur-Oise, France, in April 1945. The group identity band had previously been used on its B-26s.

Above: Natural metal had become the normal finish for operational aircraft of the USAAF by the time the A-26s entered service. Early evaluation of the A-26 in the SWPA showed problems, but European experience with the type proved more favourable, and A-20 units in the 9th Air Force were progressively re-equipped.

Right: Operating from Great Dunmow, Essex, the 386th Bombardment Group flew the first A-26 missions in September 1944, and found the type superior to both the A-20 and B-26. Four A-26B-20-DLs of the 522nd BS here share apron space with B-26s at Beaumont-sur-Oise, May 1945.

1945. Some 67 Invaders were lost to all causes in the European theatre, but A-26s also chalked up seven confirmed air-to-air kills.

In the Pacific war, the Invader also progressed from an inauspicious beginning to respectable achievement. With its 2,000-hp (1491-kW) Pratt & Whitney R-2800-27 Double Wasp engines and sea-level speed of no less than 373 mph (600 km/h), the Invader was a potent anti-shipping and ground-attack weapon, but crews did not immediately take to it. A-20 pilots who had reigned supreme in their high, single-seat cabins now found themselves with a YOT ('you over there') in the navigator's right-hand jump-seat, essentially a co-pilot without controls. When rockets and bombs were expended in unison in a low-level pass, debris from the rockets' explosions damaged the underside of the Invader. In the belief that the new machine was unsuited for low-level work, the 5th Air Force commander, General George Kenney, actually requested not to convert from the A-20 to the A-26. But conversions went ahead, the A-26 also replacing North American B-25 Mitchells in some units. The A-26 served with the USAAF's 3rd, 41st and 319th Bomb Groups in operations against Formosa, Okinawa and Japan itself. Invaders were active near Nagasaki when it was razed by the war's second atomic bomb on 9 August 1945.

An A-26B-35-DL from a training unit in the ZI (Zone of the Interior) in the US displays the eight-gun nose armament and two-gun remotely-controlled dorsal turret. The large propeller spinners flown on the prototypes were discarded for all production models.

Following the conversion of one A-26B to target-tug configuration under the designation XJD-1, the Navy procured 140 JD-1s (converted from A-26Cs). Some of these were subsequently converted for the launch and direction of drones.

After VJ-Day the aircraft which may have arrived one war too soon became a familiar sight at Far East air bases, including those in Korea. Many were converted to other tasks as **CB-26B** (transport), **TB-26B/C** (trainer), **VB-26B** (staff transport), **EB-26C** (missile test vehicle) and **RB-26B/C** (reconnaissance). The type went on to compile an impressive combat record in many post-war conflicts, including Korea, Vietnam and Algeria.

The **XA-26D** and **XA-26E** were one-off prototypes for Invader variants cancelled at the war's end, the latter variant being a glazed-nose high-performance model with R-2800-83 radials and designed to match the performance of the XA-26D solid-nose model with 2,100-hp (1566-kW) R-2800-83s. In a post-war attempt to capitalise on the jet engine, a single Invader (4434586) was converted to **XA-26F** with the addition of a 1,600-lb (7.12-kN) thrust General Electric I-16 (or J31) jet engine in the rear fuselage.

Specification
Douglas A-26C
Type: three-seat light attack bomber
Powerplant: two 2,000-hp (1491-kW) Pratt & Whitney R-2800-79 Double Wasp radial piston engines
Performance: maximum speed 373 mph (600 km/h); service ceiling 22,100 ft (6735 m); range 1,400 miles (2253 km)
Weights: empty 22,850 lb (10365 kg); maximum take-off 35,000 lb (15876 kg)
Dimensions: wing span 70 ft 0 in (21.34 m); length 51 ft 3 in (15.62 m); height 18 ft 3 in (5.56 m); wing area 540 sq ft (50.17 m²)
Armament: six 0.50-in (12.7-mm) machine-guns (two each in nose, dorsal and ventral positions) plus up to 4,000 lb (1814 kg) of bombs internally

Above: This eight-gun Invader of the 89th Bomb Squadron, 3rd Bomb Group, bellied in on Okinawa following one of the last strikes of the war on 11 August 1945. The 3rd BG was the only 5th Air Force group to convert to the A-26 by war's end. Its olive drab Invader squadrons were identified by fin-tip colour, the 89th being green with a white band.

Douglas A-26B Invader cutaway drawing key

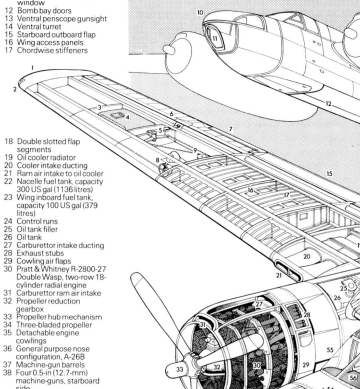

1 Starboard wing tip
2 Starboard navigation light
3 Water tank
4 Water tank filler cap
5 Aileron hinge control
6 Starboard aileron
7 Aileron tab
8 Landing and taxiing light
9 Control cables
10 Bombardier nose configuration, A-26C
11 Optically flat bomb sight window
12 Bomb bay doors
13 Ventral periscope gunsight
14 Ventral turret
15 Starboard outboard flap
16 Wing access panels
17 Chordwise stiffeners
18 Double slotted flap segments
19 Oil cooler radiator
20 Cooler intake ducting
21 Ram air intake to oil cooler
22 Nacelle fuel tank, capacity 300 US gal (1136 litres)
23 Wing inboard fuel tank, capacity 100 US gal (379 litres)
24 Control runs
25 Oil tank filler
26 Oil tank
27 Carburettor intake ducting
28 Exhaust stubs
29 Cowling air flaps
30 Pratt & Whitney R-2800-27 Double Wasp, two-row 18-cylinder radial engine
31 Carburettor ram air intake
32 Propeller reduction gearbox
33 Propeller hub mechanism
34 Three-bladed propeller
35 Detachable engine cowlings
36 General purpose nose configuration, A-26B
37 Machine-gun barrels
38 Four 0.5-in (12.7-mm) machine-guns, starboard side
39 Spent cartridge case chutes
40 Gun bay bracing strut
41 Two 0.5-in (12.7-mm) machine-guns, port side
42 Ammunition feed chutes
43 Ammunition boxes
44 Pitot tube
45 Nosewheel torque scissors
46 Rearward retracting nosewheel
47 Shock absorber leg strut
48 Nosewheel doors
49 Nosewheel bay/flight deck floor support construction
50 Rudder pedals
51 Interchangeable nose joint bulkhead
52 Autopilot controls
53 Back of instrument panel
54 Fixed foresight
55 Windscreen panels
56 Instrument panel shroud
57 Reflector sight
58 Clear vision panel
59 Control column
60 Pilot's seat
61 Pilot's side window panel/ entry hatch
62 Bomb release controls
63 Bombardier/navigator's seat
64 Canopy hatch handles
65 Bombardier/navigator's side canopy/entry hatch
66 Oxygen regulator
67 Radio racks
68 Radio receivers and transmitters
69 Bomb-bay armoured roof panel
70 Wing root fillet
71 Armoured wing spar bulkhead
72 Hydraulic accumulators
73 Air filter
74 De-icing valve
75 Aerial mast
76 Double slotted flap inboard section
77 Wing de-icing fluid reservoir
78 De-icing fluid pump
79 Starboard bomb rack, five 100-lb (45-kg) HE bombs

Left: An A-26C-30-DT undergoes an engine test at the maker's airfield. Douglas built 2,236 A-26s in the 'B' and 'C' versions at its Tulsa plant (DT), and 210 at Long Beach (DL). Extensive production of the A-26D was cancelled, but many Invaders survived to serve in Korea.

Right: An early-model A-26B shows the strangely offset arrangement of the six guns in the nose. Later A-26Bs had eight guns in a symmetrical pattern. Douglas mocked up a nose section, combining the two to mount 14 guns, but this did not progress to the hardware stage. Six guns – three in each wing – later replaced the drag-producing underwing packs.

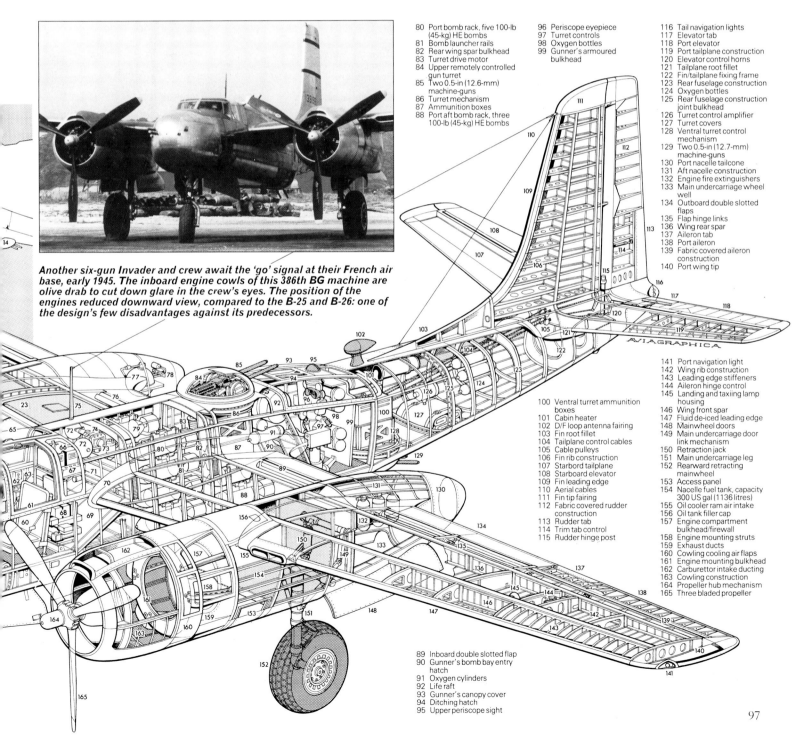

Another six-gun Invader and crew await the 'go' signal at their French air base, early 1945. The inboard engine cowls of this 386th BG machine are olive drab to cut down glare in the crew's eyes. The position of the engines reduced downward view, compared to the B-25 and B-26: one of the design's few disadvantages against its predecessors.

80 Port bomb rack, five 100-lb (45-kg) HE bombs
81 Bomb launcher rails
82 Rear wing spar bulkhead
83 Turret drive motor
84 Upper remotely controlled gun turret
85 Two 0.5-in (12.6-mm) machine-guns
86 Turret mechanism
87 Ammunition boxes
88 Port aft bomb rack, three 100-lb (45-kg) HE bombs
89 Inboard double slotted flap
90 Gunner's bomb bay entry hatch
91 Oxygen cylinders
92 Life raft
93 Gunner's canopy cover
94 Ditching hatch
95 Upper periscope sight
96 Periscope eyepiece
97 Turret controls
98 Oxygen bottles
99 Gunner's armoured bulkhead
100 Ventral turret ammunition boxes
101 Cabin heater
102 D/F loop antenna fairing
103 Fin root fillet
104 Tailplane control cables
105 Cable pulleys
106 Fin rib construction
107 Starbord tailplane
108 Starboard elevator
109 Fin leading edge
110 Aerial cables
111 Fin tip fairing
112 Fabric covered rudder construction
113 Rudder tab
114 Trim tab control
115 Rudder hinge post
116 Tail navigation lights
117 Elevator tab
118 Port elevator
119 Port tailplane construction
120 Elevator control horns
121 Tailplane root fillet
122 Fin/tailplane fixing frame
123 Rear fuselage construction
124 Oxygen bottles
125 Rear fuselage construction joint bulkhead
126 Turret control amplifier
127 Turret covers
128 Ventral turret control mechanism
129 Two 0.5-in (12.7-mm) machine-guns
130 Port nacelle tailcone
131 Aft nacelle construction
132 Engine fire extinguishers
133 Main undercarriage wheel well
134 Outboard double slotted flaps
135 Flap hinge links
136 Wing rear spar
137 Aileron tab
138 Port aileron
139 Fabric covered aileron construction
140 Port wing tip
141 Port navigation light
142 Wing rib construction
143 Leading edge stiffeners
144 Aileron hinge control
145 Landing and taxiing lamp housing
146 Wing front spar
147 Fluid de-iced leading edge
148 Mainwheel doors
149 Main undercarriage door link mechanism
150 Retraction jack
151 Main undercarriage leg
152 Rearward retracting mainwheel
153 Access panel
154 Nacelle fuel tank, capacity 300 US gal (1136 litres)
155 Oil cooler ram air intake
156 Oil tank filler cap
157 Engine compartment bulkhead/firewall
158 Engine mounting struts
159 Exhaust ducts
160 Cowling cooling air flaps
161 Engine mounting bulkhead
162 Carburettor intake ducting
163 Cowling construction
164 Propeller hub mechanism
165 Three bladed propeller

97

Douglas XA/XB-42 Mixmaster

Under the initial designation **XA-42** for an attack bomber, redesignated subsequently **XB-42** as a bomber, Douglas designed and built two prototypes and one static test airframe under a contract received from the US Army Air Force on 25 June 1943. Named **Mixmaster** by the company, this unusual aircraft had a mid-set cantilever monoplane wing, cruciform tail surfaces and tricycle landing gear, whose main units retracted aft to be housed in the sides of the fuselage. The broad and deep fuselage provided accommodation for a crew of three, consisting of a bomb-aimer/navigator in the nose, with the pilot and co-pilot in a side-by-side cockpit well forward on the fuselage, each beneath an individual canopy; the fuselage also incorporated a large internal bomb bay, as well as housing the twin-engined powerplant in a compartment immediately to the rear of the pilot's cockpit. The two Allison V-1710 engines drove, via shafting and a reduction gear-

box in the tailcone, two three-bladed contra-rotating pusher propellers to the rear of the tail unit.

Despite its unusual features, when first flown on 6 May 1944 the Mixmaster more than lived up to expectations. The second prototype was flown for the first time on 1 August 1944, soon afterwards being modified by the addition of a single canopy over the pilot/co-pilot cockpit. This prototype was destroyed in a crash during December of that year, but by that time the USAAF had decided not to proceed with production of this design, awaiting instead the development of higher-performance turbojet-powered bombers. As an interim step to allow evaluation of turbine power, the first prototype was given mixed powerplant comprising two 1,375-hp (1025-kW) Allison V-1710-133 piston engines to drive the propellers, plus two 1,600-lb (7.12-kN) thrust Westinghouse 19XB-2A turbojets mounted in underwing

nacelles. Redesignated **XB-42A**, this aircraft was used for performance testing over several months before being retired at the end of June 1949. The XB-43 Jetmaster was an all-jet conversion of the XB-42.

Specification
Douglas XB-42
Type: three-seat bomber prototype
Powerplant: two 1,325-hp (988-kW) Allison V-1710-125 V-12 piston engines
Performance: maximum speed 410 mph (660 km/h) at 29,400 ft (8960 m); cruising speed 312 mph (502 km/h); service ceiling 29,400 ft (8960 m);

The XB-42 demonstrated a spectacular performance with a large bombload and a four-gun defensive armament. The advent of jet bombers and the ending of the war halted its development.

standard range 1,800 miles (2897 km) **Weights:** empty 20,888 lb (9475 kg); maximum take-off 35,700 lb (16193 kg) **Dimensions:** span 70 ft 6 in (21.49 m); length 53 ft 8 in (16.36 m); height 18 ft 10 in (5.74 m); wing area 555.0 sq ft (51.56 m²) **Armament:** two 0.5-in (12.7-mm) machine-guns in each of two remotely-controlled wing turrets, plus an internal bombload of 8,000 lb (3629 kg)

Douglas B-18 Bolo

Faced with a US Army Air Corps requirement of early 1934 for a bomber with virtually double the bombload and range capability of the Martin B-10, which was then the USAAC's standard bomber, Douglas had little doubt that it could draw upon engineering experience and design technology of the DC-2 commercial transport which was then on the point of making its first flight.

Private venture prototypes to meet the US Army's requirements were evaluated at Wright Field, Ohio, in August 1935, these including the Boeing Model 299, Douglas DB-1 and Martin 146. The first was to be

Lacking dedicated maritime patrol aircraft when the war started, the USAAF had 122 B-18As modified during 1942 to this B-18B version, with ASV radar in the nose and Mk IV MAD in a tail 'sting'.

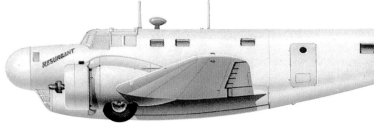

built as the B-17 Flying Fortress, the last was produced as an export variant of the Martin B-10/B-12 series, and the **DB-1** (Douglas Bomber 1) was ordered into immediate production under

the designation **B-18** in January 1936. Derived from the commercial DC-2, the DB-1 prototype retained a basically similar wing, tail unit and powerplant. There were, however, two differences

in the wing: while retaining the same basic planform of the DC-2, that of the DB-1 had a 5-ft 6-in (1.68-m) reduction in span and was mounted in a mid-wing instead of low-wing position. The powerplant comprised two 930-hp (694-kW) Wright R-1820-45 Cyclone 9 engines, each driving a three-bladed constant-speed metal propeller. The entirely new fuselage was considerably deeper than that of the commercial transport, to provide adequate accommodation for a crew of six, and to include nose and dorsal turrets, a bomb aimer's

First to operate the pug-nosed B-18 medium bombers was the 7th Bombardment Group at Hamilton Field, California, in 1937. Improved B-18As were issued later, but the advent of the B-17 and B-24 limited the usefulness of the Bolo in the bombing role.

position, and an internal bomb bay; there was, in addition, a third gunner's position, with a ventral gun discharging via a tunnel in the underfuselage structure.

A total of 133 B-18s was covered by the first contract, this number including the single DB-1 which had served as a prototype. True production aircraft, however, had a number of equipment changes, producing an increase in the normal loaded weight. The last B-18 to come off the production line differed by having a power-operated nose turret, and carried the company identification **DB-2**, but this feature did not become standard on subsequent production aircraft.

The next contracts, covering 217 **B-18A**s, were placed in June 1937 (177) and mid-1938 (40). This version differed by having the bomb aimer's position

extended forward and over the nose gunner's station, and the installation of more powerful Wright R-1820-53 engines. Most of the USAAC's bomber squadrons were equipped by B-18s or B-18As in 1940, and the majority of the 33 B-18As which equipped the USAAC's 5th and 11th Bomb Groups, based on Hawaiian airfields, were destroyed when the Japanese launched their attack on Pearl Harbor.

When B-18s were replaced in first-line service by B-17s in 1942, some 122 were equipped with search radar and magnetic anomaly detection (MAD) equipment for deployment in the Caribbean on anti-submarine patrol. The Royal Canadian Air Force also acquired 20 B-18As which, under the designation **Digby I**, were employed on

B-18As of the 7th Bombardment Group gather on the flight line at March Field in May 1940 for a Wing Exercise. The extended nose for improved bomb-aiming was an obvious distinguishing feature of the 'A' model Bolo, of which 217 examples were built.

maritime patrol. The designation **B-18C** applied to two other aircraft reconfigured for ASW patrol. Another two aircraft were converted for use in a transport role as **C-58**s, but many others were used similarly without conversion or redesignation.

Specification

Type: medium bomber and ASW aircraft
Powerplant: (B-18A) two 1,000-hp (746-kW) Wright R-1820-53 Cyclone 9 radial piston engines
Performance: maximum speed 215 mph (346 km/h) at 10,000 ft (3050 m); cruising speed 167 mph (269 km/h); service ceiling 23,900 ft (7285 m); range 1,200 miles (1931 km)
Weights: empty 16,321 lb (7403 kg); maximum take-off 27,673 lb (12552 kg)
Dimensions: span 89 ft 6 in (27.28 m); length 57 ft 10 in (17.63 m); height 15 ft 2 in (4.62 m); wing area 965 sq ft (89.65 m²)
Armament: three 0.30-in (7.62-mm) machine-guns (in nose, ventral and dorsal positions), plus up to 6,500 lb (2948 kg) of bombs

Generally similar to the B-18A, the Digby I was a version of the Douglas DB-1 for Canada. The RCAF acquired 20 of these in 1939-40 and used them to equip No. 10 (BR) Squadron for East Coast anti-submarine patrols from Gander until 1943.

Douglas XB-19A/XBLR-2

In 1934 the USAAC's Materiel Division issued its Project 'D' specification for a long-range bomber which could be used, if necessary, to provide support to troops in Alaska, Hawaii or Panama, this requiring the carriage of a 2,000-lb (907-kg) bombload at a speed of 200 mph (322 km/h) over a range of 5,000 miles (8047 km). It was certainly

very much of a challenge at a time when aircraft manufacturers had not then succeeded in creating a civil airliner to cope with the North Atlantic.

Boeing responded with its Model 294, of which a prototype was ordered under the designation XBLR-1 (Experimental Bomber Long Range - 1), later XB-15. The proposal received

from Douglas was for a very much larger aircraft, and a single prototype of this was contracted as the **XBLR-2**, later **XB-19**. When completed, it was then the largest aircraft built, with accommodation for a crew of 10 and maximum bombload of 36,000 lb (16329 kg). It flew for the first time on 27 June 1941. Powered by four Wright R-3350-5

Cyclone 18 engines, each with a take-off rating of 2,000 hp (1491 kW) and maximum continuous rating of 1,700 hp (1268 kW) at

Built to investigate the 'outer limits' of possible bomber development in the mid-1930s under USAAC sponsorship, the XB-19 was completed three years behind schedule, by which time such types as the B-17 and B-24 had already entered production.

Douglas XB-19A/XBLR-2

5,700 ft (1740 m), it was underpowered for the duty required of it, and had to await the availability of more powerful engines. When these eventually materialised the requirement had changed, and the Douglas giant was provided instead with four Allison inline engines and operated in a transport role during World War II under the designation **XB-19A**.

Specification
Type: long-range heavy bomber prototype

Powerplant: (XB-19A) four 2,600-hp (1939-kW) Allison V-3420-11 inline engines
Performance: (XB-19) maximum speed 209 mph (336 km/h); cruising speed 186 mph (299 km/h); service ceiling 22,000 ft (6705 m); maximum range 7,750 miles (12472 km)
Weights: (XB-19) empty 82,253 lb (37309 kg); maximum take-off 164,000 lb (74389 kg)
Dimensions: span 212 ft 0 in (64.62 m); length 132 ft 0 in (40.23 m); height 42 ft 9 in (13.03 m); wing area 4,492 sq ft (417.31 m²)
Armament: (XB-19) two 37-mm cannon, five 0.50-in (12.7-mm) machine-guns and six 0.30-in (7.62-mm) guns, plus up to 36,000 lb (16329 kg) of bombs

At one time called the Douglas Flying Behemoth, the XB-19 flew six months before the US was brought into the war by Japan's attack on Pearl Harbor. Following that event, the XB-19 was given regulation olive drab/grey finish and was armed for a few test flights over the Pacific.

Douglas B-23 Dragon

The Douglas B-18, designed to meet a US Army Air Corps requirement of 1934 for a high-performance medium bomber, was clearly not in the same league as the Boeing B-17 Flying Fortress, which was built to the same specification: 350 B-18s were procured in total, by comparison with almost 13,000 B-17s. In an attempt to rectify the shortcomings of their DB-1 design, in 1938 Douglas developed an improved version, and the proposal seemed sufficiently attractive for the US Army to award a contract for 38 of these aircraft under the designation **B-23** and with the name **Dragon**.

Although the overall configuration was similar to the earlier design, when examined in detail it was revealed as virtually a new aircraft. Wingspan was increased, the fuselage entirely different and of much improved aerodynamic form, and the tail unit had a much higher vertical fin and rudder. Landing gear was the same retractable tailwheel type, but the engine nacelles had been extended so that when the main units were raised in flight they were faired by the nacelle extensions and created far less drag. Greatly improved performance was expected from these refinements, plus the provision of 60 per cent more power by the use of two Wright R-2600-3 Cyclone 14 engines, each with a three-bladed constant-speed propeller. An innovation was the provision of a tail gun position, this being the

Several B-23s served in special roles, after it became clear that they had little value as bombers when newer types were already available. Here, the second production B-23 (serial 39-28) is engaged in snatch pickup trials with a Waco CG-4A troop-carrying glider.

Although it differed considerably from the B-18A it was designed to replace, the B-23 was ordered by the USAAC as a contract change affecting the final 38 B-18As already on order. This illustration shows the first aircraft, with temporary unglazed nose.

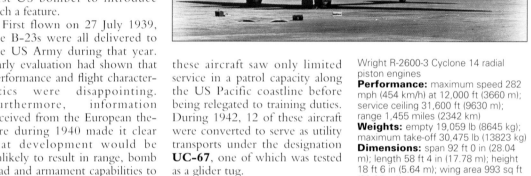

first US bomber to introduce such a feature.

First flown on 27 July 1939, the B-23s were all delivered to the US Army during that year. Early evaluation had shown that performance and flight characteristics were disappointing. Furthermore, information received from the European theatre during 1940 made it clear that development would be unlikely to result in range, bomb load and armament capabilities to compare with the bomber aircraft then in service with the combatant nations, or already beginning to emerge in the USA. As a result

these aircraft saw only limited service in a patrol capacity along the US Pacific coastline before being relegated to training duties. During 1942, 12 of these aircraft were converted to serve as utility transports under the designation **UC-67**, one of which was tested as a glider tug.

Specification
Type: four/five-seat medium bomber
Powerplant: two 1,600-hp (1193-kW)

Wright R-2600-3 Cyclone 14 radial piston engines
Performance: maximum speed 282 mph (454 km/h) at 12,000 ft (3660 m); service ceiling 31,600 ft (9630 m); range 1,455 miles (2342 km)
Weights: empty 19,059 lb (8645 kg); maximum take-off 30,475 lb (13823 kg)
Dimensions: span 92 ft 0 in (28.04 m); length 58 ft 4 in (17.78 m); height 18 ft 6 in (5.64 m); wing area 993 sq ft (92.25 m²)
Armament: one 0.50-in (12.7-mm) machine-gun in tail position and three 0.30-in (7.62-mm) guns in nose, dorsal and ventral positions

Douglas BTD Destroyer

Long before the Douglas SBD Dauntless proved itself to be an excellent dive-bomber at the Battles of Coral Sea and Midway, the US Navy was planning its successor. Douglas developed a two-seat advanced dive-bomber, of which two prototypes were ordered in June 1941 under the designation **XSB2D-1 Destroyer**. The aircraft introduced several new features, including an internal weapons bay and, for the first time on a carrierborne aircraft, a tricycle undercarriage.

By the time the aircraft first flew on 8 April 1943, the XSB2D-1 was seen not as a prototype for production but as a basis for a single-seat torpedo-bomber, as this role had by then been identified as being of greater

importance to the Pacific war. Accordingly the Destroyer was reworked with a single-seat cockpit, the addition of wing-mounted cannon, enlargement of the bomb bay to take a torpedo and the addition of airbrakes on each side of the fuselage.

The new aircraft received the designation **BTD-1**, and by 31 August 1943 orders stood at 358. The first production aircraft was delivered in June 1944, but only 28 had been delivered before the cancellation of the entire order shortly after VJ-Day. The type proved to have disappointing performance, and it never reached an operational unit.

Specification
Type: single-seat torpedo-bomber
Powerplant: one 2,300-hp (1715-kW) Wright R-3350-14 Cyclone 18 radial

piston engine
Performance: maximum speed 344 mph (554 km/h); service ceiling 23,600 ft (7195 m); range 1,480 miles (2382 km)
Weights: empty 11,561 lb (5244 kg); maximum take-off 19,000 lb (8618 kg)
Dimensions: wing span 45 ft 0 in (13.72 m); length 38 ft 7 in (11.76 m); height 13 ft 7 in (4.14 m); wing area 373 sq ft (34.65 m²)

The XSB2D-1 showed promise, but the Navy asked Douglas to eliminate planned dorsal and ventral turrets and provide a single-seat BTD-1 instead. This is one of the 28 BTD-1s completed before cancellation.

Armament: two 20-mm cannon in wings plus one torpedo or up to 3,000 lb (1451 kg) of bombs in internal bay

Douglas C-32/33/34/38/39/41/42

When TWA, needing to replace its Fokker airliners, found itself behind United Air Lines in the queue for Boeing's Model 247, it drew up a specification for an all-metal three-engined airliner with seats for at least 12 passengers and able to cruise at 146 mph (235 km/h) for more than 1,000 miles (1609 km). Douglas responded within a fortnight, having convinced TWA adviser Charles Lindbergh that the required performance could be achieved safely on only two engines. The prototype, identified as the **DC-1**, was rolled out on 22 June 1933 and, powered by two Wright R-1820 Cyclones, made its maiden flight at on 1 July.

The DC-1 never entered service, but was used for promotional purposes by TWA. An initial contract was signed for 25 production aircraft, with some structural changes which resulted

A military cargo version of the DC-2, the C-33 had enlarged vertical tail surfaces, cargo-loading door and strengthened floor. Producing 18 for the USAAC gave Douglas a useful basis for development of the ubiquitous C-47 Skytrain/Dakota.

in redesignation to **DC-2**, and the first example was delivered to TWA on 14 May 1934, entering service four days later.

The US Army Air Corps opened its purchases for fiscal year 1936 with a 16-seat DC-2, which was evaluated as the **XC-32** and which led to orders for two externally similar **YC-34**s and 18 **C-33**s, the latter type having enlarged vertical surfaces and a cargo door. In 1937 a C-33 was fitted with a DC-3 tail unit and redesignated **C-38**; from it was developed the **C-39**, with other DC-3 components, which included the wing centre-section

and landing gear, and 975-hp (727-kW) R-1820-55 engines. Thirty-five were ordered for the army's transport groups, entering service in 1939.

The fourth and fifth C-39s were converted while still on the production line to **C-41** and **C-42** standard, respectively. The first was fitted with 1,200-hp (895-kW) Pratt & Whitney R-1830-21 Twin Wasps and cleared to operate at a gross weight of 25,000 lb (11340 kg), while the second was powered by 1,200-hp (895-kW) Wright R-1820-53 Cyclones and cleared at 23,624 lb (10716 kg). Two more C-39s were later converted to **C-42**s, while 24 civil DC-2s impressed

in 1942 received the designation **C-32A**. These aircraft lacked cargo doors. Navy use was restricted to a single **R2D** procured in 1934, later augmented by four **R2D-1**s.

The DC-2s in military service were used extensively, especially in the early years of World War II, and are remembered especially for their role in carrying US survivors from the Philippines to Australia in December 1941.

Specification
Type: 18-seat cargo and passenger transport
Powerplant: (C-39) two 975-hp (727-kW) Wright R-1820-55 radial piston engines
Performance: maximum speed 210 mph (338 km/h) at 5,000 ft (1525 m); cruising speed 155 mph (249 km/h); service ceiling 20,600 ft (6280 m); range 900 miles (1448 km)
Weights: empty 14,729 lb (6681 kg); maximum take-off 21,000 lb (9525 kg)
Dimensions: span 85 ft 0 in (25.91 m); length 61 ft 6 in (18.75 m); height 18 ft 8 in (5.69 m); wing area 939 sq ft (87.23 m²)

With many of the features of the DC-3/C-47 series but retaining the smaller fuselage and outer wings of the DC-2, the C-39 was a major step in the evolution of the immortal Dakota. This Army Air Corps transport is seen over the US at the end of 1939, in the days before camouflage.

Douglas C-47 Skytrain

T he word 'ubiquitous' has been associated with a number of aircraft in wide-scale use during World War II, but the most ubiquitous of all has to be the Douglas C-47/C-53/R4D/ Skytrain/Skytrooper Dakota/'Gooney Bird'. Use any name you like for this superlative wartime transport aircraft, produced in greater numbers than any other in this category, with almost 11,000 manufactured by the time production ended in 1945: whatever you choose, it can be spelled 'dependable', for this was the secret of the type's greatness and enduring service life.

Its design originated from the DC-2/DST/DC-3 family of commercial transports that followed in the wake of the DC-1 prototype flown for the first time on 1 July 1933. The US Army had gained early experience of the basic aircraft after the acquisition of production DC-2s in 1936, followed by more specialised conversions for use as cargo and personnel transports. In August 1936 the improved DC-3 began to enter service with US domestic airlines, its larger capacity and enhanced performance making it an even more attractive proposition to the US Army, which very soon advised Douglas of the changes in configuration which were considered desirable to make it suitable for operation in a variety of military roles. These included the provision of more powerful engines, a strengthened rear fuselage to cater for the inclusion of large cargo doors, and reinforcement of the cabin floor to enable it to carry heavy cargo loads. Much of the basic design work had already been completed by Douglas, for a C-41 cargo prototype had been developed by the installation of 1,200-hp (895-kW) Pratt & Whitney Twin Wasp engines in a C-39 (DC-2) fuselage. In 1940, when the US Army began to issue contracts for the supply of these new transport aircraft under the designation **C-47**, the company was well prepared to meet the requirements and to get production under way. The only serious problem was lack of productive capacity at Santa Monica, where European demands for the DB-7 light bomber had already filled the factory floor, resulting in the C-47 being built in a new plant at Long Beach, California.

Obviously on a training mission over the American Midwest, probably in 1942, C-47s of the original Long Beach contract tow Waco CG-4A gliders. As seen here, the C-47 could be fitted with a glider towing attachment. With the C-53 the pointed tailcone was omitted and a neater towing cleat made integral with the fuselage, and this soon became standard on the C-47B also.

The most numerous of all versions was the C-47B. This example was from the single block of 300 aircraft, called C-47B-1-DL, manufactured at Long Beach. The main source, producing 3,064, was the other newly-built plant, at Kansas City. The colour was olive drab overall, with the Goodrich rubber de-icers on the leading edges left black.

Left: This aircraft, photographed on 9 January 1942, was the second C-47 to be built. At another Douglas plant, El Segundo, Ed Heinemann had produced the DC-5. This had better performance than the DC-3, tricycle landing gear and a flat level floor nearer the ground. General 'Hap' Arnold said, "Ed, we can afford only one transport. The DC-3 is further along in production, so we've decided that'll be the one for this war. Sorry."

Above: If General Arnold had picked the DC-5, hundreds of thousands of cargoes, such as this Jeep trailer, would have been much easier and quicker to load. This photograph was taken at an English airfield of the 9th Troop Carrier Command on D-Day, 6 June 1944. Aircraft 4315677 was one of 2,954 C-47A Skytrains built at Long Beach.

Right: A weatherbeaten C-47A of the Army Air Force 9th Troop Carrier Command is painted with the black/ white stripes hastily applied to every Allied aircraft that took part in the invasion of Hitler's Europe on 6 June 1944. This armada included well over 1,000 C-47s, C-47As, C-47Bs and C-53s.

Initial production version was the C-47, of which 953 were built at Long Beach, and since the basic structural design remained virtually unchanged throughout the entire production run this version will serve for a description of the structure and powerplant. Of all-metal light alloy construction, the cantilever monoplane wing was set low on the fuselage, and was provided with hydraulically operated split-type trailing-edge flaps; the ailerons comprised light alloy frames with fabric covering. The fuselage was almost circular in cross-section. The tail unit was conventional but, like the ailerons, the rudder and elevators were fabric-covered. Pneumatic de-icing boots were provided on the leading edges of wings, fin and tailplane. Landing gear comprised semi-retractable main units which were raised forward and upward to be housed in the upper half of the engine nacelles, with almost half of the main wheels exposed. The powerplant of the C-47 comprised two Pratt & Whitney R-1830-92 Twin Wasp engines, supercharged to provide an output of 1,050 hp (783 kW) at 7,500 ft (2285 m), and

each driving a three-bladed constant-speed metal propeller. The crew consisted of a pilot and co-pilot/navigator situated in a forward compartment, with the third member, the radio operator, in a separate compartment.

The all-important cabin could be equipped for a variety of roles. For the basic cargo configuration, with a maximum load of 6,000 lb (2722 kg), pulley blocks were provided for cargo handling and tie-down rings to secure it in flight. Alternative layouts could provide for the transport of 28 fully-armed paratroops, accommodated in folding bucket-type seats along the sides of the cabin, or for 18 stretchers and a medical team of three. Racks and release mechanism for up to six parachute pack containers could be mounted beneath the fuselage, and there were also underfuselage mountings for the transport of two three-bladed propellers.

The first C-47s began to equip the USAAF in 1941, but initially these were received only slowly and in small numbers, as a result of

This Skytrain was another of the single block of 300 C-47Bs built at Long Beach. It is ironic that, while the prototype B-17 had Pratt & Whitney engines yet the production bomber had Wright R-1820 Cyclones, most of the pre-war civil DC-3s had Cyclones, whereas the mass-produced wartime transports all had the Pratt & Whitney R-1830 Twin Wasp. The one firm that couldn't lose was another division of United Aircraft, Hamilton Standard, who provided the propellers. These were almost the only parts that got damaged in a belly landing, because the retracted main wheels were designed to support the aircraft.

Douglas C-47 Skytrain

The robust airframe of the Douglas transports was dramatically demonstrated by the safe return to its base in the Pacific theatre of this C-47, which in 1944 was attacked by a Japanese fighter. After exhausting all his ammunition the Japanese pilot deliberately rammed the C-47 in kamikaze style. The only aircraft not to return to base was the Japanese fighter. Note the external supply containers.

the establishment of the new production line at Long Beach which, like any other, needed time to settle down to routine manufacture. With US involvement in World War II in December 1941, attempts were made to boost production, but in order to increase the number of aircraft in service as quickly as possible DC-3s already operating with US airlines, or well advanced in construction for delivery to operators, were impressed for service with the USAAF.

As Douglas began to accumulate contracts calling for production of C-47s in thousands, it was soon obvious that the production line at Long Beach would be quite incapable of meeting requirements on such a large scale, so a second production line was established at Tulsa, Oklahoma. The first model to be built at Tulsa was the second production version, the **C-47A**, which differed from the C-47 primarily by the provision of a 24-volt, in place of a 12-volt, electrical system. Tulsa was to build 2,099 and Long Beach 2,832 of the type, 962 of them being delivered to the RAF which designated them Dakota IIIs. Last of the major production variants was the **C-47B**, which was provided with R-1830-90 or -90B engines that

Thanks to air supremacy gained by fighters (mainly F4Us) of the Marine Corps, R4D transports of the SCAT (South Pacific Combat Air Transport) were able to fly supply missions throughout the Solomon Islands without fighter escort. These R4D-3s were in March 1943 en route from Bougainville to Green Island. No. 81 is being flown by SCAT commander, Marine Colonel Allen Clark Koonce.

Douglas C-47 Skytrain cutaway key

1 Hinged nose cone, access to instruments and controls
2 Rudder pedals
3 Instrument panel
4 Windscreen de-icing fluid spray nozzle
5 Starboard propeller
6 Windscreen panels
7 Co-pilot's seat
8 Engine throttles
9 Control column
10 Cockpit floor level
11 Access panels to control cable runs
12 Pitot static tubes
13 Aerial cables
14 Propeller de-icing fluid tank
15 Pilot's seat
16 Cockpit bulkhead
17 Cockpit roof escape hatch
18 Whip aerial
19 Starboard landing/taxiing lamp
20 Windscreen de-icing fluid tank

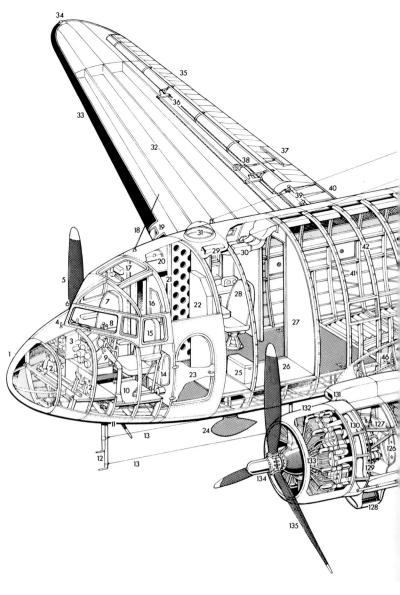

Douglas C-47 Skytrain

Left: Photographed off California in 1942 from an SBD, AAF 42-15887 was a C-53 Skytrooper. This troop transport had a single door, unlike the C47, which had wide double doors for Jeeps and similar bulky loads. Usually there were 28 inward-facing seats along the sides of the cabin. Unusually, this example does not have the 'cut-off' tailcone for glider-towing, first seen on the C-53.

Left: This photo dated 22 September 1943 shows the prototype XC-47C. Originally a normal C-47-DL, 42-5671 was converted into an amphibian by fitting two Edo Model 78 floats, each with front and rear retractable wheels and a 300-US gal fuel tank. Several field conversions into C-47Cs were carried out, but the expected need in the Pacific theatre did not materialise.

C-47-DL conversion 41-18496 became the sole XCG-17 glider. The Army Air Force test centre at Wright Field first carried out engine-off landings with C-47s, then used one C-47 to tow another (the towed aircraft using partial power on take-off) and finally tests with the glider conversion. The XCG-17 began testing in summer 1944 from Clinton County airport. Even with the nacelles left in place it had the flattest glide of any cargo glider tested up to that time, but a true glider version was never ordered.

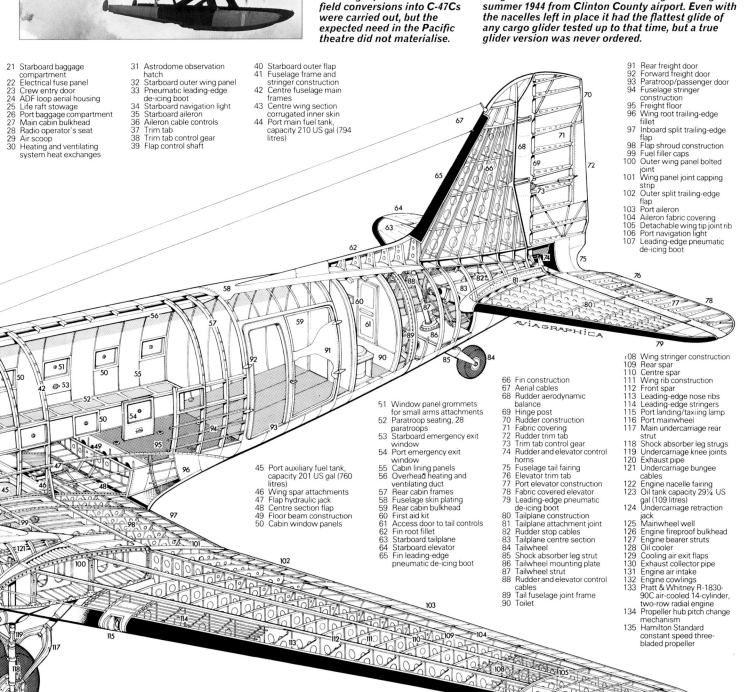

21 Starboard baggage compartment
22 Electrical fuse panel
23 Crew entry door
24 ADF loop aerial housing
25 Life raft stowage
26 Port baggage compartment
27 Main cabin bulkhead
28 Radio operator's seat
29 Air scoop
30 Heating and ventilating system heat exchanges
31 Astrodome observation hatch
32 Starboard outer wing panel
33 Pneumatic leading-edge de-icing boot
34 Starboard navigation light
35 Starboard aileron
36 Aileron cable controls
37 Trim tab
38 Trim tab control gear
39 Flap control shaft
40 Starboard outer flap
41 Fuselage frame and stringer construction
42 Centre fuselage main frames
43 Centre wing section corrugated inner skin
44 Port main fuel tank, capacity 210 US gal (794 litres)

45 Port auxiliary fuel tank, capacity 201 US gal (760 litres)
46 Wing spar attachments
47 Flap hydraulic jack
48 Centre section flap
49 Floor beam construction
50 Cabin window panels
51 Window panel grommets for small arms attachments
52 Paratroop seating, 28 paratroops
53 Starboard emergency exit window
54 Port emergency exit window
55 Cabin lining panels
56 Overhead heating and ventilating duct
57 Rear cabin frames
58 Fuselage skin plating
59 Rear cabin bulkhead
60 First aid kit
61 Access door to tail controls
62 Fin root fillet
63 Starboard tailplane
64 Starboard elevator
65 Fin leading-edge pneumatic de-icing boot

66 Fin construction
67 Aerial cables
68 Rudder aerodynamic balance
69 Hinge post
70 Rudder construction
71 Fabric covering
72 Rudder trim tab
73 Trim tab control gear
74 Rudder and elevator control horns
75 Fuselage tail fairing
76 Elevator trim tab
77 Port elevator construction
78 Fabric covered elevator
79 Leading-edge pneumatic de-icing boot
80 Tailplane construction
81 Tailplane attachment joint
82 Rudder stop cables
83 Tailplane centre section
84 Tailwheel
85 Shock absorber leg strut
86 Tailwheel mounting plate
87 Tailwheel strut
88 Rudder and elevator control cables
89 Tail fuselage joint frame
90 Toilet

91 Rear freight door
92 Forward freight door
93 Paratroop/passenger door
94 Fuselage stringer construction
95 Freight floor
96 Wing root trailing-edge fillet
97 Inboard split trailing-edge flap
98 Flap shroud construction
99 Fuel filler caps
100 Outer wing panel bolted joint
101 Wing panel joint capping strip
102 Outer split trailing-edge flap
103 Port aileron
104 Aileron fabric covering
105 Detachable wing tip joint rib
106 Port navigation light
107 Leading-edge pneumatic de-icing boot
108 Wing stringer construction
109 Rear spar
110 Centre spar
111 Wing rib construction
112 Front spar
113 Leading-edge nose ribs
114 Leading-edge stringers
115 Port landing/taxiing lamp
116 Port mainwheel
117 Main undercarriage rear strut
118 Shock absorber leg strugs
119 Undercarriage knee joints
120 Exhaust pipe
121 Undercarriage bungee cables
122 Engine nacelle fairing
123 Oil tank capacity 29¼ US gal (109 litres)
124 Undercarriage retraction jack
125 Mainwheel well
126 Engine fireproof bulkhead
127 Engine bearer struts
128 Oil cooler
129 Cooling air exit flaps
130 Exhaust collector pipe
131 Engine air intake
132 Engine cowlings
133 Pratt & Whitney R-1830-90C air-cooled 14-cylinder, two-row radial engine
134 Propeller hub pitch change mechanism
135 Hamilton Standard constant speed three-bladed propeller

had two-stage superchargers to offer high-altitude military ratings of 1,050 hp (783 kW) at 13,100 ft (3990 m) or 900 hp (671 kW) at 17,400 ft (5305 m) respectively. These were required for operation in the China-Burma-India (CBI) theatre, in particular for the 'Hump' operations over the 16,500-ft (5030-m) high Himalayan peaks, carrying desperately needed supplies from bases in India to China. Long Beach built only 300 of the model, but Tulsa provided 2,808 C-47Bs plus 133 **TC-47B**s which were equipped for service as navigational trainers. The UK received a total of 896 C-47Bs, which in RAF service were designated **Dakota Mk IV**.

Cargo-carrying deployment

The availability of such large numbers, in both US and British service, meant that it was possible to begin to utilise the C-47s on a far more extensive basis. The formation in mid-1942 of the USAAF's Air Transport Command saw the C-47s' wide-scale deployment as cargo transports, carrying an almost unbelievable variety of supplies into airfields and airstrips which would have been complimented by the description 'primitive'. Not only were the C-47s carrying in men and materials, but they were soon involved in a two-way traffic, serving in a casualty-evacuation role as they returned to their bases. These were the three primary missions for which these aircraft had been intended when first procured: cargo, casualty evacuation, and personnel transports.

However, their employment by the USAAF's Troop Carrier Command from mid-1942, and the RAF's Transport Command, was to provide two new roles, arguably the most important of their deployment in World War II, as carriers of airborne troops. The first major usage in this capacity came with the invasion of Sicily in July 1943, when C-47s dropped something approaching 4,000 paratroops. RAF Dakotas of Nos 31 and 194 Squadrons were highly active in the support of Brigadier Orde Wingate's Chindits, who infiltrated the Japanese lines in Burma in an effort to halt their advance during the winter of 1942-43, their only means of supply being from the air. Wingate (by then a major general) died on 24 March 1944 when a Dakota in which he was a passenger crashed into cloud-covered jungle-clad mountains.

Troop transport

The other important role originated with the **C-53 Skytrooper** version, built in comparatively small numbers as the **C-53B/-53C/-53D**; seven C-53s supplied to the RAF were redesignated **Dakota Mk II**. These were more nearly akin to the original DC-3 civil transport, without a reinforced floor or double door for cargo, and the majority had fixed metal seats to accommodate 28 fully-equipped paratroops. More importantly, they were provided with a towing cleat so that they could serve as a glider tug, a feature soon to become standard with all C-47s, and it is in this capacity that they served conspicuously in both USAAF and RAF service during such operations as the first

airborne invasion of Burma on 5 March 1944 and the D-Day invasion of Normandy some three months later. In this latter operation more than 1,000 Allied C-47s were involved, carrying paratroops and towing gliders laden with paratroops and supplies. In the initial stage of this invasion 17,262 US paratroops of the 82nd and 101st Airborne Divisions and 7,162 men of the British 6th Airborne Division were carried across the English Channel in the greatest airlift of assault forces up to that time. Not all, of course, were carried in or towed by C-47s, but these aircraft played a very significant role in helping to secure this first vital foothold on European soil: in fewer than 60 hours, C-47s alone airlifted more than 60,000 paratroops and their equipment to Normandy.

Other C-47 variants of World War II included the **XC-47C**, prototype of a projected version to be equipped as a floatplane or, as was the prototype, with convertible amphibious floats. Of all-metal construction, these single-step Edo floats each had two retractable wheels, and housed a 300-US gal (1136-litre) fuel tank. While this version was not built as such by Douglas, a small number of similar conversions were made by USAAF maintenance units for service in the Pacific. Douglas was also contracted to build 131 staff transports under the designation **C-117**, these having the airline-standard cabin equipment of

a commercial DC-3, plus the improvements which were current on the C-47. Their numbers, however, had reached only 17 (one **C-117B** built at Long Beach and 16 **C-117A**s from Tulsa) when VJ-Day brought contract cancellation. The requirement for a large-capacity high-speed transport glider, to be towed by a C-54, resulted in experimental conversion of a C-47 to serve in this role under the designation **XCG-17**. Early tests had been conducted with a C-47 making unpowered approaches and landings to confirm the feasibility of the project, followed by a series of flights in which one C-47 was towed by another: for take-off the towed aircraft used some power, but shut down its engines when airborne. Conversion of a C-47 to XCG-17 configuration began after completion of these tests, with engines, propellers and all unnecessary equipment removed and the forward end of the engine nacelles faired over. This was undoubtedly aerodynamically inefficient, and contributed to a reduction in performance of the XCG-17, but it was a USAAF requirement that any production aircraft should be capable of easy reconversion to powered C-47s. Despite any inefficiency, the embryo cargo glider had a successful test programme, demonstrating a towed speed of 290 mph (467 km/h), stalling speed of only 35 mph (56 km/h) and a glide ratio of 14:1. Payload was 14,000 lb (6350 kg), permitting the transport of 40 armed paratroops. No production aircraft were built, however, as a result of changing requirements.

US Navy versions

In addition to the C-47s which served with the USAAF and RAF, approximately 600 were used by the US Navy. These comprised the **R4D-1** (C-47), **R4D-3** (C-53), **R4D-4** (C-53C), **R4D-5** (C-47A), **R4D-6** (C-47B) and **R4D-7** (TC-47B). US Navy and US Marine Corps requirements resulted in several conversions with designations which include the **R4D-5E/-6E** with special-purpose electronic equipment; the winterised and usually ski-equipped **R4D-5L/-6L**; the **R4D-4Q/-5Q/-6Q** for radar countermeasures; cargo versions re-equipped for passenger carrying as the **R4D-5R/-6R**; the air-sea war-fare training **R4D-5S/-6S**; the navigational training **R4D-5T/-6T**; and the VIP-carrying **R4D-5Z/-6Z**. R4Ds were used initially by the Naval Air Transport Service that was established within five days of the attack on Pearl Harbor, equipping its VR-1, VR-2 and VR-3 squadrons, and soon after this by the South Pacific Combat Air Transport Service which provided essential supplies to US Marine Corps units as they forced the Japanese to vacate islands which stretched across the seas and led like stepping stones to that nation's home islands.

In addition to US production, the type was built in the USSR as the Lisunov Li-2 (2,000 examples or more) and in Japan as the Showa (Nakajima) L2D (485 examples).

C-47s had been involved from the beginning to the end of World War II, and that is but a small portion of their history in both military and civil service. Since VJ-Day, military C-47s have supported the Berlin Airlift, Korean and Vietnam Wars.

A technique unknown at the start of the war was 'snatching' a glider. Recognising that a glider might be used more than once, a way was found to hitch it to a towrope whose far end was suspended between two poles. The tug then extended a long hinged arm – in principle exactly like the message pick-ups used by RAF aircraft between the wars – which snagged the rope and ran along to a stop at its end. Here a C-47 of the 9th Troop Carrier Command picks a CG-4A out of a field in Normandy.

Below: Paratroops by the score – indeed, 28 per aircraft – drop in tight sticks behind C-53s of the USAAF. In World War II far more paratroops dropped from C-47s and C-53s of the USAAF than from all other Allied aircraft combined. The first time they were used in numbers was on 10 July 1943 when 4,381 assault troops parachuted onto Sicily. Far larger numbers were used in Burma, in the invasion of Normandy, the unfortunate assault on Arnhem and the crossing of the Rhine.

Specification

Type: military transport and glider tug
Powerplant: (C-47A) two 1,200-hp (895-kW) Pratt & Whitney R-1830-93 Twin Wasp radial piston engines
Performance: maximum speed 229 mph (369 km/h) at 7,500 ft (2285 m); cruising speed 185 mph (298 km/h) at 10,000 ft (3050 m); service ceiling 23,200 ft (7070 m); range 1,500 miles (2414 km)
Weights: empty 16,970 lb (7698 kg); maximum take-off 26,000 lb (11793 kg)
Dimensions: span 95 ft 0 in (28.96 m); length 64 ft 2 in (19.57 m); height 16 ft 11 in (5.16 m); wing area 987 sq ft (91.69 m²)

Douglas C-47A-65-DL
81st Troop Carrier Squadron
436th Troop Carrier Group

The 436th Troop Carrier Group, based at Membury, Berkshire, England, from 1944-45, received a Distinguished Unit Citation for its efforts during Operation Overlord. It also took part in the airborne assault on southern France, based at Voltone, Italy, during July and August 1944. The mission tally on 'Bugs Bunny', together with invasion stripes, suggests participation in the Normandy, southern France, Nijmegen and Bastogne operations, both as a paratrooper and glider tug. The aircraft was delivered on 1 November 1943 and served with the 8th Air Force from 21 January 1944 to 16 July 1945.

Structure

The exceptional service longevity of the DC-3 in all versions is due to its fatigue-resistant structure, entirely of stressed skin and with a multi-spar wing. When the DC-3 was designed in 1934-35 many of the technical advances in flaps, landing gear, propellers, radial cowlings and de-icer boots on the leading edges were all developed and available off the shelf. The C-47 Skytrain had large side doors, a reinforced fuselage floor with tie-down fittings, a glider tow attachment, and folding wooden seats along the sides of the cabin. The glider towing cleat, initially exclusive to the C-53, became a standard fitting on all C-47s. Racks and release mechanism for six parachute pack containers were fitted under the fuselage. An astrodome was fitted above and behind the flight deck.

Powerplants

The five distinctive series built for civilian customers before World War II were powered by two 1,000-hp (746-kW) to 1,200-hp (895-kW) Wright Cyclone SGR-1820-G2, -G-2E, -G-102, -G-103 or -G-202A engines. The C-47 Skytrain and C-53 Skytrooper had two Pratt & Whitney R-1830-92, 14-cylinder, two-row, air-cooled radial engines. These had a capacity of 1,830 cu in (30 litres) each rated at 1,050 hp (783 kW) at 7,500 ft (2290 m) and with 1,200-hp (895-kW) available for take-off. Three-bladed Hamilton Standard constant-speed propellers were fitted. Two main fuel tanks (210 US gal/794 litres) were located forward of the centre-section spar and two auxiliary tanks (201 US gal/760 litres) aft of the spar. One oil tank of 33¼ US gal (126 litres) was in each engine nacelle. The early C-47s had a 12-volt system, whereas the later C-47A had a 24-volt electrical system.

Wartime variants

C-41: a single C-39 (DC-2 version) re-engined with R-1830-21 engines
C-41A: single DC-3A with R-1830-21 engines fitted with VIP interior
C-47: basic transport model of DC-3A with up to 27 seats or 10,000 lb of cargo; R-1830-92 engines; 965 built, of which some transferred to US Navy as R4D-1
C-47A: similar to C-47 but with 24-volt electrical system; 5,254 built, some transferred to Navy as R4D-5
C-47B: similar to C-47A but with R-1830-90, 90B or 90C supercharged engines; 3,364 built, some transferred to Navy as R4D-6
TC-47B: 133 C-47Bs completed as navigation trainers
XC-47C: single conversion of C-47 with twin-float undercarriage
C-47C: a handful of aircraft field-modified with float undercarriage
C-48/A/B/C, C-49/A/B/C/D/E/ F/G/H/J/K, C-50, C-50A/B/C/D, C-51, C-52/A/B/C/D, C-68, C-84, R4D-2, R4D-3, R4D-4: designations applied to impressed civilian DC-3s
C-53: troop transport version of C-47 with port-side passenger door; 219 built
XC-53A: single aircraft tested with full-span leading-edge flaps and hot air de-icing
C-53B: winterised version of C-53 with extra fuel and separate navigator station; eight built
C-53C: similar to C-53 but with larger passenger door; 17 built
C-53D: as C-53C but with 24-volt electrics; 159 built
C-117A: passenger transport version of C-47 with 24 airliner-type seats; 24 built
CG-17: single C-47 tested as a glider with engines removed and cowlings faired over

C-47B version
The C-47B was the third major production version, with R-1830-90 or -90B engines with high-altitude blowers and provision for extra fuel. This version began operating over the 'Hump' in 1942, climbing to 25,000 ft (7620 m) over the Himalayan peaks. Much of the terrain was unexplored and uncharted, and during the monsoon season ground and air conditions were appalling. Crosswinds of up to 150 mph (240 km/h), severe icing, turbulence and severe up- and down-draughts were common. By the end of the war 650,000 tons of supplied had been airlifted over the 'Hump'.

Floatplane
One of the most interesting developments of the C-47 involved the installation of twin Edo Model 78 floats on SC-47C-DL (42-5671). Each single-step metal float was fitted with two retractable wheels. It was only able to operate from smooth water, but did see limited service in Alaska and New Guinea.

Interior
The Skytrain had folding seats, and the C-53 Skytrooper was the troop transport version with a small door, wood floor and fixed metal seating for 28 fully-armed airborne or parachute troops. The crew of three comprised pilot, co-pilot and radio operator. The fuselage was divided into six compartments – for the pilot, port and starboard baggage, radio operator, main passenger/cargo hold, and lavatory. The pilot's compartment seated two side by side, with dual controls. An automatic pilot control system was standard. In the cabin there were alternative fittings for 18 stretchers together with provision for a medical crew of three.

Glider tug
In 1942 the C-47 entered service with the USAAF Troop Carrier Command. Its first major operation was during the invasion of Sicily in July 1943. The airborne invasion of Burma in March 1944 involved C-47s towing Waco CG-4A gliders, and during the D-Day operations of 6 June 1944 1,000 C-47s (including RAF Dakotas) were airborne. Subsequent major operations were in August 1944 in southern France, in September 1944 at Arnhem, in March 1945 in support of the Rhine crossing, and in March and May 1945 in Burma.

Douglas C-54 Skymaster

Like its stablemate the C-47, the Douglas C-54 was derived from the prototype of a civil airliner, the DC-4E, which was built to a specification initially drawn up by United Air Lines. United was joined quickly by American Airlines, Eastern Airlines, Pan American Airways and TWA, all five carriers agreeing to share the cost with Douglas in return for early delivery positions.

Powered by four of the newly developed 1,400-hp (1044-kW) Pratt & Whitney R-2180 Twin Hornet 14-cylinder radial engines, the DC-4E flew for the first time on 7 June 1938, with Carl Cover in command. The design was innovative, incorporating such relatively untried features as cabin pressurisation, power-boosted controls, a 115-volt AC electrical system and an auxiliary power unit. This very complexity, problems with the engines, and the growing realisation that the aircraft was too large for its payload-carrying capacity led to increasing lack of interest on the part of the sponsoring airlines. Although certification was achieved on 5 May 1939 and United carried out some route-proving trials, Douglas terminated development and the DC-4E was later sold to Dai Nippon Koku Kabushiki Kaisha in Japan.

Work started immediately on a redesigned DC-4 which, at 50,000-lb (22680-kg) gross weight and with seats for 42 passengers, was slightly smaller than the prototype. The cabin pressurisation system, power-boosted controls and auxiliary power unit were deleted and the engines were replaced by four Pratt & Whitney Twin Wasps. The landing gear was also modified, the mainwheels retracting forwards into the engine nacelles rather than sideways into the wings. Orders for 61 production standard **DC-4A**s were placed by American, Eastern, Pan American and United on 26 January 1940, but war in Europe and the apparent inevitability of increased United States' involvement led the Roosevelt administration to boost the US Army Air Corps' transport capability with orders which included nine **C-54**s and 62 **C-54A**s. The nine C-54s were part of the initial batch of 24 civil DC-4As laid down at Santa Monica, and the remaining 15 were diverted to the USAAC order early in 1942. The first production C-54 made its maiden flight on 26 March 1942 and all 24 were in service with the Air Transport Command's Atlantic Wing by October. They were slightly modified for military service by the addition of four 464-US gal (1756-litre) fuel tanks in the fuselage, to bring the total capacity to 3,700 US gal (14006 litres), conferring a range of 2,500 miles (4023 km) with a 9,600-lb (4354-kg) payload that included 26 passengers.

The C-54A, 77 of which were built in Santa Monica and 117 at a new factory at Orange Place, Chicago, appeared in January 1943, featuring 33 bucket seats for troops, a large cargo door, stronger floor, cargo boom hoist and slightly larger wing tanks. The last increased total fuel capacity to 3,734 US gal 14134 litres) and gross weight rose to 68,000 lb (30844 kg), allowing a payload of 9,000 lb (4082 kg) to be carried for more than 3,000 miles (4828 km).

After the first C-54 had flown at Santa Monica on 14 February 1942, the second aircraft was handed over to the USAAF on 20 March – surely a record for speedy delivery of a new military aircraft. By the time the war ended, more than 830 C-54s were in service with Air Transport Command, providing the backbone for US long-range transport operations.

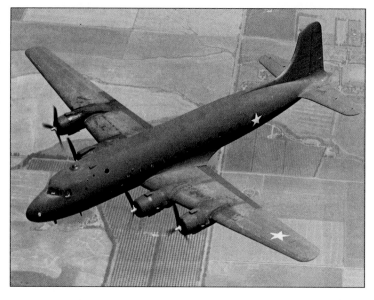

When the US entered the war, Douglas was close to completing the first DC-4 four-engined airliner, with orders in hand for 61. However, all the aircraft under construction were taken over by the USAAF, which gave the designation C-54 to the first 24 off the line; illustrated is the ninth of these. With four additional fuel tanks in the main cabin, the C-54 seated 26 military personnel.

Douglas DC-4 cutaway drawing key

1 Nose cone
2 Radio homing aerial
3 Fire extinguisher bottles
4 Nosewheel doors
5 Nose undercarriage bay construction
6 Cockpit front bulkhead
7 Pitot tubes
8 Windscreen panels
9 Instrument panel shroud
10 Instrument panel
11 Rudder pedals
12 Nosewheel hydraulic retraction jack
13 Steering jacks
14 Nosewheel
15 Torque scissors
16 Battery bay
17 Cockpit floor level
18 Control column handwheel
19 Captain's seat
20 Opening side window panel
21 First Officer's seat
22 Starboard side crew entry door
23 Navigator's folding chart table
24 Cockpit bulkhead

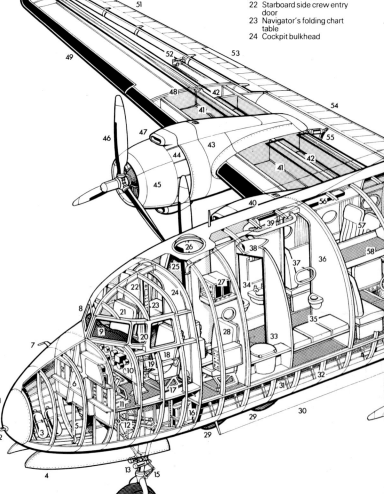

Above: Introduction of the C-54B, of which 100 examples were built, brought integral fuel tanks in the outer wing panels, allowing an increase in passenger seating in the main cabin. One C-54B went to the RAF.

Right: Worldwide transport flights were shared with the USAAF by the US Navy, which began flying Skymasters when 56 C-54As were transferred for use by Naval Air Transport Service, with the designation R5D-1.

25 Forward upper deck cargo hold, capacity 135 cu ft (3.82 m³)
26 Astrodome observation hatch
27 Radio racks
28 Radio operator's seat
29 D/F loop aerials
30 ADF sense aerial cable
31 Forward underfloor cargo hold, capacity 150 cu ft (4.25 m³)
32 Lower section fuselage frames
33 Forward toilet
34 Wash basin
35 Men's cloakroom
36 Cabin bulkhead
37 Aft facing forward seat row
38 Heater intake
39 Cabin combustion heater
40 Starboard inner engine air intake duct
41 Starboard wing integral fuel tanks; fuel capacity, 2,012 US gal (7614 litres)
42 Wing panel walkways
43 Starboard outer engine nacelle
44 Engine cooling air outlet flaps
45 Detachable engine cowlings

46 Hamilton Standard three-bladed propeller
47 Engine air intake
48 Outer wing panel joint rib
49 Leading edge de-icing boots
50 Starboard navigation light
51 Starboard fabric covered aileron
52 Aileron hinge control
53 Aileron tab
54 Starboard single slotted flap
55 Flap hydraulic jack
56 Cabin heater air distribution roof duct
57 Forward cabin seats
58 Port overhead luggage rack
59 Floor beam construction
60 Wing centre section carrying-through
61 Fuselage frame and stringer construction

62 Starboard emergency exit window
63 Wing/fuselage attachment main frames
64 Port emergency exit window
65 Main cabin four-abreast passenger seating, 44-seat layout
66 Starboard overhead luggage rack
67 HF aerial cable
68 Fuselage skin plating
69 Food and coat stowage locker
70 Aft toilet
71 Fin root fillet

72 Starboard tailplane
73 Starboard elevator
74 Leading edge de-icing boots
75 Tailfin construction
76 VHF aerial cable
77 Fin tip fairing

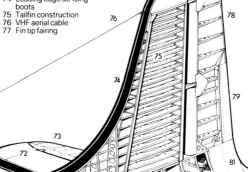

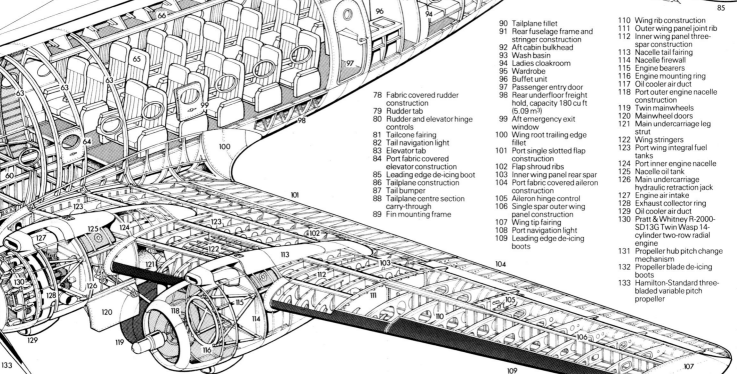

78 Fabric covered rudder construction
79 Rudder tab
80 Rudder and elevator hinge controls
81 Tailcone fairing
82 Tail navigation light
83 Elevator tab
84 Port fabric covered elevator construction
85 Leading edge de-icing boot
86 Tailplane construction
87 Tail bumper
88 Tailplane centre section carry-through
89 Fin mounting frame

90 Tailplane fillet
91 Rear fuselage frame and stringer construction
92 Aft cabin bulkhead
93 Wash basin
94 Ladies cloakroom
95 Wardrobe
96 Buffet unit
97 Passenger entry door
98 Rear underfloor freight hold, capacity 180 cu ft (5.09 m³)
99 Aft emergency exit window
100 Wing root trailing edge fillet
101 Port single slotted flap construction
102 Flap shroud ribs
103 Inner wing panel rear spar
104 Port fabric covered aileron construction
105 Aileron hinge control
106 Single spar outer wing panel construction
107 Wing tip fairing
108 Port navigation light
109 Leading edge de-icing boots

110 Wing rib construction
111 Outer wing panel joint rib
112 Inner wing panel three-spar construction
113 Nacelle tail fairing
114 Nacelle firewall
115 Engine bearers
116 Engine mounting ring
117 Oil cooler air duct
118 Port outer engine nacelle construction
119 Twin mainwheels
120 Mainwheel doors
121 Main undercarriage leg strut
122 Wing stringers
123 Port wing integral fuel tanks
124 Port inner engine nacelle
125 Nacelle oil tank
126 Main undercarriage hydraulic retraction jack
127 Engine air intake
128 Exhaust collector ring
129 Oil cooler air duct
130 Pratt & Whitney R-2000-SD13G Twin Wasp 14-cylinder two-row radial engine
131 Propeller hub pitch change mechanism
132 Propeller blade de-icing boots
133 Hamilton-Standard three-bladed variable pitch propeller

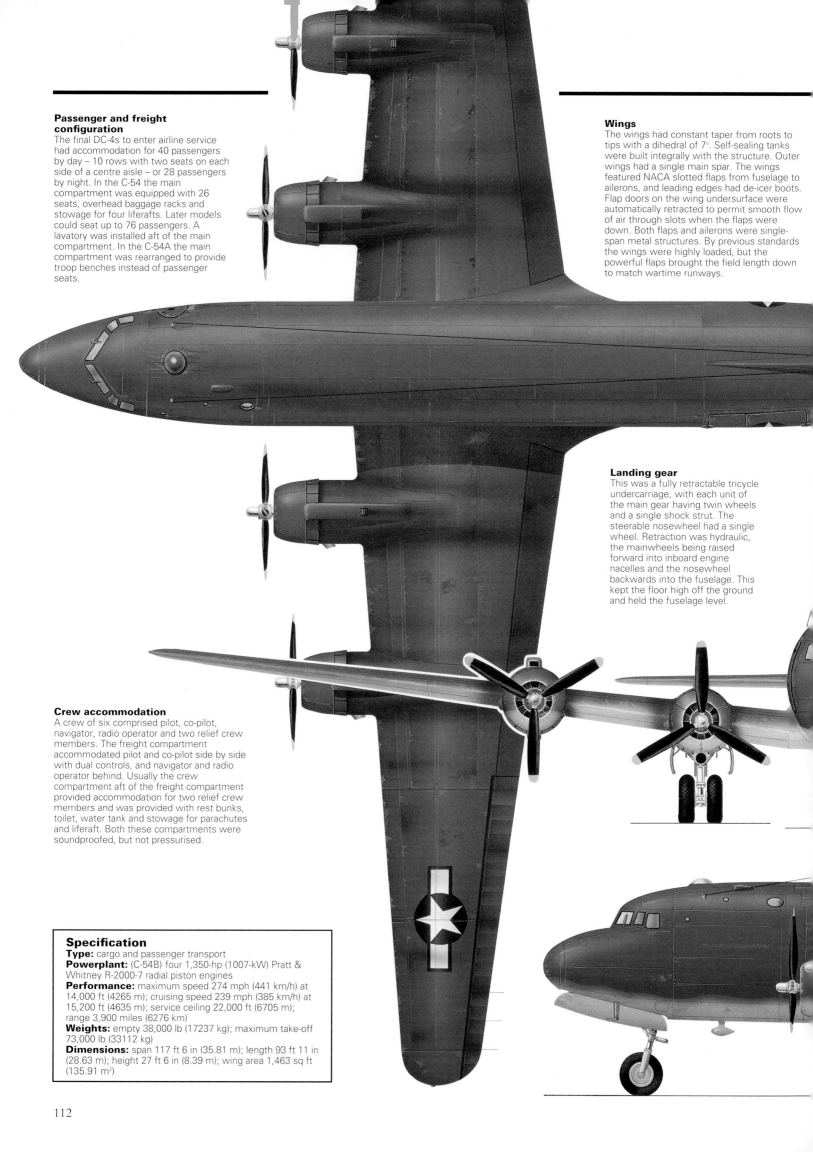

Passenger and freight configuration
The final DC-4s to enter airline service had accommodation for 40 passengers by day – 10 rows with two seats on each side of a centre aisle – or 28 passengers by night. In the C-54 the main compartment was equipped with 26 seats, overhead baggage racks and stowage for four liferafts. Later models could seat up to 76 passengers. A lavatory was installed aft of the main compartment. In the C-54A the main compartment was rearranged to provide troop benches instead of passenger seats.

Wings
The wings had constant taper from roots to tips with a dihedral of 7°. Self-sealing tanks were built integrally with the structure. Outer wings had a single main spar. The wings featured NACA slotted flaps from fuselage to ailerons, and leading edges had de-icer boots. Flap doors on the wing undersurface were automatically retracted to permit smooth flow of air through slots when the flaps were down. Both flaps and ailerons were single-span metal structures. By previous standards the wings were highly loaded, but the powerful flaps brought the field length down to match wartime runways.

Landing gear
This was a fully retractable tricycle undercarriage, with each unit of the main gear having twin wheels and a single shock strut. The steerable nosewheel had a single wheel. Retraction was hydraulic, the mainwheels being raised forward into inboard engine nacelles and the nosewheel backwards into the fuselage. This kept the floor high off the ground and held the fuselage level.

Crew accommodation
A crew of six comprised pilot, co-pilot, navigator, radio operator and two relief crew members. The freight compartment accommodated pilot and co-pilot side by side with dual controls, and navigator and radio operator behind. Usually the crew compartment aft of the freight compartment provided accommodation for two relief crew members and was provided with rest bunks, toilet, water tank and stowage for parachutes and liferaft. Both these compartments were soundproofed, but not pressurised.

Specification
Type: cargo and passenger transport
Powerplant: (C-54B) four 1,350-hp (1007-kW) Pratt & Whitney R-2000-7 radial piston engines
Performance: maximum speed 274 mph (441 km/h) at 14,000 ft (4265 m); cruising speed 239 mph (385 km/h) at 15,200 ft (4635 m); service ceiling 22,000 ft (6705 m); range 3,900 miles (6276 km)
Weights: empty 38,000 lb (17237 kg); maximum take-off 73,000 lb (33112 kg)
Dimensions: span 117 ft 6 in (35.81 m); length 93 ft 11 in (28.63 m); height 27 ft 6 in (8.39 m); wing area 1,463 sq ft (135.91 m²)

A need to carry larger loads over shorter sectors led to the development of the **C-54B**, in which two of the fuselage tanks were deleted in favour of a 499-US gal (1889-litre) integral tank in each outer wing panel. Gross weight rose again, to 73,000 lb (33112 kg), and up to 49 troops or 36 casualty stretchers could be accommodated. C-54B production totalled 89 at Santa Monica and 100 at Chicago.

A single **VC-54C**, with the C-54A's fuselage tanks and C-54B outer wing panels, with tanks to give it a range of 5,500 miles (8850 km), was delivered in June 1944 for the use of President Roosevelt. In the same month, a C-54B was delivered to the Royal Air Force for the use of Winston Churchill, fitted out with a 10-seat VIP cabin by Armstrong Whitworth Aircraft and operated by No. 24 Squadron until November 1945, when it was returned to the United States.

Replacement of the C-54B's Pratt & Whitney R-2000-7 engines by -11 models produced the **C-54D**, 304 of which were built for the USAAF at Chicago. Ten were supplied to the Royal Air Force under Lend-Lease, serving with No. 47 Group's Nos 232 and 246

Douglas C-54A-DO Skymaster
ATC, US Army Air Force

The first production C-54 flew early in 1942 without a prototype, and ultimately 1,242 were built; the end of World War II saw 839 C-54s in service with Air Transport Command. It was, for its time, an ideal long-range heavy logistic transport with a payload of up to 22,000 lb (9980 kg). 41-37273 came from the second production batch, which was the first entirely for the military, the initial batching having been commandeered from a civil order on the production lines.

Powerplants

The DC-4 was initially offered to US airlines with a choice of powerplant – either four 1,000-hp (746-kW) Wright SGR-1820-G205A Cyclone nine-cylinder radials or four 1,050 hp (783-kW) Pratt & Whitney Twin Wasp S1C3-G 14-cylinder radials. When four 1,450 hp (1081-kW) Pratt & Whitney Twin Wasp (R-2000) 2SD1-G 14-cylinder radials were offered, airlines were much more enthusiastic. Twenty-four C-54-DOs were built as military personnel transports and featured 1,350-hp (1007-kW) R-2000-3s. The C-54A-DO was the fully militarised version, and had R-2000-7s. The C-54D-DC, the Skymaster version delivered in the largest numbers, was powered by four R-2000-11s. Normal fuel capacity was 2,868 US gal (10866 litres), but could be increased to 3,592 US gal (13596 litres). Two-speed superchargers were common to all engine variations, as were three-bladed Hamilton Standard Hydromatic propellers to early versions; later variants had four-bladed propellers of 13 ft 2 in (4.01-m) diameter.

M. Badrocke
84

Douglas C-54 Skymaster

Known irreverently as 'Sacred Cow', this modified C-54A-5-DO became the VC-54C-DO transport for President Roosevelt. With the same integral tanks as the C-54B, it featured an electric lift into the fuselage for the President's wheelchair, and was arranged with a stateroom and three conference rooms. Flags on the fuselage showed countries visited.

Squadrons on routes to the Far East.

Between January and June 1945, the Santa Monica plant manufactured 105 USAAF **C-54E**s, a long-range version with 3,600 US gal (13627 litres) of fuel wholly contained in wing tanks. The final production version was the **C-54G**, with 1,450-hp (1081-kW) R-2000-9 engines, which was developed for the India-China Wing's operations over the 'Hump', the 10,000-16,500-ft (3050-5030-m) mountain ranges between the US bases on the plains of Assam and the Chinese air force bases, principally that at Kunming. USAAF procurement of C-54Gs totalled 162, all built at Santa Monica. In August 1945, USAAF Air Transport Command was operating 839 C-54s of all models on a worldwide route network.

The US Navy, with a particular responsibility for air transport in the Pacific, acquired 183 aircraft from the USAAF production lines between 1943 and 1945. This total comprised 19 **R5D-1**s (C-54A), 11 **R5D-2**s (C-54B) and 20 **R5D-4**s (C-54E) built at Santa Monica; and 38 R5D-1s, 19 R5D-2s and 76 **R5D-3**s (C-54D) built at Chicago. The aircraft equipped squadrons of the Naval Air Transport Service until that formation was disbanded in July 1948, some units then becoming part of the combined Military Air Transport Service.

The **R5D-5** was a planned US Navy version of the C-54G, but none was delivered as such, although some R5D-2s and -3s were later converted to that standard, with R-2000-9 engines. Cargo aircraft converted to passenger configuration were given an -R suffix, as in the case of the **R5D-4R** and **R5D-5R**, and the -Z suffix denoted aircraft with much improved interior furnishing. Redesignation of the R5D fleet in 1962 resulted in the R5D-1, R5D-2, R5D-3, R5D-4R, R5D-5 and R5D-5R becoming the **C-54N**, **C-54P**, **C-54Q**, **C-54R**, **C-54S** and **C-54T** respectively. Two single-example conversions for the US Coast Guard were the **EC-54U**, with special electronic equipment, and the **RC-54V** photographic surveillance variant. Post-war USAF versions included an experimental **XC-54K** with 1,425-hp (1063-kW) Wright R-1820-HD engines, a **C-54L** with a modified fuel system, 38 **C-54M**s stripped to increase payload by 2,500 lb (1135 kg) for coal-carrying operations during the Berlin Airlift, and 30 C-54Es converted in 1951 as **MC-54M** ambulance aircraft for the evacuation of wounded personnel from Korea. Other specialised-role conversions included 38 **SC-54D**s modified for the USAF Air Rescue Service in 1955, nine **JC-54** range support aircraft used for missile nosecone recovery, and a small number of **AC-54D**s for navaid calibration.

Above: Although designations up to C-54M were applied to versions of the Skymaster, the C-54G was the final production version, its features being a cabin to carry 50 troops in bucket canvas seats, and later engine variants. Bag-type fuel tanks in the inner wing took the place of the two cabin tanks retained in the C-54B and C-54D. Douglas built 162 C-54Gs at Santa Monica, of which 13 were transferred to the Navy as R5D-5s; 235 more on order were cancelled, and the last Skymaster was delivered to the USAAF on 22 January 1946.

Below: The '17' on the nose indicates the production line position of this C-54, the 17th of 24 that the USAAF sequestered from Douglas at Santa Monica in 1942. By August 1945, Skymasters had completed nearly 80,000 transocean flights, and in January 1945 they made up the bulk of a fleet of 34 four-engined transports that flew delegates to the Yalta conference, taking off at intervals from Malta and escorted by P-38s of the USAAF. With World War II over, Skymasters were still in service to participate in the Berlin Airlift and the Korean War.

Douglas DC-5

Designed at Douglas Aircraft Company's El Segundo facility, the **DC-5** was developed as a 16/22-passenger commercial transport for local service operations out of the smaller airports. Interestingly, at a time when the low-wing configuration was in the ascendancy, it was a high-wing monoplane, although it also featured the then relatively novel tricycle-type landing gear. With a design gross weight of 18,500 lb (8391 kg), the DC-5 was offered with either Pratt & Whitney R-1690 or Wright Cyclone radial engines which, on 550 US gal (2082 litres) of fuel, in two wing tanks, gave the aircraft a range of 1,600 miles (2575 km) at a cruising speed of 202 mph (325 km/h). The engine nacelles for-

Three Dutch DC-5s that survived Japanese attacks on Batavia escaped to Australia and were flown by the RAAF. In 1944 they were impressed by the USAAF and designated C-110 for operation by the 374th TCG.

ward of the firewalls, collector rings, control runs, rudder pedals and the pilot's seats were among the components used in the DC-3.

The prototype, powered by two 850-hp (634-kW) Wright GR-1820-F62 Cyclones, flew for the first time on 20 February 1939, piloted by Carl Cover.

Three were purchased by the US Navy as the **R3D-1**, but the first crashed before delivery. The remaining pair were delivered in July 1940, and served throughout the war. In 1942 they were joined by the prototype, which adopted the **R3D-3** designation. A further four aircraft were bought for Marine Corps use as **R3D-2**s, delivered in late 1940.

Civilian orders were placed by

With the DC-3 well established in airline service by 1938, Douglas turned its attention to a larger longer-range transport (the DC-4) and a smaller short-haul transport (the DC-5). Launched as a company venture, the DC-5 enjoyed only limited success commercially, but the Navy bought three R3D-1s and the Marines four R3D-2s (above).

KLM (four aircraft), Pennsylvania Central Airways (six) and SCADTA of Colombia (two), but the programme was overtaken by the war and only the KLM aircraft were delivered. Although intended for service in Europe, two went first to the Netherlands West Indies to link Curacao and Surinam and the other two to Batavia in the Netherlands East Indies. All four were used to evacuate civilians from Java to Australia in 1942 and one, damaged at Kemajoran Airport, Batavia, on 9 February 1942, was captured by the Japanese and extensively test flown at Tachikawa air force base. The three surviving DC-5s were

operated in Australia by the Allied Directorate of Air Transport and were given the USAAF designation C-110.

Specification
Type: cargo and passenger/paratroop transport
Powerplant: (DC-5) two 850-hp (634-kW) Wright GR-1820-F62 radial piston engines
Performance: maximum speed 221 mph (356 km/h) at 7,700 ft (2345 m); cruising speed 202 mph (325 km/h) at 10,000 ft (3050 m); service ceiling 23,700 ft (7225 m); range 1,600 miles (2575 km)
Weights: empty 13,674 lb (6202 kg); maximum take off 20,000 lb (9072 kg)
Dimensions: span 78 ft 0 in (23.77 m); length 62 ft 6 in (19.05 m); height 19 ft 10 in (6.05 m); wing area 824 sq ft (76.55 m²)

Douglas Dolphin

In 1930 Douglas introduced a new twin-engined commercial amphibian flying-boat which it had named **Dolphin**. Powered by two radial engines, strut-mounted above the high-set cantilever monoplane wing, it provided accommodation for a pilot, co-pilot and six passengers. An unusual feature was the use of an aerofoil section structure to brace together the two engines. An attractive-looking boat, it soon aroused the interest of the US armed forces, which were seeking transport amphibians to supplement the Loening observation amphibians then in service with both the US Army and US Navy.

First to acquire the Dolphin, however, was the US Coast Guard, which ordered three of the standard commercial aircraft in 1931 under the designation **RD**, the first of these being delivered on 9 March 1931. The next service to procure these aircraft was the US Army Air Corps, which in 1932 ordered eight **Y1C-21**s, with 350-hp (261-kW) Wright R-975-3 Whirlwind engines and accommodation for a crew of seven, plus two eight-seat **Y1C-26**s with 300-hp (224-kW) Pratt & Whitney R-985-1 Wasp Juniors.

Subsequent orders covered eight **Y1C-26A**s and six **C-26B**s, powered by R-985-5 and R-985-9 engines respectively, both types being rated at 350 hp (261 kW). In 1934, two C-26Bs were converted to accommodate a crew of two and seven passengers, being redesignated **C-29**. In that same year the US Army changed the role of the aircraft, using them as observation amphibians with a crew of four; this brought designation changes with Y1C-21, Y1C-26, Y1C-26A and C-26B versions becoming, respectively, **OA-3**, **OA-4**, **OA-4A** and **OA-4B**. One OA-4 was provided experimentally with non-retractable tricycle-type landing gear; this enabled the USAAC to evaluate the potential of this landing gear configuration, leading to its specification for use initially on the Douglas C-54 transport.

US Navy use of the Dolphin began with the procurement of one aircraft, comparable with the US Coast Guard RD and US Army Y1C-21, which was delivered in December 1931 and designated **XRD-1**. Three **RD-2**s followed, these differing by having strengthened mounting struts for the overwing engines, which

were higher-powered Pratt & Whitney R-1340-96 Wasps, and six additional **RD-3**s of generally similar configuration were next procured. From these aircraft the US Navy subsequently allocated one RD-2 and two RD-3s for service with the US Marine Corps. Final procurement covered the production of 10 **RD-4**s for the US Coast Guard, these being virtually identical to the US Navy's RD-3s except for minor changes in detail and equipment.

In American service the US Army's Dolphins were used primarily for transport or patrol duties, and those of the US Navy

Between 1931 and 1934 Douglas built 58 Dolphin amphibians, in 17 variants. Among them were 46 for the USAAC and USN with six different designations. This is an RD-4, flying with the Coast Guard at San Francisco in 1942.

as personnel transports, being of great value for communications between ship and shore. The US Coast Guard, however, used its small fleet in a search and rescue role. When the USA became involved in the war, all services used these aircraft extensively in the early years for transport and rescue, as well as for security patrols along the nation's coastline.

Specification
Type: general-purpose amphibian flying-boat
Powerplant: (RD-4) two 450-hp (336-kW) Pratt & Whitney R-1340-96 Wasp radial piston engines
Performance: maximum speed 156 mph (251 km/h); cruising speed 135 mph (217 km/h); service ceiling 17,000 ft (5180 m); range 720 miles (1159 km)
Weights: empty 7,000 lb (3175 kg); maximum take-off 9,530 lb (4323 kg)
Dimensions: span 60 ft 0 in (18.29 m); length 45 ft 1 in (13.74 m); height 14 ft 0 in (4.27 m); wing area 592 sq ft (55.00 m²)

Douglas O-46

Anxious to retain its position as chief supplier of observation aircraft to the US Army Air Corps, the Douglas company developed a proposal for a high-wing monoplane to succeed the biplane types which in the late 1920s were nearing the end of their development potential. A contract was signed in January 1930 for two Douglas XO-31 aircraft, the first of them being flown in December of that same year. A gull-wing monoplane, it had open tandem cockpits for the pilot and observer, a slim fuselage with a 600-hp (447-kW) Curtiss Conqueror V-1570-25 V-12 engine, and split-axle landing gear with provision for large wheel fairings. The wing was wire-braced above to a four-strut cabane over the fuselage and below to the lower section of the fuselage itself. The all-metal aircraft had excellent lines, somewhat marred by the corrugated duralumin skinning which covered the fuselage aft of the engine cowling.

Five Y1O-31A service-test aircraft were ordered in the summer of 1931 being delivered to the USAAC in the spring of 1933 under the designation Y1O-43. They differed consider-ably from the final configuration of the O-31As, with wire-braced parasol wings and a revised tail unit with a new fin and rudder. They went into service under the designation O-43.

The 24th airframe of the O-43A contract was completed as the **XO-46** prototype, which differed from the O-43A in having its wing braced on each side by parallel streamlined struts, thus dispensing with the cabane-type wire bracing of all the earlier Douglas high-wing observation aircraft. And, for the first time, a radial engine (the Pratt & Whitney R-1535-7) replaced the previously favoured V-12 power-plant. The XO-46 passed its tests with flying colours and an order for 71 **O-46A** production air-craft was subsequently increased to 90 machines, delivered between May 1936 and April 1937. The O-46As differed externally from the XO-46 in having their crew canopies faired into the raised rear fuselage decking.

O-46As served with US Army Air Corps observation squadrons until 1940, when most were transferred to reserve National Guard units before being finally withdrawn for training duties in 1942. The last front-line USAAC unit to operate the O-46A was the 2nd Observation Squadron which had several on charge when the Japanese attacked its base at Nichols Field in the Philippines in December 1941.

This immaculate O-46A was serving in 1940 with the 119th Observation Squadron, New Jersey National Guard. Note the D/F loop antenna underneath.

Specification
Douglas O-46A
Type: two-seat observation monoplane
Powerplant: one 725-hp (541-kW) Pratt & Whitney R-1535-7 radial piston engine
Performance: maximum speed 200 mph (322 km/h); cruising speed 171 mph (275 km/h); service ceiling 24,150 ft (7360 m); range 435 miles (700 km)
Weights: empty equipped 4,776 lb (2166 kg); maximum take-off 6,639 lb (3011 kg)
Dimensions: span 45 ft 9 in (13.94 m); length 34 ft 64 in (10.53 m); height 10 ft 8 in (3.25 m) wing area 332.0 sq ft (30.84 m²)
Armament: one fixed forward-firing 0.3-in (7.62-mm) machine-gun in leading edge of starboard wing and one similar gun on ring mounting in the observer's cockpit

Douglas SBD/A-24 Dauntless

Underpowered, vulnerable, lacking in range and exhausting to fly for any length of time, the Douglas **SBD Dauntless** bore its fair share of derogatory appellations. But it was a war-winner, playing a vital part in the early battles of the Pacific, and went on to sink a greater tonnage of Japanese shipping than any other aircraft.

The dive-bomber turned the tide of war at the Battle of Midway on 4 June 1942. But to the men involved, the size of their success may not have been immediately evident: their aircraft had a low power-to-weight ratio, giving it only fair climbing and manoeuvring characteristics; and their arming systems malfunctioned, at times pitching their centreline-mounted 500-lb (227-kg) bombs uselessly into the sea.

Launched from Admiral Chester Nimitz's carrier groups to seek out those of Admiral Isoroku Yamamoto, they were running out of fuel, running out of daylight, and stretched to the limits of range and endurance when they came upon the enemy fleet and attacked. Lieutenant Commander C. Wade McClusky, Commander Max Leslie and the other Dauntless fliers from squadrons VS-5 and VB-3 on USS *Yorktown*, VS-6 and VB-6 on USS *Enterprise*, and VS-8 and VB-8 on USS *Hornet* lost 40 of their 128 dive-bombers.

But when they swarmed down from the late-afternoon sun to send the *Kaga*, *Akagi*, *Hiryu* and *Soryu* to the bottom of the sea they reversed the trend of the Pacific conflict. Few other aircraft types, perhaps none but the Supermarine Spitfire and Hawker Hurricane, can lay claim to have so altered history as the Dauntless dive-bomber, 5,936 of which were produced before the end of World War II.

The Dauntless owes its origin to the low-wing, two-seat tandem Northrop BT-1 dive-bomber of 1938, and to the superb design work of Jack Northrop and of the mild-tempered but brilliant Edward H. Heinemann. When the El Segundo, California manufacturer became a division of Douglas Aircraft with Jack Northrop's January 1938 depar-ture, a development of the BT-1, known as the XBT-2, was being tested but seemed to offer only limited potential. Heinemann's design team reworked the sole XBT-2 (BuAer No. 0627), powering it with the 1,000-hp (746-kW) Wright XR-1830-32 engine which would become the world-famous Cyclone, driving a three-bladed propeller. The tail of the aircraft was redesigned following extensive wind tunnel tests, and the XBT-2 was redesignated **XSBD-1**. Accepted by the US

SBD-3s of scouting squadron VS-3, from USS Yorktown, are about to dive on a Japanese ship which is already burning during the fighting around Midway Island in June 1942. The very powerful perforated dive brakes show up clearly.

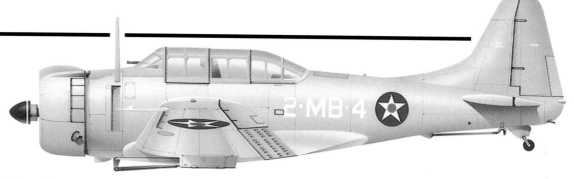

Most of the earliest deliveries went to the Marine Corps, including all the 57 SBD-1s. This SBD-1 was assigned to VMSB-232 (Marine Scout Bomber Squadron 232) of Air Group 21, based at Ewa, Hawaii, at the time of the Pearl Harbor attack in December 1941.

Navy in February 1939, while parallel work was under way on the Curtiss SB2C Helldiver, the SBD was to become the standard by which all other carrierborne dive-bombers (scout bombers' in the jargon of the time) would be judged.

On 8 April 1939, Douglas received an order for 57 **SBD-1** and 87 **SBD-2** airplanes. The SBD-1, with the definitive fin and rudder shape for the Dauntless type, was armed with two forward-firing 0.3-in (7.62-mm) guns in the engine cowling and a single 0.3-in (7.62-mm) gun for the radio-operator/gunner, who sat with his back to the pilot. Not yet fully cleared for carrier operations, the SBD-1 was earmarked instead for the US Marine Corps and was delivered between April 1939 and June 1940. The SBD-2 model, which differed in having self-sealing rubber-lined metal fuel tanks and two additional 65-US gal (246-litre) tanks in the outer wing panels, went to US Navy squadrons between November 1940 and May 1941.

The fall of France, punctuated by the scream of descending Stukas, impressed the Washington authorities with the value of the dive-bomber (although the Truman Committee of the US Congress recommended in 1941 against procuring such aircraft) and a further 174 Dauntlesses were ordered as the **SBD-3**. The SBD-3 variant had a second 0.3-in (7.62-mm) gun for the rear crewmen, improved armour and electrical system, and bladder-type self-sealing fuel tanks. By now the familiar Dauntless shape was established: the not ungraceful machine had a maximum speed of 252 mph (406 km/h) in level flight, going up to 276 mph (444 km/h) in a dive, a range of 1,225 miles (1971 km) with or 1,370 miles (2205 km) without a bombload, and a service ceiling of 27,100 ft (8260 m).

Coral Sea success

US Marine Corps Dauntlesses were destroyed on the ground during the 7 December 1941 attack on Pearl Harbor. During the Battle of Coral Sea on 7 May 1942 the airwaves were cluttered with radio transmissions, and anxious crewmen aboard USS *Lexington* and *Yorktown* could not tell how the battle was going until a clear voice blasted through: 'Scratch one flat-top! Dixon to carrier. Scratch one flat-top!' Lieutenant Commander Robert E. Dixon, commander of Bombing Two (VB-2), was reporting the sinking of the Japanese carrier *Shoho* with 545 of her crew after a 30-minute battle at the cost of only three US aircraft, a triumph for the SBD-2 and SBD-3 models of the Dauntless, to be exceeded only during the pivotal Midway battle a few weeks later.

A carrier air group aboard a typical US Navy carrier usually comprised two squadrons of fighters (Grumman F4F Wildcats, or later F6F Hellcats), one of torpedo-bombers (Douglas TBD Devastators, later Grumman TBF Avengers) and two Dauntless squadrons, one in the bombing role and one for the scout mission. These were designated VB and VS squadrons respectively. The scouting mission had been conceived before it was clear that American carriers would have the protection of radar, which they enjoyed from the outset of the conflict while Japanese carriers did not. In practice, there was little distinction and scouting pilots trained and prepared for dive-bombing missions just as their colleagues in the VB squadrons did.

The next model of the Dauntless was the **SBD-4**, delivered between October 1942 and April 1943. The SBD-4 had improved radio navigation aids, an electric fuel pump, and an improved Hamilton Standard Hydromatic constant-speed, fully-feathering propeller. A total of 780 was built before production at El Segundo shifted to the **SBD-5**, powered by an improved R-1820-60 engine delivering 1,200 hp (895 kW); 2,965 examples of this variant were produced between February 1943 and April 1944, one of which became the **XSBD-6** with installation of a 1,350-hp (1007-kW) Wright R-1820-66, the 'ultimate' Cyclone. Some 450 **SBD-6**s were built.

By late in the war, the Dauntless had been supplanted in the dive-bomber role by the more advanced Curtiss SB2C Helldiver, though

This SBD-1 (BuNo. 1626) was flown by the commanding officer of Marine bomber squadron VMB-2, with red nose and fuselage stripe. Later this unit was redesignated VMSB-232, and thus this could possibly be the same aircraft as shown above.

this troublesome aircraft never won the recognition accorded the Douglas product. The Dauntless was relegated to less glamorous anti-submarine patrol and close air support duties. The SBD also served with no less than 20 US Marine Corps squadrons. Many hundreds of SBDs were retrofitted with Westinghouse ASB radar, the first to be used by the US Navy.

The pilot of an SBD-6 Dauntless found himself sitting high up front in a machine of all-metal construction with fabric-covered control surfaces. His cantilever, low-mounted wing had a rectangular centre section with outer panels tapering in chord and thickness to detachable wing tips. The 'Swiss cheese' pierced flaps and dive-brakes, above and below the trailing edge of the outer wings and below the trailing edge only of the centre section beneath the fuselage, together with the 'multi-cellular' construction of the wing itself, were hallmarks of the design's indebtedness to Jack Northrop The oval duralumin monocoque fuselage was built in four sections, and the crew was housed beneath a continuous transparent canopy with a bullet-proof windshield and armour plate. A swinging bomb cradle with a maximum capacity of 1,000 lb (454 kg) was centred beneath the fuselage, and a bomb rack was mounted under each outer-wing section.

Flying the Dauntless, pilots found it a forgiving machine of few vices, although it had a troublesome tendency to stall in tight turns. On dive-bombing missions the pilot approached his target at 15,000 to 20,000 ft (4570 to 6095 m), took position almost directly overhead, pulled up the nose, and deployed upper and lower dive flaps. He then

By 1943, security considerations had resulted in unit insignia no longer being painted on aircraft, but only individual aircraft numbers within the unit. These SBD-3s, in the sea green and pale grey scheme of the day, are described as "returning to their carrier after a dive-bombing mission", though only one gunner has his twin 0.30-in Brownings ready.

Marine Corps Scout Squadron VMS-3 is shown in echelon formation, one favoured for approaching a dive-bombing target. The aircraft are SBD-5s, and the gull grey and off-white colour scheme was adopted in early 1944 for the North Atlantic theatre, but this unit was based in the Caribbean.

'rolled in', the Dauntless accelerating less rapidly than might be expected while plummetting at over 70°. Using the Mk VIII reflector sight which, from the SBD-5 model on, had replaced the earlier extended telescope (this had a tendency to fog over in a dive as a result of temperature changes), the pilot aimed his bombload literally by pointing his aircraft at the target. His bomb release was a red button marked 'B' on the top of the stick, and he could drop his ordnance singly or in salvo.

US Navy legend has it that pilots were prone to 'target fascination', which could lull them into failing to pull out of the dive in time. With its bombload gone, the Dauntless pulled out quite handily, with an easy motion on the stick. The machine generally handled well in normal flight and the pilot's visibility was excellent, both when level and when descending for a tricky landing on a carrier deck. Few aircraft were tougher or more reliable, the Dauntless often coming home with severe battle damage.

In the US Army Air Forces, where it was officially given the name **Banshee** but still called Dauntless, this aircraft type seemed unglamorous from the beginning. In January 1941, the USAAF placed an order for 78 A-24s similar to the US Navy's SBD-3 but for the deletion of carrier landing equipment. In addition, 90 SBD-3s from a US Navy contract were modified to land-based standard and delivered to the USAAF as the **SBD-3A** (A for Army). Eventually the USAAF ordered 100 **A-24A**s identical to the SBD-4, and 615 **A-24B**s equivalent to the SBD-5 but manufactured at the Douglas plant in Tulsa.

Although A-24s served with the 27th Bombardment Group at New Guinea and with the 531st Fighter Bomber Squadron at Makin, USAAF pilots could not outmanoeuvre aggressive Japanese fighters. Where the rear-seat gunner had been highly effective in the US Navy machine – one US Navy crew shot down seven Mitsubishi Zeroes in two days – he was less potent aboard the A-24. Casualties were so high that the type was quickly withdrawn from front-line service. Since US Navy pilots at Coral Sea and Midway had demonstrated the ability to handle themselves against the Zero, the US Army's less satisfactory performance with the Dauntless is usually attributed to the inexperience and lower morale of its flight crews.

In July 1943, No. 25 Squadron of the Royal New Zealand Air Force received 18 SBD-3s from US Marine Corps inventory. Later to receive 27 SBD-4s and 23 SBD-5s, the RNZAF squadron fought at Bougainville. Another foreign user of the Dauntless was France, which equipped two units of the Free French navy, Flottille 3B and Flottille 4B, with A-24s and SBD-3s at Agadir, Morocco, in the autumn of

1944. Dauntlesses went into operation in metropolitan France against retreating German forces and fought in dwindling numbers until VE-Day. Though production of the type ended on 22 July 1944, French SBDs were used at the fighter school at Meknes until 1953.

The UK obtained nine SBD-5 aircraft and named them Dauntless DB.Mk I. By this time – 1944 – it was regarded as underpowered and slow. British pilots also found the Dauntless fatiguing, noisy and draughty. There was never to be general agreement about the type's vulnerability to fighters; the Pacific war indicated that it was not unduly vulnerable, but RAF test pilots considered that it was. The British machines were evaluated extensively, but it was too late for the Dauntless to have an operational career in British service. In American service, where the A-24 was redesignated F-24 in 1947, an unpiloted **QF-24A** drone and its **QF-24B** controller aircraft (both rebuilds with 1948 serial numbers) kept the Dauntless type in service until 1950.

A few A-24B Dauntlesses found their way, post-war, into the hands of the Mexican air force, which was apparently the last user of this type, employing it until 1959.

Douglas SBD-3 Dauntless cutaway drawing key

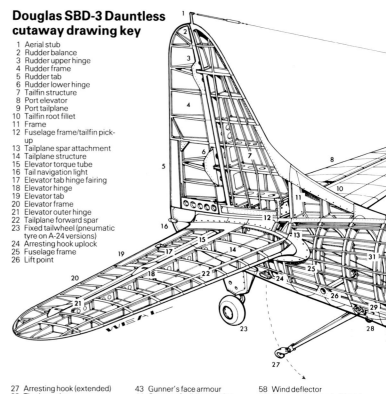

1 Aerial stub
2 Rudder balance
3 Rudder upper hinge
4 Rudder frame
5 Rudder tab
6 Rudder lower hinge
7 Tailfin structure
8 Port elevator
9 Port tailplane
10 Tailfin root fillet
11 Frame
12 Fuselage frame/tailfin pick-up
13 Tailplane spar attachment
14 Tailplane structure
15 Elevator torque tube
16 Tail navigation light
17 Elevator tab hinge fairing
18 Elevator hinge
19 Elevator tab
20 Elevator frame
21 Tailplane outer hinge
22 Tailplane forward spar
23 Fixed tailwheel (pneumatic tyre on A-24 versions)
24 Arresting hook uplock
25 Fuselage frame
26 Lift point

27 Arresting hook (extended)
28 Tie-down ring
29 Arresting hook pivot
30 Control cables
31 Fuselage structure
32 Bulkhead
33 Section light
34 Radio bay
35 Radio bay access door
36 Wingroot fairing frame
37 Stringers
38 Life-raft cylindrical stowage (access door port side)
39 Dorsal armament stowage
40 Hinged doors
41 Aerial
42 Twin 0.30-in (7.62-mm) Browning machine-guns

43 Gunner's face armour
44 Canopy aft sliding section (open)
45 Gun mounting
46 Ammunition feed
47 Canopy aft sliding section (closed)
48 Ammunition box
49 Oxygen cylinder
50 Oxygen rebreather
51 Oxygen spare cylinder
52 Entry hand/foothold
53 Aft cockpit floor
54 Radio controls
55 Gunner's position
56 Gun mounting
57 Canopy fixed centre section

58 Wind deflector
59 Armoured centre bulkhead
60 Angled support frame
61 Gunner's emergency flight controls
62 Control direct linkage
63 Hydraulics controls
64 Entry hand/foothold
65 Oxygen rebreather
66 Map case
67 Pilot's seat and harness
68 Back armour
69 Catapult headrest
70 Canopy forward sliding section
71 Compass
72 Perforated dive flap
73 Aerial mast

Demonstrating the awesome spread of its dive brakes, 42-54372 was an Army A-24B. Most A-24s had various camouflage schemes, reverting to natural metal late in the war. Like the SBD, they served in almost every war theatre and saw action in several.

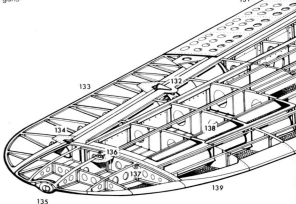

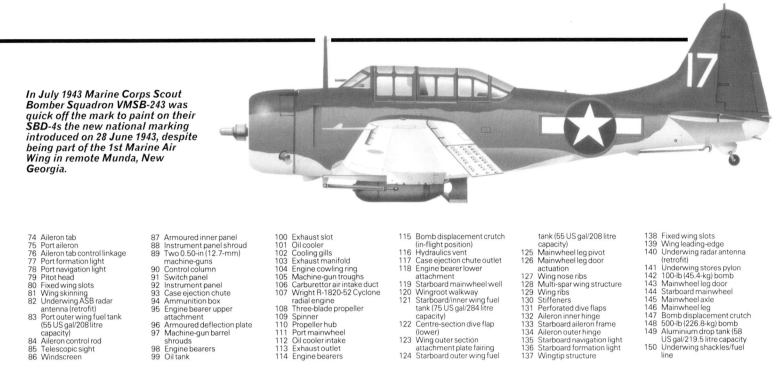

In July 1943 Marine Corps Scout Bomber Squadron VMSB-243 was quick off the mark to paint on their SBD-4s the new national marking introduced on 28 June 1943, despite being part of the 1st Marine Air Wing in remote Munda, New Georgia.

74 Aileron tab
75 Port aileron
76 Aileron tab control linkage
77 Port formation light
78 Port navigation light
79 Pitot head
80 Fixed wing slots
81 Wing skinning
82 Underwing ASB radar antenna (retrofit)
83 Port outer wing fuel tank (55 US gal/208 litre capacity)
84 Aileron control rod
85 Telescopic sight
86 Windscreen

87 Armoured inner panel
88 Instrument panel shroud
89 Two 0.50-in (12.7-mm) machine-guns
90 Control column
91 Switch panel
92 Instrument panel
93 Case ejection chute
94 Ammunition box
95 Engine bearer upper attachment
96 Armoured deflection plate
97 Machine-gun barrel shrouds
98 Engine bearers
99 Oil tank

100 Exhaust slot
101 Oil cooler
102 Cooling gills
103 Exhaust manifold
104 Engine cowling ring
105 Machine-gun troughs
106 Carburettor air intake duct
107 Wright R-1820-52 Cyclone radial engine
108 Three-blade propeller
109 Spinner
110 Propeller hub
111 Port mainwheel
112 Oil cooler intake
113 Exhaust outlet
114 Engine bearers

115 Bomb displacement crutch (in-flight position)
116 Hydraulics vent
117 Case ejection chute outlet
118 Engine bearer lower attachment
119 Starboard mainwheel well
120 Wingroot walkway
121 Starboard/inner wing fuel tank (75 US gal/284 litre capacity)
122 Centre-section dive flap (lower)
123 Wing outer section attachment plate fairing
124 Starboard outer wing fuel

tank (55 US gal/208 litre capacity)
125 Mainwheel leg pivot
126 Mainwheel leg door actuation
127 Wing nose ribs
128 Multi-spar wing structure
129 Wing ribs
130 Stiffeners
131 Perforated dive flaps
132 Aileron inner hinge
133 Starboard aileron frame
134 Aileron outer hinge
135 Starboard navigation light
136 Starboard formation light
137 Wingtip structure

138 Fixed wing slots
139 Wing leading-edge
140 Underwing radar antenna (retrofit)
141 Underwing stores pylon
142 100-lb (45.4-kg) bomb
143 Mainwheel leg door
144 Starboard mainwheel
145 Mainwheel axle
146 Mainwheel leg
147 Bomb displacement crutch
148 500-lb (226.8-kg) bomb
149 Aluminium drop tank (58 US gal/219.5 litre capacity
150 Underwing shackles/fuel line

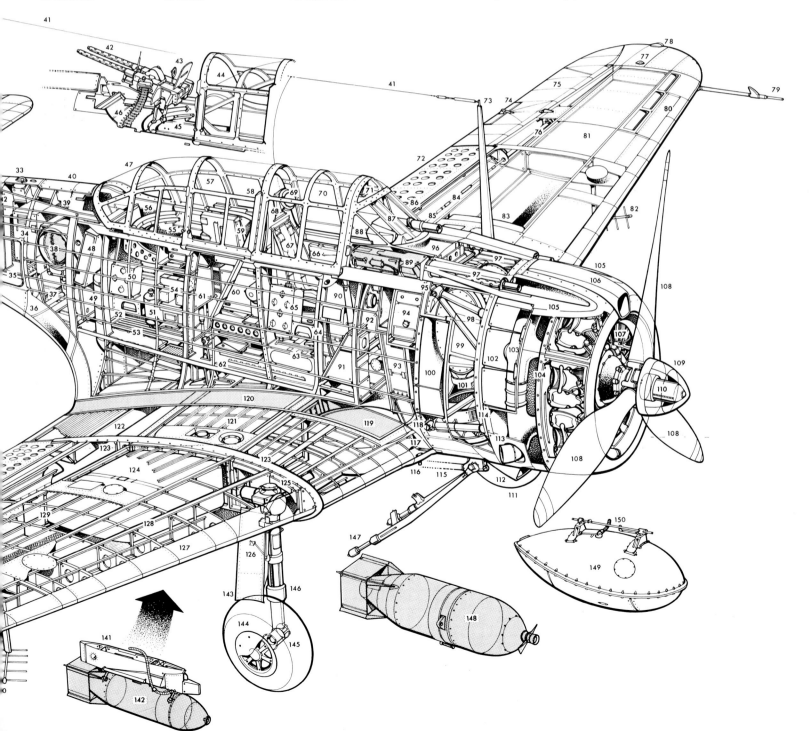

Douglas SBD Dauntless

Pilot
The pilot enjoyed an excellent view from his high-set seat, and was protected by armour plate to the rear. A telescopic sight with three zoom settings was provided for both gun and bomb aiming.

Observer/gunner
The rear cockpit had a rear-facing seat and sliding canopy to allow the firing of defensive weapons. In early variants one drum-fed 0.3-in (7.62-mm) machine-gun was fitted, but the SBD-3 introduced a pair of belt-fed weapons. These were stowed in the upper fuselage under doors when not in use.

Fuel
Early variants had four centre-section tanks holding 210 US gal (795 litres). The SBD-3 also had four self-sealing wing tanks which added a further 260 US gal (984 litres). A 58-US gal (220-litre) drop tank could be carried on the centreline in place of the bomb.

Powerplant
The SBD-3 was powered by the 1,000-hp (746-kW) Wright R-1820-52 radial engine. Exhaust gases were collected by a manifold and ejected through two outlet ducts in the lower cowling sides or through a shallow flush slot behind the cooling gills.

Douglas SBD Dauntless variants

XSBD-1: conversion of single Northrop XBT-2, BuAer no. 0627
SBD-1: initial production version, BuAer nos. 1596/1631 and 1735/1755; total 57
SBD-1P: eight conversions to reconnaissance role
SBD-2: improved armour, self-sealing tanks, BuAer nos. 2102/2188; total 87
SBD-2P: 14 conversions to reconnaissance role
SBD-3: improved production version, BuAer nos. 4518/4691, 03185/03384 and 06492/06701; total 584
SBD-3A: aircraft from US Navy contract diverted to USAAF as A-24
SBD-3P: 43 conversions to reconnaissance role and 24-V
SBD-4: production aircraft, improved propeller and electrical systems, BuAer nos. 06702/06991 and 10317/10806: total 780
SBD-5: production aircraft, R-1820-60 engine, BuAer nos. 10807/10956 10957/11066, 28059/ 28829, 28831/29213, 35922/36421, 36433/36932 and 54050/54599; total 2,965

SBD-5A: aircraft from USAAF contract, originally intended for US Army as A-24B but delivered to US Navy, BuAer nos. 09693/09752; total 60
XSBD4: single prototype for SBD-6, BuAer no. 28830
SBD-6: final production version R-1820-66, one converted from SBD-5 (BuAer no. 35950); others BuAer nos 54600/55049; total 450
A-24: originally designated SBD-3A, delivered to USAAF, serial numbers 41-15746/15823 and 42-6682/6771; total 168
A-24A: USAAF version of SBD-4, serials 42-6772/6831 and 42-60772/60881; total 170
A-24B: USAAF version of SBD-5, serials 42-54285/54899; total 615
RA-24A: redesignation after 1942 to indicate obsolescence
RA-24B: redesignation after 1942, to indicate obsolescence
F-24A: redesignation after 1947
F-24B: redesignation after 1947
QF-24A: one rebuilt as target drone, serial 48-44
QF-24B: one rebuilt as drone controller aircraft; serial 48-45

Fuselage guns
Firing through troughs in the upper fuselage decking was a pair of Browning 0.5-in (12.7-mm) machine-guns, each provided with 360 rounds in ammunition containers behind the engine bulkhead.

Wing slots
Three 'letterbox' slots were incorporated into the outer wing forward of the ailerons. These improved airflow over the control surfaces at low speeds.

Specification
Douglas SBD-5 Dauntless
Type: two-seat carrier-based scout bomber and dive-bomber
Powerplant: one 1,200-hp (895-kW) Wright R-1820-60 Cyclone air-cooled radial piston engine
Performance: maximum speed 252 mph (406 km/h) at 10,000 ft (3050 m); initial climb rate 1,700 ft (518 m) per minute; service ceiling 26,100 ft (7955 m); range 1,115 miles (1794 km) on a bombing mission or 1,565 miles (2519 km) on a scouting mission
Weights: empty 6,533 lb (2963 kg); maximum take-off 10,700 lb (4854 kg)
Dimensions: span 41 ft 6½ in (12.66 m); length 33 ft 1½ in (10.09 m); height 13 ft 7 in (4.14 m); wing area 325.0 sq ft (30.194 m²)
Armament: two 0.5-in (12.7-mm) fixed machine-guns in the nose and two 0.3-in (7.62-mm) manually-aimed machine-guns in the rear crewman's position, plus up to 1,600 lb (726 kg) of bombs under the fuselage and 650 lb (295 kg) of bombs under the wings

Undercarriage
The mainwheels of the Dauntless were inward-retracting to give a wide track for stability on the carrier. The wheels occupied wells forward of the front spar on retraction, and were left exposed.

Bombload
The standard bombload consisted of a single weapon of up to 1,600 lb (726 kg) carried on the centreline and two smaller weapons under the wings outboard of the main undercarriage. Most bombs were of the simple box-fin type. The central weapon was mounted in a cradle which swung forward on bomb release to ensure the bomb dropped clear of the propeller arc. This was only used for dive attacks; during level bombing attacks the bomb would drop free of its own accord.

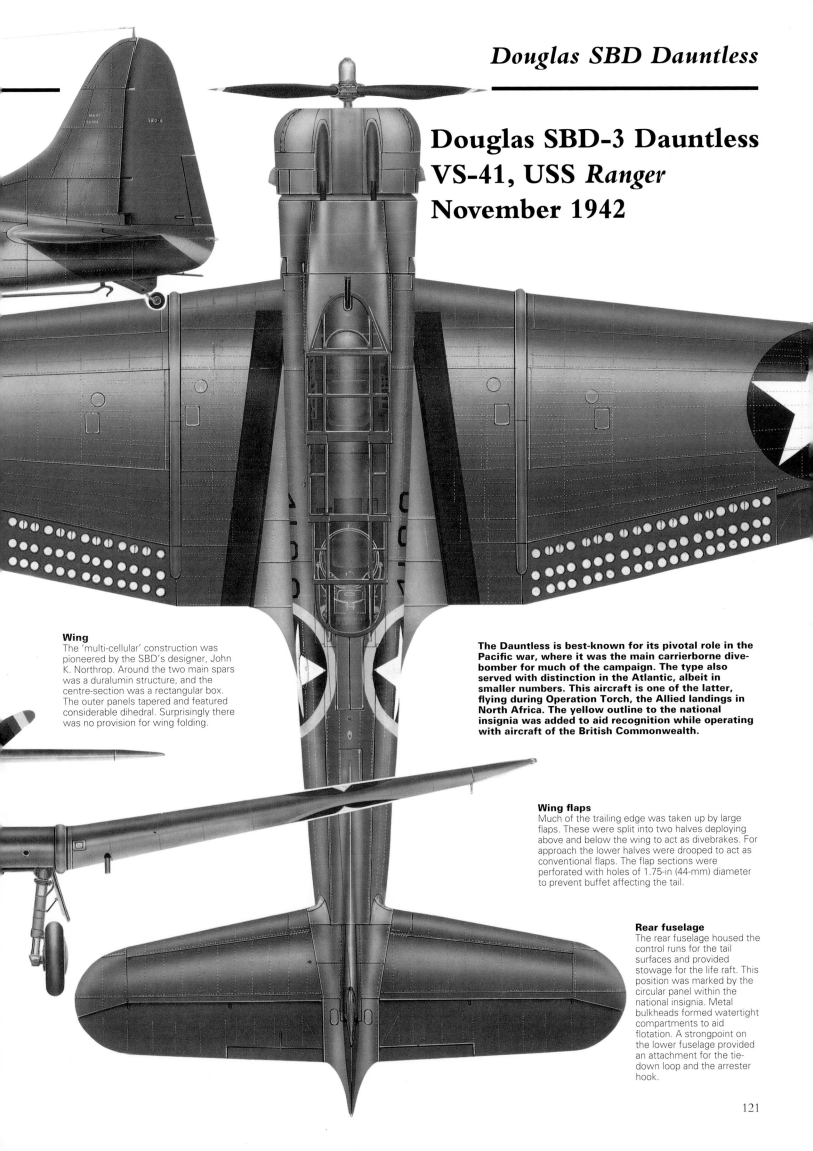

Douglas SBD-3 Dauntless
VS-41, USS *Ranger*
November 1942

Wing
The 'multi-cellular' construction was pioneered by the SBD's designer, John K. Northrop. Around the two main spars was a duralumin structure, and the centre-section was a rectangular box. The outer panels tapered and featured considerable dihedral. Surprisingly there was no provision for wing folding.

The Dauntless is best-known for its pivotal role in the Pacific war, where it was the main carrierborne dive-bomber for much of the campaign. The type also served with distinction in the Atlantic, albeit in smaller numbers. This aircraft is one of the latter, flying during Operation Torch, the Allied landings in North Africa. The yellow outline to the national insignia was added to aid recognition while operating with aircraft of the British Commonwealth.

Wing flaps
Much of the trailing edge was taken up by large flaps. These were split into two halves deploying above and below the wing to act as divebrakes. For approach the lower halves were drooped to act as conventional flaps. The flap sections were perforated with holes of 1.75-in (44-mm) diameter to prevent buffet affecting the tail.

Rear fuselage
The rear fuselage housed the control runs for the tail surfaces and provided stowage for the life raft. This position was marked by the circular panel within the national insignia. Metal bulkheads formed watertight compartments to aid flotation. A strongpoint on the lower fuselage provided an attachment for the tie-down loop and the arrester hook.

Douglas TBD Devastator

Early in 1934 the US Navy initiated a design competition for the development of a new torpedo-bomber for service on board US aircraft carriers and, in particular, for USS *Ranger,* which was due to be commissioned that year. From the proposals received, prototypes were ordered from Douglas and the Great Lakes Aircraft Corporation; the Douglas **XTBD-1** represented the first carrier-based monoplane to be produced for the US Navy. On the other hand, the Great Lakes XTBG-1, of which only a single prototype was built, was the last biplane in the torpedo-bomber category to be procured by the US Navy.

The prototype XTBD-1, which flew for the first time on 15 April 1935, was of fairly conventional configuration and construction. The low-set cantilever monoplane wing could be folded mechanically at approximately mid-span and construction was all-metal, except that the rudder and elevators were fabric-covered. The deep fuselage housed an internal weapons bay which could accommodate a torpedo or a large armour-piercing bomb. Only the main units of the tail-wheel-type landing gear were semi-retractable, the mainwheels being half exposed below the wing's lower surface when retracted. An arrester hook was mounted forward of the tailwheel. Powerplant of the prototype consisted of an 800-hp (597-kW) Pratt & Whitney XR-1830-60 radial engine. Accommodation was provided for a crew of three (pilot, bomb-aimer/navigator and gunner) housed beneath a long transparent cockpit enclosure.

TBD-1 Devastators of US Navy Torpedo Squadron VT-6 prepare to take off from CV-6 USS Enterprise at the start of the Battle of Midway on 3 June 1942. Three days later, of 41 TBDs launched from the three US carriers engaged, just five remained; but the four Japanese carriers had all been sunk.

Below: Dated 6 January 1941, this photograph shows a TBD in pre-war silver, with chrome-yellow wings. The underwing oil cooler shows up prominently.

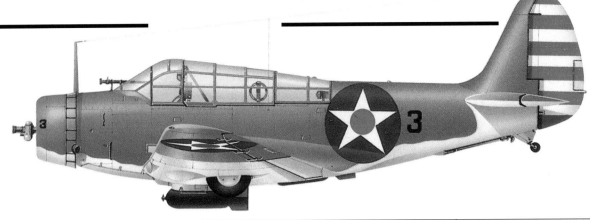

Shown as it would have appeared during the Battle of the Coral Sea, this TBD-1 flew with VT-6 aboard USS Enterprise. Devastators sunk the Japanese carrier Shoho during the battle.

Initial testing of the prototype went so well that within nine days of the first flight Douglas was able to hand it over to the US Navy for service trials. These were carried out over a period of nine months and resulted in contracts for a total of 129 examples of the **TBD-1 Devastator** production model, the first awarded to Douglas on 3 February 1936. When delivery of these aircraft began, on 25 June 1937 the US Navy had in its possession what was then, unquestionably, the most advanced torpedo-bomber in the world.

The first US Navy squadron to receive its TBD-1s, on 5 October 1937, was VT-3. Squadrons VT-2, VT-5, and VT-6 were equipped during the following year. The TBD-1 remained in first-line service with the US Navy until after the Battle of Midway. The main clash of this battle came on 4 June 1942, when 35 TBD-1s were shot to pieces, caught between blistering anti-aircraft fire and the guns of Mitsubishi A6M Zero naval fighters. Soon afterwards it was withdrawn from combat service, no longer able to survive against modern fighter and anti-aircraft opposition. Devastators were used for some time afterwards on communications and training duties.

Specification
Type: three-seat torpedo-bomber
Powerplant: one 900-hp (671-kW) Pratt & Whitney R-1830-64 Twin Wasp radial piston engine
Performance: maximum speed 206 mph (332 km/h) at 8,000 ft (2440 m); cruising speed 128 mph (206 km/h); service ceiling 19,700 ft (6005 m); range with 1,000-lb (454-kg) bomb or torpedo 416 miles (669 km)
Weights: empty 6,182 lb (2804 kg); maximum take-off 10,194 lb (4624 kg)
Dimensions: span 50 ft 0 in (15.24 m); length 35 ft 0 in (10.67 m); height 15 ft 1 in (4.60 m); wing area 422.0 sq ft (39.20 m²)
Armament: one 0.3-in (7.62-mm) forward-firing machine-gun and one 0.3-in (7.62-mm) gun on flexible mounting, plus one torpedo or 1,000-lb (454-kg) armour-piercing bomb

Above: Newly painted in sea green and pale grey, this aircraft of VT-6 is seen during the heroic defence of Wake Island in February 1942. The red/white rudder stripes were overpainted three months later.

Below: BuNo. 0275 was the eighth production aircraft. It is seen as aircraft No. 4 of VT-3, the first unit to receive the TBD. No. 4 in each squadron was distinguished by having a white nose and tail.

Above: Dated 4 November 1936, this photograph shows the XTBD-1 prototype (BuNo. 9720), modified with a higher canopy and the oil cooler relocated under the starboard wing but still with the original small fin and rudder.

Fairchild UC-61/86 Argus

When Sherman Fairchild withdrew from The Aviation Corporation in 1931, he retained control of the subsidiary Kreider-Reisner Company of Hagerstown, Maryland, renamed Fairchild Aircraft Corporation in 1935. Kreider-Reisner's Model 24C three-seat touring aircraft, first introduced in 1933, remained in production, its versions including the Models 24C8-C, 24C8-E and 24C8-F. The four-seat 24J was introduced in 1937, and was built with both Ranger and Warner engines. The Ranger-engined version was superseded by the 24K in 1938. The main production variants, however, were the 24R and 24W, respectively Ranger- and Warner-powered, and produced from 1939.

The 24W-41, with a 165-hp (123-kW) Super Scarab, was developed for service with the US Army Air Corps as the **UC-61 Forwarder** but, of 163 built, only two were retained. The rest were supplied to the UK under Lend-Lease and were known as

Already established as a light transport in the commercial market in 1941, the Fairchild F-24W-41 was ordered by the AAF as the UC-61 and UC-61A. All but 150 of the 675 acquired were supplied to Britain.

the Argus Mk I. The type was adopted as the Air Transport Auxiliary's standard transport for the carriage of ferry pilots; the ATA also received a large number of Argus Mk IIs, which were equipped with new radios and had a 24-volt electrical system rather than the 12-volt system of the Mk I. Of the RAF allocation of 364 Argus Mk IIs from the 512 **UC-61A**s built to USAAC order, a number were used in India and the Middle East, as were many of the RAF Argus Mk IIIs which comprised the entire USAAC order for 306 **UC-61K**s, developed from the 24R with a 175-hp (130-kW) Ranger L-440-7 engine. Civil aircraft impressed by the USAAF in 1942 were allocated designations **UC-61B** to **UC-61J**, according to civil model number,

while nine Model 24R-40s were impressed as the **UC-86**. Two of these were subsequently re-engined to become the **XUC-86A** and **XUC-86B** respectively.

Specification
Type: four-seat liaison and communications aircraft, or instrument trainer
Powerplant: (UC-61) one 165-hp (123-kW) Warner R-500 Super Scarab radial piston engine
Performance: maximum speed 132 mph (212 km/h); cruising speed 117 mph (188 km/h); service ceiling 15,700 ft (4785 m); range 640 miles (1030 km)
Weights: empty 1,613 lb (732 kg); maximum take-off 2,562 lb (1162 kg)
Dimensions: span 36 ft 4 in (11.07 m); length 23 ft 9 in (7.24 m); height 7 ft 7 in (2.32 m); wing area 193.3 sq ft (17.96 m²)

Fairchild AT-21 Gunner

Heavy firepower had been a distinguishing feature of the fighter aircraft which faced each other in Europe when World War II began, and progressive development aimed to increase this as much as possible. To neutralise the advantage held by attacking fighters, power-operated multi-gun turrets were evolved, to provide fast aiming and ranging of their concentrated firepower. These steps did not, however, cover deficiencies in the training schedule; not only were there no air gunners with the experience to use a gun turret, if and when provided, but there were also no

specialised air gunnery training schools. Neither were there any suitable aircraft in which pupils could gain the essential air-to-air firing practice.

To resolve this latter shortcoming, the USAAC ordered two specialised gunnery training prototypes from the Fairchild Engine & Airplane Corporation. The first **XAT-13** was intended to serve for the training of all members of a bomber's crew working as a team, and the single prototype (41-19500) was powered by two 600-hp (447-kW) Pratt & Whitney R-1340-AN-1 radial engines. The second

XAT-14 prototype (41-19503) was powered by two 520-hp (388 kW) Ranger V-770-6 inline engines and was generally similar in layout, but was adapted subsequently as a more specialised trainer for bomb-aimers under the designation **XAT-14A**, with its defensive guns removed. Testing of these aircraft served to crystallise ideas, resulting in the procurement of a special gunnery trainer under the designation **AT-21** and given the name Gunner.

Of the 175 AT-21s constructed, 106 were built by Fairchild and, to speed deliveries to the

USAAF, 39 were built by Bellanca Aircraft Corporation and 30 by McDonnell at St Louis. Entering service with newly established air gunnery schools, they remained in service until 1944, displaced eventually by the production of training examples of the operational type in which the air gunners would eventually serve. One was tested as a remotely-controlled aerial bomb under the designation **XBQ-3**.

Specification
Type: specialised gunnery trainer
Powerplant: two 520-hp (388-kW) Ranger V-770-15 inline piston engines
Performance: maximum speed 225 mph (362 km/h) at 12,000 ft (3660 m); cruising speed 196 mph (315 km/h) at 12,000 ft (3660 m); service ceiling 22,150 ft (6750 m); range 910 miles (1464 km)
Weights: empty 8,654 lb (3925 kg); maximum take-off 11,288 lb (5120 kg)
Dimensions: span 52 ft 8 in (16.05 m); length 38 ft 0 in (11.58 m); height 13 ft 1 in (4.00 m); wing area 378 sq ft (35.12 m²)
Armament: one 0.30-in (7.62-mm) machine-gun in fuselage nose and two 0.30-in (7.62-mm) guns in power-operated dorsal turret

Another in the series of specialised training aircraft acquired by the USAAF to cope with rapid wartime expansion, the Fairchild AT-21 had facilities to train bombardiers, navigators, gunners and radio operators, with gunnery as the pre-eminent role.

Fairchild PT-19/23/26 Cornell

In 1939 the USAAC carried out an evaluation of the Fairchild company's M62 two-seat monoplane. By comparison with the US Army's most advanced biplane trainer then in service (the Stearman PT-13), maximum speed, rate of climb and service ceiling were very nearly the same. The wing loading of the M62 was almost 43 per cent higher, however, which meant that its stalling speed was also higher and its low-speed handling characteristics just that little more critical. It seemed to be exactly what was needed, and in 1940 an initial order was placed for these trainers under the designation **PT-19**.

Construction of this aircraft was fairly typical of its type and period, the cantilever monoplane wing mounted low on the fuselage being a conventional two-spar wooden structure with plywood skins. The ailerons comprised light alloy frames with fabric covering, and manually-operated split type trailing-edge flaps were provided. Fuselage structure was of welded steel tube, with mainly fabric covering, but the tail unit was all-wood, except for metal-frame fabric-covered rudder and elevators, and landing gear was of the non-retractable tailwheel type. The powerplant of the initial PT-19 version consisted of a 175-hp (130-kW) Ranger L-440-1 inverted inline engine, driving a two-bladed fixed-pitch propeller. Two open cockpits accommodated pupil and instructor, and although dual controls were standard, instrumentation of the PT-19 was only very basic.

A total of 270 PT-19s was built before a new **PT-19A** version was introduced on the production lines of Fairchild, Aeronca and St Louis, these companies turning out 3,182, 477 and 33 respectively. The only significant change in this version was the introduction of the slightly more powerful Ranger L-440-3 engine and some refinements in detail. The PT-19A, like the original version, had only basic instrumentation and so was unsuitable for blind-flying or instrument flight training. This shortcoming was rectified in the subsequent **PT-19B**, which was

Rapid production of the PT-19 left Ranger struggling to match demand for engines. As a stopgap, the Continental R-670 radial was used to power 1,169 PT-23s, including 93 by Fleet in Canada, and 256 PT-23As.

When the USAAC ordered the Fairchild M-62 primary trainer in 1940, it broke with its preference for biplanes in this role. Launching a prolific family, the PT-19 was built by the thousand in three factories; the PT-19B is illustrated, equipped to give blind-flying instruction.

provided with full blind-flying instrumentation and a hood to cover the pupil's front cockpit when such training was in progress. Production totalled 774 by Fairchild and 143 by Aeronca.

The combination of production contracts covering numbers far in excess of those which Fairchild had anticipated with the urgency of the US Army's requirements, resulted in 1942 in a famine of Ranger engines. To resolve the situation the company produced an **XPT-23** prototype by the installation of an uncowled Continental R-670 radial engine and, after evaluation, this was put into production with the designation PT-23. A total of 869 was built by Fairchild (two), Aeronca (375), Howard (199) and St Louis (200), as well as 93 by Fleet Aircraft Ltd of Fort Erie, Ontario, for use in the Commonwealth Air Training Scheme which had been established in Canada. A version of the **PT-23**, with the blind-flying instrumentation and hood which had been introduced on the PT-19B, was built by Howard (150) and St Louis (106) under the designation **PT-23A**. This was the last version to be built for the

USAAF in America, with almost 6,000 delivered before the production lines closed down.

The PT-23s which Fleet in Canada had built for service under the Commonwealth Air Training Scheme had resulted in the request for a slightly more advanced version, and this reverted to the use of a Ranger L-440-C5 engine. Improvements included a continuous transparent canopy covering both cockpits, with all controls and blind-flight and navigation instruments duplicated in each. And since the temperature in Canada could often be lower than in the USA, cockpit heating and ventilation was provided. Fleet built 1,057 of

these in Canada under the designations **PT-26A** and **PT-26B**, while Fairchild built another 670 for supply to the RCAF under Lend-Lease: designated **PT-26**, these had the name **Cornell II** in RCAF service.

Specification

Type: two-seat primary trainer
Powerplant: (PT-26A) one 200-hp (149-kW) Ranger L-440-C5 inline piston engine
Performance: maximum speed 122 mph (196 km/h); cruising speed 101 mph (163 km/h); service ceiling 13,200 ft (4025 m); range 400 miles (644 km)
Weights: empty 2,022 lb (917 kg); maximum take-off 2,736 lb (1241 kg)
Dimensions: span 36 ft 0 in (10.97 m); length 27 ft 8 in (8.45 m); height 7ft 7 in (2.32 m); wing area 200 sq ft (18.58 m²)

Federal AT-20 (Avro Anson)

In RAF hands the **Avro Anson** undertook a wide variety of roles, including coastal patrol, but the type is best remembered as a utility transport and trainer. To satisfy the huge demand for the type in the latter role, Federal Aircraft Ltd was established in Canada to produce the type, marshalling the efforts of several manufacturers. The first Canadian-built version was the Anson Mk II, which featured the Jacobs L-6BM engine in place of the Armstrong-Siddeley Cheetah, and was completed with a moulded plywood nose which incorporated a bombardier position, plus hydraulically-retracting flaps and undercarriage.

Of the 1,832 Anson Mk IIs produced, 50 were supplied to the USAAF as the Federal **AT-20**, and were used as crew trainers for the bomber force.

Specification
Federal AT-20
Type: three/five-seat bomber crew trainer
Powerplant: two Jacobs L-6BM radial piston engines, each rated at 330 hp
Performance: maximum speed 178 mph; service ceiling 19,000 ft; range 790 miles
Weights: empty 5,375 lb; maximum take-off 8,000 lb
Dimensions: wing span 56 ft 5 in; length 42 ft 3 in; height 13 ft 1 in; wing area 410 sq ft

The Avro Anson entered production in Canada as the Anson Mk II in 1941; 1,832 were built. Several companies shared in Canadian production, the 50 Anson Mk IIs acquired by USAAF in 1942 being identified as Federal AT-20s.

Fisher P-75 Eagle

The **XP-75 Eagle** fighter manufactured by Fisher Body Division of General Motors, built to a 1942 USAAF specification for a single-seat fighter with a high rate of climb, was in fact an 'oddball' assortment of parts from existing production aircraft. The builder's wish for an appealing designation number is said to account for the USAAF's failure to allocate the P-73 and P-74 appellations. Fisher's design team under Don Berlin, formerly with Curtiss, believed that components of other machines could be combined with the 2,885-hp (2151-kW) Allison V-3420-23 engine at greatly reduced cost, the result being a fighter easy to manufacture in a short time to cope with the war's urgent demands. The

first of two prototype XP-75s (43-46950 and 44-32162), which flew on 17 November 1943, was built with P-51 Mustang outer wing panels, F4U Corsair landing gear, and A-24 Dauntless empennage. Production of 2,500 machines was authorised before it became apparent that this hybrid was not going to work.

There followed a contract for six production XP-75As which had bubble canopy rather than the braced hood on earlier machines.

The **XP-75A**s introduced a number of changes brought about by a shift in primary mission from the interceptor to the escort-fighter role. The XP-75As also had more components designed and built new from the

outset. By the time the first XP-75A (44-44550) flew in September 1944, it was clear that the type was a disappointment and that, in any event, the escort role was being carried out more effectively by the P-51 Mustang. Eventually three Eagles were lost in crashes, two of them fatal, and on 27 October 1944 the USAAF cancelled the programme so abruptly that the sixth and final XP-75A never flew. One immaculate XP-75A (44-44553) has survived in a non-flying condition and is displayed in the Air Force Museum at Dayton, Ohio.

Specification
Fisher XP-75A
Type: single-seat long-range escort fighter
Powerplant: one 2,885-hp (2151-kW)

An order for 2,500 P-75As was placed by USAAF months before the XP-75 prototype flew. This is the second of only five completed before cancellation.

Allison V-3420-23 liquid-cooled 24-cylinder banked Vee piston engine driving a six-bladed contra-rotating propeller unit
Performance: maximum speed about 400 mph (643 km/h) at sea level; cruising speed 310 mph (499 km/h); service ceiling 36,000 ft (10973 m); range 3,000 miles (4828 km)
Weights: empty 11,495 lb (5214 kg); maximum take-off 18,210 lb (8260 kg)
Dimensions: span 49 ft 4 in (15.04 m); length 40 ft 5 in (12.32 m); height 15 ft 6 in (4.72 m); wing area 347 sq ft (32.24 m²)
Armament: 10 0.5-in (12.7-mm) forward-firing machine-guns (six in wings and four in fuselage), plus provision for two 500-lb (227-kg) bombs on racks beneath the wing centre section

Fleetwings BT-12

US involvement in World War II, following the Japanese attack on Pearl Harbor in December 1941, was to highlight the unprepared state of the USAAF. Although some preparations had been made before the 'day of infamy' on 7 December, they were too little and too late. After the event, manufacturers could not produce aircraft fast enough to meet the demands of the nation's armed forces, and the requirement for training aircraft was insatiable.

This helps to explain why Fleetwings Inc., of Bristol, Pennsylvania, a specialist in the fabrication of stainless steel and a manufacturer of components and assemblies in this material for the US aviation manufacturers, came to build a basic trainer for the USAAF under the designation **BT-12**.

Identified by the company as the **Model 23**, the aircraft was in appearance a fairly conventional low-wing monoplane, with fixed tailwheel-type landing gear and the powerplant consisting of one

Pratt & Whitney R-985 radial engine. Accommodation was provided for instructor and pupil in separate fully duplicated cockpits with a continuous transparent canopy covering both.

The unconventional feature of the BT-12 lay in its construction which (with the exception of 65 per cent of the wing skin, ailerons, flaps, part of the fuselage skin, rudder and elevators, which were fabric-covered) was entirely of stainless-steel construction.

Fabrication was almost entirely of spot or seam welding.

A single **XBT-12** prototype (39-719) was flown and evaluated, and a contract for an additional 24 BT-12 aircraft was awarded, these being produced and delivered in 1942-43.

Specification
Type: two-seat basic trainer
Powerplant: one 450-hp (336-kW) Pratt & Whitney R-985-25 Wasp Junior radial piston engine
Performance: maximum speed 195

In the rush to plug gaps in its inventory after the Japanese attack on Pearl Harbor, the USAAF sought extra production sources. One such was Fleetwings, which offered this BT-12 trainer, but only 25 were purchased.

mph (314 km/h); cruising speed 175 mph (282 km/h); service ceiling 23,800 ft (7255 m); range 550 miles (885 km)
Weights: empty 3,173 lb (1439 kg); maximum take-off 4,410 lb (2000 kg)
Dimensions: span 40 ft 0 in (12.19 m); length 29 ft 2 in (8.89 m); height 8 ft 8 in (2.64 m); wing area 240.4 sq ft (22.33 m²)

Grumman F3F

With the FF and F2F, Grumman had established an enviable reputation for providing the US Navy with biplane fighters, and the F3F continued the tradition. It was based on the F2F but featured a lengthened fuselage and greater wingspan. The **XF3F-1** prototype first flew on 20 March 1935, but was destroyed two days later due to structural failure, prompting a strengthening modification. The crash of a second prototype resulted in aerodynamic improvements. The first of 54 **F3F-1**s entered service in January 1936, and the type had a brief career as a carrierborne fighter before being replaced by the F4F Wildcat. Eighty-one **F3F-2**s with supercharged engines and 27 **F3F-3**s with some drag-reducing features followed the initial batch. The final operational unit was Marine squadron VMF-211, which retired its aircraft on 10 October 1941. Approximately 100 F3Fs were subsequently used for fighter training during the early years of the war, the last flying example being struck off charge in November 1943 and relegated to ground instruction.

Specification
F3F-3
Type: single-seat shipboard fighter
Powerplant: one 950-hp (708-kW)

Wright R-1820-22 9-cylinder radial piston engine
Performance: maximum speed 264 mph (425 km/h); service ceiling 33,200 ft (10120 m); range 980 miles (1577 km)
Weights: empty 3,285 lb (1490 kg);

maximum take-off 4,795 lb (2175 kg)
Dimensions: wing span 32 ft 0 in (9.75 m); length 23 ft 2 in (7.06 m); height 9 ft 4 in (2.84 m); wing area 260 sq ft (24.15 m²)
Armament: two 0.3-in (7.62-mm) Browning machine-guns

Grumman F3F biplanes were in process of being transferred to training units when the US entered the war, with nearly 180 still in Navy and Marine inventory. This F3F-2, newly finished in olive drab and grey, was at NAS Corpus Christi until 1943 in the training role.

Grumman F4F Wildcat

With US naval aviation heavily reliant on biplanes in the 1930s, the introduction of monoplane designs was bound to meet with scepticism from traditionalists. Add to this a series of teething troubles, and the Grumman-designed **F4F Wildcat** would appear to have stood little chance of success. In reality it went on to become one of the most effective and successful of carrierborne fighters.

It was known universally as the Grumman Wildcat, although most were not built by Grumman and many in foreign use were known as Martlets. It is best remembered in the hands of outnumbered American pilots pitted against the Mitsubishi Zero in 1942-3, although its combat debut had come in the hands of the British when a naval pilot from HMS *Audacity* shot down a four-engined Focke-Wulf Fw 200 Condor near Gibraltar as early as 20 September 1941. It was the fighter used by Lieutenant Edward (Butch) O'Hare of squadron VF-42 from the USS *Lexington* who shot down five Mitsubishi G4M bombers in five minutes near Rabaul on 20 February 1942, becoming the US Navy's first ace of World War II and earning the Medal of Honor. Yet O'Hare, for all his achievement, was only the second man to win this medal while flying the Wildcat.

Battle-winner

All things to all men, the Grumman Wildcat (7,815 of them built before VJ-Day, most by the Eastern Division of General Motor Corporation) has one principal claim to fame that no other American aircraft can make: it was the fighter flown by US Navy and US Marine Corps airmen in the dark hours at Pearl Harbor, Coral Sea and Wake Island, and at Guadalcanal when the first hints appeared that the war might be turned against an until-then unbeaten Japanese enemy. The Wildcat never outperformed the Zero, but it won battle after battle nonetheless, and when those battles were over the war had turned in the direction of an Allied victory.

Like many great aircraft, the Wildcat was almost not built at all. A 1936 US Navy requirement for a new carrier-based fighter went not to Leroy Grumman's well-established Bethpage, Long Island, firm but to the forgettable Brewster Aeronautical Corporation for its XF2A-1 Buffalo. The F2A-1 thus became the US Navy's first operational monoplane fighter, but US Navy planners were so sceptical of its promise (wisely so) that they authorised one prototype of Grumman's competing biplane design, the **XF4F-1**. Later, the biplane proposal was shelved and on 28 July 1936 an order was placed for a prototype Grumman monoplane fighter, the **XF4F-2**.

First flown by company pilot Robert L. Hall on 2 September 1937 and almost immediately moved to NAS Anacostia, Washington DC for tests, the XF4F-2 was powered by a 1,050-hp (783-kW) Pratt & Whitney R-1830-66 Twin Wasp engine and was able to demonstrate a maximum speed of 290 mph (467 km/h). Of all-metal construction with a riveted monocoque fuselage, its cantilever monoplane wing set in mid-position on the fuselage and equipped with retractable tailwheel landing gear, the XF4F-2 proved to be marginally faster than

*The batsman (landing signals officer) of a **CVE** (**US** Navy escort carrier, or 'Woolworth flat-top') ducks as an **F4F-4**, with six 0.5-in guns, is about to hit the deck. It is painted in the 1944 livery of semi-gloss sea blue (a quite different colour from the previous sea green) and insignia white.*

the Brewster prototype in a 1938 'fly-off' evaluation at Anacostia and Dahlgren, Virginia. It also outperformed the Seversky XFN-l, a derivative of the USAAC's P-35. But speed was the XF4F-2's only advantage over the Brewster product, and the latter was ordered into production on 11 June 1938.

Clearly, the US Navy believed the XF4F-2 had hidden potential, for it was returned to Grumman in October 1938 together with a new contract for its further development. The company introduced major improvements and changed its own designation from G-18 to G-36 before this prototype flew again in March 1939 under the designation **XF4F-3**. Changes included the installation of a more powerful version of the Twin Wasp (the XR-1830-76 with a two-stage supercharger), increased wing span and area, redesigned tail surfaces, and a modified machine-gun installation. When tested in this form the XF4F-3 was

*Probably taken aboard a **US** Navy escort carrier in early 1943, this photograph shows **F4F-4**s which had taken part in **Operation Torch**, the invasion of North Africa in November 1942. The yellow ring around the national insignia can be seen overpainted to merge with the background colour of non-specular blue-grey.*

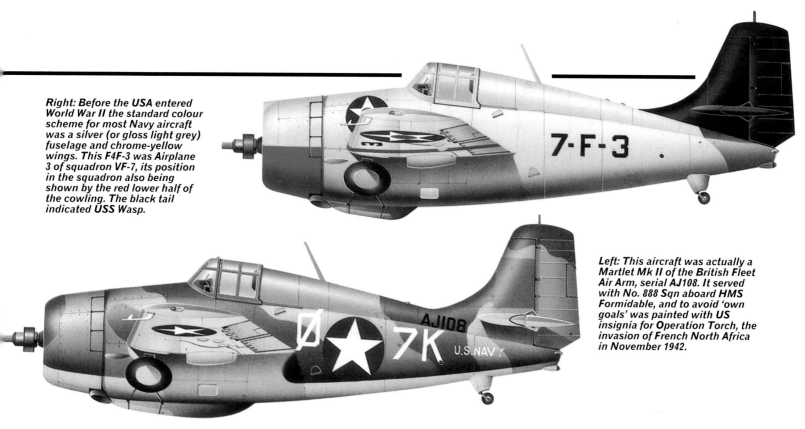

Right: Before the USA entered World War II the standard colour scheme for most Navy aircraft was a silver (or gloss light grey) fuselage and chrome-yellow wings. This F4F-3 was Airplane 3 of squadron VF-7, its position in the squadron also being shown by the red lower half of the cowling. The black tail indicated USS Wasp.

Left: This aircraft was actually a Martlet Mk II of the British Fleet Air Arm, serial AJ108. It served with No. 888 Sqn aboard HMS Formidable, and to avoid 'own goals' was painted with US insignia for Operation Torch, the invasion of French North Africa in November 1942.

found to have considerably improved performance. A second prototype was completed and introduced into the test programme, with a redesigned tail unit in which the tailplane was moved higher up the fin, and the profile of the vertical tail was changed again. In this final form the XF4F-3 was found to have good handling characteristics and manoeuvrability, and a maximum speed of 335 mph (539 km/h) at 21,300 ft (6490 m). Faced with such performance, the US Navy ordered 78 **F4F-3** production aircraft on 8 August 1939.

With war seemingly imminent in Europe, Grumman offered the G-36A design for export, receiving orders for 81 and 30 aircraft from the French and Greek governments respectively. The first of those intended for the French navy, powered by a 1,000-hp (746-kW) Wright R-1820 Cyclone radial engine, flew on 27 July 1940, but by then, of course, France had fallen. The British Purchasing Commission agreed to take these aircraft, increasing the order to 90, and the first began to reach the UK in July 1940 (after the first five off the line had been supplied to Canada), and were designated **Martlet Mk I**.

Two aircraft flown by No. 804 Squadron were the first American-built fighters in British service to destroy a German fighter during World War II. Later variants of the Grumman fighter served with 11 Royal Navy squadrons, mostly on board small escort carriers, like the *Audacity*, in the Battle of the Atlantic.

Subsequent versions of the Martlet to serve with the Fleet Air Arm included the Twin Wasp-powered folding-wing **Martlet Mk II**; 10 F4F-4As and the Greek contract G-36A aircraft as **Martlet Mk III**;

and Lend Lease **F4F-4B**s with Wright R-1820 Cyclone engines as **Martlet Mk IV**. In March 1944, all were redesignated Wildcats in a major policy decision to standardise names of US and British aircraft. All retained their distinguishing mark numbers.

Wildcat variants

The name 'Wildcat' was in use in US service from 1 October 1941. The first **F4F-3 Wildcat** for the US Navy was flown on 20 August 1940, and at the beginning of December the type began to equip US Navy squadrons VF-7 and VF-41. Some 95 **F4F-3A** aircraft were ordered by the US Navy, powered by the R-1830-90 engine with single-stage supercharger, and deliveries began in 1941. An **XF4F-4** prototype was flown in May 1941, incorporating refinements which resulted from Martlet combat experience in the UK including six-gun armament, armour, self-sealing tanks, and (above all) folding wings. Delivery of production **F4F-4 Wildcat** fighters began in November 1941, and by the time that the Japanese launched their attack on Pearl Harbor a number of US Navy and US Marine Corps squadrons had been equipped. As additional Wildcats entered service, they went to sea aboard the carriers USS *Enterprise* (CV-6), USS *Hornet* (CV-12) and USS *Saratoga* (CV-3), being involved with conspicuous success in the battles of the Coral Sea and Midway, and the operations at Guadalcanal, and were at the centre of all significant actions in the Pacific until superseded by more advanced aircraft in 1943. They also saw action with the US Navy in North Africa late in 1942.

Above: US Navy BuNo. 0383 was the original XF4F-2 prototype, first flown on 2 September 1937. It was later rebuilt into the XF4F-3, looking much more like the production F4F-3 Wildcat.

Right: On 10 April 1942, when this photograph was taken over the Pacific, not many Allied pilots could expect to win if they met Japanese fighters. Two exceptions were Lt Cdr J.S. Thach (nearest) and Lt Edward H. O'Hare, of VF-3. Flying these F4F-3s, with four guns, they already had three and four victories respectively.

Grumman F4F Wildcat

The **XF4F-5** and **XF4F-6** designations went to experimental variants of the Wildcat, and the **F4F-6** designation was initially applied to the machine which became the F4F-3A.

The first Wildcat pilot to win the Medal of Honor belonged to US Marine squadron VMF-211, which lost nine F4F-3s on the ground during the 7 December 1941 attack on Pearl Harbor and seven more on the ground at Wake Island on the next day. The battered defenders of Wake fought on, and on 9 December two VMF-211 pilots teamed up to shoot down a Japanese bomber, the first American Wildcat 'kill'. Before Wake was overwhelmed, Captain Robert McElrod achieved a direct hit on a Japanese destroyer with a bomb dropped from his Wildcat, sinking the ship and losing his life and winning the Medal of Honor posthumously.

Legendary exploits

Wildcat-Zero dogfights at Wake, Coral Sea and Midway are the stuff of legend. At Midway, Lieutenant Commander John S. Thach of squadron VF-3 on *Yorktown* devised a criss-cross dogfighting tactic which compensated for the Wildcat's inferior manoeuvrability, and the 'Thach Weave' became part of Wildcat lore forever. 'Butch' O'Hare did more than win the Medal of Honor; he shook President Roosevelt's hand and got an airport in Chicago named after him.

The carrier war was tough and brutal; merely landing the easily-stalled Wildcat on a pitching carrier deck amounted to a supreme achievement. But to many men, the Wildcat earned its spurs not aboard ship but in the heat, stench and muck at Henderson Field on Guadalcanal where America mounted its first major offensive action of the Pacific conflict.

Major John L. Smith's VMF-223, the 'Rainbow' Squadron, was launched from the escort carrier USS *Long Island* (CVE-1) on 20 August 1942 and landed at Henderson. The next day, the squadron was strafing Japanese troops at the Tenaru river. On 24 August, accompanied by five USAAF Bell P-39 Airacobras, Smith's aircraft intercepted an enemy flight of 15 bombers and 12 fighters. VMF-223 pilots shot down 10 bombers and six fighters, Captain Marion Carl scoring three of the kills. Soon Carl had become the first US Marine ace of the war, Smith became the third Wildcat pilot to rate the Medal of Honor, and the men who flew from Henderson Field ('a bowl of black dust or a quagmire of mud' according to its official history) had

Grumman F4F-4 Wildcat cutaway drawing key

1 Starboard navigation light
2 Wingtip
3 Starboard formation light
4 Rear spar
5 Aileron construction
6 Fixed aileron tab
7 All riveted wing construction
8 Lateral stiffeners
9 Forward canted main spar
10 'Crimped' leading edge ribs
11 Solid web forward ribs
12 Starboard outer gun blast tube
13 Carburettor air duct
14 Intake
15 Curtiss three-blade constant-speed propeller
16 Propeller cuffs
17 Propeller hub
18 Engine front face
19 Pressure baffle
20 Forward cowling ring
21 Cooler intake
22 Cooler air duct
23 Pratt & Whitney R-1830-86 radial engine
24 Rear cowling ring/flap support
25 Controllable cowling flaps
26 Downdraft ram air duct
27 Engine mounting ring
28 Anti-detonant regulator unit
29 Cartridge starter
30 Generator
31 Intercooler
32 Engine accessories
33 Bearer assembly welded cluster joint
34 Main beam
35 Lower cowl flap
36 Exhaust stub

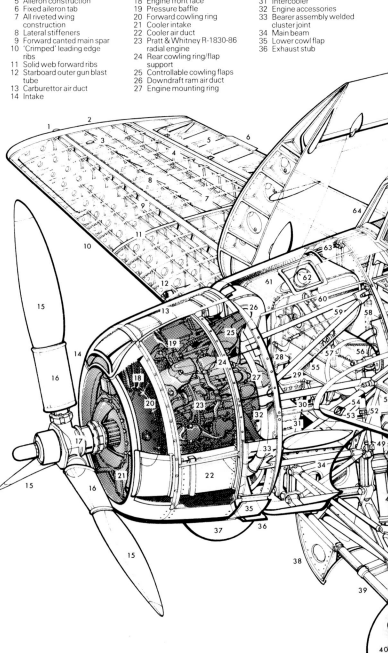

Grumman F4F Wildcat variants

XF4F-1: Grumman G-16 biplane proposal; not built
XF4F-2: Grumman G-18 monoplane prototype; first flew on 2 September 1937; one built
XF4F-3: Grumman G-36 prototype with XR-1830-76 radial; first flew on 2 February 1939; one conversion
F4F-3: first production version, with R-1830-76 radial; first flew in February 1940; 285 built
F4F-3A: production version, with R-1830 90 radial; 95 built
F4F-3P: conversions to reconnaissance role; few converted
F4F-3S: unofficial designation for two conversions to floatplane configuration with Edo floats; first flew on 28 February 1943
XF4F-4: prototype of an improved model, with R-1830-86 radial and folding wings; first flew on 14 April 1941
F4F-4: principal Grumman-built production model with folding wings; 1,169 built
F4F-4A: Lend-Lease designation of Martlet Mk III, with fixed wings
F4F-4B: Lend-Lease designation of Martlet Mk IV, with fixed wings
F4F-4P: designation of a few conversions to the reconnaissance role
XF4F-5: designation of two Grumman G-36A prototypes with Wright R-1820-40 radials; first flew in June 1940
XF4F-6: single prototype for F4F-3A

production
F4F-6: initial designation of F4F-3A
F4F-7: designation of Grumman G-52 reconnaissance variant with cameras and increased fuel; first flew on 30 December 1941; 21 built
XF4F-8: experimental prototypes with new flaps and cowlings; first flew on 8 November 1942; two built
FM-1: General Motors production version of F4F-3; first flew on 31 August 1942; 1,151 built
FM-2: General Motors production version of XF4F-8; 4,777 built
XF2M-1: proposed development by General Motors; none built
Martlet Mk I: British designation of Grumman G-36A fighters ordered by France; first flew on 11 May 1940; 181 built; later redesignated Wildcat Mk I
Martlet Mk II: British designation of Grumman G-36B fighters with folding wings; first flew in October 1940; 100 supplied; later redesignated Wildcat Mk II
Martlet Mk III: British designation of F4F-4A supplied to Fleet Air Arm with fixed wings; 30 supplied; later redesignated Wildcat Mk III
Martlet Mk IV: British designation of Lend-Lease F4F-4B; 220 built; later redesignated Wildcat Mk IV
Martlet Mk V: British designation of Lend-Lease FM-2; 312 built; later redesignated Wildcat Mk V
Wildcat Mk VI: British designation of FM-2; 370 supplied

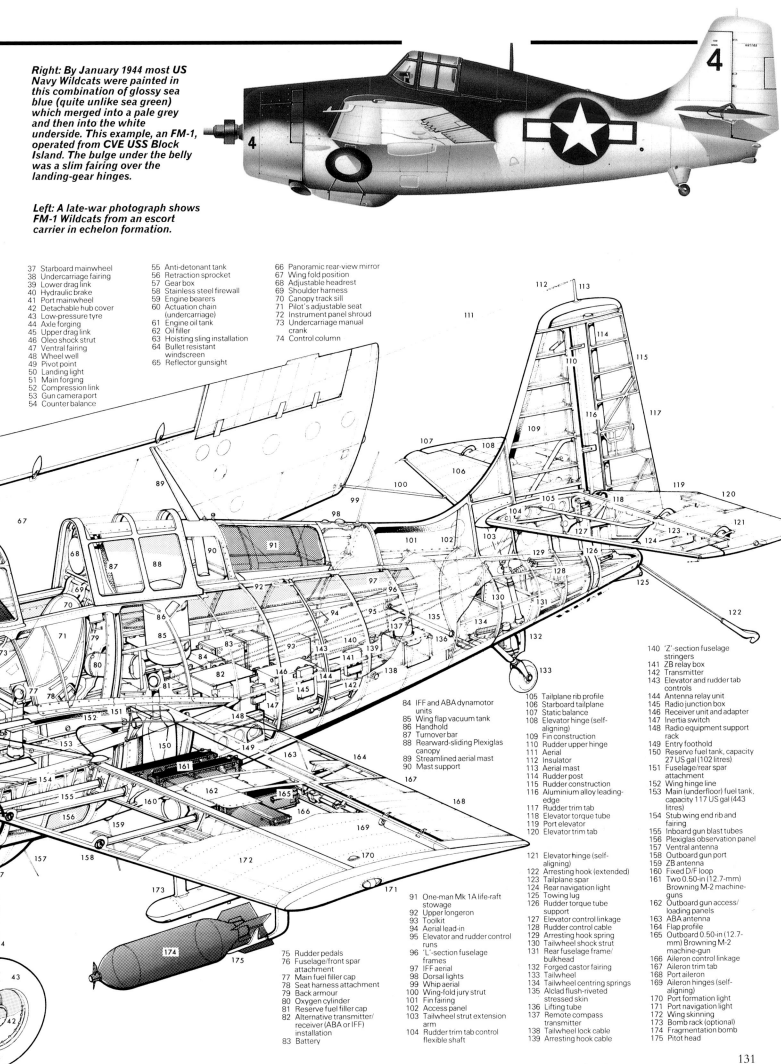

Right: By January 1944 most US Navy Wildcats were painted in this combination of glossy sea blue (quite unlike sea green) which merged into a pale grey and then into the white underside. This example, an FM-1, operated from CVE USS Block Island. The bulge under the belly was a slim fairing over the landing-gear hinges.

Left: A late-war photograph shows FM-1 Wildcats from an escort carrier in echelon formation.

37 Starboard mainwheel
38 Undercarriage fairing
39 Lower drag link
40 Hydraulic brake
41 Port mainwheel
42 Detachable hub cover
43 Low-pressure tyre
44 Axle forging
45 Upper drag link
46 Oleo shock strut
47 Ventral fairing
48 Wheel well
49 Pivot point
50 Landing light
51 Main forging
52 Compression link
53 Gun camera port
54 Counter balance

55 Anti-detonant tank
56 Retraction sprocket
57 Gear box
58 Stainless steel firewall
59 Engine bearers
60 Actuation chain (undercarriage)
61 Engine oil tank
62 Oil filler
63 Hoisting sling installation
64 Bullet resistant windscreen
65 Reflector gunsight

66 Panoramic rear-view mirror
67 Wing fold position
68 Adjustable headrest
69 Shoulder harness
70 Canopy track sill
71 Pilot's adjustable seat
72 Instrument panel shroud
73 Undercarriage manual crank
74 Control column

75 Rudder pedals
76 Fuselage/front spar attachment
77 Main fuel filler cap
78 Seat harness attachment
79 Back armour
80 Oxygen cylinder
81 Reserve fuel filler cap
82 Alternative transmitter/ receiver (ABA or IFF) installation
83 Battery

84 IFF and ABA dynamotor units
85 Wing flap vacuum tank
86 Handhold
87 Turnover bar
88 Rearward-sliding Plexiglas canopy
89 Streamlined aerial mast
90 Mast support

91 One-man Mk 1A life-raft stowage
92 Upper longeron
93 Toolkit
94 Aerial lead-in
95 Elevator and rudder control runs
96 'L'-section fuselage frames
97 IFF aerial
98 Dorsal lights
99 Whip aerial
100 Wing-fold jury strut
101 Fin fairing
102 Access panel
103 Tailwheel strut extension arm
104 Rudder trim tab control flexible shaft

105 Tailplane rib profile
106 Starboard tailplane
107 Static balance
108 Elevator hinge (self-aligning)
109 Fin construction
110 Rudder upper hinge
111 Aerial
112 Insulator
113 Aerial mast
114 Rudder post
115 Rudder construction
116 Aluminium alloy leading-edge
117 Rudder trim tab
118 Elevator torque tube
119 Port elevator
120 Elevator trim tab

121 Elevator hinge (self-aligning)
122 Arresting hook (extended)
123 Tailplane spar
124 Rear navigation light
125 Towing lug
126 Rudder torque tube support
127 Elevator control linkage
128 Rudder control cable
129 Arresting hook spring
130 Tailwheel shock strut
131 Rear fuselage frame/ bulkhead
132 Forged castor fairing
133 Tailwheel
134 Tailwheel centring springs
135 Alclad flush-riveted stressed skin
136 Lifting tube
137 Remote compass transmitter
138 Tailwheel lock cable
139 Arresting hook cable

140 'Z'-section fuselage stringers
141 ZB relay box
142 Transmitter
143 Elevator and rudder tab controls
144 Antenna relay unit
145 Radio junction box
146 Receiver unit and adapter
147 Inertia switch
148 Radio equipment support rack
149 Entry foothold
150 Reserve fuel tank, capacity 27 US gal (102 litres)
151 Fuselage/rear spar attachment
152 Wing hinge line
153 Main (underfloor) fuel tank, capacity 117 US gal (443 litres)
154 Stub wing end rib and fairing
155 Inboard gun blast tubes
156 Plexiglas observation panel
157 Ventral antenna
158 Outboard gun port
159 ZB antenna
160 Fixed D/F loop
161 Two 0.50-in (12.7-mm) Browning M-2 machine-guns
162 Outboard gun access/ loading panels
163 ABA antenna
164 Flap profile
165 Outboard 0.50-in (12.7-mm) Browning M-2 machine-gun
166 Aileron control linkage
167 Aileron trim tab
168 Port aileron
169 Aileron hinges (self-aligning)
170 Port formation light
171 Port navigation light
172 Wing skinning
173 Bomb rack (optional)
174 Fragmentation bomb
175 Pitot head

131

Grumman F4F-4 Wildcat
VGR-28
USS *Suwannee*

VGR-28 was involved in Operation Torch, the Allied invasion of French North Africa, in November 1942. *Suwannee*'s F4F-4s carried only aircraft numbers, usually partly obscured by the orange-yellow 'Torch' surround. After removal of red from markings on US Navy (and USAAF) aircraft, there was some concern in England that the white star insignia might be mistaken for enemy markings; in consequence an order was issued on 25 September 1942 requiring the addition of identification yellow surrounds to the insignia on the fuselage and beneath the wings of Army and Navy aircraft participating in the invasion. The standard fighter colour scheme of non-specular blue/grey and light grey was used. A contemporary of the Japanese Zero, the F4F had an inferior performance in several respects, yet proved capable of holding its own thanks to its superior armament, rugged construction and well-trained pilots.

Fuselage/wing
The Wildcat had the same rotund but finely streamlined fuselage as earlier Grumman naval biplanes, with an oval section semi-monocoque construction and mill-riveted metal skin. The typical Grumman undercarriage retracted manually into the fuselage, by now a distinguishing feature of Grumman fighters, in the F4F's case positioned just under the wing leading edge. The arrester hook also retracted into the fuselage, while the tailwheel was fixed. The unusual mid-wing, with a NACA 23015 wing section, was rectangular-shaped with a generous area. It had skewed hinges to fold the wings alongside the fuselage, the upper surface outwards. All-metal vacuum-operated, split trailing-edge flaps were fitted. The FM-2 had a lighter airframe and taller fin and, with the more powerful engine, gave improved take-off performance from shorter carrier decks. The enclosed cockpit had a sliding transparent canopy top over the centre of the wing with a bulletproof windshield, and armour behind the pilot.

Carrier operation
Wildcats were especially valuable for their ability to operate from small escort carriers, the pioneer work having been done with the Royal Navy Martlets in November 1940, using the 5,000-ton captured German vessel *Audacity*, on which a flat deck had been built. The first USN F4F-3s were allocated to VF-4 USS *Ranger* and VF-7 USS *Wasp*.

Armament
Initially the F4F-3 had two 0.3-in (7.62-mm) fuselage Colt-Browning guns and two 0.5-in (12.7-mm) guns in the wings. Subsequently four 0.5-in (12.7-mm) guns in the wings became standard. The F4F-4 and FM-1/2 had six forward-firing 0.5-in (12.7-mm) guns in the outer wings and could carry a bombload of 200 lb (91 kg). The FM-2 had underwing racks for two 250 lb (113-kg) bombs.

Powerplant
The XF4F-2 was powered by a Pratt & Whitney R-1830-66 Twin Wasp 14-cylinder double-row engine, rated at 1,050 hp (782.9 kW). The F4F-3 featured a supercharged R-1830-76/86 and the -3A a R-1830-90, both rated at 1,200 hp (894.8 kW). The F4F-4, FM-1 (General Motors-built) and F4F-7 each had the R-1830-36, whereas the FM-2 was fitted with the Wright Cyclone R-1820-56/56A/56W/56WA rated at 1,350 hp (1006.7 kW). In some early models the two-stage blower was giving trouble, and it was replaced with a single-stage one. At various times during the course of test flights a spinner was fitted to the propeller, but this was deleted on production aircraft. Some later FM-2s had an engine water injection system to enhance power. The fuel capacity was 160 US gal (606 litres) in self-sealing tanks in the wings, and droppable fuel tanks could be carried on the wing bomb racks.

Floatplane conversion
The F4F-3S was a conversion of F4F-3 (4038) and had the distinction of being the US Navy's first floatplane since the Curtiss F6C-3 of 1929. Though it had a maximum speed of 266 mph (428 km/h) at 20,300 ft (6096 m), its unladen weight was 886 lb (402 kg) heavier than the F4F-3. It did not enter production. The US Navy thought it would require a seaplane fighter until the small escort carrier plan proved unsuccessful, which in the event was much earlier than expected.

Specification
Grumman F4F-4 Wildcat
Type: single-seat carrier-based fighter
Powerplant: one 1,200-hp (895-kW) Pratt & Whitney R-1830-36 Twin Wasp 14-cylinder radial piston engine
Performance: maximum speed 318 mph (512 km/h) at 19,400 ft (5915 m); cruising speed 155 mph (249 km/h); initial climb rate 1,950 ft (594 m) per minute; service ceiling 39,400 ft (12010 m); range 770 miles (1239 km)
Weights: empty 5,758 lb (2612 kg); maximum take-off 7,952 lb (3607 kg)
Dimensions: span 38 ft 0 in (11.58 m); length 28 ft 9 in (8.76 m); height 9 ft 2 in (2.81 m); wing area 260.0 sq ft (24.15 m²)
Armament: six fixed 0.5-in (12.7-mm) Browning machine-guns, plus two 100-lb (45-kg) bombs

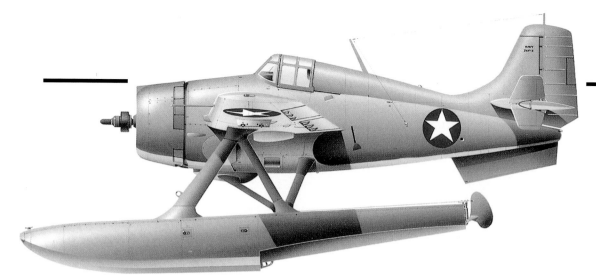

A single F4F-3, BuNo. 4038, was fitted experimentally with two Edo floats, becoming the sole F4F-3S. Like seaplane Spitfires, it was an attempt to counter Japanese fighter seaplanes. First flown on 28 February 1943, it was later fitted (as shown) with a large ventral fin.

taken the measure of their Mitsubishi nemesis.

Piloting the Wildcat was experience enough: its stalky landing gear gave it dubious ground-handling characteristics; it could be 'mushy' when manoeuvrability counted most; there was a violent draught if the cockpit hood was slid open in flight; there existed no provision at all for jettisoning the hood; and the pilot's seat was cramped and too low relative to the location of his head and his need for visibility. In short, the Wildcat could be tricky and unforgiving.

Fighting the Zero was something else. US Marines and US Navy men learned early in the war not to dogfight with the more agile Zero any time that the situation could be resolved in some other way. Where possible, they sought instead to break through a screen of Mitsubishis and attack the enemy's big bombers directly. At times, a brace of Zeroes could be lured into an overshoot, making it easier to break through to the bombers.

Hit-and-run tactics

At Guadalcanal, the bombers would approach in Vee formations more than 20 strong, and the Wildcats aimed to dive on the bombers and destroy some before the Zeroes pounced them. These hit-and-run tactics forced the Japanese pilots to over-use precious fuel. Reliance on one's wingman was crucial: once the dogfighting started a Wildcat pilot had to depend on his wingman to shoot the enemy off his tail. No 'lone wolf' survived very long, although some individual Wildcat pilots excelled. Major John L. Smith was credited with downing 19 Japanese aircraft and Major Marion Carl with 18 1/2.

One of the more intriguing tests involving the Wildcat was a 1942 effort in Philadelphia to evaluate the idea of fighters being towed by bombers, to serve as long-range escorts. The idea was one which recurred throughout the 1940s, although it was never tried in actual operations. The Wildcat was an ideal candidate because its three-blade Curtiss Electric propeller could be easily feathered and the engine restarted in flight. A hook-on and break-off system was devised to enable the Wildcat to be towed from an attachment point beneath the wing; the Wildcat pilot could connect and disconnect at will. In May 1942, an F4F was towed by a Douglas BD-1 (the US Navy version of the A-20 Havoc) and later two Wildcats were towed by a Boeing B-17 over a 1,200-mile (1930-km) eight-hour course.

The system worked; the Wildcat pilot could remain idle while his aircraft flew effectively as a glider, its range thus being limited only by the endurance of the tow aircraft. But no practical application of the arrangement was ever made.

The final production variant built by Grumman was the long-range reconnaissance F4F-7 with increased fuel capacity, camera installations in the lower fuselage, and no armament. Only 21 were built, but Grumman also produced an additional 100 F4F-3s and two XF4F-8 prototypes. With an urgent need to concentrate on development and production of the more advanced F6F Hellcat, Grumman negotiated with General Motors to continue production of the F4F-4 Wildcat under the designation **FM-1**. Production by General Motors' Eastern Aircraft Division began after finalisation of a contract on 18 April 1942, and the first of this company's FM-ls was flown on 31 August 1942. Production totalled 1,151, of which 312 were supplied to the UK under the designation **Martlet Mk V** (later **Wildcat Mk V**).

At the same time, General Motors was working on the development of an improved version, designated **FM-2**, which was the production version of the two Grumman XF4F-8 prototypes. Its major change was the installation of a 1,350-hp (1007-kW) Wright R-1820-56 Cyclone 9 radial engine, but a larger vertical tail was introduced to maintain good directional stability with this more powerful engine, and airframe weight was reduced to the minimum. A total of 4,777 FM-2s was built, 370 of them supplied to the UK and designated **Wildcat Mk VI** from the outset, the only British machines never to bear the Martlet name.

Seen here on company test in midnight blue livery, the General Motors FM-2 outnumbered all other versions combined. Its chief distinguishing feature was a taller vertical tail. This example is BuNo. 16570.

Grumman XF5F-1 Skyrocket and XP-50

The Grumman G-34 proposal of 1938 for a single-seat twin-engine shipboard fighter anticipated the realisation of an operational production example of such a type by quite a few years. In fact, the idea of flying a high-performance twin-engined aircraft off a carrier deck was then considered to be so advanced that it bordered on the revolutionary: yet only four years later, on 18 April 1942, 16 North American B-25 twin-engine bombers were flown off USS *Hornet* to attack Tokyo.

Not only was the G-34 an advanced concept; in its original form it was a most unusual-looking aircraft, with the leading edge of its low-set monoplane wing forward of the fuselage nose. The tail unit had twin endplate fins and rudders, and the landing gear was of the retractable tailwheel type, with the main units retracting aft into the wing-mounted engine nacelles. Powerplant comprised two Wright R-1820 Cyclones, each with a three-bladed propeller, these being geared to counter-rotate to offset the effects of propeller torque.

The US Navy was first to order a prototype, the **XF5F-1**, on 30 June 1938, which was flown for the first time on 1 April 1940. A number of modifications were introduced subsequently, the most noticeable being an extension of the fuselage nose so that it terminated forward of the

wing. Although failing to win a production order, the XF5F-1 soldiered on until withdrawn from use in December 1944, having done some useful work as a development prototype for the more advanced Grumman F7F.

A land-based version of Grumman's design interested the US Army Air Force, which ordered a single **XP-50** prototype. Although generally similar to the naval version, it differed by having a lengthened nose to accommodate the nosewheel of the tricycle landing gear and had as powerplant two Wright R-1820-67/-69 turbocharged engines.

First flown on 14 May 1941, the XP-50 was plagued with engine overheating problems and

was eventually written off after suffering serious damage when a turbocharger exploded. No further examples of the XP-50 were built.

Specification
Grumman XF5F-I
Type: single-seat carrier-based fighter prototype
Powerplant: two 1,200-hp (895-kW) Wright XR-1820-40/-42 Cyclone 9-cylinder radial piston engines
Performance: maximum speed 383 mph (616 km/h); cruising speed 210 mph (338 km/h); service ceiling 33,000 ft (10060 m); range 1,200 miles (1931 km)
Weights: empty 8,107 lb (3677 kg); maximum take-off 10,138 lb (4599 kg)
Dimensions: span 42 ft 0 in (12.80 m); length 28 ft 8 in (8.75 m); height 11 ft 4 in (3.45 m); wing area 303.5 sq ft (28.20 m²)
Armament: provision for two 23-mm Madsen cannon

Seen here on test over the Long Island coast, the XP-50 was potentially outstanding, and a significant improvement over the Navy XF5F. It would have been armed with two 20-mm cannon, two 0.50-in Brownings and two 100-lb bombs.

First flown on 1 April 1940, the XF5F-1 was visually striking, but emerged at a time of rapid technical development. Prolonged snags ensured that it became obsolete while still under development, but it led the way for the F7F.

Grumman F6F Hellcat

The **Grumman F6F Hellcat** was not the fastest fighter of World War II, or the most agile, or the most heavily armed. But in the war against Japan the F6F was by far the most important single aircraft, because it quickly turned the tables on what had previously been an unbroken run of almost too-easy success, and it struck fear into the heart of every Japanese pilot. Of the total score of 6,477 confirmed victories by US Navy carrier-based pilots, the F6F (which only entered the fray on 31 August 1943) gained 4,947.

Most of the other victories were gained with great skill and courage by pilots flying the Grumman F4F Wildcat. This had begun life as a biplane but eventually matured in 1940 as a tough and agile mid-wing monoplane, which did all that could be expected of an engine in the 1,000-hp (746-kW) class. Used by the UK's Fleet Air Arm as the Martlet, this type shot down a Ju 88 as early as Christmas Day 1940. Toughness, good turn radius, reliability and the powerful armament of six 0.5-in (12.7-mm) guns added up to a great deal, but the F4F was deficient in level speed and climb and could not fight the Messerschmitt Bf 109E on level terms. Against the Mitsubishi A6M Zero-Sen it was the same story, but long before that Grumman and the US Navy had decided to build an improved fighter.

Prototype contract

There was no direct attempt to rival the Vought F4U, which was in a different class; merely to build an improved F4F, and that was the way the new fighter was described in the prototype contract of 30 June 1941. The obvious engine was the Wright R-2600, or two-row Cyclone 14, already in production for bombers and for Grumman's own TBF Avenger. The contract was for two aircraft, an **XF6F-1** (BuAer No. 02981) with the 1,600-hp (1194-kW) R-2600-10 and an **XF6F-2** (02982) with the new turbocharged R-2600-16. The F6F was initially intended to be a minimum-change improvement of the F4F, but all the reports from the Royal and US Navies cried out for much higher flight performance, to the point that Grumman increasingly looked at a more powerful engine, the great Pratt & Whitney R-2800 Double Wasp. Also used in the F4U, this was starting life in the 2,000-hp (1492-kW) class, but it could never fit an F4F.

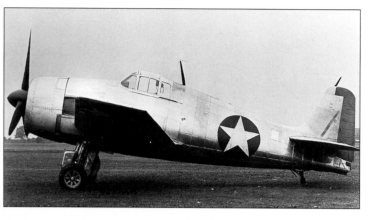

Representative in most respects of all production Hellcats that were to follow, the XF6F-1 prototype in June 1942 differed primarily in being powered by a Wright XR-2600-10 engine. The basic F6F design owed much to the F4F Wildcat.

To maximise the potential performance of the F6F airframe, a Pratt & Whitney R-2800-10 was selected to power the second prototype, ordered as the XF6F-2 but completed as the XF6F-3 shown here and flown a month after the first. The latter also became an XF6F-3.

Serving in the Pacific early in 1945, this F6F-5 of VF-12 served aboard the USS Randolph (CV-15), as indicated by the white stripes on the fin and rudder. The so-called 'G' symbols, to distinguish between aircraft operating from different carriers, were patterns of white and were rationalised only in January 1945.

Grumman's management comprised mainly engineers, notable examples being president Leroy R. Grumman, executive vice-president Leon A. Swirbul and vice-president engineering W.T. 'Bill' Schwendler. Before Pearl Harbor on 7 December 1941 these men had roughed out a scheme for a completely new F6F, larger and much stronger than the F4F and not only offering higher performance but also much greater fuel and ammunition capacity. The wing was made larger than on any other major single-engined fighter of World War II, at 334 sq ft (31.03 m²) compared with 314 sq ft (29.17m²) for the F4U, 300 sq ft (27.87 m²) for the P-47 and below 250 sq ft (23.23 m²) for most other fighters. This immense squarish wing had three spars, fabric-skinned ailerons and split flaps, and was pivoted on skewed axes at the front spar at each end of the horizontal centre section to fold back beside the fuselage with upper surface outward. Each folding outer panel contained three 0.5-in (12.7-mm) machine-guns each with 400 rounds. The wing was moved down from the F4F's mid-position to the mid-low position, which improved accommodation of fuel under the floor of the cockpit and shortened the landing gears, despite a great and welcomed increase in track. Each main gear, stressed for 14 ft (4.27 m) per second vertical descent, pivoted to the rear with the wheel rotating 90° to lie flat in the wing ahead of the flap. The fuselage was much larger than that of the F4F, the pilot

being perched in the top of a cross-section changed from a circle to a pear shape, giving great width in the lower part but leaving a narrow dorsal region similar to early 'razorback' P-47s. (Unlike the US Army fighter the F6F never received a moulded bubble canopy, and its rearward view was always a weak point.)

Successful engine testing

Design of an R-2800 installation went ahead in early 1942 but the Wright engine was installed in the first aircraft, the XF6F-1, which was flown by Selden Converse on 26 June 1942, less than a year after the go-ahead. Results were good, though longitudinal stability was excessive for a fighter, and trim changes on varying engine power or cycling gear or flaps were unacceptably large. Fortunately there was nothing calling for substantial redesign, because in May 1942 the US Navy had begun placing massive production contracts for the chosen R-2800 aircraft as the **F6F-3**. Only a month after the first, the second prototype flew on 30 July with the 2,000-hp (1492-kW) R-2800-10 driving a Curtiss Electric propeller with spinner, with the designation **XF6F-3**. This was a superior aircraft, and it is remarkable that Grumman was able to fit the larger and heavier engine into an aircraft of basically unchanged dimensions or fuel capacity while still preserving centre of gravity position.

Left: A pair of Hellcats is prepared for action during operations in the Pacific area. Each aircraft carries a 150-US gal (568-litre) drop tank on the fuselage centreline. The blue border to the star-and-bar insignia dates this photograph later than September 1943.

Right: Finished in the Navy's 1943 scheme of non-specular blue-grey graduated from top to bottom to a light grey-blue, these F6F-3s bear the markings of Navy Squadron VF-8. Hellcats would continue to fly actively with the Navy until 1954, and then for several more years in the target drone role.

Grumman F6F Hellcat

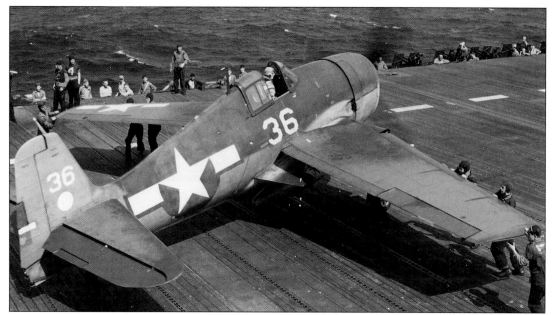

Right: A pair of Hellcats in their element over the Pacific, where the Grumman fighter became one of the most feared of Allied aircraft among Japanese fliers. In nearly two years of operations, USN and USMC Hellcats were credited with 5,156 victories, with a 19:1 kill-to-loss ratio.

Left: Immediately after landing aboard the USS Hornet (CV-12) after a raid over the Marianas in the spring of 1944, this F6F has its wings folded. The action was wholly manual; the wings pivoted as they were folded aft to lie, upper surfaces outwards, along the fuselage sides.

Grumman was a hive of activity in early 1942, with constant feedback from combat units, a colossal load of production on high priority and the need to build a complete new plant at Bethpage alongside the original works to build the F6F. A plan to build under licence at Canadian Vickers never bore fruit. In spring 1942 the company bought up thousands of steel girders from the old 2nd Avenue elevated railroad and a World's Fair pavilion, thus speeding up the new factory. F6F-3s were on the line long before the plant was finished. Little redesign was needed, though the main-gear fairings were simplified (the lower part of the wheel being left exposed in the wing), the engine attitude was slightly altered (though it was still 3° nose-down) and the propeller was changed to a Hamilton Hydromatic with no spinner. The tilt of the engine was matched with a zero-incidence wing setting, which meant that at take-off or in cruising flight the engine was horizontal while the rest of the aircraft was tail-down. At full power the fuselage became horizontal for minimum drag.

Prototype flies

On 2 October 1942 the first prototype flew as the **XF6F-4** with a two-speed R-2800-27, but this engine was not adopted. The second aircraft was brought up to production F6F-3 standard, except for the landing-gear fairings, and among other things was used for trials with drop tanks and other stores under the fuselage. From the start both prototypes had bulletproof windscreens and 212 lb (96 kg) of cockpit armour, and very few changes were needed to the Hellcat for the rest of its career except in armament and equipment. One of the puzzles is that, though both prototypes had structural provision for the six guns, they were not installed and the wing leading edges had no apertures!

A factory-fresh F6F-5. In this wartime print, the barrel protrusions of the machine-guns have been crudely obliterated. The six-gun armament remained the standard for all Hellcats, but some late-production F6F-5s had two 20-mm cannon replacing a pair of machine-guns.

Grumman F6F-5 Hellcat cutaway key

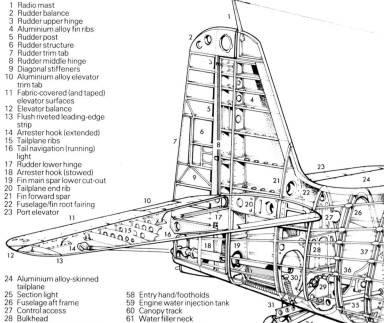

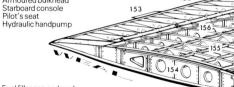

1 Radio mast
2 Rudder balance
3 Rudder upper hinge
4 Aluminium alloy fin ribs
5 Rudder post
6 Rudder structure
7 Rudder trim tab
8 Rudder middle hinge
9 Diagonal stiffeners
10 Aluminium alloy elevator trim tab
11 Fabric-covered (and taped) elevator surfaces
12 Elevator balance
13 Flush riveted leading-edge strip
14 Arrester hook (extended)
15 Tailplane ribs
16 Tail navigation (running) light
17 Rudder lower hinge
18 Arrester hook (stowed)
19 Fin main spar lower cut-out
20 Tailplane end rib
21 Fin forward spar
22 Fuselage/fin root fairing
23 Port elevator

24 Aluminium alloy-skinned tailplane
25 Section light
26 Fuselage aft frame
27 Control access
28 Bulkhead
29 Tailwheel hydraulic shock-absorber
30 Tailwheel centering mechanism
31 Tailwheel steel mounting arm
32 Rearward-retracting tailwheel (hard rubber tyre)
33 Fairing
34 Steel plate door fairing
35 Tricing sling support tube
36 Hydraulic actuating cylinder
37 Flanged ring fuselage frames
38 Control cable runs
39 Fuselage longerons
40 Relay box
41 Dorsal rod antenna
42 Dorsal recognition light
43 Radio aerial
44 Radio mast
45 Aerial lead-in
46 Dorsal frame stiffeners
47 Junction box
48 Radio equipment (upper rack)
49 Radio shelf
50 Control cable runs
51 Transverse brace
52 Remote radio compass
53 Ventral recognition lights (3)
54 Ventral rod antenna
55 Destructor device
56 Accumulator
57 Radio equipment (flower rack)

58 Entry hand/footholds
59 Engine water injection tank
60 Canopy track
61 Water filler neck
62 Rear-view window
63 Rearward-sliding cockpit canopy (open)
64 Headrest
65 Pilot's head/shoulder armour
66 Canopy sill (reinforced)
67 Fire-extinguisher
68 Oxygen bottle (port fuselage wall)
69 Water tank mounting
70 Underfloor self-sealing fuel tank (60 US gal/227 litres)
71 Armoured bulkhead
72 Starboard console
73 Pilot's seat
74 Hydraulic handpump

75 Fuel filler cap and neck
76 Rudder pedals
77 Central console
78 Control column
79 Chart board (horizontal stowage)
80 Instrument panel
81 Panel coaming
82 Reflector gunsight
83 Rear-view mirror
84 Armoured glass windshield
85 Deflection plate (pilot forward protection)

86 Main bulkhead armour-plated upper section with hoisting sling attachments port and starboard)
87 Aluminium alloy aileron trim tab
88 Fabric covered (and taped) aileron surfaces

89 Flush riveted outer wing skin
90 Aluminium alloy sheet wing tip (riveted to wing outer rib)
91 Port navigation (running) light
92 Formed leading-edge (approach/landing light and camera gun inboard)
93 Fixed cowling panel
94 Armour plate (oil tank forward protection)

July 1943 the national insignia grew the side rectangles with red border, changed to dark blue a month later, and the usual finish became overall midnight blue.

Features standardised in production included a self-sealing tank for 60 US gal (227 litres) under the cockpit and one of 87.5 US gal (331 litres) in each inner wing for a total of 235 US gal (889 litres), armour around the oil tank and cooler under the engine, retractable tailwheel with solid rubber tyre, sting-type hook extended to the rear from the extreme tail (this area required strengthening because of failures), fabric-skinned control surfaces with pilot-operated metal trim tabs, and a regular B-series R-2800-10 Double Wasp with a 13 ft 1 in (3.99 m) propeller. Most fighting in the Pacific was at medium or low altitudes, and although turbochargers were studied they were never adopted. In late 1943 an F6F-3 (66244) was diverted as a test aircraft with a turbocharged R-2800-21. The installation required a deepened lower duct for the turbocharger and cooling air, with waste gates on the underside of the fuselage just aft of the leading edge, and a special four-bladed propeller with root cuffs was fitted. Eventually this aircraft, which was given the defunct earlier designation of XF6F-2, was given the BuAer number 43137 as a standard F6F-3 (and in fact the last of this model) in April 1944. Despite the enormous numbers of Hellcats built, no attempt was ever made to fit any engine other than the R-2800 into any subsequent F6F.

Armament was certainly present on the first production F6F-3, from the block 04775-04958, which flew on 4 October 1942. The finish was graduated shades of blue, ranging from greenish blue (called medium sea blue) above, through a paler blue to an underside that was pale blue in the first block and later gull grey or insignia white. These were low-contrast colours, strongly resembling some in use today. In

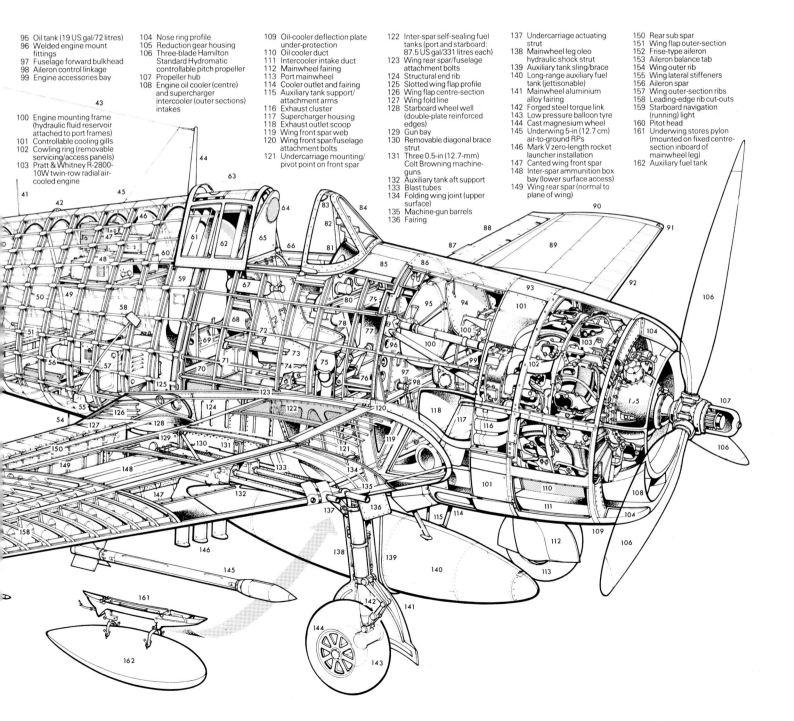

95 Oil tank (19 US gal/72 litres)
96 Welded engine mount fittings
97 Fuselage forward bulkhead
98 Aileron control linkage
99 Engine accessories bay

100 Engine mounting frame (hydraulic fluid reservoir attached to port frames)
101 Controllable cooling gills
102 Cowling ring (removable servicing/access panels)
103 Pratt & Whitney R-2800-10W twin-row radial air-cooled engine
104 Nose ring profile
105 Reduction gear housing
106 Three-blade Hamilton Standard Hydromatic controllable pitch propeller
107 Propeller hub
108 Engine oil cooler (centre) and supercharger intercooler (outer sections) intakes

109 Oil-cooler deflection plate under-protection
110 Oil cooler duct
111 Intercooler intake duct
112 Mainwheel fairing
113 Port mainwheel
114 Cooler outlet and fairing
115 Auxiliary tank support/attachment arms
116 Exhaust cluster
117 Supercharger housing
118 Exhaust outlet scoop
119 Wing front spar web
120 Wing front spar/fuselage attachment bolts
121 Undercarriage mounting/pivot point on front spar

122 Inter-spar self-sealing fuel tanks (port and starboard: 87.5 US gal/331 litres each)
123 Wing rear spar/fuselage attachment bolts
124 Structural end rib
125 Slotted wing flap profile
126 Wing flap centre-section
127 Wing fold line
128 Starboard wheel well (double-plate reinforced edges)
129 Gun bay
130 Removable diagonal brace strut
131 Three 0.5-in (12.7-mm) Colt Browning machine-guns
132 Auxiliary tank aft support
133 Blast tubes
134 Folding wing joint (upper surface)
135 Machine-gun barrels
136 Fairing

137 Undercarriage actuating strut
138 Mainwheel leg oleo hydraulic shock strut
139 Auxiliary tank sling/brace
140 Long-range auxiliary fuel tank (jettisonable)
141 Mainwheel aluminium alloy fairing
142 Forged steel torque link
143 Low pressure balloon tyre
144 Cast magnesium wheel
145 Underwing 5-in (12.7 cm) air-to-ground RPs
146 Mark V zero-length rocket launcher installation
147 Canted wing front spar
148 Inter-spar ammunition box bay (lower surface access)
149 Wing rear spar (normal to plane of wing)

150 Rear sub spar
151 Wing flap outer-section
152 Frise-type aileron
153 Aileron balance tab
154 Wing outer rib
155 Wing lateral stiffeners
156 Aileron spar
157 Wing outer-section ribs
158 Leading-edge rib cut-outs
159 Starboard navigation (running) light
160 Pitot head
161 Underwing stores pylon (mounted on fixed centre-section inboard of mainwheel leg)
162 Auxiliary fuel tank

Grumman F6F Hellcat

Adding ground-attack to the Hellcat's primary air-fighting role, provision was made on later F6F-5s for up to 1,000-lb (454-kg) bombs or – shown here – a pair of 11.75-in (29.8-cm) Tiny Tim rockets under the centre section and six HVARs under the outer wings.

Deliveries began on 16 January 1943 to US Navy fighter squadron VF-9, embarked aboard USS *Essex*. At this time Vought's F4U had been flying almost three years, yet was still not qualified for carrier operation; indeed, competition from the rapidly produced F6F is held to have acted as a major spur to the Vought team, which had to make major changes to its basically superior aircraft. By January 1943 prolonged trials had been held with various kinds of external ordnance under F6Fs, but so far as is known none of the 4,402 (not 4,403, for, as noted, nos 66244 and 43137 were the same aircraft) F6F-3s built had provision for any external load except the 150-US gal (568-litre) drop tank, though some were given bomb or rocket attachments.

Reception to the Hellcat was very positive and, despite the rather poor forward view, tendency to weathercock on the ground unless the tailwheel was locked, and long-stroke legs which could allow the big propeller to hit the ground, pilots soon converted and found few problems in operating even from light escort carriers. By August 1943 many Hellcats were at readiness aboard the fleet carriers USS *Essex*, *Yorktown* and *Independence*, and aboard the light carriers USS *Belleau Wood* and *Princeton*. The first combat mission was flown by VF-5 in the second attack on Marcus Island on 31 August, operating from USS *Yorktown*, followed on the same day by VF-9 from USS *Essex*. Many good results were obtained, including improved cruise control for greater mileage per gallon, procedures for rapid strike-down on deck and high reliability in intensive operations involving two missions per aircraft per day. In the first big air battle, in the Kwajalein/Roi area on 4 December 1943, 91 Hellcats met 50 A6Ms and destroyed 28 for the loss of two.

By the end of 1943 deliveries had reached 2,555, with only minor deficiencies becoming apparent. None of the aircraft in action in that year had bomb racks, but an extremely important new development, following a few months later than the same development on the F4U, was the installation of radar for night interceptions. The story of the US Navy radars working on the short wavelength of 3 cm is a long one, and of course began with the British gift of the magnetron in 1940. There were eventually nine different sets, four of which went into production. That for the F6F was derived from the AI Mk III (SCR-537) by Sperry with designation AIA (it was the progenitor of the ASH set used in British naval aircraft). The production sets derived from it were the APS-4 and APS-6 families, both of which had the main power units, timebase and other items in the fuselage but the scanner in a pod far out on the right wing, where it rotated at 1,200 rpm while sweeping through a 60° spiral scan. No tremors were felt in the cockpit and aircraft handling was little affected, though the pod reduced maximum speed by some 20 mph (32 km/h) and in a sideslip gave a falsely high airspeed reading.

The first night-fighter version was the field-converted **F6F-3E**,18 of which were converted at MCAS Quonset Point, which had hand-built the first night-fighter Corsairs three months earlier in June 1943. The F6F-3Es had the AIA with a Philco RF head originally tailored for ASV (air-to-surface vessel) use with a wide but shallow scan. Other changes included red cockpit lighting and removal of the curved Plexiglas fairing ahead of the bulletproof windscreen, which experience had shown easily became scratched and progressively less transparent. Then followed a factory-built **XF6F-3N** and 205 production **F6F-3N** night-fighters with the APS-6 radar, radio altimeter and IFF. At one time it was planned to fit APS-6 to half of all future Hellcat production (limiting factors were insufficient radars and insufficient qualified night-fighter pilots). The 3-cm story is a great one, but 1943 was full of Japanese activity at night and while waiting for the proper night-fighters both the US Navy and US Marines tried alternative schemes.

Night action success

The one best-remembered was the hunter/killer team of from one to three single-seat fighters in formation with a TBF Avenger with ASV radar or a Dauntless with ASB. Teams had to work as a unit and practise together, and the first major night action took place on 26 November 1943, led by Lieutenant Commander 'Butch' O'Hare. He destroyed a Mitsubishi G4M but was shot down by Japanese fighters while the F6F-3s were making mincemeat of the main Japanese force. The world's busiest airport (at Chicago) is named in his memory.

Above: From mid-1943 onwards, many Hellcats were adapted or produced for the night-fighting role. Both F6F-3N (illustrated) and F6F-5N variants were fitted with the 3-cm AN/APS-6 radar in a pod on the starboard wing leading edge.

Left: Production of the Hellcat peaked at 20 aircraft a day, and all 12,274 F6Fs came from a single Grumman factory on Long Island, New York. This F6F-5 in early post-war service differed little from the prototype, and all Hellcat variants retained the R-2800 powerplant.

Like all 1944 F6F-3s, the F6F-3Ns had several improvements, the most important being the R-2800-10W engine rated at 2,200 hp (1641kW) with water injection. The water tank was behind the cockpit, with a long duct from a filler in the top of the rear spine. This engine arrived at Bethpage right at the end of F6F-3 production, and is regarded mainly as one of the key features of the **F6F-5** which from 21 April 1944 followed on the production line. Another standard modification was removal of the curved windshield fairing, which as noted earlier spoilt forward view for no significant gain in speed. Other changes included spring-tab ailerons, a changed design of main gear leg, a smaller upright radio mast and omission of the gun fairings, cockpit rear window and lower cowl flaps.

Impact in every theatre

Thus the F6F-5, which poured from the Bethpage line at the rate of roughly 20 per day, was almost identical to the F6F-3. It is difficult to find any other aircraft made only in one factory to the tune of 12,274 examples, all substantially identical, in 2½ years. For cost-effectiveness and impact on a world war the F6F is right in the very front rank. Almost all the major air combats of the Pacific theatre from August 1943 onwards were dominated by it, and it was flown by all the US Navy aces of that period. From February 1945 it was flown by four US Marine carrier squadrons. Its superiority over the Japanese had by late 1944 become so absolute it maintained a continuous presence by day and night over the combat zones and Japanese airfields in what was called 'The Big Blue Blanket'. On the basis of contemporary unit records, the ratio of F6F kills to losses exceeded 19:1.

Variants are listed separately, those produced in quantity being the **F6F-5N** night-fighter and **F6F-5P** photo aircraft. All had armament, and a substantial proportion of F6F-5 production, apparently including all F6F-5Ns and F6F-5Ps, had the innermost 0. 5-in (12.7-mm) guns replaced by 20-mm cannon, each with 200 rounds. All F6F-5s had provision for an external load of ordnance, though as this was also

As one Hellcat strives to gain height, two more are readied for launch, using port and starboard catapults alternately. This is the scene aboard the USS Randolph (CV-15) as the war against Japan neared its end.

a feature of many F6F-3s it cannot be regarded as a distinguishing feature. The centreline attachments could carry a 1,000-lb (454-kg) bomb or a 150-US gal (682-litre) tank. A similar rack was provided under each wing root for a 1,000-lb (454-kg) bomb or Tiny Tim rocket. The outer wings could each carry three HVARs (high-velocity aircraft rockets).

Many other armament fits were investigated, and in the UK the trials programme included eight rails for 60-lb (27-kg) rocket projectiles. The Fleet Air Arm received 252 F6F-3s under Lend-Lease from late April 1943, the service at first calling the type **Grumman Gannet Mk I** until the name Hellcat was standardised. All had British camouflage and saw much action, initially with Nos 800 and 804 Squadrons, off Norway and in the Mediterranean. They were followed by 930 **Hellcat Mk II** (F6F-5) and 80 **Hellcat NF.Mk II** (F6F-5N), delivered in midnight blue and almost all used in the Pacific with blue/white theatre roundels and often with white bands round nose, wings and tail. Some were camera-equipped **Hellcat FR.Mk II**s, and a few had guns removed to become **Hellcat PR.Mk II**s. They operated throughout the East Indies, Malaya, Burma and in the final assault on Japan. By late 1945 all but two of 12 active squadrons had re-equipped, but one aircraft, KE209, was used by the commander of RNAS Lossiemouth as his personal mount until well into 1953.

At least 120 ex-USN Hellcats were supplied to France's Aéronavale for use in Indo-China, and survivors later served in North Africa. Other operators included the navies of Argentina and Uruguay (to 1961). Over 300 were converted as **F6F-5K** remotely-piloted targets and explosive-packed missiles, six of the latter being guided to North Korean targets in August 1952.

Above: Although the US Navy caption for this photograph locates the scene aboard the USS Randolph, the F6F-5 awaiting launch for a strike against Japanese targets displays the stylised arrowhead marking associated with the USS Bennington (CV-20).

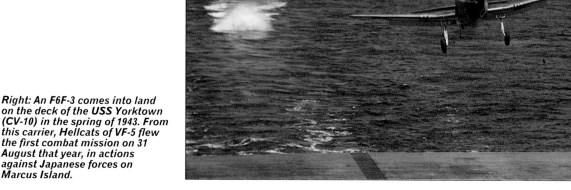

Right: An F6F-3 comes into land on the deck of the USS Yorktown (CV-10) in the spring of 1943. From this carrier, Hellcats of VF-5 flew the first combat mission on 31 August that year, in actions against Japanese forces on Marcus Island.

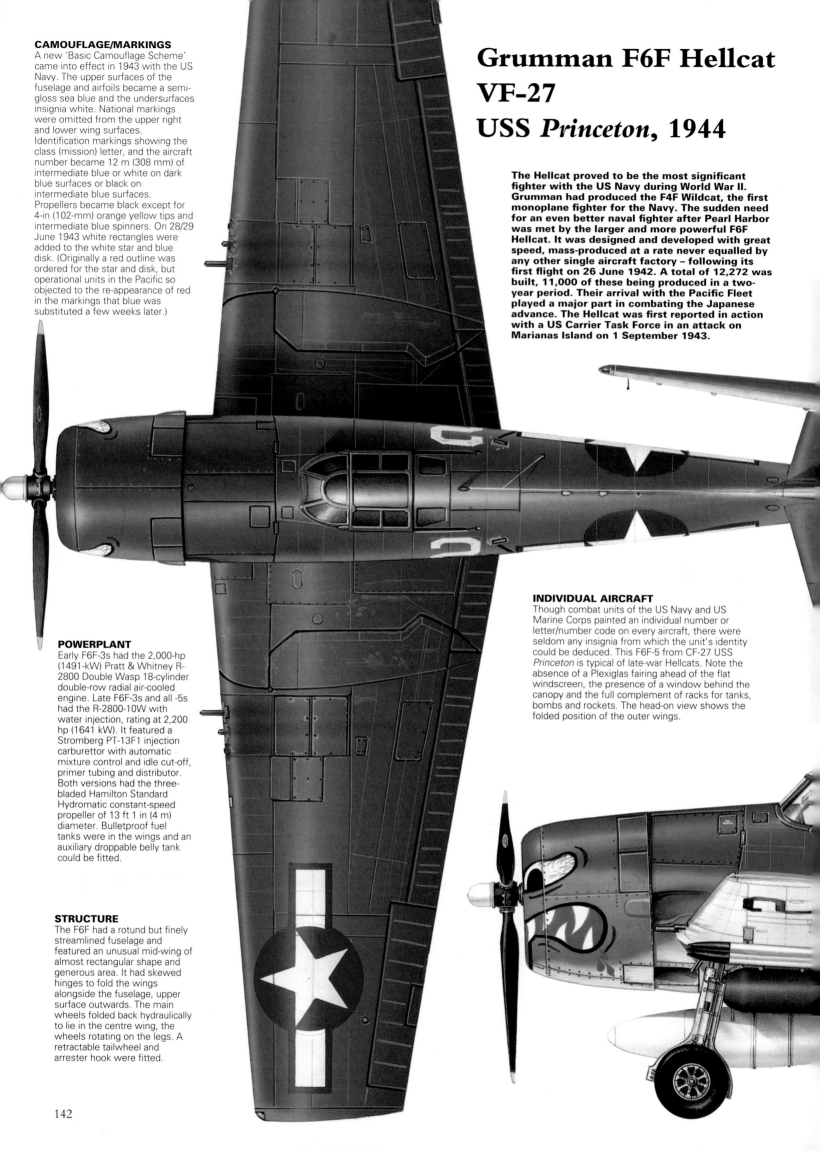

CAMOUFLAGE/MARKINGS

A new 'Basic Camouflage Scheme' came into effect in 1943 with the US Navy. The upper surfaces of the fuselage and airfoils became a semi-gloss sea blue and the undersurfaces insignia white. National markings were omitted from the upper right and lower wing surfaces. Identification markings showing the class (mission) letter, and the aircraft number became 12 m (308 mm) of intermediate blue or white on dark blue surfaces or black on intermediate blue surfaces. Propellers became black except for 4-in (102-mm) orange yellow tips and intermediate blue spinners. On 28/29 June 1943 white rectangles were added to the white star and blue disk. (Originally a red outline was ordered for the star and disk, but operational units in the Pacific so objected to the re-appearance of red in the markings that blue was substituted a few weeks later.)

Grumman F6F Hellcat
VF-27
USS *Princeton*, 1944

The Hellcat proved to be the most significant fighter with the US Navy during World War II. Grumman had produced the F4F Wildcat, the first monoplane fighter for the Navy. The sudden need for an even better naval fighter after Pearl Harbor was met by the larger and more powerful F6F Hellcat. It was designed and developed with great speed, mass-produced at a rate never equalled by any other single aircraft factory – following its first flight on 26 June 1942. A total of 12,272 was built, 11,000 of these being produced in a two-year period. Their arrival with the Pacific Fleet played a major part in combating the Japanese advance. The Hellcat was first reported in action with a US Carrier Task Force in an attack on Marianas Island on 1 September 1943.

POWERPLANT

Early F6F-3s had the 2,000-hp (1491-kW) Pratt & Whitney R-2800 Double Wasp 18-cylinder double-row radial air-cooled engine. Late F6F-3s and all -5s had the R-2800-10W with water injection, rating at 2,200 hp (1641 kW). It featured a Stromberg PT-13F1 injection carburettor with automatic mixture control and idle cut-off, primer tubing and distributor. Both versions had the three-bladed Hamilton Standard Hydromatic constant-speed propeller of 13 ft 1 in (4 m) diameter. Bulletproof fuel tanks were in the wings and an auxiliary droppable belly tank could be fitted.

INDIVIDUAL AIRCRAFT

Though combat units of the US Navy and US Marine Corps painted an individual number or letter/number code on every aircraft, there were seldom any insignia from which the unit's identity could be deduced. This F6F-5 from CF-27 USS *Princeton* is typical of late-war Hellcats. Note the absence of a Plexiglas fairing ahead of the flat windscreen, the presence of a window behind the canopy and the full complement of racks for tanks, bombs and rockets. The head-on view shows the folded position of the outer wings.

STRUCTURE

The F6F had a rotund but finely streamlined fuselage and featured an unusual mid-wing of almost rectangular shape and generous area. It had skewed hinges to fold the wings alongside the fuselage, upper surface outwards. The main wheels folded back hydraulically to lie in the centre wing, the wheels rotating on the legs. A retractable tailwheel and arrester hook were fitted.

COMBAT SERVICE

Hellcats destroyed more than 6,000 enemy aircraft – 4,947 by US Navy carrier squadrons, 209 by land-based USMC units and the rest by 1,182 Hellcats of the Fleet Air Arm. Deliveries to USS *Essex* began in early 1943, only 18 months after the first contract was placed. By mid 1944 the Hellcat, and its Chance Vought contemporary, the Corsair, had become standard US Navy equipment through the Pacific. In June 1944 Hellcats achieved a major victory in the Battle of the Philippine Sea. By the end of the war Hellcats had been credited with almost 75 per cent of the Navy's air-to-air victories. Production ended in November 1975 with a grand total of 12,275.

Specification
Grumman F6F-5 Hellcat
Type: single-seat carrier-based fighter/bomber
Powerplant: one 2,000-hp (1492-kW) Pratt & Whitney R-2800-10W Double Wasp 18-cylinder radial piston engine
Performance: maximum speed 386 mph (621 km/h) at medium altitudes; initial climb rate (clean) 3,410 ft (1039 m) per minute; service ceiling 37,300 ft (11369 m); range on internal fuel 1,040 miles (1674 km)
Weights: empty 9,153 to 9,239 lb (4152 to 4191 kg); normal take-off 12,500 lb (5670 kg); maximum take-off 15,413 lb (6991 kg)
Dimensions: span 42 ft 10 in (13.08 m) or (folded) 16 ft 2 in (4.93 m); length 33 ft 7 in (10.23 m); height (propeller as shown) 13 ft 1 in (3.99 m); wing area 334 sq ft (31.03 m²)
Armament: six 0.5-in (12.7-mm) Browning machine-guns each with 400 rounds, plus provision for two or three bombs up to maximum total of 2,000 lb (907 kg) and six 5-in (127-mm) HVAR rockets

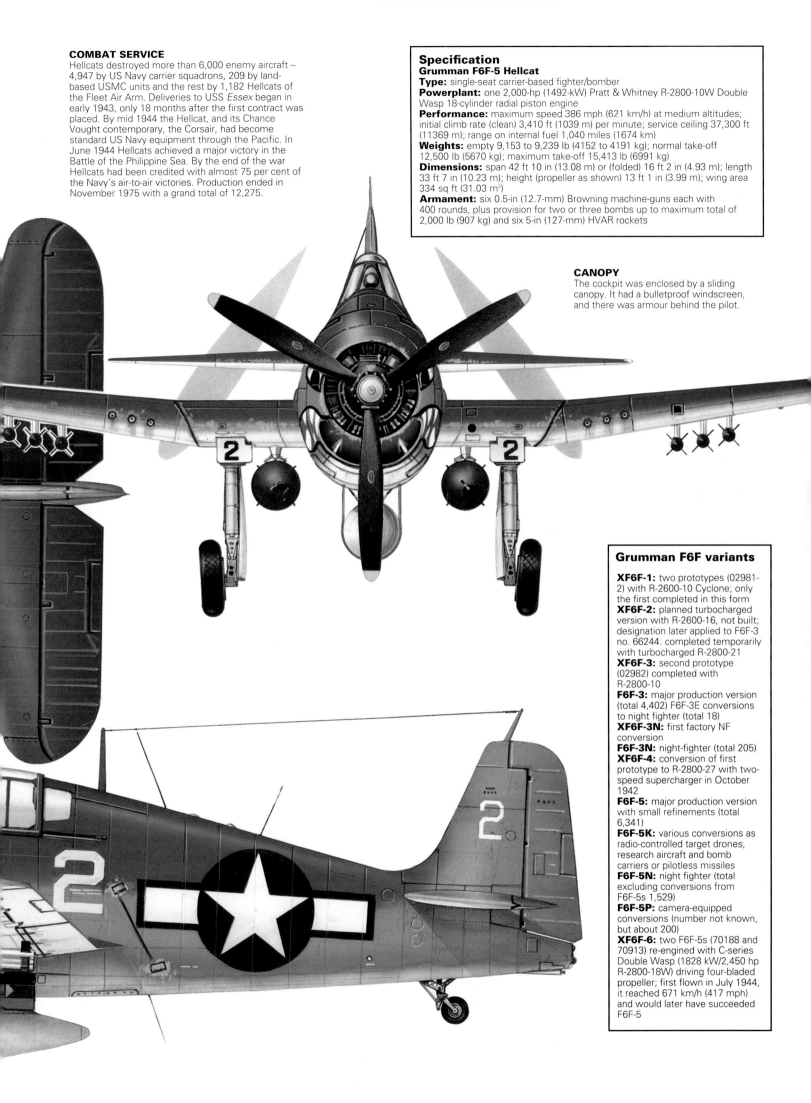

CANOPY

The cockpit was enclosed by a sliding canopy. It had a bulletproof windscreen, and there was armour behind the pilot.

Grumman F6F variants

XF6F-1: two prototypes (02981-2) with R-2600-10 Cyclone; only the first completed in this form
XF6F-2: planned turbocharged version with R-2600-16, not built; designation later applied to F6F-3 no. 66244. completed temporarily with turbocharged R-2800-21
XF6F-3: second prototype (02982) completed with R-2800-10
F6F-3: major production version (total 4,402) F6F-3E conversions to night fighter (total 18)
XF6F-3N: first factory NF conversion
F6F-3N: night-fighter (total 205)
XF6F-4: conversion of first prototype to R-2800-27 with two-speed supercharger in October 1942
F6F-5: major production version with small refinements (total 6,341)
F6F-5K: various conversions as radio-controlled target drones, research aircraft and bomb carriers or pilotless missiles
F6F-5N: night fighter (total excluding conversions from F6F-5s 1,529)
F6F-5P: camera-equipped conversions (number not known, but about 200)
XF6F-6: two F6F-5s (70188 and 70913) re-engined with C-series Double Wasp (1828 kW/2,450 hp R-2800-18W) driving four-bladed propeller; first flown in July 1944, it reached 671 km/h (417 mph) and would later have succeeded F6F-5

Grumman F7F Tigercat

Grumman's **XF5F-1** twin-engine carrier-based fighter prototype failed to gain a production contract, but in the process of its evolution the company gained a far wider appreciation of the problems involved in the creation of such a machine. In early 1941 work was initiated on the design of a new twin-engine fighter for operation from the planned larger carriers in the 'Midway' class. Identified by the company as the Grumman **G-51 Tigercat**, there was little resemblance to its predecessor, for the US Navy by then wanted to procure a high-performance fighter with unprecedented firepower.

Grumman's proposal resulted in the award of a contract for two **XF7F-1** prototypes on 30 June 1941, the first of them flown during December 1943. Of all-metal construction, the Tigercat was of cantilever shoulder-wing monoplane configuration, the outer panels of the wings folding for carrier stowage. Fuselage and tailplane were conventional, but the retractable landing gear was of tricycle type. A retractable deck arrester hook was mounted in the aft fuselage. Powerplant comprised two Pratt & Whitney R-2800-22W Double Wasp engines, installed in large under-wing nacelles.

Before the first flight of the prototype, Grumman had received a contract for 500 production aircraft under the designation **F7F-1** for supply to the US Marine Corps which, by then, was already engaged in landing operations on Japanese-held islands in the Pacific. Operating from land bases, these aircraft would provide the US Marines with their own close-support. However, the Tigercat materialised too late to see operational service with the USMC before the end of the war.

Though often identified as an F7F-2N because of the second cockpit, this photograph, taken on 3 May 1945, actually shows an F7F-3. The bold number on the Double Wasp cowling is the last three digits of the Bureau number, 80401. Note the boarding ladder, which did not extend automatically when weight was on the landing gear.

Above: This Tigercat was F7F-2N night-fighter BuNo. 80320, assigned to VMF(N)-533, the first twin-engined Marine Corps (or Navy) night-fighter squadron. They were based at Eagle Mountain Lake, west of Houston, Texas. This was the first production version in which nose guns were replaced by radar.

The first production F7F-1 was generally similar to the prototypes, as were the 33 aircraft which followed, and delivery of these began in April 1944. The 35th aircraft on the production line was modified for use in a night-fighter role, under the designation **XF7F-2N**, and 30 production examples followed under the designation **F7F-2N** during 1944. These differed from the F7F-1 by deletion of the aft fuselage fuel tank (to provide space for the radar operator's cockpit) and removal of the nose armament. There followed production of a new single-seat version, the **F7F-3 Tigercat**, of which 189 were built. This differed from the F7F-1 in having R-2800-34 engines to provide increased power at altitude, slightly increased vertical tail surface areas to cater for this, and a seven per cent increase in fuel capacity.

These aircraft were the last produced under the original contract, with the balance cancelled after VJ-Day.

Post-war production included 60 **F7F-3N** and 13 **F7F-4N** night-fighters, both with a lengthened nose housing advanced radar, the latter 13 aircraft being the only examples with strengthening, arrester hook, and specialised equipment for carrier-based operation. A small number of F7F-3s were modified after delivery for use in electronic (**F7F-3E**) and photo-reconnaissance (**F7F-3P**) roles. Some squadrons remained in service with the US Marines in the immediate post-war years, but were soon displaced by higher-performance turbine-powered aircraft.

Specification
Grumman F7F-3
Type: twin-engine carrier-based fighter-bomber
Powerplant: two 2,100 hp (1566-kW) Pratt & Whitney R-2800-34W Double Wasp 18-cylinder radial piston engines
Performance: maximum speed 435 mph (700 km/h) at 22,200 ft (6765 m), cruising speed 222 mph (357 km/h); initial climb rate 4,530 ft (1380 m) per minute; service ceiling 40,700 ft (12405 m), normal range 1,200 miles (1931 km)
Weights: empty 16,270 lb (7380 kg); maximum take-off 25,720 lb (11666 kg)
Dimensions: span 51 ft 6 in (15 70 m), length 45 ft 4½ in (13.83 m), height 16 ft 7 in (5.05 m); wing area 455.0 sq ft (42.27 m²)
Armament: four 20-mm cannon in wing roots and four 0.5-in (12.7-mm) machine-guns in nose, plus one torpedo beneath the fuselage and up to 1,000 lb (454 kg) of bombs under each wing

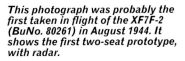

This photograph was probably the first taken in flight of the XF7F-2 (BuNo. 80261) in August 1944. It shows the first two-seat prototype, with radar.

Grumman F8F Bearcat

Last of the line of piston-engine carrier-based fighters which Grumman began with the FF of 1931, the Grumman F8F Bearcat was designed to be capable of operation from aircraft carriers of all sizes and to serve primarily as an interceptor fighter. It was a role which demanded excellent manoeuvrability, good low-level performance and a high rate of climb. To achieve these capabilities for the two **XF8F-1** prototypes ordered on 27 November 1943 Grumman adopted the big R-2800 Double Wasp that had been used to power the F6F and F7F, but ensured that the smallest and lightest possible airframe was designed to accommodate the specified armament, armour and fuel.

First flown on 21 August 1944, the XF8F-1 was not only smaller than the US Navy's superb Hellcat but was some 20 per cent lighter, resulting in a rate of climb about 30 per cent greater than that of its predecessor. Grumman had more than achieved the specification requirements, and then crowned their achievement by starting delivery of production aircraft in February 1945, only six months after the first flight of the prototype.

A cantilever low-wing monoplane of all-metal construction, the **F8F-1** had wings which

Right at the war's end, Grumman produced the prototype of the fighter which might have helped to shorten the conflict. This was the XF8F-1, distinguished by the big TEST label and also by lack of a tailfin.

folded at about two-thirds span for carrier stowage, retractable tailwheel landing gear, armour, self-sealing fuel tanks and, by comparison with prototypes, a very small dorsal fin had been added. Powerplant of these production aircraft was the Pratt & Whitney R-2800-34W and armament comprised four 0.5-in (12.7-mm) machine-guns.

Shortly after initiation of the prototype's test programme in 1944 the US Navy placed a contract for 2,023 production F8F-1s, and the first of these began to equip US Navy Squadron VF-19 on 21 May 1945. This squadron, and other early recipients of Bearcats, were still in the process of familiarisation with their new fighters when VJ-Day put an end to World War II. It also cut 1,258 aircraft from Grumman's contract and brought complete cancellation of an additional 1,876 **F8M-1 Bearcat** fighters contracted from General Motors.

When production ended in May 1949, Grumman had built 1,266 Bearcats: 765 of the F8F-1; 100 of the **F8F-1B**, which differed in having the four machine-

guns replaced by 20-mm cannon; 36 of the **F8F-1N** variant, equipped as night-fighters; 293 of the **F8F-2**, with redesigned engine cowling, taller fin and rudder, plus some changes in detail design and adoption of the 20-mm cannon as standard armament; 12 of the night-fighter **F8F2N**; and 60 photo-reconnaissance **F8F-2P** aircraft, this last version carrying only two 20-mm cannon. In late post-war service, some aircraft were modified to serve in a drone control capacity under the designations **F8F-1D** or **F8F-2D**.

By the time production ended, Bearcats were serving with some 24 US Navy squadrons, but all had been withdrawn by late 1952. Some of these, with a modified fuel system, were supplied to the French Armée de l'Air for service in Indo-China

under the designation F8F-lD. One hundred similar F8F-lDs and 29 **F8F-lB**s were also supplied to the Thai air force.

Specification
Grumman F8F-1B
Type: single-seat carrier-based interceptor fighter
Powerplant: one 2,100-hp (1566-kW) Pratt & Whitney R-2800-34W Double Wasp 18-cylinder radial piston engine
Performance: maximum speed 421 mph (678 km/h) at 19,700 ft (6005 m); cruising speed 163 mph (262 km/h); initial climb rate 4,570 ft (1395 m) per minute, service ceiling 38,700 ft (11795 m); range 1,105 miles (1778 km)
Weights: empty 7,070 lb (3207 kg); maximum take-off 12,947 lb (5873 kg)
Dimensions: span 35 ft 10 in (10.92 m); length 28 ft 3 in (8.61 m); height 13 ft 10 in (4.22 m), wing area 244.0 sq ft (22.67 m²)
Armament: four 20-mm cannon plus underwing hardpoints for two 1,000-lb (454-kg) bombs, or four 5-in (127-mm) rocket projectiles, or two 150-US gal (568-litre) drop tanks

Grumman G-21 Goose

In 1937 Grumman produced a twin-engine amphibian flying-boat known as the Grumman G-21 Goose. The first of a long line of such machines, it was powered by two 450-hp (336-kW) Pratt & Whitney R-985 radial engines.

The Goose was a high-wing monoplane, the wing serving also to mount the engines and carry underwing stabilising floats. The deep two-step hull was of conventional construction, and the tail unit included a braced tailplane. Amphibious capability was provided by tailwheel type landing gear, all three units of which retracted into the hull.

Built pre-war for commercial use as the **G-21A**, which had accommodation for up to seven passengers, the Navy ordered one evaluation example, which was given the designation **XJ3F-1**. A production order followed, and delivery of 20 aircraft, redesignated JRF, began in 1939. The first batch were used by the Navy and

the Marine Corps for transport, target towing, and photography and were designated **JRF-1A**. The next 10 could carry bombs or depth charges and were designated **JRF-4**. A further batch of 10 were ordered for the Coast Guard and were known as **JRF-2**s, or with the provision of de-icing equipment for use in the Arctic as **JRF-3**s.

In the build-up to war in 1941, Grumman introduced the **JRF-5**, with uprated engines and other refinements. Total production was 184, including 24 **JRF-5G**s for the Coast Guard, 16 for Canada and four which were sold to Britain as the **Goose Mk I**. Fifty further aircraft were assigned to Britain under Lend-Lease and were designated JRF-6B. Five were delivered to the USAAF where they were known as **OA-9**s.

At the end of the war, surviving commercial and war-surplus aircraft which came onto the

market were to prove of value for certain post-war air services, and McKinnon Enterprises in the USA began to specialise in Goose refurbishment and the development of turbine-engined conversions, many of which are still flying half a century later.

Specification
Grumman JRF-5 Goose
Type: utility amphibian flying-boat
Powerplant: two 450-hp (335-kW) Pratt & Whitney R-985-AN-6 radial piston engines
Performance: maximum speed 201 mph (323 km/h) at 5,000 feet (1524 m); cruising speed 191 mph (307 km/h);

Apart from national 1942-43 insignia, no markings are visible on this JRF-5, which was probably photographed over the Aleutians in 1942. It is painted in the standard sea green and grey livery, with a red stripe to warn of the propellers.

service ceiling 21,300 feet (6492 m); range 640 miles (1030 km)
Weights: empty 5425 lb (2461 kg); maximum loaded 8,000 lb (3629 kg)
Dimensions: span 49 ft (14.94 m); length 38 ft 6 in (11.73 m); height 16 ft 2 in (4.93 m); wing area 375 sq. ft (34.84 m²)
Armament: normally none, but the earlier JRF-4 could carry two 25-lb (113 kg) bombs or depth charges.

Grumman G-44 Widgeon

The success of the Grumman Goose eight-seat commercial amphibian, and the obvious market for a smaller and cheaper version, led directly to development of the five-seat Grumman G-44 Widgeon, powered by two 200-hp (149-kW) Ranger L-440C-5 engines. The prototype Widgeon was test-flown by Roy Grumman and Bud Gillies at Bethpage on 28 June 1940, and 10 examples had been sold to civil buyers before the first production aircraft was delivered on 21 February 1941. The initial production batch of 44 Widgeons was intended for the civil market, although 11, which had been built to fulfil a Portuguese contract, plus four other examples, were impressed for service with the USAAC under the designation **OA-14**.

The second production run, of 25 aircraft, was earmarked for the US Coast Guard and, designated **J4F-1** these were delivered between 7 July 1941 and 29 June 1942. In August 1942, a Widgeon of Coast Guard Squadron 212, based at Houma, Louisiana, sank the U-boat *U-166* off the Passes of the Mississippi, scoring the first US Coast Guard kill of an enemy submarine.

Grumman then built a total of 131 **J4F-2** aircraft for the US

Navy, these being delivered between 13 July 1942 and 26 February 1945. Operated by a crew of two and with up to three passengers in the utility transport role, the J4F-2 was used also for coastal patrol and anti-submarine duties. Fifteen J4F-2s were supplied under Lend-Lease to the Royal Navy and used for communications, principally in the West Indies where (at Piarco, Trinidad for example) observer training schools were maintained. Royal Navy J4F-2s were known initially under the name **Gosling**, later taking the American name.

An improved **G-44A** was introduced by Grumman in 1944, flying first on 8 August. It had a revised hull with a deeper keel and incorporated hydrody-

namic improvements. A total of 76 was built, the last being delivered on 13 January 1949, and some of these were later re-engined with Continental W-670s or Avco Lycoming 90-435As. During 1948/9 some 41 G-44As were built under licence by Société de Construction Aéro-Navale (SCAN) at La Rochelle, France as the **SCAN 30**. Subsequently McKinnon Enterprises at Sandy, Oregon, initiated a conversion scheme for the Widgeon. The resulting **Super Widgeon**, of which more than 70 conversions were completed, introduced 270-hp (201-kW) Avco Lycoming GO-480BlD engines, improvements to the hull and interior, and the provision of increased fuel capacity.

Photographed by Grumman off Long Island, this publicity shot has a J4F-1 boldly toting a 200-lb depth charge under its starboard wing. The colour scheme would have been sea green and grey.

Specification
Grumman J4F-2
Type: five-seat light transport or coastal/anti-submarine patrol aircraft
Powerplant: two 200-hp (149-kW) Ranger L-440C-5 6-cylinder inline piston engines
Performance: maximum speed 153 mph (246 km/h); cruising speed 138 mph (222 km/h); service ceiling 14,600 ft (4450 m); maximum range 920 miles (1481 km)
Weights: empty 3,189 lb (1447 kg) maximum take-off 4,500 lb (2041 kg)
Dimensions: span 40 ft 0 in (12.19 m); length 31 ft 1 in (9.47 m) height 11 ft 5 in (3.48 m); wing area 245.0 sq ft (22.76 m²)
Armament: none

Grumman JF/J2F Duck

This recently-taken photograph shows a restored J2F-6 which, after starring in the 1974 movie 'Murphy's War', was repainted to resemble a Duck of the 1930s. It is, however, totally dissimilar in design details.

Grumman's FF-1 and F2F carrier-based fighters for the US Navy, the company's first production aircraft, had introduced some new ideas including retractable tailwheel landing gear, making them the first of their kind to enter US Navy service. The FF-1 was also the fastest fighter operational with the US Navy but, because of the limited procurement that was possible in the years between the wars, was acquired in limited numbers.

With the FF-1 nearing production, Grumman began the development of a new utility amphibian which would combine the better features of the FF-1 and the Loening OLs then in service, and in late 1932 submitted its proposal for review by the US Navy. This resulted in the award of a contract for the supply of a Grumman **XJF-1** prototype, which flew for the first time on 4 May 1933. Flight testing found no serious problems, and an

uncomplicated evaluation by the US Navy resulted in an initial production order for 27 **JF-1** aircraft, the first of these being delivered in late 1934.

Intended to fulfil a general utility role, the type was used first to replace ageing Loening OL-9 observation and general-purpose aircraft in US Navy service, and it was not until 1936 that they began to reach squadrons. Their performance by comparison with the similarly configured Loenings was quite staggering, with maximum speed, rate of climb and service ceiling increased by more than 40 per cent, 50 per cent and 65 per cent respectively.

The equal span biplane wings had a basic structure of light alloy with fabric covering, the fuselage

was a conventional stressed-skin light alloy structure, and the large monocoque central float housed the main wheel units when retracted. Stabiliser floats were strut-mounted beneath each lower wing, and a crew of two or three could be carried in the tandem cockpits. Pilot forward and observer aft was standard, but a radio operator could also be accommodated in the observer's cockpit. Powerplant of the prototype and the first batch of JF-1 production aircraft consisted of a 700-hp (522-kW) Pratt & Whitney R-1830 Twin Wasp engine.

The second production contract was for 14 **JF-2** (Grumman **G-4**) aircraft for the US Coast Guard, these having equipment changes and 750-hp (559-kW) Wright R-1820 Cyclone engines. Four were transferred subsequently to the US Navy, which service also acquired five new aircraft with similar powerplant under the designation **JF-3**.

This profile shows a J2F-3, powered by an 850-hp Cyclone in a Townend-ring cowl, BuNo. 1569. Assigned to a senior flag officer, it has a blue fuselage and float and the officer's two-star marker inserted into a slotted receptacle on each side of the fuselage.

There were few major changes in later production examples, the 20 **J2F-1** machines of 1937 and the later 21 **J2F-2**, 20 **J2F-3** and 32 **J2F-4** types differing in only minor detail. Nine **J2F-2A** float-planes for Marine Squadron VMS-3 were armed with machine-guns and carried under-wing bomb racks.

The last version to be built by Grumman was ordered in 1940, and comprised 144 of the **J2F-5** model, which was the first to be officially given the name **Duck**. Generally similar to previous util-ity models, this was powered by the 850-hp (634-kW) Wright R-1820-50 engine. Final production version, the **J2F-6**, was built by Columbia Aircraft Corporation of Long Island, New York, from which company the US Navy ordered 330 after the USA had become involved in World War II. These were generally similar

to the Grumman-built Ducks except for the installation of a more powerful R-1820-54 engine.

Most of the JF/J2F Ducks remained in service throughout the war, operated both from car-riers and land bases in a variety of roles, including patrol, photo-survey, rescue and target towing.

Specification
Grumman J2F-6
Type: two/three-seat utility amphibian
Powerplant: one 900-hp (671-kW) Wright R-1820-54 Cyclone 9 nine-cylinder radial piston engine
Performance: maximum speed 190 mph (306 km/h); cruising speed 155 mph (249 km/h); service ceiling 25,000 ft (7620 m); range 750 miles (1207 km)
Weights: empty 4,400 lb (1996 kg); maximum take-off 7,700 lb (3493 kg)
Dimensions: span 39 ft 0 in (11.89 m), length 34 ft 0 in (10.36 m); height 13 ft 11 in (4.24 m); wing area 409.0 sq ft (38.00 m²)
Armament: normally none, but provision for two 325-lb (147-kg) depth bombs

The final and by far the most numerous version was the J2F-6, built by Columbia, not far from Grumman at Valley Stream. They incorporated every modification needed for a very wide range of roles, including racks for bombs or depth charges and provision for towing gunnery targets.

Grumman TBF Avenger

For over 50 years Grumman has provided some of the world's best carrier-based aircraft, typified by generous wings, amiable han-dling and such strength that the company is colloquially known as 'The Iron Works'. No aircraft better exemplifies Grumman than the Avenger, chief torpedo-bomber of the Pacific war in 1942-45.

On the Avenger's first combat mission six new **TBF-1s** thundered off into the Battle of Midway on 4 June 1942. Only one came back, and that had the pilot flying a shattered aircraft on the trimmers, one crewman injured and the other dead. This seemed almost a repetition of what had been happening with the previous-generation Douglas TBD-1 Devastator, which was simply not survivable in World War II. In fact, nothing could have been more wrong, and the Avenger was to be one of the great war-winners of the conflict.

When Douglas had produced the TBD in 1935 it had been as mod-ern as the hour, with all-metal stressed-skin construction, enclosed cockpits and retractable gear. As early as October 1939, however, it was clear that a single 900-hp (671-kW) engine was inadequate for the ship-based torpedo-bomber mission, and in that month the US Navy began organising plans for an industry competition for a replacement aircraft. The key to the development lay in the existence of such pow-erful engines as the Pratt & Whitney R-2800 and the Wright R-2600 and R-3350. Grumman was well placed to win what was certain to be a major programme.

Avengers of Navy Task Force 58 head for Saipan at the start of the campaign to retake the islands in June 1944. They are Grumman-built TBF-1s, and are all from the same carrier. Their forte was torpedoes and level bombing, rather than the SBD technique of steep dive-bombing.

This photograph is believed to show the first production TBF-1 in January 1942, painted in sea green and grey. The striped rudder was soon discontinued.

The US Navy's requirements were no pushover, however, and the numerical requirements for mission radius with particular weapon loads could only just be met. In an intensive five weeks at the turn of the Year 1941 the engineering team under chief experimental engineer Bob Hall roughed out the shape that was later to be called 'The Pregnant Beast' or, more kindly, 'The Turkey'. That portly fuselage, giant angular wing and distinctive tail could only have come from Grumman, but what might not have been expected were the internal weapons bay and the gun turret. Project engineer R. Koch was first to decide on an internal bay, partly because this fitted in with the lower rear defensive gun position. There was no problem with the pilot, who sat in lofty state in a roomy and comfortable cockpit above the leading edge, where his view was perfect. The other two crew were less obvious.

A door on the right side aft of the wing gave access into the rear fuselage, which was packed with equipment, flares, parachutes and ammunition. At the lower level the bombardier was provided with a folding seat from which he could either man the lower rear machine-gun, a Browning of 0.3-in (7.62-mm) calibre, or face forward and aim

the aircraft for medium-altitude level bombing.

During development in 1942 radar was introduced to the US Navy, and the Westinghouse ASB radar became standard equipment on some versions. Another common fit was the APG-4 'Sniffer' low-level auto-bombing radar which used a dipole Yagi array toed out at 40° under each outer wing. The radar viewing scope was ahead of the bombardier, whose compartment thus became somewhat crowded. The radar scope was in fact directly under the turret, which in itself was an innovation where the US Navy was concerned (though a turret had been fitted to a few other single-engine attack types such as the Soviet BB-1/Su-2).

Improved turret mounting

The US Navy had specified a turret, to mount a single 0.5-in (12.7-mm) gun, and Grumman handled the development in-house Though almost everything on the TBF was hydraulic, it eventually found itself with an electrically driven turret, chiefly because the job was assigned to Oscar Olsen whose entire background (mainly with General Electric) had been electrical. He was aware of the problems caused by flight manoeuvres which could impose totally different loads on different parts of the turret mount ring. The best answer appeared to Olsen to be the Amplidyne form of control, which can govern both the torque and speed of an electric motor with great precision. He was thus able to equip the turret with synchronised motors which, no matter what the attitude of the turret or aircraft might be, always gave fingertip gun-pointing accuracy.

In contrast, most of the other movable items were hydraulic, including the massive main landing gears (which could take a bone-crushing arrival at 16 ft/4.88 metres per second vertical velocity onto a hard deck), the folding outer wings, the big split flaps and the double-fold bomb doors.

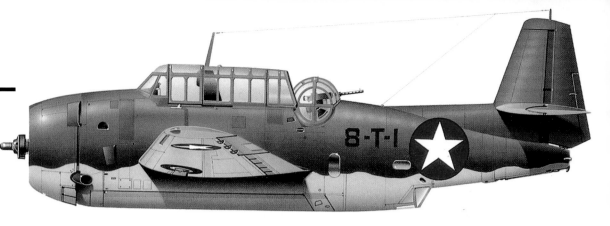

This TBF-1 was one of those that went into action with Navy squadron VT-8, on 4 June 1942, and failed to return. Fortunately the Navy already had no doubt that in this aircraft they had the world's best carrier-based attack aircraft.

Right: This Avenger is a TBF-1C, with two 0.5-in guns in the wings. It was photographed in 1944 in midnight blue livery flying over a Pacific task force. Pilots generally liked to fly with the canopy open.

Below: A loose gaggle of TBF-1s is seen during the Coral Sea battle of early May 1942. Despite the prominent Mk 13-2 torpedo here being released, this engagement and the Battle of Midway suggested that dive-bombers can sink more ships than torpedo-bombers.

Leroy Grumman himself had hit on the wing fold only a year earlier, and this feature was first applied to production models of the F4F Wildcat then just coming off the line. He had foreseen the clearance problem caused by conventional upward-hinged wings on carrier hangar decks, and so experimented with two partly unfolded paper-clips stuck into the sides of a draughtsman's soap-eraser. Eventually he got the two clips at just the right skewed angle so that the 'wings' folded neatly alongside the 'body'. In the folded position the upper surfaces faced outwards. For the big TBF power folding was essential; no crew of men could have handled such wings, loaded with radar, tanks and rockets, on a pitching deck. The only other item driven electrically was the giant sting arrester hook, normally housed inside the rear fuselage but extended on rails by a cable and pulley track when needed.

Weapon fit

As well as the two rear guns, a 0.3-in (7.62-mm) gun was mounted high on the right side of the nose, firing through the propeller disc. It was always considered good practice to give the pilot a gun, not only to improve morale but for sound offensive reasons. Though the bombardier could aim bombs from altitude it was the pilot who managed torpedo attacks, using the illuminated torpedo sight on the left side of the coaming. Ahead he had merely a ring-and-bead sight for the gun, though this could also be used for dive-bombing, the bombardier then being a mere passenger. The main gears could be extended as airbrakes to hold dives to about 300 mph (482 km/h), though the controls became exceedingly heavy and a great deal of effort and fast re-trimming was needed both in the dive and the pull-out .

The first of two **XTBF-1** prototypes, BuNo. 2539, made a highly successful first flight on 1 August 1941. The pilot, as with most experimental Grumman aircraft at the time, was the chief experimental engineer himself, Bob Hall. He had only recently been fished from the ocean after deciding that the XP-50 was no longer a safe place to stay, and he found the XTBF-1 a welcome contrast, seemingly as safe as houses with the trusty 14-cylinder Cyclone rumbling lustily ahead of his feet. Grumman was fast becoming overloaded with work and was well into the construction of Plant 2, a complete new factory twice as big as the first. Here would be built the 286 TBFs ordered 'off the drawing board' back in December 1940. Then, as often happens, trouble came out of the blue. On 28 November 1941 the XTBF-1 was flying in the hands of Bob Cook and engineer Gordon Israel. Near

These early TBF-1s, seen in 1942, are believed to be from CV-16 (the second Lexington), although there is no means of positive identification. Almost all US Navy Avengers that saw action were carrier-based, though this was not true of the Marines and Britain's Fleet Air Arm.

Brentwood, about 10 miles (16 km) east of the Bethpage plant, they found the bomb bay was burning fiercely. (The only cause anyone could think of was an electrical fault.) Cook and Israel hit the silk, and the flaming torpedo-bomber dived into some woods.

This did not damage the programme, and by this time the US Navy had changed its order for 286 to an open-ended contract which was to last until 31 December 1943, 2,291 aircraft later (and with even bigger numbers built by others).

On an unseasonably hot Sunday morning, 7 December 1941, all was bustle at Bethpage as, amid colourful ceremony, the vast new Plant 2 was dedicated. Spotlighted in the middle was the gleaming new second prototype XTBF-1, which was to be the priority product. Suddenly the company vice-president, Clint Towl, was called to the telephone by the public address system. He picked up the instrument to be told, "The Japs have attacked Pearl Harbor; we're at war." Towl prohibited any announcement, and the public began to go home; then, when the last of the thousands had gone through the gate, the plant was locked and searched for any saboteurs. It was to be a secure place for the next four years; and the TBF was appropriately named Avenger.

Into service

By this time Plant 2 was already full of production TBF-1s, and the number one off the line, BuNo. 00373, flew on 3 January 1942. So few engineering changes had been needed that by the end of six months another 145 had been delivered, with half of US Navy squadron VT-8 already nearing the end of its conversion course at NAS Norfolk, Virginia. From here the six new TBFs were flown, with 270-US gal (1022-litre) tanks in the bomb bays, right across the USA and over the 10-hour ocean sector to Pearl Harbor. Their ship, USS Hornet, had already departed, so they rumbled on all the way to Midway island. It was here that all six aircraft were shot to pieces, as noted at the opening of this account; it was perhaps the only occasion on which the TBF came off second-best. From that time on it was to be the destroyer not only of the Japanese navy but also of Hitler's U-boats.

With the normal internal load of a Mk 13-2 torpedo or four 500-lb (227-kg) bombs, and full internal fuel of 335 US gal (1268 litres) in three wing tanks, the TBF-1 could attack targets up to 260 miles (418 km) distant. It was always pleasant to fly, though spinning was prohibited. When flown with determination by a strong pilot it could almost

By chance, the first public showing of the XTBF-1 took place on the day Japan attacked the US Fleet at Pearl Harbor. From the two prototypes, one of which is seen here, came 9,937 further aircraft which lived up to their name of 'Avenger'.

Grumman TBM-1C Avenger cutaway drawing key:

1 Starboard elevator
2 Fabric covered aileron construction
3 Elevator trim tab
4 Elevator horn balance
5 Tailplane construction
6 Rudder tab
7 Trim tab control jack
8 Tail navigation light
9 Fabric covered rudder construction
10 Aerial cable rear mounting
11 Fin construction
12 Port elevator
13 Port tailplane
14 Elevator hinge controls
15 Tailplane support frames
16 Deck arrester hook (lowered)
17 Arrester hook guide rails
18 Rudder hinge control
19 Rear fuselage frames
20 Flush-riveted aluminium skin covering
21 Fin root fairing
22 Tailplane control cables
23 Arrester hook retraction drive motor
24 Lifting tube
25 Rear fuselage frame and stringer construction
26 Tailwheel shock absorber strut
27 Catapult 'hold-back' shackle
28 Retractable tailwheel
29 Crew compartment rear bulkhead
30 Search flares
31 Parachute flare launch tube
32 Ventral gun turret
33 Ammunition magazine
34 Browning 0.3-in (7.62-mm) machine-gun
35 Machine-gun mounting
36 Gun camera switch box
37 Crew door
38 Parachute stowage
39 Rear fuselage production break point
40 Spare coil stowage rack
41 Bombardier's side window
42 Upper turret spare ammunition magazines
43 Bombardier's folding seat
44 Gun turret mounting ring
45 Gun elevating mechanism
46 Ammunition feed chute
47 Browning 0.5-in (12.7-mm) machine-gun
48 Upper rotating gun turret
49 Bullet proof windscreen
50 Gunner's armoured seat back

51 Aerial cable
52 Port wing folded position
53 Canopy aft glazing
54 Emergency life raft stowage
55 Hydraulic reservoir
56 Radio communications equipment
57 ASB weapons aiming controller
58 Bomb release levers
59 Cabin heater duct
60 Aft end of bomb bay
61 Fixed wing root construction
62 Wing fold joint line
63 Browning 0.5-in (12.7-mm) fixed machine-gun
64 Ammunition feed chute
65 Ammunition magazine (320 rounds)
66 Trailing edge flap shroud construction
67 Lattice wing ribs
68 Starboard, fabric covered aileron construction
69 Aileron hinge control
70 Aileron trim tab
71 Starboard wing tip
72 Starboard navigation light
73 Leading edge ribs
74 Fixed leading edge slot
75 ASB aerial
76 RT-5/APS-4 search radar pod
77 Radar mounting sway braces
78 Rocket launching pylons
79 Jettisonable fuel tank (58 US gal/219.5 litre capacity)
80 Main undercarriage wheel well
81 Sloping main spar
82 Wing fold hinge axis
83 Twin hydraulic folding jacks
84 Machine-gun blast tube

85 Starboard main fuel tank (90 US gal/340.7 litre capacity)
86 Centre section main spar
87 Oxygen bottle
88 Autopilot controls
89 Rear cockpit entry hatch
90 ASB equipment rack
91 Aerial mast
92 Roll-over crash pylon
93 Second cockpit control column provision
94 Propeller de-icing fluid tank
95 Seat-back armour
96 Headrest
97 Safety harness
98 Pilot's seat
99 Emergency hydraulic handpump
100 Centre main fuel tank (145 US gal/549 litre capacity)
101 Fuel tank filler cap
102 Main undercarriage retraction jack
103 Wing fold locking cylinder
104 Machine-gun muzzle
105 Centre section leading edge construction
106 Front fuselage frames
107 Rudder pedals
108 Back of instrument panel
109 Control column
110 Pilot's sliding entry hatch
111 Illuminated torpedo sight
112 Instrument panel shroud
113 Windscreen panels
114 Ring-and-bead gunsight
115 Gun camera
116 Port split trailing edge flaps

117 Remote compass transmitter
118 Aileron control rods
119 Aileron hinge control
120 Fabric covered port aileron
121 Aileron trim tab
122 Formation light
123 Pitot tube
124 Port navigation light
125 Fixed leading edge slot
126 Wing 'tie-down' shackle
127 ASB aerial mounting
128 Retractable landing lamp
129 Red, white and green approach lights
130 Port ASB aerial

131 Ground attack rockets (5-in/12.7-cm)
132 Oil tank filler cap
133 Engine oil tank (13 US gal/49 litre capacity)
134 Engine compartment bulkhead
135 Engine mounting struts
136 Cowling air exit flap
137 Twin carburettors
138 Carburettor air trunking

139 Wright R-2600-8 Cyclone 14-cylinder two-row radial engine
140 Carburettor air intake
141 Propeller governor
142 Reduction gearbox
143 Hamilton Standard three-bladed variable-pitch propeller
144 Engine cooling intake
145 Engine cowlings
146 Cowling air flap control lever
147 Lower cowling air flap
148 Batteries
149 Starboard exhaust pipe
150 Oil cooler
151 Oil cooler air exit flap
152 Bomb release shackle
153 Four 500-lb (226.8-kg) bombs
154 Bomb bay door construction
155 Bomb doors (open)
156 Port mainwheel
157 Bomb bay jettisonable fuel tank (270 US gal/1,022 litres capacity)
158 Main undercarriage leg door
159 Retraction strut
160 Shock absorber leg strut
161 Torque scissor links
162 Hydraulic brake pipe
163 Starboard mainwheel
164 Removable wheel disc cover
165 Torpedo stabilizing vanes
166 Mk 13-2 torpedo

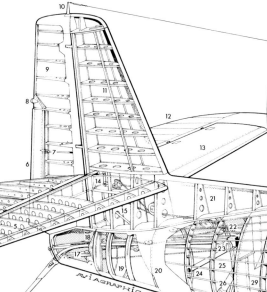

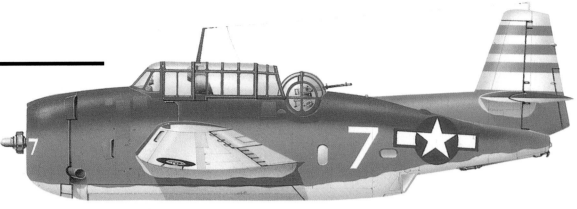

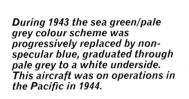

During 1943 the sea green/pale grey colour scheme was progressively replaced by non-specular blue, graduated through pale grey to a white underside. This aircraft was on operations in the Pacific in 1944.

The Avenger, whether a **TBF** or **TBM**, was perhaps the least difficult of all wartime aircraft to land on a carrier. Here two **TBFs** with gear and hooks lowered approach their '**Essex**' class carrier in 1944.

Armourers run a **Mk 13-2** torpedo up to a **G**eneral **M**otors (**E**astern Aircraft) **TBM**-1, with weapon-bay doors folded open, aboard USS **S**an **J**acinto during the battle of **Leyte Gulf** in October 1944.

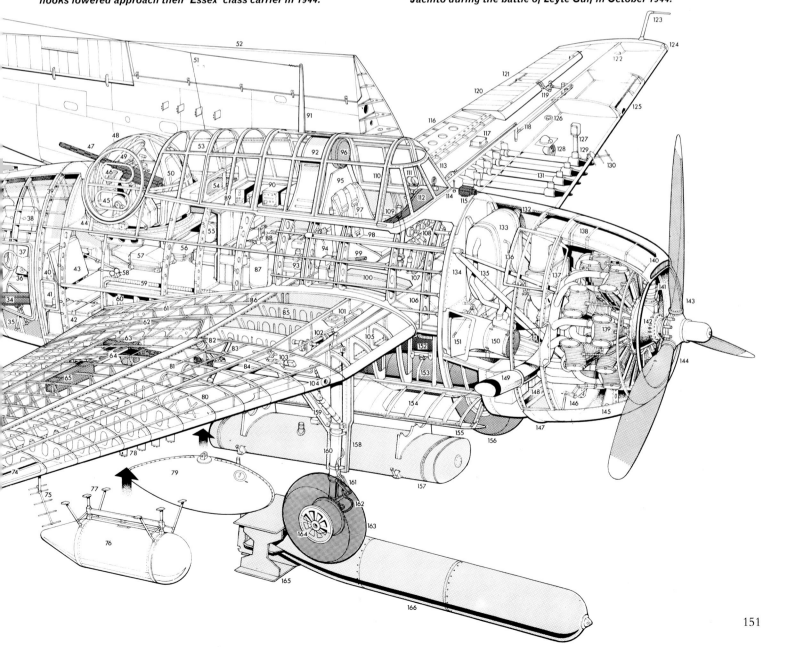

Gruman TBF Avenger

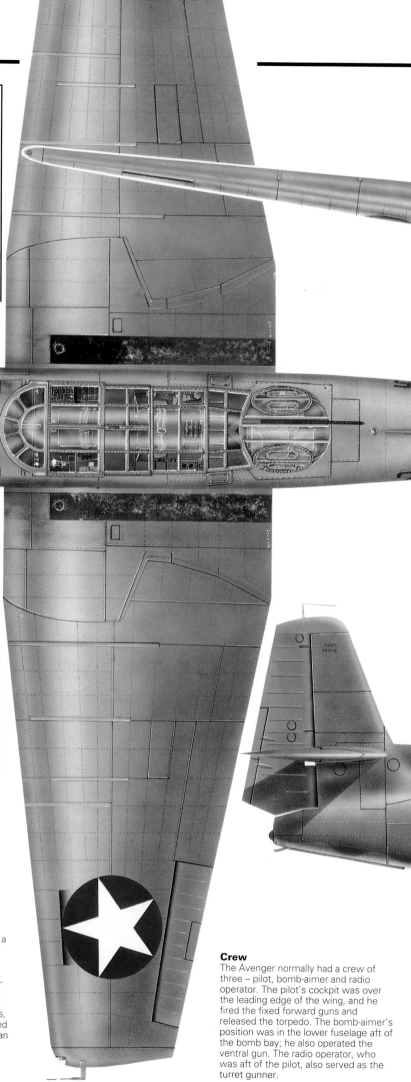

Gruman Avenger variants

XTBF-1: two prototypes, R-2600-8 engine

TBF-1: initial production version similar to second prototype; total 2,291 excluding prototypes but including -1Bs and -1Cs

TBF-1B: designation of Grumman variant for British with detail differences; initially designated Tarpon TR.Mk 1; total 395

TBF-1C: as TBF-1 but maximum fuel capacity increased from 335 to 726 US gal (1268 to 2748 litres) with two wing drop tanks and bomb bay ferry tank, two 0.5-in (12.7-mm) wing guns

TBF-1CP: conversions of TBF-1C with trimetrogen reconnaissance cameras in fan to give wide coverage

TBF-1D: conversion with RT-5/APS-4 radar in wing pod; TBF-1CD similar conversion of TBF-1C

TBF-1E: conversion with special radar and additional avionics

TBF-1J: new-build version (included in TBF-1 total) with bad-weather avionics and lighting, and special ice protection

TBF-1L: sub-type with searchlight on retractable mount extending from bomb bay

TBF-1P: TBF-1 conversion as TBF-1CP

XTBF-2: conversion of TBF-1 No. 00393 with 1,900-hp (1417-kW) XR-2600-10 engine

XTBF-3: two TBF-1s completed with engine installation of TBF-3

TBF-3: second major production series with R-2600-20; manufacture mostly at Eastern as TBM-3

TBM-1: similar to TBF-1: total 550

TBM-1C: similar to TBF-1C: total 2,336

TBM-1D/E/J/L/P: similar to corresponding TBFs

TBM-2: conversion of TBM-1 No, 24580 with XR-2600-10 engine

XTBM-3: conversions of four TBM-1Cs with R-2600-20

TBM-3: major production model with R-2600-20 engine and outer wing drop tanks or rockets: total 4,657

TBM-3D: conversion with APS-4 radar on right

TBM-3E: conversions with strengthened structure and RT-5/APS-4 in pod under right wing

TBM-3E2: updated TBM-3E with extra avionics

TBM-3H: conversions with surface-search radar

TBM-3J: conversions as TBF-1J

TBM-3L: conversions as TBF-1L

TBM-3M: conversions for missile launching (various programmes) post-war

TBM-3M2: updates with extra equipment

TBM-3N: conversions (1945/46) for special night attack missions

TBM-3P: photo-reconnaissance conversions, differing from TBF-1P

TBM-3Q: various rebuilds for post-war ECM and EW research and combat duty with prominent additions on belly, cockpit, fin and in some cases wings for reception and/or jamming

TBM-3R: conversions for seven passenger or cargo transport in at least three configurations, all without guns and with door on right

TBM-3S: major post-war conversion programme for ASW strike, most being further updated as TBM-3S2 with TBM 3E2 avionics

TBM-3U: conversions for utility and target towing

TBM-3W: major post-war conversion programme for AEW (radar picket) duty with APS-20 radar, no armament and extra fins; most updated as TBM-3W2 with upgraded displays for two rear operators and other changes

XTBM-4: three new-build aircraft with redesigned wing with different fold system and re-stressed to 5g manoeuvres, production of 2,141 TBM-4 cancelled at VJ-Day

Avenger Mk I: British designation of TBF-1B; total 402

Avenger Mk II: British designation of TBM-1; total 334

Avenger Mk III: British designation of TBM-3; total 222

Avenger AS.Mk 4: British designation (post-war) of TBM-3S; total 100

Fuselage/wings

The chunky fuselage had an oval-section, semi-monocoque structure, built up of a series of angle frames and stamped bulkheads, all covered by a smooth metal skin. The mid-wing had a rectangular centre-section and equally-tapered folding outer wing sections. It was of all-metal single-spar structure with a flush-rivet smooth metal skin, with split trailing-edge flaps between the ailerons and centre-section. There was hydraulic folding and unfolding of the outer wings. Cantilever undercarriage oleo legs were hinged at the extremities of the centre section and were raised outwards into recesses in the undersides of the outer wing-sections, and the tailwheel was fully retractable. Catapult points and an electrically-operated retractable arrester hook were fitted at the rear. Like all products of the 'Grumman Iron Works', the TBF was well-engineered and almost unbreakable.

Crew

The Avenger normally had a crew of three – pilot, bomb-aimer and radio operator. The pilot's cockpit was over the leading edge of the wing, and he fired the fixed forward guns and released the torpedo. The bomb-aimer's position was in the lower fuselage aft of the bomb bay; he also operated the ventral gun. The radio operator, who was aft of the pilot, also served as the turret gunner.

Grumman TBF-1 Avenger
US Navy, 1942

Grumman received a Navy contract for two prototypes of a torpedo-bomber, designated XTBF-1, in April 1940. The type was destined to become the US Navy's standard torpedo-bomber of World War II, and remained in operational service for some 15 years. The illustration shows one of the first TBF-1s to come off the line at Bethpage early in 1942, bearing the number 25. Only about 200 were delivered with the national insignia as shown, a red border with white rectangles being added in June 1943. The colour scheme of sea blue, fading through grey to a white underside, was introduced in 1943; all earlier TBFs had the original scheme of sea green above and light grey below. A total of 9,839 Avengers was built.

Powerplant

The prototype XTBF-1 had a Wright R-2600-8 engine. This 1,700-hp (1268-kW) 14-cylinder radial, air-cooled engine, with a two-speed supercharger, was fitted to most variants. The TBM-4 had a 1,900-hp (1417-kW) R-2600-20 engine and a three-bladed propeller. Three main fuel tanks were built into the centre section – a centre tank of 150 US gal (568 litres) within the fuselage, and two outer tanks of 90 US gal (340 litres) each in the centre-section stubs. Auxiliary streamlined droppable tanks (58 US gal/220 litres each) could be carried under each outer wing, and a droppable long-range ferry tank (275 US gal/1040 litres) could be carried in the bomb bay. The oil tank (32 US gal/120 litres)) was carried in the engine compartment.

Specification
Grumman TBF-1 Avenger

Type: three-seat carrier-based torpedo-bomber

Powerplant: one 1,700-hp (1268-kW) Wright R-2600-8 Cyclone 14-cylinder two-row radial piston engine

Performance: maximum speed 271 mph (436 km/h); typical long-range cruise 145 mph (233 km/h); range on internal fuel 1,105 miles (1778 km); climb rate 1,430 ft per minute (7.3 m per sec); service ceiling 22,400 ft (6830 m)

Weights: empty (TBF-1C) 10,555 lb (4788 kg); maximum loaded 17,364 lb (7876 kg)

Dimensions: span 54 ft 2 in (16.51 m); length 40 ft 0.2 in (12.2 m); height 16 ft 5 in (5.00 m); wing area 490 sq ft (45.52 m²)

Armament: one 0.3-in (7.62-mm) gun firing ahead (in TBF-1C, two 0.5-in/12.7-mm), one 0.5-in (12.7-mm) in turret and one 0.3-in (7.62-mm) in lower rear position; internal bay for one 22.7-in (577-mm) torpedo or up to 2,000 lb (907 kg) of other stores

Armament

The TBF-1 had one fixed forward-firing 0.3-in (7.62-mm) gun in the engine cowling (the TBF-1C two 0.5-in/12.7-mm guns), one 0.5-in (12.7-mm) gun in the electrically controlled spherical dorsal turret, and one 0.3-in (7.62-mm) gun in the ventral turret position, and each had a bomb/torpedo load of 1,600 lb (726 kg). The TBF-3's armament was increased to two forward-firing 0.5-in (12.7-mm) and 0.5-in (12.7-mm) guns in the dorsal turret and ventral position. The bomb/torpedo (a USN short air-torpedo – 22 in/558-mm Mk XII) load was 2,000 lb (907 kg). Underwing racks for eight 60-lb (27-kg) rockets could be fitted. The special anti-submarine detection radar in the TBM-3E made this variant of particular value to the US Navy in the early post-war years, and it became the principal operational version of the Avenger after 1945. The hydraulically-operated bomb doors could be controlled by the pilot or bomb-aimer. A smokescreen tank could be inserted in the bomb bay, and the TBF-1L had a retractable searchlight in there also.

Gruman TBF Avenger

turn like a fighter. and quite early in production it was decided to increase the forward-firing armament, the **TBF-1C** having the 0.3-in (7.62-mm) nose gun replaced by two of 0.5-in (12.7-mm) calibre in the outer wings, each with 600 rounds. These are included in the Grumman total of 2,291, no breakdown being possible. This total also includes 395 **TBF-1B**s, which were fitted with British radio and several other different equipment items for the Fleet Air Arm.

Altogether the British received no fewer than 921 Avengers (the original British name Tarpon being dropped), which equipped no less than 33 first- and second-line squadrons. These served on literally dozens of carriers, numerous UK bases and many other shore stations from Canada to Ceylon and the Far East.

In December 1941 the urgent need for TBFs made it essential to find a second-source producer. General Motors had five plants on the east coast (Tarrytown, Linden, Bloomfield, Trenton and Baltimore), which were without work. Quickly they were organised into a powerful team called Eastern Aircraft Division, and they tooled up to build not only Wildcat fighters under the designation FM but also Avengers, the latter being designated **TBM**. By December 1943 the 1,000th Eastern TBM had been delivered, and the final total by VJ-Day from this builder was no fewer than 7,546 in more than 20 variants. Most were of the **TBM-3** type, with more power and an external arrester hook, often with no turret TBF and in all cases with provision for outer-wing rockets or drop tanks. The Dash-**1D** (TBF and TBM) and the **TBM-3D** and **-3E** had the RT-5/APS-4 search radar, operating at 3-cm wavelength, in a pod well outboard on the right wing.

Thus by the end of the war 9,836 Avengers had been produced, including small numbers of many special variants, of which perhaps the most significant was the Project Cadillac testbed, first of the **TBM-3W** series, which in November 1946 became the first aircraft to fly the APS-20 surveillance radar in a giant 'Guppy' radome. After 1945

the dominant model was the **TBM-3E**, used both with and without a turret, and supplied under the Mutual Assistance Program to many friendly navies, including those of Canada, France, the Netherlands and, later, Japan (the country against which most Avengers had fought!). In the US Navy and also in Britain the anti-submarine Dash-**3S** served in hunter/killer pairs with the Dash-**3W** and **-3W2** with 'Guppy' radars and triple fins until June 1954, several utility models going on for years longer.

These post-war aircraft were Eastern-built TBM-3E Avengers, seen in midnight blue livery in the late 1940s. Though not specifically an anti-submarine version, as was the TBM-3S, they were assigned to shore-based squadron VS-25.

Howard GH/NH/UC-70 Nightingale

Ben Howard, who had designed and built his first aircraft (identified as the DGA-1 – Damned Good Airplane) in 1923, established Howard Aircraft Corporation on 1 January 1937. A series of successful designs linked those years, and his DGA-6 *Mister Mulligan* had won all three of the major American air races in 1935. Direct developments of *Mister Mulligan* led to

the **DGA-15** which, in 1941, was ordered for the US Navy for service in a general utility role under the designation **GH-1**.

Of mixed construction, the GH-1 was a braced high-wing monoplane; the wing structure was of wood, with plywood and fabric skins, the fuselage and tail unit were frameworks of welded steel tube with light alloy and fabric covering. The landing gear

The most numerous of the DGA-15 variants was the NH-1, a US Navy navigation trainer; at the front were two seats with dual controls. At the rear on the left was the navigation pupil.

was of the fixed tailwheel type, with low-pressure main wheels enclosed in streamlined fairings. The cabin seated four and full blind-flying instrumentation and radio equipment was standard. The powerplant comprised a Pratt & Whitney R-985 Wasp Junior driving a two-bladed constant-speed propeller.

Initially the GH-1s, which began to enter US Navy service in late 1941, were used in the transport role, but with the availability in greater numbers a number were reroled as air ambulances under the name **Nightingale**. Some 29 GH-1s were procured, followed by 131 **GH-2** ambulance aircraft and 115 improved **GH-3**s. The final Navy version was the **NH-1**, 205 of this navigation trainer

version being acquired.

After entry into the war, the USAAC impressed 20 civilian Howards. These consisted of 11 **UC-70**s (DGA-15P), two **UC-70A**s (DGA-12), four **UC-70B**s (DGA-15J), one **UC-70C** (DGA-8) and two **UC-70D**s (DGA-9).

Specification
Howard GH-1
Type: four-seat cabin monoplane
Powerplant: one Pratt & Whitney R-985 Wasp Junior radial piston engine rated at 450 hp (336 kW)
Performance: maximum speed 201 mph (323 km/h); service ceiling 21,500 ft (6555 m); range 1,260 miles (2028 km)
Weights: empty 2,700 lb (1225 kg); maximum take-off 4,350 lb (1973 kg)
Dimensions: wing span 38 ft 0 in (11.58 m); length 25 ft 8 in (7.82 m); height 8 ft 5 in (2.57 m); wing area 210 sq ft (19.51 m²)

Hughes XF-11

No purpose-built photo-reconnaissance aircraft flew during World War II, but among those designed for the role was the mighty **Hughes XF-11** (later redesignated **XR-11**). This had been developed from the private-venture Hughes D-2, which had first flown at Harper Lake on 20 June 1943. Dissatisfied with this aircraft, which was destroyed in a hangar fire in November, Hughes designed a more sophisticated aircraft, the **D-5**. With the USAAF designation XF-11, the aircraft was developed purely for the long-range high-altitude reconnaissance role, and was intended as a replacement for the Lockheed F-5 (P-38), which it resembled in configuration. The slender wing

mounted two long tailbooms and a central nacelle where the pilot and cameras were accommodated. The tailbooms continued forward of the wing to mount 3,000-hp Pratt & Whitney R-4360-31 engines.

The first prototype (44-70155) was fitted with contra-rotating propellers, and flew for the first time on 7 July 1946. Although showing sufficient promise to warrant an order for 98 production F-11s, the programme was terminated after the first aircraft crashed when one of the contra-rotating propellers went into reverse pitch. The pilot, Howard Hughes himself, was almost killed. When the second aircraft (44-70156) flew in April 1947, it had

In principle the XF-11 – heavier and much more powerful than a B-17E – was a world-beater, but it was held back by the company management and by ill luck. This is the second aircraft, with reliable single-rotation propellers.

standard four-bladed propellers. It was evaluated post-war by the USAF's Reconnaissance Section, but the advent of the jet aircraft rendered the design obsolete.

Specification
Type: long-range high-altitude photo-reconnaissance platform
Powerplant: two Pratt & Whitney R-4360-31 Double Wasp radial piston

engines, each rated at 3,000 hp (2238 kW)
Performance: maximum speed 450 moh (724 km/h); service ceiling 44,000 ft (13411 m); range approximately 5,000 miles (8000 km)
Weights: empty 37,103 lb (16830 kg); maximum take-off 58,800 lb (26672 kg)
Dimensions: wing span 101 ft 5 in (30.91 m); length 65 ft 5 in (19.94 m); height 23 ft 3 in (7.09 m); wing area 983 sq ft (91.32 m²)

Interstate L-6 Grasshopper

In 1940 the Interstate Aircraft and Engineering Corporation entered the two-seat high-wing

lightplane market with its **S-1A Cadet**, offered with a choice of four engines (65-hp Continental

Originally given the Army Air Corps designation XO-63, this aircraft did so well on test that Interstate received a substantial production order. From this angle it is possible to see the sharp outward slope of the large cabin side windows, giving an undistorted view straight downwards. Interstate also received an order for eight S-1A Cadets, with Army designation L-8, but these were passed on to Bolivia.

or 65, 85 or 90 hp Franklin). The company also produced components for military aircraft, and saw that a military order could improve the commercial sales of the Cadet. Accordingly the company produced the **S-1B**, with extended cabin glazing and more powerful engine. A single aircraft was procured by the Army for evaluation as the **XO-63**. This was subsequently redesignated **XL-6**.

As a result of a successful evaluation, a batch of 250 **L-6**s was ordered, these being given the name **Grasshopper** (along with L-2s, L-3s and L-4s). Although

built in much smaller numbers than its competitiors, the L-6s nevertheless proved of some use during the conflict.

Specification
Type: two-seat observation and liaison aircraft
Powerplant: one 102-hp (76-kW) Franklin O-200-5 inline piston engine
Performance: maximum speed 114 mph (183 km/h); service ceiling 16,500 ft (5030 m); range 540 miles (869 km)
Weights: empty 1,103 lb (500 kg); maximum take-off 1,650 lb (748 kg)
Dimensions: wing span 35 ft 6 in (10.82 m); length 23 ft 5¹/₂ in (7.15 m); height 7 ft 0 in (2.13 m); wing area 173.8 sq ft (16.15 m²)

Lockheed Model 10 Electra

Lockheed's reputation was founded on its outstanding series of fast single-engined Vega, Air Express, Sirius, Altair and Orion monoplanes, but the impact of twin-engined designs, such as Boeing's Model 247 and the Douglas DC-1, forced the Lockheed Aircraft Corporation to follow suit. Work on such a design began at the end of 1932, and the prototype **Model 10 Electra** was rolled out on 23 February 1934, making its first flight later that day. Flight testing occupied almost three months, at the end of which the Bureau of Air Commerce awarded the Model 10 Approved Type Certificate No. 551 on 11 August 1934.

In 1936 two Electras were supplied to the US Navy and US Coast Guard, designated **XR2O-1** and **XR3O-1** respectively. The former was a Model 10-A for the use of the Secretary of the Navy and the latter a Model 10-B used by the Secretary of the Treasury. Four Lockheed 10-As were also purchased by the US Army Air

In 1937 no other passenger transport could approach the performance of the XC-35. Thanks to its pressurised fuselage and turbocharged engines it could cruise at 285 mph at 25,000 ft.

Corps; three were delivered in 1936 under the designation **Y1C-36** and the fourth, in 1937, as a **Y1C-37** for the National Guard Bureau. In 1942 26 civil Electras were impressed for communications duties, comprising 15 10-As which became designated **UC-36A**, four 10-Es (**UC-36B**) and seven 10-Bs (**UC-36C**).

Of particular importance was the single **XC-35** which, powered by two 550-hp (410-kW) Pratt & Whitney XR-1340-43 engines, was first flown on 7 May 1937. Built to USAAC order for experiments with cabin pressurisation and engine supercharging, this had a redesigned fuselage of circular cross-section and had the standard cabin windows eliminated. For the sponsorship of this development, and its use in what proved to be a valuable research

programme, the US Army was later awarded the Collier Trophy.

Specification
Type: twin-engined light transport aircraft
Powerplant: (Y1C-36) two 450-hp (336-kW) Pratt & Whitney R-985-13 Wasp Junior radial piston engines
Performance: maximum speed

201 mph (323 km/h) at 5,000 ft (1525 m); cruising speed 194 mph (312 km/h) at 5,000 ft (1525 m); service ceiling 24,000 ft (7315 m); range 666 miles (1072 km)
Weights: empty 7,100 lb (3221 kg); maximum take-off 10,500 lb (4763 kg)
Dimensions: span 55 ft 0 in (16.76 m); length 38 ft 7 in (11.76 m); height 10 ft 1 in (3.07 m); wing area 458.3 sq ft (42.58 m²)

Lockheed Model 12

The improved financial stability that the Model 10 Electra had conferred upon Lockheed enabled the company to embark upon a new project in 1935. This evolved as another twin-engined design, outwardly similar to the Electra but of slightly smaller dimensions. Identified as the **Model 12**, it was one of the first aircraft intended for business use, seating six passengers in a well-furnished cabin.

From the start, the company was committed to a first flight target date of 27 June 1936, to enable the type to compete in the 1936 Department of Commerce design competition. That target was achieved, test pilot Marshall Headle taking off at 1212 on 27 June, and the aircraft subsequently won the competition.

In 1937-38 the US services acquired Lockheed 12-As for transport duties, initially in seven-seat configuration. The US Navy took a single **JO-1** and two **JO-2**s, three additional examples of the latter serving with the US Marine Corps. Three for the US Army Air Corps were designated **C-40** and 10 five-passenger machines were known as **C-40A**s. Impressed

civil aircraft taken on charge in 1942 became **UC-40D**s. The US Navy and US Air Corps each operated a single 12-A trainer with fixed tricycle-type landing gear, designated respectively **XJO-3** and **C-40B**.

An armed version evolved in 1938 and the prototype flew in the following February, featuring a 0.50-in (12.7-mm) machine-gun in the nose, another in a dorsal turret, and with underfuselage racks for up to eight 250-lb (113-kg) bombs. Sixteen were ordered by the Royal Netherlands Indies Army's Air Division for crew training duties in support of the division's Martin 139

bombers, and to form a Java-based maritime patrol squadron. Thirteen Lockheed 12-A transports had also been ordered, and eight of these were still undelivered when the Dutch East Indies fell into Japanese hands. Together with four similarly undelivered aircraft intended for KNILM (Royal Dutch East Indies Airways), they were used instead by the Netherlands Military Flying School at Jackson, Mississippi.

Specification
Type: six/seven-seat commercial and military light transport, and gunnery trainer
Powerplant: two 450-hp (336-kW)

Pratt & Whitney R-985-SB Wasp Junior radial piston engines
Performance: maximum speed 225 mph (362 km/h); cruising speed 212 mph (341 km/h); service ceiling 22,900 ft (6980 m); range 800 miles (1287 km)
Weights: empty 5,960 lb (2703 kg); maximum take-off 9,200 lb (4173 kg)
Dimensions: span 49 ft 6 in (15.09 m); length 36 ft 4 in (11.07 m); height 9 ft 9 in (2.97 m); wing area 352 sq ft (32.70 m²)
Armament: (military trainer) two 0.50-in (12.7-mm) machine-guns (one in nose and one in dorsal turret), plus up to 2,000 lb (907 kg) of bombs carried externally

From 1941 this C-40 was used by the US Embassy in London. It is seen here over England in British camouflage and with pre-1942 Army insignia.

Lockheed Model 18 Lodestar

Last in the line of Lockheed twin-engined commercial transports, the **Model 18 Lodestar** was developed from the Model 14 and the prototype, flown for the first time on 21 September 1939, was a conversion from a standard Lockheed 14-H2. With a longer fuselage seating 14 passengers and having a crew of three, the Lodestar was built in a number of versions, principally the Models 18-07 with 750-hp (559-kW) Pratt & Whitney S1E-3G Hornet engines, 18-08 with 900-hp (671-kW) Pratt & Whitney SC-3G Twin Wasps, 18-14 with 1,050-hp (783-kW) S4C-4G Twin Wasps, 18-40 with 900-hp (671-kW) GR-1820-G102A Wright Cyclones, 18-50 with 1,000-hp (746-kW) GR-1820-G202A Cyclones, and 18-56 with similarly powered GR-1820-G205A Cyclones.

US military interest in the Lodestar was first shown in 1940, when the US Navy ordered a single **XR5O-1** and two **R5O-1** command transports, a similar aircraft being delivered to the US Coast Guard. These were powered by Wright R-1870 engines, as were 12 **R5O-4**s, 41 **R5O-5**s and 35 **R5O-6**s. These last three models were, respectively, four- to seven-seat executive transports, 12/14-seat personnel transports, and 18-seat troop carriers used by the US Marine Corps for paratroop operations. Pratt & Whitney R-1830 engines powered the single R5O-2 and three **R5O-3**s built for the US Navy.

The US Army Air Corps ordered a single Wright R-1820-29-engined aircraft in May 1941, under the designation **C-56**, this being the military version of the civil Model 18-50. At the same time three Model 18-14s were ordered, with Pratt & Whitney R-1830-53 engines. These were supplemented by later orders for seven and three aircraft respectively, all 13 machines being designated **C-57**.

An impressed civil aircraft was designated **C-57A**, seven troop carriers were known as **C-57B**s and three of the later model **C-60A**s were re-engined with Pratt & Whitney R-1830-43 radials to become **C-57C**s; one of these three became a **C-57D** with R-1830-92 engines.

The greater number of aircraft taken over from the US internal airlines from December 1941, however, were given designations in the C-56 series, comprising one **C-56A**, 13 **C-56B**s, 12 **C-56C**s, seven **C-56D**s and two **C-56E**s.

Ten Model 18-07s and 15 Model 18-56s were acquired as **C-59**s and **C-60**s respectively, later supplemented by another 21 C-60s and 325 **C-60A**s; one of the latter became a **C-60B** with an experimental hot-air de-icing system. A single Model 18-10, with 1,200-hp (895-kW) R-1830-53 engines and seats for 11 passengers, was purchased in 1942 and designated **C-66**.

Specification
Type: 17-seat personnel and cargo transport
Powerplant: (C-56) two 1,200-hp (895-kW) Wright R-1820-71 radial piston engines
Performance: maximum speed

This Lodestar is one of the Navy R5O versions. Almost forgotten today, the similar C-60 variant was the AAF's most important glider tug-pilot trainer.

253 mph (407 km/h); cruising speed 200 mph (322 km/h); service ceiling 23,300 ft (7100 m); range 1,600 miles (2575 km)
Weights: empty 11,650 lb (5284 kg); maximum take-off 17,500 lb (7938 kg)
Dimensions: span 65 ft 6 in (19.96 m); length 49 ft 10 in (15.19 m); height 11 ft 1 in (3.38 m); wing area 550 sq ft (51.10 m²)

Lockheed A-29 Hudson

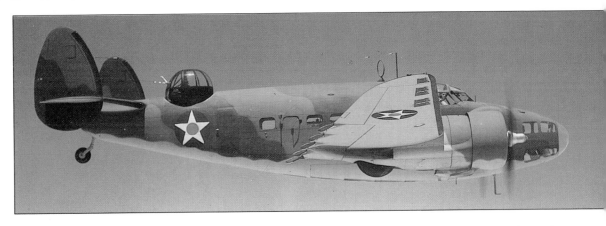

British contracts for Hudsons catapulted Lockheed into the ranks of giant aircraft companies, putting the company and its subsidiary Vega into a position to fulfil even bigger US orders. This immaculate aircraft, devoid of any marking except the pre-1942 US insignia, was probably one of the first Hudsons to be repossessed as an A-29. Cyclone-powered, unlike many of the RAF Hudsons, which had Twin Wasps, it retains British camouflage and the Boulton Paul dorsal turret. Almost all later A-29s had the turret replaced by an open cockpit with (usually) a 0.50-in gun.

The first American-built aircraft to be used operationally by the RAF during World War II, the Lockheed Hudson was a design which stemmed from the urgent British requirement for a maritime patrol/navigational trainer aircraft. Faced with the problem of producing these aircraft as quickly as possible for Britain, Lockheed offered a militarised version of the Lockheed 14 Super Electra civil airliner, identified by Lockheed as the Model 414. While the aircraft's general configuration differed little from that of the civil airliner, there were a number of specific changes to provide suitable armament, plus the installation of more powerful engines. With approval accorded, production went ahead to such good effect that the first of these aircraft, to which the RAF had given the name Hudson, was able to record its initial flight on 10 December 1938.

Of all-metal construction, the wings were set in a mid position and featured a Lockheed-modified version of the Fowler-type trailing-edge flap. The fuselage was conventional, but included a bomb bay to provide internal stowage for up to 1,400 lb (635 kg) of bombs, a new bomb-aimer's position in the fuselage nose, and provision for two forward-firing machine-guns mounted in the upper fuselage forward of the pilot, plus a power-operated dorsal turret sited well aft, near the tail unit which had twin vertical fins and rudders. Landing gear was of the tailwheel type, with the main units retracting aft to be housed in the engine nacelles. The powerplant, wing-mounted in long nacelles, comprised two 1,100-hp (820-kW) Wright GR-1820-G102A Cyclone engines, each driving a three-bladed variable-pitch propeller. Standard accommodation was for a crew of four, comprising pilot, navigator, bomb-aimer and radio operator/air gunner.

Procurement for the RAF and RAAF amounted to something like 1,500 aircraft before introduction of the Lend-Lease programme, and subsequent requirements were procured by the USAAF for supply to Britain.

The first USAAF order was for 52 **A-28**s, all supplied to Britain, as were the 450 **A-28A**s which followed, and these were designated **Hudson Mks IV** and **VI** respectively, by the RAF. The A-28s had 1,050-hp (783-kW) Pratt & Whitney R-1830-45 Twin Wasp engines, but the A-28As not only had 1,200-hp (895-kW) R-1830-67

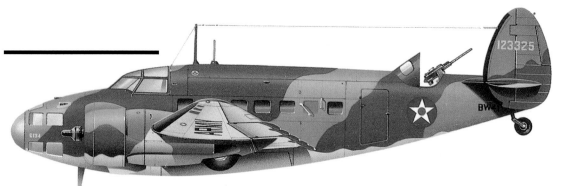

Twin Wasps but also convertible interiors for alternative use as troop transports. Other versions procured by the USAAF included 416 **A-29**s with 1,200-hp (895-kW) Wright R-1820-87 engines and 384 **A-29A**s with the same engines, the latter having the convertible interiors of the A-28A. All were allocated to the RAF, but only 382 were received by that service and designated **Hudson Mk IIIA**. The balance were impressed for service by the USAAF for bomber crew training and anti-submarine patrol, and 20 went to the US Navy which designated them **PBO-1**. Some 24 of the US Army's A-29s were converted in 1942 for use in a photo-reconnaissance role, and were accordingly redesignated **A-29B**. The designation **C-63** was allocated by the USAAF for a projected cargo variant, but this was cancelled before any were built. The final variant procured by the USAAF was required as a trainer for air gunners, or as a target tug. These were generally similar to A-29As and were equipped with a Martin dorsal turret. Lockheed built 217 of them as **AT-18**s, followed by 83 **AT-18A**s, as navigation trainers, with different internal equipment and the turret deleted. Three civilian Model 14s were impressed as **C-111**s.

One of the USAAF'S A-29s was the first US Army aircraft to sink a German U-boat in World War II, and the PBO-1s of the US Navy's VP-82 Squadron based at Ventia, Newfoundland, sank the first two U-boats credited to that service in World War II on 1 and 15 March 1942.

Specification

Type: twin-engined maritime patrol-bomber
Powerplant: (A-29) two 1,200-hp (895-kW) Wright R-1820-87 Cyclone 9 radial piston engines
Performance: maximum speed 253 mph (407 km/h) at 15,000 ft (4570 m); cruising speed 205 mph (330 km/h); service ceiling 26,500 ft (8075 m); range 1,550 miles (2494 km)
Weights: empty 12,825 lb (5817 kg); maximum take-off 20,500 lb (9299 kg)
Dimensions: span 65 ft 6 in (19.96 m); length 44 ft 4 in (13.51 m); height 11 ft 11 in (3.63 m); wing area 551 sq ft (51.19 m²)
Armament: two 0.30-in (7.62-mm) machine-guns in fuselage nose, one 0.30-in (7.62-mm) gun in ventral position and two 0.30-in (7.62-mm) guns in optional dorsal turret, plus up to 1,600 lb (726 kg) of bombs

This A-29 was one of a line-up of B Flight, 2nd Recon Sqn, USAAF, at Manaos in the heart of the Brazilian jungle in 1943. They were used on anti-U-boat patrol over the Atlantic, and also for bomber crew training, transport and reconnaissance. There was no need for defensive guns, but they carried depth charges and various bombloads.

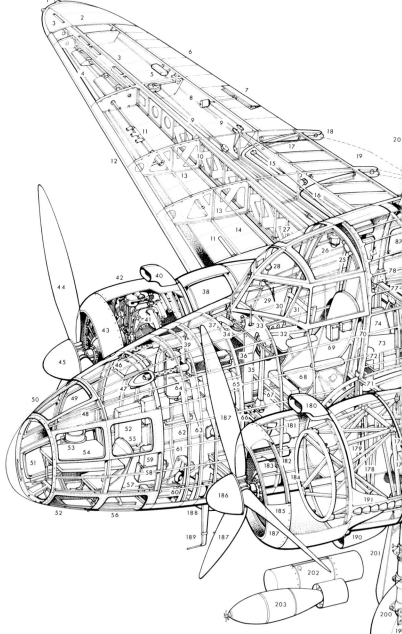

These A-29s were from the original ex-RAF batch, with Army serials 41-23223/23638, and with the rear fuselage contoured to take a turret. Had they gone to the RAF they would have been flown to the Canadian border and towed across by a horse, under the terms of the Lend-Lease Act.

Lockheed A-29 Hudson cutaway key

1 Starboard navigation/identification lights
2 Starboard wingtip
3 De-icing slots
4 Internal vanes
5 Aileron internal mass balance
6 Starboard aileron
7 Aileron tab
8 Tab mechanism
9 Control cables
10 Wing main spar structure
11 De-icing tubes
12 Leading-edge de-icing boot
13 Main wing rib stations
14 Wing skinning

38 Starboard engine oil tank
39 Fixed forward-firing 0.303-in (7.7-mm) Browning machine-guns (two)
40 Carburettor intake
41 Wright R-1820-G102A radial engine
42 Starboard nacelle
43 Cowling nose ring
44 Three-blade propeller
45 Spinner

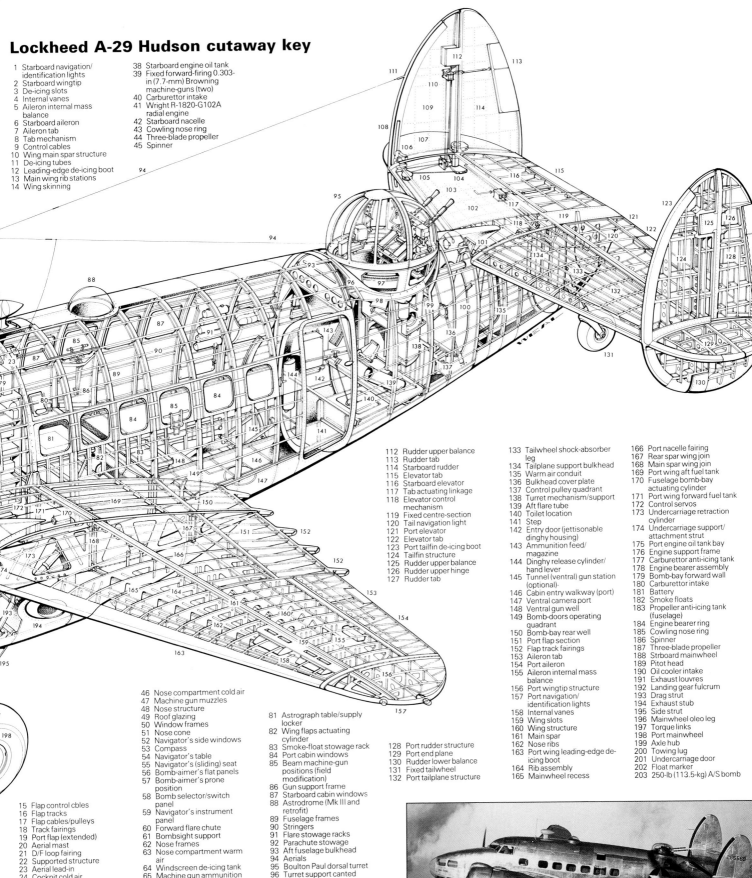

112 Rudder upper balance
113 Rudder tab
114 Starboard rudder
115 Elevator tab
116 Starboard elevator
117 Tab actuating linkage
118 Elevator control mechanism
119 Fixed centre-section
120 Tail navigation light
121 Port elevator
122 Elevator tab
123 Port tailfin de-icing boot
124 Tailfin structure
125 Rudder upper balance
126 Rudder upper hinge
127 Rudder tab

133 Tailwheel shock-absorber leg
134 Tailplane support bulkhead
135 Warm air conduit
136 Bulkhead cover plate
137 Control pulley quadrant
138 Turret mechanism/support
139 Aft flare tube
140 Toilet location
141 Step
142 Entry door (jettisonable dinghy housing)
143 Ammunition feed/magazine
144 Dinghy release cylinder/hand lever
145 Tunnel (ventral) gun station (optional)·
146 Cabin entry walkway (port)
147 Ventral camera port
148 Ventral gun well
149 Bomb-doors operating quadrant
150 Bomb-bay rear well
151 Port flap section
152 Flap track fairings
153 Aileron tab
154 Port aileron
155 Aileron internal mass balance
156 Port wingtip structure
157 Port navigation/identification lights
158 Internal vanes
159 Wing slots
160 Wing structure
161 Main spar
162 Nose ribs
163 Port wing leading-edge de-icing boot
164 Rib assembly
165 Mainwheel recess

166 Port nacelle fairing
167 Rear spar wing join
168 Main spar wing join
169 Port wing aft fuel tank
170 Fuselage bomb-bay actuating cylinder
171 Port wing forward fuel tank
172 Control servos
173 Undercarriage retraction cylinder
174 Undercarriage support/attachment strut
175 Port engine oil tank bay
176 Engine support frame
177 Carburettor anti-icing tank
178 Engine bearer assembly
179 Bomb-bay forward wall
180 Carburettor intake
181 Battery
182 Smoke floats
183 Propeller anti-icing tank (fuselage)
184 Engine bearer ring
185 Cowling nose ring
186 Spinner
187 Three-blade propeller
188 Strboard mainwheel
189 Pitot head
190 Oil cooler intake
191 Exhaust louvres
192 Landing gear fulcrum
193 Drag strut
194 Exhaust stub
195 Side strut
196 Mainwheel oleo leg
197 Torque links
198 Port mainwheel
199 Axle hub
200 Towing lug
201 Undercarriage door
202 Float marker
203 250-lb (113.5-kg) A/S bomb

46 Nose compartment cold air
47 Machine gun muzzles
48 Nose structure
49 Roof glazing
50 Window frames
51 Nose cone
52 Navigator's side windows
53 Compass
54 Navigator's table
55 Navigator's (sliding) seat
56 Bomb-aimer's flat panels
57 Bomb-aimer's prone position
58 Bomb selector/switch panel
59 Navigator's instrument panel
60 Forward flare chute
61 Bombsight support
62 Nose frames
63 Nose compartment warm air
64 Windscreen de-icing tank
65 Machine gun ammunition magazine
66 Rudder pedal assembly
67 Pilot's control column
68 Pilot's seat
69 Pilot's radio control boxes
70 Forwrd (canted) fuselage frame
71 Frame/wing pick-up
72 Hydraulics reservoir
73 Wireless-operator's table
74 Wireless-operator's seat
75 Transmitter
76 Receiver
77 Main spar centre-section carry-through
78 Spar/frame attachment
79 Wireless bay racks
80 Cabin cold air

81 Astrograph table/supply locker
82 Wing flaps actuating cylinder
83 Smoke-float stowage rack
84 Port cabin windows
85 Beam machine-gun positions (field modification)
86 Gun support frame
87 Starboard cabin windows
88 Astrodrome (Mk III and retrofit)
89 Fuselage frames
90 Stringers
91 Flare stowage racks
92 Parachute stowage
93 Aft fuselage bulkhead
94 Aerials
95 Boulton Paul dorsal turret
96 Turret support canted frame
97 Turret ring
98 Dorsal cut-out former
99 Bulkhead
100 Rear bulkhead/tailplane support
101 Tail surface control linkage
102 Starboard tailplane
103 Twin 0.303-in (7.7-mm) machine-guns
104 Rudder control quadrant
105 Cable linkage
106 De-icing tube
107 Starboard end plane
108 Tailfin de-icing boot
109 Tailfin skinning
110 Rudder tab actuator
111 Aerial attachment

128 Port rudder structure
129 Port end plane
130 Rudder lower balance
131 Fixed tailwheel
132 Port tailplane structure

15 Flap control cbles
16 Flap tracks
17 Flap cables/pulleys
18 Track fairings
19 Port flap (extended)
20 Aerial mast
21 D/F loop fairing
22 Supported structure
23 Aerial lead-in
24 Cockpit cold air
25 Flight deck sun-blind frames
26 Windscreen wiper motor
27 Jettisonable canopy hatch
28 Console light
29 Windscreen wipers
30 Second-pilot's jump seat
31 Adjustable quarterlight
32 Windscreen frame support member
33 External gunsight
34 Second-pilot's (back-up) control column (cantilevered)
35 Central instrument console
36 Starboard nose compartment entry tunnel
37 Bulkhead

Army 42-55569 was the second of 217 AT-18 trainers. Normally they carried two pilots and a pupil gunner who manned a Martin electrically-powered turret with twin 0.50-in guns. Powered like the A-29 by 1,200-hp R-1820-87 Cyclone engines, they were also equipped to tow targets. Some also trained navigators (note the D/F loop and astrodome).

Lockheed C-69 Constellation

Lockheed's **C-69 Constell-ation** military transport was destined to become perhaps the most elegant and certainly one of the most successful airliners ever produced by the US industry. Indeed, the aircraft was designed originally to meet a Transcontinental and Western Airlines (TWA) specification for a pressurised airliner capable of flying the US transcontinental routes without a stop, carrying a 6,000-lb (2722-kg) payload over a range of 3,500 miles (5633 km) and cruising at up to 300 mph (483 km/h) at an altitude of 20,000 ft (6095 m).

The Constellation was launched with an initial TWA order for nine aircraft, and construction of the prototype was initiated in 1940. Completed in December, the first Model 49 was quickly readied for its maiden flight which took place on 9 January 1943, flown by Lockheed chief test pilot Miro Burcham and his Boeing opposite number Eddie Allen. Powered by four 2,200-hp (1641-kW) Wright R-3350-35 Cyclone 18 two-row radials, the prototype lifted from the runway at Burbank and, after an hour in the air, landed at Muroc Field (now known as Edwards Air Force Base). The test programme quickly established that design performance had been achieved, with a maximum speed of 347 mph (558 km/h), a cruising speed of 275 mph (443 km/h) achieved on 52.5 per cent power at one US gal per mile (2.4 litres

per km) fuel consumption.

TWA's order had been increased to 40, and was followed by one from Pan American Airways for a similar number of a transoceanic version. However, both airlines waived their rights to the first batches of aircraft from the production line in favour of the USAAF, which needed fast troop transports. The prototype, despite its civil registration, had been painted with military green upper surfaces and grey undersides, and was handed over to the USAAF on 28 July 1943.

The first production **C-69**, although bearing its military serial, was painted in TWA livery and, at 0356 on 17 April 1944, co-captains Howard Hughes and Jack Frye of TWA took off from Burbank on delivery to the USAAF, flying to Washington National in a new transcontinental record time of a few seconds under six hours 58 minutes. On 23 January 1945 TWA's

Prime mover behind the Constellation was Howard Hughes, who worked with Lockheed on a project called the Excalibur. This grew into the heavier Model 049, powered by the most powerful engine available, the Duplex Cyclone. At last the prototype flew in January 1943, when the photograph above was taken. By this time it had become the first Army C-69, painted olive drab.

Finished in natural metal, Army 43-10315 was the seventh of nine Model 049-39-10 transports originally ordered by TWA and PanAm. Lockheed built a further 13 C-69s on direct Army order, with Fiscal Year 1942 serials (94549/94561). The original prototype (top of page), c/n 1961, was later used by Lockheed for many tests, with different engines and stretched to become the first 1049 Super Constellation.

Intercontinental Division was contracted to see the C-69 into regular service with USAAF Air Transport Command. During this period the first Constellation transatlantic flight took place, nonstop from New York to Paris, in a record time of 14 hours 12 minutes.

After VJ-Day the USAAF's transport requirements were drastically reduced, and the C-69 programme was cancelled. Twenty C-69-1-LO or -5-LO

63-seat troop transports and one **C-69C** 43-seat personnel transport were completed to USAAF order, although some did not enter service. With the exception of one which crashed at Topeka, Kansas, on 18 September 1945 and one destroyed in static tests at Wright Field, all C-69s were sold to civil operators and many aircraft which had been at an advanced state of construction when cancellation took place were completed as civil Model 049s. This version was awarded the US Civil Aeronautics Board Approved Type Certificate No. 763 on 11 December 1945 after only 27 hours of test flying.

This C-69, 43-10314, immediately preceded the example seen above. It was photographed a little later, after the USAAF Air Transport Command badge had been applied to the rear fuselage. The beautiful fish-like shape of the 'Connie' was retained in the much longer Super Constellation, which was also distinguished from the wartime version by having square passenger windows.

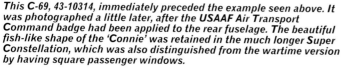

Specification
Type: cargo and passenger transport
Powerplant: four 2,200-hp (1641-kW) Wright R-3350-35 Cyclone 18 radial piston engines
Performance: maximum speed 330 mph (531 km/h); cruising speed 300 mph (483 km/h); service ceiling 25,000 ft (7620 m); range 2,400 miles (3862 km)
Weights: empty 50,500 lb (22906 kg); maximum take-off 72,000 lb (32659 kg)
Dimensions: span 123 ft 0 in (37.49 m); length 95 ft 2 in (29.01 m); height 23 ft 8 in (7.21 m); wing area 1,650 sq ft (153.29 m²)

Lockheed PV Ventura/Harpoon and B-34 Lexington

The early success of its Hudsons in operational service with the RAF induced Lockheed to initiate the design of a more advanced version. This was based on the company's somewhat larger Model 18 Lodestar civil airliner, but the resulting aircraft was very similar in appearance to the Hudson. The design was duly investigated and approved by the British Purchasing Commission, and 675 were ordered from Lockheed. Produced by the company's Vega division, the first of these flew on 31 July 1941. Its design had benefitted from the company's manufacturing and British operational experience with the Hudson, so there were no major problems discovered during the flight test programme, and the first examples began to enter service with the RAF's No. 21 Squadron in October 1942.

Designated **Ventura Mk I**, the new aircraft differed from the Hudson in having a wider and deeper fuselage with a length increase of 16 per cent, more powerful Pratt & Whitney engines each rated at 2,000 hp (1491 kW), the introduction of a proper ventral gun position with two 0.303-in (7.7-mm) machine-guns and, because of the more voluminous fuselage and greater engine power, a bomb bay able to accommodate a maximum bombload of 2,500 lb (1134 kg). Two fuel drop tanks, two 500-lb (227-kg) bombs or two depth charges could be carried beneath the wings, outboard of the engine nacelles, and the bomb bay was long enough to contain a standard short 22-in

Humid oceanic air and vortices from the tips of the Hamilton Standard 'paddle-blade' propellers combine to leave white vortices as this PV-1 flies at low level. It is fully operational with one of the VP patrol squadrons. These had previously been exclusively equipped with flying-boats, but such aircraft proved vulnerable to Japanese fighters.

(559-mm) torpedo. After 188 Ventura Mk Is had been delivered, changes in armament and the installation of R-2800-31 engines brought redesignation as **Ventura Mk II**.

Venturas were first used operationally by RAF Bomber Command on 3 November 1942, and during this and subsequent daylight raids the new bombers were not considered to be well suited to such a role, although an additional 200 had been ordered under Lend-Lease as **Ventura Mk IIA** by this time. Consequently, those then in service were transferred for operation with Coastal Command under the des-

Wartime Navy aircraft seldom displayed any prominent Bureau number, though the white 47 on the rudder of this PV-1 may have been the last two digits. This example has the unglazed nose of aircraft ordered directly as PV-1 s, and not transferred from an RAF Ventura contract. All were equipped to carry external drop tanks, of each either 150 or 300 US gal capacity.

Lockheed PV Ventura/Harpoon and B-34 Lexington

Dated 25 January 1944, this photograph shows a PV-1 of the 1st Marine Air Wing at Bougainville, New Guinea. It is one of the glazed-nose versions originally ordered as an RAF Ventura or Army B-34 Lexington. Note the fixed 'letter box' slots along the outer leading edge, a feature of all aircraft derived from the Model 14 transport.

PV-1s, probably from Navy bomber squadron VB-135, are shown over the Aleutian island chain in 1944. They are carrying drop tanks, but – surprisingly, as this was a front-line theatre – have no lower rear guns.

ignation **Ventura GR.Mk I** and outstanding orders were cancelled. Thus only about 300 of the total on order were delivered.

When the Ventura was included in the Lend-Lease programme it was procured initially for the RAF under the designation **B-34**, but with the cancellation of British orders the outstanding aircraft began to enter USAAF service initially as **R-37**s, based on the manufacturer's model number, and later as **B-34A Lexingtons**, and these were used mainly for maritime patrol. In addition a small number were procured as navigational trainers, and these were allocated the designation **B-34B**. In 1942 the US Army ordered 550 examples of a new version with 1,700-hp (1 268-kW) Wright R-2600-31 Cyclone 14 engines, for use in a patrol/reconnaissance role under the designation **O-56**, but only 18 of these aircraft had been received, becoming instead **B-37**, before the balance of 532 on order were cancelled.

The two cancellations would suggest that there was no further use for Lockheed's Model 37, but this was not the case, for towards the end of 1942 the US Navy requisitioned 27 of the Lend-Lease B-34s then still in the process of supply to the UK. These entered service with the US Navy under the designation **PV-3**, for training and familiarisation, pending the receipt of the first quantities of a larger batch of aircraft then in production for the USAAF as B-34s, and

which the US Navy had designated **PV-1**. Following the RAF and USAAF cancellations of B-34s and O-56s respectively, all subsequent production was transferred to the US Navy, and it was this service which continued also to procure Lend-Lease requirements.

The first of the US Navy's PV-1s were delivered in December 1942, these entering service first with US Navy Squadron VP-82 and replacing the PBO-1s (Hudsons) which had been requisitioned from Lend-Lease production for the UK in the autumn of 1941. Approximately 1,600 PV-1s were procured by the US Navy, of which 388 were supplied to the UK under Lend-Lease. These were designated **Ventura GR.Mk V**s, and the majority served with the Commonwealth air forces in Australia, Canada, New Zealand and

This PV-1 was painted in all-white livery, normally used only over the North Atlantic. This made the black rubber de-icer boots stand out prominently. The maximum offensive load of the PV-1 was six 500-lb bombs or mines, or various depth charges or one torpedo internally, plus (usually as an overload) two 1,000-lb bombs under the wings as an alternative to drop tanks.

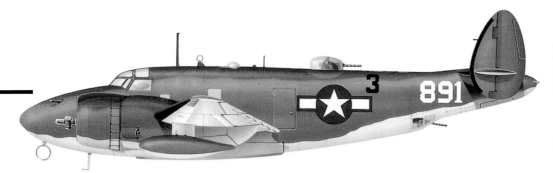

South Africa. Some of the US Navy's PV-1s were modified subsequently to serve in a reconnaissance role, under the designation **PV-1P**. On 30 June 1943 the US Navy ordered a new version under the changed designation **PV-2** and with the name **Harpoon**. While retaining the same general appearance as the earlier Model 37, it differed in several respects. General configuration and powerplant was unchanged, but the wing span was increased by 9 ft 5 in (2.87 m), this giving a wing area of 686 sq ft (63.73 m²). Other changes included increased fuel capacity, greater fin and rudder area, and much improved armament. In the basic PV-2 this consisted of five 0.50-in

(12.7-mm) forward-firing machine-guns in the fuselage nose and two flexibly-mounted 0.50-in (12.7-mm) guns in both dorsal turret and ventral position, plus up to four 1,000-lb (454-kg) bombs carried in the bomb bay and two similar bombs carried externally. The final production version, of which 33 were built, had the designation **PV-2D**, and in these aircraft the nose armament was increased to a total of eight 0.50-in (12.7-mm) machine-guns.

Orders for the PV-2 totalled 500, and initial delivery of these to US Navy squadrons began in March 1944. One of the aims of the increased wing span of this version was to provide considerably increased fuel capacity by use of the wing structure to form integral tanks, but great difficulty was experienced in making these fuel-tight. The first 30 aircraft were withdrawn from service and the integral tanks in the outer wings sealed off; the aircraft were then used in a training role with the designation **PV-2C**. The problem of the leaking outer tanks was beyond solution at that time, and all of the 470 production PV-2s had leak-proof fuel cells installed within the integral tanks.

The PV-2 served primarily in the Pacific theatre as a patrol-bomber, until VJ-Day brought its withdrawal from front-line service. However, operated by US Navy Reserve units, the type remained in use for several years after the war.

Specification

Type: four/five-seat medium bomber
Powerplant: (B-34A) two 2,000-hp (1491-kW) Pratt & Whitney R-2800-31 Double Wasp radial piston engines
Performance: maximum speed 315 mph (507 km/h) at 15,500 ft (4725 m); cruising speed 230 mph (370 km/h); service ceiling 24,000 ft (7315 m); range 950 miles (1529 km)
Weights: empty 17,275 lb (7836 kg); maximum take-off 27,250 lb (12360 kg)
Dimensions: span 65 ft 6 in (19.96 m); length 51 ft 5 in (15.67 m); height 11 ft 11 in (3.63 m); wing area 551 sq ft (51.19 m²)
Armament: two forward-firing 0.50-in (12.7-mm) machine-guns in fuselage nose and six 0.30-in (7.62-mm) guns on flexible mounts in nose, dorsal and ventral position, plus up to 2,500 lb (1134 kg) of bombs in bomb bay

Above: Like the RAF, the Army Air Force decided the B-34 Lexington would be unsuitable for bombing missions against heavily defended targets. Accordingly, the B-34 was used as a crew trainer, with limited use on anti-submarine patrol off the US coast. These 'reverse Lend-Lease' Lexingtons, painted with RAF camouflage, are training bomber crews at Randolph Field, Texas. The nearest aircraft is 41-38165.

Below: Extending the wings and enlarging the tail of the PV-2 Harpoon degraded flight performance except for take-off and landing. On the other hand, it improved handling and enabled heavier loads to be carried. This was the first example, on test from Vega Aircraft at Burbank.

The new outer wings of the PV-2 Harpoon no longer incorporated fixed 'letter box' slots, of the kind seen on the Model 14, Hudson, Lodestar, Ventura and all derived aircraft. This view of an early PV-2 emphasises the short nose, with the cockpit well behind the closely spaced engines. After 1945 many Harpoons were converted into PV-2T crew trainers, while others were passed to friendly countries.

Lockheed PV-2 Harpoon
US Navy Squadron VPB-142
Marianas Islands, 1945

Vega Aircraft, a subsidiary of Lockheed, was awarded a contract by the British Purchasing Commission in June 1940 for 875 of a new design of bomber derived from the Lockheed Lodestar airliner. Called the Lockheed V-146, or Vega 37, it resembled a more powerful Hudson, with a longer fuselage provided with a ventral gun position. Known as the PV-1 Ventura, B-34/B-37 Lexington and PV-2 Harpoon, the versions were based on a basic configuration. The PV-2, as illustrated here, was one of the original and most common variants with a forward-firing armament of five guns, two high in the nose and three below. Later the number was increased to eight. The larger Harpoon differed from the Ventura in almost every detail except for small sections of the fuselage, inboard wing ribs and the engine cowlings. The B-34/B-37 Lexington was a USAAF designation given to early Lend-Lease examples of the PV-1 Ventura for service on overwater patrols.

Powerplant
The PV-2 Harpoon had Pratt & Whitney R-2800-31 Double Wasp 18-cylinder, two-row, radial air-cooled engines with two-speed superchargers. These developed 1491 kW (2,000 hp) each. Three-bladed Hamilton Standard Hydromatic broad-blade constant-speed propellers, 10 ft 7 in (3.23 m) in diameter, were fitted. The main fuel system comprised four tanks on the centre section, two in the outer sections and two cabin tanks, all self-sealing. Two external droppable tanks could be carried under the outer wings. There was provision for long-range ferry tanks, housing 780 US gal (2953 litres), in the bomb bay. The main oil tanks were carried on each nacelle with a reserve tank in the fuselage. In the late 1930s there was increased interest in high-performance liquid-cooled inline engines then being developed. Pratt & Whitney stated that they could build an equally powerful conventional radial engine. In the event, the Double Wasp proved one of the most successful aero engines of World War II.

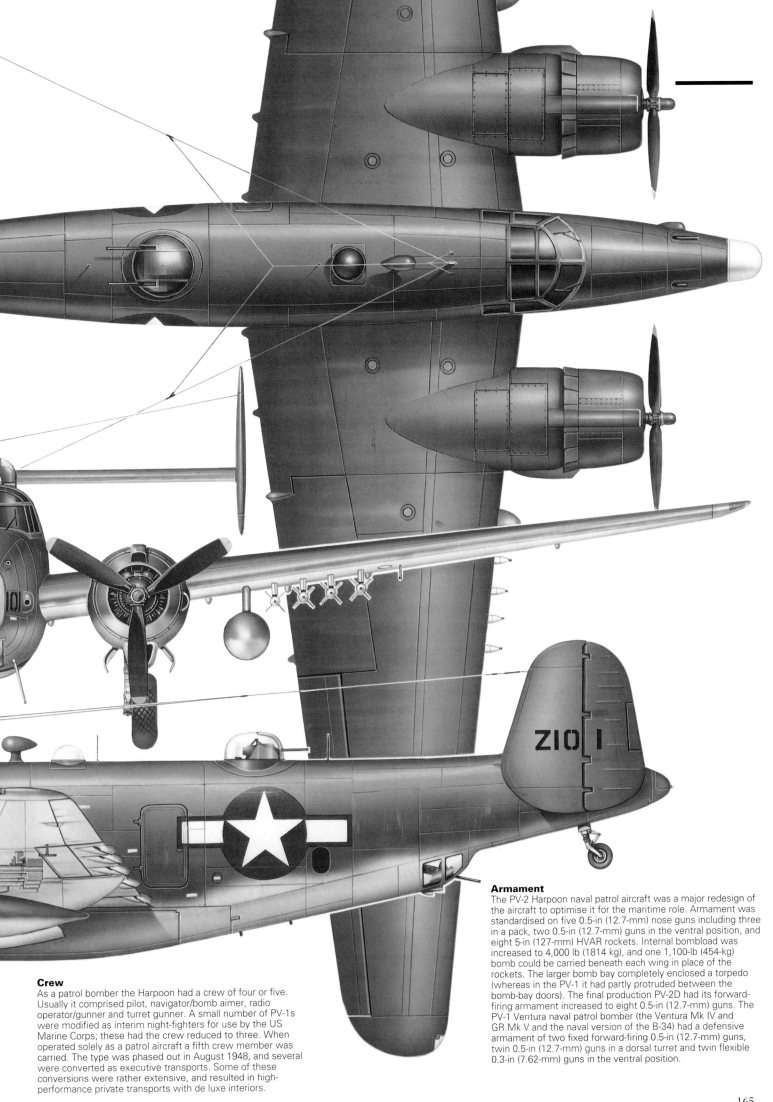

Crew
As a patrol bomber the Harpoon had a crew of four or five. Usually it comprised pilot, navigator/bomb aimer, radio operator/gunner and turret gunner. A small number of PV-1s were modified as interim night-fighters for use by the US Marine Corps; these had the crew reduced to three. When operated solely as a patrol aircraft a fifth crew member was carried. The type was phased out in August 1948, and several were converted as executive transports. Some of these conversions were rather extensive, and resulted in high-performance private transports with de luxe interiors.

Armament
The PV-2 Harpoon naval patrol aircraft was a major redesign of the aircraft to optimise it for the maritime role. Armament was standardised on five 0.5-in (12.7-mm) nose guns including three in a pack, two 0.5-in (12.7-mm) guns in the ventral position, and eight 5-in (127-mm) HVAR rockets. Internal bombload was increased to 4,000 lb (1814 kg), and one 1,100-lb (454-kg) bomb could be carried beneath each wing in place of the rockets. The larger bomb bay completely enclosed a torpedo (whereas in the PV-1 it had partly protruded between the bomb-bay doors). The final production PV-2D had its forward-firing armament increased to eight 0.5-in (12.7-mm) guns. The PV-1 Ventura naval patrol bomber (the Ventura Mk IV and GR.Mk V and the naval version of the B-34) had a defensive armament of two fixed forward-firing 0.5-in (12.7-mm) guns, twin 0.5-in (12.7-mm) guns in a dorsal turret and twin flexible 0.3-in (7.62-mm) guns in the ventral position.

Lockheed P-38 Lightning

Fighter, bomber, night-fighter, reconnaissance aircraft, air ambulance, torpedo-bomber and even glider tug: there seemed no limit to the adaptability of the Lockheed P-38. It was one of the brilliant trio of 'pursuit' fighters produced by the USA during World War II, and the only one to remain in series production throughout the entire period of American participation in the war.

Originally conceived to meet a 1937 requirement for a high-altitude fighter capable of 360 mph (580 km/h) at 20,000 ft (6095 m), and a full-throttle endurance of one hour at this altitude, the Lockheed design team under H.L. Hibbard (undertaking its first military task) embarked on a radical twin-engined, twin-boom design, there being no engine available to meet the performance demands in a single-engined layout. After examination of other alternatives, it was found that the twin-boom configuration bestowed numerous advantages, such as accommodation of engines, main landing gear, superchargers and radiators, as well as providing the benefits of endplate effect on the tailplane with twin vertical surfaces. Although the nose was thus left free for armament without synchronisation, the foreshortened central nacelle always proved difficult to adapt for additional equipment. The original gross weight of 14,800 lb (6713 kg) was higher than that of most contemporary American light bombers.

Prototype flown

The Lockheed Model 22 design was accepted by the USAAC on 23 June 1937 and a single **XP-38** prototype ordered. This was flown by Lieutenant B.S. Kelsey at March Field on 27 January 1939. Two weeks later the aircraft was flown across the continent in 7 hours 2 minutes with two refuelling stops, but was destroyed when it undershot on landing at Mitchell Field.

A batch of 13 **YP-38** pre-production test aircraft had already been ordered, and the first of these was flown on 16 September 1940, powered by 1,150-hp (858-kW) Allison V-1710-27/29 engines with spur reduction gear driving outward-rotating propellers in place of the prototype's 960-hp (716-kW) V-1710-IV15 engines with epicyclic gear driving inward-rotating propellers. Armament provision was also changed from one 23-mm Madsen cannon and four 0.5-in (12.7-mm) Browning machine-guns to one 37-mm Oldsmobile cannon, two 0.5-in (12.7-mm) machine-guns and two 0.3-in (7.62-mm) machine-guns.

Delivery of the YP-38s was completed from Burbank, California, in March 1941. Long before, in September 1939, an initial production order for 66 **P-38**s had been signed, followed quickly by another for 607. The P-38 reverted to the armament of the XP-38 and, with the

addition of some armour around the cockpit, grossed up to 15,340 lb (6958 kg), with a top speed of 395 mph (636 km/h) at 19,800 ft (6035 m). Deliveries of the first 30 aircraft were completed in mid-1941, but these aircraft were largely confined to training duties. One P-38 was modified as the **XP-38A** with an experimental pressure cabin, but the **P-38B** and **P-38C** projects remained unbuilt.

The first fully combat-standard version was the **P-38D**, which incorporated many features recommended in reports of air fighting in Europe, the first deliveries to the USAAC starting in August 1941 with the 27th Pursuit Squadron, 1st Pursuit Group, at Selfridge Field, Michigan. This version, of which 36 were produced, featured self-sealing fuel tanks and introduced increased tailplane incidence which led to improved elevator control and reduced buffeting at low speeds; a retractable landing light and low-pressure pilot's oxygen system were also introduced. At the time of Pearl Harbor the USAAC had on inventory a total of 47 P-38s and P-38Ds.

As production at Burbank switched to the P-38E (of which 210

When it flew in January 1939, the XP-38 became the first dedicated fighter in the world to have a tricycle undercarriage. It was also notable for the metal-covered, rather than fabric-covered, control surfaces, and the use of exhaust-driven turbo-superchargers for the engines. Other claims to fame would include its longevity, remaining in production throughout the war, and its destruction of the first German aircraft claimed by a USAAF fighter. This illustration shows a P-38H-5-LO in mid-1943 finish and markings.

*Above: A flight of P-38H-1s in **USAAF** service. This model followed closely upon the P-38G, from which it differed primarily in having automatic oil radiator flaps, needed to overcome a serious engine overheating problem at high altitudes.*

were built) in November 1941, three P-38s were experimentally modified as RP-38s to include a second cockpit in the port tail boom (the supercharger gear being removed) to test pilot experience of asymmetric flight, although the reason for this interest remains unknown. The **P-38E** dispensed with the 37-mm gun, instead featuring a 20-mm Hispano with increased ammunition capacity; later sub-variants introduced Curtiss Electric propellers with solid dural blades in place of Hamilton Standard Hydromatic propellers with hollow steel blades, revised electrical and hydraulic systems and SCR-274N radio. P-38Es served with a total of 12 squadrons of the USAAF during 1942 and 1943, the majority of them in the south-west Pacific theatre and in the Aleutians.

RAF order

Meanwhile, the Royal Air Force had expressed interest in the P-38 (now named the Lightning, the name Atlanta – at one time favoured – having been discarded), a British Purchasing Mission had signed a cash purchase order for 667 aircraft in March 1940. A small number of **Lightning Mk I**s was shipped to the UK early in 1942 and flew at Boscombe Down and Farnborough, where pilots recommended that further deliveries be suspended. Accordingly, about 130 of the first 143 Lightning Mk Is were repossessed by the USAAF for use as trainers (known as **P-322**s) or fully modified as **P-38F-13**s or **-15**s. The remainder of the British order (**Lightning Mk II**s) was completed with V-1710-F2R engines but, following the USA's entry into the war, all were repossessed by the USAAF and most were modified at a Dallas plant to become **P-38G-15**s.

In March 1942 the USAAF received the first deliveries of a reconnaissance version, the **F-4** (converted from P-38Es), in which all armament had been replaced by four K-17 cameras; a drift sight and

Right: To give trainee pilots a taste of the Lightning's performance, in 1942 Lockheed developed this 'piggyback' two-seater based on a P-38F-1-LO retained for demonstration purposes. The trainee behind the pilot could only observe, having no controls.

Right: For high-speed photo-reconnaissance, P-38s were fitted with five cameras and had armament removed. Those based on the P-38G airframe took the new designation -5A and relevant block number (this is a -10-LO).

Right: The Lightning was a prominent player with the 8th Air Force, offering greater range than the P-47 that preceded it into action. First to see combat was the 55th Fighter Group, including the 38th FS, with which this P-38J-10-LO served in 1944.

Lockheed P-38 Lightning

Right: Shark's teeth markings, first seen on the Hawk Mk 81As of the AVG in China, became popular on several other types of aircraft. Here they are displayed on a P-38F-5-LO of the 39th Fighter Squadron, 35th FG, assigned to fly in the defence of Guadalcanal in February 1943.

Left: Fighters flying escort for the bombers of the 8th Air Force adopted a system of two-letter codes to identify squadrons, similar to that used by the RAF. This is a P-38J-5-LO of the 79th FS, 20th FG, serving at Kingscliffe, Northants, in 1944.

Above: Among the first Lightnings to arrive at Isley Field, Saipan, in the Marianas, on 10 July 1944, 'Stinky' was an F-5B-1-LO photographic reconnaissance variant. An unarmed, camera-equipped version of the P-38J-5-LO, the F-5B was the final production PR version.

Above: Lockheed's final production Lightning was the P-38L; more than 3,800 were built. Batteries of 5-in (12.7-cm) HVARs were added to the armament, but the 14-rocket arrangement shown here was less than satisfactory, and 10-missile 'trees' followed.

Right: Of the 10,037 Lightnings built, Lockheed completed all but 113 P-38Is produced by Vultee. This Lockheed-built P-38L-5 represents the final production form of the twin-boom fighter, which could also have a glazed or radar-carrying nose.

autopilot were also introduced as standard. Some 99 F-4s were converted, first joining the 5th and 7th Photographic Squadrons in the USA.

The P-38F joined the Burbank line early in 1942 with 1,325-hp (988-kW) V-1710-49/53 engines which maintained the top speed at 395 mph (636 km/h) at 25,000 ft (7620 m) at an all-up weight increased to 18,000 lb (8165 kg). The additional weight was the result of introducing underwing bomb racks for two 1,000-lb (454-kg) bombs, a smoke-laying installation or long-range drop tanks. The last bestowed a maximum range of 1,750 miles (2816 km), a useful performance attribute for warfare in the Pacific theatre.

The P-38F-5-LO introduced A-12 oxygen equipment, the F-13-LO was the repossessed Lightning Mk I with instrument display to BS.2338, and the P-38F-15-LO featured provision for a combat flap setting of 8 degrees that allowed tighter turning at combat speeds by increasing the lift coefficient. At least one P-38F-13 was test-flown with a pair of 22-in (559-mm) torpedoes on the underwing racks. The P-38F was the first version to undergo modification as a two-seater, a small number having the radio removed and a second seat installed on

the wing main spar; no controls were fitted in this cockpit, and the variant was intended only to provide air experience for pilots who were unaccustomed to a nosewheel landing gear, and in any case would have been extremely cramped and uncomfortable. A total of 527 P-38Fs was produced, this number including 20 reconnaissance F-4As which, apart from the later engines, were similar to the F-4.

Overseas deployment

P-38F-1-LOs with SCR-522 and SCR-535 radio were the first American fighters to be flown to the UK across the Atlantic, aircraft of the 1st and 14th Fighter Groups (accompanied by Boeing B-17s as navigator/escort ships) flying from the USA to Goxhill and Atcham respectively in July and August 1942 before being assigned to the 12th Air Force in North Africa later in that year. Another group flew to North Africa by way of the South Atlantic. The first German aircraft to be shot down by a P-38 had, however, long before been claimed by the pilot of a P-38E of an Iceland-based group, who had disposed of a Focke-Wulf Fw 200 Condor within hours of the USA's declaration of war.

The **P-38G** was little changed from the F-series. It featured 1,325-hp (988-kW) V-1710-51/55 engines, boost-governed to deliver no more than 1,150 hp (858 kW) at 27,000 ft (8230 m) owing to inadequate radiator area; it also reverted to the SCR-274N radio. The P-38G-3-LO had B-13 superchargers and the P-38G-15 was the repossessed RAF Lightning Mk II. Of the 1,082 P-38Gs built, 181 were converted to F-5A reconnaissance aircraft and 200 to F-5Bs (similar to the F-5As but with intercoolers). Whereas the earlier F-4s equipped 20 reconnaissance squadrons between 1942 and 1945 (including the 18th Combat Mapping Squadron, the 111th Tactical Reconnaissance Squadron and the 154th Weather Reconnaissance Squadron), the F-5

sub-variants reached 33 squadrons, remaining on some after the war.

P-38Gs joined 27 USAAF squadrons in the Pacific theatre during 1943, and it was the drop tank-equipped aircraft of a detachment from the 339th Fighter Squadron, 347th Fighter Group, based on Guadalcanal, that intercepted and destroyed the Japanese aircraft carrying Admiral Isoroku Yamamoto 550 miles (885 km) from their base. The P-38 pilot who claimed this victory was Lieutenant Thomas G. Lanphier, who later flew with Lockheed as a test pilot.

Increased all-up weight to 19,200 lb (8709 kg) and 1,425-hp (1063-kW) V-1710-89/91 engines identified the **P-38H**, of which Lockheed built 601 and which entered service in May 1943, reaching the European theatre the following month. The increased weight resulted from re-stressing the underwing pylons to carry bombs or other stores of up to a total of 3,200 lb (1452 kg). Later sub-variants introduced automatically-operating oil cooler flaps in an effort to cure persistent overheating troubles, while the P-38H-5-LO featured the General Electric B-33 supercharger which provided high boost at altitude. Maximum speed of the P-38H-5 was 418 mph (673 km/h).

Meanwhile the P-38 was in constant action in Europe and the Mediterranean theatre, earning the German sobriquet *'der gabelschwanzer Teufel'* (the fork-tailed devil). Despite the obvious benefit of the combat flap, the P-38 did not prove entirely suitable for combat with the single-engined fighters of the Luftwaffe. This was learned at some cost during the first bomber-escort flights to Berlin from bases in England. Nevertheless, the reconnaissance F-5s of the 12th Photographic Reconnaissance Squadron, 3rd Photographic Group, based at La Marsa, Tunisia, succeeded in mapping some 80 per cent of the Italian mainland before the invasion of that country. There were 128 conversions of P-38Hs to F-5C reconnaissance standard.

The first externally-obvious alteration to the P-38 was made in the **P-38J** series, which entered combat service in August 1943. Powered by 1,425-hp (1063-kW) V-1710-89/91 engines (like the previous version), this series introduced 'chin' fairings under the nose to enclose the intercooler intakes sandwiched between the oil radiator intakes. On the P-38J-5-LO the space previously occupied by the intercoolers

Named 'Information, Please', this P-38J-20-LO of the 28th Photo Reconnaissance Squadron is flying with Marine Corps F4Us on a strike against Kushi-Take, central Okinawa, in June 1945. It carries cameras and a crewman in the Plexiglas-nosed belly tank.

in the wing leading edges now accommodated two additional 55-US gal (208-litre) fuel tanks, thereby increasing the total internal fuel capacity to 410 US gal (1552 litres). When carrying two 360-US gal (1363-litre) drop tanks, the P-38J had a range of 2,300 miles (3701 km) with a 10-minute combat allowance, thereby permitting long-distance penetration flights to the heart of Europe.

Shortcomings in the fighter-versus-fighter combat role proved largely academic with the build-up of P-47 and P-51 squadrons in Europe, and henceforth the P-38 tended increasingly to be committed to ground-attack tasks in this theatre. In the Pacific and Far East, however, the P-38 continued to give unsurpassed service as a long-range fighter; Lightning pilots were credited with the destruction of more Japanese aircraft than those of any other fighter. America's highest-scoring pilot, Major Richard Bong, who flew with the 9th Fighter Squadron, 49th Fighter Group, and the 39th Fighter Squadron, 35th Fighter Group, and later as gunnery officer with V Fighter Command, achieved his entire score of 40 enemy aircraft destroyed while flying

Above: Adding to the Lightning's versatility, Lockheed working groups in Britain developed a two-seat variant to serve as a navigation/bomb-aiming lead ship. With a glazed droop-snoot nose containing Norden bombsight and bombardier, modified P-38Js entered service in April 1944.

As an alternative to the droop-snoot version, Lockheed also designed a P-38L conversion that incorporated AN/APS-15 BTO (Bombing Through Overcast) radar plus a radar operator in a lengthened nose. Small numbers served in both European and CBI theatres.

P-38s (he also later flew as a Lockheed test pilot but was killed in a P-80). Runner-up in the Far East was another P-38 pilot, Major Thomas Buchanan McGuire, who destroyed 38 Japanese aircraft while with the 9th and 431st Fighter Squadrons. Both pilots won the Medal of Honor.

Maximum speed of the P-38J was 414 mph (666 km/h) at 25,000 ft (7620 m) without external stores, and combat experience showed that the aircraft could be dived at speeds of around 550 mph (885 km/h), although this was accompanied by a strong pitch-down movement. To overcome this the P-38J-25-LO introduced a small electrically-actuated flap under each wing; at the same time hydraulically-boosted control systems were incorporated to alleviate aileron reversal – one of the earliest instances of power-assisted controls in an operational aircraft. One P-38J was modified to become the **P-38K**, powered by V-1710-75/77 engines driving larger-diameter propellers.

Major variant

In 1944 production of the P-38J gave place to the **P-38L**, numerically the most important of all Lightnings. Lockheed completed 3,810 at Burbank and a Vultee plant at Nashville, Tennessee, produced another 113, but contract cover for 1,887 other P-38Ls was cancelled on VJ-Day in 1945. The P-38L, powered by 1,600-hp (1194-kW) V-1710-111/113 engines and with a maximum all-up weight of 21,600 lb (9798 kg), was the first Lightning to be armed with underwing rocket projectiles, 10 5-in (127-mm) weapons being mounted on 'tree' tiers outboard of the engine nacelles.

By the end of 1944 P-38s had reached 101 squadrons, the majority of earlier versions having made way for P-38Js and P-38Ls. Of these, 34 squadrons were serving in the west Pacific and Southeast Asia, 16 in the south-west Pacific, 12 in the North Pacific and the Aleutian Islands, and 24 in Europe and the Mediterranean, the remainder being in the USA and Panama Canal Zone. Among the reconnaissance versions, F-5 sub-variants were serving with 44 photographic and tactical reconnaissance squadrons throughout the Pacific, and in Burma, India, China, Australia, Puerto Rico, Panama, Italy, France, England and North Africa, some units such as the 21st Photo Reconnaissance Squadron in India retaining their F-5s until the end of the war.

In Europe, as the emphasis shifted from use of the P-38 as a fighter in 1944, Lightning squadrons came to be used more and more in the tactical bombing role, and a tactic was evolved by which large formations of Lightnings released their bombloads (by now increased to two 2,000-lb/907-kg bombs) simultaneously with the lead aircraft's release. These leading aircraft were two-seat adaptations of the P-38J and P-38L in which a bombardier, complete with Norden bomb sight, was located in a transparent nose (all gun armament having been

Lockheed P-38J Lightning cutaway drawing key

1 Starboard navigation light
2 Wingtip trailing edge strake
3 Landing light (underwing) location
4 Starboard aileron
5 Aileron control rod/quadrant
6 Wing outer spar
7 Aileron tab drum
8 Aileron tab control pulleys
9 Aileron tab control rod
10 Aileron trim tab
11 Fixed tab
12 Tab cable access
13 Flap extension/retraction cables
14 Control pulleys
15 Flap outer carriage
16 Fowler-type flap (extended)
17 Control access panel
18 Wing spar transition
19 Outer section leading-edge fuel tanks (P-38J-5 and subsequent) capacity 46 Imp gal (208 litres) each
20 Engine bearer/bulkhead upper attachment
21 Firewall
22 Triangulated tubular engine bearer supports
23 Polished mirror surface panel (undercarriage visual check)
24 Cantilever engine bearer
25 Intake fairing
26 Accessories cooling intake
27 Oil radiator (outer sections) and intercooler (centre section) tripleintake
28 Spinner
29 Curtiss-Electric three-blade (left) handed propeller
30 Four machine gun barrels
31 Cannon barrel
32 Camera-gun aperture
33 Nose panel
34 Bulkhead
35 Machine gun blast tubes
36 Four 0.5-in (12.7-mm) machine guns
37 Cannon flexible hose hydraulic charger
38 Chatellerault-feed cannon magazine (150 rounds)
39 Machine gun firing solenoid
40 Cannon ammunition feed chute
41 Nose armament cowling clips
42 Case ejection chute (port lower machine gun)
43 Ammunition box and feed chute (port lower machine gun)
44 Case ejection chute (port upper machine gun)
45 Ammunition box and feed chute (port upper machine gun)
46 Radio antenna
47 Ejection chute exit (shrouded when item 52 attached)
48 Nosewheel door
49 Nosewheel shimmy damper assembly and reservoir
50 Torque links
51 Towing eye
52 Type M10 triple-tube 4.5-in (11.4-cm) rocket-launcher
53 Rearward-retracting nosewheel
54 Alloy spokes cover plate
55 Fork
56 Rocket-launcher forward attachment (to 63)
57 Nosewheel lower drag struts
58 Nosewheel oleo leg
59 Nosewheel pin access
60 Side struts and fulcrum
61 Actuating cylinder
62 Upper drag strut
63 Rocket-launcher forward attachment bracket
64 Rudder pedal assembly
65 Engine controls quadrant
66 Instrument panel

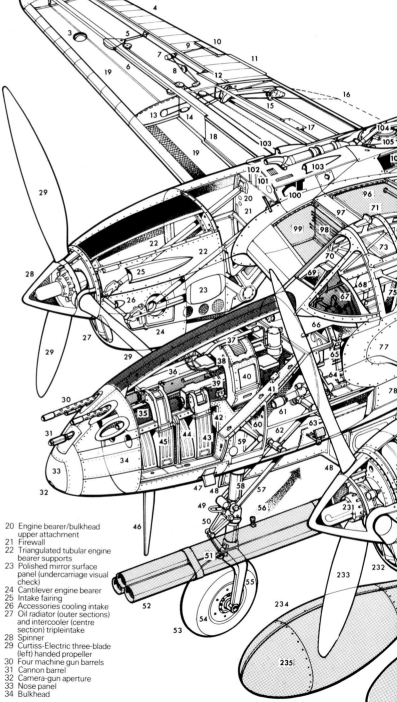

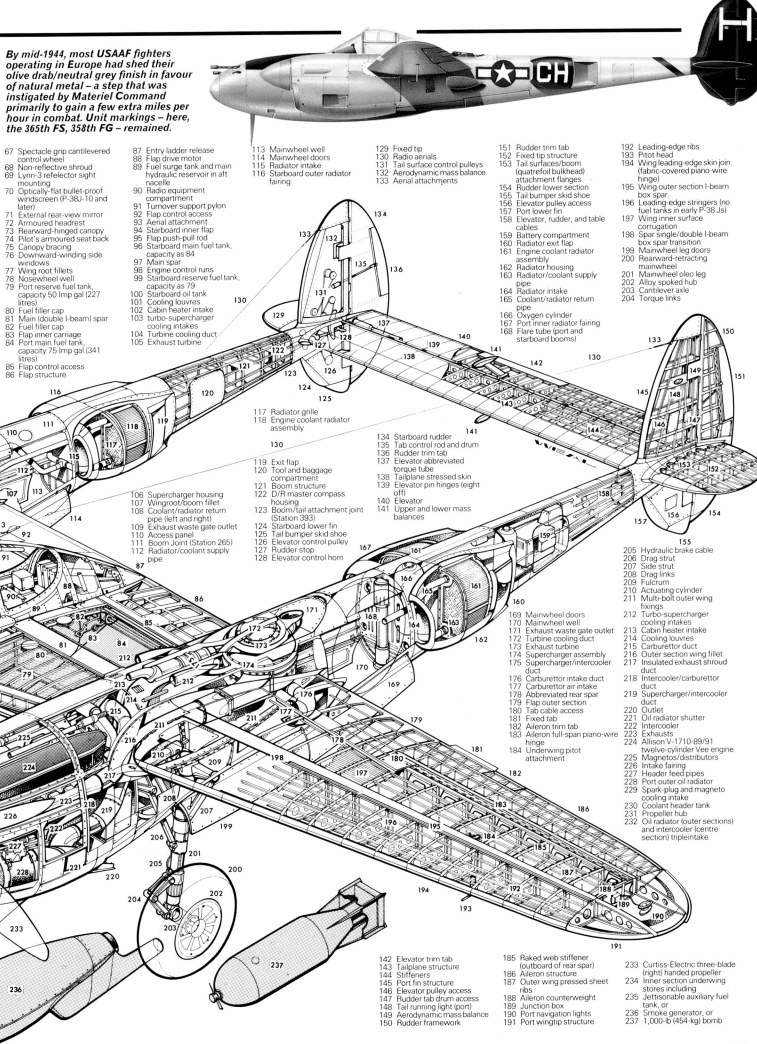

By mid-1944, most *USAAF* fighters operating in Europe had shed their olive drab/neutral grey finish in favour of natural metal – a step that was instigated by *Materiel Command* primarily to gain a few extra miles per hour in combat. Unit markings – here, the 365th *FS*, 358th *FG* – remained.

67 Spectacle grip cantilevered control wheel
68 Non-reflective shroud
69 Lynn-3 reflector sight mounting
70 Optically-flat bullet-proof windscreen (P-38J-10 and later)
71 External rear-view mirror
72 Armoured headrest
73 Rearward-hinged canopy
74 Pilot's armoured seat back
75 Canopy bracing
76 Downward-winding side windows
77 Wing root fillets
78 Nosewheel well
79 Port reserve fuel tank, capacity 50 Imp gal (227 litres)
80 Fuel filler cap
81 Main (double I-beam) spar
82 Fuel filler cap
83 Flap inner carriage
84 Port main fuel tank, capacity 75 Imp gal (341 litres)
85 Flap control access
86 Flap structure

87 Entry ladder release
88 Flap drive motor
89 Fuel surge tank and main hydraulic reservoir in aft nacelle
90 Radio equipment compartment
91 Turnover support pylon
92 Flap control access
93 Aerial attachment
94 Starboard inner flap
95 Flap push-pull rod
96 Starboard main fuel tank, capacity as 84
97 Main spar
98 Engine control runs
99 Starboard reserve fuel tank, capacity as 79
100 Starboard oil tank
101 Cooling louvres
102 Cabin heater intake
103 turbo-supercharger cooling intakes
104 Turbine cooling duct
105 Exhaust turbine

106 Supercharger housing
107 Wingroot/boom fillet
108 Coolant/radiator return pipe (left and right)
109 Exhaust waste gate outlet
110 Access panel
111 Boom Joint (Station 265)
112 Radiator/coolant supply pipe

113 Mainwheel well
114 Mainwheel doors
115 Radiator intake
116 Starboard outer radiator fairing

117 Radiator grille
118 Engine coolant radiator assembly

119 Exit flap
120 Tool and baggage compartment
121 Boom structure
122 D/R master compass housing
123 Boom/tail attachment joint (Station 393)
124 Starboard lower fin
125 Tail bumper skid shoe
126 Elevator control pulley
127 Rudder stop
128 Elevator control horn

129 Fixed tip
130 Radio aerials
131 Tail surface control pulleys
132 Aerodynamic mass balance
133 Aerial attachments

134 Starboard rudder
135 Tab control rod and drum
136 Rudder trim tab
137 Elevator abbreviated torque tube
138 Tailplane stressed skin
139 Elevator pin hinges (eight off)
140 Elevator
141 Upper and lower mass balances

142 Elevator trim tab
143 Tailplane structure
144 Stiffeners
145 Port fin structure
146 Elevator pulley access
147 Rudder tab drum access
148 Tail running light (port)
149 Aerodynamic mass balance
150 Rudder framework

151 Rudder trim tab
152 Fixed tip structure
153 Tail surfaces/boom (quatrefoil bulkhead) attachment flanges
154 Rudder lower section
155 Tail bumper skid shoe
156 Elevator pulley access
157 Port lower fin
158 Elevator, rudder, and table cables
159 Battery compartment
160 Radiator exit flap
161 Engine coolant radiator assembly
162 Radiator housing
163 Radiator/coolant supply pipe
164 Radiator intake
165 Coolant/radiator return pipe
166 Oxygen cylinder
167 Port inner radiator fairing
168 Flare tube (port and starboard booms)

169 Mainwheel doors
170 Mainwheel well
171 Exhaust waste gate outlet
172 Turbine cooling duct
173 Exhaust turbine
174 Supercharger assembly
175 Supercharger/intercooler duct
176 Carburettor intake duct
177 Carburettor air intake
178 Abbreviated rear spar
179 Flap outer section
180 Tab cable access
181 Fixed tab
182 Aileron trim tab
183 Aileron full-span piano-wire hinge
184 Underwing pitot attachment

185 Raked web stiffener (outboard of rear spar)
186 Aileron structure
187 Outer wing pressed sheet ribs
188 Aileron counterweight
189 Junction box
190 Port navigation lights
191 Port wingtip structure

192 Leading-edge ribs
193 Pitot head
194 Wing leading-edge skin join (fabric-covered piano-wire hinge)
195 Wing outer section I-beam box spar
196 Leading-edge stringers (no fuel tanks in early P-38 Js)
197 Wing inner surface corrugation
198 Spar single/double I-beam box spar transition
199 Mainwheel leg doors
200 Rearward-retracting mainwheel
201 Mainwheel oleo leg
202 Alloy spoked hub
203 Cantilever axle
204 Torque links

205 Hydraulic brake cable
206 Drag strut
207 Side strut
208 Drag links
209 Fulcrum
210 Actuating cylinder
211 Multi-bolt outer wing fixings
212 Turbo-supercharger cooling intakes
213 Cabin heater intake
214 Cooling louvres
215 Carburettor duct
216 Outer section wing fillet
217 Insulated exhaust shroud duct
218 Intercooler/carburettor duct
219 Supercharger/intercooler duct
220 Outlet
221 Oil radiator shutter
222 Intercooler
223 Exhausts
224 Allison V-1710-89/91 twelve-cylinder Vee engine
225 Magnetos/distributors
226 Intake fairing
227 Header feed pipes
228 Port outer oil radiator
229 Spark-plug and magneto cooling intake
230 Coolant header tank
231 Propeller hub
232 Oil radiator (outer sections) and intercooler (centre section) tripleintake

233 Curtiss-Electric three-blade (right) handed propeller
234 Inner section underwing stores including
235 Jettisonable auxiliary fuel tank, or
236 Smoke generator, or
237 1,000-lb (454-kg) bomb

171

Lockheed P-38 Lightning

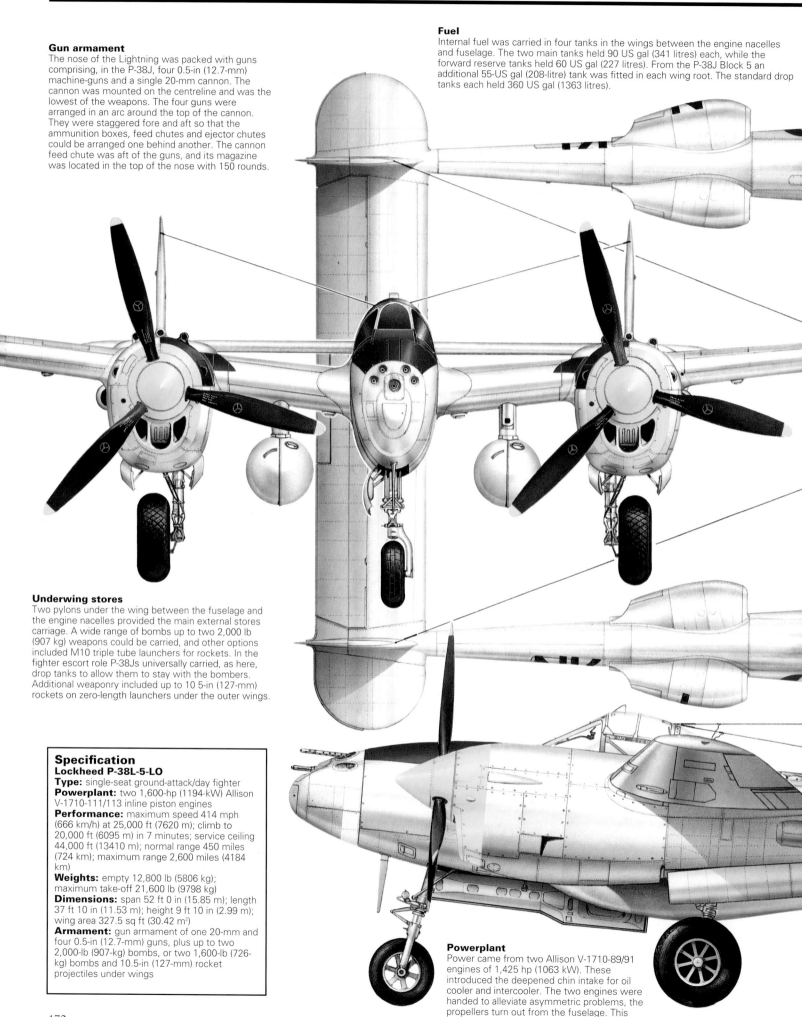

Gun armament
The nose of the Lightning was packed with guns comprising, in the P-38J, four 0.5-in (12.7-mm) machine-guns and a single 20-mm cannon. The cannon was mounted on the centreline and was the lowest of the weapons. The four guns were arranged in an arc around the top of the cannon. They were staggered fore and aft so that the ammunition boxes, feed chutes and ejector chutes could be arranged one behind another. The cannon feed chute was aft of the guns, and its magazine was located in the top of the nose with 150 rounds.

Fuel
Internal fuel was carried in four tanks in the wings between the engine nacelles and fuselage. The two main tanks held 90 US gal (341 litres) each, while the forward reserve tanks held 60 US gal (227 litres). From the P-38J Block 5 an additional 55-US gal (208-litre) tank was fitted in each wing root. The standard drop tanks each held 360 US gal (1363 litres).

Underwing stores
Two pylons under the wing between the fuselage and the engine nacelles provided the main external stores carriage. A wide range of bombs up to two 2,000 lb (907 kg) weapons could be carried, and other options included M10 triple tube launchers for rockets. In the fighter escort role P-38Js universally carried, as here, drop tanks to allow them to stay with the bombers. Additional weaponry included up to 10 5-in (127-mm) rockets on zero-length launchers under the outer wings.

Specification
Lockheed P-38L-5-LO
Type: single-seat ground-attack/day fighter
Powerplant: two 1,600-hp (1194-kW) Allison V-1710-111/113 inline piston engines
Performance: maximum speed 414 mph (666 km/h) at 25,000 ft (7620 m); climb to 20,000 ft (6095 m) in 7 minutes; service ceiling 44,000 ft (13410 m); normal range 450 miles (724 km); maximum range 2,600 miles (4184 km)
Weights: empty 12,800 lb (5806 kg); maximum take-off 21,600 lb (9798 kg)
Dimensions: span 52 ft 0 in (15.85 m); length 37 ft 10 in (11.53 m); height 9 ft 10 in (2.99 m); wing area 327.5 sq ft (30.42 m²)
Armament: gun armament of one 20-mm and four 0.5-in (12.7-mm) guns, plus up to two 2,000-lb (907-kg) bombs, or two 1,600-lb (726-kg) bombs and 10.5-in (127-mm) rocket projectiles under wings

Powerplant
Power came from two Allison V-1710-89/91 engines of 1,425 hp (1063 kW). These introduced the deepened chin intake for oil cooler and intercooler. The two engines were handed to alleviate asymmetric problems, the propellers turn out from the fuselage. This accounted for the two sub-marks applied to the otherwise identical engines.

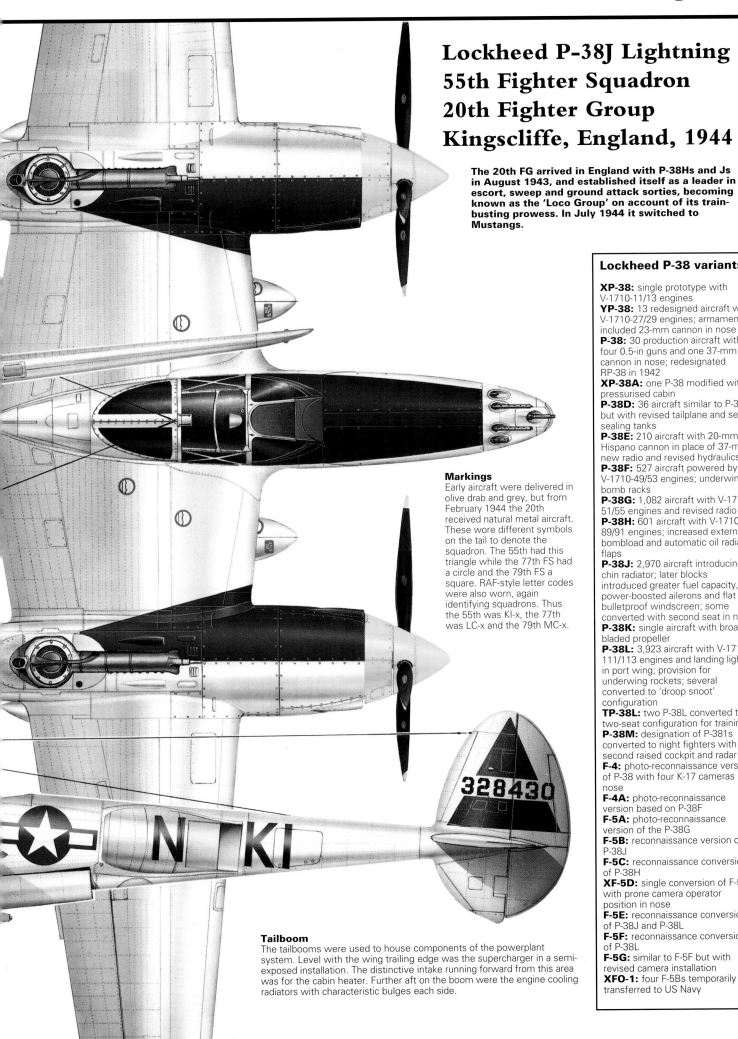

Lockheed P-38J Lightning
55th Fighter Squadron
20th Fighter Group
Kingscliffe, England, 1944

The 20th FG arrived in England with P-38Hs and Js in August 1943, and established itself as a leader in escort, sweep and ground attack sorties, becoming known as the 'Loco Group' on account of its train-busting prowess. In July 1944 it switched to Mustangs.

Lockheed P-38 variants

XP-38: single prototype with V-1710-11/13 engines

YP-38: 13 redesigned aircraft with V-1710-27/29 engines; armament included 23-mm cannon in nose

P-38: 30 production aircraft with four 0.5-in guns and one 37-mm cannon in nose; redesignated RP-38 in 1942

XP-38A: one P-38 modified with pressurised cabin

P-38D: 36 aircraft similar to P-38 but with revised tailplane and self-sealing tanks

P-38E: 210 aircraft with 20-mm Hispano cannon in place of 37-mm; new radio and revised hydraulics

P-38F: 527 aircraft powered by V-1710-49/53 engines; underwing bomb racks

P-38G: 1,082 aircraft with V-1710-51/55 engines and revised radio

P-38H: 601 aircraft with V-1710-89/91 engines; increased external bombload and automatic oil radiator flaps

P-38J: 2,970 aircraft introducing chin radiator; later blocks introduced greater fuel capacity, power-boosted ailerons and flat bulletproof windscreen; some converted with second seat in nose

P-38K: single aircraft with broad-bladed propeller

P-38L: 3,923 aircraft with V-1710-111/113 engines and landing light in port wing; provision for underwing rockets; several converted to 'droop snoot' configuration

TP-38L: two P-38L converted to two-seat configuration for training

P-38M: designation of P-38Ls converted to night fighters with second raised cockpit and radar

F-4: photo-reconnaissance version of P-38 with four K-17 cameras in nose

F-4A: photo-reconnaissance version based on P-38F

F-5A: photo-reconnaissance version of the P-38G

F-5B: reconnaissance version of P-38J

F-5C: reconnaissance conversion of P-38H

XF-5D: single conversion of F-5A with prone camera operator position in nose

F-5E: reconnaissance conversion of P-38J and P-38L

F-5F: reconnaissance conversion of P-38L

F-5G: similar to F-5F but with revised camera installation

XFO-1: four F-5Bs temporarily transferred to US Navy

Markings

Early aircraft were delivered in olive drab and grey, but from February 1944 the 20th received natural metal aircraft. These wore different symbols on the tail to denote the squadron. The 55th had this triangle while the 77th FS had a circle and the 79th FS a square. RAF-style letter codes were also worn, again identifying squadrons. Thus the 55th was KI-x, the 77th was LC-x and the 79th MC-x.

Tailboom

The tailbooms were used to house components of the powerplant system. Level with the wing trailing edge was the supercharger in a semi-exposed installation. The distinctive intake running forward from this area was for the cabin heater. Further aft on the boom were the engine cooling radiators with characteristic bulges each side.

328430

The final photographic variant of the Lightning was designated *F-5G-6-LO* and was a conversion of the *P-38L-5-LO*, modification work being completed at Dallas. Clearly shown here are the so-called 'compressibility' flaps under the wing to improve diving control.

Responding to a March 1939 USAAC request for a new interceptor, Lockheed offered a P-38 derivative, featuring a pressure cabin and more powerful engines. A single prototype was built, as the XP-49, but after protracted development its performance was found inferior to the P-38J.

removed). Following the success of these so-called 'droop-snoot' P-38s, the next expedient was to replace the visual bomb-aiming position by 'Mickey' or BTO (bombing-through-overcast) radar; use of these P-38 Pathfinders enabled targets to be attacked despite being obscured by cloud. Neither of these P-38 versions was much used outside Europe.

On the other hand, the **P-38M**, which was produced too late for the war in Europe, saw limited service during the final weeks of the war in the Pacific. This was a two-seat night-fighter in which a radar operator was squeezed into a raised rear cockpit and a radar pod was mounted beneath the nose. About 80 such aircraft were prepared as conversions of P-38Ls, and served with V Fighter Command's 421st and 457th Night-Fighter Squadrons on Luzon, XIII Fighter Command's 419th and 550th Night-Fighter Squadrons at Mindanao and Leyte respectively, and with the 10th Bomb Wing's 418th Night-Fighter Squadron at Okinawa from July 1945. Another two-seat conversion of the P-38L was the **TP-38L-LO** trainer, of which a few were produced in 1945.

Adaptability of the P-38 was allowed full rein during the last year of the war. Cargo and personnel pods were developed which could be mounted on the underwing store pylons, enabling P-38 units to remain self-supporting by moving ground personnel and spares forward to new bases with the pilots and aircraft. Casualty evacuation was

performed in the same manner, using modified drop tanks with transparent nose sections, each of which could carry two stretcher cases. Another P-38J was flown with a retractable ski landing gear to prepare for possible use in the Aleutians, while others were tested as glider tugs, the P-38 proving capable of towing three fully-laden light assault gliders into the air.

Although the P-38 largely disappeared from front-line squadron use in 1946, and was officially declared surplus to military requirements in 1949, mention should be made of two P-38 developments.

The **XP-49** flew in November 1942 with 1,350-hp (1007-kW) Continental XIV-1430-13/15 engines, a pressurised cabin and an armament of two 20-mm and four 0.5-in (12.7-mm) guns; it was employed in high-altitude research. The **XP-58** (dubbed the 'Chain Lightning') was in effect an enlarged P-38 with an all-up weight of 43,000 lb (19505 kg), and featured 3,000-hp (2240-kW) Allison V-3420-11 engines, a four-gun turret plus an interchangeable nose armament of a 75-mm or two 20-mm and four 0.5-in (12.7-mm) guns, and had a top speed of 702 km/h (436 mph) at 7620 m (25,000 ft). It was flown in June 1944 but, with the P-38 then assuming the role of ground-attack fighter, no requirement was seen for this very large fighter.

Total production of all variants derived from the Model 22 was 10,037.

Lockheed P-80 Shooting Star

The P-80 was the first genuinely successful American jet fighter and could, in fact, have been available earlier. Clarence L. ('Kelly') Johnson's design team at Burbank, California, had proposed a jet fighter in 1939, only to have its L-133 design quashed by lack of an engine and official indifference. Pressured by wartime exigencies, the USAAF

Product of a rapid development programme in 1944, the XP-80 prototype was one of the first products of what was to become famous as Lockheed's 'Skunk Works'.

in 1943 asked Johnson to produce the **XP-80**, a low-wing, tricycle-gear, conventional single-seat jet fighter, in just 180 days! Put together in a scant 143 days, the prototype XP-80 (44-83020), nicknamed 'Lulu Belle', was powered by a 3,000-lb (13.34-kN) thrust de Havilland-built Goblin centrifugal-flow turbojet engine.

The spinach-green XP-80 made its first flight on 8 January 1944 with Milo Burcham at its controls. Urgent testing was undertaken at Muroc Dry Lake,

California. By VE-Day, two **P-80**s were in Italy readying for combat, two had reached England, and in all no fewer than 16 examples were flying. Early P-80 accidents claimed the lives of Burcham on 20 October 1944 and of America's top ace, Major Richard I. Bong, on 6 August 1945, but the overall programme was exceedingly successful and an improved engine was to make it more so. Developed from British technology by General Electric but manufactured by Allison, the 4,000-lb (17.79-kN) thrust J33-A-11, 5,200-lb (23.07-kN) thrust J33-A-19 and

The second of the 13 service-test YP-80As shows the revised tail geometry adopted for production Shooting Stars. With cameras in the nose, this became the XFP-80 (later XF-14) recce version.

5,400-lb (24.02-kN) thrust J33-A-25 centrifugal-flow turbojet powered the similar **P-80A**, **P-80B** and **P-80C** variants of the Lockheed Shooting Star.

The designation **F-14A** was assigned to the photo-reconnaissance version of the Lockheed fighter which developed into the **RF-80A** and **RF-80C**, and served as an intelligence-gathering platform during the 1950-53

Korean War. The designation **P-80R** was used for an ultra-streamlined, one-off racing aircraft which set a speed record in the late 1940s but was otherwise not a success.

Specification
Type: single-seat fighter
Powerplant: one 5,400-lb (24.02-kN) thrust Allison J33-A-35 axial-flow turbojet engine
Performance: maximum speed 594 mph (955.9 km/h) at sea level; service ceiling 46,800 ft (14265 m); range 825 miles (1328 km)
Weights: empty 8,420 lb (3819.3 kg); maximum take-off 16,856 lb (7645.9 kg)

Shooting Star variants included the F-14A photo reconnaissance version, which had three cameras in the nose in place of six 0.5-in (12.7-mm) machine-guns. F-14As became FP-80As in 1945 and then RF-80As, seeing service in Korea.

Dimensions: span 38 ft 9 in (11.81 m); length 34 ft 5 in (10.49 m); height 11 ft 3 in (3.43 m); wing area 237.6 sq ft (22.07 m²)
Armament: six 0.5-in (12.7-mm) fixed forward-firing nose machine-guns, plus provision for two 1,000-lb (454-kg) bombs and eight underwing rockets

Martin A-30 Baltimore

Developed from the Model 167 Maryland, the **Martin Model 187 Baltimore** was produced to British specifications, and featured a deeper fuselage for better crew communications and more powerful engines. Direct orders from Britain resulted in 50 **Baltimore Mk I**s, 100 **Mk II**s and 250 **Mk III**s. The passing of the Lend-Lease Act allowed the USAAF to procure the type on behalf of the RAF, resulting in 281 **Mk IIIA**s with an electrically-actuated dorsal turret, 294 **Mk IV**s with minor detail changes and 600 **Mk V**s which introduced slightly uprated engines.

The Baltimore was purchased by the RAF, but also supplied to other nations, notably Free France, South Africa and Australia. Only a few remained on USAAC charge, designated A-30. This is one of those aircraft, displaying 'Army' titles under the wing.

The Lend-Lease aircraft received the designations **A-30** (Mk IIIA) and **A-30A** (Mks IV and V) in USAAF nomenclature. A small number were retained in the United States for trials and training purposes.

Specification
Martin A-30A Baltimore
Type: four-seat light bomber
Powerplant: two Wright R-2600-19

Cyclone 14-cylinder radial piston engines, each rated at 1,660 hp (1238 kW)
Performance: maximum speed 305 mph (490 km/h); service ceiling 23,300 ft (7100 m); range 1,082 miles (1741 km) with 1,000-lb (454-kg) bombload
Dimensions: wing span 61 ft 4 in (18.69 m); length 48 ft 5½ in (14.77

m); height 17 ft 9 in (5,41 m); wing area 538.5 sq ft (50 m²)
Armament: four 0.303-in machine-guns in wings and either two or four in dorsal turret; two 0.3-in machine-guns in ventral position and provision for four similar guns in fixed rearward-firing position; bombload of up to 4,000 lb (1814 kg)

Martin B-10/B-12

After being unsuccessful in several design competitions, in 1930 the Glenn L. Martin Company decided to build an advanced bomber as a private venture. The US Army contracted for 48 production aircraft on 17 January 1933. The **B-10** was a mid-wing monoplane of all-metal construction, except for fabric-covered control surfaces. The tailwheel-type landing gear was manually retractable, and the standard powerplant was two Wright Cyclones. The crew of four or five was accommodated in three separate cockpits with the bomb aimer/gunner in the nose, pilot and radio operator just forward of the wing leading edge, and gunners or a gunner and navigator in the aft cockpit. The nose position was covered by a cupola to permit deployment of the gun, and the other two cockpits each had a transparent canopy.

The first 14 production aircraft, with 675-hp (503-kW) R-

1820-25 engines, were designated **YB-10**; the seven **YB-12**s which followed had 775-hp (578-kW) Pratt & Whitney R-1690-11 Hornets. The next 25 production **B-12A**s also had the Hornet engines, and provision was made for an extra fuel tank to be carried in the bomb bay. Late procurement, in 1934 and 1935, resulted in 88 and 15 **B-10B**s respectively. These Martin bombers remained in service with the USAAC until replaced

by Boeing B-17s and Douglas B-18s in the late 1930s, although a handful were still in service in 1941 in the Philippines.

Specification
Type: four/five-seat twin-engined light bomber
Powerplant (B-10B): two 775-hp (578-kW) Wright R-1820-33 Cyclone 9 radial piston engines
Performance: maximum speed 213 mph (343 km/h) at 6,000 ft (1830 m); cruising speed 193 mph (311 km/h); service ceiling 24,200 ft (7375 m); range 1,240 miles (1996 km)
Weights: empty 9,681 lb (4391 kg);

Martin B-10Bs had seen USAAC service since 1934. A few lingered in the Philippines, where this example was flying in November 1939 with the 28th BS.

maximum take-off 16,400 lb (7439 kg)
Dimensions: span 70 ft 6 in (21.49 m); length 44 ft 9 in (13.64 m); height 15 ft 5 in (4.70 m); wing area 678 sq ft (62.99 m²)
Armament: three 0.30-in (7.62-mm) machine-guns (one each in nose and rear turrets and one in ventral position), plus up to 2,260 lb (1025 kg) of bombs carried internally

Martin B-26 Marauder

uring the last years of the 1930s the US Army Air Corps was singularly poorly equipped with medium bombers, dependence being laid almost exclusively upon the aged Douglas B-18 and Martin B-10, neither of which possessed the performance, bombload or defensive armament comparable with modern aircraft in service in Europe. When in January 1939 the AAC circulated among American manufacturers outline proposals for a new medium bomber, emphasis was given to high speed, long range and a bombload of 2,000 lb (907 kg), it being tacitly accepted that achievement of these characteristics would likely result in high wing-loading and therefore high landing speed and lengthy take-off run.

Prepared by Peyton M. Magruder and submitted to the Air Board by the Glenn L. Martin Company on 5 July 1939, the **Martin 179** design was adjudged the best of all competing tenders and, despite the highest-ever wing-loading of an aircraft intended for the AAC, was ordered into production immediately after the design had been accepted, an expedient prompted by the worsening international situation. With a five-man crew, the Martin 179 was to be powered by two 1,850-hp (1380-kW) Pratt & Whitney R-2800 Double Wasp radials in nacelles underslung from a shoulder-mounted wing of only moderate area. Two 0.3-in (7.62-mm) and two 0.5-in (12.7-mm) machine-guns constituted the defensive armament, and the centre portion of the beautifully streamlined, circular-section fuselage featured an unrestricted bay to accommodate the bombload.

Hazardous training

Designated **B-26**, 1,100 aircraft were ordered in September 1939 and the first aircraft (40-1361) was flown by William K. Ebel on 25 November 1940. There were no prototypes as such. The first 201 examples were powered by R-2800-5 engines and most were retained for experimental and training purposes, the latter proving to be a lengthy and somewhat hazardous procedure as a result of pilot unfamiliarity with the nosewheel type of landing gear and the high landing speed; at a gross weight of 32,000 lb (14515 kg) and wing area of 602.0 sq ft (55.93 m²), the wing loading was 53.2 lb/sq ft (260 kg/m²) and at a normal landing weight the touchdown speed was around 96 mph (154 km/h). The maximum bombload of 5,800 lb (2631 kg) far exceeded the original requirement, and the top speed of 315 mph (507 km/h) was the highest of all B-26 variants.

Photographed soon after making its maiden flight on 25 November 1940, the first Marauder was built on a production contract but served as a prototype. The circular fuselage cross-section was a prominent feature of the design, which was also notable for its high wing loading.

First deliveries to the AAF started in 1941, and during the second half of that year production switched to the **B-26A** which, introducing provision for optional bomb-bay fuel tanks, shackles for a 22-in (5.88-cm) torpedo under the fuselage and 0.5-in (12.7-mm) guns in place of the 0.3-in (7.62-mm) guns in nose and tail, had a maximum all-up weight of 32,200 lb (14606 kg). At the same time the electrical system was changed from 12 volt to 24 volt.

A total of 139 B-26As was built, and it was with this version that the 22nd Bomb Group (Medium) moved to Australia immediately after Pearl Harbor in December 1941; with extra fuel replacing part of the bombload these aircraft flew attacks against targets in New Guinea the following April. In June that year torpedo-carrying B-26As went into action during the great Battle of Midway, as others of the 73rd and 77th Bomb Squadron attacked shipping in the Aleutians.

Production of the B-26A continued at the Baltimore, Maryland, factory until May 1942 when the first **B-26B**s appeared. With a total of 1,883 built, the B-26B was the most-produced version. The B-

'DeeFeater' was a Martin B-26B-55-MA operating in 1944 with the 598th Bomb Squadron, 397th BG, as part of the 9th Air Force based at Dreux in France. Black and white invasion markings have been partly obliterated to render the aircraft less conspicuous from above.

26B-1 introduced increased armour protection, improved engine cowling shape (without propeller spinners), a ventral gun position and a twin 0.5-in (12.7-mm) tail gun position. These alterations increased the gross weight to 36,500 lb (16556 kg) without any change in powerplant, but in the B-2, -3 and -4 production blocks the engines were the uprated 1,920-hp (1432-kW) R-2800-41 or -43 version.

The B-26B-4 sub-variant introduced a lengthened nosewheel leg as an attempt to provide increased wing incidence on take-off, and single 0.5-in (12.7-mm) beam guns replaced the ventral gun. The B-5 featured slotted flaps to improve landing approach handling. A total of 641 B-1s, -2s, -3s, -4s and -5s was produced.

Still the B-26 attracted harsh comment from the service, and the B-10 (and subsequent versions) featured a wing span increased to 71 ft 0 in (21.64 m) to reduce the wing loading, but this was accompanied by yet further weight increases (to a gross weight of 38,200 lb/17328 kg) by the addition of four 0.5-in (12.7-mm) 'package' machine-guns on the sides of the nose, and a Martin-Bell power-operated tail turret. Far from being significantly reduced, the wing loading at all-up weight had advanced to 58.05 lb/sq ft (283.4 kg/m³) and the normal touchdown speed to 103 mph (166 km/h). As a means of limiting the critical speed and of improving lateral stability, the vertical tail was also increased in height and area.

The Baltimore plant produced 1,242 B-10s and their derivatives, and Martin went on to open a new facility at Omaha, Nebraska, late in 1942, where 1,235 **B-26C**s (equivalent to the B-10 and subsequent blocks) were produced.

Wartime service

War operations by the B-26 during the USA's first 11 months of war were confined to the Pacific theatre but, in support of the campaign following the 'Torch' landings, the 17th, 319th and 320th Bomb Groups (Medium), comprising the 34th, 37th, 95th, 432nd, 437th, 438th, 439th, 440th, 441st, 442nd, 443rd and 444th Squadrons operated with the 12th Air Force in North Africa with B-26Bs and B-26Cs from December 1942, thereafter accompanying and supporting the Allied armies in Sicily, Italy, Sardinia, Corsica and southern France.

In northern Europe the B-26's early operations were disappointing. Following a partly successful baptism by the 8th Air Force's first B-26 group, the 322nd, in an attack on the Velsen generating station at Ijmuiden on 14 May 1943, a second attack by 10 aircraft led by Colonel Robert M. Stillman on the same target three days later resulted in the loss of the entire formation to flak, German fighters and collision. In recognition of the B-26's apparent vulnerability to ground fire, operations moved to medium and high altitudes. The Marauder's full potential was not realised, however, until it was assigned to the newly formed 9th Air Force at the end of 1943, when the aircraft

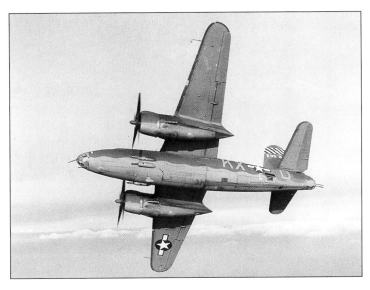

Above: This B-26B-50-MA served with the 558th Bomb Squadron, 387th BG, in the UK. This Group flew only 29 missions as part of the 8th Air Force, between August and October 1943. It was then transferred to the 9th Air Force, and eventually moved to France in August 1944.

Above: The original olive drab finish, with neutral grey undersides, gave way to natural metal in early 1944. Both finishes can be seen on these B-26C-MOs of the 454th Bomb Squadron, 323rd BG, 9th Air Force, over France in late 1944.

Left: Final production variant of the Marauder was the B-26G, which introduced numerous but quite minor changes in the name of standardisation. The heavily-armed Marauder packed 11 (sometimes 12) 0.5-in (12.7-mm) Colt Brownings and carried up to 5,200 lb (2359 kg) of bombs internally.

Martin B-26 Marauder

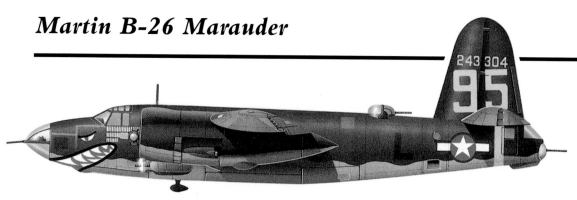

Left: During the final months of the war, all the B-26Bs of the 444th Bomb Squadron, 320th BG, based at Decimomannu, Sardinia, acquired 'shark mouth' markings. The large numeral on the tail was the 'battle number' that was widely used on aircraft in the Mediterranean theatre.

assumed the role of medium-altitude strategic attack (albeit under fighter escort) against targets in preparation for the forthcoming invasion of Europe. By May 1944 the 9th Air Force operated eight B-26 groups, the 322nd, 323rd, 344th, 386th, 387th, 391st, 394th and 397th, comprising 28 squadrons.

Meanwhile the B-26 had entered service with the Royal Air Force. In July 1942 the first **Marauder Mk I**s (equivalent to the 65-ft/19.81-m span B-26A) had reached Egypt, and the following month No. 14 Squadron started disposing of its Bristol Blenheims in favour of the American aircraft. However, the RAF repeated the criticisms voiced elsewhere, and these were confirmed by trials with an aircraft in the United Kingdom, with the result that deliveries to the Middle East were stockpiled at Maintenance Units. No. 14 Squadron for many months remained the only RAF Marauder-equipped squadron, persevering with their aircraft until September 1944.

South African Mk II

The rapid expansion and deployment of the South African Air Force in North Africa resulted in the long-span **Marauder Mk II** (equivalent to the B-26C-30-MO) being issued to Nos 12, 21, 24, 25 and 30 Squadrons SAAF. Nineteen short-span B-26Bs remained on RAF charge. In 1944, **Marauder Mk III**s (equivalent to the B-26F and B-26G) arrived in the Mediterranean theatre and joined the SAAF as well as six squadrons of the newly reconstituted French air force. In all, a total of 525 Marauders was acquired by the UK on Lend-Lease.

Production of the B-26B ended at Baltimore in February 1944 with delivery of the last B-26B-55-MA. In addition, Martin produced 208 **AT-23A**s for the USAAF, these being a target tug/trainer version of the B-26B without armour, guns or turret, but with a C-5 target winch. Omaha production ended in April 1944 with the B-26C-45-MO and 350 **AT-23B** target tug/trainers; 225 of the target tugs were delivered to the US Navy and US Marine Corps under the designation **JM-1**. The USAAF aircraft were redesignated **TB-26**s in 1944.

A single **XB-26D** was produced after modification of an early aircraft to test anti-icing systems, but the planned **B-26E**, with reduced weight and the dorsal turret moved forward to the navigator's compartment, was not built.

Two other production versions were produced. Both featured the long-span wings, and the wing incidence was increased by 3.5°; this was considered by most pilots to improve take-off and landing characteristics and certainly resulted in better approach handling, but sharply reduced the maximum speed to 277 mph (446 km/h). Production of the **B-26F** started late in 1943, with the first deliveries to the USAAF being made the following February. Some 300 B-26Fs were complet-

ed, of which 200 were delivered to the Middle East under Lend-Lease as Marauder Mk IIIs (equivalent to the B-26F-2 and B-26F-6).

Numerous minor changes in equipment and fittings identified the **B-26G**, of which Martin produced 893, with 150 purchased by the UK also as Marauder Mk IIIs. Some 57 **TB-26G**s were also produced in 1944, of which the last 15 went to the US Navy and US Marine Corps as the **JM-2**.

With the take-off and landing problems largely sorted out, a second RAF squadron, No. 39, started to receive Marauder Mk IIIs at Alghero, Italy, in February 1945, retaining them in the Middle East

In the basic olive drab and neutral grey finish of the USAAF in 1942, this is an early B-26, as indicated by the short wing span, short fin and small engine intakes. Operational use of the Marauder in its early B-26A version began in the spring of 1942.

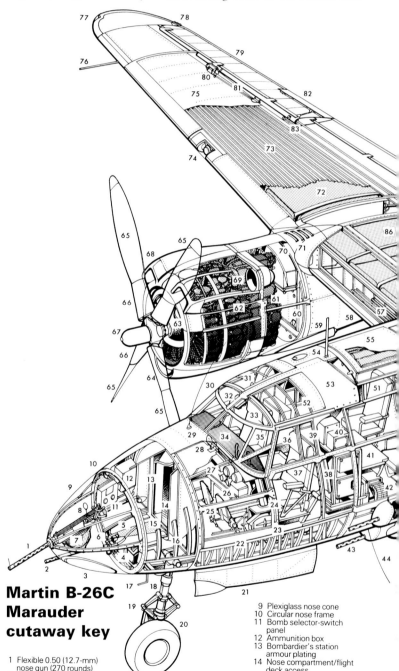

Martin B-26C Marauder cutaway key

1 Flexible 0.50 (12.7-mm) nose gun (270 rounds)
2 Fixed 0.50 (12.7-mm) nose gun (200 rounds)
3 Optically flat bomb-sight window
4 Bomb door control quadrant
5 Nose cone warm-air/demist
6 Bomb sights
7 Cartridge collector bag
8 Ring sight
9 Plexiglass nose cone
10 Circular nose frame
11 Bomb selector-switch panel
12 Ammunition box
13 Bombardier's station armour plating
14 Nose compartment/flight deck access
15 Bombardier's station
16 Nose wheel pivot
17 Pitot head
18 Nosewheel oleo
19 Channel-section torque scissors

Martin B-26 Marauder

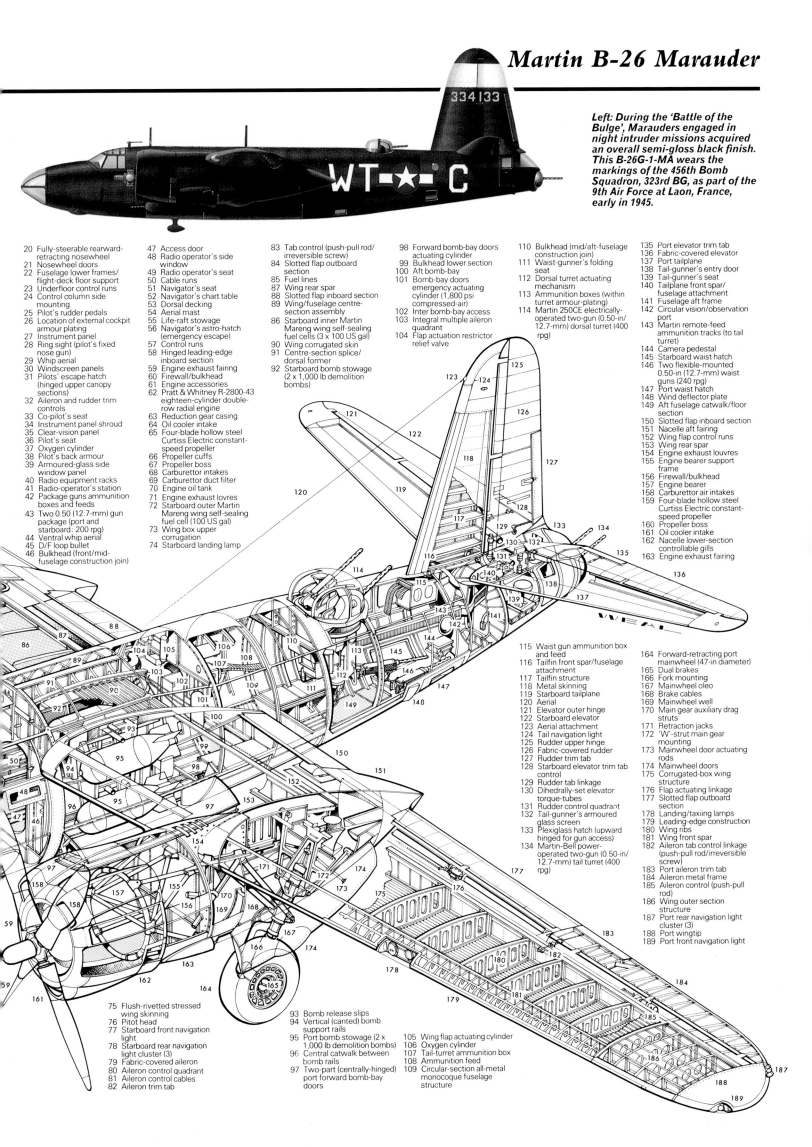

Left: During the 'Battle of the Bulge', Marauders engaged in night intruder missions acquired an overall semi-gloss black finish. This B-26G-1-MA wears the markings of the 456th Bomb Squadron, 323rd BG, as part of the 9th Air Force at Laon, France, early in 1945.

20 Fully-steerable rearward-retracting nosewheel
21 Nosewheel doors
22 Fuselage lower frames/flight-deck floor support
23 Underfloor control runs
24 Control column side mounting
25 Pilot's rudder pedals
26 Location of external cockpit armour plating
27 Instrument panel
28 Ring sight (pilot's fixed nose gun)
29 Whip aerial
30 Windscreen panels
31 Pilots' escape hatch (hinged upper canopy sections)
32 Aileron and rudder trim controls
33 Co-pilot's seat
34 Instrument panel shroud
35 Clear-vision panel
36 Pilot's seat
37 Oxygen cylinder
38 Pilot's back armour
39 Armoured-glass side window panel
40 Radio equipment racks
41 Radio-operator's station
42 Package guns ammunition boxes and feeds
43 Two 0.50 (12.7-mm) gun package (port and starboard: 200 rpg)
44 Ventral whip aerial
45 D/F loop bullet
46 Bulkhead (front/mid-fuselage construction join)

47 Access door
48 Radio operator's side window
49 Radio operator's seat
50 Cable runs
51 Navigator's seat
52 Navigator's chart table
53 Dorsal decking
54 Aerial mast
55 Life-raft stowage
56 Navigator's astro-hatch (emergency escape)
57 Control runs
58 Hinged leading-edge inboard section
59 Engine exhaust fairing
60 Firewall/bulkhead
61 Engine accessories
62 Pratt & Whitney R-2800-43 eighteen-cylinder double-row radial engine
63 Reduction gear casing
64 Oil cooler intake
65 Four-blade hollow steel Curtiss Electric constant-speed propeller
66 Propeller cuffs
67 Propeller boss
68 Carburettor intakes
69 Carburettor duct filter
70 Engine oil tank
71 Engine exhaust lovres
72 Starboard outer Martin Mareng wing self-sealing fuel cell (100 US gal)
73 Wing box upper corrugation
74 Starboard landing lamp

83 Tab control (push-pull rod/irreversible screw)
84 Slotted flap outboard section
85 Fuel lines
87 Wing rear spar
88 Slotted flap inboard section
89 Wing/fuselage centre-section assembly
86 Starboard inner Martin Mareng wing self-sealing fuel cells (3 x 100 US gal)
90 Wing corrugated skin
91 Centre-section splice/dorsal former
92 Starboard bomb stowage (2 x 1,000 lb demolition bombs)

98 Forward bomb-bay doors actuating cylinder
99 Bulkhead lower section
100 Aft bomb-bay
101 Bomb-bay doors emergency actuating cylinder (1,800 psi compressed-air)
102 Inter bomb-bay access
103 Integral multiple aileron quadrant
104 Flap actuation restrictor relief valve

110 Bulkhead (mid/aft-fuselage construction join)
111 Waist-gunner's folding seat
112 Dorsal turret actuating mechanism
113 Ammunition boxes (within turret armour-plating)
114 Martin 250CE electrically-operated two-gun (0.50-in/12.7-mm) dorsal turret (400 rpg)

135 Port elevator trim tab
136 Fabric-covered elevator
137 Port tailplane
138 Tail-gunner's entry door
139 Tail-gunner's seat
140 Tailplane front spar/fuselage attachment
141 Fuselage aft frame
142 Circular vision/observation port
143 Martin remote-feed ammunition tracks (to tail turret)
144 Camera pedestal
145 Starboard waist hatch
146 Two flexible-mounted 0.50-in (12.7-mm) waist guns (240 rpg)
147 Port waist hatch
148 Wind deflector plate
149 Aft fuselage catwalk/floor section
150 Slotted flap inboard section
151 Nacelle aft fairing
152 Wing flap control runs
153 Wing rear spar
154 Engine exhaust louvres
155 Engine bearer support frame
156 Firewall/bulkhead
157 Engine bearer
158 Carburettor air intakes
159 Four-blade hollow steel Curtiss Electric constant-speed propeller
160 Propeller boss
161 Oil cooler intake
162 Nacelle lower-section controllable gills
163 Engine exhaust fairing

115 Waist gun ammunition box and feed
116 Tailfin front spar/fuselage attachment
117 Tailfin structure
118 Metal skinning
119 Starboard tailplane
120 Aerial
121 Elevator outer hinge
122 Starboard elevator
123 Aerial attachment
124 Tail navigation light
125 Rudder upper hinge
126 Fabric-covered rudder
127 Rudder trim tab
128 Starboard elevator trim tab control
129 Rudder tab linkage
130 Dihedrally-set elevator torque-tubes
131 Rudder control quadrant
132 Tail-gunner's armoured glass screen
133 Plexiglass hatch (upward hinged for gun access)
134 Martin-Bell power-operated two-gun (0.50-in/12.7-mm) tail turret (400 rpg)

164 Forward-retracting port mainwheel (47-in diameter)
165 Dual brakes
166 Fork mounting
167 Mainwheel oleo
168 Brake cables
169 Mainwheel well
170 Main gear auxiliary drag struts
171 Retraction jacks
172 'W'-strut main gear mounting
173 Mainwheel door actuating rods
174 Mainwheel doors
175 Corrugated-box wing structure
176 Flap actuating linkage
177 Slotted flap outboard section
178 Landing/taxiing lamps
179 Leading-edge construction
180 Wing ribs
181 Wing front spar
182 Aileron tab control linkage (push-pull rod/irreversible screw)
183 Port aileron trim tab
184 Aileron metal frame
185 Aileron control (push-pull rod)
186 Wing outer section structure
187 Port rear navigation light cluster (3)
188 Port wingtip
189 Port front navigation light

75 Flush-rivetted stressed wing skinning
76 Pitot head
77 Starboard front navigation light
78 Starboard rear navigation light cluster (3)
79 Fabric-covered aileron
80 Aileron control quadrant
81 Aileron control cables
82 Aileron trim tab

93 Bomb release slips
94 Vertical (canted) bomb support rails
95 Port bomb stowage (2 x 1,000 lb demolition bombs)
96 Central catwalk between bomb rails
97 Two-part (centrally-hinged) port forward bomb-bay doors

105 Wing flap actuating cylinder
106 Oxygen cylinder
107 Tail-turret ammunition box
108 Ammunition feed
109 Circular-section all-metal monocoque fuselage structure

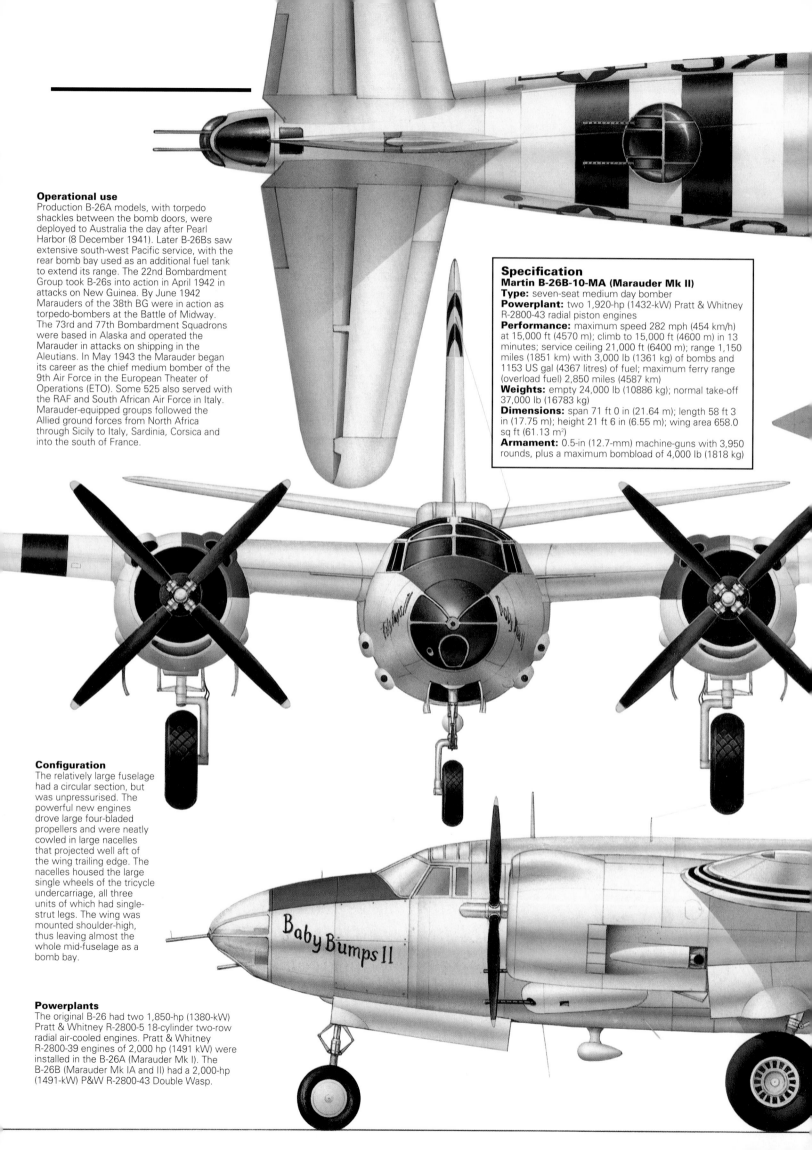

Operational use

Production B-26A models, with torpedo shackles between the bomb doors, were deployed to Australia the day after Pearl Harbor (8 December 1941). Later B-26Bs saw extensive south-west Pacific service, with the rear bomb bay used as an additional fuel tank to extend its range. The 22nd Bombardment Group took B-26s into action in April 1942 in attacks on New Guinea. By June 1942 Marauders of the 38th BG were in action as torpedo-bombers at the Battle of Midway. The 73rd and 77th Bombardment Squadrons were based in Alaska and operated the Marauder in attacks on shipping in the Aleutians. In May 1943 the Marauder began its career as the chief medium bomber of the 9th Air Force in the European Theater of Operations (ETO). Some 525 also served with the RAF and South African Air Force in Italy. Marauder-equipped groups followed the Allied ground forces from North Africa through Sicily to Italy, Sardinia, Corsica and into the south of France.

Specification
Martin B-26B-10-MA (Marauder Mk II)
Type: seven-seat medium day bomber
Powerplant: two 1,920-hp (1432-kW) Pratt & Whitney R-2800-43 radial piston engines
Performance: maximum speed 282 mph (454 km/h) at 15,000 ft (4570 m); climb to 15,000 ft (4600 m) in 13 minutes; service ceiling 21,000 ft (6400 m); range 1,150 miles (1851 km) with 3,000 lb (1361 kg) of bombs and 1153 US gal (4367 litres) of fuel; maximum ferry range (overload fuel) 2,850 miles (4587 km)
Weights: empty 24,000 lb (10886 kg); normal take-off 37,000 lb (16783 kg)
Dimensions: span 71 ft 0 in (21.64 m); length 58 ft 3 in (17.75 m); height 21 ft 6 in (6.55 m); wing area 658.0 sq ft (61.13 m²)
Armament: 0.5-in (12.7-mm) machine-guns with 3,950 rounds, plus a maximum bombload of 4,000 lb (1818 kg)

Configuration

The relatively large fuselage had a circular section, but was unpressurised. The powerful new engines drove large four-bladed propellers and were neatly cowled in large nacelles that projected well aft of the wing trailing edge. The nacelles housed the large single wheels of the tricycle undercarriage, all three units of which had single-strut legs. The wing was mounted shoulder-high, thus leaving almost the whole mid-fuselage as a bomb bay.

Powerplants

The original B-26 had two 1,850-hp (1380-kW) Pratt & Whitney R-2800-5 18-cylinder two-row radial air-cooled engines. Pratt & Whitney R-2800-39 engines of 2,000 hp (1491 kW) were installed in the B-26A (Marauder Mk I). The B-26B (Marauder Mk IA and II) had a 2,000-hp (1491-kW) P&W R-2800-43 Double Wasp.

Martin B-26C
557th BS, 387th BG
Chipping Ongar
Essex 1944

In the 1930s Glenn L. Martin Co. pulled out all the stops to win the 1939 Medium Bomber competition for the US Army. It boldly chose a wing optimised for high-speed cruise efficiency, rather than for take-off and landing. With the unprecedented high wing loading it proved difficult for inexperienced pilots to handle, particularly with its high landing speed. Eventually the wing and vertical tail were extended and the B-26 went on to set a record for the lowest loss rate of any US Army bomber in Europe. The last Marauder was delivered in April 1945 after a production of 5,157 aircraft. In 1948 the Marauder was withdrawn from service and the B-26 designation passed to the Douglas Invader.

Crew
As a medium bomber the Marauder crew varied from five to seven. One gunner manually operated a 0.5-in machine-gun in the nose (later increased to two), another operated a Martin 250CE electrically-operated dorsal turret equipped with two 0.50-in machine-guns, another operated a Martin-Bell power-operated tail turret with two 0.50-in guns and there were two manually-aimed 0.50-in waist guns.

Wing
On its entry into service the Marauder had the highest wing loading of any aircraft then designed for the USAAF. Because of its high landing speed (inevitable with the chosen wing loading) conversion training was lengthy. The nosewheel strut was lengthened to improve the take-off performance by increasing the wing incidence.

Camouflage/markings
The standard USAAF colours were olive drab on top and neutral grey underneath for land-based aircraft. Because of the urgency in camouflaging a large number of aircraft much unsatisfactory paint was used pending the formulation of dark olive drab with better weathering characteristics. Aircraft painted in the early part of World War II eventually weathered considerably to a variety of colours depending on local conditions: when freshly applied olive drab was darker than the greens, but the OD faded noticeably faster.

Martin B-26 Marauder

This JM-1 is one of 225 ex-USAAF AT-23Bs that went to the US Navy and Marines to serve as target tugs. The aircraft wears an overall yellow finish for that role.

The 'Middle River Stump Jumper', a TB-26G converted to XB-26H, had tandem mainwheels and outriggers to test bicycle undercarriages for jet bombers.

This is one of 208 AT-23As completed on the Baltimore production line. They were used as target tugs by the USAAF, trailing sleeve or drogue targets.

until September 1946.

The final B-26 was delivered on 30 March 1945 for a total of 5,157 Marauders completed. (One other aircraft, the **XB-26H**, 44-28221, was produced to test the four-wheel bicycle landing gear planned for the Boeing B-47 and Martin XB-48 bombers.)

Despite the problems stemming from the relatively advanced design philosophy, the B-26 had an impressive war record, including a total of 129,943 operational sorties flown in the European and Mediterranean theatres alone, during which B-26s dropped 169,382 tons of bombs; their crews claimed the destruction of 402 enemy aircraft, while the loss of 911 aircraft in combat represented an overall loss rate of less than one per cent. The USAAF's B-26 inventory peaked in March 1944 when 11 groups were operational (comprising 43 squadrons), and 1,931 B-26s were on charge in the ETO alone.

When first introduced to service the B-26 cost $261,000, and by 1944 this had dropped to $192,000 (compared with $142,000 for a B-25). It was a robust aeroplane whose semi-monocoque fuselage was

constructed in three sections with four main longerons, transverse circular frames and longitudinal stringers; the centre-section with bomb bay was constructed integrally with the wing section. The box-type wing structure, formed by two heavy main spars with heavy-gauge skin, was reinforced by spanwise members to provide torsional stiffness; the entire leading edge was hinged to the front spar to facilitate servicing. Only the rudder was fabric-covered. All units of the hydraulically-operated tricycle landing gear retracted rearwards, the nosewheel pivoting 90° to lie flat in the fuselage nose.

The seven-man crew included two pilots, navigator, radio operator, front gunner/bombardier, turret and tail gunners. The 11 0.5-in (12.7-mm) machine-guns (single nose gun, four in nose packs, two in the turret, two hand-held flexible beam guns and two in the extreme tail) were provided with a total of 3,950 rounds. The maximum bombload of two 1,600-lb (726-kg) bombs and a single 2,000-lb (907-kg) torpedo was seldom carried, most sorties being flown with eight 500-lb (227-kg) or 16 250-lb (113-kg) bombs.

Martin B-26 Marauder variants

B-26: initial production model, of which 201 built (40-1361 to 40-1561); powered by R-2800-5 engines; redesignated **RB-26** to signify obsolescence and mostly used for training or tests
B-26A: 139 aircraft (41-7345 to 41-7483) similar to B-26 but with 0.5-in (12.7-mm) guns in nose and tail and two more in dorsal turret; 24-volt electrical system and provision for extra fuel tanks in bomb bay; provision for one externally carried torpedo; R-2800-9 or -39 engines; 52 to RAF as **Marauder Mk I**; subsequently redesignated **RB-26A**
B-26B: major production model with improved armour protection; first 791 with R-2800-5 engines, remainder with R-2800-41; aircraft up to Block 3 had 0.3-in gun, while Block 4 and subsequent had two 0.5-in beam guns; Block 5 introduced slotted flaps while Block 10 introduced longer

wings, taller fin, additional nose gun and four fuselage-side gun packs; 1,883 built (41-17544 to 18334, 41-31573 to 32072, 42-43260 to 42-43357, 42-43360 to 42-43361, 42-43459, 42-95738 to 96228) of which 123 transferred to RAF as **Marauder Mk IA**; surviving B-26Bs redesignated **ZB-26B** in 1948
CB-26B: a handful of B-26Bs converted to transports
TB-26B: redesignation of AT-23A
B-26C: similar to B-26B but built at Omaha rather than Baltimore; 1,210 aircraft were built (41-34673 to 41-35370, 41-35372, 41-35374 to 41-35515, 41-35517 to 41-35538, 41-35540, 41-35548 to 41-35551, 41-35553 to 41-35560, 42-107497 to 42-107830) of which 123 transferred to RAF as **Marauder Mk II**
TB-26C: redesignation of AT-23B
XB-26D: single B-26 with hot air de-icing equipment

B-26E: single B-26B with dorsal turret moved to the forward fuselage; not proceeded with
B-26F: similar to B-26B but with increased wing incidence and other minor improvements; 300 built (42-96229 to 42-96528) of which 200 supplied to RAF as **Marauder Mk III**
B-26G: similar to B-26F with R-2800-43 engines as standard and detail changes; 893 were built (43-34115 to 43-34614, 44-67805 to 44-67944, 44-67970 to 44-68221, 44-68254)
TB-26G: unarmed target tug/trainers, primarily for US Navy; 57 built (44-67945 to 44-67969, 44-68222 to 44-68253) of which 44-67960 to 44-67969 retained by USAAF
XB-26H: one TB-26G (44-28221) converted with bicycle undercarriage with outriggers under the engine nacelles to test the undercarriage

layout for the B-47 and B-48 jet bombers; redesignated **ZXB-26H** in 1948
AT-23A: gunnery trainer version of B-26B; 208 delivered (42-43358 to 42-43359, 42-43362 to 42-43458, 42-95629 to 42-95737); redesignated TB-26B
AT-23B: trainer version of B-26C; 375 delivered (41-35371, 41-35373, 41-35516, 41-35539, 41-35541 to 41-35547, 41-35552, 41-35561 to 41-35872, 42-107471 to 42-107496, 42-107831 to 42-107855); 225 transferred to US Navy/Marine Corps; redesignated TB-26C
JM-1: 225 AT-23B for USN/USMC utility training target tug duties (BuNo. 66595 to 66794, 75183 to 75207)
JM-1P: a few JM-1s were converted for photo-reconnaissance
JM-2: 47 TB-26Gs transferred to USN/USMC (BuNo 90507 to 90521, 91962 to 91993)

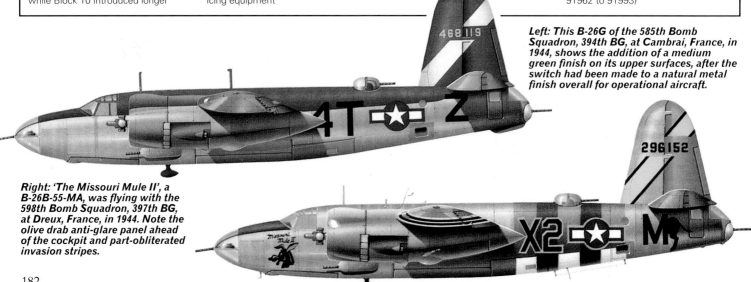

Left: This B-26G of the 585th Bomb Squadron, 394th BG, at Cambrai, France, in 1944, shows the addition of a medium green finish on its upper surfaces, after the switch had been made to a natural metal finish overall for operational aircraft.

Right: 'The Missouri Mule II', a B-26B-55-MA, was flying with the 598th Bomb Squadron, 397th BG, at Dreux, France, in 1944. Note the olive drab anti-glare panel ahead of the cockpit and part-obliterated invasion stripes.

Martin BTM Mauler

As 1943 drew to a close the US Navy began to plan a new breed of attack aircraft, drawing on its experience of two years' active service carrier operations and reflecting the changing demands upon naval air power. The intention was to combine the formerly separate roles of the scout and torpedo bombers, as exemplified by the Curtiss SB2C Helldiver and Grumman TBF Avenger.

The emphasis was to be on load-carrying ability and performance, and the resulting specification was for a single-seater, designed around the most powerful engine then available, which was to carry its offensive load on external hardpoints rather than in an internal bay, saving both in airframe weight and complexity.

Among the designs submitted to the US Navy was Martin's **Model 210**, two prototypes of which were ordered on 31 May 1944. Designated **XBTM-1**, the first aircraft was flown on 26 August 1944, powered by a 3,000-hp (2237-kW) Pratt & Whitney XR-4360-4 engine. Four 20-mm cannon were mounted in the folding outer panels of the wings, which also incorporated 14 hardpoints that, together with one beneath the

fuselage, could carry up to 4,500 lb (2040 kg) of bombs and rockets. A production order for 750 **BTM-1**s was placed on 15 January 1945, but the designation was changed to **AM-1** before the first production aircraft flew on 16 December 1946. Type acceptance trials were flown in 1947, and the first deliveries were made to VA-17A on 1 March 1948.

The end of the war robbed the **Mauler** of its original urgency, and only 149 Cyclone-powered AM-1s were delivered. The aircraft were passed swiftly to Reserve units as sufficient Douglas Skyraiders (designed to

the same specification) became available, and their service careers were short.

Specification
Martin BTM-1 Mauler
Type: single-seat carrier-based attack bomber
Powerplant: one 2,975-hp (2218-kW) Wright R-3350-4 Cyclone 18 radial piston engine
Performance: maximum speed 367 mph (591 km/h); service ceiling 30,500 ft (9295 m); range 1,800 miles (2897 km)
Weights: empty 14,500 lb (6577 kg); maximum take-off 23,386 lb (10608 kg)
Dimensions: wing span 50 ft 0 in (15.24 m); length 41 ft 2 in (12.55 m); height 16 ft 10 in (5.13 m); wing area 496 sq ft (46.08 m²)
Armament: four 20-mm cannon in wings; up to 4,500 lb (2040 kg) of assorted bombs, rocket projectiles or torpedoes

The two XBTM-1 prototypes were powered by 28-cylinder Pratt & Whitney XR-4360-4 Wasp Major engines. This example was the unpainted second aircraft, BuNo 85162. Though an impressive performer, the production aircraft was largely redesigned, among other things switching to the same Wright engine as its Douglas competitor, which was eventually judged superior. Another rival was the Kaiser-Fleetwings XBTK-1.

Martin PBM Mariner

The first production PBM-1s had unpainted Alclad hulls, but the graceful gull wings were painted chrome yellow. This aircraft, with floats retracted, bears the markings of VP-55 patrol squadron.

Developed to replace Martin's earlier open-cockpit P3M flying-boats which had served the US Navy as patrol aircraft since 1931, the **Martin 162** was designed in 1937 and a single-seat quarter-scale model, known as the **162A**, was built to test its flight characteristics. On 30 June 1937 the US Navy ordered a single development prototype which, as the **XPBM-1**, was flown on 18 February 1939, powered by two 1,600-hp (1193-kW) Wright R-2600-6 Cyclone engines. These were mounted in large nacelles which included weapons bays to accommodate a combined total of up to

2,000 lb (907 kg) of bombs or depth charges, and the XPBM-1 had provision for five 0.50-in (12.7-mm) and one 0.30-in (7.62-mm) gun in nose, dorsal and tail turrets and at waist positions. The underwing floats were retractable and the tailplane was originally without dihedral, although this was later modified to follow the angle of the inboard section of the gull wing.

Twenty production **PBM-1**s were ordered on 28 December and these were completed by April 1941, together with a single **XPBM-2** with additional fuel capacity and provision for catapult launching. They were ini-

tially delivered to US Navy Squadron VP-74, formed from the merged VP-55 and VP-56.

The **PBM-3** which followed had 1,700-hp (1268-kW) R-2600-12 engines in elongated nacelles each able to house four 500-lb (227-kg) bombs or depth charges, and larger non-retractable floats were introduced. A total of 379 was ordered on 1 November 1940, but the first 50 aircraft were unarmed **PBM-3R** transports with strengthened cargo floor, cargo loading doors, and able to seat 20 passengers. These were followed by 274 armed **PBM-3C**s and 201 **PBM-3D**s,

the latter with 1,900-hp (1417-kW) R-2600-22 engines driving four-bladed propellers. The -3Ds also had increased armour protection for the crew and additional armament which comprised two 0.50-in (12.7-mm) guns in each of the bow, dorsal and tail turrets and a similar weapon in each of the waist positions. Bombload in the nacelle bays was also increased and could include eight 500-. 1,000- or 1,600-lb (227-, 454- or

Take-off from Martin's Middle River plant of the much later PBM-5A amphibian. This version, the last to be produced in quantity, was too late for the war.

Martin PBM Mariner

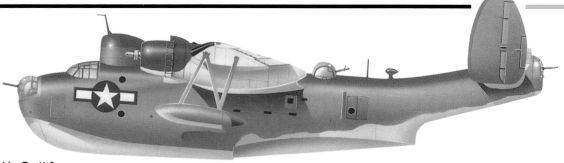

Right: This is a PBM-5, but the radar-equipped PBM-3 versions were almost identical. One way of distinguishing between the two is that on the PBM-3 the Wright R-3350 carburettor inlet extended to the front lip of the cowling.

Below: PBM-5 BuNo. 59228, powered by Pratt & Whitney R-2800 Double Wasp engines, was fitted with the same type of bulky surface search radar in a dorsal 'doghouse' as the PBM-3C and -3D.

Above: A PBM-3C afloat after being launched from NAS Norfolk, Virginia, in late 1942. This 'C' version had powered turrets in the bow and dorsal positions but a single hand-aimed 0.50-in gun in the tail. This example has not yet been fitted with radar.

726-kg) bombs or eight depth bombs. Alternative offensive loads were four mines or two torpedoes, the latter carried beneath the wings. Fuel tanks were self-sealing, with the exception of auxiliary tanks which could be fitted in the nacelle bomb bays.

Examples of both -3C and -3D variants were fitted with search radar, mounted dorsally just behind the cockpit, and a specialised long-range anti-submarine version, the **PBM-3S**, was developed in 1944. Some 156 were built, with R-2600-12 engines and additional fuel capac-

ity to provide increased range. A weight reduction programme resulted in the removal of most of the armour plating and the deletion of the power-operated nose and dorsal turrets, armament being limited to four hand-held 0.50-in (12.7-mm) guns.

The projected **PBM-4**, which was to have been powered by R-3350-8 engines, was not produced, despite the fact that 180 had been ordered in 1941. However, in 1943 the **XPBM-5** was evolved, and this version was ordered instead on 3 January 1944. Powered by 2,100-hp (1566-kW) R-2800-34 engines

and with eight 0.50-in (12.7-mm) guns, **PBM-5**s were delivered from August 1944. Some were fitted with APS-15 radar and redesignated **PBM-5E**, and others specially equipped for anti-submarine warfare were identified as **PBM-5S**s. Production totalled 631.

The last of the Mariner line was the **PBM-5A** amphibian, which was used principally for air-sea rescue duties by the US Navy and US Coast Guard after World War II, 36 being manufactured before production ceased in April 1949.

Twenty-seven **PBM-3B**s, with some British equipment, were supplied to the Royal Air Force as **Mariner GR.Mk I**s, the first aircraft arriving at Beaumaris, Anglesey in August 1943. A special operational experience and training unit, No. 524 Squadron,

was set up on 20 October at Oban, but after only a few weeks it was decided that the Mariner would not be used operationally by the Royal Air Force and the squadron was disbanded on 7 December 1943, its aircraft passing to HQ Transport Command. The remaining Mariners were stored at No. 57 Maintenance Unit, Wig Bay, near Stranraer, awaiting return to the United States. The Royal Australian Air Force received 12 Mariners between 1943 and 1946, for operation by No. 41 Squadron.

Post-war deliveries from US Navy stocks included three PBM-5s for the Uruguayan navy, some similar aircraft for the Argentine navy and 17 for the Netherlands navy.

Taxiing out for a mission over the North Atlantic, this PBM-3S is finished in the all-white scheme used from 1943 by anti-submarine patrol units in that theatre. This version was fitted with radar, sonobuoys and anti-submarine torpedoes and depth charges, but had no gun turrets.

Specification

Type: seven/eight-seat patrol flying-boat
Powerplant: (PBM-3D) two 1,900-hp (1417-kW) Wright R-2600-22 Cyclone radial piston engines
Performance: maximum speed 211 mph (340 km/h) at 1,500 ft (455 m); service ceiling 19,800 ft (6035 m); range 2,240 miles (3605 km)
Weights: empty 33,175 lb (15048 kg); maximum take-off 58,000 lb (26308 kg)
Dimensions: span 118 ft 0 in (35.97 m); length 79 ft 10 in (24.33 m); height 27 ft 6 in (8.38 m); wing area 1,408 sq ft (130.80 m²)
Armament: eight 0.50-in (12.7-mm) machine-guns (in nose and dorsal turrets and at waist and tail positions), plus up to 8,000 lb (3629 kg) of bombs or depth charges

Martin PB2M Mars

Developed to meet a US Navy specification for a long-range patrol bomber, the **Martin Model 170 Mars** was at the time of its construction the world's largest flying-boat. Ordered on 23 August 1938, the prototype **XPB2M-1** made its first flight on 3 July 1943, this having been delayed by an accident during preparatory tests. In its reconnaissance role the Mars had provision for power-operated nose and tail turrets, but these were deleted during 1943 and the positions faired over.

With reinforced floors, enlarged hatches and with loading equipment installed, the machine was redesignated **XPB2M-1R** to denote its transport role. In this form it made its first flight in December 1943, from Patuxent River Naval Air Station to Natal, Brazil, carrying a payload of 13,000 lb (5897 kg) for the 4,375-mile (7041-km) journey. Early in the following year it flew a 4,700-mile (7564-km) mission to Hawaii and

back, in a time of 27 hours 26 minutes and carrying a load of 20,500 lb (9299 kg).

In January 1945, 20 purpose-built cargo aircraft were ordered under the US Navy designation **JRM-1**, although only five were completed. These were redesigned with a single fin in place of the original endplate fins. The first JRM-1, named *Hawaii Mars*, took off on its maiden flight on 21 July 1945 but proved to be short-lived by crashing in Chesapeake Bay on 5 August. The other four were named after Pacific Islands as *Philippine Mars*, *Marianas Mars*, *Marshall Mars* and (again) *Hawaii Mars*.

A sixth production Mars, completed in November 1947, had structural changes to permit operation at a gross weight of 165,000 lb (74843 kg): this was designated **JRM-2** and named *Caroline Mars*. The four surviving JRM-1s were retrospectively converted to JRM-2 standard, becoming redesignated **JRM-3**. *Marshall Mars* was destroyed in a

In a unique combination, the XPB2M-1R prototype is seen here formating on the first production JRM-1, named 'Hawaii Mars', which in turn holds station on the PBM photographic aircraft while an SNJ formates on the far side.

fire at Honolulu on 5 April 1950, but the remaining aircraft were flown by US Navy Squadron VR-2 from Alameda Naval Air Station, California, until withdrawn in November 1956, the largest flying-boats ever to have seen service with the US Navy. In July 1959 they were sold to Canada for use as firefighting water-bombers, fitted with tanks which had a capacity of 7,000 US gal (26497 litres). These could be

filled in 15 seconds, with the aircraft skimming the surface of a suitable lake.

Specification
Type: seven-seat long-range passenger/cargo transport flying boat
Powerplant: (JRM-2) four 2,200-hp (1641-kW) Wright R-3350-18 Duplex Cyclone radial piston engines
Performance: maximum speed 221 mph (356 km/h) at 4,500 ft (1370 m); cruising speed 149 mph (240 km/h); service ceiling 14,600 ft (4450 m); range 4,945 miles (7958 km)
Weights: empty 75,573 lb (34279 kg); maximum take-off 165,000 lb (74843 kg)
Dimensions: span 200 ft 0 in (60.96 m); length 117 ft 3 in (35.74 m); height 38 ft 5 in (11.71 m); wing area 3,683 sq ft (342.15 m²)

McDonnell XP-67

The **XP-67** 'Bomber Destroyer' or 'Moonbat' emanated from a little-known St Louis, Missouri, firm established by James S. McDonnell in 1939. Although there was strong interest in twin-engined fighters in the immediate pre-war period and the McDonnell Aircraft Company would later make an indelible mark on history with just such an aircraft, the XP-67 was hampered by so many delays and tribulations that, when it flew on 6 January 1944, it had been bypassed by history.

The original design for an engine located behind the pilot, driving a pair of pusher propellers through right-angle extension shafts, was rejected by the US Army at the very time in 1940 when it was ordering three not dissimilar and wholly unsuccessful machines (Vultee XP-54, Curtiss XP-55, Northrop XP-56). McDonnell engineers redesigned a more conventional twin-engined fighter powered by twin 1,150-hp (857-kW) Continental XI-1430-17/19 engines with augmentor stacks providing additional thrust beyond that afforded by the four-bladed propeller. The sleek engine nacelles blended smoothly into the wings, as did the fuselage shape at the wing roots, thus

posing minimal drag but not providing additional lift. The company received a go-ahead on 22 May 1941 to build two XP-67s (42-11677/11678).

Rolled out at St Louis 29 November 1943 – more than a year after the builder had originally hoped to fly it – the XP-67 was plagued with engine problems and, once, by a ground fire which nearly destroyed the airframe. In its early 1944 flight tests, the machine handled well but every measure of its performance fell short of expectations. Engines were each to provide 1,400 hp (1044 kW), providing 448 mph (721 km/h) at 20,000 ft (6096 m), but actual top speed was 405 mph (651 km/h).

Ferried to Wright Field, Ohio, the XP-67 was undergoing an official US Army Air Force evaluation on 6 September 1944 when the right engine caught fire. The pilot landed safely but the blaze engulfed the XP-67. A plan to complete the second prototype with an unusual four-engined configuration consisting of two 1,695-hp (1264-kW) Packard V-1650 licence-built Rolls-Royce Merlins and two unspecified 2,300-lb (10.23-kN) thrust jet engines proved too ambitious, and the project had to be shelved. Available earlier, the

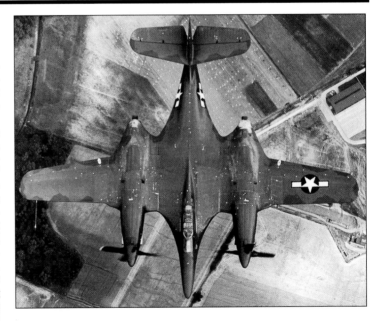

Though McDonnell Aircraft had already mass-produced the Fairchild AT-21 Gunner, the curiously shaped XP-67 was the first aircraft of its own design to be built. It was also one of only two aircraft to be powered by the troubled XI-1430 engine, the other being the Lockheed XP-49.

XP-67 might not have been needed to destroy bombers but could have escorted Fortresses and Liberators to Berlin. It was not the first time that an aircraft type with some promise was denied production status partly because of the loss of the only prototype.

Specification
Type: single-seat fighter
Powerplant: two 1,150-hp (857-kW) Continental XI-1430-17/19 liquid-cooled

12-cylinder inverted-Vee piston engines driving four-bladed propellers
Performance: maximum speed 405 mph (651 km/h) at 20,000 ft (6096 m); initial climb rate 2,100 ft (640 m) per minute; service ceiling 37,000 ft (11278 m); range 2,100 miles (3380 km)
Weights: empty 16,395 lb (7436 kg); maximum take-off 23,115 lb (10,485 kg)
Dimensions: span 55 ft 0 in (16.76 m); length 42 ft 0 in (12.80 m); height 14 ft 9 in (4.50 m); wing area 414 sq ft (38.46 m²)
Armament: six 37-mm fixed forward-firing cannon planned but not installed

Naval Aircraft Factory N3N

The Naval Aircraft Factory (NAF), established in the Philadelphia Navy Yard, Pennsylvania, in 1918, was created to provide the US Navy with its own manufacturing and test facilities. However, in 1918 the most urgent requirement of the US Navy was an adequate supply of aircraft, so the NAF was immediately involved in what, for the size of the facility, was quite large-scale production. This continued until 1922, after which the NAF functioned more or less as had been intended from the beginning, building prototypes only of US Navy-designed aircraft, carrying out modification and overhaul of machines in service, as well as providing testing of anything from components to complete aircraft.

This period was of short duration, however, for in the mid-1930s the NAF began construction of 10 per cent of the aircraft procured by the US Navy, to keep a check on costs and manufacturing techniques,

Navy BuNo. 0056 was one of 180 N3N-1 Canary primary trainers, seen here as a centrefloat seaplane. The derivation of the name is obvious, but they were also commonly dubbed Yellow Perils. All N3N-1s were delivered with cowled engines, but these were removed in 1941 to improve accessibility.

and with American involvement in World War II the NAF again became involved in the design and construction of aircraft on a large scale.

In 1934 the US Navy had designed a new primary trainer which offered superior performance to the Consolidated NY-2s and NY-3s then in service, and construction of a prototype **XN3N-1** resulted in a first flight in August 1935. Following

Also seen in seaplane configuration, the N3N-3 never did have a cowled engine, and the engine itself was the less-obsolescent R-760-96. This example, on its beaching trolley, is BuNo. 4480. Until 1961 midshipmen at Annapolis were taught to handle these piston-engined seaplanes and also sailing ships.

successful tests in both landplane and seaplane configurations, the decision was made to order it into production, and the NAF began immediately the manufacture of the first batch of **N3N-1**s, of which 179 had been ordered. The N3N was a neat single-bay biplane with staggered wings, conventional fuselage, braced tail unit and fixed tailwheel type landing gear as standard, and 158 aircraft of this initial order were to be powered by a 220-hp (164-kW) Wright J-5 radial engine which the US Navy had held in store. An additional prototype was ordered as **XN3N-2** and one production aircraft was converted to **XN3N-3** prototype configuration, both powered by 240-hp (179-kW) US Navy-built versions of the Wright R-760-96 radial engine. This was considered desirable to evaluate the suitability of the R-760 engine as a replacement for the J-5 which was obsolescent, and when found to be suitable the last 20 production N3N-1s were provided with the US Navy-built R-760.

At a later date all remaining N3N-1s had their J-5 engines

replaced by 235-hp (175-kW) R-760-2s.

Production of 816 **N3N-3**s followed from 1938, these having amended tail units and landing gear, and four of these were transferred to the US Coast Guard in 1941. Used extensively in US Navy primary flying training schools throughout World War II, the majority became surplus immediately the war ended. The exception was due to a small number of the seaplane version retained for primary training at the US Naval Academy and these, when retired in 1961, were the last biplanes to be used in US military service.

Specification

Type: two-seat primary trainer
Powerplant: (N3N-3) one 235-hp (175-kW) Wright R-760-2 Whirlwind 7 radial piston engine
Performance: maximum speed 126 mph (203 km/h); cruising speed 90 mph (145 km/h); service ceiling 15,200 ft (4 635 m); range 470 miles (756 km)
Weights: empty 2,090 lb (948 kg); maximum take-off 2,792 lb (1266 kg)
Dimensions: span 34 ft 0 in (10.36 m); length 25 ft 6 in (7.77 m); height 10 ft 10 in (3.30 m); wing area 305 sq ft (28.33 m²)

Naval Aircraft Factory/Hall PH

Few aircraft of World War II can trace a direct lineage back to the fighting aircraft of the previous conflict, so dramatic were the advances made in aviation in the intervening period. One of those was the **Hall PH**, an antiquated biplane flying-boat which served in small numbers on patrol duties.

The derivation of the PH began with the Curtiss flying-boat of 1914, which led directly to the Felixstowe F-5, developed in Britain and destined to become one of the most successful flying-boats of World War I. The Naval Aircraft Factory built

The PH-2 was the penultimate variant of a basic design dating back to 1914. The Wright R-1820 Cyclone engines had Townend ring cowls. This was a Coast Guard aircraft.

this design in the USA as the F-5L. In 1922 the aircraft was redesignated as the PN-5, and was subsequently developed through a series of variants, culminating in the PN-11 (later redesignated P4N), which introduced a wider metal hull than its predecessors. The Naval Aircraft Factory's production capability was severely limited, so contracts were placed with other compa-

nies. Variants of the PN series were also built by Douglas (as the PD), Martin (PM) and Keystone (PK).

The final development of the series was entrusted to the Hall Aluminium Aircraft Corporation, which built a version based on the PN-11, but with a larger fin and rudder. The prototype **XPH-1**, first flown in December 1929, was powered by two 537-hp (400-kW) Wright GR-1750 engines, but the nine **PH-1**s which followed had the 620-hp (462-kW) Wright R-1820-86. The PH-1 also introduced a rudimentary enclosure for the pilot's cockpit, and was armed with two Lewis guns in open bow and dorsal positions. A US Coast Guard order followed for 14 unarmed aircraft, split between seven **PH-2**s with 750-hp (559-kW) Wright R-1820F-51 engines, and seven similarly-powered **PH-3** with further refinements to the pilot's enclosure and long-chord engine cowlings. On entry into World War II, a handful of these USCG aircraft were rearmed and employed on anti-submarine patrol duties around the US coast, flying from Elizabeth City, Miami, Brooklyn, Biloxi, San Diego and San Francisco. The PH-2s were retired in 1941, but the PH-3s soldiered on until 1944.

Generally similar to the PH-2, the final seven Hall patrol flying-boats were designated PH-3. The most obvious differences were that the cockpit canopy was redesigned for lower drag and the engines had long-chord cowlings. The USCG used this aircraft until 1944.

Specification
Hall PH-3
Type: six-crew patrol flying-boat
Powerplant: two 750-hp (559-kW) Wright R-1820-F51 Cyclone 9 radial piston engines
Performance: maximum speed 159 mph (256 km/h); service ceiling 21,350 ft (6505 m); range 1,937 miles (3117 km)
Weights: empty 9,614 lb (4361 kg); maximum take-off 17,679 lb (8019 kg)
Dimensions: wing span 72 ft 10 in (22.20 m); length 51 ft 0 in (15.54 m); height 19 ft 10 in (6.05 m); wing area 1,170 sq ft (108.69 m²)
Armament: up to 1,000 lb (454 kg) of depth bombs

Noorduyn C-64 Norseman

Noorduyn Aircraft Ltd, soon changed to Noorduyn Aviation Ltd, was established in Canada in 1935, occupying the former Curtiss-Reid factory near Montreal. Work had started in 1934, before formation of the company, on the design of a medium-size transport aircraft that would appeal to a wide civil and/or military market, be suitable for operation in the severe Canadian winter, and have optional float, ski or wheel landing gear to give it go-anywhere capability. Named **Noorduyn Norseman I**, the prototype (CF-AYO) was flown first on 14 November 1935, a braced high-wing monoplane with fixed tailwheel landing gear and powered by a Canadian-built 420-hp (313-kW) Wright R-975-E3 radial engine.

Initial production version was the **Norseman II** with only minor changes from the prototype, but it was soon discovered that the aircraft was underpowered with the Wright engine, leading first to the **Norseman III** with a 450-hp (336-kW) Pratt & Whitney Wasp SC (only three built), and the **Norseman IV** with the 550-hp (410-kW) Pratt & Whitney S3H1 or R-1340-AN-1 Wasp engine. The same powerplant was used in the **Norseman V** and **Norseman VI**, the latter designation being used for the aircraft produced during World War II for the RCAF and USAAF. The major buyer was the US Army Air Force which, after testing a single Norseman IV, acquired it and six others as **YC-64**s. Subsequent contracts for Norseman Vs reached a total of 749, designated initially **C-64A** and later **UC-64A**. Three of this total were transferred to the US Navy, which designated them **JA-1**, and six with twin floats, designated **UC-64B,** were used by the US Army Corps of Engineers.

Specification
Noorduyn UC-64A (landplane)
Type: utility transport
Powerplant: one 550-hp (410-kW) Pratt & Whitney R-1340-AN-1 Wasp radial piston engine
Performance: maximum speed 155 mph (249 km/h); service ceiling 17,000 ft (5180 m); range 1,150 miles (1851 km)
Weights: empty 4,680 lb (2123 kg); maximum take-off 7,400 lb (3357 kg)
Dimensions: span 51 ft 6 in (15.70 m); length 32 ft 0 in (9.75 m); height 10 ft 3 in (3.12 m); wing area 325.0 sq ft (30.19 m²)

Towards the end of World War II, a UC-64A or two might be found on almost every US military airfield. In December 1944 one (bearing 'invasion stripes' like the example below) vanished while taking famed USAAF bandleader Major Glenn Miller to Paris.

North American B-25 Mitchell

In 1938 the US Army Air Corps issued a requirement for a medium bomber, a design for which North American Aviation Inc. at Inglewood, California, had already started work at private expense. This **NA-40** design was a twin-engine, three-seat shoulder-wing aircraft with tricycle landing gear, designed for two 1,100-hp (821-kW) Pratt & Whitney R-1830-56C3G radials. By chance this prototype was first flown by Paul Balfour in January 1939, the same month that the USAAC announced a competition for medium bomber designs to be submitted by 5 July that year. With engines changed to 1,350-hp (1007-kW) Wright GR-2600-A71s, the prototype (now the **NA-40B**) was delivered for tests at Wright Field in March.

The NA-40B was destroyed in an accident after only two weeks at Wright Field, but had already so impressed USAAC pilots that North American was instructed to continue development, specifying a number of changes. A wider fuselage allowed the bombload to be doubled; the wing was moved to mid-fuselage position and the top line of the cockpit was re-drawn to be flush with the upper line of the fuselage; the crew was increased from three to five and the armament increased to three 0.3-in (7.62-mm) guns in nose, dorsal and ventral positions, and one 0.5-in (12.7-mm) gun in the extreme tail. The new design, designated **B-25**, was not completed until September 1939, but already North American had (on 10 August) received an $11,771,000 contract for 184 production aircraft.

Flight tests

The first aircraft was a static test airframe, completed in July 1940, and the first flight by a production B-25 took place on 19 August with 1,700-hp (1268-kW) R-2600-9s at a gross weight of 27,310 lb (12388 kg), an increase of more than 7,800 lb (3538 kg) compared with the original NA-40 prototype. Early flight tests with the first B-25 disclosed a marked lack of directional stability, a shortcoming that was quickly and effectively cured by almost eliminating the dihedral of the wings outboard of the engines, a change that gave the B-25 its characteristic gull wing. Only the first nine B-25s (40-2165 to 40-2173) were completed with the straight dihedral wing, followed by 15 with the modified wing, no differentiation being made in the basic designation.

Early wartime combat experience in Europe had demonstrated the need for protection from gunfire, and 1941 saw the widespread modification of many American aircraft to benefit from this rather obvious lesson. The next B-25s on the Inglewood production line were 40 **B-25A**s (**NA-62A**) with armour protecting the pilots and with self-sealing fuel tanks. First service deliveries were made in the spring of 1941 to the 17th Bombardment Group (Medium), commanded by Lieutenant Colonel (later Brigadier General) Walter R. Peck, whose component squadrons (the 34th, 37th and 95th) were based at Lexington County Airport, South Carolina. At the end of that year the group moved to the west coast of the USA for coastal anti-shipping patrols after the Japanese attack at Pearl Harbor, and one of its B-25As sank a Japanese submarine on 24 December.

Meanwhile the original 1939 production contract was completed in 1941 with the production of 120 **B-25B**s (although one aircraft, 40-

Above: This aircraft is one of the first nine North American B-25s, which had constant dihedral from wingroot to tip. All subsequent aircraft in the Mitchell series had flat outer wing panels, with dihedral restricted to the centre section, inboard of the engine nacelles.

The B-25B version of the Mitchell was the first variant to reach a three-figure production total. It introduced Bendix electrically-operated dorsal and ventral twin-gun turrets. Of 120 B-25Bs built, 23 went to the RAF as Mitchell Mk Is.

2243, crashed and was written off before delivery). This version featured electrically operated Bendix dorsal and ventral turrets, each with a pair of 0.5-in (12.7-mm) machine-guns; the tail gun was deleted, however, and the gross weight increased to 28,460 lb (12909 kg). With considerably accelerated production already planned for further improved versions, the American government was able to supply 23 B-25Bs to the UK under Lend-Lease. However, only one such aircraft (termed the **Mitchell Mk I** in the Royal Air Force) arrived in the United Kingdom, the remainder being shipped to North Africa. Inadequate maintenance facilities existed to introduce them into service with an operational unit, and late in 1942 they were moved to India, where they eventually joined No.681 Squadron at Dum Dum in January 1943 and later flew reconnaissance sorties over Burma and Siam. A small number of other B-25Bs were shipped to the North

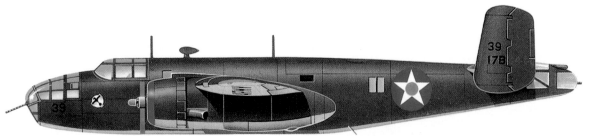

Left: This B-25A served in 1941 at McChord Field with the 34th Bombardment Squadron (Medium), 17th Bomb Group – the first in the USAAF to fly the new North American twin-engined bomber. The Group was in action before the end of 1941.

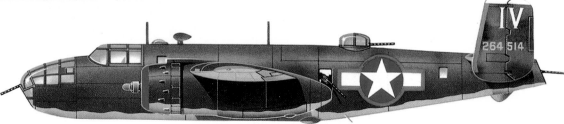

Right: Flying from Gerbini, Sicily, in August 1943, this B-25C-20-NA featured a Roman numeral 'IV' on the tail, indicating service with the fourth squadron (81st BS) in the 12th Bomb Group (Medium) as part of the 12th Air Force.

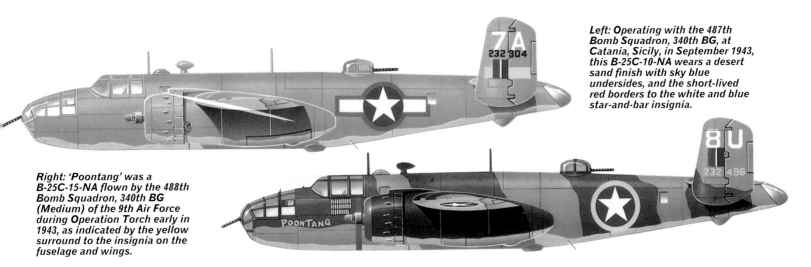

Left: Operating with the 487th Bomb Squadron, 340th BG, at Catania, Sicily, in September 1943, this B-25C-10-NA wears a desert sand finish with sky blue undersides, and the short-lived red borders to the white and blue star-and-bar insignia.

Right: 'Poontang' was a B-25C-15-NA flown by the 488th Bomb Squadron, 340th BG (Medium) of the 9th Air Force during Operation Torch early in 1943, as indicated by the yellow surround to the insignia on the fuselage and wings.

Left: This is one of 16 B-25Bs from the 17th BG that took off from USS Hornet on 18 April 1942 to strike targets on the Japanese mainland, including Tokyo, going on to land in China or the USSR.

Above: 'El Diablo IV', a B-25D-10-NC, flies over New Britain Island while operating with the 5th Air Force to attack Cape Gloucester. More than 5,000 lb (2268 kg) of bombs could be carried.

Russian ports as deck cargo in the early PQ convoys.

About 40 B-25Bs were scheduled for delivery to the Dutch in the Netherland East Indies, but as a result of the rapidly deteriorating situation facing the Americans in the South West Pacific, all were diverted to the 13th and 19th Squadrons of the 3rd Bombardment Group, USAAF, at Brisbane, Australia, commanded by Robert F. Strickland (who rose from first lieutenant to full colonel in only nine months, in 1942). Other aircraft were delivered to the 17th Bombardment Group (Medium), replacing the earlier B-25As.

It was in April 1942 that the B-25 leapt into the headlines with one of the war's most daring epics, when 16 B-25Bs made an extraordinary attack on the Japanese mainland. Using aircraft from the 17th Group, modified to carry 1,141 US gal (4319 litres) of fuel compared with the standard 694 US gal (2627 litres), these B-25Bs were crewed by volunteers led by Lieutenant Colonel James H. Doolittle, one of America's greatest airmen, who as long ago as 1925 had won a

Mounting an M4 75-mm cannon to fire 15-lb (6.8-kg) shells, plus two 0.5-in (12.7-mm) machine-guns to assist aiming, this converted B-25C-25-NA was a forerunner of 405 productionised B-25Gs. The latter lacked the ventral turret of this conversion.

Schneider Trophy race and who later in the war commanded the 8th, 12th and 15th US Air Forces. The B-25's ventral turrets and Norden bombsights were removed and two wooden 'guns' fitted in the tail for deception purposes, yet the gross weight rose to 31,000 lb (14062 kg). Carried to within 800 miles (1290 km) of the Japanese mainland aboard the carrier USS *Hornet*, Doolittle led his aircraft in low-level attacks on targets in Tokyo, Kobe, Yokohama and Nagoya on 18 April. All the raiders either crashed or force-landed, the majority of crews being repatriated by the Russians or Chinese.

Major modifications

Extensive detail redesign identified the **B-25C**, of which deliveries started just before the end of 1941, 1,619 being produced at the parent plant at Inglewood and 2,290 (designated **B-25D**) at a second North American factory at Dallas, Texas. The aircraft were powered by 1,700-hp (1268-kW) R-2600-13s and were equipped with autopilots; external racks on the fuselage could increase the fuel capacity to 1,100 US gal (4164 litres), while this and a bomb-bay fuel tank carrying 585 US gal (2214 litres) took the maximum gross weight to 41,800 lb (18960 kg). Maximum bombload of 5,200 lb (2359 kg) comprised

Finished in desert sand overall, this 9th Air Force B-25 (a 'B' or 'C' model) flies over the featureless Western Desert, accompanying the shadows of a preceding six-ship formation. Mitchells were also used in the Middle East by RAF and SAAF squadrons.

3,200 lb (1452 kg) internally plus eight 250-lb (113-kg) bombs on wing racks. B-25Cs and B-25Ds occasionally carried a 2,000-lb (907-kg) torpedo externally for shipping attacks. Maximum speed of this version was 284 mph (457 km/h) at 15,000 ft (4570 m).

A total of 455 B-25Cs and 40 B-25Ds was supplied to the UK, serving with Nos 98, 180, 226, 305, 320 and 342 Squadrons of the RAF based in the UK under the designation **Mitchell Mk II**. Some 182 B-25Cs were supplied to the Soviet Union (although eight were lost at sea in transit), as well as 688 B-25Ds. Others were delivered to Canada, mainly for use as trainers.

Anti-shipping variant

The next production version was the **B-25G**, developed from the **XB-25G** prototype which had been taken from the B-25C production line and modified to mount a standard US Army 75-mm field gun in the nose. The production B-25G, of which 405 were produced, carried an M4 75-mm gun with 21 15-lb (6.81-kg) shells, and was developed for anti-shipping strikes in the Pacific theatre. Loaded by the navigator/bombardier by hand, the big gun could seldom fire more than four shots in a single attack. The four-crew B-25G was not regarded as successful, but a great improvement was made in the **B-25H**, of which 1,000 were produced with the lighter T13E1 75-mm gun and a crew of five. With four 0.5-in (12.7-mm) guns in the extreme nose, four more in blister packs on the sides of the nose, two in each of the dorsal and tail positions and two in the fuselage waist, plus a bombload of 3,000 lb (1361 kg) and up to eight 5-in (12.7-cm) underwing rockets, the B-25H was indeed a formidable aircraft and was highly successful in operations against the Japanese.

The main and by far the most widely-used version of the B-25 was the **B-25J** variant, of which 4,318 (as B-25J-NCs) were built at a new

factory at Kansas City, Kansas. This reverted to a six-man crew and a glazed nose, without 75-mm gun but retaining the four 'blister' guns, and the dorsal turret was moved forward to a position immediately aft of the pilots' cockpit; power was provided by two R-2600-29 radials.

In 1944 an analysis of B-25 operations in the Far East disclosed that most attacks were being carried out at low level and that the bombardier was seldom needed. His station was accordingly deleted and a 'solid' nose re-introduced, first as a field modification and later on the production line. In place of the two hand-held machine-guns previously fitted, a battery of eight 0.5-in (12.7-mm) guns was mounted, bringing to a total of 18 the number of guns carried by later B-25Js.

Two hundred and ninety-five B-25Js were purchased by the UK, but 20 of these were transferred back to the USAAF in North Africa; in the RAF this version was termed the **Mitchell Mk III**, and served almost exclusively with the UK-based squadrons already listed. Despite the large number of B-25s built, the USAAF inventory at no time exceeded 2,500, the balance being composed of large numbers

North American B-25J Mitchell cutaway key

1 Flexible 0.50-in (12.7-mm) machine-gun
2 Fixed nose machine-gun
3 Bomb sight
4 Nose compartment glazing
5 Bomb fusing and release switch panel
6 Bombardier's instrument panel
7 Cabin heater blower
8 Nose undercarriage leg strut
9 Nosewheel
10 Undercarriage torque scissors
11 Aerial mast
12 Heating air ducting
13 Bombardier's seat
14 Nose compartment emergency escape hatch
15 Armoured cockpit bulkhead
16 Windscreen panels
17 Instrument panel shroud
18 Pilot's gunsight
19 Windscreen de-misting air ducting
20 Instrument panel
21 Rudder pedals
22 Control column
23 Cockpit armoured skin plating
24 Crawlway to nose compartment
25 D/F loop aerial
26 Ventral aerial cable
27 Extending ladder
28 Forward entry hatch
29 Machine-gun blister fairing
30 0.50-in (12.7-mm) fixed machine-guns
31 Ammunition boxes
32 Ammunition feed chutes
33 Fire extinguisher
34 Pilot's seat
35 Safety harness
36 Co-pilot/navigator's seat
37 Seat back armour plating
38 Cockpit roof ditching hatch
39 Starboard fixed gun ammunition boxes
40 Radio racks
41 Turret foot pedals
42 Ammunition boxes
43 Hydraulic reservoir
44 Turret mounting ring
45 Front/centre fuselage joint frame

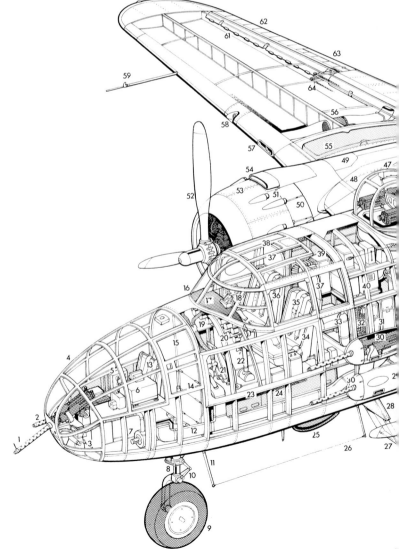

Transferred by the USAAF to the Marine Corps, 255 B-25Js took the Navy designation PBJ-1J. Operating in the South Pacific area, Marine PBJ-1s were usually fitted with ASV radar in a podded installation on the port outer wing; these PBJ-1Js also have underwing HVAR mounts.

Features of the B-25D-35-NC – the final 'D' model built is illustrated – included a forward-mounted dorsal turret, waist gun positions and a raised tail gunner's cupola. Built at a new North American factory at Dallas, the B-25D was equivalent to the B-25C built at Inglewood.

Based on the B-25D airframe, the B-25H had the bombardier nose section replaced with the 75-mm cannon mounting of the B-25G. Four 0.5-in (12.7-mm) machine-guns were also mounted in the nose itself, adding to the forward firepower of the fuselage-side package guns.

46 Twin 0.50-in (12.7-mm) machine-guns
47 Upper rotating gun turret
48 Starboard inner wing panel
49 Nacelle top fairings
50 Engine cooling air flaps
51 Sjector type exhaust pipes
52 Starboard Hamilton Standard constant-speed propellor
53 Detachable engine cowlings
54 Carburettor air intake
55 Outboard auxiliary fuel tank
56 Oil coolers
57 Oil cooler ram air intake
58 Landing/taxiing lamp
59 Pitot tube
60 Starboard navigation light
61 Aileron balance weights
62 Starboard fabric covered aileron
63 Aileron tab
64 Aileron hinge control
65 Starboard outer slotted flap
66 Oil cooler air outlets
67 Nacelle tail fairing
68 Starboard inner slotted flap
69 Gun deflector plates
70 Bomb bay roof crawlway
71 Bomb hoisting frame

72 Vertical bomb rack
73 Port bomb stowage, maximum bomb load 3,000 lb (1360 kg)
74 Gun turret motor amplidyne
75 Centre/rear fuselage joint frame
76 Rear fuselage heater unit
77 Starboard 0.50-in (12.7-mm) waist machine-gun
78 Dinghy stowage
79 Fuselage skin plating
80 Ammunition feed chute
81 Starboard waist gun ammunition box
82 Starboard tail gun ammunition box
83 Tail gun feed chute
84 Tailplane centre section

85 Starboard tailplane construction
86 Starboard tailfin
87 Aerial cable
88 Fabric covered rudder
89 Rudder horn balance
90 Rudder tab
91 Starboard fabric covered elevator construction

92 Elevator tab
93 Tail gunner's enclosure
94 Armour plating
95 Tail barbette
96 Twin 0.50-in (12.7-mm) machine guns
97 Elevator tab
98 Port elevator

99 Port rudder construction
100 Rudder tab
101 Tailfin construction
102 Fin/tailplane attachment joint
103 Port tailplane
104 Tail-gunner's seat
105 Rear fuselage/tailplane attachment frame
106 Tail bumper
107 Fuselage frame construction
108 Port tail gun ammunition box
109 Port waist gun ammunition box
110 Air scoop
111 Fuselage walkway
112 Emergency stores pack
113 Rear entry hatch
114 Extending boarding ladder
115 Port waist gun gondola
116 Flexible canvas seal

117 0.50-in (12.7-mm) machine-gun
118 Spent cartridge case collector box
119 Port inboard slotted flap
120 Flap emergency actuator
121 Inner wing rear spar
122 Fuselage/inner wing joint strip
123 Rear main fuel tank, 164 US gal (621 litres)
124 Forward main fuel tank, 151 US gal (572 litres)
125 Auxiliary fuel tanks, 152 US gal (575 litres) in three fuel cells per wing
126 Flap actuator links
127 Flap hydraulic jack
128 Port oil coolers
129 Oil cooler exhaust ducts
130 Nacelle tail fairing
131 Port outer slotted flap construction

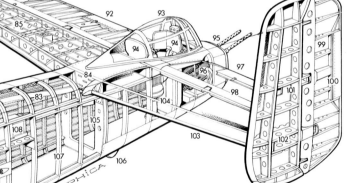

Final production version of the Mitchell, the B-25J reverted to the bombardier nose of the 'D' model, but was otherwise similar to the B-25H. Used by the RAF, this variant was the Mitchell Mk III.

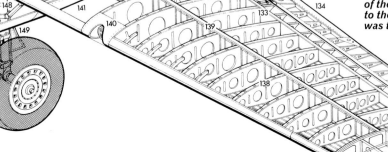

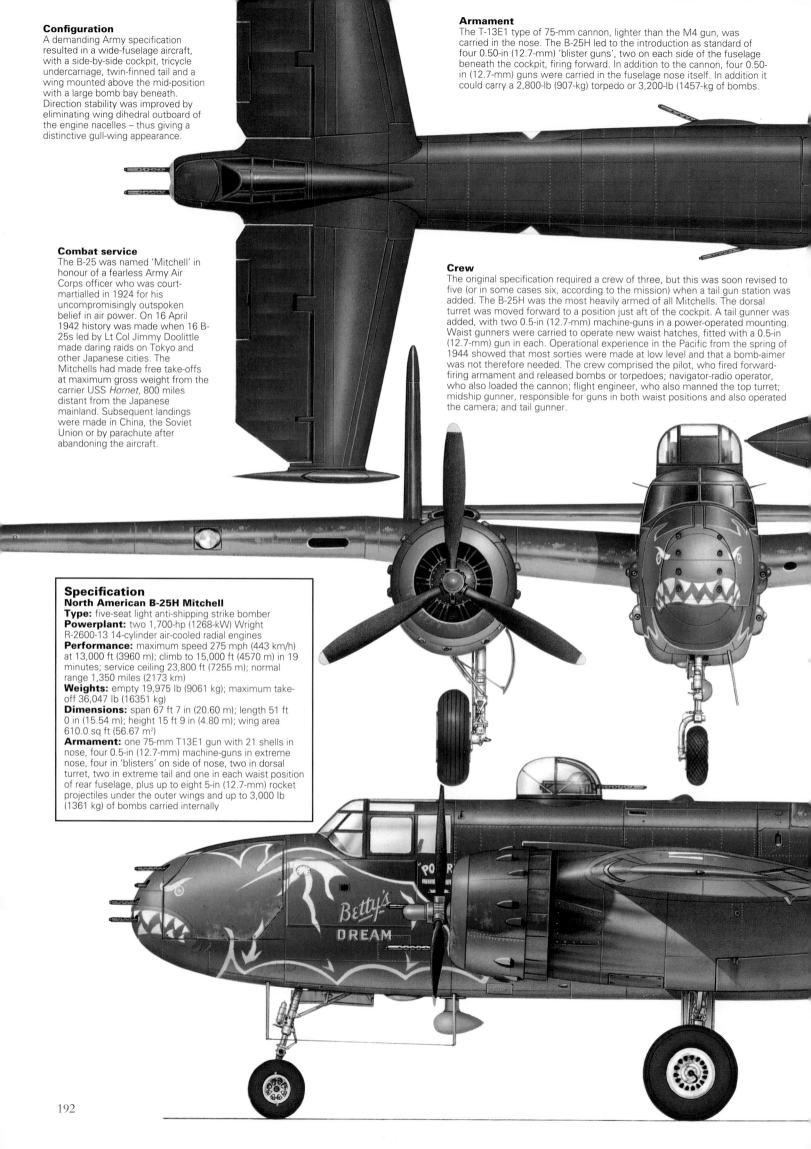

Configuration
A demanding Army specification resulted in a wide-fuselage aircraft, with a side-by-side cockpit, tricycle undercarriage, twin-finned tail and a wing mounted above the mid-position with a large bomb bay beneath. Direction stability was improved by eliminating wing dihedral outboard of the engine nacelles – thus giving a distinctive gull-wing appearance.

Armament
The T-13E1 type of 75-mm cannon, lighter than the M4 gun, was carried in the nose. The B-25H led to the introduction as standard of four 0.50-in (12.7-mm) 'blister guns', two on each side of the fuselage beneath the cockpit, firing forward. In addition to the cannon, four 0.50-in (12.7-mm) guns were carried in the fuselage nose itself. In addition it could carry a 2,800-lb (907-kg) torpedo or 3,200-lb (1457-kg) of bombs.

Combat service
The B-25 was named 'Mitchell' in honour of a fearless Army Air Corps officer who was court-martialled in 1924 for his uncompromisingly outspoken belief in air power. On 16 April 1942 history was made when 16 B-25s led by Lt Col Jimmy Doolittle made daring raids on Tokyo and other Japanese cities. The Mitchells had made free take-offs at maximum gross weight from the carrier USS *Hornet*, 800 miles distant from the Japanese mainland. Subsequent landings were made in China, the Soviet Union or by parachute after abandoning the aircraft.

Crew
The original specification required a crew of three, but this was soon revised to five (or in some cases six, according to the mission) when a tail gun station was added. The B-25H was the most heavily armed of all Mitchells. The dorsal turret was moved forward to a position just aft of the cockpit. A tail gunner was added, with two 0.5-in (12.7-mm) machine-guns in a power-operated mounting. Waist gunners were carried to operate new waist hatches, fitted with a 0.5-in (12.7-mm) gun in each. Operational experience in the Pacific from the spring of 1944 showed that most sorties were made at low level and that a bomb-aimer was not therefore needed. The crew comprised the pilot, who fired forward-firing armament and released bombs or torpedoes; navigator-radio operator, who also loaded the cannon; flight engineer, who also manned the top turret; midship gunner, responsible for guns in both waist positions and also operated the camera; and tail gunner.

Specification
North American B-25H Mitchell
Type: five-seat light anti-shipping strike bomber
Powerplant: two 1,700-hp (1268-kW) Wright R-2600-13 14-cylinder air-cooled radial engines
Performance: maximum speed 275 mph (443 km/h) at 13,000 ft (3960 m); climb to 15,000 ft (4570 m) in 19 minutes; service ceiling 23,800 ft (7255 m); normal range 1,350 miles (2173 km)
Weights: empty 19,975 lb (9061 kg); maximum take-off 36,047 lb (16351 kg)
Dimensions: span 67 ft 7 in (20.60 m); length 51 ft 0 in (15.54 m); height 15 ft 9 in (4.80 m); wing area 610.0 sq ft (56.67 m²)
Armament: one 75-mm T13E1 gun with 21 shells in nose, four 0.5-in (12.7-mm) machine-guns in extreme nose, four in 'blisters' on side of nose, two in dorsal turret, two in extreme tail and one in each waist position of rear fuselage, plus up to eight 5-in (12.7-mm) rocket projectiles under the outer wings and up to 3,000 lb (1361 kg) of bombs carried internally

North American B-25 Mitchell 499th Bomb Squadron 345th Bomb Group Leyte, 1944

The B-25 Mitchell was regarded by many as the best aircraft in its class in World War II. Less ambitious than the B-26 Marauder, it did not have quite the performance of the Martin bombers. Some 11,000 B-25s were built between 1940 and 1945, of which the USAAF received 9,816. The Mitchell served on every major front during the war, where it established an unrivalled reputation.

Powerplants

The early B-25s had two 1,700-hp (1258 kW) Wright R-2600-9 14-cylinder two-row radial engines, each driving a Hamilton Standard propeller of 12 ft 7 in (3.84 in) diameter. The Wright R-2600-13 or -29 of similar power were substituted from the B-25C. Two-speed superchargers were standard equipment. Each engine was fitted with independent fuel system consisting of two interconnected fore and aft compartments equipped with bulletproof self-sealing fuel cells located between the fuselage and nacelles. R-2600-92 were installed in the B-25J.

Camouflage

Illustrated is a B-25H, one of the most colourfully decorated aircraft of World War II. Commanded by Colonel Glenn A. Doolittle, the 345th Bomb Group (Medium) moved to Leyte in the Philippines in November 1944, its B-25Hs marked with the Group's 'Air Apache' badge prominently on their tailfins. Among its component squadrons were the 498th 'Falcons' and the 499th 'Bats Outa Hell', the latter displaying enormous bat wings enveloping the aircraft's noses, as typified by this 18-gun B-25H 'Betty's Dream'. By April 1945 they were operating from Luzon in the Philippines.

Keith Fretwell.

North American B-25 Mitchell

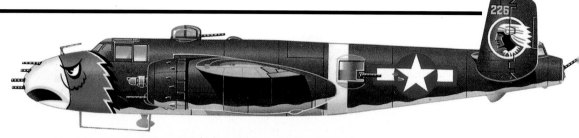

Right: Flamboyant artwork characterised the B-25s operated by 'The Falcons', the 498th Bomb Squadron, 345th BG. The Group's 'Air Apache' marking appeared on the tail. This B-25J was at Luzon in April 1945.

Left: Most of the 706 Mitchells that became PBJ-1s were operated by the Marine Corps, which formed at least eight squadrons on the type for use in the Pacific theatre. This is a PBJ-1H, armed like the equivalent B-25H with a 75-mm cannon.

Below: Unlike the B-26 Marauders operational in the ETO, B-25 Mitchells retained camouflage finishes until the end of hostilities. This B-25J-22-NC in natural metal finish was photographed in 1945; service in the training role ended in 1959.

North American B-25 variants

NA-40 (later NA-40B and NA-42): private-venture prototype; Pratt & Whitney R-1830-56 radials, later Wright GR 2600-A71s

B-25 (NA-62): 24 aircraft (40-2165 to 40-2188) first nine with straight wing dihedral remainder with gull wing; Wright R-2600-9 radials

B-25A (NA-62A): 40 aircraft (40-2189 to 40-2228), self-sealing tanks and pilot armour, to 17th Bomb Group; Wright R-2600-9 radials

B-25B (NA-62B): 120 aircraft (40-2229 to 40-2242 and 40-2244 to 40-2348, 40-2243 crashed before delivery; 23 to RAF as Mitchell Mk I; some to USSR

B-25C (NA-82): 1,625 aircraft built at Inglewood (41-12434 to 41-13038, 41-13039 to 41-13296, 42-32233 to 42-32532, 42-53332 to 42-53493, 42-64502 to 42-64801); 856 to USAAF; 555 purchased by the UK as **Mitchell Mk II** but 45 retained in Canada; 25 to Brazil; 182 to USSR (including eight lost in transit); some to China and Netherlands Indies Air Corps (two of these later to RAF); R-2600-13 radials; survivors redesignated **ZB-25C** in 1948

TB-25C: redesignation of AT-24C

B-25D (NA-82A): 2,290 aircraft built at Dallas (41-29648 to 41-30847, 42-87113 to 42-87612, 43-3280 to 43- 3869); all purchased for USAAF but 40 B-25D-15s passed to RAF; 29 delivered to Canada; 688 to USSR; some to Indonesia post-war; the few still on charge in 1948 were redesignated **ZB-25D**

RB-25D: redesignation of F-10

TB-25D: redesignation of AT-24D

XB-25E: one B-25C (42-32281) with hot air de-icing of wing leading edge; later redesignated **ZXB-25E**

XB-25F: one converted B-25C with electric de-icing of wing leading edge

XB-25G: one B-25C (41-13296) converted with standard US Army 75-mm field gun in nose

B-25G (NA-96): production version with M4 gun and many with gun packs on fuselage sides; ventral turret often omitted; five B-25C conversions (42-32384 to 42-32388) and 400 new-build aircraft (42-64802 to 65201)

TB-25G: redesignation of AT-24B

B-25H (NA-98): similar to B-25G but with T13E1 cannon; numerous gun configurations but usually had four 0.5-in (12.7-mm) nose guns; dorsal turret moved forwards; R-2600-13 or -29 engines; 1,000 built (43-4105 to 43-5104)

B-25J (NA-108): as B-25H but with glazed nose housing one fixed and two moveable 0.5-in (12.7-mm) guns; R-2600-29 engines; B-25J-27 and -32NC conversions had eight-gun solid noses; 4,318 were built (43-3870 to 43-4104, 43-27473 to 43-28222, 43-35946 to 43-36245, 44-28711 to 31510, 44-86692 to 44-86897, 45-8801 to 45-8899) although some were cancelled in the final batch; 295 to RAF as **Mitchell Mk III**

CB-25J: small number of B-25Js converted for utility transport tasks

TB-25J: redesignation of AT-24D; many post-war conversions to TB-25J trainer standard

VB-25J: staff transport conversion of B-25J

TB-25K: 117 B-25Js converted with E1 radar fire control system as radar trainers

TB-25L: 90 B-25Js converted for pilot training

TB-25M: 40 B-25J radar trainer conversions with E5 radar system

TB-25N: 47 B-25J pilot trainer conversions

AT-24A/B/C/D: 60 B-25s converted for advanced crew training; redesignated TB-25 in 1945

F-10: 10 B-25Ds converted to reconnaissance role with extra fuel and chin and rear fuselage camera installations; redesignated RB-25D

PBJ-1C: 50 B-25C equivalents for USMC (BuNo 34998 to 35047)

PBJ-1D: 152 B-25D equivalents (BuNo 35048 to 35096, 35098 to 35193, 35196 to 35202)

PBJ-1G: one B-25G equivalent (BuNo 35097)

PBJ-1H: 248 B-25H equivalents (BuNo 35250 to 35297, 88872 to 89071)

PBJ-1J: 255 B-25J equivalents (BuNo 35194 to 35195, 35203 to 35249, 35798 to 35920, 38980 to 39012, 64943 to 64992)

supplied to other friendly air forces during the last year of the war and shortly afterwards.

The B-25 was also widely used by the USAAF as a reconnaissance aircraft, early B-25s (mostly Bs) being given rudimentary camera installations in the field and issued to the 89th Reconnaissance Squadron in December 1941; others followed to the 5th Photographic Reconnaissance Group in the Mediterranean early in 1943 and the 26th Observation Group in the USA. A dedicated photographic reconnaissance version, the **F-10**, with a fan of three cameras for trimetrogen photography in a 'chin' fairing, was not developed until 1943; all guns were removed and fuel tanks were installed in the bomb bay.

Late-war trainer conversions

During the latter half of the war 60 B-25Cs, B-25Ds, B-25Gs and B-25Js were stripped of all operational equipment and converted for use as trainers, being given designations in the AT (later TB) categories. After the war this conversion continued with the B-25J until more than 600 had been delivered to the USAF. Some of these went on to become **TB-25K**s, **TB-25L**s, **TB-25M**s and **TB-25N**s. Others were converted to become utility and staff transports with CB, VB and ZB designations, some serving with Strategic Air Command for communications duties from 1946 onwards. The last USAF unit to fly the B-25 in service was based at Reese Air Force Base, whose TB-25L and TB-25N pilot trainers were eventually declared obsolete in January 1959.

Finally, the third largest operator of the B-25 (after the USAAF and RAF) was the US Navy, following the policy decision reached in July 1942 to allow the US Navy to take a share of land-based bomber production. Deliveries started in January 1943; of the first 50 **PBJ-1C**s (equivalent to the B-25C) delivered, the US Marine Corps Bombing Squadron VMB-413 was the first to receive 20. These were followed by 152 **PBJ-1D**s, one **PBJ-1G**, 248 **PBJ-1H**s and 255 **PBJ-1J**s (US Navy equivalents to the B-25D, B-25G, B-25H and B-25J respectively).

North American XB-28

Envisaged originally as a high-altitude version of the B-25 Mitchell, the **NA-63** emerged as an almost entirely different aircraft. Designated **XB-28** by the USAAF, the aircraft had a single fin and a circular-section fuselage (with pressure cabin for five crew), and was powered by two R-2800 engines. The bomb bay capacity was for 4,000 lb (1814 kg). Defensive armament consisted of dorsal, ventral and tail turrets, each armed with two 0.5-mm (12.7-mm) machine-guns, and aimed remotely from the cockpit. Three fixed forward-firing guns were fitted for strafing work.

Three prototypes were ordered in February 1940, the first of which flew in April 1942. The second prototype was cancelled and the third was completed as the **XB-28A** with a reconnais-

sance installation, no armament and R-2800-27 engines. Following the crash of this aircraft early in the test programme, plans for production were terminated.

Specification
Type: five-crew medium bomber
Powerplant: two 2,000-hp (1491-kW) Pratt & Whitney R-2800-11 radial piston engines

Performance: maximum speed 372 mph (599 km/h); service ceiling 34,600 ft (10545 m); range 2,040 miles (3283 km) with bombload
Weights: empty 25,573 lb (11600 kg); maximum take-off 37,200 lb (16874 kg)
Dimensions: wing span 72 ft 7 in (22.12 m); length 56 ft 5 in (17.20 m); height 14 ft 0 in (4.27 m); wing area 676 sq ft (62.80 m²)
Armament: three 0.5-in (12.7-mm) machine-guns firing forward, six similar

The first XB-28 is seen here amidst snow, which suggests Wright Field rather than California, before it crashed into the Pacific. Ed Heinemann's similarly-powered A-26 Invader was preferred.

weapons in dorsal, ventral and tail turrets; up to 4,000 lb (1814 kg) of bombs carried internally

North American BT-9/14 Yale

In 1935 North American produced a privately-funded prototype for a basic trainer under the company designation **NA-16**. This trainer proved to have performance very similar to contemporary combat aircraft, and following evaluation at Wright Field the USAAC swiftly ordered the type as a basic trainer with the designation **BT-9**. These 42 aircraft were powered by the 400-hp (298-kW) Wright R-975-7 radial. The US Navy took a similar type as the **NJ-1**, resulting in 40 aircraft featuring the 500-hp (373-kW) Pratt & Whitney R-134C radial. The 40 **BT-9A**s that followed introduced a fixed forward gun (with gun camera) and a trainable gun

in the rear cockpit. Only small changes were made in the 117 **BT-9B**s and 67 **BT-9C**s.

A single aircraft was modified as the **BT-9D** with BC-1A type wing panels and tail surfaces, while a single BT-9C was fitted with a 600-hp R-1340-41 engine to become the **Y1BT-10**.

Experience with the BT-9D led to the **BT-14**, of which 251 were built with the 450-hp (336-kW) Pratt & Whitney R-985-25 radial. These had wings of greater chord and with angular wingtips, and redesigned fins. Some 27 were later converted to **BT-14A** standard with the 400-hp (298-kW) R-985-11 engine. Canada operated the BT-14 as the **Yale Mk I**.

This is a BT-9 of the 46th School Squadron. In the revised designator system, training units carried suffix ED, from Education. Note the slats on the outer wings. This was one of the first of over 20,000 trainers of NAA design made in dozens of variants for many nations.

Specification:
North American BT-9B
Type: two-seat basic trainer
Powerplant: one 400-hp (298-kW) Wright R-975-7 radial piston engine
Performance: maximum speed 170 mph (274 km/h) at sea level; service ceiling 19,750 ft (6020 m); range 882 miles (1420 km)
Weights: empty 3,314 lb (1500 kg); maximum take-off 4,471 lb (2030 kg)
Dimensions: wing span 42 ft 0 in (12.80 m); length 27 ft 7 in (8.39 m); height 13 ft 7 in (4.13 m); wing area 248 sq ft (23.03 m²)
Armament: two 0.3-in (7.62-mm) Browning machine-guns

This BT-14 was assigned to the 52nd School Squadron at Randolph Field, Texas. Among many other changes from the BT-9, the slats were omitted.

North American BC-1

Above: Army 38-379 was one of the third and last block of BC-1 basic combat trainers. The demand for trainers was huge, so in April 1941 long-lasting aluminium dope (instead of blue/yellow) was used, despite the slightly increased risk of mid-air collision.

Below: The prototype NA-26 in its original form. This was the first of some 19,000 advanced trainers of NAA design to have retractable landing gear.

Above: This is one of the final three aircraft on the BC-1 contract, completed as BC-2 (NA-54) prototypes with a metal-skinned fuselage, integral fuel tanks, blunt-tipped wings, a straight-edged rudder and an R-1340-45 engine driving a three-bladed Hamilton propeller.

Although the BC-1 designation is today unfamiliar, the airplane to which it applied is one of the best-known shapes in the sky. In 1935, General Aviation (soon to be renamed North American) had flown the NA-16 trainer prototype, from which had been developed the BT-9 basic trainer. In 1937 the Army Air Corps ran a competition for a basic combat trainer, and North American returned to the NA-16 prototype for inspiration. A big Wasp engine was fitted, driving a variable-pitch propeller and a hydraulic system, the latter allowing a retractable undercarriage to be fitted. This retracted inwards into uncovered wells under the leading edge and centre-section, necessitating the

fitment of characteristic circular fairings at the wingroot. Provision was made for light armament for weapons training and radio. Under the company designation **NA-26**, the new prototype easily won the competition, and was rewarded with an order for 41 aircraft under the military designation **BC-1** (**NA-36**). An additional 139 were built for the Air Corps, of which 30 were modified to act as instrument trainers under the designation **BC-1I**. The final three aircraft were built with wings and rudder redesigned to facilitate production, and with the Pratt & Whitney R-1340-45 engine driving a three-bladed propeller. These were known as **BC-2**s (NA-54).

The major production version was the **BC-1A** (NA-55), which had revised wings and was the first of the series to introduce a straight trailing edge to the rudder. Ninety-two were ordered, of which one became the **BC-1B** with a redesigned centre-section, and nine were delivered with a new designation that would be far more famous than the original: AT-6. Although it had a different company number (NA-59), the initial batch of AT-6s was no different to the preceding BC-1As, reflecting only the 1940 decision to drop the Basic Combat (trainer) category and revive the dormant Advanced Trainer category. Of course the AT-6 became the best-known trainer of

the war, and served in this role into the 1990s. AT-6 variants are described under that heading.

Specification
Type: two-seat basic combat trainer
Powerplant: one Pratt & Whitney R-1340-49 radial piston engine, rated at 600 hp (447 kW)
Performance: maximum speed 207 mph (333 km/h); service ceiling 24,100 ft (7345 m); range 665 miles (1070 km)
Weights: empty 4,050 lb (1837 kg); maximum take-off 5,200 lb (2358 kg)
Dimensions: wing span 43 ft 0 in (13.10 m); length 27 ft 9 in (8.44 m); height 14 ft 0 in (4.26 m); wing area 225.0 sq ft (29.90 m²)
Armament: one fixed forward-firing 0.30-in (7.62-mm) machine-gun and similar weapon on flexible mount in rear cockpit

North American AT-6

Almost certainly the most universally used military training aircraft of all time, the North American Texan was derived from the NA-16 prototype, built at the General Aviation Factory at Dundalk, Maryland, to a US Army Air Corps specification for a basic trainer which was the forerunner of more than 17,000 examples of a number of derivatives. Development of service trainers began with the BT-9 and BT-14, leading to the BC-1 and BC-2 with retractable undercarriage.

When the USAAC changed the role designations to advanced trainer, subsequent production carried AT designations, the series commencing with 94 **AT-6** Texans which included the last nine of the BC-1A order. A development of the AT-6 for export was armed

Above: With the AT-6A, North American approached close to the mass-produced wartime Texan/Harvard/SNJ family. One of the few visible differences is the design of the windscreen. In October 1941 this example was serving with the 62nd (Air Corps Advanced Flying) School at Victoria, Texas. This was the final version built at the Inglewood, California, plant.

Above: Unlike any other members of this prolific family, the NA-69 was an attack aircraft built for Siam (today Thailand), powered by a 785-hp Wright Cyclone R-1820-75 engine and armed with five 0.30-in guns and 400 lb of bombs. The 10 ordered were impressed into the US Army Air Corps as A-27 attack trainers, painted olive drab.

with two 0.3-in guns in the nose, two in the wings and one in the rear cockpit. Ten of these destined for Thailand were impressed by the USAAC under the designation **A-27**.

Replacement of the centre-section integral fuel tank by removable tanks and installation of the R-1340-49 engine produced the **AT-6A**, 517 of which were built at Inglewood before all production was transferred to Dallas, Texas, where North American had already established a second line. Dallas-built aircraft to USAAF contracts included 1,330 AT-6As, 400 of the gunnery trainer **AT-6B** version, 2,970 **AT-6C**s, 3,404 **AT-6D**s and 956 **AT-9F**s. The AT-6C arose from the need to alleviate an anticipated shortage of light alloy and approximately 1,250 lb (567 kg) per aircraft was saved by the use of other light metals, bonded plywood construction for the rear fuselage, and ply-covered tail surfaces. Although the AT-6D marked a return to all-metal construction, it featured also a 24-volt rather than a 12-volt electrical system, and the AT-6F had a redesigned rear fuselage and strengthened wings.

Below: This AT-6A is pictured while serving in 1942 with the Gunnery School at Harlingen, Texas (today the home of the Confederate Air Force). The 0.30-in Browning in the rear cockpit would be fired against sleeve targets over the Gulf of Mexico. In 1941 the serial numbers became too long to fit on the fin, and some were stencilled below the canopies.

Air Corps serial 41-16069 was an AT-6A built at Dallas. It is seen being flown on 6 March 1942 by Mo Cjing Yung, one of a group of Chinese Air Force cadets going through the regular US Army syllabus at Phoenix, Arizona. They were said to have "exceptional aptitude", and upon graduation were assigned to combat duty in China. The colour of the cowling is not recorded. Like almost all tandem-seat trainers, the pupil or solo pilot always sat in the front cockpit.

Possibly on a formation exercise (part of the syllabus at schools equipped with the AT-6) in May 1943, these Dallas-built Texans were among the last batches to AT-6C standard. These were constructed with as little aluminium and its alloys as possible, no less than 1,246 lb of the potentially scarce metal being saved in each aircraft. The Navy SNJ-4 had a similar steel and plywood structure.

US Navy aircraft were designated **SNJ**. The **SNJ-1** and **-2** corresponded to the BC-1, the SNJ-2 featuring an R-1340-56 engine. The **SNJ-3** was similar to the AT-6A while the **SNJ-4** corresponded to the AT-6C, this being the major production version for the Navy with 2,400 built. The **SNJ-5** designation covered no fewer than 1,573 AT-6D aircraft transferred from the USAAF, while 931 of the US Army's 956 AT-6Fs were actually procured on behalf of the US Navy, which used them as the **SNJ-6**. Some SNJs were converted with arrester hooks for deck landing practice, these being denoted by the 'C' suffix (e.g. SNJ-4C). **AT-16** was the designation given to 2,610 aircraft built by Noorduyn Aviation Ltd of Montreal for the RAF and RCAF, these corresponding to USAAF AT-6As. In 1948, the AT, BT and PT designations were superseded by a catch-all 'T' for all trainers, so the AT-6 became the **T-6**.

Throughout the conflict, the AT-6 and SNJ were used to turn out thousands of pilots for the war effort. For both the USAAF and US Navy the type was the principal advanced trainer, and many Allied pilots, principally those of the RAF and RCAF, were trained on the type. Its performance and handling made it an ideal lead-in trainer for fighter aircraft, although it retained sufficiently docile handling to avoid too many losses of young pilots.

The T-6's success story lasted long after the war's end. From 1949, 2,068 T-6s were remanufactured as **T-6G**s for the US Air Force or **SNJ-7** for the US Navy with a revised cockpit layout, an improved

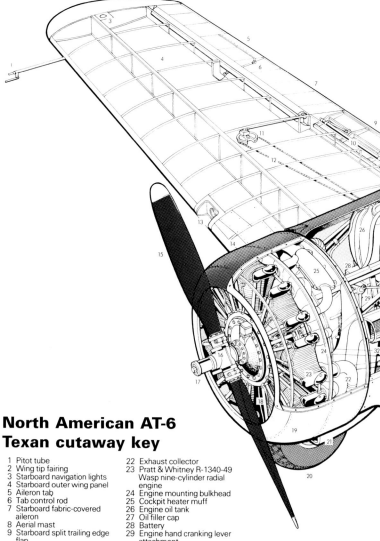

North American AT-6 Texan cutaway key

1 Pitot tube
2 Wing tip fairing
3 Starboard navigation lights
4 Starboard outer wing panel
5 Aileron tab
6 Tab control rod
7 Starboard fabric-covered aileron
8 Aerial mast
9 Starboard split trailing edge flap
10 Flat control rod
11 Aileron hinge control
12 Aileron cables
13 Starboard landing/taxiing lamp
14 Detachable engine cowling panels
15 Hamilton Standard two-bladed variable-pitch propeller
16 Feathering bobweights
17 Propeller hub pitch change mechanism
18 Engine oil tank sump
19 Bottom cowling panels
20 Starboard mainwheel
21 Carburettor air intake duct

22 Exhaust collector
23 Pratt & Whitney R-1340-49 Wasp nine-cylinder radial engine
24 Engine mounting bulkhead
25 Cockpit heater muff
26 Engine oil tank
27 Oil filler cap
28 Battery
29 Engine hand cranking lever attachment
30 Engine bearer struts
31 Filtered air intake
32 Air intake heater duct
33 Lower engine bearers
34 Mainwheel well
35 Fuel pump
36 Intake fairing
37 Engine control rod runs
38 Fireproof bulkhead
39 Forward rudder pedals
40 Fuse box
41 Generator control unit
42 Electrical control panel
43 Front pilot's instrument panel
44 Instrument panel shroud
45 Aerial cable lead-in

46 Windscreen panels
47 Forward sliding canopy section
48 Front pilot's seat
49 Safety harness
50 Throttle mixture and propeller control levers
51 Cockpit light
52 Tailplane trim control wheels
53 Footboards
54 Wing spar/fuselage attachment joint
55 Fuel contents gauge
56 Hydraulic system emergency handpump

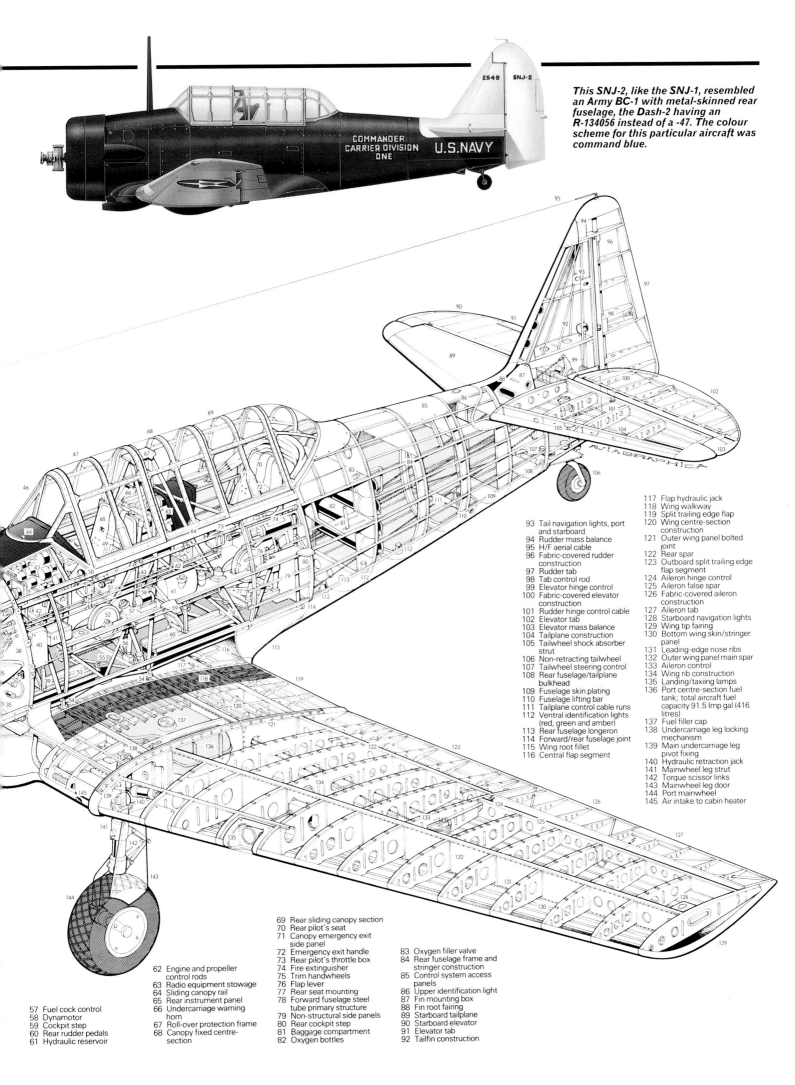

This SNJ-2, like the SNJ-1, resembled an Army BC-1 with metal-skinned rear fuselage, the Dash-2 having an R-134056 instead of a -47. The colour scheme for this particular aircraft was command blue.

93 Tail navigation lights, port and starboard
94 Rudder mass balance
95 H/F aerial cable
96 Fabric-covered rudder construction
97 Rudder tab
98 Tab control rod
99 Elevator hinge control
100 Fabric-covered elevator construction
101 Rudder hinge control cable
102 Elevator tab
103 Elevator mass balance
104 Tailplane construction
105 Tailwheel shock absorber strut
106 Non-retracting tailwheel
107 Tailwheel steering control
108 Rear fuselage/tailplane bulkhead
109 Fuselage skin plating
110 Fuselage lifting bar
111 Tailplane control cable runs
112 Ventral identification lights (red, green and amber)
113 Rear fuselage longeron
114 Forward/rear fuselage joint
115 Wing root fillet
116 Central flap segment

117 Flap hydraulic jack
118 Wing walkway
119 Split trailing edge flap
120 Wing centre-section construction
121 Outer wing panel bolted joint
122 Rear spar
123 Outboard split trailing edge flap segment
124 Aileron hinge control
125 Aileron false spar
126 Fabric-covered aileron construction
127 Aileron tab
128 Starboard navigation lights
129 Wing tip fairing
130 Bottom wing skin/stringer panel
131 Leading-edge nose ribs
132 Outer wing panel main spar
133 Aileron control
134 Wing rib construction
135 Landing/taxiing lamps
136 Port centre-section fuel tank; total aircraft fuel capacity 91.5 Imp gal (416 litres)
137 Fuel filler cap
138 Undercarriage leg locking mechanism
139 Main undercarriage leg pivot fixing
140 Hydraulic retraction jack
141 Mainwheel leg strut
142 Torque scissor links
143 Mainwheel leg door
144 Port mainwheel
145 Air intake to cabin heater

69 Rear sliding canopy section
70 Rear pilot's seat
71 Canopy emergency exit side panel
72 Emergency exit handle
73 Rear pilot's throttle box
74 Fire extinguisher
75 Trim handwheels
76 Flap lever
77 Rear seat mounting
78 Forward fuselage steel tube primary structure
79 Non-structural side panels
80 Rear cockpit step
81 Baggage compartment
82 Oxygen bottles

83 Oxygen filler valve
84 Rear fuselage frame and stringer construction
85 Control system access panels
86 Upper identification light
87 Fin mounting box
88 Fin root fairing
89 Starboard tailplane
90 Starboard elevator
91 Elevator tab
92 Tailfin construction

62 Engine and propeller control rods
63 Radio equipment stowage
64 Sliding canopy rail
65 Rear instrument panel
66 Undercarriage warning horn
67 Roll-over protection frame
68 Canopy fixed centre-section

57 Fuel cock control
58 Dynamotor
59 Cockpit step
60 Rear rudder pedals
61 Hydraulic reservoir

North American AT-6 Texan

This photograph was taken during the mid-war years at NAS Pensacola, Florida, one of the Navy's biggest training schools. This section of ramp housed SNJ-3s, painted in the usual silver and chrome yellow livery and with various coloured cowlings. An indication of the intensity of activity is provided by the fact that all but one of the aircraft has its engine running. A few SNJs of various sub-types were fitted with an arrester hook for training in deck landing, and most SNJ-5s were equipped for training in fixed and free gunnery and occasionally for bombing and observer photography.

canopy, relocated aerial masts, a square-tipped propeller, F-51-type landing-gear and flap-actuating levers, and steerable tailwheel. Some were converted to **LT-6G** standard for service as forward air control aircraft in Korea from July 1950, operating with the 6147th Tactical Air Control Squadron. The **T-6H** designation covered a few AT-6F aircraft modified to T-6G standard. The final variant was the **SNJ-8** for the Navy, which was due to enter service as the **TJ-8**. The 240 on order were eventually cancelled.

Canadian Car and Foundry, which had taken over Noorduyn in 1946, manufactured 270 similar-standard Harvard 4s for the RCAF and 285 T-6Js for USAF Mutual Aid programmes.

Specification
Type: two-seat advanced trainer, or close air support aircraft
Powerplant: (AT-6D) one 550-hp (410-kW) Pratt & Whitney R-1340-AN-1 Wasp radial piston engine
Performance: maximum speed 205 mph (330 km/h) at 5,000 ft (1525 m); cruising speed 170 mph (274 km/h) at 5,000 ft (1525 m); service ceiling 21,500 ft (6555 m); range 750 miles (1207 km)
Weights: empty 4,158 lb (1886 kg); maximum take-off 5,300 lb (2404 kg)
Dimensions: span 42 ft 0 in (12.8 m); length 29 ft 6 in (8.99 m); height 11 ft 9 in (3.58 m); wing area 253.7 sq ft (23.57 m²)
Armament: (AT-6) one fixed forward-firing and one rear cockpit-mounted 0.30-in (7.62-mm) machine-gun, plus underwing pylons for machine-gun pods or light bombs (COIN conversions)

North American O-47

Developed by General Aviation (the precursor of North American Aviation) to meet a US Army specification for an observation aircraft, the **GA-15** represented a radical change in design for such a role in that, unlike its predecessors, it was a low-wing monoplane with an enclosed cockpit seating a three-man crew. Powered by an 850-hp (634-kW) Wright R-1820-41 Cyclone engine, the **XO-47** prototype (36-145) flew in mid-1935, and to provide an acceptable field of view for the observer a glazed nose position was located under the fuselage. North American put the type into production to meet a USAAC contract for 109 North American **O-47A** aircraft ordered in February 1937, later increased to 164 (37-260 to 37-368 and 38-271 to 38-325). They were powered by 975-hp (727-kW) Cyclones, while 74 **O-47B** aircraft (39-65 to 39-138) had 1,060-hp (790-kW) R-1820-57 engines and additional fuel

capacity. A handful were still serving in the observation role at US overseas outposts at the beginning of World War II, but for the remainder of the conflict they served mainly as trainers and target tugs.

Specification
North American O-47A
Type: three-seat observation aircraft
Powerplant: one 975-hp (727-kW) Wright R-1820-49 radial piston engine
Performance: maximum speed 221 mph (356 km/h); service ceiling 23,200 ft (7070 m); endurance 2.1 hours
Weights: empty 5,980 lb (2712 kg); maximum take-off 7,636 lb (3464 kg)
Dimensions: wing span 46 ft 4 in (14.12 m); length 33 ft 7 in (10.17 m); height 12 ft 2 in (3.70 m); wing area 350 sq ft (32.5 m²)
Armament: one 0.3-in (7.62-mm) machine-gun in starboard wing and one 0.3-in (7.62-mm) gun in rear cockpit

Dated 10 February 1939, this photograph shows an O-47A over the Sierras, operating from Elko, Nevada. The fuselage badge is that of the 82nd Observation Squadron.

North American P-51

The **P-51 Mustang**, arguably the greatest American fighter of all time and among the greatest from any nation, was not requested by the US Army. It began as the company **NA-73X** (civil registry NX 19998), designed and assembled with remarkable haste in the mid-1940s by a company, North American Aviation of Los Angeles, that had never before made a fighter. North American, established in 1934 and presided over by J. H. 'Dutch' Kindelberger, was contacted by the British Purchasing Commission in 1940 as a potential new supplier of the Curtiss P-40. Company designers

Raymond Rice and Edgar Schmued, the latter a veteran of service with Messerschmitt and Fokker, wanted instead to create a new fighter powered by the 1,150-hp (857.6-kW) Allison V-1710-39 inline engine used in the P-40. The coolant section for the powerplant would be located behind and below the pilot, a configuration tried on the prototype P-40 but not on subsequent production machines, and tried again on the Curtiss XP-46. The designers' decision turned out to be half right, since a later engine change would be needed to assure the Mustang's greatness. The British agreed on the proviso that the NA-73 fighter be completed within 120 days. Kindelberger's fighter team actually conceived, designed and constructed the prototype in 102 days and had to wait three weeks longer for Allison to deliver an engine. Test pilot Vance Breese took the unpainted, unmarked NA-73X aloft on its maiden flight on 26 October 1940.

On 29 May 1940, the UK ordered 320 of the yet-unflown NA-73 fighters under an arrangement which called for two examples to be given to the USAAF without cost as the **XP-51**. Much, much later, USAAF chief of staff General H. H. 'Hap' Arnold would acknowledge that it had been an extraordinary error not to have entered the fighter into American squadron service immediately. The first production RAF **Mustang Mk I** (AG345) flew within a year of the prototype and the second (AG346) was first to arrive in the United Kingdom, in

Above: The original NA-73X prototype had gun apertures painted on the wing and USAAC rudder stripes drawn in on issued photographs, but this picture actually shows 41-39, the second true XP-51 for the Army Air Corps. The tenth Mustang to come off the production line, it had the extended carburettor inlet and full armament.

Right: 43-6013 was the 11th P-51A, from the first contract placed by the US Army for the fighter version. It was painted olive drab and (like all Army P-51s, A-36s and P-51As) with the serial painted large in yellow on the fuselage. This version had only four 0.50-in guns, two in each wing, as did the P-51B.

Left: This aircraft was the third P-51, distinguished from the P-51A by having four 20-mm cannon. It was converted as a P-51-1 with two K24 cameras, and is seen in North African November 1942 markings.

Right: This P-51A-10, 43-6199, was the aircraft of Colonel Philip Cochrane, CO of the 1st Air Commando Group at Hailakandi, India, in early 1944. The individual white-stripe marking partly obliterated the serial.

North American P-51 Mustang

In common with the P-38, P-40, P-47 and P-63, the P-51 was tested with skis for possible use in Arctic theatres. The only installation flown was made on the third P-51A, and it was extremely neat, all three units being retractable (unlike those of the P-47). Together with the P-38, this was the only fully successful installation; testing at Grenier Field, New Hampshire, and Ladd Field, Alaska, presented no problems.

November 1941. Although the two XP-51s (41-38/39) were soon flying in US markings, American planners preoccupied with the Lightning and Thunderbolt paid not nearly enough attention to the new design – although, in fact, more than has been generally suggested.

Major improvements

The Mustang was a low-wing single-seater, a sleek, all-metal, stressed-skin fighter not unlike the Messerschmitt Bf 109 but much larger and considerably more advanced. It was one of the first fighters to employ a laminar-flow wing which had its maximum thickness well aft and resulted in greatly reduced drag. It differed from nearly all fighters of its time in having square-cut tips to both wing and tail surfaces. The liquid-cooled engine with the radiator far back under the rear fuselage, as noted, further reduced drag. The big fighter reached 382 mph (615 km/h), a speed not then possible even for the smaller, sleeker Spitfire which carried half as much fuel.

The RAF Mustang Mk I flew its first combat mission on 27 July 1942 and, three weeks later, flew close support for the Dieppe landings. Despite the fighter's superb potential, the limitations of its Allison engine relegated the RAF's 620 Mustang Mk I and **Mk IA**s to ground-attack and reconnaissance duties. Meanwhile, still moving with undue caution, the USAAF ordered 150 **P-51**s armed with four 20-mm wing cannon; 310 **P-51A**s were then ordered, with 1,200-hp (895-kW) V-1710-81 engine, four wing 0.5-in (12.7-mm) machine-guns and underwing racks for two 500-lb (227-kg) bombs or two 150-US gal (568-litre) drop tanks.

In England, the dramatic step which would assure the Mustang's place in history occurred when Rolls-Royce proposed installing the Merlin engine in this excellent airframe. Thought was given to locating the engine behind the cockpit in the manner of the Bell P-39 Airacobra, but a more conventional layout was decided upon. Four RAF Mustangs (AL963, AL975, AM203 and AM208) were equipped

On General H.H. Arnold's initiative, the Mustang was ordered for the USAAF, the first buy being 500 A-36A dive-bombers. The prototype is seen here, with an SBD and barrage balloon, in late 1942. This version introduced the V-1710-87, giving high power at low level, but its main new features were racks for two 500-lb bombs, hydraulically opened airbrakes and armament of six 0.50-in guns, one pair replacing the four 0.30-in of the Mustang I.

North American P-51 Mustang cutaway key

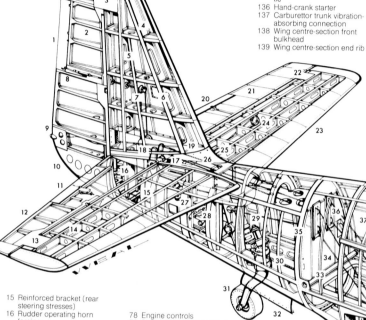

1 Plastic (Phenol fibre) rudder trim tab
2 Rudder frame (fabric covered)
3 Rudder balance
4 Fin front spar
5 Fin structure
6 Access panel
7 Rudder trim-tab actuating drum
8 Rudder trim-tab control link
9 Rear navigation light
10 Rudder metal bottom section
11 Elevator plywood trim tab
12 Starboard elevator frame
13 Elevator balance weight
14 Starboard tailplane structure
15 Reinforced bracket (rear steering stresses)
16 Rudder operating horn forging
17 Elevator operating horns
18 Tab control turnbuckles
19 Fin front spar/fuselage attachment
20 Port elevator tab
21 Fabric-covered elevator
22 Elevator balance weight
23 Port tailplane
24 Tab control drum
25 Tab control drum
26 Elevator cables
27 Tab control access panels
28 Tailwheel steering mechanism
29 Tailwheel
30 Tailwheel leg assembly
31 Forward-retracting steerable tailwheel
32 Tailwheel doors
33 Lifting tube
34 Fuselage aft bulkhead/break point
35 Fuselage break point
36 Control cable pulley brackets
37 Fuselage frames
38 Oxygen bottles
39 Cooling-air exit flap actuating mechanism
40 Rudder cables
41 Fuselage lower longeron
42 Rear tunnel
43 Cooling-air exit flap
44 Coolant radiator assembly
45 Radio and equipment shelf
46 Power supply pack
47 Fuselage upper longeron
48 Radio bay aft bulkhead (plywood)
49 Fuselage stringers
50 SCR-695 radio transmitter-receiver (on upper sliding shelf)
51 Whip aerial
52 Junction box
53 Cockpit aft glazing
54 Canopy track
55 SCR-552 radio transmitter-receiver
56 Battery installation
57 Radiator/supercharger coolant pipes
58 Radiator forward air duct
59 Coolant header tank/radiator pipe
60 Coolant radiator ventral access cover

61 Oil-cooler air inlet door
62 Oil radiator
63 Oil pipes
64 Flap control linkage
65 Wing rear spar/fuselage attachment bracket
66 Crash pylon structure
67 Aileron control linkage
68 Hydraulic hand pump
69 Radio control boxes
70 Pilot's seat
71 Seat suspension frame
72 Pilot's head/back armour
73 Rearward-sliding clear-vision canopy
74 External rear-view mirror
75 Ring and bead gunsight
76 Bullet-proof windshield
77 Gyro gunsight
78 Engine controls
79 Signal-pistol discharge tube
80 Circuit-breaker panel
81 Oxygen regulator
82 Pilot's footrest and seat mounting bracket
83 Control linkage
84 Rudder pedal
85 Tailwheel lock control
86 Wing centre-section
87 Hydraulic reservoir
88 Port wing fuel tank filler point
89 Port Browning 0.5-in guns
90 Ammunition feed chutes
91 Gun-bay access door (raised)
92 Ammunition box troughs
93 Aileron control cables
94 Flap lower skin (Alclad)
95 Aileron profile (internal aerodynamic balance diaphragm)
96 Aileron control drum and mounting bracket
97 Aileron trim-tab control drum
98 Aileron plastic (Phenol fibre trim tab)
99 Port aileron assembly
100 Wing skinning
101 Outer section sub-assembly
102 Port navigation light
103 Port wingtip
104 Leading-edge skin
105 Landing lamp
106 Weapons/stores pylon
107 500 lb (227 kg) bomb
108 Gun ports
109 Gun barrels
110 Detachable cowling panels
111 Firewall/integral armour
112 Oil tank
113 Oil pipes
114 Upper longeron/engine mount attachment
115 Oil-tank metal retaining straps
116 Carburettor
117 Engine bearer assembly

118 Cowling panel frames
119 Engine aftercooler
120 Engine leads
121 1,520 hp Packard V-1650 (R-R Merlin) twelve-cylinder liquid-cooled engine
122 Exhaust fairing panel
123 Stub exhausts
124 Magneto
125 Coolant pipes
126 Cowling forward frame
127 Coolant header tank
128 Armour plate
129 Propeller hub
130 Spinner
131 Hamilton Standard Hydromatic propeller
132 Carburettor air intake, integral with (133)
133 Engine-mount front-frame assembly
134 Intake trunk
135 Engine-mount reinforcing tie
136 Hand-crank starter
137 Carburettor trunk vibration-absorbing connection
138 Wing centre-section front bulkhead
139 Wing centre-section end rib
140 Starboard mainwheel well
141 Wing front spar/fuselage attachment bracket
142 Ventral air intake (radiator and oil cooler)
143 Starboard wing fuel tank
144 Fuel filler point
145 Mainwheel leg mount/pivot
146 Mainwheel leg rib cut-outs
147 Main gear fairing doors
148 Auxiliary fuel tank (plastic/pressed-paper composition, 90 gal/409 litres)
149 Auxiliary fuel tank (metal 62.5 gal/284 litres)
150 27-in smooth-contour mainwheel
151 Axle fork
152 Towing lugs
153 Landing-gear fairing
154 Main-gear shock strut
155 Blast tubes

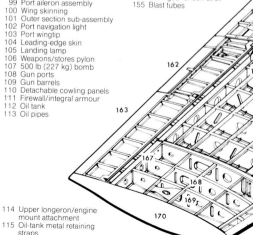

North American P-51 Mustang

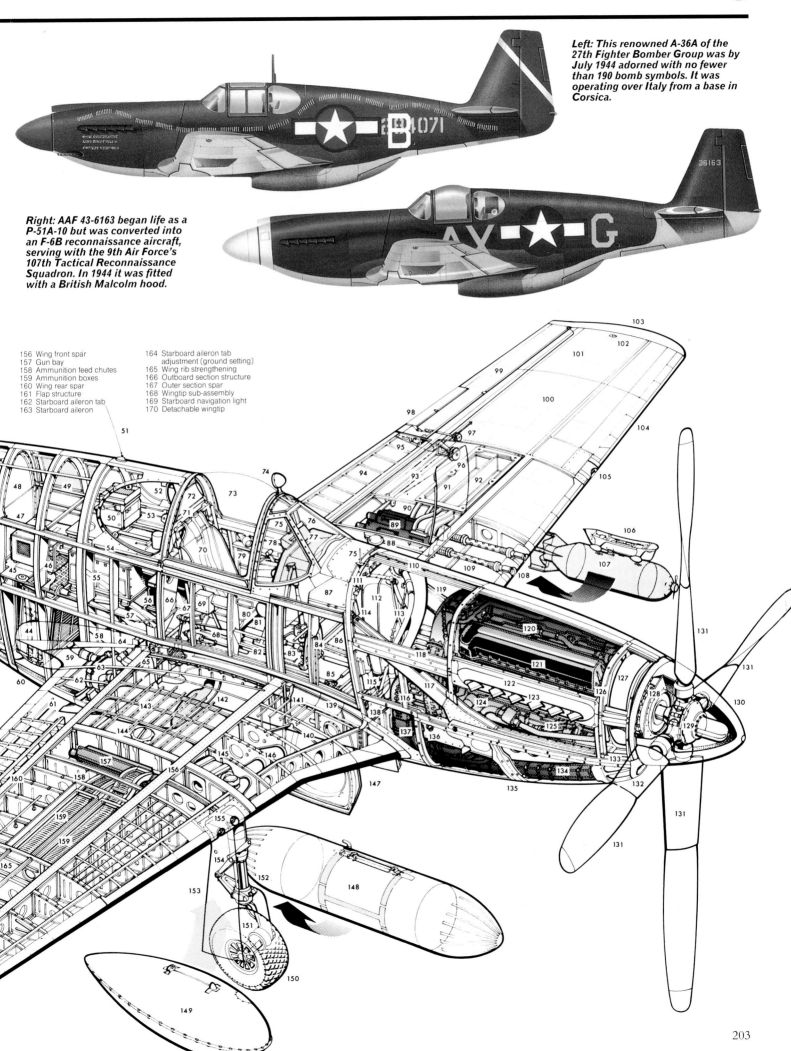

Left: This renowned A-36A of the 27th Fighter Bomber Group was by July 1944 adorned with no fewer than 190 bomb symbols. It was operating over Italy from a base in Corsica.

Right: AAF 43-6163 began life as a P-51A-10 but was converted into an F-6B reconnaissance aircraft, serving with the 9th Air Force's 107th Tactical Reconnaissance Squadron. In 1944 it was fitted with a British Malcolm hood.

156 Wing front spar
157 Gun bay
158 Ammunition feed chutes
159 Ammunition boxes
160 Wing rear spar
161 Flap structure
162 Starboard aileron tab
163 Starboard aileron
164 Starboard aileron tab adjustment (ground setting)
165 Wing rib strengthening
166 Outboard section structure
167 Outer section spar
168 Wingtip sub-assembly
169 Starboard navigation light
170 Detachable wingtip

North American P-51 Mustang

with Merlins and four-bladed propellers and performed so well, exceeding 400 mph (644 km/h), that North American began plans for P-51 variants powered by the 1,520-hp (1134-kW) licence-built Merlin 61, the Packard V-1650-3.

The USAAF ordered 500 Allison-powered **A-36** aircraft, identical to the P-51A but for dive brakes which overstressed the airframe and had to be wired inoperative. The **A-36A** was never really wanted for the attack role, but was used as a device to keep production going while the merits of the basic design were still being argued. To confuse things further, the A-36A was known initially as the **Apache** and later as the **Invader** until the Mustang name stuck. The airplanes were moderately successful in Sicily and southern Italy, and claimed their share of Luftwaffe victims in air-to-air combat despite the 'attack' appellation.

Some P-51s were converted for the photo-reconnaissance role as **F-6A**s. Finally, a Merlin-powered variant, the **XP-51B**, took to the air on 30 November 1942 with Bob Chilton at the controls. The US Army had ordered 2,200 **P-51B**s before that maiden flight. A bit more cantankerous than earlier Mustangs, reliable but not as easy to fly, the P-51B retained a flush pattern framed canopy, as did the **P-51C**, armed with six 0.5-in (12.7-mm) guns. Most Mustangs were to come from North American's Inglewood, California, facility but the P-51C,

During the mid-war years NAA's engineers totally redesigned the P-51 to reduce weight. The last of the lightweight prototypes, and the first powered by a return to the Allison engine, was this XP-51J, first flown by Joe Barton on 23 April 1945. All nose inlets were eliminated, engine air being piped from the radiator duct.

Below: The first of the lightweights was 43-43332, the first of two XP-51Fs powered by the Packard V-1650-7 driving a three-bladed propeller. First flown by Bob Chilton on 14 February 1944, it led to the P-51H.

Above: 43-43335 was the first of two XP-51G lightweights, powered by a Rolls-Royce Merlin RM.14SM (Mk 145) driving a five-bladed Rotol propeller. First flown by Ed Virgin on 10 August 1944, it had an airframe similar to the XP-51F, with a new fuselage and wing, small mainwheels and long teardrop canopy. Armament was four 0.5-in machine-guns.

Right: Changing to the Packard-built Merlin (initially as the V-1650-3) completely altered the powerplant installation. This well-worn P-51B shows the inlet for engine air below the spinner of the 11 ft 2 in Hamilton Standard propeller with four broad blades with root cuffs. Armament of the P-51B was four 0.50-in machine-guns, all in the wings.

Here seen on production test off the California coast, 43-12201 was one of the 400 P-51B1 Mustangs, the first production type with the Merlin engine. In this view the pitot head is prominent, but in later versions it was found that accurate readings could be obtained by a pressure head closer to the wing. The most important future changes were to redesign the armament installation and fit improved types of canopy.

reflecting wartime expansion of the aircraft industry, was produced at the firm's Dallas, Texas, plant.

England to Berlin

The **P-51D** variant first ordered in 1943 introduced the bubble canopy and a dorsal fin to correct stability problems. In later P-51Ds, an 85-US gal (322-litre) fuel cell was added behind the pilot's seat, bringing total fuel capacity to the point where the P-51D could range all the way from England to Berlin, as it did by March 1944 with Lieutenant Colonel Donald L. Blakeslee's 4th Fighter Group. The long-range fighters weaving above massed formations of B-17 and B-24 bombers greatly complicated the Third Reich's air defence burden and, once drop tanks were discarded, could fight on equal or better terms with anything belonging to the Luftwaffe. By 1944, early P-51Bs were operating in Burma, and later machines would range against the Japanese homeland from Ie Shima and Iwo Jima, but it was in Europe where the type excelled. First Lieutenant Urban L. Drew of the 361st Fighter Group illustrated this by shooting down two Messerschmitt Me 262 jet fighters.

Following **F-6B** and **F-6C** variants of flush-canopy Mustangs, good results were obtained with the bubble-canopy **F-6D** tactical reconnaissance craft, 136 of which were converted from P-51D standard at Dallas with hatches for oblique and vertical cameras in the rear fuselage and additional radio (including DF) gear. Although the

earlier Malcolm hood which improved visibility on the **Mustang Mk II** and **Mk III** was also employed by the USAAF, the bubble canopy became the accepted feature and a few so-equipped P-51Ds operated in British service as the **Mustang Mk IV**. One hundred P-51D airframes were assembled in Australia by Commonwealth, and 226 more were manufactured there. Ten USAAF machines were converted to two-seat trainers as the **TP-51D**.

Minimising weight

The P-51E designation was not used. Three **XP-51F** airframes (4343332/43334) came from Inglewood as the first lightweight Mustang, with the V-1650-7 Merlin but with major internal redesign which lowered maximum take-off weight to 9,060 lb (4110 kg) and introduced new wing and landing-gear features. One of these (FR409) reached the RAF as the **Mustang Mk V**. Two further lightweight Mustang test ships, designated **XP-51G** (43-43335/43336), were powered by the 1,500-hp (1119-kW) Rolls-Royce Merlin 145 with an unusual Rotol five-bladed propeller. The XP-51G grossed a mere 8,765 lb (3975 kg) and reached a top speed of 468 mph (753 km/h) in level flight. One (FR410) was flown by the RAF. These efforts to

Right: 43-12173 was the 81st P-51B-1, and was included in the first batch of Merlin Mustangs to arrive in England in October 1943. It served with the 355th Fighter Squadron, 354th Fighter Group, the first group to take the P-51B into action. Note the 75-US gal drop tanks.

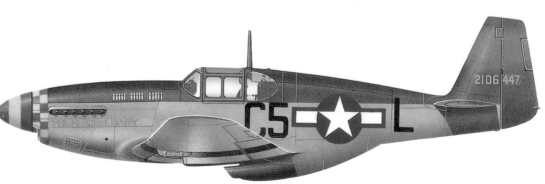

Left: 'Shoo Shoo Baby', title of a 1944 hit tune, served with the 364th Fighter Squadron, 357th Fighter Group, based at Leiston, Suffolk. Several fighter groups retained some olive drab into the 'unpainted' era.

North American P-51 Mustang

lower the Mustang's weight culminated in the taller-tailed production **P-51H**, 555 of which were built. The P-51H had a shorter bubble canopy, a four-bladed Aeroproducts propeller, and an increase in overall length to 33 ft 4 in (10.16 m). One (KN987) was evaluated in the UK. The P-51H did get into combat in World War II, a few flying missions from the Philippines before VJ-Day.

Two experimental **XP-51Js** (44-76027/76028) were similar to the lightweight XP-51F but for the 1,500-hp (1119-kW) Allison V-1710119. The **P-51K** was the Dallas-built production equivalent of Inglewood's P-51D, differing only in having an Aeroprop propeller, and 1,500 were delivered during the war years, 163 performing the reconnaissance role as the **F-6K**. The **P-51L** was a production machine cancelled at the war's end, and the sole **P-51M** (45-11743)

In the Pacific theatre, P-51Ds of a USAAF fighter group escort a special B-29 – possibly 'Enola Gay' or 'Bock's Car' – wearing the insignia of the 509th Group. The World War II missions were unescorted, but P-51Ds did escort B-29s during the Korean War of 1950-53.

Below. Whereas an early P-51 was transferred to the Navy as BuNo. 57987, P-51D-5-NA no. 44-14017 was fitted with a hook for deck trials aboard the escort carrier Shangri-La (CV38), flown by Lt R.M. Elder USN. It never left the AAF, and later it became the ETF-51D with a P-51H tail.

Though familiar, this is one of the best photographs ever taken of P-51s on an operational flight in World War II. Three of the aircraft, 44-13926, 13410 and 13568, are all Inglewood-built P-51D-5s, 13926 having the dorsal fin which was added to many P-51Ds built without it. Furthest away is P-51B-15 42-106811, with the original canopy. They flew with the 8th Air Force's 375th Fighter Squadron, 361st Fighter Group.

was another lightweight variant powered by a 1,400-hp (1044-kW) V-1650-9A.

The P-51 was essential to wartime victory. About 40 USAAF fighter groups and 31 RAF squadrons operated the type; the P-51 was also among the most widely used post-war fighters. The P-51D fought in Israel's war for independence and in China on both sides, an example being on display today in a Beijing museum. The Korean War of 1950-53 brought the type back into combat in US markings, Mustangs serving the USAF and Air National Guard to the end of the 1950s. Hundreds of flyable examples remain in the world today. The first USAAF machine, XP-51 41-38, was prudently saved for the US Air Force Museum at Dayton, Ohio.

"Getting a fully-loaded Mustang off the ground on a long-range mission was one bear of a job," says former First Lieutenant David Jones of the USAAF 4th Fighter Group. The P-51D loaded with maximum fuel, including drop tanks, tipped the scales at 11,600 lb (5262 kg) and "could scarcely be handled until you'd burned an initial amount of that fuel away," says Jones.

The high risk of take-off on a maximum escort mission to Berlin is dramatised in a key crash scene in Len Deighton's novel *Goodbye Mickey Mouse*. Jones and Deighton, members of Mustang International, a private group devoted to P-51 history and preservation today, agree that, however beautiful, the aircraft was difficult to get going and suffered from serious lateral stability problems. "The pilot had to be constantly alert to the need for opposite rudder to prevent a skid or

P-51 D-15-NA no. 44-15459, 'American Beauty', is seen serving with the 308th Fighter Squadron, 31st Fighter Group, of the 15th Air Force in the Mediterranean theatre, ranging widely over southern Europe. Code letters of the 31st's three squadrons (MX, HL and WZ) duplicated those of the 8th Air Force's 78th Fighter Group.

sideslip which could throw the P-51 into a spin." A dorsal fin corrected this tendency, but reduced manoeuvrability in combat. "But when you'd pickled off the drop tanks," says Jones, "you were on equal terms with the other guy. The Mustang could manoeuvre with and outgun even the latest models of the Focke-Wulf Fw 190. With a teardrop-shaped canopy, you had super visibility and could spot the other guy first." Lieutenant Urban Drew, air ace and killer of Messerschmitt Me 262 jets, flew both the P-51D and the later P-47N. Drew says that he greatly preferred the P-51D and wished that more had been available in the Pacific, where he flew after his European successes.

Best armament

Colonel Hubert A. ('Hub') Zemke, the only man to command P-38, P-47 and P-51 fighter groups in Europe, considered the P-51D the best air-to-air fighter of the three below 25,000 ft (7620 m) and found its armament adequate, although he preferred the Thunderbolt for its ruggedness, its eight 0.5-in (12.7-mm) guns (compared with six on the P-51D) and its better performance at higher altitude. Captain Henry Lawrence of the all-black 332nd Fighter Group had only the P-39 to compare with the P-51D, and considered the Mustang "as fine a flying machine as men could make, most of the bugs worked out of it by late in the war." On 24 March 1945, escorting bombers to

Several features, particularly the large port in the rear fuselage for a reconnaissance camera, identify 44-84540 as an F-6D-25-NT, a Dallas-built photo ship. Usually two K24 or one K17 and one K22 cameras were installed. Note also the direction-finding loop antenna immediately to the rear of the radio mast, which in these aircraft did secure the front end of the wire antenna from the fin. In P-51Ds and Ks the wire passed through the canopy.

Left: 42-106942 was an Inglewood-built P-51B-15, later fitted as shown with the Malcolm sliding hood. It served with the 8th Air Force's 374th Fighter Squadron, 361st Fighter Group.

Right: 'Bonnie B' was an early P-51B-1-NA, later modified with not only the bulged Malcolm hood but also (uncommon on a P-51B) a dorsal fin. It served with the 353rd Fighter Squadron of the 354th Fighter Group, the first to fly Merlin-Mustangs.

North American P-51D
361st Fighter Group
8th Air Force
Bottisham
Cambridgeshire
UK, 1944

The Mustang was designed very quickly to meet a British requirement for a fighter for service in Europe, and its outstanding qualities made it the leading US fighter in the European theatre during the final months of the war. Rolled out in 117 days and first flown on 26 October 1940, the P-51 combined every contemporary aerodynamic, structural and systems advance, the chief results of which were exceptional internal fuel capacity and low drag. It passed all tests satisfactorily and was put into production before the end of 1940. This aircraft's fighter group began to arrive in the UK in May 1944. Bottisham's Mustangs were extremely busy during that summer, operating mainly over France. When the A-20 fighter group left Little Walden in Essex in September the 361st moved to this better-equipped station, where its three squadrons, Nos 374, 375 and 376, continued their escort and ground support operations until early 1945 when they were relocated to St Dizier in France, returning to Little Walden in April.

Canopy
The P-51B had the 'birdcage' type of cockpit cover, with a restricted rear view. P-51Bs and Cs delivered to the RAF had a modification undertaken in the UK, introducing a Malcolm backward-sliding bulged cockpit head. A further canopy change distinguished the P-51D. The fuselage was redesigned with a lowered rear decking, and a large one-piece rearward-sliding 'bubble' canopy fitted to improve the rearward view. The windshield incorporated an optically-flat five-ply laminated bulletproof glass front panel, with safety glass side panels.

Serial number
USAAF serials were presented on the fin. The first digit was the last digit of the Fiscal Year of procurement (in this case, 1944). The next digits were the individual serial number of the aircraft.

Markings
All Mustangs operated by the 361st Fighter Group had yellow spinners and yellow around the machine-gun housing. The front part of the engine cowling was also yellow. Upper surfaces were finished in light olive drab with light grey undersides. This aircraft has invasion stripes on the undersurfaces of the wing, but not on the top, as was more usual, together with fuselage stripes under the national insignia.

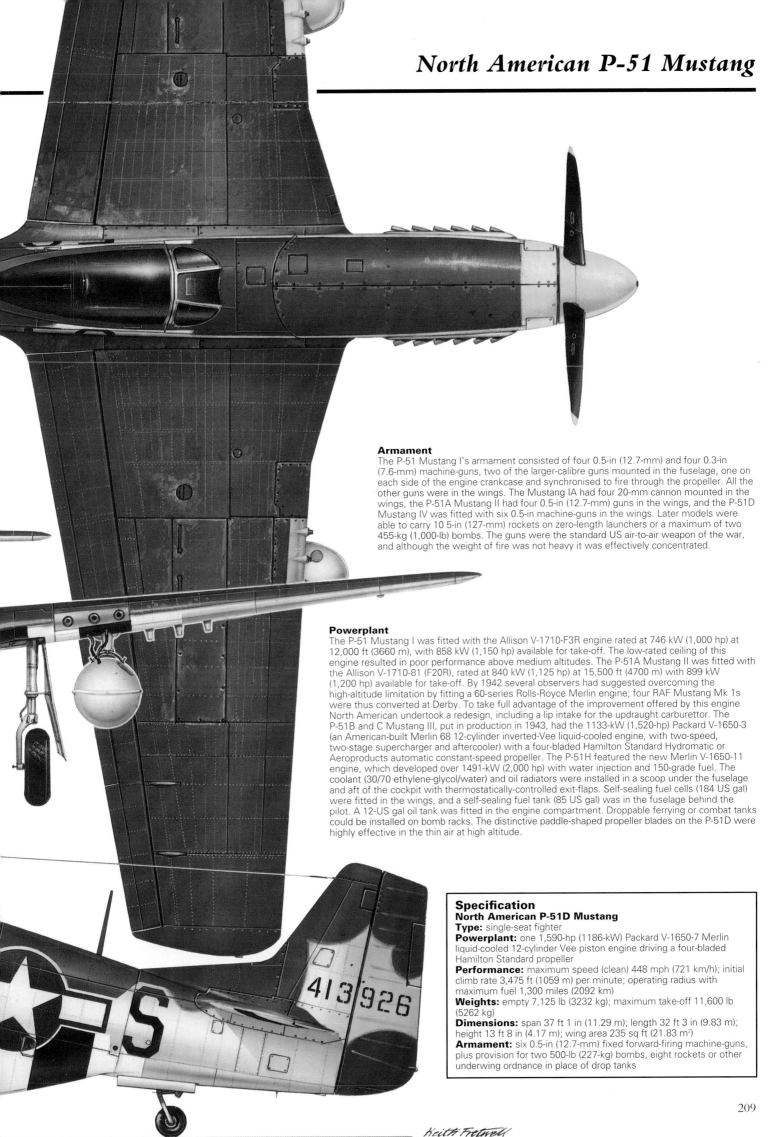

North American P-51 Mustang

Armament
The P-51 Mustang I's armament consisted of four 0.5-in (12.7-mm) and four 0.3-in (7.6-mm) machine-guns, two of the larger-calibre guns mounted in the fuselage, one on each side of the engine crankcase and synchronised to fire through the propeller. All the other guns were in the wings. The Mustang IA had four 20-mm cannon mounted in the wings, the P-51A Mustang II had four 0.5-in (12.7-mm) guns in the wings, and the P-51D Mustang IV was fitted with six 0.5-in machine-guns in the wings. Later models were able to carry 10 5-in (127-mm) rockets on zero-length launchers or a maximum of two 455-kg (1,000-lb) bombs. The guns were the standard US air-to-air weapon of the war, and although the weight of fire was not heavy it was effectively concentrated.

Powerplant
The P-51 Mustang I was fitted with the Allison V-1710-F3R engine rated at 746 kW (1,000 hp) at 12,000 ft (3660 m), with 858 kW (1,150 hp) available for take-off. The low-rated ceiling of this engine resulted in poor performance above medium altitudes. The P-51A Mustang II was fitted with the Allison V-1710-81 (F20R), rated at 840 kW (1,125 hp) at 15,500 ft (4700 m) with 899 kW (1,200 hp) available for take-off. By 1942 several observers had suggested overcoming the high-altitude limitation by fitting a 60-series Rolls-Royce Merlin engine; four RAF Mustang Mk 1s were thus converted at Derby. To take full advantage of the improvement offered by this engine North American undertook a redesign, including a lip intake for the updraught carburettor. The P-51B and C Mustang III, put in production in 1943, had the 1133-kW (1,520-hp) Packard V-1650-3 (an American-built Merlin 68 12-cylinder inverted-Vee liquid-cooled engine, with two-speed, two-stage supercharger and aftercooler) with a four-bladed Hamilton Standard Hydromatic or Aeroproducts automatic constant-speed propeller. The P-51H featured the new Merlin V-1650-11 engine, which developed over 1491-kW (2,000 hp) with water injection and 150-grade fuel. The coolant (30/70 ethylene-glycol/water) and oil radiators were installed in a scoop under the fuselage and aft of the cockpit with thermostatically-controlled exit-flaps. Self-sealing fuel cells (184 US gal) were fitted in the wings, and a self-sealing fuel tank (85 US gal) was in the fuselage behind the pilot. A 12-US gal oil tank was fitted in the engine compartment. Droppable ferrying or combat tanks could be installed on bomb racks. The distinctive paddle-shaped propeller blades on the P-51D were highly effective in the thin air at high altitude.

Specification
North American P-51D Mustang
Type: single-seat fighter
Powerplant: one 1,590-hp (1186-kW) Packard V-1650-7 Merlin liquid-cooled 12-cylinder Vee piston engine driving a four-bladed Hamilton Standard propeller
Performance: maximum speed (clean) 448 mph (721 km/h); initial climb rate 3,475 ft (1059 m) per minute; operating radius with maximum fuel 1,300 miles (2092 km)
Weights: empty 7,125 lb (3232 kg); maximum take-off 11,600 lb (5262 kg)
Dimensions: span 37 ft 1 in (11.29 m); length 32 ft 3 in (9.83 m); height 13 ft 8 in (4.17 m); wing area 235 sq ft (21.83 m²)
Armament: six 0.5-in (12.7-mm) fixed forward-firing machine-guns, plus provision for two 500-lb (227-kg) bombs, eight rockets or other underwing ordnance in place of drop tanks

Keith Fretwell

North American P-51 Mustang

Above: 24 swastikas, each denoting a confirmed kill, adorned the P-51D-20-NA of Lt Col G.T. Eagleston, CO of the 354th Fighter Group. This was all the more remarkable since the 9th Air Force's two P-51 groups specialised in ground attack.

Below: The 325th FG in Italy used code numbers only, and overpainted their serial numbers by a yellow/black chequerboard. This aircraft served with the group's 317th FS. An earlier '30' had been a P-51B Dorothy II.

Berlin, Lawrence joined the ranks of pilots who have shot down Me 262 jet fighters.

Although the lightweight P-51H did see limited combat in the Pacific, contrary to most published reports, the best Japanese fighters were no longer available as competitors by late 1945. Post-war tests showed the P-51H to be faster and more manoeuvrable than the Mitsubishi A6M5 Zero in all performance regimes. The P-51H had been relegated to second-line duties by 1950, however, and it was the more popular P-51D which went to war in Korea. The Mustang's 0.5-in (12.7-mm) guns and 5-in (127-mm) high-velocity aircraft rockets (HVAR) were of marginal effectiveness against North Korean T-34 tanks, but in the air P-51Ds cleared the skies with remarkable ease of North Korean Yakovlev fighters. Major Dean Hess, who instructed Republic of Korea Air Force (RoKAF) pilots in the P-51D, said that "the Mustang was remarkably easy for an inexperienced pilot to learn how to fly."

On 7 November 1950, Captain Howard Tanner of the 36th Fighter-Bomber Squadron at Kimpo AB, Korea, was flying a 'sweep' near the Yalu River when three MiG-15 jet fighters tore into his formation of F-51D Mustangs (as the P-51D had been redesignated on 1 June 1948). A fourth MiG locked onto Tanner and began firing from too far out. Tanner was able to turn inside the MiG, pull lead,

and strike the newer, faster jet. Surprised by the American's aggressiveness, the MiGs pulled away, but then re-engaged. Tanner and his wingmen scored further hits on MiGs without themselves sustaining damage, although they could not confirm any certain kills. This was early evidence of the coming Chinese entry into the Korean War, a conflict that was waged by another North American product, the F-86 Sabre.

Last of the production Mustangs, the P-51H was perhaps the fastest piston-engined aircraft ever produced in large numbers (555 built, 1,445 incomplete or never started), with a maximum speed of 487 mph at 25,000 ft. An unusual feature was a twin antenna mast.

P-51 Mustang variants

NA-73X: single privately funded prototype with 1,100-hp Allison V-1710-39 engine; provision for four 0.5-in and four 0.3-in guns but armament not fitted

NA-73 Mustang Mk I: first production batch of 320 aircraft for RAF; 1,150-hp V-1710-F3R engine; four 0.5-in and four 0.303-in guns fitted; many fitted with oblique cameras for reconnaissance role

XP-51: two early production (Nos 4 and 10) NA-73 aircraft for US evaluation

NA-83 Mustang Mk I: second production batch (300) for RAF with minor changes; one aircraft later fitted with Merlin 61 and two fitted with Merlin 65 as Mustang Mk X; one armed with two 40-mm Vickers 'S' cannon

NA-91 Mustang IA: 93 aircraft supplied by Lend-Lease to RAF (from batch of 150) with four 20-mm cannon in wings

P-51 (NA-91): remainder of Mustang IA batch (57 aircraft) retained by US after Pearl Harbor; all subsequently fitted with two K24 cameras as P-51-1s but later redesignated F-6A

P-51A (NA-99): similar to P-51 but with nose guns deleted, leaving four 0.5-in wing guns; pylons for two 500-lb bombs but no divebrakes;

powered by Allison V-1710-81 (export V-1710-F20R); 310 built of which 50 passed to RAF as Mustang Mk II

XP-51B (NA-101): two P-51s re-engined with Packard V-1650-3 Merlin of 1,450 hp; armament removed; originally designated XP-78

P-51B (NA-102/104): production model of XP-51B with 1,450-hp V-1650-3 (V-1650-7 in later production) and four 0.5-in wing guns; last 550 aircraft also had 75-US gal rear fuselage tank, a feature retrofitted to some earlier machines; NA-104 had wing hardpoints strengthened for 1,000-lb bombs; 1,988 built, of which 25 passed to RAF as Mustang Mk III

P-51C (NA-103/111): similar to P-51B but built at Dallas plant rather than Inglewood; 1,750 built

XP-51D (NA-106): two P-51B airframes completed with teardrop canopy and cut-down rear fuselage and provision for six 0.5-in wing guns

P-51D (NA-109/111/122/124): production version of XP-51D with 1,490-hp V-1650-7 Merlin and six wing guns; all but initial production fitted with dorsal fin, a feature retrofitted to many aircraft (including Bs and Cs); from Block 25 provision for four 5-in rockets added; production total 6,502 (Inglewood) and 1,454 (Dallas) of which 280 to RAF as Mustang Mk IV; redesignated F-51D in 1948

FP-51D: post-war redesignation of

F-6D, redesignated RF-51D in 1948

TP-51D: two-seat conversion trainer with second seat in place of radio equipment; armament reduced to four guns; 10 built as such by Dallas, followed by several conversions; redesignated TF-51D in 1948

ETF-51D: single TF-51D converted for carrier landing trials

P-51E: designation reserved for Dallas-built P-51D but not taken up, aircraft being completed as P-51D-NT

XP-51F (NA-105): lightweight model powered by V-1650-7 Merlin; new low-drag wing with straight leading edge and other modifications; three completed, of which one passed to RAF

XP-61G (NA-105): two aircraft similar to XP-51F with 1,675-hp Merlin 145M engines and five-bladed propellers; one to RAF

P-51H (NA-126/129): lightweight version based on XP-51F but with longer fuselage and taller fin; powered by V-1650-9A engine offering 1,380 hp for take-off and 2,218 hp at altitude with water injection; six 0.5-in wing guns; 555 completed (NA-126) but 1,445 NA-129s cancelled

XP-51J (NA-105): two experimental aircraft similar to XP-51F but powered by 1,720-hp Allison V-1710-119 engines

P-51K (NA-111): Dallas-built version of P-51D with Aeroproducts

propeller of smaller diameter; Block 10 onwards introduced four stubs for 5-in rockets; 1,500 built of which 594 to RAF as Mustang Mk IVA; redesignated F-51K in 1948

P-51L (NA-129): intended production version based on P-51H with V-1650-11 engine; 1,700 cancelled

P-51M (NA-124): Dallas-built version of P-51H with V-1650-9A; only one aircraft completed with an order for 1,628 cancelled

A-36A (NA-97) Apache: dive bomber version with six 0.5-in wing guns, divebrakes and pylons for two 500-lb bombs; Allison V-1710-87 engine; 500 built, of which three supplied to RAF for evaluation

F-6A: 57 P-51s fitted with two K24 cameras in fuselage; armament retained

F-6B: 35 P-51As fitted with two K24 cameras; armament retained

F-6C: tactical reconnaissance version of P-51B/C with either two K24 cameras or one K17 and one K22; 71 P-51Bs and 20 P-51Cs converted

F-6D: 136 P-51Ds fitted with rear fuselage cameras; several further conversions made from P-51Ds; redesignated FP-51D and then RF-51D; some converted to two-seat configuration designated TRF-51D

F-6K: 163 P-51Ks completed with camera installation; subsequently redesignated FP-51K and then RF-51K

North American P-64

The **P-64** designation falls out of chronological order and belongs to a North American product the USAAC never intended to use. The company **Model NA-50A**, ordered by Siam (Thailand) on 30 December 1939, was little more than a single-seat pursuit ship patterned after the Harvard trainer and developed from the NA-50 used by Peru. The six examples of this strictly export aircraft were built at Inglewood and painted in Siamese markings, and were en route to Siam when the US Army confiscated them, removed the armament, and assigned them to training duties at Luke Field, Arizona. A widely-published report that the Siam-bound aircraft were caught at Pearl Harbor during the 7

The P-64 was North American's only fighter design before they went on to produce the Mustang. This example is parked among Valiants.

December 1941 Japanese attack is inaccurate; the NA-50As were apparently embargoed in October 1940 and a camouflaged example in USAAF markings was noted at Luke AFB as early as 16 September 1941.

Never really a fighter in USAAF service, the six P-64s were essentially base 'hacks' and used for liaison duties without weapons. The aircraft were allocated serial numbers 41-19082/19087), but these may not have been taken up.

Specification
Type: single-seat trainer
Powerplant: one 870-hp (648-kW) Wright R-1820-77 air-cooled nine-cylinder radial piston engine driving a three-bladed propeller
Performance: maximum speed 270 mph (434 km/h) at 8,700 ft (2652 m); initial climb rate 1,200 ft (366 m) per minute; service ceiling 14,000 ft (4267 m); range 860 miles (1384 km)
Weights: empty 4,660 lb (2113 kg); maximum take-off 5,990 lb (2717 kg)
Dimensions: span 37 ft 3 in (11.35 m); length 27 ft 0 in (8.23 m); height 9 ft 0 in (2.74 m); wing area 228 sq ft (21.18 m²)
Armament: none

North American P-82 Twin Mustang

The North American P-82 Twin Mustang was not, as is often stated, two P-51 aircraft joined to a single wing. Rather, the P-82 was a virtually new design, ultimately to be powered by twin 1,600-hp (1193-kW) Allison V-1716-143/145 piston engines, using the twin-boom configuration to achieve long range and good endurance. Conceived as early as 1943 for the Pacific war where pilots often spent six to eight hours in their cockpits on maximum-distance missions, the two-man P-82 was intended to provide a navigator who, while not equipped with full flight controls, could 'spell' the pilot for brief periods. The two booms or 'fuselages', although based on the XP-51F, were in fact entirely new structures. The pilot was located on the port side of the aircraft. The first of two **XP-82** aircraft (44-83887/83888) first flew on 15 April 1945, powered by Merlin engines.

These were followed by the sole **XP-82A**, which introduced the Allison powerplant. Testing of the three prototypes led to a USAAF order for 500 Merlin-powered **P-82B** fighters, but only 20 had been built when the war ended. Two of this number were converted as night-fighters designated **P-82C** and **P-82D**, with SCR-720 and APS-4 radar respectively. Successful trials with the night-fighters led to orders for 100 **F-82E** day escort fighters, 100 **F-82F** night-fighters with SCR 720 radar, and 50 **F-82G** night-fighters with APS-4 radar. The last version to enter

service was the **F-82H**, a winterised variant for service in Alaska. By the end of 1949 the Twin Mustang was in wide operational use, its night-fighter variants having replaced the Northrop F-61 Black Widow.

Specification
North American F-82G
Type: two-seat fighter
Powerplant: two 1,600-hp (1193-kW) Allison V-1710-143/145 liquid-cooled 12-cylinder Vee piston engines driving four-bladed propellers
Performance: maximum speed 461 mph (742 km/h) at 21,000 ft (6401 m); initial climb rate 3,770 ft (1149 m) per minute; service ceiling 38,900 ft (11857 m); range 2,240 miles (3605 km)
Weights: empty 15,997 lb (7256 kg); maximum take-off 25,591 lb (11608 kg)
Dimensions: span 51 ft 3 in (15.62 m); length 42 ft 5 in (12.93 m); height 13 ft 10 in (4.22 m); wing area 408 sq ft (37.9 m²)

AAF 44-83887 was the second of the two XP-82 prototypes. The post-war production versions were powered by the Allison V-1710 engine.

Armament: six 0.5-in (12.7-mm) fixed forward-firing wing machine-guns, plus provision for up to four 1,000-lb (454-kg) bombs or four auxiliary fuel tanks on underwing racks

Northrop A-13/16/17/33

Northrop used the Gamma transport as the basis of a private-venture design for a light attack bomber, identifying this as the Northrop Gamma 2C which, powered by a 735-hp (548-kW) Wright SR-1820F radial engine, was acquired for evaluation by the US Army Air Corps in June 1934 under the designation **YA-13**. Subsequently re-engined with a 950-hp (708-kW) Pratt & Whitney R-1830 Twin Wasp, this aircraft was redesignated **XA-16** (Northrop Gamma 2F). Following tests of the YA-13 and XA-16, Northrop received a $2 million contract for 110 attack bombers designated **A-17**, but because testing of the XA-16 had shown that the aircraft was overpowered, the Gamma 2F was re-engined with a 750-hp (559-kW) Pratt & Whitney R-1535 Twin Wasp Junior serving as the prototype for the A-17. Following the incorporation of several other modifications, the first of 109 production A-17 aircraft was delivered in December 1935. A contract was received in the same month for an improved **A-17A**, introducing retractable tailwheel landing gear and the 825-hp (615-kW) Pratt & Whitney R-1535-13 engine. Some 129 were built, initially by Northrop, but in 1937 Douglas acquired the remaining 49 per cent of

Northrop Corporation's stock, and it was the Douglas Company which completed production of these aircraft. Of the total, 93 served with the USAAC for only 18 months and were returned to Douglas for sale to the UK and France. The Royal Air Force received 60, designating them **Nomad Mk I**, and all were transferred to the South African Air Force. Douglas also built this aircraft for export under the designation **Douglas Model 8A**, supplying them to Argentina, Iraq, the Netherlands and Norway. A batch of 34 **Model**

8A-5 aircraft was also built for Peru, 31 of them being commandeered by the US Army Air Force in early 1942 for use in an attack role. Armed with six 0.3-in (7.62-mm) machine-guns and able to carry up to 1,800 lb (816 kg) of bombs, all were used in a training role under the designation **A-33**.

Specification
Northrop A-17A
Type: two-seat attack aircraft
Powerplant: one 825-hp (615-kW) Pratt & Whitney R-1535-13 radial piston engine
Performance: maximum speed 220

Apparently photographed at Boeing Field, Seattle, this A-17AS (the three-seat modification) wears the 'Capitol' insignia of the 14th Bomb Squadron, usually based at Bollina Field, DC.

mph (354 km/h); service ceiling 19,400 ft (5915 m); range 730 miles (1175 km)
Weights: empty 5,106 lb (2316 kg); maximum take-off 7,543 lb (3421 kg)
Dimensions: span 47 ft 9 in (14.55 m); length 31 ft 8 in (9.65 m); height 12 ft 0 in (3.66 m); wing area 362.0 sq ft (33.63 m²)
Armament: five 0.3-in (7.62-mm) machine-guns (four forward-firing and one on a trainable mount in rear cockpit), plus four 100-lb (45-kg) bombs

Northrop XP-56

The Northrop **XP-56**, informally called 'Black Bullet', was the third of the pusher fighters conceived in 1940 (together with the Vultee XP-54 and Curtiss XP-55). First flown on 6 September 1943 in secrecy at Muroc Dry Lake, California, with John Myers as pilot, the

XP-56 was the only one of the three designs to employ contra-rotating propellers. It was also the first true flying wing tested by the US Army, and the first of many flying wing designs to come from Northrop's facility at Hawthorne, California.

The US Army ordered two

XP-56 airframes (41-786 and 42-38353) and, after initially considering other powerplants, had them built with the 2,000-hp (1491-kW) Pratt & Whitney R-2800-9 air-cooled radial. The aircraft flew well despite its revolutionary configuration, but proved unable to manoeuvre effectively in a dogfight situation. The unpressurised cockpit was positioned immediately ahead of the engine and posed interesting problems to any pilot thinking of bailing out with two three-bladed Curtiss Electric contra-rotating airscrews behind him.

After the all-silver first XP-56 was wrecked in a mishap which injured Myers, the camouflaged second ship flew on 23 March 1944 at Hawthorne with Harry

Crosby at the controls. This machine had a greatly enlarged dorsal vertical stabiliser (not actually a rudder, since steering was done from blown-air jets at the wingtips) to improve yaw tendencies. The machine proved underpowered and, because it was nose-heavy, difficult to handle during the take-off roll.

Specification
Northrop XP-56
Type: single-seat fighter
Powerplant: one 2,000-hp (1491-kW) Pratt & Whitney R-2800-9 air-cooled 18-cylinder radial piston engine driving two three-bladed Curtiss Electric contra-rotating propellers
Performance: maximum speed 465 mph (748 km/h) at 25,000 ft (7620 m); climb to 20,000 ft (6096 m) in 7.2 minutes; service ceiling 33,800 ft (10302 m); range 660 miles (1062 km)
Weights: empty 8,700 lb (3946 kg); maximum take-off 12,143 lb (5508 kg)
Dimensions: span 43 ft 7 in (13.28 m); length 27 ft 7 in (8.41 m); height 11 ft 0 in (3.35 m); wing area 307 sq ft (28.52 m²)
Armament: two 20-mm cannon and four 0.5-in (12.7-mm) machine-guns planned but not installed

Visibly different from the second prototype, Army 41-786 runs up its Double Wasp and contraprops at Muroc in 1943. It proved a disappointment.

Northrop P-61 Black Widow

If the RAF had had the **Northrop Black Widow** in 1940, the story of the night Blitz would have been very different. In that particular conflict the giant Northrop night-fighter would have been able to destroy every aircraft onto which it was vectored. Unfortunately, it did not reach the squadrons until almost four years later, and by that time not only were hostile aircraft becoming scarce (both over Europe and in the Pacific) but they had far higher performance and were elusive enough to make victories scarcer still. Nevertheless, the P-61 deserves its place in history as the first aircraft ever designed (as distinct from being modified) for use as a night-fighter, using radar and all other electronic devices.

The US Army Air Corps had previously used primitive night-fighters, starting with the Curtiss PN-1 of 1921, and in 1940 was busy with a programme to convert A-20 bombers into P-70 night-fighters, keeping a close eye on the RAF's similar conversion into Havocs. The USAAC knew about the British development of AI (airborne interception) radar, and in fact 60 sets of this radar were shortly supplied for incorporation in the production P-70s, even though the USA was strictly neutral. Even more significantly, the Tizard mission sent to the USA in August 1940 gave preliminary details of the most important single technical secret then possessed by the UK: the cavity magnetron. This totally new device was the key to radars operating on centimetric wavelengths (previous radars had wavelengths measured in metres) and enabled H2S bombing radar, and also superior AI radars for fighters, to be created. The amazing disclosure was made on 28 September 1940, and on 18 October the USA decided to go ahead at top priority with a world-beating AI radar and a fighter to carry it.

Radar success

The radar was assigned to a large team headed by the Radiation Laboratory, a specially created subsidiary of the Massachusetts Institute of Technology (MIT). The work went ahead with a joint US/UK team, with astonishing rapidity. Two days ahead of the 'impossible' schedule, on 4 January 1941, the first microwave radar built in the USA was displaying a picture of the Boston skyline across the Charles River from an MIT roof. It had one of the vital British (GEC) magnetrons, a Westinghouse pulser, Sperry power-driven dish aerial, fixed receiver aerial, Bell Telephone Laboratories receiver (with IF unit by RCA) and General Electric oscilloscope display. It first flew in a Douglas B-18A on 10 March and eventually matured as the production SCR-720, which was also used in many British night-fighters as the AI.Mk X.

First flown on 26 May 1942, the XP-61 was fitted with a mock-up of the dorsal barbette, which was designed to accommodate four 0.5-in (12.7-mm) machine-guns and gave the night-fighting Black Widow a formidable punch.

While the challenging radar needed the resources of all the chief companies in the emergent US electronics industry, the aircraft to carry it, which was launched three days later in a letter of 21 October 1940, was assigned to Northrop Aircraft of Hawthorne (Los Angeles) in California. Northrop lacked nothing in skill and dedication, but had never had a major production programme, nor anything in such an exceptionally difficult field. In October 1940 the US Army Air Corps mission to the UK, headed by General Emmons, had just returned to Washington. Among a host of recommendations it urged development of a purpose-designed night-fighter, and the arrival of the British magnetron was a large bonus. With the benefit of hindsight, while SCR-720 was unquestionably a war weapon of the very highest importance which the RAF was glad to use in post-war night-fighters into the 1950s, the 'clean sheet of paper' night-fighter arrived late and was no better than a modification of (for example) the Douglas A-26 Invader for the same purpose. Indeed, the considered opinion of many experts, in both the RAF and USAF, was that it offered little that the compromised lash-up night-fighter versions of the Bristol Beaufighter and de Havilland Mosquito had not been doing since 1941. Many who flew both the British aircraft and Black Widows considered the

The 23rd production P-61A flies over the environs of Los Angeles, in a somewhat faded olive drab and neutral grey finish. This was used for a few early aircraft, before the more appropriate overall black was adopted for the night-fighting role.

Northrop P-61 Black Widow

This late-production P-61B-20-NO, in high-gloss black finish, carries four drop tanks, which could enhance internal fuel capacity by as much as 1,240 US gal (4692 litres) and provided for a range of up to 1,350 miles (2172 km).

The second YP-61, delivered to the USAAF in the autumn of 1943, had two guns removed from the dorsal barbette after early flight trials revealed that serious buffet occurred when all four guns in the barbette were elevated or rotated in azimuth.

P-61 a first-class aircraft whose only fault was the burden it placed on everyone concerned with maintaining and flying it.

It was not meant to be like that. John K. Northrop expected to get into production inside a year. His right-hand man on design was Walt Cerny, who came with him to present the outline NS-8A proposal to a small group under Dr William Sears, who came on the payroll in 1942. From the start the US Army insisted on a crew of three, exceptional all-round view and armament including a power-driven turret or turrets. The original scheme comprised a central nacelle with twin-boom tail, and three crew in a row: pilot, radar/gunner above and behind and thus able to use a gunsight directly ahead as could the pilot, and a gunner in the rear of the nacelle to cover the aft hemisphere. As in the US Navy Grumman F7F, which had the same tremendous power of two R-2800 engines, four 20-mm cannon were to be in the inboard wing or in the outer panels. In addition, there was to be a dorsal turret with four 0.5-in (12.7-mm) guns and a ventral turret with two more such guns.

In those days, even with telephones, Wright Field was a long way from Los Angeles. At the mock-up review board, on 2 April 1941, no fewer than 76 engineering changes were called for, the most serious

By the beginning of 1945, no fewer than 10 squadrons of Black Widows – the heaviest of any fighters used by the USAAF, and the largest to carry a 'P for Pursuit' designation – were operating in the Central Pacific. These two P-61Bs have fully reinforced barbettes.

Northrop P-61 Black Widow cutaway key

1 Starboard navigation light
2 Starboard formation light
3 Aileron hinge fairing
4 Conventional aileron
5 Aileron tab
6 Full span flaps
7 Retraction aileron (operable as spoiler)
8 Wing skinning
9 De-icer boot
10 Intercooler controllable shutters
11 Intercooler and supercharger induction
12 Fuel filler cap
13 Starboard outer wing fuel tank
14 Nacelle fairing
15 Cooling gills
16 Pratt & Whitney R-2800-65 engine
17 Nacelle ring
18 Starboard outer auxiliary tank
19 Four-bladed Curtiss Electric propeller
20 Propeller cuffs
21 Propeller boss
22 Heater air induction
23 Front spar
24 Plexiglas canopy
25 Cannon access bulkhead cut-out
26 Front gunner's compartment
27 Sighting station
28 Bullet resistant windshield
29 Inter-cockpit/ compartment armour (shaded)
30 Pilot's canopy
31 Pilot's seat
32 Control column
33 Gunsight (fixed cannon)
34 Bullet resistant windshield
35 Fuselage structural joint (armour plate deleted for clarity)
36 Radar modulator
37 Di-electric nose cone
38 SCR-720 radar scanner
39 Gun camera (gunsight aiming point)

40 Mast
41 Pitot head
42 Radar equipment steel support tube
43 Bulkhead (centre joint)
44 Rudder pedals
45 Drag strut
46 Torque link
47 Towing eye
48 Nosewheel
49 Cantilever steel strut
50 Mudguard (often deleted)
51 Taxi lamp

52 Air-oil shock strut (shimmy damper on forward face)
53 Nosewheel door
54 Cockpit floor
55 Radar aerials
56 Gunner compartment floor (stepped)
57 Forward gunner's seat-swivel mechanism
58 Cannon ports
59 Heater air induction
60 Cannon ammunition magazines
61 Ammunition feed chute
62 20-mm cannon in ventral compartment
63 Magazine forward armour plate
64 Front-spar fuselage cut-out
65 Magazine rear armour plate
66 Rear-spar fuselage cut-out
67 Dorsal turret support/drive motor
68 Front spar carry-through
69 Turret support forward armour plate
70 Flush-riveted aluminium alloy skin
71 Gun mantlet (four 0.50-in
72 General Electric remote-control power turret
73 Turret drive ring
74 Rear spar carry-through
75 Turret support rear armour plate

Northrop P-61 Black Widow

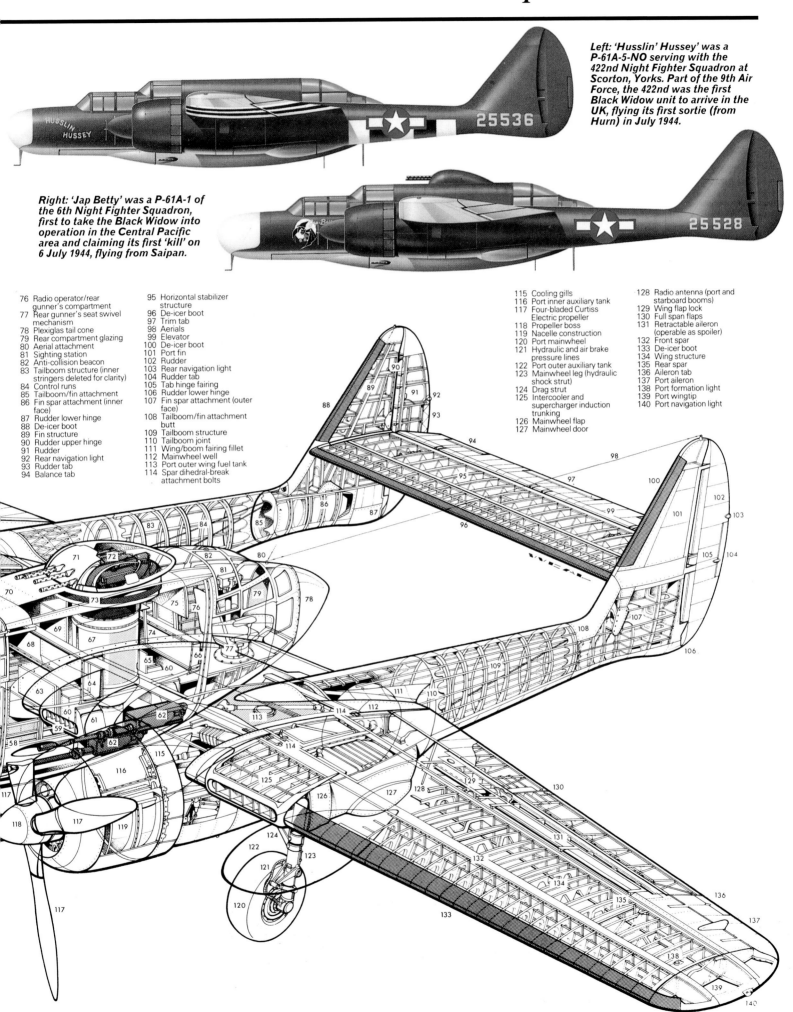

Left: 'Husslin' Hussey' was a P-61A-5-NO serving with the 422nd Night Fighter Squadron at Scorton, Yorks. Part of the 9th Air Force, the 422nd was the first Black Widow unit to arrive in the UK, flying its first sortie (from Hurn) in July 1944.

Right: 'Jap Betty' was a P-61A-1 of the 6th Night Fighter Squadron, first to take the Black Widow into operation in the Central Pacific area and claiming its first 'kill' on 6 July 1944, flying from Saipan.

76 Radio operator/rear gunner's compartment
77 Rear gunner's seat swivel mechanism
78 Plexiglas tail cone
79 Rear compartment glazing
80 Aerial attachment
81 Sighting station
82 Anti-collision beacon
83 Tailboom structure (inner stringers deleted for clarity)
84 Control runs
85 Tailboom/fin attachment
86 Fin spar attachment (inner face)
87 Rudder lower hinge
88 De-icer boot
89 Fin structure
90 Rudder upper hinge
91 Rudder
92 Rear navigation light
93 Rudder tab
94 Balance tab

95 Horizontal stabilizer structure
96 De-icer boot
97 Trim tab
98 Aerials
99 Elevator
100 De-icer boot
101 Port fin
102 Rudder
103 Rear navigation light
104 Rudder tab
105 Tab hinge fairing
106 Rudder lower hinge
107 Fin spar attachment (outer face)
108 Tailboom/fin attachment butt
109 Tailboom structure
110 Tailboom joint
111 Wing/boom fairing fillet
112 Mainwheel well
113 Port outer wing fuel tank
114 Spar dihedral-break attachment bolts

115 Cooling gills
116 Port inner auxiliary tank
117 Four-bladed Curtiss Electric propeller
118 Propeller boss
119 Nacelle construction
120 Port mainwheel
121 Hydraulic and air brake pressure lines
122 Port outer auxiliary tank
123 Mainwheel leg (hydraulic shock strut)
124 Drag strut
125 Intercooler and supercharger induction trunking
126 Mainwheel flap
127 Mainwheel door

128 Radio antenna (port and starboard booms)
129 Wing flap lock
130 Full span flaps
131 Retractable aileron (operable as spoiler)
132 Front spar
133 De-icer boot
134 Wing structure
135 Rear spar
136 Aileron tab
137 Port aileron
138 Port formation light
139 Port wingtip
140 Port navigation light

Northrop P-61 Black Widow

being relocation of the fixed cannon to the underfloor area of the nacelle, the ventral barbette being omitted. Countless other factors conspired to delay the programme, which had been designated **XP-61** in December 1940, including argument over the engine installation, structural materials, flight controls and tankage; and Northrop's priority task of building 400 Vengeance dive-bombers for the RAF and US Army did not help either. Despite this the original contract of 11 January 1941, amounting to $1,167,000 for design, development and two prototypes, was augmented in September 1941 by an order for 150 production P-61s, followed on 12 February 1942 by 410 more! This was a backlog of over $26 million, about 26 times anything Northrop had known before, and still the first prototype was incomplete.

Prototype problems

Eventually the unpainted XP-61 (41-19509) was completed in early May 1942, and flown by Vance Breese with generally excellent results. It was certainly an odd-looking machine, enormous for a fighter with a wing of 662.36 sq ft (61.53 m²) area, even bigger than the wing of today's F-15, and with a crew area considerably more spacious than most medium bombers despite the mass of controls and switchgear. The second XP-61 (19510) followed on 18 November 1942, painted from the start in the glossy black dope which helped give the fighter its name. Altogether it was a very fine machine, though there were enough major problems to prevent the initiation of

Newly arrived at Saipan in June 1944, a P-61A-1 of the 6th Night Fighter Squadron awaits installation of the dorsal barbette, which Northrop had redesigned and strengthened to overcome the early difficulties. Beyond, a C-87 transport version of the Liberator is seen landing.

full production. The original fuel system, with a 270-US gal (1023-litre) flexible cell between the wing spars in the engine nacelles, was augmented by two further 120-US gal (455-litre) tanks and provision for 310-US gal (1173-litre) drop tanks on underwing pylons (these were not introduced until well into production). The rectangular tailplane and elevators were redesigned aerodynamically to improve pitch control, the welded-magnesium tailbooms were replaced by conventional flush-rivetted light alloy, and the Zap flaps (pioneered by Northrop with an OS2U Kingfisher in May 1941) had to be replaced by double-slotted flaps, which were a practical production job. Even then, flap flutter caused major difficulties (and frightening vertical acceleration readings of +9g/-6g, which says much for the strength of the wing). The flaps were extremely powerful. Northrop had long understood better than most designers that lift coefficient is very important, and the P-61 had flaps over almost the whole span. The conventional ailerons were very small, but roll control was backed up when needed by four sections of differential spoiler an each wing. This enabled the P-61 to be amazingly agile considering its size and weight. It would have stood little chance in daylight against Fw 190s, but at night it easily outmanoeuvred every twin it met.

The radar finally got into the second prototype in late April 1943,

'Tabitha', a barbette-less P-61A-10-NO, was operating with the 425th NFS in France a few weeks after D-Day when this photograph was taken. The 425th was the second Widow-equipped squadron to reach the UK, to work up alongside the 422nd at Scorton in June 1944. During July, both units flew successful night intercept missions against V-1 flying-bombs launched against southern England.

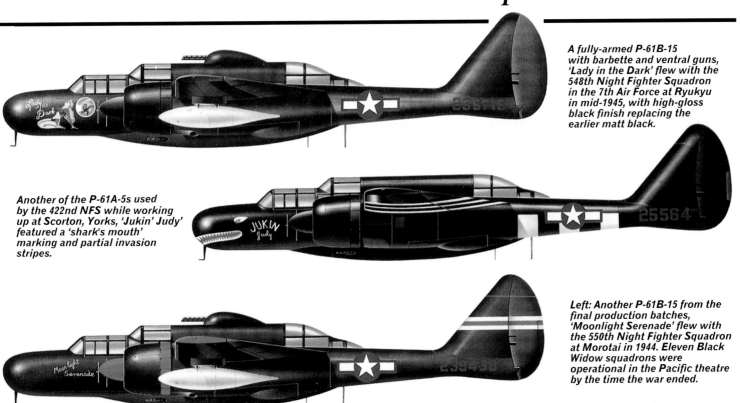

A fully-armed P-61B-15 with barbette and ventral guns, 'Lady in the Dark' flew with the 548th Night Fighter Squadron in the 7th Air Force at Ryukyu in mid-1945, with high-gloss black finish replacing the earlier matt black.

Another of the P-61A-5s used by the 422nd NFS while working up at Scorton, Yorks, 'Jukin' Judy' featured a 'shark's mouth' marking and partial invasion stripes.

Left: Another P-61B-15 from the final production batches, 'Moonlight Serenade' flew with the 550th Night Fighter Squadron at Morotai in 1944. Eleven Black Widow squadrons were operational in the Pacific theatre by the time the war ended.

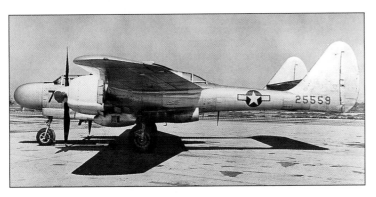

Above: First of two XP-61Ds, this was a P-61A-5 modified (by Goodyear) to have Navy-type R-2800-14 engines with CH-5 turbo-superchargers, as a possible alternative to the P-61C, which also featured CH-5s. Development ended when the P-61C proved successful.

Above: The XF-15A conversion of a P-61C-1-NO was the second Black Widow adapted for the photographic reconnaissance role, fitted with six cameras in the lengthened nose. Production of 175 similar F-15As was ordered, but only 36 were built.

Below: A pair of Black Widows play 'chase me Charlie' in the wide blue yonder. Although plagued by early service problems and initially thought to be sluggish and unresponsive because of strict flight limitations, the P-61s became highly regarded in the night-fighting role.

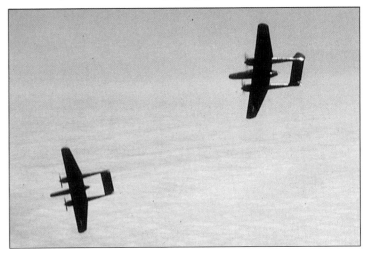

at Wright Field, by which time the 13 service-test **YP-61**s (numbered sequentially earlier than the prototypes at 41-18876/18888) were visible on the line. These all flew in August and September, and though they incorporated reinforced skin over the nose gear and many other areas to withstand the firing of the cannon, it was found that an operative dorsal turret could, when slewed to the beam position, cause severe tail buffet. Accordingly the turret was fitted to only the first 37 production P-61As (numbers from 42-5485); moreover, the structure was stiffened and often had only the outboard guns fitted. From the 38th the turret was omitted, and it is remarkable that the gain in speed was a mere 3 mph (4.8 km/h). Later at least 10, and possibly many more, of the remaining 163 P-61As had the turret installed after the buffet trouble had been eradicated.

It seemed that every day there were at least a dozen new problems, and this if anything got worse after the start of service deliveries in March 1944 to the 348th Night Fighter Squadron of the 481st Night Fighter Group, which sweltered in Florida training future Black Widow crews. The troubles were due almost entirely to the fact that there was so much to go wrong; for example, there were 229 design changes in the cannon installation alone between early 1942 and spring 1944. Once crews had got over the shock of the size of the 'Widow' they were pleased at the way it could be flung around the sky, the only prohibited manoeuvres being stalls, spins, flick rolls and sustained inverted flight. Other unpopular features were the fact the 12 ft 2 in (3.71 m) Curtiss Electric four-bladed propellers were in line with the pilot, and the absence (at first) of any way for a trapped

Northrop P-61 Black Widow

The final Black Widow variant was the XP-61E-NO, featuring a revised clear-view canopy over the two tandem cockpits and four 0.50-in (12.7-mm) machine-guns in the nose in place of the dorsal barbette. Two P-61C were converted to this configuration.

force-landed crew to be released from outside.

From June 1944 the floodgates were opened and aircraft came through at about three a day to the ETO (European Theater of Operations) and CPA (Central Pacific Area). The first P-61 'kill' was scored in the latter area on 6 July, when the 6th NFS bagged a Mitsubishi G4M 'Betty'. In the UK the first units were the 422nd and 425th NFS, which arrived in May and continued what they had done before: endless, slogging training in classrooms. On 6 June (D-Day) the 425th watched endless streams of Douglas C-47s pulling Airspeed Horsa and Waco CG-4 gliders to France from their base at Charmy Down; then in the full light of day they went back to their own war effort in the classroom. On 28 June things got worse: IX Fighter Command had decided the Mosquito could outfight the big 'Widow'. Lieutenant Colonel Oris B. Johnson of the 422nd and Major Leon G. Lewis of the 425th gathered their best crews and arranged a show-down fly-off at Hurn. The beefy P-61 held its own, and by July both units were in business with 16 'Widows', a North American AT-6 Texan and a Cessna UC-78 Bobcat, even though to save time and fuel they had been relocated 200 miles (322 km) to the north at RAF Scorton!

Deep intruder operations

It says much for the power and strength of the P-61 that in its first ETO actions it succeeded in catching and shooting down nine flying bombs, one of them from a mere 100 ft (30 m) dead astern, which almost took the Black Widow with it. From August the 422nd and 425th NFS got into real action in deep intruder missions, bagging not only large numbers of locomotives, supply convoys and even the odd bridge but also Bf 109s, Bf 110s, Me 410s, Fw 190s, Do 217s and various unidentified types. In Italy the 12th Air Force got the 414th converted from the trusty Beaufighter by January 1945 and got five kills, but the 415th, 416th and 417th NFSs did not convert until March, by which time the show was over. In the Pacific units were luckier, the 418th and 421st NFS seeing a lot of action from mid-1944, and in China the 426th and 427th NFS converted in late 1944 and were used mainly on ground-attack with rocket tubes.

From July 1944 deliveries were of the **P-61B** version, which had not only the R-2800-65 engine with a 2,250-hp (1679-kW) wet rating (this had been introduced on the 46th P-61A) but also the four-gun dorsal turret (of an improved type from the P-61B-20 onwards) and, from the B-10 block, four wing pylons each stressed for a tank or a 1,600-lb (726-kg) bomb. The **P-61C** introduced further uprated engines, but only a few were completed before the war's end. Other variants are listed separately. Certainly the best-looking of the whole family were the **XP-61E** and **F-15A**, because these had slim nacelles with graceful teardrop canopies. The F-15A Reporter reconnaissance aircraft turned the '3' figures of the Black Widow into '4' figures: 440 mph (708 km/h), 41,000 ft (12495 m) and 4,000 miles (6437 km), all extremely impressive for a 1945 aircraft. As for the P-61, 674 were built by VJ-Day and 706 altogether, and the P-61C did not pass from the scene until the 68th and 339th NFSs (347th FG in the Pacific) finally re-equipped in 1950.

Northrop P-61 variants

XP-61: two prototypes (41-19509/19510) with R-2800-10 engines
YP-61: 13 pre-production/service test aircraft with R-2800-10 engines (41-18876/18888)
P-61A: first production model, of which 200 built (42-5485/5634 and 42-39348/39397); first 45 powered by R-2800-10 and subsequent aircraft by R-2800-65; first 37 completed with dorsal turret and subsequent aircraft without, although many had the turret retrofitted; redesignated **F-61A** and **ZF-61A** in 1948
P-61B: 450 production aircraft (42-39398/39757 and 43-8231/8320) with minor improvements; most were completed with dorsal turret and four underwing hardpoints for air-to-ground weapons; later redesignated F-61B
P-61C: 41 production aircraft (43-8321/8361) with R-2800-73 engines and CH-5 turbochargers, emergency wet rated at 2,800 hp (2089 kW); Curtiss Electric paddle blade hollow steel propellers; top speed 430 mph (692 km/h) at altitude; 476 aircraft cancelled at end of war; redesignated F-61C in 1948
XP-61D: two P-61As (42-5559 and 42-5587) re-engined with 2,100-hp (1567-kW) R-2800-77 turbocharged engines
XP-61E: two P-61Bs (42-39549 and 42-39557) rebuilt with a slim fuselage nacelle, dorsal turret deleted, and large Plexiglas bubble hood over a two-man cockpit; nose; radar deleted and replaced by four 0.5-in (12.7-mm) machine-guns; four 20-mm cannon in ventral pack; fuel capacity increased to 1,158 US gal (4382 litres)
XP-61F: one P-61C (43-8338) scheduled for conversion to similar standard to XP-61E but not completed
P-61G: designation applied to weather reconnaissance aircraft modified from P-61Bs in 1945
XF-15 Reporter: one XP-61E (42-39549) further modified with photo-reconnaissance nose containing six cameras
XF-15A: one P-61C (43-8335) fitted with camera nose; distinguishable from XF-15 by supercharger ducts under engines
F-15A: production version of XF-15 powered by R-2800-65; 175 ordered but only 36 completed (45-59300/59335); redesignated R-15A in 1947 and RF-61C in 1948
F2T-1N: 12 P-61Bs were transferred to the Marine Corps for use as night-fighter trainers (BuNos 52750/52761)

Configuration

The P-61 was a shoulder-wing monoplane of all-metal construction; twin tailbooms extended aft from engine nacelles. The fins were built integral with the tailbooms and the tailplane located between the fins. Th unique twin-boom configuration housed a crew of three in a large pod mounted to a sturdy centre section.

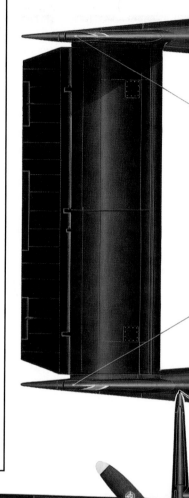

Service

The first production P-61As went to the 348th Night Fighter Squadron for training at Orlando Air Base in Florida. The P-61 was involved in the D-Day landings as well as subsequent action over northern France, the Rhineland, Ardennes, Alsace and central Eurpe. The number of German aircraft roaming the night sky at this time was, by then, past history and the pickings for the Black Widow were relatively slim, and the Army reasoned that the P-61 should be employed as a night intruder, attacking enemy rolling stock and positions that was a dangerous proposition in daylight. The Pacific theatre, however, produced more action for the P-61.

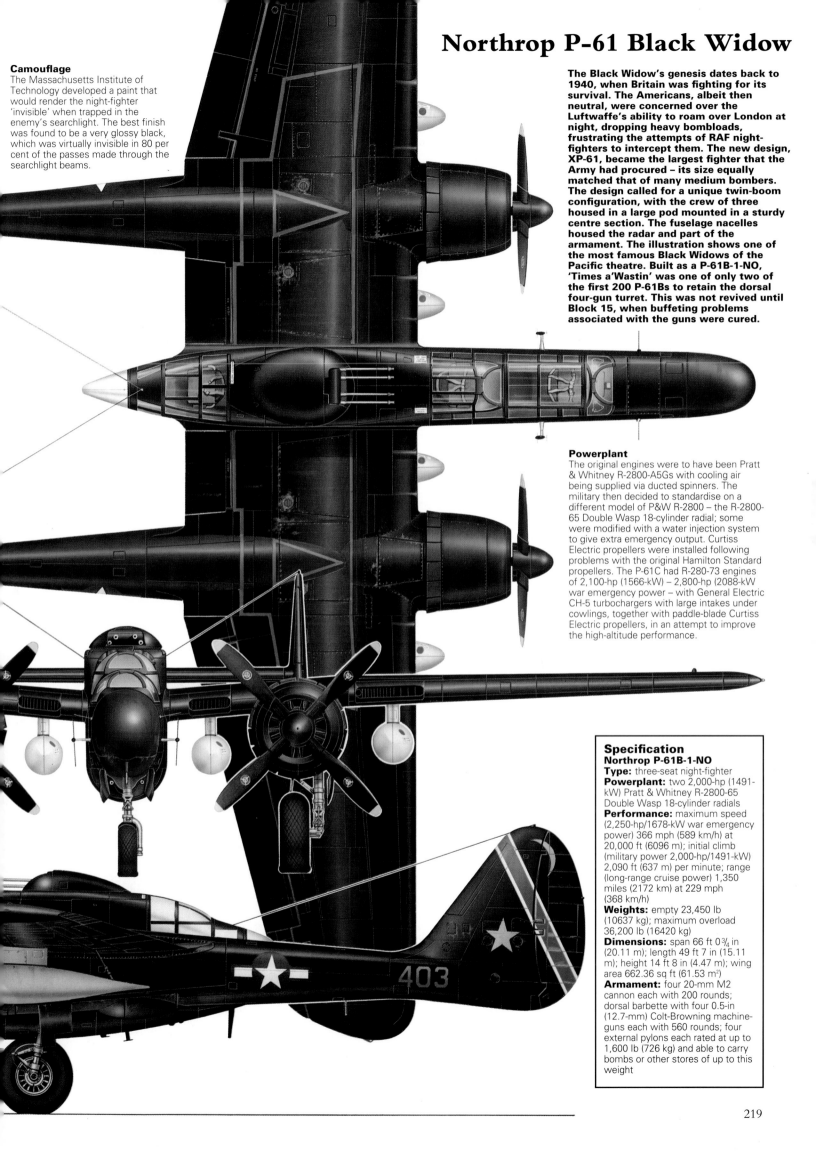

Northrop P-61 Black Widow

Camouflage
The Massachusetts Institute of Technology developed a paint that would render the night-fighter 'invisible' when trapped in the enemy's searchlight. The best finish was found to be a very glossy black, which was virtually invisible in 80 per cent of the passes made through the searchlight beams.

The Black Widow's genesis dates back to 1940, when Britain was fighting for its survival. The Americans, albeit then neutral, were concerned over the Luftwaffe's ability to roam over London at night, dropping heavy bombloads, frustrating the attempts of RAF night-fighters to intercept them. The new design, XP-61, became the largest fighter that the Army had procured – its size equally matched that of many medium bombers. The design called for a unique twin-boom configuration, with the crew of three housed in a large pod mounted in a sturdy centre section. The fuselage nacelles housed the radar and part of the armament. The illustration shows one of the most famous Black Widows of the Pacific theatre. Built as a P-61B-1-NO, 'Times a'Wastin' was one of only two of the first 200 P-61Bs to retain the dorsal four-gun turret. This was not revived until Block 15, when buffeting problems associated with the guns were cured.

Powerplant
The original engines were to have been Pratt & Whitney R-2800-A5Gs with cooling air being supplied via ducted spinners. The military then decided to standardise on a different model of P&W R-2800 – the R-2800-65 Double Wasp 18-cylinder radial; some were modified with a water injection system to give extra emergency output. Curtiss Electric propellers were installed following problems with the original Hamilton Standard propellers. The P-61C had R-280-73 engines of 2,100-hp (1566-kW) – 2,800-hp (2088-kW) war emergency power – with General Electric CH-5 turbochargers with large intakes under cowlings, together with paddle-blade Curtiss Electric propellers, in an attempt to improve the high-altitude performance.

Specification
Northrop P-61B-1-NO
Type: three-seat night-fighter
Powerplant: two 2,000-hp (1491-kW) Pratt & Whitney R-2800-65 Double Wasp 18-cylinder radials
Performance: maximum speed (2,250-hp/1678-kW war emergency power) 366 mph (589 km/h) at 20,000 ft (6096 m); initial climb (military power 2,000-hp/1491-kW) 2,090 ft (637 m) per minute; range (long-range cruise power) 1,350 miles (2172 km) at 229 mph (368 km/h)
Weights: empty 23,450 lb (10637 kg); maximum overload 36,200 lb (16420 kg)
Dimensions: span 66 ft 0¾ in (20.11 m); length 49 ft 7 in (15.11 m); height 14 ft 8 in (4.47 m); wing area 662.36 sq ft (61.53 m²)
Armament: four 20-mm M2 cannon each with 200 rounds; dorsal barbette with four 0.5-in (12.7-mm) Colt-Browning machine-guns each with 560 rounds; four external pylons each rated at up to 1,600 lb (726 kg) and able to carry bombs or other stores of up to this weight

Northrop XP-79

The **XP-79** designation was assigned at first to a Northrop flying-wing fighter of all-magnesium construction with a prone position for the pilot, powered by one 2,000-lb (8.89-kN) thrust Aerojet rocket engine. As early as January 1943, it was foreseen that this rocket-propelled aircraft would attain 518 mph (833 km/h) at 40,000 ft (12192 m). After development of the rocket powerplant was delayed to the extent that two prototypes had to be cancelled, Northrop built the sole **XP-79B** 'Flying Ram', propelled by two 2,000-lb (8.89-kN) thrust Westinghouse axial-flow turbojets eventually designated J30. Combining Northrop's ongoing work in the flying-wing field with a twin tail, the XP-79B was intended to succeed in battle in a unique fashion; although not a suicide aircraft, it was designed to slice off portions of enemy aircraft with the sturdily-built leading edge of its wing. In addition, an armament of four 0.5-in (12.7-mm) machine-guns would have been installed on a production version.

In early taxi tests at Muroc Dry Lake, California, the XP-79B encountered various problems, including frequent tyre blow-outs. On 12 September 1945 Northrop test pilot Harry Crosby took the aircraft aloft for its tragic first and only flight. After narrowly missing a fire truck which inadvertently blocked his runway, Crosby made a seemingly normal take-off. He made a sweeping circle over on watchers at 10,000 ft (3048 m) and, on a second pass, went into a stall. The XP-79B plunged into a nose-down spin and Crosby attempted to parachute to safety. He was struck by a portion of the aircraft and his parachute never opened.

Although the airframe was too badly burned for an accident investigation, it is believed that a trim tab failure caused the violent manoeuvre which resulted in Crosby's death.

Specification
Type: single-seat fighter
Powerplant: two 2,000-lb (8.89-kN) thrust Westinghouse J30 axial-flow turbojet engines
Performance: maximum speed 547 mph (880 km/h) at 20,000 ft (6096 m); cruising speed 480 mph (772 km/h); initial climb rate 4,000 ft (1219 m) per minute; service ceiling 40,000 ft (12192

The XP-79 was not only a flying-wing twin-jet but designed deliberately to collide with enemy aircraft. In this view one can see the four landing-gear wheels, and also one of the wingtip ducts which supplied ram air to the bellows which worked the control spoilers.

m); range 993 miles (1598 km)
Weights: empty 6,250 lb (2835 kg); maximum take-off 8,669 lb (3932 kg)
Dimensions: span 38 ft 0 in (11.58 m); length 14 ft 0 in (4.27 m); height 7 ft 0 in (2.13 m); wing area 278 sq ft (25.83 m²)
Armament: four 0.5-in (12.7-mm) machine guns planned but not installed

Piper L-4 Grasshopper

Evaluated for the role of artillery spotting and front-line liaison, as were the Aeronca L-3 and Taylorcraft L-2, four examples of the Piper Aircraft Corporation's Cub Model J-3C-65 were acquired for this purpose by the US Army Air Corps in mid-1941. These were allocated the designation **YO-59** and, almost simultaneously, 40 additional examples were ordered as **O-59s**. These were all delivered quickly enough for the US Army to employ them on a far wider evaluation basis than had been anticipated, using them in the field as if on operational service during annual manoeuvres held at the end of 1941.

There was no doubt at all after this very practical test that the little Cubs were of more value than had been envisaged, and this useful experience made it possible to procure a new version more specifically tailored to the US Army's requirements. This, designated **O-59A**, was of braced high-wing monoplane configuration and was of composite construction comprising wooden spars, light alloy ribs and fabric covering. The fuselage and braced tail unit had basic structures of welded steel tube and were fabric-covered. Landing gear was of the fixed tailwheel type, and the powerplant of the O-59A comprised a 655-hp (48-kW) Continental O-170-3 flat-four engine. Primary requirement of the O-59A specification was improved accommodation for pilot and observer, which was achieved with a modified enclosure for the tandem cockpits to provide better all-round visibility.

Orders for this version totalled 948, but designation changes resulted in all becoming **L-4As**, the previously applied YO-59s and O-59s becoming **L-4s**. Subsequent procurement covered 980 **L-4Bs** with reduced radio equipment, 1,801 **L-4Hs** which had only detail changes, and 1,680 **L-4Js** which introduced a variable-pitch propeller that made a significant improvement to take-off performance. In addition to the various L-4 Grasshoppers procured specifically for the US Army, more than 100 were impressed from civil sources and designated **L-4C** (J-3C-65s), **L-4D** (J-3F-65s), **L-4E** (J-4Es),

L-4F (J-5As), and **L-4G** (J-5Bs). Those impressed for use in Panama received the designations **UC-83** (four J5As), **UC-83A** (two J3Ls) and **UC-83B** (one J4A).

In 1942 Piper was requested to develop a training glider from the basic L-4 design, this involving the removal of the powerplant and landing gear. In its modified form it had a simple cross-axle landing gear with hydraulic brakes, and the powerplant was replaced by a new front fuselage to accommodate an instructor; he and both pupils were provided with full flying controls. A total of 250 was built for the USAAF under the designation **TG-8**, plus three for evaluation by the US Navy which designated them **XLNP-1**.

Apart from the three XLNP-1s, which the US Navy acquired for evaluation, this service also procured 230 **NE-1s**, basically similar to the US Army's L-4s, and these were used as primary trainers. Twenty similar aircraft procured at a later date were

Olive drab overall, AAF serial 43-1053 was one of the 980 L-4B versions. These had provision for dual control and a first-aid kit, but no radio.

designated **NE-2**, and 100 examples of the Piper J-5C Cub which were acquired for ambulance use (carrying one stretcher) were originally **HE-1**.

L-4 developments included the **YL-14**, of which five were produced. This was an enlarged three-seater with a 130-hp O-290-3 engine, but plans for 845 production **L-14s** were cancelled.

Specification
Type: two-seat lightweight liaison aircraft
Powerplant: (L-4) one 65-hp (48-kW) Continental O-170-3 flat-four piston engine
Performance: maximum speed 85 mph (137 km/h); cruising speed 75 mph (121 km/h); service ceiling 9,300 ft (2835 m); range 190 miles (306 km)
Weights: empty 730 lb (331 kg); maximum take-off 1,220 lb (533 kg)
Dimensions: span 35 ft 3 in (10.74 m); length 22 ft 0 in (6.71 m); height 6 ft 8 in (2.03 m); wing area 179 sq ft (16.63 m²)

The insignia shows that this L-4B was snapped later in the war, but still in the USA. The Army never asked for the side windows to slope outwards to improve downwards view.

Republic XF-12 Rainbow

Like the Hughes XF-11, the Republic **XF-12** was developed during World War II as a high-altitude photo-reconnaissance aircraft.

The Rainbow was developed in response to a USAAF requirement for a very fast and high-flying reconnaissance aircraft with sufficient range to survey targets in Japan in support of the strategic bombing campaign. The XF-12 featured a very slender cigar-shaped fuselage, with no cockpit step; instead, the crew sat behind glazed panels which were moulded to the shape of the fuselage, which housed cameras and fuel.

The extremely clean fuselage shape, highly efficient wings and very powerful engines (which utilised exhaust gases to provide additional jet thrust) combined to give outstanding performance.

Two prototypes were built, but despite the programme being accorded great urgency they did not fly before the end of the war. With the main requirement removed, the Rainbow programme proceeded far slower, and the first aircraft did not fly until 2 July 1946. The second followed in 1947, and following the loss of this aircraft the already waning interest died completely.

The advanced features of the two XF-12As (44-91002/91003) meant a high pilot workload. Their unrivalled performance led to PanAm interest in the RC-2 pressurised airline version, for 46 passengers.

Specification
Type: high-altitude strategic reconnaissance platform
Powerplant: four 3,500-hp (2611-kW) Pratt & Whitney R-4360 radial engines
Performance: maximum speed 490 mph (788 km/h); service ceiling 42,000 ft (12800 m); range 4,100 miles (6600 km)
Weight: maximum take-off 116,500 lb (52844 kg)
Dimensions: wing span 129 ft 2 in (39.37 m); length 93 ft 9½ in (28.59 m); height 30 ft 0 in (9.14 m); wing area 1,640 sq ft (152.36 m²)

Republic P-43 Lancer

The **Republic P-43 Lancer** was designer Alexander Kartveli's follow-up to the P-35 and XP-41, and was built by the Farmingdale, Long Island, manufacturer which in October 1939 changed its name from Seversky to Republic. Kartveli had made an attempt to put a streamlined cowl around a radial engine, in the fashion of the Curtiss XP-42, using the experimental company Model AP-4. The concept was stymied by cooling problems, and Kartveli's P-43 was a company Model AP-4 with a return to traditional radial-engine configuration. Although this meant accepting the drag imposed by a broad open cowl, Kartveli hoped to compensate with an otherwise clean aerodynamic design and brute power. This worked moderately well with the P-43 Lancer and would achieve real success with the Thunderbolt to follow.

Powered by a 1,200-hp (894-kW) Pratt & Whitney R-1830-35 Twin Wasp radial, the P-43 began flying in 1939 and offered some improvement in performance over the Seversky P-35 and Curtiss P-36 then in use. The US Army placed a 12 May 1939 contract for 13 service-test **YP-43** airframes. Meanwhile, studies aimed at finding a more powerful engine resulted in Republic's proposal for the R-2180-powered P-44 Rocket. In September 1940, planned purchases of the latter machine were redirected to the P-43 Lancer as a stopgap measure, while the P-44 was cancelled and the Farmingdale line was tooled up in anticipation of the P-47 Thunderbolt.

The 13 service-test YP-43s were followed by 54 production **P-43**s with R-1830-47 engines, 80 **P-43A**s with the R-1830-49 ordered in lieu of the P-44 and 125 **P-43A-1**s with the R-1830-57. The 272 airframes served eminently forgettable careers with the US Army 1st Pursuit Group and other units, being used in 1940 to simulate the enemy in war games. Some 150 machines were converted to **P-43B** standard for the reconnaissance role with cameras, and a further two airframes were converted to **P-43C**, also a reconnaissance variant. Even as a photoplane, the Republic P-43 Lancer never saw significant action with US forces. Some appear to have been delivered to India. About 180 P-43s reached the Chinese Nationalist air force and saw combat against Japanese forces.

Specification
Type: single-seat fighter
Powerplant: one 1,200-hp (894.8-kW) Pratt & Whitney R-1830-49 Twin Wasp air-cooled 14-cylinder radial piston engine driving a three-blade propeller
Performance: maximum speed 355 mph (571 km/h) at 20,000 ft (6096 m); initial climb rate about 2,700 ft (823 m) per minute; service ceiling 26,000 ft (7925 m); range 800 miles (1287 km)
Weights: empty 5,730 lb (2599 kg); maximum take-off 7,800 lb (3538 kg)
Dimensions: span 36 ft 0 in (10.97 m); length 28 ft 6 in (8.67 m); height 14 ft 0 in (4.27 m); wing area 224 sq ft (20.81 m²)
Armament: two cowl 0.3-in (7.62-mm) and two wing 0.5-in (12.7-mm) fixed forward-firing machine-guns, plus provision for six 20-lb (9-kg) or two 200-lb (90-kg) bombs

Seen at the Farmingdale plant, painted in 1941 olive drab, Army Air Corps 41-31449 was the second of 125 P-43A-1 Lancers, fitted with fuselage guns of 0.50-in calibre. In 1942 180 Lancers were shipped to China, while many other examples were converted to P-43B, C or D standard with a reconnaissance camera in the rear fuselage. In October 1942 they were redesignated as RP-43s.

Republic P-47 Thunderbolt

Built in larger numbers than any other fighter in American history, the mighty P-47 - popularly called the 'Jug', short for Juggernaut - was the exact opposite of the Russian philosophy of making fighters small and agile. Today even the smallest fighters make the P-47 look like a midget, but in World War II it was a monster. RAF pilots said the driver of a P-47 could escape enemy fire by running around in the cockpit, and the shock its laden weight of 13,500 lb (6124 kg) provoked would have been turned to amazement had people then (in 1942) known that by 1945 later versions would turn the scales at 20,700 lb (9390 kg) - considerably heavier than a loaded Dornier Do 17 bomber! One can argue indefinitely about small and large fighters, but the 'T-bolt' was to prove itself one of the most useful Allied aircraft, in all theatres.

Certainly the question of small or large fighters was far from resolved in the US Army Air Corps in 1940. One of its chief fighter builders, Republic Aviation Corporation (successor to Seversky Aircraft) had a heritage of rotund radial-engined fighters with elliptical wings and tails, and was in production with the P-35 and about to produce the P-43 Lancer with inward-retracting landing gear and a turbocharged Twin Wasp engine. For the future there were various AP-4 projects with the 1,400-hp (1044-kW) R-2180 or the massive new 1,850-hp (1380-kW) R-2800 Double Wasp, as well as the lightweight AP-10 with liquid-cooled Allison engine and two 0.5-in (12.7-mm) machine-guns. Combat reports from Europe suggested none would make the grade, and on 12 June 1940 chief engineer Alex Kartveli submitted a dramatically more formidable machine which technically was probably the most advanced then in existence. It was quickly accepted by the worried Army Air Corps and allotted the designation **XP-47B**, the original XP-47 and XP-47A having been versions of the totally different AP-10.

The new fighter was an exceptionally severe challenge. For a start, the engine installation was so complex Kartveli designed this first, and then schemed the rest around it. The chosen engine, the big 18-cylin-

Above: Designations XP-47 and XP-47A having applied to an earlier fighter proposal from Republic, the prototype of the Thunderbolt was the XP-47B. When first flown on 6 May 1941, the XP-47B was by a substantial margin the USAAC's largest and heaviest fighter in its class.

Above: The early production P-47Bs closely resembled the prototype, although they sported a sliding cockpit hood, and were distinguished by the raked-forward radio aerial mast. The P-47Bs were used to equip the 56th Fighter Group while it trained in the US.

P-47B Thunderbolts of the 56th Fighter Group fly formation during training in the US. Aircraft '1' is flown by the CO of the Group; pilots of the 61st Fighter Squadron fly the other aircraft. Using P-47Cs, this Group was the first to fly Thunderbolts in the European Theater of Operations.

Above: An external clue to the identity of this P-47C is provided by the upright radio aerial mast. Less obvious is the 8-in (20-cm) lengthening of the fuselage ahead of the firewall to improve handling by moving the CG forwards. A water-injection system was fitted to increase engine power.

Left: Despite its size and weight, the P-47 posed few difficulties for pilots converting from earlier aircraft types. There was little demand for a two-seat version, but two Curtiss-built P-47Gs became TP-47Gs with added second seats, as seen here.

Above: Serving with the 379th FS, 362nd FG in the 9th Air Force, this is a P-47D-II, equipped to carry a bomb on the fuselage centreline. Two 150-US gal (568-litre) wing drop tanks could be carried in place of the centreline tank, when a bomb was fitted.

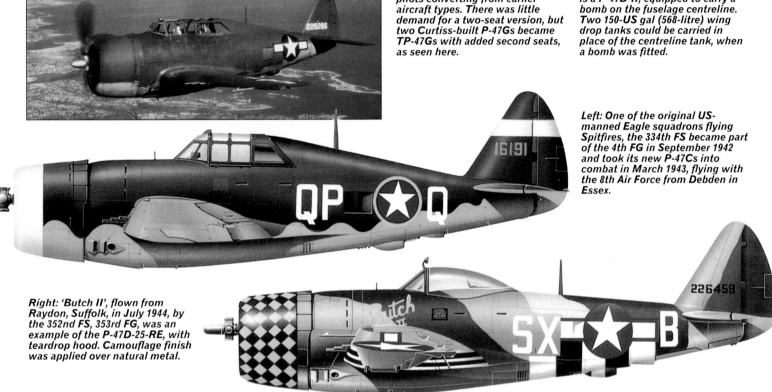

Left: One of the original US-manned Eagle squadrons flying Spitfires, the 334th FS became part of the 4th FG in September 1942 and took its new P-47Cs into combat in March 1943, flying with the 8th Air Force from Debden in Essex.

Right: 'Butch II', flown from Raydon, Suffolk, in July 1944, by the 352nd FS, 353rd FG, was an example of the P-47D-25-RE, with teardrop hood. Camouflage finish was applied over natural metal.

der R-2800, was supplied by a turbocharger which, for various aerodynamic and efficiency reasons, was mounted under the rear fuselage instead of close to the engine. The multiple exhausts were grouped into two monster pipes, which at their upstream ends glowed red-hot at full power and which led back beneath the wing to the turbocharger itself. Here a variable valve system called a waste gate either expelled the hot gas to the atmosphere or, as altitude was increased, diverted it to drive the turbine. The latter spun a centrifugal compressor at some 60,000 rpm to feed high-pressure air to the engine via even larger ducts which incorporated intercoolers to increase the density of the air, and thus give further-enhanced engine power. The mass of large pipes and ducts made the fuselage deep, and put the wing well above its bottom.

This was just what Kartveli did not want, because the great power of the engine needed an enormous propeller; even with the novel use of four blades in a constant-speed Curtiss electric propeller, the diameter had to be no less than 12 ft 2 in (3.71 m). To provide safe clearance between the tips and the ground on take-off, the landing gear had to be exceptionally long, especially because the wing was not in the low position and had to have dihedral. Long landing gears are not only very heavy (if they are not to get a reputation for breaking) but also need long spaces in the wings when retracted. Again, this was just what Kartveli did not want, because he proposed to use the phenome-

nal armament of not two but eight of the big 0.5-in (12.7-mm) Browning guns, all in the wings outboard of the landing gear legs. It was a technical triumph to design main gears which on retraction shortened by 9 in (22.86 cm) to fit into normal-size bays in the wing between the spars. Immediately outboard of the landing gears were four guns in each wing, staggered so that the four bulky ammunition belts (each of at least 350 rounds) could lie in boxes side-by-side extending very nearly to the tip of the wing.

Enormous fuel load

The bluff nose cowl was not circular but extended below into a pear shape to accommodate the ducts for left and right oil coolers and for the bulky intercooler air which was then discharged through a large rectangular valve on each side of the rear fuselage. It was then necessary to find somewhere to put an exceptionally large fuel capacity, and main and auxiliary tanks for 205 and 100 US gal (776 and 379 litres), both of self-sealing construction, were installed above the wing between the supercharger air ducts and in the rear fuselage under the cockpit. The cockpit was extremely well equipped; it was packed with controls for systems and devices not then found in other fighters, such as electric fuel-contents transmitters, cabin air-conditioning, variable gun-bay heating and anti-icing by an Eclipse pump. There was a deep Vee windscreen, upward-hinged canopy and sharp upper line to the

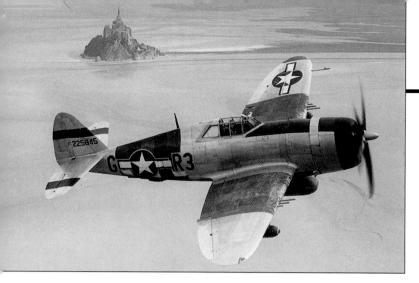

St Michael's Mount, off the coast of Normandy, provides an impressive backdrop for a P-47D-22-RE enjoying the freedom of French skies soon after the Allied invasion. This, and later, versions could carry two 1,000-lb (454-kg) bombs on the wings as well as the fuselage bomb.

rear fuselage which caused all early P-47s later to be called 'razor-backs'.

Completely unpainted, the prototype XP-47B flew on 6 May 1941, exactly eight months after it was ordered. It was clearly a potential world-beater, but gave a lot of trouble. Handicapped by its sheer size and weight, it suffered problems with fabric-covered flight-control surfaces, canopies which jammed, and snags with the guns, fuel system and engine installation. Despite agonised misgivings, the US Army ordered 171 of the new fighters and soon followed with orders for 602 of an improved model, designated **P-47C**. The first production **P-47B** left the assembly line at Farmingdale, Long Island, in March 1942. This had a sliding canopy with jettison system, metal-skinned control surfaces (not yet standard), sloping radio mast mounted farther aft, blunt-nose ailerons, balance/trim rudder tab and production R-2800-21 engine. The first deliveries went to the 56th Fighter Group of what by this time was the US Army Air Force. After suffering severely from control problems, tyre bursts and other difficulties, the 56th FG went on to become the top-scoring fighter group in all US forces. With the 78th FG, the 56th joined the 8th Air Force in England and flew its first escort mission on 13 April 1943. With 305 US gal (1155 litres), the big fighters could not accompany the bombers very far, and they found life tough in close combat with the smaller Messerschmitt Bf 109s and Focke-Wulf Fw 190s. The unmatched diving speed of the P-47 meant they could always break off, but that after all was not the basic objective, which was to shoot down the Luftwaffe.

Additional drop tank

The last P-47B had a pressurised cockpit and was designated **XP-47E**. The 172nd was the first P-47C, with a fundamental problem of balance removed by mounting the engine nearly 1 ft (0.3 m) further forward and for the first time fitting an attachment under the fuselage for a 500-lb (227-kg) bomb or a 200-US gal (757-litre) drop tank, an important addition. Externally, the most obvious change was the shorter vertical radio mast. Recognising the P-47 should have presented no problem, but in the European theatre standards of recognition were so poor that the first Thunderbolts (which were painted

Serving with the 355th FS, 354th F-B Group in the 9th Air Force, a P-47D-25-RE taxis in with the aid of a 'wingman' who has met the Thunderbolt at the end of its landing run. Fuselage markings on this aircraft record 18¹/₂ victories claimed by the pilot.

Republic P-47D-10 Thunderbolt cutaway key

1 Rudder upper hinge
2 Aerial attachment
3 Fin flanged ribs
4 Rudder post/fin aft spar
5 Fin front spar
6 Rudder trim tab worm and screw actuating mechanism (chain driven)
7 Rudder centre hinge
8 Rudder trim tab
9 Rudder structure
10 Tail navigation light
11 Elevator fixed tab
12 Elevator trim tab
13 Starboard elevator structure
14 Elevator outboard hinge
15 Elevator torque tube
16 Elevator trim tab worm and screw actuating mechanism
17 Chain drive
18 Starboard tailplane
19 Tail jacking point
20 Rudder control cables
21 Elevator control rod and linkage
22 Fin spar/fuselage attachment points
23 Port elevator
24 Aerial
25 Port tailplane structure (two spars and flanged ribs)
26 Tailwheel retraction worm gear
27 Tailwheel anti-shimmy damper
28 Tailwheel oleo
29 Tailwheel doors
30 Retractable and steerable tailwheel
31 Tailwheel fork
32 Tailwheel mount and pivot
33 Rudder cables
34 Rudder and elevator trim control cables
35 Lifting tube
36 Elevator rod linkage
37 Semi-monocoque all-metal fuselage construction
38 Fuselage dorsal 'razorback' profile

39 Aerial lead-in
40 Fuselage stringers
41 Supercharger air filter
42 Supercharger
43 Turbine casing
44 Turbosupercharger compartment air vent
45 Turbosupercharger exhaust hood fairing (stainless steel)
46 Outlet louvres
47 Intercooler exhaust doors (port and starboard)
48 Exhaust pipes
49 Cooling air ducts
50 Intercooler unit (cooling and supercharged air)
51 Radio transmitter and receiver packs (Detrola)
52 Canopy track
53 Elevator rod linkage
54 Aerial mast
55 Formation light
56 Rearward-vision frame cut-out and glazing
57 Oxygen bottles
58 Supercharged and cooling air pipe (supercharger to carburettor) port
59 Elevator linkage
60 Supercharged and cooling air pipe (supercharger to carburettor) starboard
61 Central duct (to intercooler unit)
62 Wingroot air louvres
63 Wingroot fillet
64 Auxiliary fuel tank (100 US gal/379 litres)
65 Auxiliary fuel filler point
66 Rudder cable turnbuckle
67 Cockpit floor support
68 Seat adjustment lever
69 Pilot's seat
70 Canopy emergency release (port and starboard)
71 Trim tab controls
72 Back and head armour
73 Headrest
74 Rearward-sliding canopy
75 Rear-view mirror fairing
76 'Vee' windshields with central pillar
77 Internal bulletproof glass screen

78 Gunsight
79 Engine control quadrant (cockpit port wall)
80 Control column
81 Rudder pedals
82 Oxygen regulator
83 Underfloor elevator control quadrant
84 Rudder cable linkage
85 Wing rear spar/fuselage attachment (tapered bolts/bushings)
86 Main fuel tank (205 US gal/776 litres)
87 Wing supporting lower bulkhead section
88 Fuselage forward structure
89 Stainless steel/Alclad firewall bulkhead
90 Cowl flap valve
91 Main fuel filler point
92 Anti-freeze fluid tank
93 Hydraulic reservoir
94 Aileron control rod
95 Aileron trim tab control cables
96 Aileron hinge access panels
97 Aileron and tab control linkage

98 Aileron trim tab (port wing only)
99 Frise-type aileron
100 Wing rear (No. 2) spar
101 Port navigation light
102 Pitot head
103 Wing front (No. 1) spar
104 Wing stressed skin
105 Four-gun ammunition troughs (individual bays)
106 Staggered gun barrels
107 Removable panel
108 Inter-spar gun bay access panel
109 Forward gunsight bead
110 Oil feed pipes
111 Oil tank (28.6 US gal/108 litres)
112 Hydraulic pressure line
113 Engine upper bearers
114 Engine control correlating cam
115 Eclipse pump (anti-icing)
116 Fuel level transmitter
117 Generator
118 Battery junction box
119 Storage battery
120 Exhaust collector ring
121 Cowl flap actuating cylinder
122 Exhaust outlets to collector ring
123 Cowl flaps
124 Supercharged and cooling air ducts to carburettor (port and starboard)
125 Exhaust upper outlets
126 Cowling frame
127 Pratt & Whitney R-2800-59 18-cylinder twin-row engine
128 Cowling nose panel
129 Magnetos
130 Propeller governor
131 Propeller hub
132 Reduction gear casing
133 Spinner
134 Propeller cuffs
135 Four-blade Curtiss constant-speed electric propeller
136 Oil cooler intakes (port and starboard)

137 Supercharger intercooler (central) air intake
138 Ducting
139 Oil cooler feed pipes
140 Starboard oil cooler
141 Engine lower bearers
142 Oil cooler exhaust variable shutter
143 Fixed deflector
144 Excess exhaust gas gate
145 Belly stores/weapons shackles
146 Metal auxiliary drop tank (75 US gal/284 litres)
147 Inboard mainwheel well door
148 Mainwheel well door actuating cylinder
149 Camera gun port
150 Cabin air-conditioning intake (starboard wing only)
151 Wingroot fairing
152 Wing front spar/fuselage attachment (tapered bolts/bushings)
153 Wing inboard rib mainwheel well recess
154 Wing front (No. 1) spar
155 Undercarriage pivot point
156 Hydraulic retraction cylinder
157 Auxiliary (undercarriage mounting) wing spar
158 Gun bay warm air flexible duct
159 Wing rear (No. 2) spar
160 Landing flap inboard hinge
161 Auxiliary (No. 3) wing spar inboard section (flap mounting)

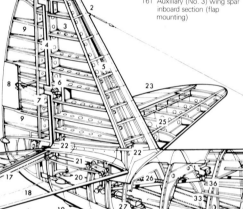

Republic P-47 Thunderbolt

Left: With the introduction of the P-47D-30-RA, a small dorsal fin was added to the distinctive contours of the Thunderbolt, helping to reduce a tail-flutter problem. This example flew with the 366th FS, 358th FG at Toul in France, 1944, and bears the red and orange tail marking of the 1st Tactical Air Force.

Right: This P-47D-30-RA of the 512th FS, 406th FG, was at Nord-Holz in Germany in the summer of 1945. The red-yellow-red fuselage band indicates that the unit had been assigned to serve with the occupation air forces after the hostilities had ended.

162 NACA slotted trailing-edge landing flaps
163 Landing flap centre hinge
164 Landing flap hydraulic cylinder
165 Four 0.5-in (12.7-mm) Browning machine guns
166 Inter-spar gun bay inboard rib
167 Ammunition feed chutes
168 Individual ammunition troughs

169 Underwing stores/weapons pylon
170 Landing flap outboard hinge
171 Flap door
172 Landing flap profile
173 Aileron fixed tab (starboard wing only)
174 Frise-type aileron structure
175 Aileron hinge/steel forging spar attachments
176 Auxiliary (No. 3) wing spar outboard section (aileron mounting)
177 Multi-cellular wing construction

178 Wing outboard ribs
179 Wingtip structure
180 Starboard navigation light
181 Leading-edge rib sections
182 Bomb shackles
183 500-lb (227-kg) M43 demolition bomb
184 Undercarriage leg fairing (overlapping upper section)
185 Mainwheel fairing (lower) section

186 Wheel fork
187 Starboard mainwheel
188 Brake lines
189 Landing gear air-oil shock strut
190 Machine gun barrel blast tubes
191 Staggered gun barrels
192 Rocket-launcher slide bar

193 Centre strap
194 Front mount (attached below front spar between inboard pair of guns)
195 Deflector arms
196 Triple-tube 4.5-in (11.5-cm) rocket-launcher (Type M10)
197 Front retaining band
198 4.5-in (11.5-cm) M8 rocket projectile

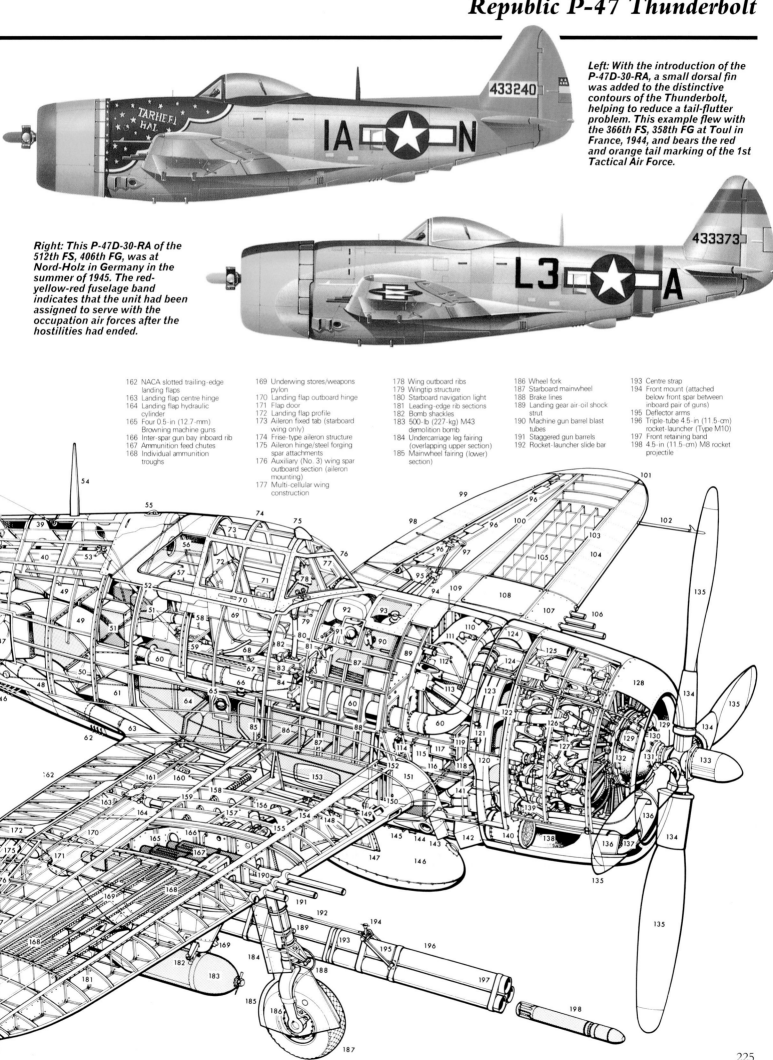

Republic P-47 Thunderbolt

The XP-47H was a conversion of a P-47D airframe, extensively re-engineered to accept the unusual Chrysler XI-2220-11, an inverted-Vee 16-cylinder engine that in the event proved unsuccessful.

First flown in November 1943, the XP-47J – this is the first of two completed – featured a lightened wing structure and used fan-assisted cooling for the R-2800 engine. It achieved 505 mph (813 km/h) in August 1944.

Using a Hawker-style all-round-view cockpit canopy, the XP-47K (illustrated) and XP-47L were modified P-47Ds. The latter, featuring an enlarged fuselage fuel tank, was production-ised as the P-47D-25.

olive drab overall) were given white bands across the tail surfaces, and a white nose so that they would not be shot down by mistake for the totally different Fw 190. By mid-1943, when the first of the **P-47D** models reached front-line units, everyone had come to respect the P-47's great strength, which often enabled it to limp home with severe damage and to effect a self-destructive belly landing without injury to the pilot.

Record number built

Although the first order for the P-47D was placed on 13 October 1941, before the United States entered the war, it was mid-1943 before the flood of production had much effect. Eventually no fewer than 12,602 of this version were built, far more than of any other US fighter, and including output from a new factory at Evansville, Indiana. A further 354 identical machines were made by Curtiss-Wright as the **P-47G**. Basically the P-47D grouped a whole package of improvements, such as a refined engine with water injection for emergency combat boost, a better turbocharger installation, improved pilot armour, and multi-ply tyres (also retrofitted to earlier P-47s) which did not burst even on rough strips when the aircraft was carrying bombs and tanks. The ability to carry both loads together came

with the P-47D-20 (and counterparts at the Evansville plant), which introduced a 'universal' wing with pylons for 1,000-lb (454-kg) bombs on each side or a 150-US gal (568-litre) tank, as well as the load on the centreline. With three tanks the P-47 could escort bombers deep into Germany, going all the way on most missions; on the return journey it became common practice to use unexpended ammunition shooting up targets of opportunity on the ground. The P-47D became the chief ground-attack aircraft of the Allied air forces in Europe in the final year of war, as well as serving in large numbers in the Pacific and with the RAF (825, mainly in Burma), Soviet Union, Brazil and Mexico (and many other air forces post-war).

In July 1943 one aircraft was given a cut-down rear fuselage and the clear-view bubble canopy from a Typhoon. This **XP-47K** was so popular that the new hood was immediately introduced to production, starting with the P-47D-25-RE and Evansville's P-47D-26-RA. Previously, Farmingdale had delivered 3,962 P-47Ds and the Indiana plant 1,461; from the Dash-25, the two factories produced 2,547 and

A pair of P-47Ns fly formation during a pre-delivery check flight. The 'N' model of the Thunderbolt was developed to operate in the Pacific area and introduced a revised wing with – for the first time in a P-47 – internal wing tankage. A range of 2,350 miles (3781 km) was achieved.

Flying from Duxford, Cambs, 1943-45, the 78th Fighter Group was unusual in that it was equipped, successively, with P-38s, P-47s and P-51s. This P-47D-23-RE has the Group's chequerboard marking and the MX codes of the 82nd Fighter Squadron. Partial invasion stripes are carried on the fuselage and under the wings; the tail band changed from white to black when the earlier olive drab finish was discarded.

4,632. By this time the aircraft were being delivered unpainted, which slightly enhanced performance. Despite the great increase in weight (to some 17,500 lb/7938 kg), the boosted engine improved performance, which gained a further fillip (such as 400 ft/122 m per minute extra climb) as a result of the fitting of a broad paddle-bladed propeller that was especially useful at high altitude. The lower rear fuselage caused slight loss in directional stability, and from the D-27-RE batch the fin area was increased by a shallow dorsal spine stretching most of the way to the canopy. From the D-35-RA block each wing was given zero-length attachments for five 5-in (12.7-cm) rocket projectiles on each side.

Long-range variant

The only other service variants were the 'hot-rod' **P-47M** and the very-long-range **P-47N**. The P-47M was quickly produced in the summer of 1944 to counter the menace of the V-1 flying bomb, which ordinary P-47s were hard-pressed to catch, and the various German jet and rocket fighters. Basically a late-model P-47D, the P-47M had the extra-powerful R-2800-57(C) engine with uprated CH-5 turbocharger which had previously been fitted to the experimental XP-47J to make it the fastest piston-engined fighter of all, at 504 mph (811 km/h). The only other significant change was the fitting of airbrakes to the wings to assist slowing down behind slower aircraft before opening fire.

The P-47N, however, was almost a new aircraft because it had a long-span wing of totally new design which not only was tailored to much-increased gross weights but also for the first time contained fuel. A 93-US gal (352-litre) tank was fitted in each, so that with external tanks no less than 1,266 US gal (4792 litres) could be carried. This resulted in a really capable long-range fighter for the Pacific war, although the loaded weight of up to 21,200 lb (9616 kg) required a strengthened landing gear and fairly good, long airstrip. Features of the production P-47N included the Dash-77 engine, enlarged ailerons and square-tipped wings for rapid roll, and zero-length rocket launchers. Farmingdale built 1,667; Evansville also managing to deliver the first 149 of an order for 5,934. Farmingdale completed the last of the P-47N series not to be cancelled in December 1945, bringing the grand total of all versions to 15,683.

In typical US style, plenty of information was published not only about the 'Jug' but also about its accomplishments. P-47s flew 546,000 combat sorties between March 1943 and VJ-Day in August 1945. They had an outstanding combat record of only 0.7 per cent losses per mission, with 4.6 enemy aircraft destroyed for each P-47 lost. They dropped 132,000 US tons (119750 tonnes) of bombs, many thousands of gallons of napalm and fired 132 million rounds of '50 calibre' and over 60,000 rockets. They burned 204 million US gal (77.5 million litres) of fuel in 1.9 million operational flight hours. The claims for ground targets knocked out were astronomical, but even more important was the European (excluding Italian front) claim of 3,752 aircraft destroyed in air combat and an additional 3,315 on the ground. These losses to the Luftwaffe bled it white; they could not be replaced.

Left: This is one of the three YP-47Ms, converted P-47D-27 airframes fitted with uprated R-2800-57 engines. Republic built 130 P-47Ms, and the 56th Fighter Group, which had been the first to take the Thunderbolt into action, began to receive this model at the end of 1944. However, the new engine installation proved troublesome, and was only eventually cured in the P-47N used in the Pacific area.

Right: By the time the P-47M was ready for service, most Thunderbolt units in the 8th AF had re-equipped on P-51s. Still flying the 'Jug', though, was the original 56th FG, now at Boxted, Essex. This attractively-coloured M-1 model was flown by the 63rd Fighter Squadron, spring 1945.

Right: In an unusual deviation from the two-letter code marking system, the 79th FG, flying Thunderbolts at Fano, Italy, in February 1945, retained the 'X-plus-number' system it had first applied to P-40s in North Africa. This P-47D was in service with the 86th FS.

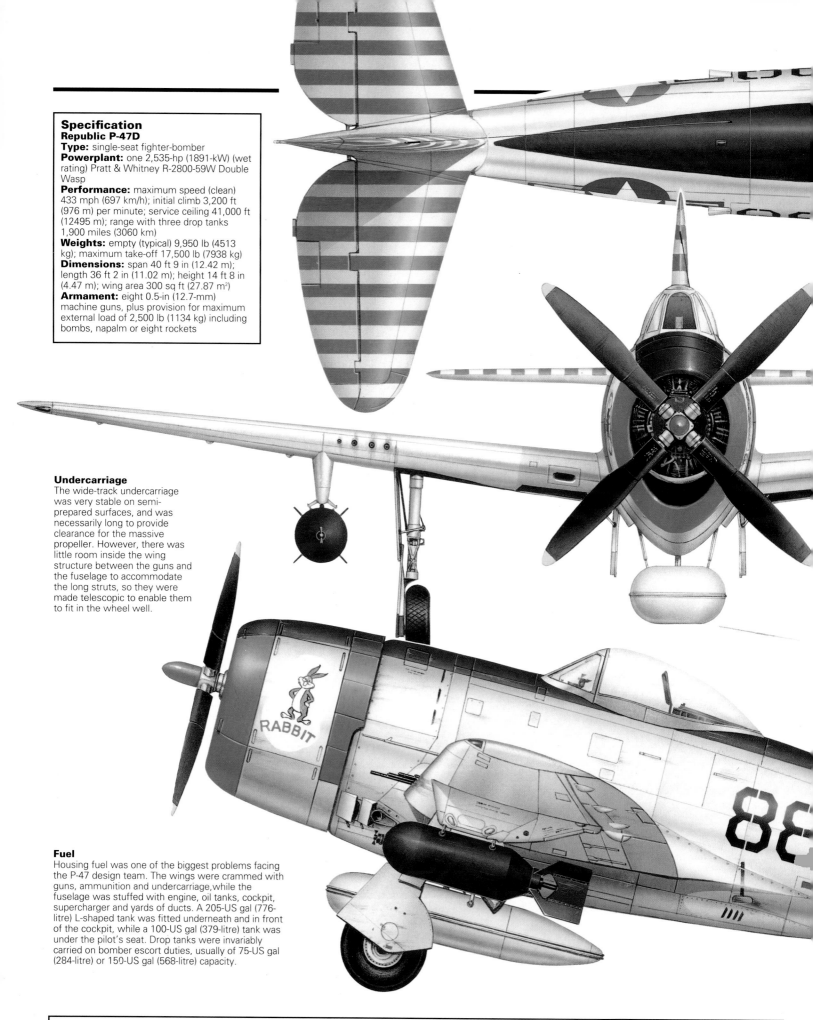

Undercarriage

The wide-track undercarriage was very stable on semi-prepared surfaces, and was necessarily long to provide clearance for the massive propeller. However, there was little room inside the wing structure between the guns and the fuselage to accommodate the long struts, so they were made telescopic to enable them to fit in the wheel well.

Fuel

Housing fuel was one of the biggest problems facing the P-47 design team. The wings were crammed with guns, ammunition and undercarriage, while the fuselage was stuffed with engine, oil tanks, cockpit, supercharger and yards of ducts. A 205-US gal (776-litre) L-shaped tank was fitted underneath and in front of the cockpit, while a 100-US gal (379-litre) tank was under the pilot's seat. Drop tanks were invariably carried on bomber escort duties, usually of 75-US gal (284-litre) or 150-US gal (568-litre) capacity.

Republic P-47 variants

XP-47 and XP-47A: projected prototypes cancelled in favour of XP-47B
XP-47B: single prototype after complete reworking of basic design
P-47B: 170 aircraft; similar to XP-47B but with sliding canopy and metal-covered control surfaces; R-2800-21 engine
P-47C: 602 aircraft; revised engine mounting and forward fuselage lengthened by 8 in; provision for ventral tank; R-2800-59 engine from Block 5
P-47D: 12,603 aircraft built; initially as P-47C but with revised turbocharger exhaust system, paddle-bladed propeller and extra armour; various armament combinations, later aircraft introducing ventral and underwing bomb racks and provision for rockets; from Block 25 P-47Ds built with cut-down rear fuselage and teardrop canopy; from Block 27 a dorsal strake was added
XP-47E: single P-47B tested with pressurised cockpit
XP-47F: single P-47B tested with laminar-flow wings
P-47G: 354 aircraft built by Curtiss,

Pylons
In addition to shackles under the belly for the carriage of fuel or weapons, the P-47D introduced underwing pylons from Block 20 onwards, these being stressed to carry 1,000-lb (454-kg) bombs or more fuel. Carrying three tanks allowed UK-based P-47Ds to escort bombers all the way into Germany, after which they would return at low level shooting targets of opportunity at will. From Block 35 the P-47D gained five zero-length launchers under each outer wing panel for 5-in (12.7-mm) rockets.

Gun armament
One of the Thunderbolt's many great attributes was its armament, which in most P-47Ds consisted of eight 0.5-in (12.7-mm) machine guns in the wings. This was a hard-hitting weapon with high muzzle velocity and rapid fire. The guns were staggered so that the ammunition belts could lay in trays one behind each other outboard of the guns. In later D models the armament was often reduced to six guns when weapons pylons were fitted.

Teardrops and Razorbacks
In 1943 a P-47D was given a cut-down rear fuselage and teardrop canopy to improve visibility from the cockpit. This was adopted from Block 25 onwards, although it was not until Block 27 that a small dorsal fillet was introduced to restore directional stability. The adoption of the teardrop canopy led to the older Thunderbolts being termed 'Razorbacks'.

Republic P-47D Thunderbolt 527th Fighter Squadron 86th Fighter Group Pisa, Italy, 1944

One of the finest fighter-bombers of the war, the P-47D had adequate range and firepower to excel in the bomber escort role, but really found its niche as a ground attack platform. Extremely fast and very tough, the Thunderbolt was a stable gunnery platform and was deadly with rockets or bombs at low level. This aircraft served in the tough Italian theatre, the Thunderbolt having replaced the 527th FS's A-36 Invaders in 1944. In addition to fighter and attack work in support of the slow advance through Italy, the 527th was also involved in bomber escort duties (primarily of B-24s) into Germany itself, even reaching Berlin. In October 1944 the squadron moved into France with the opening of the southern flank, and arrived at a southern German airfield shortly before the end of hostilities.

Powerplant
The P-47 was constructed around the giant Double Wasp engine with supercharging. The latter component was located in the rear fuselage, requiring yards of ducting. The engine was cooled through the main cowling, which also admitted ram air for the supercharger and oil coolers. The supercharger air was ducted back along the bottom of the fuselage where it was charged using exhaust gases also ducted back from the engine cylinders. The supercharged air was then passed forward through the intercooler (itself needing yet more ram air from the cowling) and then to the carburettor. Supercharged air passed through ducts along the side of the fuselage. Intercooler air was controlled by flaps on the side of the fuselage, while supercharger exhaust was vented through the fuselage undersides. In addition to the supercharger, the P-47 also had a 30-US gal (114-litre) water tank for boosting, this situated behind the engine where the 28.6-US gal (108-litre) oil tank was also located.

---

similar to early 'razorback' P-47Ds
TP-47G: two P-47Gs converted to two-seat trainer configuration
XP-47H: two P-47D re-engined with Chrysler XIV-2220 powerplant of 2,300 hp
XP-47J: single trials aircraft with close-cowled R-2800-57 with separate

turbocharger intake; lightened airframe and six guns
XP-47K: single P-47D used to test the cut-down rear fuselage
XP-47L: one P-47D with increased fuel capacity; this feature applied to production aircraft
YP-47M: three P-47Ds converted

with 2,800-hp R-2800-57 engine, improved turbocharger and underwing airbrakes
P-47M: 130 'sprint' aircraft; R-2800-57(C) engine with CH-5 turbocharger; production version with underwing shackles for bombs and gun armament often reduced to six;

maximum speed 470 mph (756 km/h)
XP-47N: single P-47D completed with redesigned wings accomodating fuel and strengthened undercarriage
P-47N: 1,816 long-range aircraft; marriage of P-47M fuselage with XP-47N wings; 2,800-hp (2089-kW) R-2800-57(C) engine

Republic XP-72

The Republic **XP-72** was based upon the P-47 airframe and was designed by Alexander Kartveli's fighter team as a 'Super Thunderbolt' around the 3,000-hp (2237-kW) Pratt & Whitney R-4360-13 Wasp Major radial engine. The powerplant was, simply, the most powerful piston engine to reach production in any country during World War II. Intended primarily to be faster than the Thunderbolt, the XP-72 was viewed in part as a remedy for the Third Reich's high-speed V-1 buzz bomb. The USAAF planned to use the fighter to intercept buzz bombs, taking advantage of its ability to reach 20,000 ft (6096 m) in just under five minutes. An armament of six 0.5-in (12.7-mm) guns would have been carried.

The first of two examples (43-6598) flew at Farmingdale on 2 February 1944 using a large

four-bladed propeller. The name of the pilot is not recorded, but C. Hart Miller was active in Republic flight test at the time. The second XP-72 (43-6599) flew in July 1944 with the intended Aeroproducts six-bladed contra-rotating propeller. The

second aircraft, however, was lost on an early flight.

With priority shifted to long-range escort fighters, this promising interceptor was not needed. The other XP-72 airframe is thought to have been scrapped at Wright Field around VJ-Day.

Powered by a mighty Wasp Major radial, the XP-72 was expected to be a world-beater. This was the first with single-rotation propeller.

Specification
Republic XP-72
Type: single-seat fighter
Powerplant: one 3,000-hp (2237-kW) Pratt & Whitney R-4360-13 Wasp Major air-cooled 28-cylinder radial piston engine driving an Aeroproducts six-bladed contra-rotating propeller unit
Performance: maximum speed 490 mph (788 km/h) at 25,000 ft (7620 m); initial climb rate 3,100 ft (945 m) per minute; climb to 20,000 ft (6096 m) in 5 minutes; service ceiling 42,000 ft (12,800 m); range 1,200 miles (1931 km)
Weights: empty 10,965 lb (4973 kg); maximum take-off 14,750 lb (6690 kg)
Dimensions: span 40 ft 11 in (12.49 m); length 36 ft 7 in (11.17 m); height 14 ft 6 in (4.42 m); wing area 300 sq ft (27.87 m²)
Armament: six 0.5-in (12.7-mm) fixed forward-firing machine-guns plus provision for two 1,000-lb (454-kg) bombs under the wings

Ryan FR Fireball

The first of a small crop of American jet-plus-propeller fighters, the FR-1 suffered from having a low-power piston engine and a low-thrust jet.

with both powerplants working. Flight testing revealed no serious flaws, and the first FR-1 was delivered to US Navy squadron VF-66 in March 1945. After the first 14 had been built, single-slotted trailing-edge flaps were added to the folding, low-set wing. By VJ-day production orders stood at 1,300, but were cancelled at the end of the war with just 66 aircraft built. These were widely used for carrier and operational trials of jet-powered aircraft, although none saw combat during the conflict.

Specification
Type: single-seat carrierborne fighter-bomber
Powerplant: one 1,425-hp (1063-kW) Wright R-1820-72W Cyclone radial piston engine and one 1,600-lb (7.12-kN) thrust General Electric J31-GE-3 turbojet
Performance: maximum speed (both engines) 426 mph (686 km/h), (Cyclone only) 295 mph (475 km/h); service ceiling 43,100 ft (13135 m); range 1,030 miles (1658 km)
Weights: empty 7,915 lb (3590 kg); maximum take-off 10,595 lb (4806 kg)
Dimensions: wing span 40 ft 0 in (12.19 m); length 32 ft 4 in (9.86 m); height 13 ft 7 in (4.15 m); wing area 275 sq ft (25.55 m²)
Armament: four 0.50-in (12.7-mm) machine-guns in wings, plus up to 1,000 lb (454 kg) of bombs or eight 5-in (127-mm) rockets externally

Unless one saw it in flight with the propeller fully feathered, the Fireball looked an entirely conventional aircraft. However, in addition to the conventionally located radial engine, it incorporated a turbojet in the rear fuselage.

The concept originated in late 1942 when the US Navy drew

up a requirement for a carrier-borne fighter-bomber which could utilise the potential of the new jet propulsion. The disadvantages of high landing speed and very short range could be offset by using a conventional powerplant for landing and cruise, which could then be augmented by the jet during the

take-off and attack phases of the sortie.

Ryan was awarded a contract for two **XFR-1** prototypes in early December 1943, followed closely by a production contract for 100 **FR-1 Fireballs**. On 25 June 1944 the first prototype flew, without a jet fitted, and the following month took to the air

Ryan PT-16/20/21/22/25 Recruit

Sensing a new demand for light-planes, T. Claude Ryan founded the Ryan Aeronautical Company in 1933-34, using as his key to the market a two-seat light monoplane which had the designation S-T. Production of this began in 1934, and it was available in three versions with engines of 95-150 hp (71-112 kW) as S-T, S-T-A or S-T-A Special. When the US Army Air Corps began to show interest in the procurement of new primary trainers, a single example of the Ryan S-T-A was acquired for evaluation under the designation **XPT-16**. When delivered in 1939, this represented something of an evolutionary step for the USAAC, for it was the first primary training monoplane to be acquired; all previous USAAC primary trainers had been biplanes.

Early evaluation resulted in considerable interest in the type, and very soon an additional 15 **YPT-16**s were procured so that a wider evaluation programme could be completed more rapidly. These differed from the XPT-16 only by the addition of an electric starter. Both of these initial versions were powered by the 125-hp (93-kW) Menasco L-365-1 inline engine, although the XPT-16 was re-engined with a 125-hp R-440-1 engine to become the XPT-16A.

An order for 40 production aircraft followed in 1940 under the designation **PT-20** and these, delivered in 1941, were generally similar to the YPT-16s except for minor structural changes such as wider cockpits and strengthened airframes.

During 1941 the US Army decided that the five-cylinder Kinner R-440 radial engine offered better performance than the Menasco inline, and the 100 **PT-21**s ordered in 1941 were powered by the 132-hp (98-kW) Kinner R-440-3 engine. The installation of this engine in a streamlined nose fairing, with its five cylinders projecting through the fairing and left uncowled, meant that the PT-21, and subsequent Kinner-engined variants, were easily identified. Their entry into service showed the superiority of this airframe/engine combination, with the result that 13 of the YPT-16s and 27 of the PT-20s were re-engined with 132-hp (98-kW) Kinner R-440-1 engines, and were redesignated **PT-16A** and **PT-20A** respectively. Three PT-20s delivered with civil (as opposed to military) versions of

Above: An impressive line-up of the 15 YPT-16 trainers of the Army Air Corps was photographed on the day World War II started at the Ryan School of Aeronautics at San Diego. Note the Navy carrier in the background.

Right: One of the 100 PT-21s is seen here with instructor and pupil. Though the Kinner radial was slightly heavier than the Menasco, it was installed further forward, making the aircraft about a foot longer.

the Menasco engine, the D-4, were designated **PT-20B**.

With the rapid expansion of aircrew training during 1941, Ryan received a contract for 1,023 examples of what was to be the final and most extensively built version, the **PT-22 Recruit**. This introduced several changes, including deletion of the wheel spats and main landing gear unit fairings which had proved troublesome with aircraft which were making far more take-offs and landings per day than had been envisaged during original design, and by installation of a 160-hp (119-kW) Kinner R-540-1 engine; in other respects these aircraft were similar to the PT-21. Two hundred and fifty aircraft re-engined with the R-540-3 engine received the **PT-22C** designation.

Ryan also built a number of S-Ts for export, and included

among these orders was one from the Netherlands for the supply of 25 S-T-3s (basically the same structurally and with the same powerplant as the USAAC PT-22s). By the time these were ready for delivery, the Netherlands had already been overrun by German forces and, with the designation **PT-22A**, they were acquired by the US Army. Used mainly at civilian-operated flying training schools throughout the US, the Ryan trainers gave valuable service before their retirement towards the end of World War II.

This demand for training aircraft was not exclusive to the USAAC, for the US Navy had initiated a similar expansion of its training programme. Following

US Army evaluation of this trainer, the US Navy also ordered 100 examples of the Ryan S-T-3 version with Kinner R-440-3 engines on 19 August 1940, these being designated **NR-1** Recruit and remaining in service until mid-1944.

Specification
Type: two-seat primary trainer
Powerplant: (PT-22) one 160-hp (119-kW) Kinner R-540-1 radial piston engine
Performance: maximum speed 131 mph (211 km/h); cruising speed 123 mph (198 km/h); service ceiling 15,500 ft (4725 m); range 352 miles (566 km)
Weights: empty 1,313 lb (596 kg); maximum take-off 1,860 lb (844 kg)
Dimensions: span 30 ft 1 in (9.17 m); length 22 ft 5 in (6.83 m); height 6 ft 10 in (2.08 m); wing area 134.25 sq ft (12.47 m²)

BuNo. 4197 was the penultimate aircraft of the first block of Navy NR-1s. Allocated to NAS Jacksonville, they had lockable tailwheels. Colour scheme was silver, with chrome-yellow wings and horizontal tail.

St Louis PT-15

Competing in one of the many prototype competitions for primary trainers in 1939-40 were the St Louis Model PT-1W and the Waco Model UPF-7, both biplane primary trainers which had been built for the civil aircraft market. They were of particular interest to the USAAC because the procurement of an aircraft which was already in production would fill the training gap far more quickly than would the issue of a contract for the design and development of an entirely new trainer.

Testing of an example of the St Louis trainer, given the designation **XPT-15**, resulted in a follow-up order for a small batch of 13 **YPT-15** pre-production aircraft. These were single-bay stagger-wing biplanes of clean appearance, with a minimum of struts and bracing wires, and provided with ailerons on the

The St Louis trainer so closely resembled the rival Stearman (Boeing) that one has to look for details such as the N-type cabane struts and downward-pointing exhaust. This was the XPT-15 prototype.

lower wing only. The basic structure was all-metal, with fabric covering on all the aerofoil surfaces and a metal skin on the fuselage. Landing gear was of the non-retractable tailwheel type, the cantilever main units being well faired to reduce drag. Powerplant consisted of a Wright R-760-1 Whirlwind 7 engine, uncowled but faired so that only the cylinder heads and a forward-mounted exhaust ring were exposed. Instructor and pupil were accommodated in tandem open cockpits, and dual controls and full instrumentation were standard.

All of the trainers were delivered in 1940, and although used in the primary training role they were regarded only as stopgaps until aircraft procured to US Army specification became available, and no additional orders ensued.

Specification
Type: two-seat biplane primary trainer

Powerplant: one 225-hp (168-kW) Wright R-760-1 Whirlwind 7 radial piston engine
Performance: maximum speed 130 mph (209 km/h); cruising speed 116 mph (187 km/h); service ceiling 15,000 ft (4570 m); range 350 miles (563 km)
Weights: empty 2,059 lb (934 kg); maximum take-off 2,766 lb (1255 kg)
Dimensions: span 33 ft 10 in (10.31 m); length 26 ft 5 in (8.05 m); height 9 ft 5 in (2.87 m); wing area 279.9 sq ft (26.00 m²)

Republic (Seversky) AT-12 Guardsman

Under the designation Seversky 2PA Guardsman, the company developed from its P-35 fighter a two-seat export version powered by a 1,000-hp (746-kW) Wright R-1820 Cyclone radial engine. Twenty were supplied to Japan and two to the USSR, but of an order received from Sweden for 52 2PAs to be equipped as fighter-bombers only two had been delivered before the balance was impressed for service with the US Army Air Corps. The US Army had no requirement for a

two-seat fighter-bomber, but with 1,050-hp (783-kW) Pratt & Whitney R-1830-45 engines they entered service as advanced trainers under the designation **AT-12**. The 50 were serialled 41-17494 to 41-17543).

Today unknown to many aviation buffs, the Guardsman was an advanced trainer that had been intended as a front-line fighter. Maximum speed was 288 mph. This example bears underwing markings of the Materiel Division at Wright Field.

Seversky BT-8

From its SEV-2XP, which had served as the first private-venture prototype for the P-35 fighter, Seversky developed for the USAAC a two-seat basic trainer which had fixed tailwheel landing gear and was powered by a Pratt & Whitney R-985-11 Wasp Junior radial of 450 hp. This was the first USAAC aircraft designed specifically as a basic trainer, and was of further significance for being the first monoplane trainer. Thirty aircraft were built (34-247 to 34-276), and saw limited service before retirement.

Specification
Type: tandem two-seat basic trainer
Powerplant: one Pratt & Whitney R-985-11 radial piston engine, rated at 450 hp (335 kW)
Performance: maximum speed 175 mph (280 km) at sea level
Weights: empty 3,017 lb (1368 kg); maximum take-off 4,050 lb (1837 kg)
Dimensions: wing span 36 ft 0 in (10.97 m); length 24 ft 4 in (7.41 m); wing area 220 sq ft (20.43 m²)

The BT-8 was only marginally an aircraft of World War II. This example was the first, 34-247. The single-row Wasp engine had a remarkably long-chord cowling.

Seversky P-35

The **P-35** marked the debut of Seversky (later Republic) of Farmingdale, Long Island, as a major builder of fighters and introduced the work of the firm's chief designer, Alexander Kartveli. The Seversky P-35 was the first single-seat all-metal pursuit plane with retractable landing gear and enclosed cockpit to go into service with the US Army Air Corps. It was a major step forward, albeit one which was short-lived as war approached. The type began as the company **SEV-IXP**, one of several machines flown as pursuit prototypes and racers in the 1930s by Major Alexander P. de Seversky, Jacqueline Cochran and others.

The P-35 won out over the Curtiss Hawk Model 75 (later P-36) for a 16 June 1936 US Army contract for 77 airframes (36-354/430), powered by the 950-hp (708-kW) Pratt & Whitney R-1830-9 Twin Wasp 14-cylinder radial engine. The final airframe in this batch was diverted to become the sole Seversky **XP-41**. The first P-35 was delivered to Wright Field, Ohio, for tests, and the remaining 75 went initially to the 1st Pursuit Group at

Little known today, the P-35 and P-35A were, with the P-36, the most important Army fighters of the late 1930s. Thanks to the revised (May 1940) designation system, this P-35A can be identified as the 10th aircraft in the 31st Pursuit Group at Minneapolis.

Selfridge Field, Michigan. There, the type was received with considerable enthusiasm which lingered even after six machines had been lost in accidents during 1938. Only by later, wartime standards would it become evident that the P-35 was unstable, underarmed and lacking both armour protection for the pilot and self-sealing fuel tanks.

The company **EP-106** export variant attracted Sweden's attention and 120 machines were ordered with the Flygvapen designation J9. These were powered by the 1,050-hp (783-kW) Pratt & Whitney R-1830-45 Twin Wasp radial. When President Roosevelt announced his 10 October 1940 embargo on fighter shipments to Scandinavia, only half (FV serials 2101/2160) had been delivered. The remainder were seized by the US Army as the **P-35A**.

P-35A pursuit ships served with various USAAC units, but by late 1941 about 50 were with First Lieutenant Joseph H. Moore's 20th Pursuit Squadron, 24th Pursuit Group, at Clark Field in the Philippines. Second Lieutenant Max Louk wrote to his parents in mid-1941 that the squadron was undergoing "a very strenuous program" of flying "up to eight hours a day" in the P-35A. Incredibly, some P-35As arrived at Clark still painted in Swedish markings and still wore them during the 8 December

This P-35A still wears the badge and '17' designator of the 17th Pursuit Squadron at Selfridge Field, Michigan, but also has the designator of the 4th Composite Group in the Philippines, to which the 17th was transferred in December 1940.

Below: Buzzing like wasps, or rather Twin Wasps, P-35s of the 27th Pursuit Squadron, 1st Pursuit Group, from Selfridge Field, hold excellent line-abreast formation.

Seversky P-35

This P-35A, painted olive drab, has '18' on its fin and possibly served with the 24th Pursuit Group at Clark Field, Philippines.

1941 Japanese assault, which was synchronised with the attack on Pearl Harbor.

The P-35 was flown by a few memorable pilots, including First Lieutenant 'Buzz' Wagner, commander of the 17th Pursuit Squadron, Nichols Field, Philippines, the first American ace of the war. By December 1941 the type had become dated and inadequate. Pilots of the P-35 started with the disadvantage of an unforgiving mount. 1939 Technical Order No. 01-65 BA-1 had imposed mind-boggling limitations on the P-35, proscribing inverted flight, inverted spins, and outside loops, and similar caveats applied to the slightly more powerful P-35A.

Americans in P-35As in the

Philippines simply could not stay with or effectively fight the Mitsubishi and Nakajima fighters that swarmed down on them. Some died tragically and unnecessarily; First Lieutenant Samuel W. Marrett, commander of the 34th Pursuit Squadron at Del Carmen Field, Philippines, was killed on 10 December 1941 when an ammunition barge he

was strafing exploded beneath him over Lingayen Gulf, northern Luzon.

Specification
Seversky P-35A
Type: single-seat pursuit aircraft
Powerplant: one 1,050-hp (783-kW) Pratt & Whitney R-1830-45 air-cooled 14-cylinder radial piston engine driving a three-bladed Hamilton Standard propeller
Performance: maximum speed 310

mph (499 km/h) at 14,300 ft (4359 m); service ceiling 31,400 ft (9571 m); maximum range 950 miles (1529 km)
Weights: empty 4,575 lb (2075 kg); maximum take-off 6,723 lb (3050 kg)
Dimensions: span 36 ft 0 in (10.97 m); length 26 ft 10 in (8.18 m); height 9 ft 9 in (2.97 m); wing area 220 sq ft (20.44 m²)
Armament: two 0.5-in (12.7-mm) and two 0.3-in (7.62-mm) fixed forward-firing machine-guns, plus provision for up to 350 lb (158 kg) of bombs carried externally

Sikorsky R-4/R-6 Hoverfly

Dated 11 April 1945, this photograph shows R-4B no. 43-46533 getting in some practice time beside the tower at Tinian, whence 'Enola Gay' and 'Bock's Car' would soon arrive plus two A-bombs.

Although Igor Sikorsky could not claim to have invented the helicopter, he most certainly developed the basic concept into a practical flying machine which was to be the foundation of an important sector of the aviation industry. His successful introduction of the anti-torque tail rotor overcame the last major control problem, following months of trials with various auxiliary rotors fitted to his **VS-300** prototype, which had made its first tethered flight on 14 September 1939.

By the spring of 1941 the VS-300 was achieving free flight

at forward speeds of up to 70 mph (113 km/h), and the Vought-Sikorsky Division of United Aircraft received a contract for the development of a two-seat version which was designated **XR-4**. It had a fabric-covered fuselage with an enclosed cockpit and was powered by a 165-hp (123-kW) Warner R-500 engine which drove both the main and tail rotors through gearboxes and driveshafts. The first flight was made at Stratford, Connecticut, on 14 January 1942, and by April Sikorsky had become sufficiently confident to

demonstrate the helicopter to governmental representatives and senior military officers.

Over the period from 13 to 18 May the XR-4 was flown to Wright Field, Ohio for evaluation, accomplishing the world's first cross-country helicopter delivery flight. During the 761-mile (1225-km) journey, which was completed in 16 hours 10 minutes' flying time, the XR-4 made 16 landings.

Thirty production **R-4**s were ordered by the USAAF, the first three being designated **YR-4A** and the rest **YR-4B**; all were

powered by the 180-hp (134-kW) Warner R-550-1 engine and were equipped with a 38-ft (11.58-m) diameter main rotor in place of the 36-ft (10.97-m) diameter rotor fitted to the prototype. Production was completed by 100 **R-4B**s with 200-hp (149-kW) R-550-3 engines.

Among the R-4's achievements was the first helicopter landing aboard ship, accomplished on 6 May 1943 when a USAAF YR-4B, flown by Colonel Frank Gregory, landed on USS *Bunker Hill*, using a deck area only 14 ft (4.27 m) greater than the rotor diameter. The type also recorded the first helicopter rescue, probably that made by a machine from Colonel P. D. Cochran's 1st Air Commando which, in April 1944, rescued the four occupants of a light aircraft which had crashed behind Japanese lines in Burma.

An earlier example of the helicopter's value in a humanitarian role was provided on 3 January 1944 when, in strong winds with sleet and snow, Commander Frank Erickson of the US Coast

Visually far more streamlined than the R-4, this was one of the YR-6A batch, which were built by Nash-Kelvinator.

Guard flew his YR-4B from Floyd Bennett Field, New York, to Sandy Hook, New Jersey, with plasma for badly-burned survivors of an explosion aboard the destroyer USS *Turner*.

The US Navy had taken a decision to acquire helicopters for evaluation in July 1942 and its first **HNS-1** (a YR-4B on loan from the USAAF) was delivered later that year, to be supplemented by two more in March 1943. A total of 25 HNS-1s was eventually to be operated by the US Navy and US Coast Guard.

British observers had been present at Sikorsky's demonstration flight in April 1941 and had been active in the later deck operation trials. Seven YR-4Bs and 45 R-4Bs were flown by Royal Air Force and Fleet Air Arm units under the designation **Hoverfly Mk I**, entering service with the Helicopter Training Flight at RAF Andover in 1945 and with No. 771 Fleet Requirements Unit at Portland in September of that year.

The R-4 helicopter was subsequently developed into the **R-6**, which retained the earlier machine's rotor and transmission system but installed in a streamlined fuselage with a semi-monocoque all-metal tail boom. Powered by a Lycoming O-435 engine of 225 hp (168 kW), the prototype **XR-6** was flown on 15 October 1943 and was followed by five **XR-6A**s with a 240-hp O-405-9 engine. The 26 **YR-6A**s were similar. Production of 193 **R-6A**s followed, of which 36 went to the US Navy as the **HOS-1** and 150 to the UK as the **Hoverfly Mk II**. The **R-6B** was a projected version with a 225-hp O-435-7 engine, but this was not proceeded with.

Specification
Sikorsky YR-4B
Type: two-seat training and rescue helicopter
Powerplant: one 180-hp (134-kW) Warner R-550-1 radial piston engine
Performance: maximum speed 75 mph (121 km/h); service ceiling 8,000 ft (2440 m); range 130 miles (209 km)
Weights: empty 2,020 lb (916 kg); maximum take-off 2,535 lb (1150 kg)
Dimensions: main rotor diameter 38 ft 0 in (11.58 m); length 48 ft 2 in (14.68 m); height 12 ft 5 in (3.78 m); disc area 1,134 sq ft (105.35 m²)

Sikorsky R-5 Dragonfly

While the R-6 was being developed, work was also in progress on a completely new helicopter, the **VS-337**, with an all-metal fuselage which provided tandem accommodation for two. Four prototypes, plus one additional at a later date, were ordered by the USAAF, and the first of these, with the designation **XR-5** and powered by the 450-hp (336-kW) Pratt & Whitney R-985-AN-5 engine, was flown at Bridgeport, Connecticut, on 18 August 1943. Total production of 65 included the remaining four XR-5s (two of which were fitted with British equipment and redesignated **XR-5A**), 26 **YR-5A**s built for USAAF evaluation, and 34 production R-5As. The last could be fitted with a stretcher carrier on each side of the fuselage, and the type was used by the Air Rescue Service. The addition of a nose-wheel, a rescue hoist, an external auxiliary fuel tank and a third seat identified the **R-5D**, 21 of which were modified from R-5As. For training duties, five YR-5As were fitted with dual controls and redesignated Y**R-5E**.

A total of 379 was built, many of them for the US armed forces. Eleven were acquired by the USAF in 1947 as **R-5F**s (redesignated **H-5F** in June 1948), supplemented by 39 H-5Gs with a rescue hoist, for use by the Air Rescue Service, and USAAF procurement was completed by 16 **H-5H**s purchased in 1949.

Following trials with two US Army YR-5As, which were redesignated **HO2S-1**, the US Navy ordered a number of **HO3S-1**s which were equivalent to the USAF R-5F, deliveries commencing in November 1946.

Specification
Type: two/four-seat rescue helicopter

Powerplant: (R-5B) one 450-hp (336-kW) Pratt & Whitney R-985-AN-5 radial piston engine

Performance: maximum speed 106 mph (171 km/h); cruising speed 85 mph (137 km/h) at 1,000 ft (305 m); service ceiling 14,400 ft (4390 m); range 360 miles (579 km)

Weights: empty 3,780 lb (1715 kg); maximum take-off 4,825 lb (2189 kg)

Dimensions: main rotor diameter 48 ft 0 in (14.63 m); length 57 ft 1 in (17.40 m); height 13 ft 0 in (3.96 m); main rotor disc area 1,810 sq ft (168.15 m²)

All variants of the R-5 were made by Sikorsky. Army 43-46623 was one of the 26 YR-5As, with the mainwheels at the front.

Stinson UC-81/AT-19/R3Q Reliant

Prior to World War II the Stinson Reliant had been produced in some quantities for civilian use and in several variants, including no less than eight engine options. A sturdy high-wing monoplane, the Reliant was in demand for both passenger and light cargo carriage.

On the entry of the US into the war, production was suspended and a number of Reliants were impressed into military service under the USAAF designation **UC-81**. Suffix letters related to the various civilian models, and reached UC-81N. Four more impressed aircraft were designated **L-12** and **L-12A**.

Use by other services was limited, although a single Reliant,

designated **RQ**, had served with the Coast Guard prior to the war. This later became the **XR3Q-1** when transferred to the Navy, and was joined by a second example. The biggest wartime operator was the Royal Navy, which procured more than 500

under the USAAF designation **AT-19**. These were used primarily as trainers. Several aircraft procured directly by the RN as the **Reliant Mk I** were used by the US Navy as trainers and communications aircraft.

Royal Navy FK881 was one of 500 Reliants which served in many roles. HMS Dipper had more than 150 on navigation training.

Specification
Type: four-seat navigation/radio trainer and communications aircraft
Powerplant: (AT-19) one 290-hp (216-kW) Lycoming R-680 radial piston engine
Performance: maximum speed 141 mph (227 km/h); service ceiling 14,000 ft (4265 m); range 810 miles (1303 km)
Weights: empty 2,810 lb (1275 kg); maximum take-off 4,000 lb (1814 kg)
Dimensions: wing span 41 ft 10½ in (12.76 m); length 30 ft 0 in (9.14 m); height 8 ft 7 in (2.62 m); wing area 258.5 sq ft (24.01 m²)

Stinson L-1/O-49 Vigilant

When, in 1940, the US Army Air Corps realised the need to reinforce its aircraft in the two-seat light observation category, specifications were circulated and these resulted in contracts for three examples each of Bellanca and Ryan designs, designated YO-50 and YO-51 respectively. Stinson, however, were awarded a contract for 142 of its design under the designation O-49. Built by Vultee after its acquisition of Stinson during the summer of 1940, the O-49 appeared as a braced high-wing monoplane, with an all-metal basic structure, part metal- and part fabric-covered. To provide the essential low-speed and high-lift performance, the whole of the wing leading edge was provided with automatically operated slats, and the entire trailing edge was occupied by wide-span (almost two-thirds) slotted flaps and large slotted ailerons which drooped 20° when the flaps were fully down. The non-retractable tail-

This L-1F (AAF 41-18912) was photographed while serving in Burma. The colours were probably olive drab and pale grey.

wheel-type landing gear was designed specially for operation from unprepared strips. The powerplant consisted of a 285-hp (213-kW) Lycoming R-680-9 radial engine with a two-bladed constant-speed propeller. An enclosed cabin seated two in tandem, and the pilot and observer had excellent vision all around, above and below.

A second contract covered the construction of 182 **O-49A**s, which differed by having a slightly longer fuselage, minor equipment changes and detail refinements. Designation changes in 1942 resulted in the O-49 and O-49A becoming the **L-1** (liaison) and **L-1A** respectively. Both versions were supplied to the RAF under Lend-Lease and these were given the British name

Vigilant. The designation **O-49B** (later **L-1B**) was applied to three O-49s converted to serve in an ambulance role; these could accommodate one stretcher and had a special loading door in the upper surface of the fuselage. Other designations included an **L-1C** ambulance converted to have a different internal arrangement; 21 **L-1D**s modified from L-1As to provide pilot training in glider pick-up techniques; seven L-1s equipped for the ambulance role and provided with amphibi-

ous floats as **L-1E**s; and five similarly-equipped L-1As, redesignated **L-1F**s.

No further production of new Vigilant aircraft followed, for the type was superseded by the more effective lightweight Grasshopper family. Nevertheless, Vigilants saw wide use in both the European and Pacific theatres, the RAF operating many of its aircraft for artillery liaison in Italy, Sicily and Tunisia.

Specification
Type: two-seat light liaison/observation aircraft
Powerplant: (L-1A) one 295-hp (220-kW) Lycoming R-680-9 radial piston engine
Performance: maximum speed 122 mph (196 km/h); service ceiling 12,800 ft (3900 m); range 280 miles (451 km)
Weights: empty 2,670 lb (1211 kg); maximum take-off 3,400 lb (1542 kg)
Dimensions: span 50 ft 11 in (15.52 m); length 34 ft 3 in (10.44 m); height 10 ft 2 in (3.10 m); wing area 329 sq ft (30.56 m²)

The L-1 was designed purely for STOL performance, with a 220-ft take-off and 145-ft landing at 31 mph airspeed. This was 40-269, serving as an Arctic rescue machine with skis and red wingtips and tail.

Stinson L-5/O-62 Sentinel

Stinson's 105 Voyager was an attractive three-seat civil lightplane, and in 1941 the US Army acquired six of these civil aircraft, which it evaluated for use in a light liaison role under the designation **YO-54**. Successful testing resulted in an initial order of 1941 for 275 similar aircraft to be powered by the Lycoming O-435-1 flat-four engine, and these were allocated the designation **O-62**. The following order covered 1,456 similar aircraft, but when delivery of these began in 1942 the designation had been changed to **L-5**, and the 275 O-62s from the earlier order were also redesignated L-5.

Construction of these L-5s was changed somewhat from the original Voyager design to follow a policy of that particular period which sought to conserve light alloy materials, which it was considered should be reserved for the construction of combat aircraft. Instead of the mixed construction which had been used for the wing and tail unit of the Voyager, those of the L-5 were all-wood, but retained the welded steel-tube fuselage structure. Other changes included rearrangement of the enclosed cabin to seat two in tandem, a reduction in height of the rear fuselage to provide improved rearward vision, and the provision of clear transparent panels in the roof. The original wing design had included leading-edge slots and slotted trailing-edge flaps, and these were retained. The main units of the non-retractable tailwheel type landing gear were modified so that the stroke of the oleo spring shock-absorbers was almost doubled.

In 1943, 688 of the L-5s were reworked to provide a 24-volt instead of 12-volt electrical system, and the streamlined fairings were removed from the main landing gear units; these aircraft were redesignated **L-5A**. Modifications, which included the installation of an upward-hinged door in the aft fuselage and provision of a stretcher, identified the 679 **L-5B**s which followed. The **L-5C**, of which 200 were built, had provisions for the installation of a K-20 reconnaissance camera. The L-5D designation was cancelled, and the ensuing 750 **L-5E**s were generally similar to the L-5C except that they introduced ailerons which drooped when the flaps were fully extended. A single **XL-5F** introduced some minor changes and an O-435-2 engine, leading to the final production version, the **L-5G**, with the 190-hp (142-kW) O-435-11 powerplant. Otherwise generally similar to the L-5E, 115 of this last version were built.

Used extensively by the USAAF throughout World War II, especially in the Pacific theatre, many L-5s were still in use to provide valuable service during the Korean War. The RAF was allocated 100 of these aircraft under Lend-Lease, and these were used widely in Burma for liaison, spotting and air ambulance duties under the name **Sentinel**. The US Marine Corps acquired a total of 306 L-5s of differing versions, but all were designated **OY-1**, the Y signifying origin from Consolidated after a merger with Vultee in early 1943. The US Marine Corps deployed its Sentinels for similar missions to those of the RAF and USAAF in support of its operations in the Pacific.

Specification
Type: two-seat light liaison aircraft
Powerplant: (L-5) one 185-hp (138-kW) Lycoming O-435-1 flat-four piston engine
Performance: maximum speed 130 mph (209 km/h); service ceiling 15,800 ft (4815 m); range 420 miles (676 km)
Weights: empty 1,550 lb (703 kg); maximum take-off 2,020 lb (916 kg)
Dimensions: span 34 ft 0 in (10.36 m); length 24 ft 1 in (7.34 m); height 7 ft 11 in (2.41 m); wing area 155 sq ft (14.40 m²)

With the manually operated flaps down, a test pilot demonstrates short landing in the second O-62 in 1941. At this time nobody suspected that the Wayne, Michigan, plant would build over 3,800, of which 3,590 went to the Army.

Army 42-98718 was another L-5, later converted into an L-5A with 24-volt electrics. Everywhere the Sentinel went it proved versatile and equal to most tasks, partly because of its extra power compared with the L-4.

Below: Another of the original batch, 42-14803, seen in 1942. The L-5 really came into its own with the later versions, which could carry stretcher casualties. After the war large numbers of L-5s and OY-1s threatened to hurt the Wayne plant's sales of new civil Voyagers.

Supermarine Spitfire

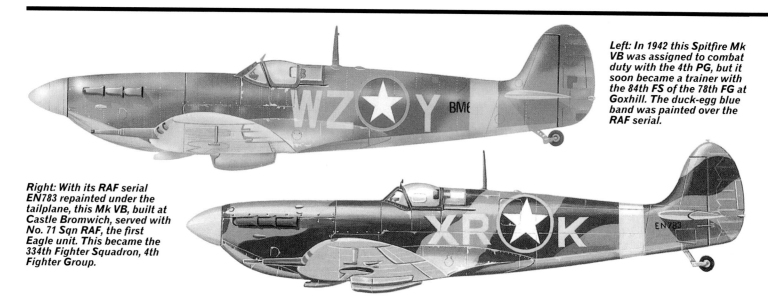

Left: In 1942 this Spitfire Mk VB was assigned to combat duty with the 4th PG, but it soon became a trainer with the 84th FS of the 78th FG at Goxhill. The duck-egg blue band was painted over the RAF serial.

Right: With its RAF serial EN783 repainted under the tailplane, this Mk VB, built at Castle Bromwich, served with No. 71 Sqn RAF, the first Eagle unit. This became the 334th Fighter Squadron, 4th Fighter Group.

One of those aircraft (such as the Douglas DC-3 and North American P-51 Mustang) which is so well known to aviation enthusiasts that it requires no description, the **Supermarine Spitfire** served in comparatively small numbers with the US Army Air Force during World War II. Its first use was by those gallant American pilots who decided to come to the aid of the 'little guy' being bullied by Hitler's Luftwaffe. They volunteered initially in numbers adequate for the Royal Air Force to establish in 1940 No. 71 'Eagle' Squadron at Church Fenton. Operational with Hawker Hurricanes in February 1941, this squadron was soon in the thick of battle and on 20 August of that year received its first **Spitfire Mk IIA**s. Subsequently, Nos 121 and 133 'Eagle' squadrons were formed with American pilots. In September 1942 all three squadrons were transferred to the US 8th Air Force in the UK, as the 4th Pursuit Group's Nos 334th, 335th and 336th Squadrons respectively. The 4th was initially based at Debden. Spitfire Mks IIA, **VA** and **VB** aircraft had been used by all three

'Eagle' squadrons, but No. 133 was the only one also to use the more advanced **Spitfire Mk IX**.

In addition to this use by American pilots in the RAF, many Spitfires saw service with the USAAF, acquired under a process known as 'Reverse Lend-Lease', and in numbers that appear to be inaccurately recorded, varying between 350 and 600 according to source. Spitfire Mks VA and VBs served for a brief period with the 31st Fighter Group at Atcham and the 52nd Fighter Group at Goxhill in the UK before embarking to take part in Operation Torch, the invasion of North Africa. The Spitfires left for Gibraltar in October 1942. Following this action these groups continued to serve there until replaced by P-51s in 1944, equipped with the tropicalised **Spitfire Mk VC**. Two other 8th Air Force units to receive the Spitfire were the 350th Fighter Group at Duxford, which also used Bell P-400 Airacobras, and the 67th Reconnaissance Group at Membury, which flew Mk VAs alongside Piper L-4s in a utility role. The 67th subsequently re-equipped with P-51A/Bs on its

transferral to the 9th Air Force, while the 350th took its Spitfires and P-39s to North Africa in January 1943. Soon after, adequate numbers of US-built aircraft became available, and sur-

Both photographs show aircraft of the 31st Pursuit (later Fighter) Group. Above, Lieutenant H.J. Connor is seen with Crew Chief Sergeant W.A. Ponder of the 309th FS, newly arrived in Tunisia in December 1942. The Spitfire is a Mk IX. In England they had flown the Mk VB, similar to 'Lima Challenger' (left), which was presented to the RAF by Mr H.L. Woodhouse of Lima, Peru, and passed on to the 307th FS; Lt R. Wooten gets ready, still at Merston, England, on 27 August 1942. Serial EN851 is tiny at the top of the fin.

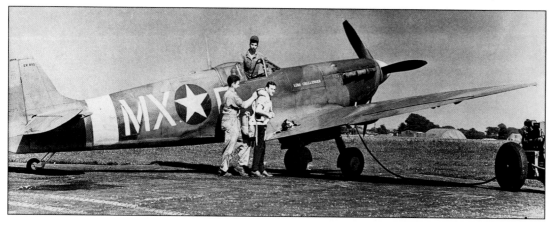

viving Spitfires of all units were returned to the RAF.

Nevertheless, the Spitfire was vital to the USAAF cause in bridging the gap during the early months in Europe and North Africa when there were no US-built fighters available.

In October 1943 a small number (around 20) **Spitfire PR.Mk XI**s were assigned to the 14th Photographic Squadron, 7th Photographic Group, based at Mount Farm in Oxfordshire. These worked closely with the RAF's PR Spitfire force, based nearby at Benson, in providing high-level photographic coverage of the European mainland. The Group's other three squadrons used the Lockheed F-4/F-5 Lightning, and while one F-5 squadron was forward deployed to France, the remaining squadrons

moved to Chalgrove in March 1945, shortly before the end of hostilities. From here the 14th PS flew the last Spitfire sortie in USAAF markings in late April.

Specification
Spitfire Mk VB
Type: single-seat fighter
Powerplant: one 1,470-hp (1096-kW) Rolls-Royce Merlin 45 Vee piston engine
Performance: maximum speed 369 mph (594 km/h) at 19,500 ft (5945 m); cruising speed 270 mph (435 km/h) at 5,000 ft (1525 m); initial climb rate 4,750 ft (1450 m) per minute; service ceiling 36,200 ft (11035 m); range 395 miles (636 km)
Weights: empty 5,050 lb (2291 kg); maximum take-off 6,650 lb (3016 kg)
Dimensions: span 32 ft 2 in (9.8 m); length 29 ft 11 in (9.12 m); height 9 ft 11 in (3.02 m); wing area 231 sq ft (21.46 m²)
Armament: four 0.303-in (7.7-mm) machine-guns and two-in (20-mm) Hispano cannon

A beautiful panorama of Spitfire Mk VBs of the 12th and 109th Reconnaissance Squadrons, 67th Reconnaissance Group, operating from Membury, England, in 1943. The 109th painted out the duck-egg blue rear-fuselage band.

This Spitfire Mk VC, JK226, was built at the vast Castle Bromwich plant with a 'B' prominent additional air filter under the engine for desert service. It was photographed over the Mediterranean in late 1942 with the 308th Fighter Squadron, 31st Fighter Group.

Left: Spitfire Mk VC of the 308th Fighter Squadron, 31st Fighter Group, showing the desert camouflage scheme. The desert filter reduced performance slightly.

Right: By 1943 the 31st Fighter Group had re-equipped with the far superior Spitfire Mk VIII. Five swastikas adorned the aircraft of Lt L.P. Molland, CO of the 308th Fighter Squadron.

Left: Distinguished by its deep jowl caused by the larger oil tank, this unarmed PR.Mk XI ranged throughout Europe from Mount Farm with the 7th Photo Group.

Taylorcraft L-2/O-57 Grasshopper

Though it was the first off-the-shelf STOL lightplane to be bought by the Army, the Taylorcraft type was eventually far outnumbered by the Piper L-4. In this photograph of an O-57 the impossible number 4210 has been drawn in (over the top of the bracing wires!).

In 1941 the US Army conducted an operational evaluation with four of each of three types of two-seat light aircraft for use in the artillery spotting and liaison roles, the three types being the **Taylorcraft YO-57**, the Aeronca YO-58 and the Piper YO-59; all were known as Grasshoppers. The successful use of the aircraft during the US Army's manoeuvres, operating directly with ground forces, resulted in increased production contracts for all three, although the Piper design was to be the most prolific.

The first four Taylorcraft YO-57s were standard civil Taylorcraft Model Ds, powered by the 65-hp (48-kW) Continental YO-170-3 flat-four engine, and were followed by 70 basically-similar **O-57s**. However, the need to provide all-round vision resulted in modifications to the cabin and rear fuselage and the introduction of trailing-edge cut-outs at the wingroots. Other alterations to fit the aircraft for its specialised tasks included an observer's seat which could be turned around to face the rear, and the installation of radio. In this form the type was designated O-57A and 336 were manufactured.

A further 140 were built under the designation **L-2A**, US Army aircraft of this class having been reclassified from observation to liaison in 1942. The YO-57s and O-57s became **L-2**s and the YO-57As were redesignated L-2A. Some 490 aircraft with special equipment, built for service with the field artillery, were designated **L-2B** and the final variant, with a production run of 900, was the **L-2M**, identified by the fully cowled engine and the fitting of wing spoilers.

Taylorcraft aircraft were also involved in the training programme for military glider pilots, involving 43 impressed civil machines which were used to provide an initial powered flying course. This total of 43 comprised nine Model DC-65s and nine BC-12-65s, both with Continental A-65 engines and designated **L-2C** and **L-2H** respectively; one DL-65, seven BL-65s and four BL-12-65s, with Lycoming O-145s and designated **L-2D**, **L-2F** and **L-2J**; and seven DF-65s, two BFT-65s, three BF-12-65s and one BF-50, all with Franklin 4AC-150s and designated **L-2E**, **L-2G**, **L-2K** and **L-2L**. Before becoming an L-2F, one aircraft impressed in Panama was assigned the designation **UC-95**. The company also developed a light training glider version which was known as the Taylorcraft ST-100 and given the designation **TG-6**. The front fuselage was extended and a 'glasshouse' canopy fitted, the landing gear simplified and a skid added under the nose; the lengthened nose necessitated increased fin area. Production totalled 253, including 10 for US Navy trials designated **XLNT-1** and 25 production **LNT-1**s.

Specification
Type: two-seat liaison aircraft/training glider
Powerplant: one 65-hp (48-kW) Continental O-170-3 flat-four piston engine
Performance: maximum speed 88 mph (142 km/h); service ceiling 10,000 ft (3050 m); range 230 miles (370 km)
Weights: empty 875 lb (397 kg); maximum take-off 1,300 lb (590 kg)
Dimensions: span 35 ft 5 in (10.79 m); length 22 ft 9 in (6.93 m); height 8 ft 0 in (2.44 m); wing area 181 sq ft (16.81 m²)

Vought F4U Corsair

The bent-wing F4U Corsair was the first carrier aircraft which could outfight not only the best fighters used by the Japanese but also those on the Allied side. Many consider the Corsair, which first flew in 1940 and was still coming off the production line in 1952, the greatest piston-engined fighter ever built.

Design of the Corsair started in February 1938. The US Navy wanted a new, high-performance shipboard fighter to follow such machines as the Brewster F2A and Grumman F-4F, the first of the fast US Navy monoplanes, with engines in the 900- to 1,000-hp (671- to 746-kW) class. The US Navy expected the new 1938 designs to use the latest Cyclone or Twin Wasp of 1,200 hp (895 kW), but Pratt & Whitney was running a larger engine, the R-2800 Double Wasp, already giving 1,850 hp (1380 kW) and good for 2,000 hp (1492 kW) with further development.

Pratt & Whitney was one of the companies of United Aircraft Corporation in Connecticut. Another UAC company, formed by a shotgun marriage of two dissimilar members, was called Vought-Sikorsky Aircraft (although by 1943 they had parted, with Sikorsky going off to make helicopters and Chance Vought Aircraft putting almost all its effort into the F4U). Vought-Sikorsky's chief engineer Rex Beisel boldly submitted a proposal to meet the 1938 fighter requirement with a fighter powered by the new R-2800. In June 1938 this was accepted, and Vought-Sikorsky received a contract for the prototype **XF4U-1**. Design progressed swiftly, and the mock-up

These aircraft, probably Marine Corps F4U-1 Ds, appear to have collided. The bulldozed airstrips on the Pacific islands were often no wider than a carrier deck, and the forward view and tendency to swing and bounce made life difficult.

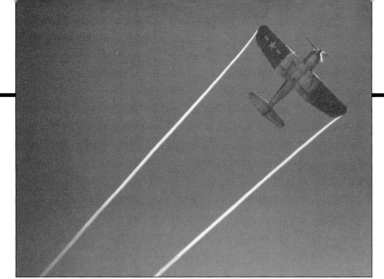

Vought F4U Corsair

*Vapour trails stream from the wingtips as an **F4U-1** of the Marines pulls out of a dive in the Solomon Islands theatre. Beyond question, the powerful bent-wing fighter gave the Japanese a severe shock. They had expected eventually to be outnumbered, but not to be beaten on a one-on-one basis.*

Below: The prototype XF4U (BuNo. 1443) had to be largely redesigned to turn it into a production aircraft. Tragically, this delayed large-scale service by two vital years.

review was successfully passed in February 1939. The silver XF4U-1 was duly flown by Lyman A. Bullard Jr at Stratford on 29 May 1940.

Though the XF4U's empty weight of 7,418 lb (3365 kg) was a technical triumph it was, in fact, considerably heavier than the laden weight of all previous US Navy carrier fighters. Compared with most fighters of World War II, and especially those of the USSR and Japan, the Vought-Sikorsky team had created a monster. The 18-cylinder radial engine was the biggest and most powerful yet put into a fighter, and it drove a three-blade Hamilton Standard (yet another UAC company) propeller with a diameter of 13 ft 4 in (4.04 m). This was easily the largest propeller so far fitted to a fighter. By comparison, the Messerschmitt Bf 109 propeller measured 9 ft 10 in (3.00 m). It was partly to give the long blades ground clearance that the wings were bent down in inverted-gull form. This made the main landing gears short enough to retract to the rear, the wheels turning 90° to lie flat in the angle of the wing just ahead of the large flaps.

The wing had to be large to provide for slow carrier landings, and this also conferred exceptional manoeuvrability. The wing of the prototype incorporated some of the earliest integral tanks, in which no less than 273 US gal (1046 litres) of fuel could be carried. In the outer wings were compartments for 20 small bombs, aimed via a sighting panel in the belly. Above the fuselage were two 0.30-in (7.62-mm) calibre synchronised guns, and two of the larger 0.50-in (12.7-mm) guns were in the outer wings. Structurally the new fighter was immensely strong, the skin of the fuselage being especially thick, and like that on the front of the wing it was attached by a new spot-welding process. Aft of the main spar, however, the wing skin was fabric, and fabric also covered the control surfaces.

Performance was even better than predicted, but on the fifth flight the valuable prototype was caught with tanks almost dry in heavy rain squalls. Pilot Boone T. Guyton decided to put it down on the Norwich golf course, but the heavy machine refused to slow down on the slippery wet grass, slammed into trees and came to rest almost demolished with just enough space under the inverted fuselage for Guyton to get out. It was then discovered that the XF4U was so strong it was repairable, though several months were lost.

From September measured performance figures were taken, and on 1 October 1940 a true speed of 405 mph (652 km/h) was recorded in level flight. This was faster than any other fighter in the world, and one important spin-off of this performance was that Pratt & Whitney

There are not many photographs of F4Us in formation with the pre-July 1943 national insignia. If these three are in the customer's hands, they are probably on test with VF-12.

sought and won US Army Air Corps permission to abandon their large and costly programme of liquid-cooled sleeve-valve engines. After all, said the engine-maker, what could these promised future engines do that the R-2800 was not doing already in the Corsair? This flight by the big US Navy fighter ensured that the Allies' biggest aero-engine maker stuck with air-cooled radials for the rest of the piston era, and it also made the Corsair the standard by which other US Navy fighter proposals would be judged.

Yet the XF4U had a very long way to go. After much argument the armament was radically changed. The fuselage guns were omitted, and the outer wings were given four extra 0.50-in (12.7-mm) guns, to make six in all. Bombs and the sighting panel were deleted. Unfortunately the heavy wing armament made it impossible to put integral tanks in the leading edge, and the rather retrograde decision was taken to put all fuel in a vast 237-US gal (896-litre) tank in the fuselage. In turn this meant moving the cockpit 32 in (0.81 m) to the rear, which made the most vital forward field of view worse. There were many other changes, such as an increase in size of the ailerons to give more rapid roll, and a change to NACA-type slotted flaps. Armour was added, along with a bulletproof windshield, protected self-sealing fuel-tank construction, folding wings, an arrester hook and the British-invented IFF ('identification friend or foe' radio). The already outstanding engine installation

was improved with 'jet thrust' exhaust stacks and efficient leading-edge ram inlets for the carburettor and oil coolers.

Final demonstrations took place early in 1941, and the first production contract, for 584 **F4U-1** Corsairs, was received in June 1941. The first F4U-1 flew a year later and was handed to the US Navy on 31 July 1942, one day after the first of the rival Grumman F6F Hellcats made its first flight, with a similar engine.

It so happened that the F6F was rushed into carrier service, while the Navy found much to criticise in the potentially much more capable F4U-1. Stalling behaviour was dangerous, and a sharp-edged metal strip was eventually added on the outer right leading edge to make that wing stall at the same time as the left. A sudden yaw called 'rudder kick' near the point of touchdown was corrected by making the tailwheel leg longer, but this made it impossible to use the full wing lift and so land more slowly. An especially tricky problem on a

Above: An F4U-1 D is photographed just off the line at Stratford, Connecticut, and ready for its first flight. Chance Vought built nearly all the 12,571 Corsairs.

Right: Four 20-mm cannon immediately identify this aircraft as an F4U-1C; it was probably BuNo. 82277. Only 200 were built, most going to VMF-311.

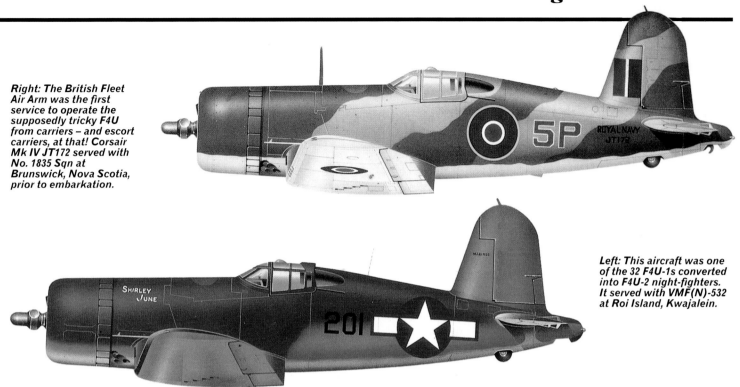

Right: The British Fleet Air Arm was the first service to operate the supposedly tricky F4U from carriers – and escort carriers, at that! Corsair Mk IV JT172 served with No. 1835 Sqn at Brunswick, Nova Scotia, prior to embarkation.

Left: This aircraft was one of the 32 F4U-1s converted into F4U-2 night-fighters. It served with VMF(N)-532 at Roi Island, Kwajalein.

carrier deck was the severe tendency to bounce.

The upshot of these factors was that the F4U was not accepted for carrier service, and all the first batches went to units of the US Marine Corps. These fine squadrons, beginning with VMF-124, all fought from narrow airstrips on Pacific islands. By the end of 1943 everyone, especially the Japanese, knew the F4U to be the premier air combat fighter in the Pacific; subsequent tests in the USA showed it on many counts to be the best everywhere else

Production slowly got into its stride, and whereas 178 were built in 1942 the total for 1943 was 2,294, of which 378 were **FG-1**s produced by Goodyear Aircraft and 136 **F3A**s by the inefficient Brewster company. After the 1,550th Corsair the more powerful R-2800-8W engine was fitted, with water injection to give 2,250 hp (1679 kW). This resulted in the designation **F4U-1A** (plus Goodyear **FG-1A**, with non-folding wings, and Brewster **F3A-1A**).

By this time pilot view had been improved by a small bulge in the top of the sliding canopy, followed by elimination of the original 'birdcage' in favour of a clear-view raised canopy in conjunction with a raised seat. The **F4U-1B** was a variant for the British Fleet Air Arm. The **F4U-1C** was a batch of 200 with four 20-mm M2 (Hispano)

With SBDs and TBFs behind, F4U-2 night fighters of VF(N)-101 prepare to take off from CVE-6 Enterprise for an operation against Truk in February 1944. This Marine squadron was the only one to fly F4U night-fighters from a wartime escort carrier.

Below: The F4U-5 was a post-war version, with a 2,450-hp Double Wasp, retractable tailwheel and other changes. These have the bold 36-in two-letter fuselage code, soon replaced by a single tail letter and the individual number on the fuselage.

cannon. The **F4U-1D** was the first model with pylons under the inner wings for two 160-US gal (606-litre) drop tanks or two 1,000-lb (454-kg) bombs, an exceptional load for a fighter. Thirty-two F4U-ls were rebuilt as **F4U-2** night fighters, with only four guns but radar, an autopilot and other special gear; these Corsairs, the first radar-equipped naval night fighters, achieved a remarkable combat record from carriers and shore bases.

Carrier flying was still prohibited in the US Navy, but the 2,012 Corsairs supplied under Lend-Lease to the British Fleet Air Arm were used aboard carriers from 1943. By April 1944 both HMS *Victorious* and *Illustrious* were launching Corsairs in action, against the German battleship *Tirpitz* in Norway and against Japanese installations in the Dutch East Indies. The British had to clip 8 in (0.203 m) off each wing, squaring off the tip, to provide stowage on their low-roofed hangar decks, yet despite this reduction in wing area the Corsair was cleared for deck operations as soon as a curving landing pattern had been devised to keep the deck in view.

Altogether there were 500 major and over 2,500 minor engineering changes made to the F4U-1 during production of 4,102 by Vought, 3,808 by Goodyear and 735 by Brewster. Only a handful of **F4U-3** high-altitude fighters were produced, with the XR-2800-16 engine and turbo-supercharger, ram air being admitted via a large ventral duct. The **F4U-4**, however, did go into production as the final wartime model, stemming from the **F4U-4XA** flown in April 1944.

Vought F4U Corsair

Differences were relatively minor, including a new R-2800-18W or -42W engine (rated at up to 2,450 hp/1828 kW with water injection and driving a 13 ft 2 in/4.01 m four-blade Hydromatic propeller) with the carburettor air duct moved from the leading edge to a new duct under the engine, which in turn meant re-routing the exhaust stacks. The **F4U-4B** had four M3 cannon, and all F4U-4s could carry any of the profusion of external loads now available including eight 5-in (12.7-cm) rockets or two of the monster Tiny Tim rockets. The F4U-4 was being built by Vought at the rate of 300 a month by 1945, and it stayed in production until 1947, by which time 2,365 had been delivered. By VJ-Day the F4U had flown 64,051 sorties, with a combat record of 2,140 confirmed enemy aircraft destroyed in air battle (plus at least as many more destroyed on the ground) for the combat loss of only 189 Corsairs.

Post-war production

Unlike almost all other US piston-engined fighters, the F4U remained a busy development and production programme after VJ-Day. On 4 April 1946 Chance Vought Aircraft flew the improved **F4U-5**, which was extensively used during the Korean war. US Marine Corps squadrons flew the bulk of the Corsair missions in Korea, though it was a US Navy carrier-based unit that opened the campaign only eight days after the war began. Corsairs were in intensive action to the last day of that war, 27 July 1953.

As in the case of the F4U-4 there were **F4U-5N** radar night-fighters and **F4U-5P** photo-reconnaissance versions, and the bitter winter in Korea led to a further variant, the **F4U-5NL** night-fighter with wing and tail de-icer boots of the Goodrich flexible pattern, de-icer shoes along the leading edges of the propeller and further improved thermal de-icing of the pilot windscreen. The **F4U-6** was a dedicated attack version of the Corsair, which by the time it flew in 1952 had been redesignated **AU-1**. The overload take-off weight of the AU-1 could be as high as 19,398 lb (8799 kg) with over 4,480 lb (2032 kg) of offensive stores under wings and fuselage, plus drop tanks.

The final model was for France's Aéronavale, which needed modern multi-role tactical aircraft for service in Indo-China. The French received 94 **F4U-7**s under the US Mutual Defense Assistance Program. Completed in December 1952, they were the last of 12,571 Corsairs of all versions and the last piston-engined fighter in production in the world apart from the S-49 in Yugoslavia and the Hispano Ha 1112 (Merlin-Messerschmitt) in Spain.

A Marine Corps F4U-1D salvoes 5-in rockets at Japanese dug in among the mountains of southern Okinawa in June 1945. The photo was taken by Marine Lt D.D. Duncan from inside a modified drop tank under a Lockheed F-5E.

Vought F4U Corsair cutaway drawing key

1 Spinner
2 Three-bladed Hamilton Standard constant-speed propeller
3 Reduction gear housing
4 Nose ring
5 Pratt & Whitney R-2800-8 Double Wasp 18-cylinder two-row engine
6 Exhaust pipes
7 Hydraulically-operated cowling
8 Fixed cowling panels
9 Wing leading-edge unprotected integral fuel tank, capacity 235 litres (62 US gal)
10 Truss-type main spar
11 Leading-edge rib structure
12 Starboard navigation light
13 Wingtip
14 Wing structure
15 Wing ribs
16 Wing outer-section (fabric skinning aft of main spar)
17 Starboard aileron
18 Ammunition boxes (max total capacity 2,350 rounds)
19 Aileron trim tab
20 Aerial mast
21 Forward bulkhead
22 Oil tank, capacity 98 litres (26 US gal)
23 Oil tank forward armour plate
24 Fire suppressor cylinder
25 Supercharger housing
26 Exhaust trunking
27 Blower assembly
28 Engine support frame
29 Engine control runs
30 Wing mainspar carry-through structure
31 Engine support attachment
32 Upper cowling deflection plate (0.25 cm/0.1 in aluminium)
33 Fuel filler cap
34 Fuselage main fuel tank, capacity 897 litres (237 US gal)
35 Upper longeron
36 Fuselage forward frames
37 Rudder pedals
38 Heelboards
39 Control column
40 Instrument panel
41 Reflector sight
42 Armour-glass windshield
43 Rear-view mirror
44 Rearward-sliding cockpit canopy
45 Handgrip
46 Headrest
47 Pilot's head and back armour
48 Canopy frame
49 Pilot's seat
50 Engine control quadrant
51 Trim tab control wheels
52 Wing-folding lever
53 Centre/aft fuselage bulkhead
54 Radio shelf
55 Radio installation
56 Canopy track
57 Bulkhead
58 Aerial lead-in
59 Aerial mast
60 Aerials
61 Heavy-sheet skin plating
62 Dorsal identification light
63 Longeron
64 Control runs
65 Aft fuselage structure
66 Compass installation
67 Lifting tube
68 Access/inspection panels
69 Fin/fuselage forward attachment
70 Starboard tailplane
71 Elevator balance
72 Fin structure
73 Inspection panels
74 Rudder balance
75 Aerial stub
76 Rudder upper hinge
77 Rudder structure
78 Diagonal bracing
79 Rudder trim tab
80 Trim tab actuating rod
81 Access panel
82 Rudder post
83 Tailplane end rib
84 Elevator control runs
85 Fixed fairing root
86 Elevator trim tabs (port and starboard)
87 Tail cone
88 Rear navigation light
89 Port elevator
90 Elevator balance
91 Port tailplane structure
92 Arrester hook (stowed)
93 Tail section frames
94 Fairing
95 Tailwheel (retracted)
96 Arrester hook (lowered)
97 Tailwheel/hook doors
98 Tailwheel/hook attachment/pivot
99 Mooring/tie-down lug
100 Rearward-retracting tailwheel
101 Tailwheel oleo
102 Support strut
103 Arrester hook actuating strut
104 Aft/tail section bulkhead
105 Arrester hook shock-absorber
106 Tailwheel/arrester hook cylinder
107 Tailwheel retraction strut
108 Bulkhead attachment points
109 Fuselage skinning
110 Bulkhead frame
111 Elevator/rudder control runs
112 Entry hand/foothold
113 Hydraulically-operated flap inboard section
114 Wing fold line
115 'Flap gap' closure plate
116 Hydraulically-operated flap outboard section

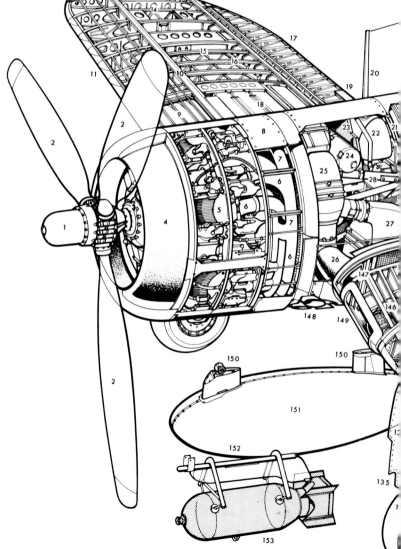

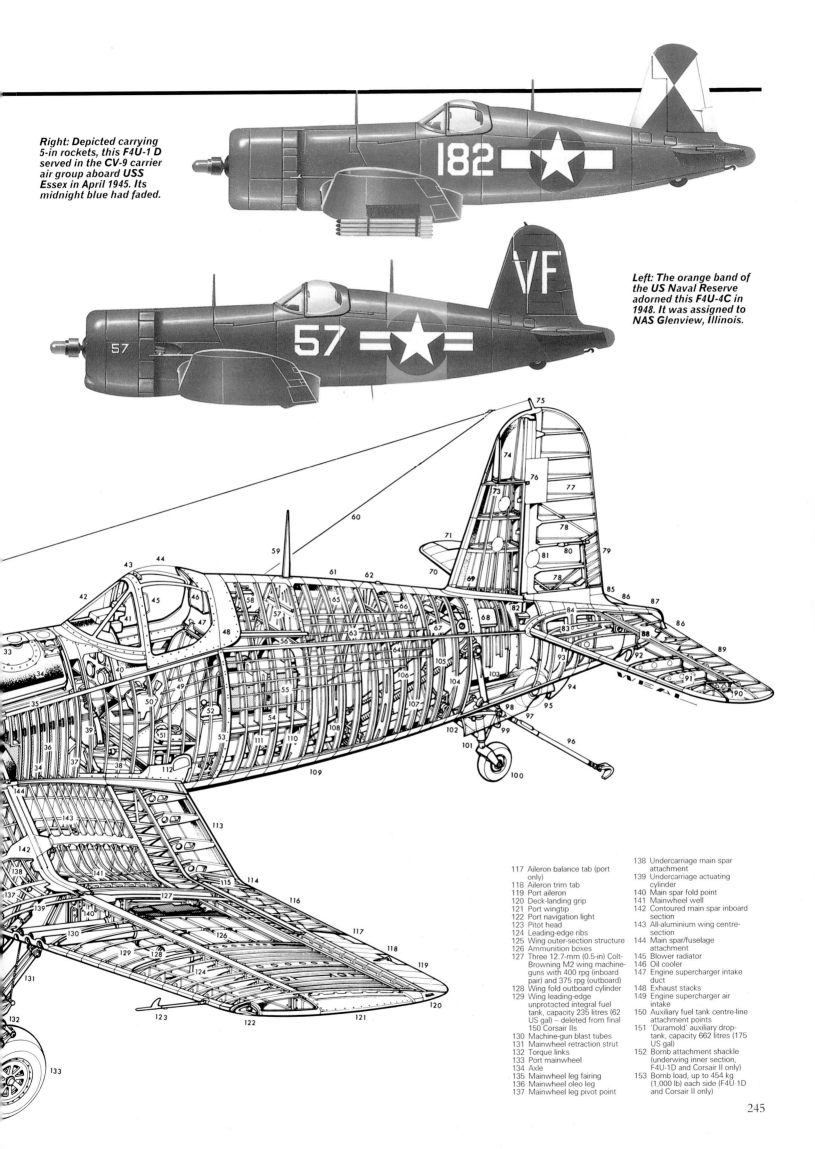

Right: Depicted carrying 5-in rockets, this F4U-1 D served in the CV-9 carrier air group aboard USS Essex in April 1945. Its midnight blue had faded.

182

Left: The orange band of the US Naval Reserve adorned this F4U-4C in 1948. It was assigned to NAS Glenview, Illinois.

VF

57

117 Aileron balance tab (port only)
118 Aileron trim tab
119 Port aileron
120 Deck-landing grip
121 Port wingtip
122 Port navigation light
123 Pitot head
124 Leading-edge ribs
125 Wing outer-section structure
126 Ammunition boxes
127 Three 12.7-mm (0.5-in) Colt-Browning M2 wing machine-guns with 400 rpg (inboard pair) and 375 rpg (outboard)
128 Wing fold outboard cylinder
129 Wing leading-edge unprotected integral fuel tank, capacity 235 litres (62 US gal) – deleted from final 150 Corsair IIs
130 Machine-gun blast tubes
131 Mainwheel retraction strut
132 Torque links
133 Port mainwheel
134 Axle
135 Mainwheel leg fairing
136 Mainwheel oleo leg
137 Mainwheel leg pivot point

138 Undercarriage main spar attachment
139 Undercarriage actuating cylinder
140 Main spar fold point
141 Mainwheel well
142 Contoured main spar inboard section
143 All-aluminium wing centre-section
144 Main spar/fuselage attachment
145 Blower radiator
146 Oil cooler
147 Engine supercharger intake duct
148 Exhaust stacks
149 Engine supercharger air intake
150 Auxiliary fuel tank centre-line attachment points
151 'Duramold' auxiliary drop-tank, capacity 662 litres (175 US gal)
152 Bomb attachment shackle (underwing inner section, F4U-1D and Corsair II only)
153 Bomb load, up to 454 kg (1,000 lb) each side (F4U-1D and Corsair II only)

Vought F4U Corsair

F4U-1A 29 Corsair VF-17 'Jolly Roger' USS *Bougainville* Nov 1943 – Feb 1944

This Corsair was flown by Lieutenant Ira C. 'Ike' Kepford, the US Navy's leading ace in the Pacific, with VF-17, the 'Jolly Roger', the first US Navy F4U squadron to see action. Kepford, who was one of 15 aces to go to war with the F4U, had 16 victories recorded by 'rising suns' on the fuselage side, forward of the cockpit.

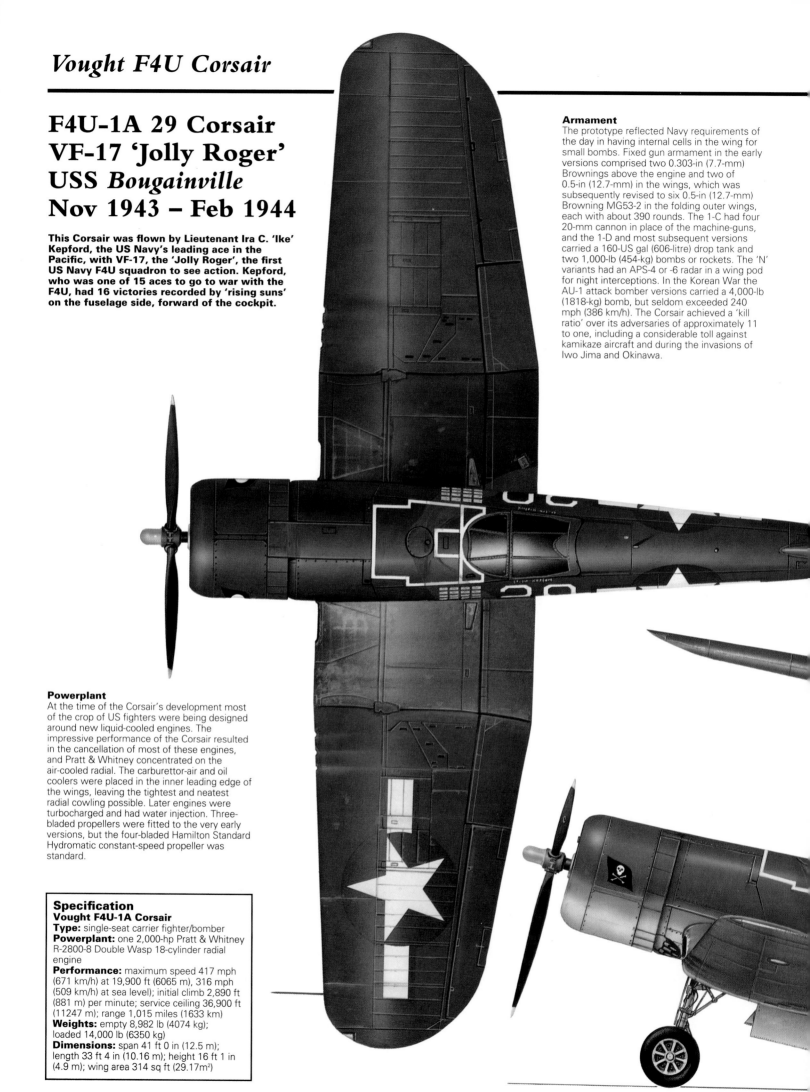

Armament
The prototype reflected Navy requirements of the day in having internal cells in the wing for small bombs. Fixed gun armament in the early versions comprised two 0.303-in (7.7-mm) Brownings above the engine and two of 0.5-in (12.7-mm) in the wings, which was subsequently revised to six 0.5-in (12.7-mm) Browning MG53-2 in the folding outer wings, each with about 390 rounds. The 1-C had four 20-mm cannon in place of the machine-guns, and the 1-D and most subsequent versions carried a 160-US gal (606-litre) drop tank and two 1,000-lb (454-kg) bombs or rockets. The 'N' variants had an APS-4 or -6 radar in a wing pod for night interceptions. In the Korean War the AU-1 attack bomber versions carried a 4,000-lb (1818-kg) bomb, but seldom exceeded 240 mph (386 km/h). The Corsair achieved a 'kill ratio' over its adversaries of approximately 11 to one, including a considerable toll against kamikaze aircraft and during the invasions of Iwo Jima and Okinawa.

Powerplant
At the time of the Corsair's development most of the crop of US fighters were being designed around new liquid-cooled engines. The impressive performance of the Corsair resulted in the cancellation of most of these engines, and Pratt & Whitney concentrated on the air-cooled radial. The carburettor-air and oil coolers were placed in the inner leading edge of the wings, leaving the tightest and neatest radial cowling possible. Later engines were turbocharged and had water injection. Three-bladed propellers were fitted to the very early versions, but the four-bladed Hamilton Standard Hydromatic constant-speed propeller was standard.

Specification
Vought F4U-1A Corsair
Type: single-seat carrier fighter/bomber
Powerplant: one 2,000-hp Pratt & Whitney R-2800-8 Double Wasp 18-cylinder radial engine
Performance: maximum speed 417 mph (671 km/h) at 19,900 ft (6065 m), 316 mph (509 km/h) at sea level; initial climb 2,890 ft (881 m) per minute; service ceiling 36,900 ft (11247 m); range 1,015 miles (1633 km)
Weights: empty 8,982 lb (4074 kg); loaded 14,000 lb (6350 kg)
Dimensions: span 41 ft 0 in (12.5 m); length 33 ft 4 in (10.16 m); height 16 ft 1 in (4.9 m); wing area 314 sq ft (29.17m²)

Production

The Corsair achieved the longest production run of any American piston-engined fighter. Despite delayed entry into production in late 1941, the last Corsair left the factory in December 1952. In the post-war period during the Korean War more than 1,800 Corsairs were involved, and altogether the total of Corsair variants built was 12,571. It was also the last piston-engined fighter to go into series production in the United States, and was still in front-line service when the first jets made their appearance.

US Marine Corps carriers

Flown by pilots of the Marine Corps, Corsairs first won air supremacy in the battle zones and then went on to prove themselves as the Marines' best friends in their secondary role as fighter-bombers as US forces advanced deep into enemy territory in the Pacific theatre. The Marines and their Corsairs became a byword for deadly firepower, and many became aces while flying their F4Us.

Vought F4U Corsair variants

XF4U-1: prototype, with R-2800-4 engine of 1,850 hp (1380 kW) and all fuel in wings

F4U-1: principal production version; usually 2,000-hp (1492 kW) R-2800-8 engine (late versions 2,250 hp/ 1879 kW); six 0.50-in (12.7-mm) guns or (-IC) four M2 cannon (total 9441)

F4U-1A: similar to F4U-1 except for canopy (heightened and in one piece); spoiler on outside edge of wings; longer tailwheel leg and minor alterations; 360 delivered to Royal Navy as Corsair Mk IIs

F4U-1C: 200 F4U-1As armed with four 20-mm cannon in place of machine-guns

F4U-1D: fighter-bomber version of F4U-1A with provision for bombs, rockets or auxiliary fuel tanks. 192 to RNZAF and 150 to Royal Navy

F4U-1P: several F4U-1s modified into photo-reconnaissance aircraft

F4U-2: conversions to first night-fighter version with APS-4 radar on right wing; usually four or five 0.50-in (12 7-mm) guns

F4U-3: high-altitude version with turbocharged R-2800- 16 (no production)

F4U-4: late-war production version; R-2800-18W or -42W engine rated at 2,450 hp (1828 kW); improved cockpit and other changes (total 2,357)

F4U-4C: 300 F4U-4s armed with 20-mm cannon in place of six machine-guns

F4U-4E: several F4U-4Cs modified into night-fighters with APS-4 radar

F4U-4K: radio-controlled target aircraft modified from F4U-4

F4U-4N: F4U-Cs modified into night-fighters with APS-6 radar

F4U-4P: F4U-4s modified into armed photo-reconnaissance aircraft

F4U-5: post-war model with 2,850 hp (2126 kW) R-2800-32W, metal-skinned wings and tail, and many other changes (total in several sub-types 568)

F5U-5N: night-fighter version of F4U-5

F5U-5NL: 72 night-fighters similar to F4U-5N except for cold-climate modification; several F5U-5Ns brought up to same standard

F5U-5P: 40 F5U-5s produced as armed photo-reconnaissance aircraft

AU-1 (F4U-6): dedicated low level attack version (total 111)

F4U-7: carrier-based fighter-bomber version for French, basically AU with F4U-4 engine (total 94)

FG-1A: 1,704 F4U-1As produced by Goodyear from February 1943; 99 to Royal Navy as Corsair Mk IV

FG-1D: F4U-1Ds produced by Goodyear; 828 to Royal Navy as Corsair Mk IV and 60 to RNZAF

Fuselage/wing

The low-set wings were of inverted-gull form, partly to achieve the ideal 90° junction with the fuselage (which would otherwise have needed a mid-wing like the F4F Wildcat) and partly to match the 13 ft 4 in (4.06 m) propeller. It also enabled the length of landing gear that could retract backwards with the wheels rotating 87° on the legs to lie neatly inside the wings; the apertures closed by hinged doors and strut fairings after the wheels were retracted. This meant that the undercarriage had to be very high, a great drawback for an aircraft that had to land on flight decks. The outer wing sections were set at a coarse dihedral angle. The wing was of single-spar, all-metal construction, with spot-welded smooth skin and the outer wings folded upwards for stowage in aircraft-carriers. Of semi-monocoque construction, the all-metal fuselage was spot-welded to produce a completely smooth finish. Subsequently an improved-visibility one-piece blown cockpit was fitted, the pilot was seated at a higher level, and the designation was changed from F4U-1 to F4U-1A.

Vought O3U/SU Corsair

Its assignation clearly marked, BuNo. 8870 was the last but one of 87 O3U-1s. All versions were Wasp-engined.

First aircraft to bear the famous Vought Corsair name was the O2U, which was little more than a developed version of the UO/FU series of observer aircraft of the 1920s, which were themselves derived from the Lewis & Vought VE trainer of 1918. The O2U incorporated an all-steel tube fuselage structure and introduced the Pratt & Whitney Wasp radial engine. Deliveries to the US Navy began in 1927 and production totalled 291 in several versions

From 1930 the O2U began to be superseded in US Navy service by the **O3U Corsair,** which was basically similar to the O2U-4, one of which was fitted experimentally with a Grumman amphibious float. O3U aircraft were built in six different versions which incorporated greater strength and more engine power. The **O3U-2** was later redesignated **SU-1**, the **O3U-4** became the **SU-2**, and with low-pressure tyres it became the **SU-3**. The **SU-4** was a new production version of the **SU-2**. A total of 289 O3Us and SUs were built for the US Navy.

By the time the USA became involved in World War II these Corsair biplanes had been withdrawn from first-line use, although 141 remained in service in secondary roles. A few O3U-6s were converted by the Naval Aircraft Factory to radio-controlled pilotless configuration for experimental use, and these were provided with fixed tricycle landing gear to simplify take-off and landing operations. Export versions included the V-65F for the Argentine navy, the V-80P for the Peruvian air force and the V-85G for Germany.

Specification
Vought SU-4 Corsair
Type: two-seat scout
Powerplant: one 600-hp (447-kW) Pratt & Whitney R-1690-42 Hornet radial piston engine
Performance: maximum speed 167 mph (269 km/h) at sea level; service ceiling 18,600 ft (5670 m); range 680 miles (1094 km)
Weights: empty 3,312 lb (1502 kg); maximum take-off 4,765 lb (2161 kg)
Dimensions: span 36 ft 0 in (10.97 m); length 27 ft 5½ in (8.37 m); height 11 ft 4 in (3.45 m); wing area 337.0 sq ft (31.31 m²)
Armament: three 0.3-in (7.62-mm) machine-guns, one forward-firing and two on trainable mount in rear cockpit

Vought OS2U Kingfisher

Designed to replace the O3U Corsair biplane, the **Vought VS-310 Kingfisher** incorporated new constructional features, including the use of spot welding. Evaluation of the design proposal led to a US Navy contract for a prototype which was powered by a 450-hp (336-kW) Pratt & Whitney R-9854 engine. It was flown for the first time in landplane configuration in March 1938 and in its intended float-plane version on 19 May 1938.

A successful conclusion to official testing brought the first production order for the **OS2U-1 Kingfisher**, and when these aircraft began to enter service from August 1940 they were the first catapult-launched monoplane observation aircraft to serve with the US Navy.

Built quite extensively, the Kingfisher was primarily intended for the scout/observation role, operating from catapults aboard the US Navy's capital ships and cruisers, But it also served with US Navy inshore patrol squadrons, where it proved very successful in the ASW and air/sea rescue roles.

The **XOS2U-l** was the original prototype, powered by a Pratt & Whitney R-985-4 engine. The first production variant was the

The OS2U was better than all its planned replacements. The launch of this OS2U-3 was watched by hundreds of the crew of the battleship Texas.

Above: Dated 11 May 1940, this official picture shows the first production OS2U-1 in landplane configuration. Colours were silver and yellow.

Left: An OS2U-3 is taxied onto the recovery sled towed by the cruiser Quincy ready for the crane to hoist it aboard.

OS2U-l, with the 450-hp (336-kW) R-985-48 engine; 54 were built. These were followed by 158 **OS2U-2s**, which introduced some equipment changes and the R-985-50 engine of the same power output. The main produc-tion version was the **OS2U-3**, with 1,006 being built. This introduced self-sealing fuel tanks, armour protection, and the R-985-AN-2 engine of the same output. The **OS2N-l** was the OS2U-3 built by the Naval Aircraft Factory, which complet-ed 300 examples. The **XOS2U-4** was a converted OS2U-2 with narrow-chord wings and other aerofoil revisions, but which never went into production.

The type was used also by the Royal Navy, which received 100 under Lend-Lease, these being operated under the designation Kingfisher Mk I, serving as catapult-launched reconnaissance aircraft and as trainers. Others were supplied to Argentina (9), Chile (15), the Dominican Republic (3), Mexico (6) and Uruguay (6). Twenty-four which were en route to the Netherlands East Indies were docked in Australia when the islands were overrun by the Japanese, and 18 of them served with the Royal Australian Air Force.

Specification
Vought OS2U-3 Kingfisher
Type: two-seat observation aircraft
Powerplant: one 450-hp (336-kW) Pratt & Whitney R-985-AN-2 radial piston engine
Performance: maximum speed 164 mph (264 km/h) at 5,500 ft (1675 m); service ceiling 13,000 ft (3960 m); range 805 miles (1296 km)
Weights: empty 4,123 lb (1870 kg); maximum take-off 6,000 lb (2722 kg)
Dimensions: span 35 ft 11 in (10.95 m); length 33 ft 10 in (10.31 m); height 15 ft 12 in (4.61 m); wing area 262.0 sq ft (24.34 m²)
Armament: two 0.3-in (7.62-mm) machine-guns (one forward-firing and one on trainable mount in rear cockpit), plus two 100-lb (45-kg) or 325-lb (147-kg) bombs on underwing racks

Vought SB2U Vindicator

This SB2U-1 is depicted in the markings of VS-41, aboard USS Ranger in August 1942, immediately before withdrawal from front-line use.

Late in 1934, Vought received a US Navy order for two proto-types of a new carrier-based scout-bomber. The Vought **XSB2U-l** was to be a mono-plane and for competitive evalua-tion the **XSB3U-l** was to be a biplane. Both machines were tested in the early summer of 1936, and there was no doubt of the superiority of the monoplane; an initial order for 54 production **SB2U-l** aircraft was placed on 26 October 1936.

The close relationship of this aircraft to the Vought SBU, a two-seat fighter then in service, was confirmed by the fact that the XSB3U-1 biplane prototype was basically an SBU-1 with retractable main landing gear units. However, the SB2U-1, while similar, differed by having an all-metal basic structure with part-fabric and part-metal cover-ing, outer wing panels that folded for carrier stowage, an arrester hook in the rear fuselage, and powerplant comprising an 825-hp (615-kW) Pratt & Whitney R-1535-96 Twin Wasp Junior engine. Subsequent orders for the US Navy included the generally similar **SB2U-2** (58 built), and the **SB2U-3** (57) which intro-duced armour protection, increased fuel, the R-1535-02 engine and heavier armament; these were the first models to be named Vindicator. One SB2U-2 tested on twin floats was given the designation **XSB2U-3**.

US Navy squadrons equipped with SB2Us saw action in the Pacific during 1942, including participation in the Battle of Midway, but the Vought scout bomber was quickly withdrawn from combat service because of

Vought SB2U Vindicator

its vulnerability to modern fighters such as the Mitsubishi A6M Zero.

Under the company designation V-156 Vought built and delivered 24 of 40 Vindicators ordered for the French navy, some of these falling into German hands when the French capitulated. Similarly, 50 with the designation V-156B-l were built for the British Fleet Air Arm, which designated them **Chesapeake Mk I**; following combat evaluation all were used in an operational training role.

Specification
Vought SB2U-3 Vindicator
Type: carrier-based scout/bomber
Powerplant: one 825-hp (615-kW) Pratt & Whitney R-1535-02 Twin Wasp Junior radial piston engine
Performance: maximum speed 243 mph (391 km/h) at 9,500 ft (2895 m); service ceiling 23,600 ft (7195 m); range 1,120 miles (1802 km)

Left: Dated 21 May 1937, this official view shows the first production SB2U-1, BuNo. 0726. It is devoid of markings.

Weights: empty 5,634 lb (2556 kg); maximum take-off 9,421 lb (4273 kg)
Dimensions: span 42 ft 0 in (12.80 m), length 34 ft 0 in (10.36 m); height 10 ft 3 in (3.12 m); wing area 305.0 sq ft (28.33 m²)

Above: These OS2U-1s were seen on 23 May 1939 in the full markings of bomber squadron VB-3, embarked aboard USS Saratoga.

Armament: two 0.5-in (12.7-mm) machine-guns (one forward-firing and one on trainable mount in rear cockpit), plus up to 1,000 lb (454 kg) of bombs

Vultee A-31/A-35 Vengeance

This V-72 was built by Northrop in 1942 as a Vengeance Mk II for the RAF, but requisitioned (with RAF camouflage and serial) as a USAAF air-gunner trainer. Later transfers were redesignated as A-31s.

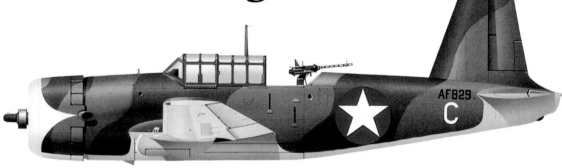

Development of the Vultee V-11/V-12 single-engined light attack bomber led to the **V-72** dive-bomber. In 1940 a British purchasing mission, which had received plenty of confirmation of the capabilities of the dive-bomber, placed an order for 700 of these aircraft under the designation **Vengeance**, and the first of these aircraft for Britain (AN838) flew initially in July 1941. A fairly large mid-wing monoplane of all-metal construction, it had hydraulically-operated air-brakes on the wings for control in the dive and hydraulically-retracted tailwheel-type

This Air Corps Materiel Division photograph shows 41-31256, a Nashville-built A-35B. Of 1,931 Vengeances, only a handful saw action in Burma with the RAF, RIAF and RAAF.

landing gear. The powerplant comprised one 1,700-hp (1268-kW) Wright GR-2600-A5 Cyclone 14 twin-row radial engine.

The British order comprised 400 Mk I aircraft and 300 Mk II, built by Northrop and Vultee respectively, since the latter had insufficient production capacity. Subsequently, under Lend-Lease, the USAAF ordered 300 more aircraft for Britain, allocating the designation **A-31**.

When the US became involved in the war, at least 243 of the aircraft intended for Britain were commandeered by the USAAF and put into service as V-72s or **RA-31**s. Further production was initiated for the USAAF, these equipped to US Army standards, and with armament comprising five 0.50-in (12.7-mm) machine-guns. Vultee built 99 under the designation **A-35A**, followed by 831 A-35Bs

with the Wright R-2600-13 engine and increased armament. Many were used as target tugs. Variants included one **XA-31B** with a 3,000-hp (2237-kW) Wright XR-4360-1 Wasp Major radial engine installed for test purposes, and five **YA-31C**s with 2,200-hp (1640-kW) R-3350-13/-37 Cyclone engines installed for development purposes.

Specification
Type: two-seat dive-bomber
Powerplant: (A-35B) one 1,700-hp (1268-kW) Wright R-2600-13 Cyclone 14 radial piston engine
Performance: maximum speed 279 mph (449 km/h) at 13,500 ft (4115 m); cruising speed 230 mph (370 km/h); service ceiling 22,300 ft (6800 m); range 2,300 miles (3701 km)
Weights: empty 10,300 lb (4672 kg); maximum take-off 16,400 lb (7439 kg)
Dimensions: span 48 ft 0 in (14.63 m); length 39 ft 9 in (12.12 m); height 15 ft 4 in (4.67 m); wing area 332 sq ft (30.84 m²)
Armament: six 0.50-in (12.7-mm) machine-guns, plus up to 2,000 lb (907 kg) of bombs

Vultee BT-13/BT-15/BC-3/SNV Valiant

A study of the designs initiated by the Vultee Company, especially from the mid-1930s, indicated the introduction of many innovative features. Perhaps one of their most revolutionary design schemes was that for four aircraft to be produced with the same basic tooling and having such assemblies as the wings, aft fuselage and tail unit in common. Variations in powerplant, forward fuselage, landing gear and equipment would ring the necessary changes to provide an advanced, basic or basic combat trainer and a lightweight fighter. While the company probably hoped that such a plan would enable them to get the maximum profit yield from the typical small-scale procurement of the inter-war years, it is unlikely that they imagined in their wildest dreams that one aircraft of that quarto would outnumber all other basic trainers produced in the USA during World War II.

It began in a very small way in 1938 when the US Army Air Corps tested Vultee's **BC-3** basic combat trainer, evolved from the **BC-51** which was one of the four aircraft mentioned above. The BC-3 had retractable landing gear and a 600-hp (447-kW) Pratt & Whitney Wasp engine and, while testing showed that it had ideal characteristics for a training role, the complexity of a retractable landing gear was unnecessary for the required basic

trainer, as was such a powerful engine. As a result, Vultee developed a new **Model 74**, which had fixed landing gear and a less powerful engine, and US Army testing resulted in an initial contract for 300 aircraft. When placed in September 1939, this was the US Army's largest ever order for basic trainers.

Designated **BT-13** by the USAAC, the new basic trainer was a low-wing cantilever monoplane of all-metal structure, with all control surfaces fabric-covered. Landing gear featured oleo-pneumatic shock-struts, a steerable tailwheel, and hydraulic brakes. Accommodation was provided for a crew of two, seated in tandem beneath a continuous transparent canopy, and dual controls and blind-flying instrumentation were standard.

BT-13s were soon established in service, and contracts were placed for very large numbers of these aircraft. They were followed on the production line by **BT-13As** with a different version of the R-985 Wasp Junior engine and detail refinements, and 6,407 of this variant were built. The **BT-13B** differed only by having a 24-volt electrical system. Production of these airframes was so rapid that the supply of engines dried up, leading to the **BT-15** with the 450-hp (336-kW) Wright R-975-11 Whirlwind 9 engine, of which 1,693 were built. The single

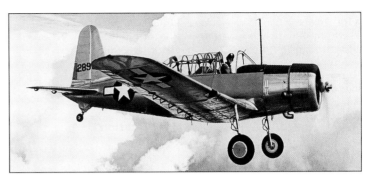

Every aviation buff knows the T-6/Harvard, yet in terms of numbers of Allied pilots trained in the USA the 11,537 Valiants made at least an equal contribution. This was one of the 6,407 of the BT-13A version.

With so many available, some Valiants reached foreign theatres. BT-13A 42-88868 was photographed in 1944 at Myitkyina, Burma. It has its AAF serial number repeated under the wing. Painted cowlings and vertical tails were featured by some schools in the USA.

Below: One of a line of BT-13Bs, distinguished mainly by having a 24-volt electrical system. Its light-alloy propeller blades appear to be painted red. Despite having 450 hp against the T-6's 600, and fixed landing gear, the all-round performance of the two aircraft was not significantly different. A substantial number are still airworthy.

Vultee BT-13/BT-15/BC-3/SNV Valiant

XBT-16 was a BT-13 constructed by Vidal in 1942 with an all-plastic fuselage.

The US Navy also had a requirement for basic trainers and, taking the US Army's lead, placed an initial order on 28 August 1940 for a version equivalent to the BT-13A except for the installation of an R-985-AN-1 engine; this had the US Navy designation **SNV-1**, and 1,350 were built. **SNV-2** was the designation of a variant that was the equivalent of the US Army's BT-13B. In all, well over 11,000 of these trainers were built for service with the USAAF and US Navy in the period 1940-44 but, with

changing ideas and the introduction of turbine-powered aircraft, all of the aircraft were retired very quickly after the war's end. A handful survived after 1948 to receive the revised designation **T-13**.

Specification
Type: two-seat basic trainer
Powerplant: (BT-13A) one 450-hp (336-kW) Pratt & Whitney R-985-AN-1 Wasp Junior radial piston engine
Performance: maximum speed 180 mph (290 km/h); service ceiling 21,650 ft (6600 m); range 725 miles (1167 km)
Weights: empty 3,375 lb (1531 kg); maximum take-off 4,496 lb (2039 kg)
Dimensions: span 42 ft 0 in (12.80 m); length 28 ft 10 in (8.79 m); height 11 ft 6 in (3.51 m); wing area 239 sq ft (22.20 m²)

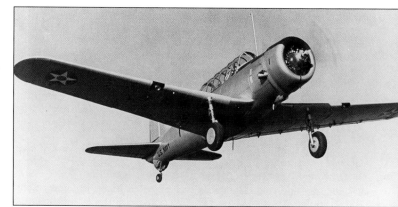

Photographed in 1941, this must have been one of the first SNV-1s delivered to the Navy. Altogether the Navy purchased exactly 2,000, the final 650 being SNV-2s with 24-volt electrics. Unlike Army Valiants, they were painted chrome yellow overall.

Vultee XP-54

The **Vultee XP-54**, or company **Model 84**, apart from being a twin-boom pusher, was by far the largest USAAF single-engined fighter of its time. The result of later thinking than the Bell XP-52 of similar layout, the twin-boom, single-seat, tricycle-gear XP-54 was ordered in late 1941 together with the closely related Curtiss XP-55 and Northrop XP-56. It was conceived for the 1,850-hp (1379-kW) Pratt & Whitney X-1800-A4G engine with contra-rotating propellers, and early cancellation of the powerplant reduced the type's performance and production prospects from the start. At the time when the smaller but similarly-configured Swedish Saab J21 was taking shape, destined for widespread use, the engine change prevented the XP-54 from reaching its planned top speed of 510 mph (820 km/h) and did not see service.

Two prototypes (41-1210/1211) were built with minor structural differences, the first flown 15 January 1943 with the alternate 2,300-hp (1715-kW) Lycoming XH-2470, the first product by this manufacturer to power a USAAF fighter. The plan to install contra-rotating propellers was dropped.

Armed with two 37-mm cannon and two 0.5-in (12.7-mm) machine-guns, the XP-54 was equipped with a nose section that could be tilted upward to 'lob' its low-velocity cannon shells at their target, while its machine-guns remained in depressed position. Another novel feature was a powered lift which raised the pilot into his cockpit 8 ft (2.44 m) off the ground. In an emergency bail-out, the pilot's seat slid downwards, a hinged panel protecting him from being hurled

back into the pusher propeller. It is unclear whether protection from the forward airstream was adequate, but the arrangement was prophetic; it would not appear again until the US Navy Douglas F-10 (F3D) Skyknight fighter of the 1950s.

The camouflaged first XP-54 (411210) made 86 flights before being ferried to Wright Field, Ohio, on 28 October 1943, where only limited further tests took place. The natural-metal second XP-54 (411211) flew only once on a test hop from the manufacturer's plant at Downey, California, to nearby Norton Field. Although the XP-54 showed awesome potential, the programme was discontinued

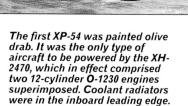

The first XP-54 was painted olive drab. It was the only type of aircraft to be powered by the XH-2470, which in effect comprised two 12-cylinder O-1230 engines superimposed. Coolant radiators were in the inboard leading edge.

after the tilting nose-gun section, dismantled from the airframe, was evaluated at Eglin Field, Florida. By late 1943, the time of innovation with propeller-driven fighters was nearing a close.

A further development of the XP-54 design, the XP-68 Tornado, was cancelled before construction could begin.

Specification
XP-54
Type: single-seat fighter
Powerplant: one 2,300-hp (1715-kW) Lycoming XH-2470-1 24-cylinder liquid-cooled H-type piston engine driving a pusher four-bladed propeller
Performance: maximum speed 403 mph (648 km/h) at 12,000 ft (3658 m); initial climb rate 2,300 ft (701 m) per minute; climb to 26,000 ft (7925 m) in 17.3 minutes; service ceiling 37,000 ft (11278 m); range 500 miles (805 km)
Weights: empty 15,262 lb (6922 kg); maximum take-off 19,335 lb (8770 kg)
Dimensions: span 53 ft 10 in (16.41 m); length 54 ft 9 in (16.69 m); height 13 ft 0 in (3.96 m); wing area 456 sq ft (42.36 m²)
Armament: two 37-mm cannon and two 0.5-in (12.7-mm) machine guns in a forward-firing installation

The second aircraft, 41-1211, was left natural metal. Though the XP-54, popularly dubbed the Swoose Goose, scored higher than any other fighter in a major AAF evaluation, it was so filled with complex and undeveloped features that it had little chance of seeing production.

Vultee P-66 Vanguard

No fighter came into USAAF livery more indirectly, had as much international 'flavour' or, in the end, failed so utterly as the **Vultee P-66 Vanguard**, which was known as the manufacturer's **Model 48** long before acquiring its fighter designation.

Ordered by Sweden, tested by the UK, used in the defence of the western USA and blooded in Chinese markings, the P-66 was conceived in 1938 by Vultee's design team under Richard Palmer as the Model 48, an all-metal, low-wing monoplane fighter with retractable landing gear and a unique, flush-fitting cowl over its 1,200-hp (894-kW) Pratt & Whitney R-1830 radial engine. The low-drag cowl design, fitted on the same engine in the Curtiss XP-42, posed cooling problems and, although tested on the fourth airframe by Vance Breese in 1939, was discarded in favour of conventional, open-air cooling. The production prototype of the Vultee **Model 48C**, as it became known, flew in September 1940 and 144 airframes were ordered by Sweden with the Flygvapen designation J10. Although one Vanguard flew with Swedish markings, the 1940 embargo on US sales to Stockholm prevented delivery, and these machines acquired US serials 42-6832/6975. In anticipation of acquisition by the UK, 100 Royal Air Force serials (BW208/BW307) were assigned but only three machines (BW208/BW210) flew bearing these serials. The yet-unfinished production run of 144 machines was again diverted, 15 Vanguards being assigned to USAAF operational training units on the American West Coast including the 14th Pursuit Group at NAS Oakland, California, and 129 being earmarked for China. The Chinese P-66 Vanguards were shipped by sea to Karachi in US markings for reassembly and onward ferrying to Chengtu, China. Some were lost en route, and others crashed during early trial flights from Karachi airfield where they were kept for a time in the aerodrome's massive hangar.

The P-66 should have been more than a match for the Nakajima Ki-43 fighters Japan would throw against it in the south-west China theatre. Formidably armed with no fewer than four 0.3-in (7.62-mm) and two 0.5-in (12.7-mm) machine-guns, the Vanguard was manoeuvrable and had good endurance. But Chinese pilots, trained in the tricycle-gear Bell P-39, found it difficult to land this unforgiving 'tail dragger', and pranged many in trial hops at Karachi. Hydraulic problems and swollen rubber seals hampered P-66s already weathered by their long sea voyage. As few as 79 aircraft of the intended 129 actually reached Chengtu, these being assigned non-sequential Chinese serials in the P-13002/P-26886 range. Worse, in a confusing 21 November 1943 air battle, Chinese pilots shot down one Japanese Ki-43 but also despatched two friendly P-66s.

Flying the P-66 in combat from Fengwaushan airfield near Chengtu was an experience, but scarcely a favourable one for beleaguered Chinese airmen. In a crosswind on the ground, the wide 13-ft (3.96-m) landing gear track of the P-66 almost invited a catastrophic ground loop. Aloft, the aircraft handled well and was comfortable, but was unstable in a high-speed dive and had poor spin stall characteristics. Many P-66s were caught on the ground by Japanese strafing and the Vanguard took longer than most types to scramble into the air. A few Chinese pilots scored air-to-air kills, but the Vanguards were retired from service by late 1943. Some were crated and may have ended up in the hands of Chinese Communist operators.

Finished in shiny metal, apart from the black anti-dazzle panel, NX-28300 was the third Vanguard built. It was the first Model 48C, and thus was the production prototype, first flown on 6 September 1940. With only 1,200 hp, it swiftly became obsolescent.

Specification
Type: single-seat fighter
Powerplant: one 1,200-hp (894-kW) Pratt & Whitney R-1830-S3C4-G Twin Wasp air-cooled 14-cylinder radial piston engine driving a Hamilton Standard 23E50 three-bladed hydromatic propeller
Performance: maximum speed 340 mph (547 km/h) at 15,000 ft (4572 m); climb to 17,000 ft (5182 m) in 9.2 minutes; service ceiling 28,200 ft (8595 m); range 850 miles (1360 km)
Weights: empty 5,235 lb (2374 kg); maximum take-off 7,400 lb (3356 kg)
Dimensions: span 35 ft 10 in (10.92 m); length 28 ft 5 in (8.66 m); height level 13 ft 0 in (3.96 m) and at rest 10 ft 0 in (3.05 in); wing area 197 sq ft (18.30 m²)
Armament: two 0.5-in (12.7-mm) Colt synchronised cowl machine-guns and four 0.3-in (7.62-mm) Colt wing machine guns, all forward-firing

The production Model 48C fighters, including the P-66s, were finished olive drab. Chinese aircraft had a three-digit fin serial in white. This example lacks the Chinese insignia.

Waco PT-14

In 1937 Waco introduced its Model **UPF-7** as an open-cockpit biplane with a 220-hp (164-kW) Continental W-670-K radial engine and seating for two or three. The type was intended for training and sport use, and as such was designed with an exceptionally sturdy airframe. This commended the type to the USAAC as a primary trainer, and a single example (39-702) was evaluated during 1939 with the designation **XPT-14**. There followed 13 **YPT-14** service trials aircraft (40-14 to 40-26), which were later redesignated **PT-14** and a single civil Model UPF-7 was impressed with the designation **PT-14A**. However, another 600 aircraft of the same basic type were ordered with three engine types for the Civilian Pilot Training Program that undertook pilot training at educational institutions to provide a pool of trained pilots in the event of war. Another 31 similar aircraft were bought by the Civil Aeronautics Authority for its own flying unit. These retained their manufacturer's designations.

Specification
Type: two-seat primary trainer
Powerplant: one Continental R-670-3, 220 hp (164 kW)
Performance: maximum speed 138 mph (222 km/h) at sea level
Weight: maximum take-off 2,650 lb (1202 kg)
Dimensions: span 30 ft 0 in (9.14 m); length 23 ft 5 in (7.16 m)

Resplendent in its blue fuselage, chrome-yellow wings and tail and striped rudder, one of the YPT-14s, with cowled engine, is seen on evaluation, probably in 1940. Waco biplanes were noted for their strength and good handling, and there could easily have been 10,346 Wacos instead of that number of Stearmans. Another candidate was the St Louis PT-1W.

INDEX

Aircraft are covered alphabetically by manufacturer throughout the book. Here they are listed under their designation and name and under the manufacturer's name. Page numbers in **bold** refer to a major entry.

INDEX

Picture acknowledgements

The following organisations have kindly supplied photographs for this book:

US Air Force
US Navy
US Marine Corps
Bell Aircraft Corporation

Lockheed
McDonnell Douglas
North American
Northrop Grumman

The MacClancy Collection
Imperial War Museum
Aerospace Publishing Ltd